VISUAL LANGUAGE

FOR DESIGNERS

Inspiring | Educating | Creating | Entertaining

Brimming with creative inspiration, how-to projects, and useful information to enrich your everyday life, Quarto Knows is a favorite destination for those pursuing their interests and passions. Visit our site and dig deeper with our books into your area of interest: Quarto Creates, Quarto Cooks, Quarto Homes, Quarto Lives, Quarto Drives, Quarto Explores, Quarto Gifts, or Quarto Kids.

First published in 2011 by Rockport Publishers,
an imprint of The Quarto Group,
100 Cummings Center, Suite 265-D,
Beverly, MA 01915, USA.
T (978) 282-9590 F (978) 283-2742
www.QuartoKnows.com

Rockport Publishers titles are also available at discount for retail, wholesale, promotional, and bulk purchase. For details, contact the Special Sales Manager by email at specialsales@quarto.com or by mail at The Quarto Group, Attn: Special Sales Manager, 401 Second Avenue North, Suite 310, Minneapolis, MN 55401, USA.

Library of Congress Cataloging-in-Publication Data
Malamed, Connie.
  Visual language for designers : principles for creating graphics that people understand / Connie Malamed.
     p. cm.
  ISBN-13: 978-1-59253-515-6
  ISBN-10: 1-59253-515-1
  1. Commercial art. 2. Graphic arts. 3. Visual communication. I. Title.
  NC997.M24 2009
  741.601'9--dc22

                                                    2008052335
                                                    CIP

ISBN: 978-1-59253-741-9

Design: Kathie Alexander

Printed in USA

VISUAL LANGUAGE

FOR DESIGNERS

PRINCIPLES FOR
CREATING GRAPHICS THAT
PEOPLE UNDERSTAND

CONNIE MALAMED

ACKNOWLEDGMENTS

My heartfelt thanks to the designers around the globe
who contributed their exceptional work to this book
and to all the professors and researchers who happily
answered my stream of questions. Thanks to everyone
at Rockport Publishers for their dedication and
hard work.

DEDICATION

To Tom for untiring support,
Hannah for invaluable help,
and Rebecca and Silas for sweet encouragement.

CONTENTS

Introduction 9

SECTION ONE GETTING GRAPHICS

An explanation of how we process
visual information 19

SECTION TWO PRINCIPLES

1 **Organize for Perception** 45
Features that Pop Out 54
Texture Segregation 58
Grouping 66

2 **Direct the Eyes** 71
Position 80
Emphasis 82
Movement 86
Eye Gaze 92
Visual Cues 96

3 **Reduce Realism** 103
Visual Noise 110
Silhouettes 113
Iconic Forms 118
Line Art 122
Quantity 125

4 **Make the Abstract Concrete** 129
Big-Picture Views 140
Data Displays 144
Visualization of Information 150
More than Geography 156
Snapshots of Time 162

5 **Clarify Complexity** 169
Segments and Sequences 178
Specialized Views 184
Inherent Structure 196

6 **Charge It Up** 203
Emotional Salience 210
Narratives 214
Visual Metaphors 220
Novelty and Humor 224

Bibliography 228
Glossary of Terms 229
Sources Cited 230
Directory of Contributors 235

"Sight is swift, comprehensive, simultaneously analytic, and synthetic. It requires so little energy to function, as it does, at the speed of light, that it permits our minds to receive and hold an infinite number of items of information in a fraction of a second."

CALEB GATTENGO, *Towards a Visual Culture*

WE HAVE NO CHOICE but to be drawn to images. Our brains are beautifully wired for the visual experience. For those with intact visual systems, vision is the dominant sense for acquiring perceptual information. We have over one million nerve fibers sending signals from the eye to the brain, and an estimated 20 billion neurons analyzing and integrating visual information at rapid speed.[1] We have a surprisingly large capacity for picture memory, and can remember thousands of images with few errors.[2]

We are also compelled to understand images. Upon viewing a visual, we immediately ask, "What is it?" and "What does it mean?" Our minds need to make sense of the world, and we do so actively. To understand something is to scan and search our memory stores, to call forth associations and emotions, and to use what we already know to interpret and infer meaning on the unknown. As we derive pleasure, satisfaction, and competence from understanding, we seek to understand more.

Acquiring a sense of our innate mental and visual capacities can enable graphic designers and illustrators to express their message with accurate intent. For example, if one's goal is to visually explain a process, then understanding how humans comprehend and learn helps the designer create a well-defined information graphic. If one's purpose is to evoke a passionate response, then an understanding of how emotions are tied to memory enables the designer to create a poster that sizzles. If one's purpose is to visualize data, then understanding the constraints of short-term memory enables the designer to create a graph or chart that is easily grasped.

In the beginning was the dot.

Maziar Zand,
M. Zand Studio, Iran

This book explores how the human brain processes visual information. It presents ways to leverage the strengths of our cognitive architecture and to compensate for its limitations. It proposes principles for creating graphics that are comprehensible, memorable, and informative. It examines the unique ways we can provide cognitive and emotional meaning through visual language. Most important, this book is meant to inspire new and creative ways of designing to inform.

We depend on visual language for its efficient and informative value. As the quantity of global information grows exponentially, communicating with visuals allows us to comprehend large quantities of data. We often find that technological and scientific information is so rich and complex, it can only be represented through imagery. Using an informative approach to visual language allows the audience to perceive concepts and relationships that they had not previously realized.

Our neurons seem to be plugged in to the digital stream, having adjusted to the continual barrage of visual information. With multiple windows, scrolling text, personal digital assistants, new media, digital imagery, video on demand, advertising banners, and pop-ups, we have come to appreciate the fact that visuals reduce the time it takes for a viewer to understand and respond to information. The sheer quantity of visual messages relayed through new technology has led some to call imagery "the new public language."

Visual communication is fitting for a multilingual, global culture. Using basic design elements, it's possible to bypass differences in symbol perception and language to convey our message through imagery. Gyorgy Kepes, influential designer and art educator, envisioned this in 1944, when he wrote, "Visual communication is universal and international; it knows no limits of tongue, vocabulary, or grammar, and it can be perceived by the illiterate as well as by the literate."

▲ *Imagery enables us to apprehend concepts that are difficult to explain. By visualizing three layers of the human form as distinct bodies and using blurred doubles to express motion, the artist provides a glimpse of how each interconnected layer of the body performs while running.*

Daniel Muller, *United States*

▲ This graphic for Vodafone pairs the complex symbols of technology with the simplicity of iconic forms to effectively convey "technology at your fingertips."

Peter Grundy, Grundini,
United Kingdom

▶ In this graphic depicting the greeting customs of four different cultures, the illustrator uses a minimum of graceful strokes and effective symbols to convey his message.

Nigel Holmes,
United States

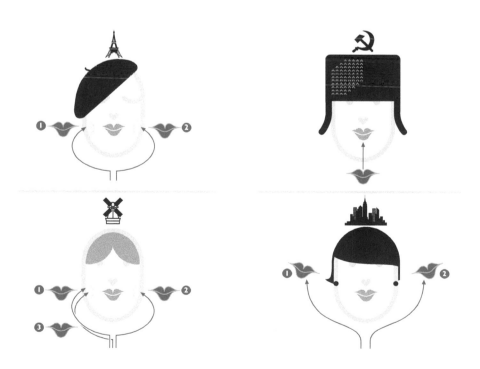

The One Campus Ecosystem: Uniting Your Academic & Administrative Enterprise

CAMPUS
MANAGEMENT

Introducing a fully unified, student-centric administrative and e-learning platform. Welcome to the One Campus Ecosystem™ from Campus Management.

Admissions Forecasting
Identify recruiting trends to predict the numbers of prospects, applicants and enrollments per program and term. Pinpoint the sources of the most qualified prospective students.

Financial Health in Real-time
Business officers can assess financial health across all institutional operations. Tuition, for example moves in real-time between the One Campus student system and financial system.

On-demand Student Services
Through a personalized web portal, students interact seamlessly with admissions, financial aid, registrar, bursar, faculty and advisors, career services, and more.

Synergize Sites and Programs:
One Campus system manages and reports on multiple sites, affiliates and programs. Share catalogs so students can register for virtually any mix of classroom and online courses.

Open Architecture
Connect third party software and create custom web applications. A suite of interfaces (APIs) provides sustainable integrations that can leverage workflows already built into the One Campus system.

Career Services
A portal for employers lets recruiters search for qualified students, interact with advisors and candidates, and schedule interviews. Reports activities and employment records.

Built-in Contact Manager
Automate text messages, emails, and To Dos. Contact manager is threaded throughout the entire system, streamlining the flow of communications, alerts and tasks for students, staff and instructors.

Managed Services and Consulting
Outsource your infrastructure to Campus Management. Services include hosting, upgrades, application support, academic consulting, and 24/7 e-learning helpdesk.

Configurable vs. Custom
Add new sites, define new programs and re-configure workflows easily, without having to write or maintain custom code.

Alumni Relations On-the-go
Manage and track campaigns and communications with your benefactors and alumni. Track complex relationships, collect, process and analyze pledges and matching gifts. Access donor profiles, documents and images remotely.

Manage Nontraditional Programs
Institutions eliminate silos, using one system to manage traditional as well as continuing and distance education programs — including those with variable terms and borrower-based academic years.

Integrated e-Learning with Moodle
Deploy Moodle enterprise-wide. Linkages to the student hub enhance retention and Learning Outcomes Management.

Proactive Retention
The system constantly scans for yellow and red flags, such as tardy submission of lessons, poor quiz scores, lack of participation in online courses. Automatically alerts the student, faculty and advisor.

- Student Services
- Administration
- Academics
- Architecture

XPLANATIONS

▲ *Visual language enables us to depict processes and systems in their entirety so we can understand the big perspective. This diagram of a campus enterprise system details each component of the system while presenting the global view.*

Taylor Marks, XPLANE,
United States

Communication through imagery has other advantages as well. To explain something hidden from view, such as the mechanics of a machine or the human body, a cross section of the object or a transparent human figure works well. When we need to describe an invisible process, such as how a mobile text message is transmitted, iconic forms interconnected with arrows can be used to represent a system and its events. To communicate a difficult or abstract concept, we may choose to depict it with a visual metaphor to make the idea concrete. Precise charts and tables help to structure information so audiences can easily absorb the facts. When we wish to instigate a call to action, we find that emotionally charged imagery is the most memorable. We see that a graphic with humor or novelty can capture our audience's attention and provide motivation and interest. And when the task calls for an immediate response, we know that a graphic will provide quick comprehension. The power of visual communication is immeasurable.

▶ *This snapshot of social media trends on the Internet was created for Business Week magazine. The clear and precise pixel graph provides the coherency we need to make comparisons, find patterns, and appreciate the richness of the data.*

Arno Ghelfi, United States

Social Media as a Percentage of Web Traffic

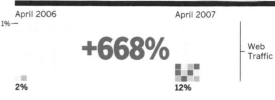

April 2006	April 2007	
1%—		Web Traffic
2%	12%	

+668%

Percentage of Upload/Edit per visit

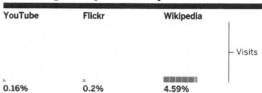

YouTube	Flickr	Wikipedia	
			Visits
0.16%	0.2%	4.59%	

Social Technographics Categories

Percent of each generation in each Social Technographics category

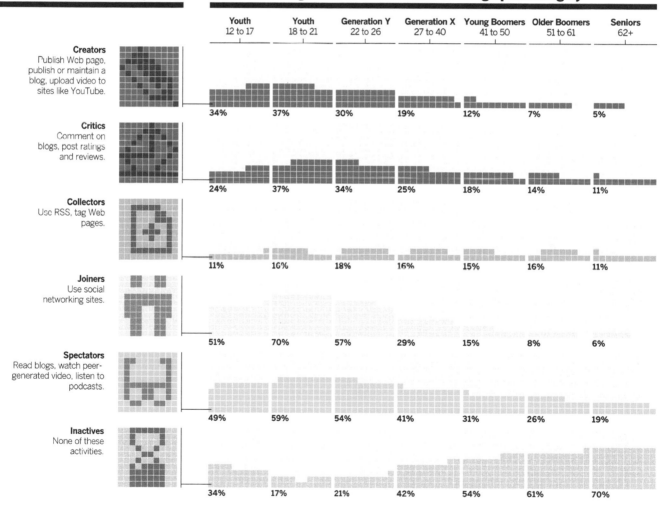

	Youth 12 to 17	Youth 18 to 21	Generation Y 22 to 26	Generation X 27 to 40	Young Boomers 41 to 50	Older Boomers 51 to 61	Seniors 62+
Creators — Publish Web page, publish or maintain a blog, upload video to sites like YouTube.	34%	37%	30%	19%	12%	7%	5%
Critics — Comment on blogs, post ratings and reviews.	24%	37%	34%	25%	18%	14%	11%
Collectors — Use RSS, tag Web pages.	11%	16%	18%	16%	15%	16%	11%
Joiners — Use social networking sites.	51%	70%	57%	29%	15%	8%	6%
Spectators — Read blogs, watch peer-generated video, listen to podcasts.	49%	59%	54%	41%	31%	26%	19%
Inactives — None of these activities.	34%	17%	21%	42%	54%	61%	70%

The Designer's Challenge

The never-ending flood of facts and data in our contemporary world has caused a paradigm shift in how we relate to information. Whereas at one time information was community based, slow to retrieve, and often the domain of experts, information is now global, instantaneous, and often in the public domain. We now want information and content in our own hands and on our own terms. We maintain an underlying belief that it is our fundamental right to have access to well-structured and organized information. As a result, information design is exploding as organizations and individuals scramble to manage an overwhelming quantity of content. Understanding the most effective ways to inform is now a principal concern. According to professor of information design Dino Karabeg, "Informing can make the difference between the technologically advanced culture which wanders aimlessly and often destructively, and a culture with vision and direction."[4]

This has profound implications for graphic communication. There is an increasing demand for the information-packed graphic, greater competition for an audience's visual attention, and ever more complex visual problems requiring original solutions. There are requirements to design for pluralistic cultures and a continuous need to design for the latest technologies.

As part of this new path, visual communicators need a sense of how the mind functions. Effective informative graphics focus on the audience. An increased awareness of how people process visual information can help the designer create meaningful messages that are understood on both a cognitive and emotional level. An informative image is not only well designed; it captures both the feeling of the content and facilitates an understanding of it. The final product affects how the audience perceives, organizes, interprets, and stores the message. The new role of a graphic designer is to direct the cognitive and emotional processes of the audience. In shaping the information space of a visually saturated world, efficient and accurate communication is of primary importance.

Step Inside

Visual Language for Designers is based on research from the interconnected fields of visual communication and graphic design, learning theory and instructional design, cognitive psychology and neuroscience, and information visualization. The imagery incorporates an expansive definition of visual design, exemplifying the diverse fields from which this research is drawn. This type of fusion is natural in a world of collaboration, interrelationships, and blurry delineations, and represents the diverse requests that contemporary designers must often fulfill.

The first section of *Visual Language for Designers* presents an overview of how we perceive, understand, and acquire visual information. The reader will also be introduced to the important concept of cognitive load, which has significant implications in the design of informative graphics.

The second section presents principles for creating graphics that accommodate the human mind and emotions. These principles are intended as a guide—as a space for exploration and discovery rather than hard-and-fast rules. The principles are meant to serve as a catalyst for finding visual solutions and fine-tuning one's work. Most important, this book is meant to inspire new and creative ways of designing to inform.

With a reflective background, this poster captures the museum experience as it receives varying images from the changing surroundings.

Boris Ljubicic, Studio International, Croatia

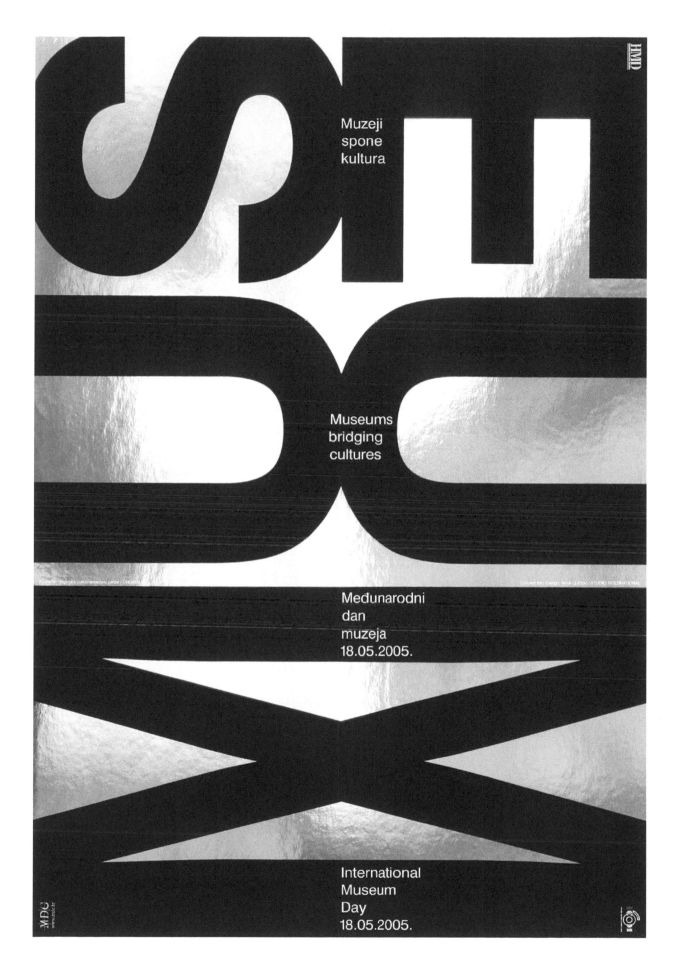

AN Emergent Mosaic OF Wikipedian Activity

Received **Honorable Mention** in 2007 NetSci Visualizing Network Dynamics Competition
http://vw.indiana.edu/07netsci/

AUTHORS
Bruce W. Herr (Visualization Expert)
Todd M. Holloway, (Data Mining Expert)
Elisha Hardy (Graphic Design)
Katy Börner (Advisor & Sponsor)
Kevin Boyack, Sandia Labs (Node Layout)
School of Library and Information Science
Department of Computer Science
Indiana University
Bloomington, IN 47405, USA
{bherr,tohollow,efhardy,katy}@indiana.edu
kboyack@sandia.gov

INTRODUCTION
This emergent mosaic supplies a macro view of all of the English Wikipedia (http://en.wikipedia.org) and reveals those areas that are currently 'hot', meaning, of late, they are being frequently revised.

ARTICLE NETWORK
The provided dataset [1,2] comprises **659,388** interconnected Wikipedia articles. One article (node) is connected to another if it links to it. There are **16,582,425** links.

POSITIONING
Articles are shown close to one another if they are similar, and far apart if they are different. Two articles are said to be similar if articles that link to one often link to the other.

MOSAIC
The **1,869** images were taken directly from Wikipedia. This represents approximately one image for every 300 articles. The images were selected automatically in a three step process. First, the layout was cut into half inch tiles. Next, the articles in each tile were ranked by their indegree, i.e., the number of articles that link to them. Finally, the first image of the highest ranked article that contains a non-icon image was selected for display. All images of controversial subject matter were kept, making it appropriate for mature audiences.

"The mosaic stunningly illustrates the broad spectrum of what I would call the diffuse focus of the masses. Its value is in its all-encompassing overview, and that it allows one to explore and compare this focus. It would be interesting to see how it changes over time, my faith in humankind would be restored to someday see that Albert Einstein and Muhammad generated more interest than Britney Spears."

Daniel Zeller (Visual Artist)
New York City

"Bruce and Todd have shown a volcanic landscape with lava pools, geysers and crusted-over areas. So far the best representation out there to show what moves mankind's minds. A true mindscape of the public."

Ingo Günther (Journalism & Art)
Tokyo National University for Fine Arts & Music, Japan

Edit Activity

few   1000's

2001 to April 6th, 2007, articles were
...imes. The red, larger nodes are those
...en revised more frequently than those
...yellow nodes. We gave more
...urrent and major revisions. The result
...ng articles which have been furiously

...Most Actively Revised Articles

...18
...Adolf Hitler
3. October 2003
4. Nintendo Revolution
5. Hurricane Katrina
6. India
7. RuneScape
8. Anarchism
9. Britney Spears
10. PlayStation 3
11. Saddam Hussein
12. Japan
13. Albert Einstein
14. 2004 Indian Ocean Earthquake
15. New York City
16. Germany
17. Muhammad
18. Pope Benedict XVI
19. Ronald Reagan
20. Hinduism

REFERENCES
[1] Denoyer, Ludovic & Gallinari, Patrick (2006). The Wikipedia
XML Corpus. SIGIR Forum.
[2] Wikipedia network downloaded from
http://www.zweipunktnull.at/Vizards07/.
Accessed on November 2006.
[3] Wikipedia edit history data downloaded from
http://download.wikimedia.org/enwiki/, Accessed on April 2007.
[4] Davidson, G. S., Wylie, B. N., & Boyack, K. W. (2001). Cluster
stability and the use of noise in interpretation of clustering. Proc.
IEEE Information Visualization 2001, 23-30.

ACKNOWLEDGEMENTS
We would like to thank the WikiMedia Foundation for freely making data dumps available for research,
the many Wikipedians who have made Wikipedia the useful resource that it is, Vladimir Batagelj for
organizing the Vizards session, Sonia Sanyal and Shashikant Penumarthy for their input to this project,
and the Cyberinfrastructure for Network Science Center at Indiana University for hosting our research.
This research is supported by the National Science Foundation under IIS-0513650 and a CAREER grant under
IIS-0238261. Any opinions, findings, and conclusions or recommendations expressed in this material are those of
the author(s) and do not necessarily reflect the views of the NSF.

Online versions available at http://scimaps.org

cyberinfrastructure for
NETWORK SCIENCE CENTER

NSF

*Combining graphic design
and data visualization,
this 5-foot (1.5 m) image
captures one moment of
Wikipedia activity. Through
visual representation, we
are able to comprehend the
colossal number of edits
made to Wikipedia every
minute.*

Visualization:
Bruce W. Herr II

Data Mining:
Todd M. Holloway

Advisor:
Katy Borner, United States

Getting lost while trying
to understand the mind is
a shared human experience.

Rhonald Blommestijn,
The Netherlands

SECTION ONE
GETTING GRAPHICS

"The brain adds information to the raw visual impressions, which gives a richness of meaning far beyond the simple stimuli it receives."

ROBERT SOLSO, *Cognition and the Visual Arts*

The Meaning of Pictures

A picture is more than a two-dimensional marked surface. It reflects the creator's intent and signifies there is information to be communicated. It is the artifact of creative play and thoughtful decisions, produced to evoke a visual experience. Designers create graphics with the assumption that viewers will understand their message—that upon viewing line, color, and shape, a communication will be transmitted. They assume the viewer will proceed through a graphic in an orderly sequence, controlled by the designer's expression of visual hierarchy.

But how can one know that a viewer will find meaning in a visual communication? How can a designer ensure that the audience will comprehend his or her intent? After all, picture perception can be a tricky affair. When looking at a picture, the viewer consciously or unconsciously experiences competing perceptions. A person perceives the two-dimensional picture surface while simultaneously viewing an illusory three-dimensional space. The viewer must reconcile these contradictory perceptions while at the same time attempting to understand and interpret a picture. A suspension of belief, however small, is often required.

Also, audience members differ in their perceptions and interpretations of a picture. We cannot know how an individual will perceive a graphic, nor what thoughts, emotions, knowledge, and expectations the viewer will bring to a visual encounter. When viewers look at a graphic, their perceptions are inevitably colored by their preconceived ideas, likes and dislikes, values, and beliefs. This can create a powerful bias toward seeing what one wishes to see, potentially missing the designer's intent. Age, gender, educational background, culture, and language are other potent influences on perception.

In a study that examined the gap between intended and perceived meaning, some audience groups misinterpreted the meaning of pictures more than half the time. The author's study concluded, "Despite what appears to be a cross-cultural ability to recognize objects depicted in pictures, the visual content of an illustration is frequently a vehicle to communicate a more complex meaning or intention. Unlike the subject content of the picture, this intended meaning may often be misunderstood or unrecognized by the viewer."[1]

The discrepancy between a designer's intention and a viewer's interpretation may also be due to the enhanced visual skills that artists possess compared to nonartists. When viewing art, the artist excels at synchronizing multiple regions of the brain, which creates a coherent and unified visual perception.[2] This advanced visual skill may be due to training in the arts, a well-developed visual imagination, and a natural inclination toward the visual. Specifically, when viewing a painting, art-trained viewers spend more time looking at background features and the relationships among elements, like shapes and color. Untrained viewers spend more time looking at central and foreground figures, focusing on objects and pictorial elements.[3] Due to this variance in perceptions between artist and nonartist, it is possible that during the act of creation, the designer cannot quite anticipate what the audience will perceive.

While viewing a graphic, we simultaneously perceive the flat two-dimensional picture plane and the three-dimensional picture space, exemplified in this catamaran information graphic for Popular Science *magazine.*

__Kevin Hand,__ United States

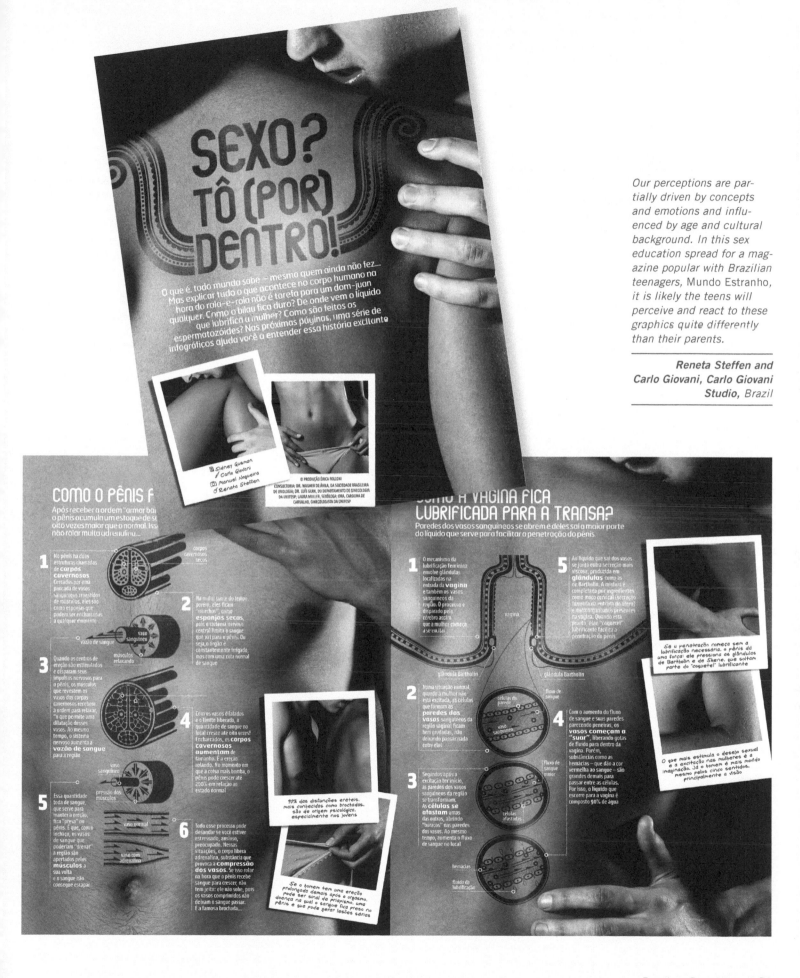

Our perceptions are partially driven by concepts and emotions and influenced by age and cultural background. In this sex education spread for a magazine popular with Brazilian teenagers, Mundo Estranho, it is likely the teens will perceive and react to these graphics quite differently than their parents.

Reneta Steffen and Carlo Giovani, Carlo Giovani Studio, *Brazil*

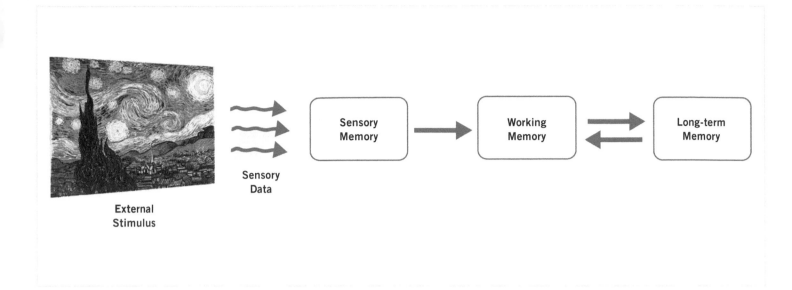

External Stimulus

Sensory Data

Sensory Memory → Working Memory ⇄ Long-term Memory

Despite these challenges, graphic designers seek to create clarity in their communications so viewers will accurately interpret the intended message. "This is the real measure of the performance of any and every piece of graphic design and the proof that graphic design cannot be understood in isolation but only within a communication context," writes Jorge Frascara in his essay "Graphic Design: Fine Art or Social Science?"[4] Understanding how people process visual information will increase the likelihood that a designer will produce graphics that audiences understand. This is because every aspect of a design and every design element is part of a visual language that conveys meaning to an audience. Fortunately, we can turn to cognitive science—the study of how we think and learn—for a plausible explanation of how people perceive and comprehend visuals.

Human Information Processing System
Cognitive science emerged from several fields, including cognitive psychology, computer science, neuroscience, philosophy, and linguistics, and makes use of the computer as a metaphor for how we process information. It relies on a model known as the *human information-processing system* to explain how raw data from the senses is transformed into meaningful information that we act upon or store away for later use. Not only does our nervous system continuously and instantaneously perform this remarkable feat, it cannot do otherwise.

Our information-processing system consists of three main memory structures—sensory memory, working memory, and long-term memory. The input to the system is raw sensory data that registers in sensory memory. A small portion of this data passes on to working memory—the equivalent of awareness—and is represented there. Some information is coded and stored in long-term memory as new knowledge; some information may simply result in performing an action. With the proper cues, we can retrieve information stored in long-term memory.

For example, when we look at *The Starry Night*, its colors, brushstrokes, and shapes register in sensory memory. The main features and elements of the scene are held in working memory. Simply seeing the painting is a cue to recall the painting's title and the painter's name from long-term memory. In addition, the experience of viewing *The Starry Night* will be stored in long-term memory. With this generic model of cognition, we can examine information processing in more detail, particularly in terms of how we extract visual information and interpret and understand pictures.

The human information-processing system is the model that cognitive scientists use to understand how people transform sensory data into meaningful information.

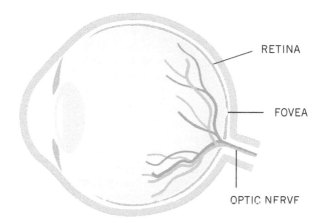

RETINA

FOVEA

OPTIC NERVE

Visual Perception: Where Bottom-Up Meets Top-Down

We are able to see a picture because reflected or emitted light focuses on the retina, composed of more than 100 million light-absorbing receptors. The job of the retina is to convert this light energy into electrical impulses for the brain to interpret. One could say that the mechanics of visual perception center on the fovea, the region of the retina that gives us sharpness of vision. The fovea allows us to distinguish small objects, detail, and color. Because the fovea is small, just a limited part of our visual world is imaged on it at any moment in time. Most visual information falls on the peripheral areas of the retina, where the sharpness of vision and detail fall off rapidly from the fovea.

Our eyes must repeatedly move to keep the object of most interest imaged on the fovea. These rapid eye movements, called saccades, allow us to select what we attend to in the visual world. The eye performs several saccades each second. In between saccades there are brief fixations—around three per second when the eyes are nearly at rest. This is when we extract visual data from a picture and process it. The visual system continuously combines image information from one fixation to the next.

Unlike data streaming into a passive computer, we perceive objects energetically, as active participants. Although our visual awareness is driven by the external stimulus, known as *bottom-up processing*, our perceptions are also driven by our memories, expectations, and intentions, known as *top-down processing*. Visual perception is the result of complex interactions between bottom-up and top-down processing.

▲ The fovea is the part of the eye that gives us the greatest acuity of vision.

▼ Visual perception results from the complex interactions of bottom-up and top-down processes.

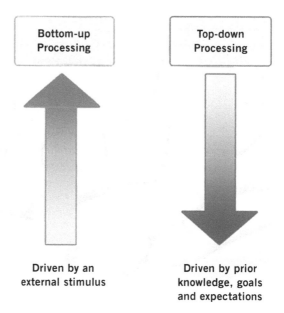

Bottom-up Processing

Top-down Processing

Driven by an external stimulus

Driven by prior knowledge, goals and expectations

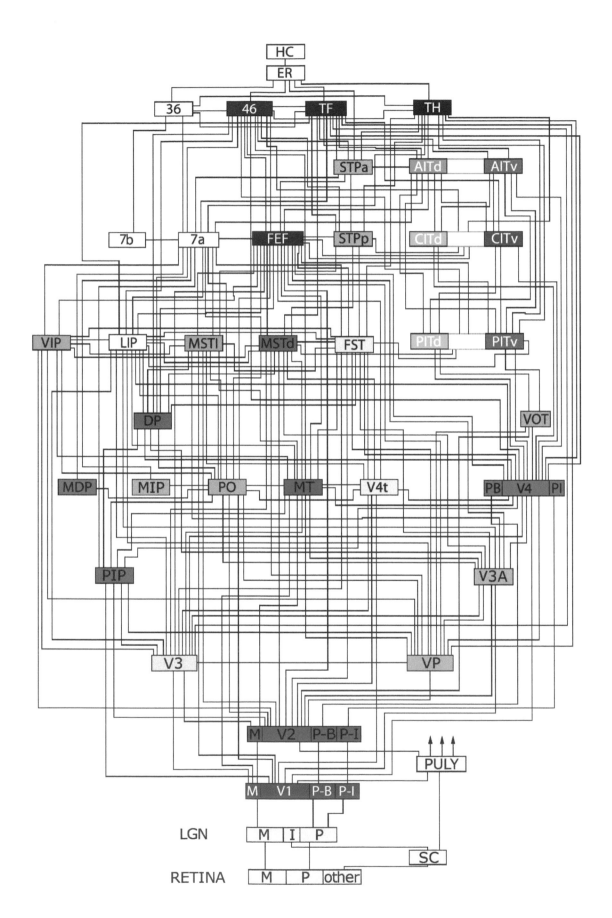

◀ Our visual system is highly attuned to visual composition. This diagram maps the many visual regions of a primate brain, which are specialized to process distinct visual attributes, such as motion, form, and color.

Published in Science magazine, for an article by David Van Essen, Charles Anderson, and Daniel Felleman

▶ In this visually rich explanation of Hindu cosmology, a viewer will preattentively see the colors and shapes through bottom-up processes. Then, using selective attention, the viewer will follow the numbered sequences and relate this information to prior knowledge through top-down processes.

Annie Bisset, Annie Bisset Illustration, United States

Bottom-up visual processing occurs early in the vision process without conscious attention or effort, propelled by the brain's persistent need to find meaningful patterns in the visual environment. When we happen to glance at a picture or a scene, we detect motion, edges of shapes, color, contours, and contrasts through bottom-up processes without conscious awareness.[5] As our brain processes these primitive features, it discriminates foreground from background, groups elements together, and organizes textures into basic forms. This occurs rapidly, helping us to recognize and identify objects. The output from bottom-up processing is quickly passed on to other areas of the brain and influences where we place our attention. This second phase of perception, top-down processing, is strongly influenced by what we know, what we expect, and the task at hand. We tend to disregard anything that is not meaningful or useful at the moment. Top down processing so affects our visual perception that some say we see more with our mind than our eyes.

Events in our information processing system occur rapidly and are measured in milliseconds or one thousandth of a second. As we interact with the world, we continually process sensory data in parallel. Different regions of the brain that are attuned to specific visual attributes of a picture, such as color or shape, are activated simultaneously. Accordingly, visual perception produces a network of activated neurons in the brain, rather than a single concentrated area of activated neurons. Massive parallel processing makes the act of perception fast and efficient. Perception and object recognition would be quite slow if data were passed from neuron to neuron in a serial fashion.

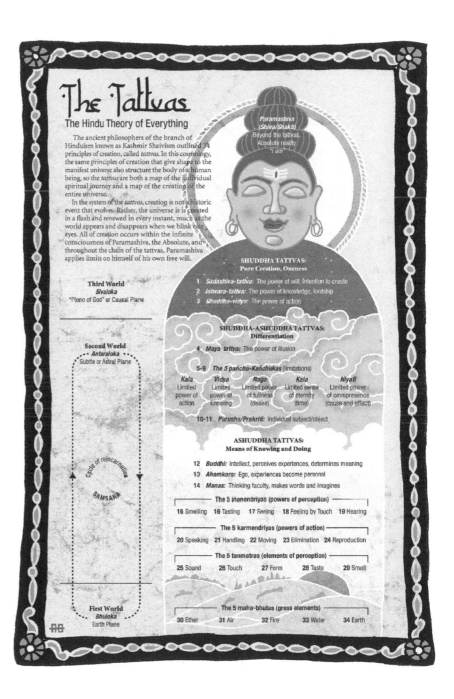

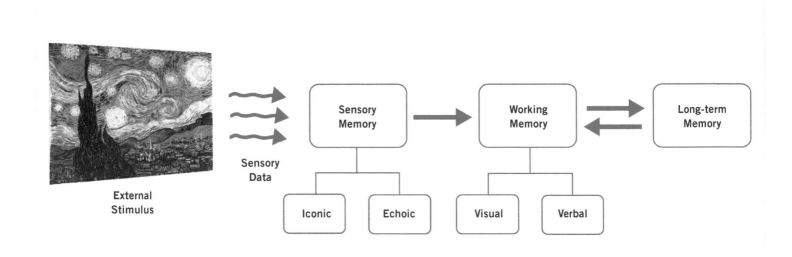

Sensory Memory: Fleeting Impressions

When we process sensory data, an impression or brief recording of the original stimulus registers in sensory memory. Sensory memory is thought to have at least two components: an iconic memory for visual information and an echoic memory for auditory information. Although the impression fades after a few hundred milliseconds, it is buffered long enough for some portion to persist for further processing.[6] In picture perception, the prominent features of the picture along with our conscious attention influence what will be retained.

Working Memory: Mental Workspace

Because we are compelled to understand what we see, we need a mental workspace to analyze, manipulate, and synthesize information. This occurs in working memory, where conscious mental work is performed to support cognition. In working memory, we maintain and manipulate information that is the focus of attention, piece together sensory information, and integrate new information with prior knowledge. Like sensory memory, working memory processes information through two systems; visual working memory processes visual information and verbal working memory processes verbal information.

A profound aspect of working memory is how it helps us make sense of the world. To understand something, we have to compare it with what we already know. Thus, as new information streams into working memory, we instantaneously search through related information in our permanent store of knowledge to find a match. If we find a match, we recognize the object or concept and identify it. If it is unfamiliar, we make inferences about it.

Both sensory memory and working memory are thought to process information in separate channels: visual and verbal.

Analyze

Studying The Social Sciences at Holy Cross

Synthesize

Studying the Humanities at Holy Cross

The ability to analyze and synthesize are important aspects of cognition, as aptly expressed in these cover graphics for a college brochure.

David Horton, Philographica, *United States*

For example, upon viewing this map, we separate figure from ground and immediately try to identify the shapes as objects. We rapidly search through our knowledge base (long-term memory) to find a match for the shapes. This activates our associated knowledge of maps and geography. If the external depiction of the map matches our generalized internal representation, we are able to recognize the landmass as "the world" and to understand the symbols from reading the legend. If we cannot identify the landmass or have no knowledge of map reading, we will not understand the graphic. The comprehension of a particular graphic is dependent on a viewer's prior knowledge and ability to retrieve that knowledge.

Two well-known constraints of working memory are its limited capacity and short duration. Although the capacity of working memory is not fixed, it appears that on average, a person can manipulate around three to five chunks of information in awareness at one time.[7] Thus, working memory is considered a bottleneck in the information-processing system. One can easily sense the limits of working memory by performing a sequential mental operation, such as multiplying two large numbers. At some point, more partial results are needed to perform the multiplication problem than working memory can handle. That is when we typically reach for paper and pencil or a calculator.

This statistical map was created for a Newsweek Education Program for high school students to learn how to interpret and analyze information.

Eliot Bergman, Japan

In addition to its limited capacity, the short duration of working memory also affects our cognitive abilities. New information in working memory decays rapidly unless the information is manipulated or rehearsed. For example, we must mentally repeat directions until we can write them down or they will quickly fade away. Individual factors also affect the constraints of working memory. Age is a factor; working memory capabilities increase with maturation but decline in old age. Working memory is also affected by the speed with which an individual processes information. Speedier processing results in a greater capacity to handle information. Distractibility is another factor. People who are adept at resisting distractions, which are known to overload working memory, have a greater functional capacity. Finally, a person's level of expertise affects working memory. With a great deal of domain-specific knowledge, an expert is not as easily overwhelmed when performing associated tasks as is a novice.[8]

Conversely, the constraints of working memory can be considered advantageous. The transitory nature of information in working memory enables us to continually change cognitive direction, providing the flexibility to shift the focus of our attention and processing to whatever is most important in the environment. In terms of picture perception, this allows a viewer to instantly perceive and consider a newly discovered area of a picture that may be easier to comprehend or of greater importance. The limited capacity of working memory creates a highly focused and uncluttered workspace that may be the perfect environment for speedy and efficient processing of information.[9]

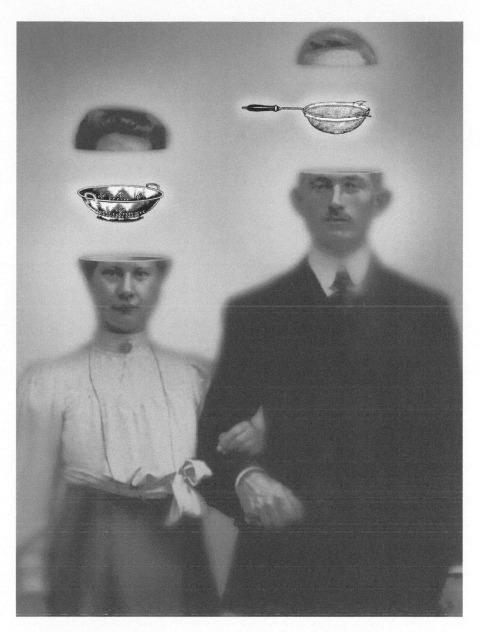

As portrayed in this graphic for Elegance magazine, information in working memory decays rapidly.

Rhonald Blommestijn,
The Netherlands

All About Stem Cells

Stem cells are the origin of all cells in the body (every cell "stems" from this type).
Under the right conditions, stem cells can become any of the body's 200 different cell types.

There are two types of stem cell	EMBRYONIC also called **early** stem cells	ADULT also called **mature** stem cells (much the rarer of the two types—only one of every 10,000 cells in bone marrow, for instance)	
	"Pluripotent" can give rise to all cell types (except cells of the placenta)	**"Multipotent"** can give rise to limited cell types	*"Unipotent" stem cells are cells that can self-replicate but not become a different type of cell.*
First isolated	**1998** at the University of Wisconsin	**1960s**	
Federal funding (1999 to 2004)	▪ $55 million	▪▪▪▪▪▪▪▪▪▪▪▪▪▪▪▪▪▪▪▪▪▪▪▪▪▪▪▪▪ ▪▪▪▪▪▪▪▪▪▪▪▪▪▪▪▪▪ ▪▪▪▪▪ $2.24 billion	
Results	**In animal trials** no human trials to date	**50+ human therapies**	

How researchers isolate stem cells

Two ways the process can start

1a In a technique called **cell nuclear replacement,** an egg is surgically removed from a woman's ovary.

Egg

The nucleus is removed.

A cell is taken from a patient.

The nucleus from the patient's cell is inserted into the egg.

The cell is activated with a tiny electrical charge to encourage development.

1b Sperm fertilizes an egg cell.

2 The cells begin to divide.

3 In approximately five days, the cells have divided into about 100 cells. They cluster together in a blastocyst.

BLASTOCYST

4 The cluster of cells is removed and placed in a culture …

5 … where the cells continue to divide. This is a **stem-cell line.** Division continues until there are several million cells.

6 Researchers decide what kind of tissue they want to recreate. For instance:
- BRAIN CELLS
- HEART-MUSCLE CELLS
- PANCREATIC-EYELET CELLS
- SKIN CELLS
- MUSCLE CELLS

7 The cells are exposed to hormones and growth factors that replicate the chemistry the cells would be exposed to if they were still in the blastocyst developing into cells needed to produce a human being.

8 New tissue or even, ultimately, whole organs could be transplanted into the patient. If the transplanted stem-cell tissue is a genetic match with the patient, the problem of tissue rejection is minimized.

The purity of this mixture is very hard to achieve, and researchers need more time to perfect the process.

Opponents of stem cell research consider a blastocyst to be an early-stage embryo, and as such, human life.

Two contentious issues

If a blastocyst were to be implanted in a woman's uterus it could theoretically lead to a pregnancy. This is called **reproductive cloning.** It is banned in all countries.

Potential U.S. recipients of stem-cell-based therapies

Cardiovascular disease	Autoimmune disease	Diabetes	Osteoporosis	Cancer	Alzheimer's disease	Parkinson's disease	Spinal-cord injuries
58 million	**30** million	**16** million	**10** million	**8.2** million	**5.5** million	**5.5** million	**0.25** million

Cognitive Load: Demands on Working Memory

While many of the cognitive tasks we perform, such as counting, make little demand on working memory, other tasks are quite taxing. Demanding tasks include such things as acquiring new information, solving problems, dealing with novel situations, consciously recalling prior knowledge, and inhibiting irrelevant information.[10] The resources we use to satisfy the demands placed on working memory are known as *cognitive load*.

When a high cognitive load impinges on working memory, we no longer have the capacity to adequately process information. This overload effect often results in a failure to understand information, a misinterpretation of information, or overlooking of important information. Many challenging tasks associated with complex visual information make high demands on working memory. Designers of visual communication can reduce cognitive load through various graphical techniques and approaches that are discussed throughout this book.

Long-Term Memory: Permanent Storage

When we selectively pay attention to information in working memory, it is likely to get transformed and encoded into long-term memory. Long-term memory is a dynamic structure that retains everything we know. It is capable of storing an unlimited quantity of information, making it functionally infinite. Knowledge in long-term memory appears to be stored perma-nently—though we may have difficulty accessing it. Educational psychologist John Sweller describes its

significance: "Because we are not conscious of the contents of the long-term memory except when they are brought into working memory, the importance of this store and the extent to which it dominates our cognitive activity tends to be hidden from us."[11]

Long-term memory is not a unitary structure because not all types of memories are the same. We remember facts and concepts, such as basic color theory; we remember childhood events, such as playing our first instrument; and we remember how to perform a task, like riding a bicycle. Accordingly, long-term memory appears to have multiple structures to accommodate different types of memories. Semantic memory is as-sociated with meaning; it stores the facts and concepts that compose our repository of general knowledge about the world. This includes the information we extract from pictures. Episodic memory is autobio-graphical. It stores events and associated emotions that relate to experiences. Procedural memory is the storehouse of how to do things. It holds the skills and procedures that enable us to accomplish a task.

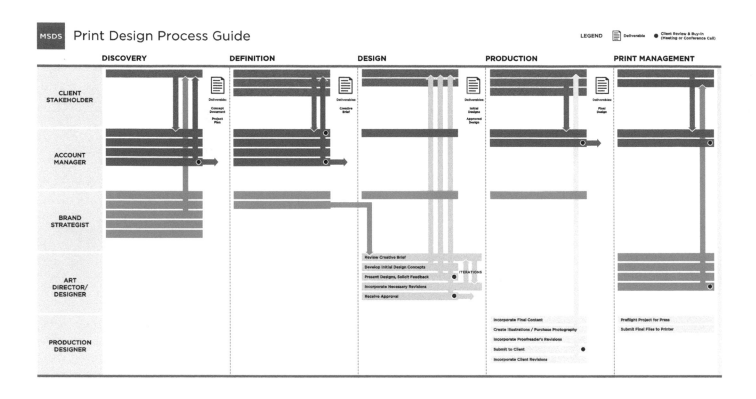

Print Design Process Guide

Encoding. Although some information is automatically processed from working memory into long-term memory without conscious effort, encoding into long-term memory generally involves some form of conscious rehearsal or meaningful association. Maintenance rehearsal is simply a matter of repeating new information until it is retained; elaborative rehearsal occurs when we analyze the meaning of new information and relate it to previously stored knowledge in long-term memory. Research suggests that the more ways we can connect new information with old information, the more likely it is to be recalled. In addition, connecting information from both the visual and verbal channels facilitates encoding to long-term memory.

Depth of processing. Cognitive researchers think that depth of processing significantly affects how likely it is that information will be recalled from long-term memory. When a viewer focuses only on the physical aspects of a word or graphic, the information is not stored as deeply as when the viewer focuses on the semantic aspects, which are those that have meaning. For example, if a viewer concentrates only on the shapes and colors of a graph, the information will not be processed as deeply as if the person studied the graph, followed the flow of explanations, and understood its meaning. Encoding at the semantic level is superior to encoding at the perceptual level. The important point that cannot be overemphasized is that we have a superior memory for anything that is processed at the level of meaning.

Depth of processing can be understood by observing this chart that depicts the processes of print design. Following the horizontal path of each process for a coherent understanding results in deeper encoding than focusing only on the layout, colors, and shapes of the elements.

Gordon Cieplak,
Schwartz Brand Group,
United States

SCHEMAS: MENTAL REPRESENTATIONS

To store a lifetime of knowledge in long-term memory, we need it in an accessible form. Not surprisingly, we achieve this by classifying and storing information in terms of what it means to us. "New information is stored in memory—not by recording some literal copy of that information but, rather, by interpreting that information in terms of what we already know. New items of information are 'fit in' to memory, so to speak, in terms of their meaning," write researchers Elizabeth and Robert Bjork.[12]

Cognitive scientists theorize that the knowledge in long-term memory is organized in mental structures called schemas. Schemas form an extensive and elaborate network of representations that embody our understanding of the world. They are the context for interpreting new information and the framework for integrating new knowledge. We rapidly activate schemas to conduct mental processes, such as problem solving and making inferences.

Unlike a perceptual experience that focuses on unique features, a schema is an abstract or generalized representation. There are schemas that represent objects and scenes and schemas that represent concepts and the relationships between concepts. When we see a house, we notice its architectural style, the materials from which it is built, its colors and textures, and the surrounding environment. Although each house is unique, each time we encounter one of these structures we are able to identify it as a house, whether it is a hut constructed of mud and straw, a farmhouse, or a townhouse. This is because we have a generalized schema of what constitutes a house. A general schema for house might include a place where people live; a structure with rooms, windows, doors and roof; and a place to sleep, eat, and bathe.

Our schemas are constantly changing, adapting, and accommodating new information, contributing to the dynamic nature of long-term memory. Every time we encounter new information and connect it to prior knowledge, we are adapting a schema to assimilate this new information. When schemas change or new schemas are constructed through analogy, we call this occurrence *learning*. And when a person becomes very skilled in a particular area, having constructed thousands of complex schemas in a particular domain, we consider the person an expert.

Retrieval. Our sole purpose in encoding information into long-term memory is to retrieve the information when we need it. Unfortunately, as we have all experienced, this is not always a straightforward process. According to the Bjorks, "The retrieval process is erratic, highly fallible, and heavily cue dependent."[13] Information recall is accomplished by a retrieval cue, which is the piece of information that activates associated knowledge stored in long-term memory. Retrieval cues can be of any form—an image, a fact, an idea, an emotion, a stimulus in the environment, or a question we ask ourselves.

When long-term memory is cued to retrieve stored memories, the cue activates associated schemas. Activation quickly spreads to other schemas in the network. A common experience occurs, for example, when a person hears an old song and tries to remember the band that recorded it. The song is the cue that retrieves associated schemas from long-term memory. If the right schemas are retrieved, the person will remember the band's name. A failure to remember something is often the result of a poor retrieval cue rather than a lack of stored knowledge.

Automaticity. Many schemas, such as word recognition, become automatic through practice. Over time and with repeated use, more complex mental operations also become automated with practice. When this happens, the procedure is processed with less conscious effort. Since working memory is the space where conscious work is performed, automaticity decreases the load on working memory.[14]

A good example of this occurs as someone learns to read. Upon one's first encounter with the word *cat*, three letters or three perceptual units are held in working memory while the word is deciphered. As a reader gains experience, the word *cat* is chunked into one perceptual unit until eventually, recognizing the word *cat* becomes an automatic process with little imposition on working memory. It is not uncommon for people with expertise in a field to perform a task without needing to pay deliberate attention to it. As the automaticity of the schema frees up cognitive resources, the expert can use working memory to competently deal with more complex tasks, such as solving problems or handling novel situations. This can be observed in experienced athletes, master teachers, and expert designers.[15]

Mental models. Whereas schemas form the underlying structure of memory, mental models are broader conceptualizations of how the world works. Mental models explain cause and effect and how changes in one object or phenomenon can cause changes in another. For example, users of graphic software have a mental model of how layers operate. The mental model contains knowledge of how a layer is affected by moving it above or below another layer and the effect of increasing or decreasing its opacity. This mental model is easily transferred to any graphic software that uses the same paradigm. Thus, mental models help us know what results to expect.

With an understanding of schemas and mental models, graphic designers can begin to consider how an audience might understand a visual form of communication. When someone looks at a graphic, the objects, shapes, and the overall scene activate associated schemas and mental models that enable the viewer to make inferences about the visual and construct an interpretation of it.

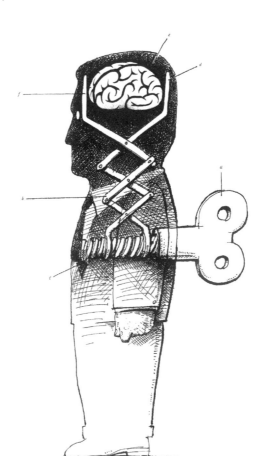

◀ *Created for the NRC Handelsblad, this graphic suggests the automaticity of many of our actions.*

Rhonald Blommestijn,
The Netherlands

▶ *This graphic portrays a novel way of seeing the interrelationships inherent in cognitive processes.*

Lane Hall, *United States*

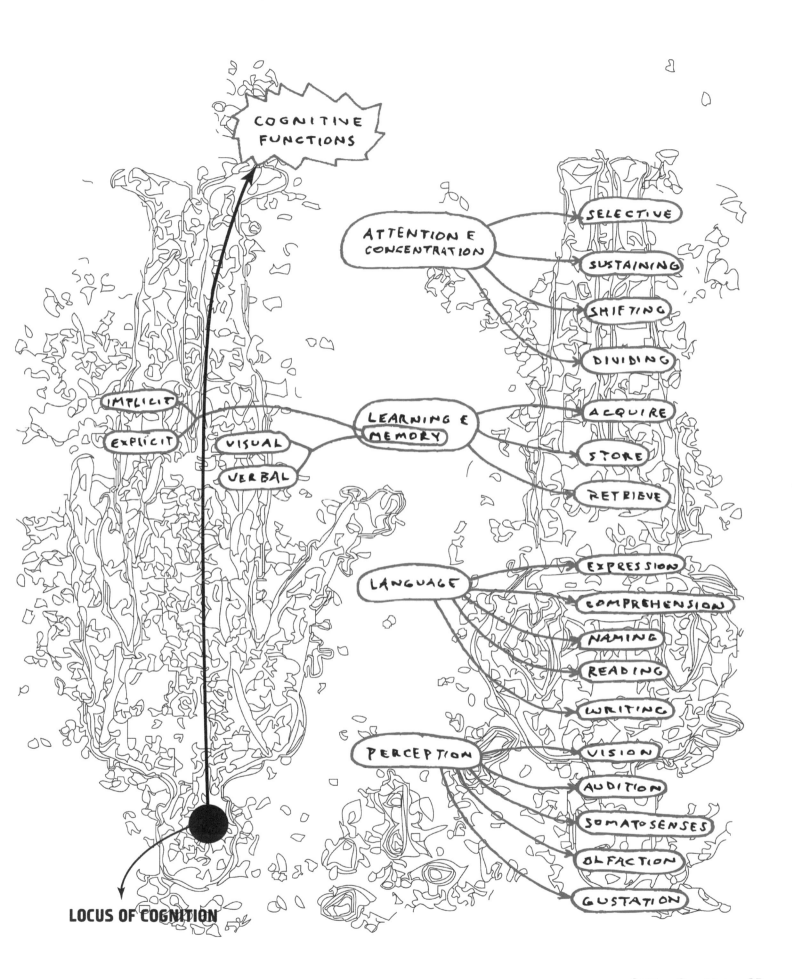

DUAL CODING: THE VISUAL AND THE VERBAL

Verbal and visual information appear to be processed through separate channels, referred to as dual coding. One channel processes visual information that retains the perceptual features of an object or picture and one channel processes verbal information and stores the information as words. Although the systems are independent, they communicate and interact, such as when both image and concept knowledge are retrieved from long-term memory. For example, upon hearing the name Salvador Dalí, a person might retrieve both image-based and verbal information from long-term memory. One might construct mental images of the artist's paintings and also recall biographical information about his life.

This dual system of processing and storage explains why memorized information is more likely to be retrieved when it is stored in both visual and verbal form. That is why associating graphics with text or using an audio track with an animation can improve information recall. Placing pictures together with words also allows these two modes of information to form connections, creating a larger network of schemas.

THE AUDIENCE'S COGNITIVE CHARACTERISTICS

It may not be possible to fully predict how an audience will perceive and interpret a picture because of the complex nature of human experience and the variable cognitive skills among individuals. Yet an awareness of an audience's cognitive characteristics can bring designers closer to this goal. In her book *Research into Illustration*, professor Evelyn Goldsmith categorizes the cognitive resources and abilities that could affect an individual's ability to comprehend a picture.

The first characteristic is developmental level. The implication is that development, rather than age, is a more accurate predictor of a person's cognitive abilities. A less skilled viewer may interpret a picture literally although the intended meaning is metaphorical. The ability to interpret more complex types of visual expression comes with mature development. Also, visual skills vary with developmental level. Visual skills such as depth perception, color differentiation, and acuity vary at different stages of development.

Distractibility is the ability to focus on what is important while inhibiting distraction from other events and information. In terms of graphic comprehension, an individual capable of inhibiting distractions will be better able to concentrate on relevant information in a visual. Not surprisingly, younger viewers find it more difficult to close their minds to extraneous information.

▶ *The cognitive characteristics of developmental level and distractibility come into play when designing for a young audience. These display graphics use bright colors and humorous illustrations for an aquarium exhibit.*

Greg Dietzenbach,
McCullough Creative,
United States

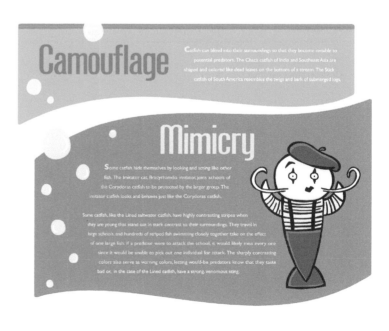

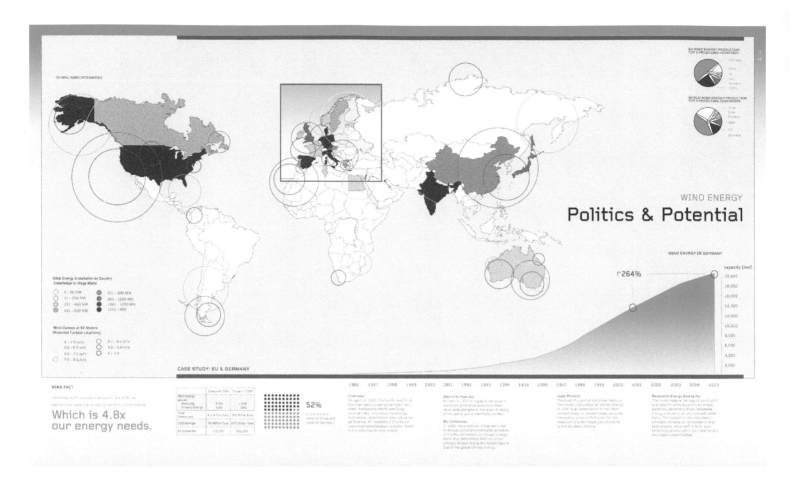

The graphic shows text including: GLOBAL WIND INTENSITIES, WIND ENERGY Politics & Potential, CASE STUDY: EU & GERMANY, WIND FACT, and "Which is 4.8x our energy needs."

This information graphic visualizes the potential global usage of wind energy depicted in maps and graphs. Advanced developmental and visual literacy levels are required to comprehend complex graphics.

Kristin Clute, University of Washington, *United States*

Another characteristic at the top of the list is visual literacy. Although it may not take training to recognize the objects in an image, a comprehensive understanding of a picture involves the ability to fully decode the visual message. Knowledge of the symbols and graphical devices used in one's culture as well as an understanding of the context are required. Learning to accurately read a picture is a result of education and experience. For example, it takes an advanced level of visual literacy to analyze and interpret an information graphic using many types of graphs.

The audience's level of expertise should significantly affect design decisions. Experience with the content of a picture is an important predictor of a viewer's ability to comprehend a graphic. Experts are known to organize complex patterns in the visual environment into fewer perceptual units, which reduces cognitive load. Thus, viewers with domain-specific experience are less likely to get overloaded when perceiving a complex visual as compared to novices.

Motivation is an important factor in whether an audience member will have an interest in a picture. A viewer's motivation is typically based on his or her goals for viewing the graphic. Is the graphic being viewed for aesthetic appreciation or is it required for performing a task, such as fixing a bicycle? Does the graphic explain a complex concept that must be learned? Or is it a bland marketing mailer for which the viewer has no use? With enough motivation, a viewer will attend to and work at understanding a graphic.

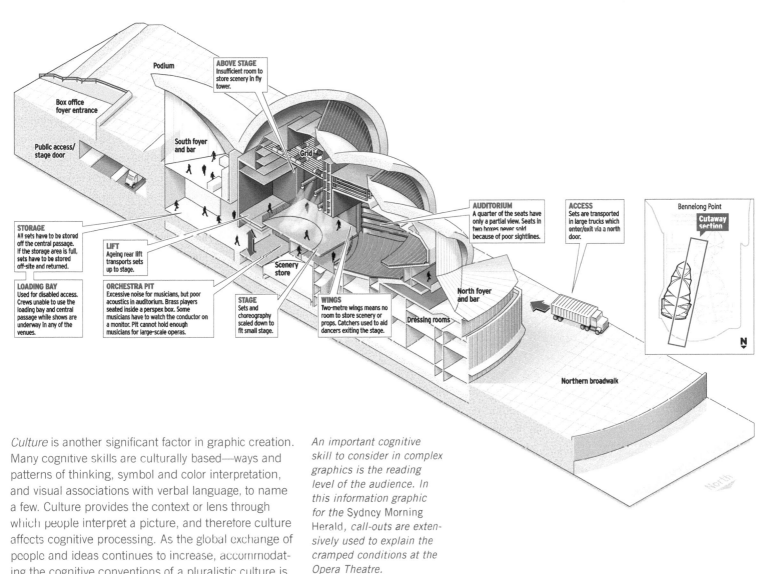

Podium

Box office foyer entrance

Public access/ stage door

ABOVE STAGE
Insufficient room to store scenery in fly tower.

South foyer and bar

Grid

STORAGE
All sets have to be stored off the central passage. If the storage area is full, sets have to be stored off-site and returned.

LIFT
Ageing rear lift transports sets up to stage.

Scenery store

LOADING BAY
Used for disabled access. Crews unable to use the loading bay and central passage while shows are underway in any of the venues.

ORCHESTRA PIT
Excessive noise for musicians, but poor acoustics in auditorium. Brass players seated inside a perspex box. Some musicians have to watch the conductor on a monitor. Pit cannot hold enough musicians for large-scale operas.

STAGE
Sets and choreography scaled down to fit small stage.

WINGS
Two-metre wings means no room to store scenery or props. Catchers used to aid dancers exiting the stage.

AUDITORIUM
A quarter of the seats have only a partial view. Seats in two boxes never sold because of poor sightlines.

ACCESS
Sets are transported in large trucks which enter/exit via a north door.

North foyer and bar

Dressing rooms

Northern broadwalk

Bennelong Point

Cutaway section

N

North

Culture is another significant factor in graphic creation. Many cognitive skills are culturally based—ways and patterns of thinking, symbol and color interpretation, and visual associations with verbal language, to name a few. Culture provides the context or lens through which people interpret a picture, and therefore culture affects cognitive processing. As the global exchange of people and ideas continues to increase, accommodating the cognitive conventions of a pluralistic culture is a fundamental requirement of effective design.

Reading skills often correspond to the user's understanding of a graphic. People with low reading levels may not be proficient at following a visual hierarchy or finding the most relevant information. They may not be experienced at allocating their visual attention to a picture in the most efficient manner and may miss important information.[16] Reading level also affects how well the viewer will read titles, captions, and call-outs and how he or she will integrate text and images.

An important cognitive skill to consider in complex graphics is the reading level of the audience. In this information graphic for the Sydney Morning Herald, *call-outs are extensively used to explain the cramped conditions at the Opera Theatre.*

Ninian Carter, *Canada*

INFORMATIVE VALUE

Another aspect of cognition relates to a graphic's informative purpose. In his book *Steps to an Ecology of the Mind*, Gregory Bateson writes that information "is a difference that makes a difference." This statement is profoundly true for visual communication. The visual language of a graphic and every compositional element it contains potentially convey a message to the viewer.

By determining a graphic's informative purpose, designers can strategically organize a graphic to invoke the most suitable mental processes. For instance, some graphics only request recognition from the viewer. They require the viewer to notice, to become aware—of an organization, an event, a product, or an announcement. These graphics must be magnetic to attract the viewer's attention and sustain it for as long as possible. The viewer's gaze must be directed to the most important information. And the graphic should be memorable, so that the viewer encodes the message into long-term memory.

Other graphics are created to extend the viewer's knowledge and reasoning abilities. The value of maps, diagrams, graphs, and information visualizations is to make things abundantly clear and move the viewer beyond what he or she could previously understand. Upon viewing one of these visuals, the viewer should be able to see new relationships. Here, the graphics must be clean and well organized and must accommodate ease of interpretation and reasoning. Then there are graphics designed to assist with a task or a procedure, such as assembling furniture. In order for the graphic to be effective when the viewer becomes a user, it must be accurate and unambiguous, leaving no room for misinterpretation.

By understanding the mental processes required to meet specific informative goals, designers can find the most suitable graphic approach for their purpose. The principles discussed in the next section of the book describe ways to achieve this.

▶ *The rich, striking textures in this promotional poster make it memorable.*

Adrian Labos, X3 Studios, *Romania*

▼ *An effective visual explanation, such as this depiction of how a digital camera operates, must be efficient and organized to promote ease of comprehension.*

Kevin Hand, *United States*

SECTION TWO
THE PRINCIPLES

1: Organize for Perception

2: Direct the Eyes

3: Reduce Realism

4: Make the Abstract Concrete

5: Clarify Complexity

6: Charge It Up

"For design is about the making of things: things that are memorable and have presence in the world of mind. It makes demand upon our ability both to consolidate information as knowledge and to deploy it imaginatively to create purpose in the pursuit of fresh information."

KROME BARRATT, *Logic & Design in Art, Science & Mathematics*

Jean-Manuel Duvivier,
Jean-Manuel Duvivier
Illustration, Belgium

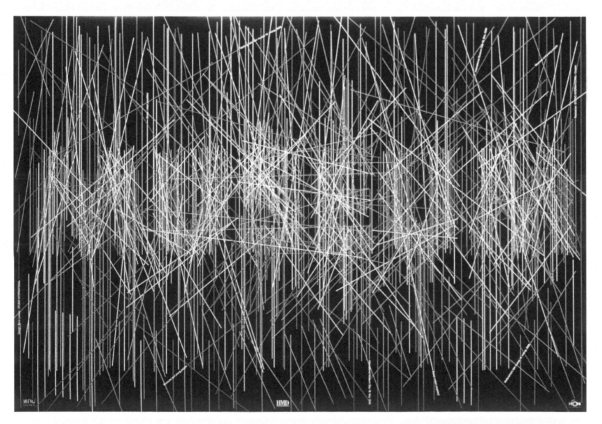

Our visual intelligence enables us to see the word museum in this poster, which is constructed using straight lines and three simple colors.

Boris Ljubicic, Studio International, *Croatia*

ORGANIZE FOR PERCEPTION

"Vision is not a mechanical recording of elements, but rather the apprehension of significant structural patterns."

RUDOLF ARNHEIM *Art and Visual Perception*

Our visual system is remarkably agile. It helps us perform tasks necessary for survival in our environment. Yet we are able to apply these same processes to perceiving and understanding pictures. For example, without conscious effort we scan our surroundings to extract information about what is "out there," noting if there is anything of importance in the environment. Similarly, without conscious effort we scan a picture to acquire information, noting if there is anything of importance in the visual display. All of this occurs effortlessly, before we have consciously focused our attention.

The processes associated with early vision, called preattentive processing, have generated a great deal of research that can be applied to graphic communication and design. By understanding how viewers initially analyze an image, designers can structure and organize a graphic so it complements human perception. The goal is to shift information acquisition to the perceptual system to speed up visual information processing. This is equivalent to giving a runner a head start before the race begins.

Early vision rapidly scans a wide visual field to detect features in the environment. This first phase of vision is driven by the attributes of an object (the visual stimulus), rather than a conscious selection of where to look. Upon detecting the presence of visual features, we extract raw perceptual data to get an overall impression. This data is most likely "mapped into different areas in the brain, each of which is specialized to analyze a different property."[1] From this rapid visual analysis, we create some form of rough mental sketch or representation.[2]

Later, vision makes use of this representation to know where to focus our attention. It is under the influence of our preexisting knowledge, expectations, and goals. For example, using the low-level visual system of early vision, we might register the shapes and color features we see in a graphic. Later, vision directs our attention to those same features and uses knowledge stored in long-term memory to recognize and identify the shapes as people. These two stages of vision form a complex and little understood interaction that provides us with a unique visual intelligence.

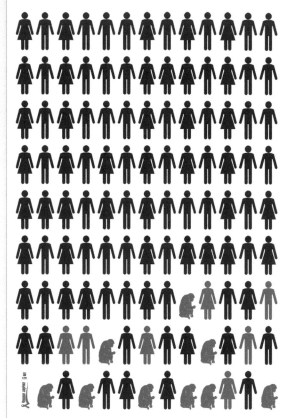

▲ Designed as a picto-graph, this poster (left) conveys the loss of life from AIDS by taking advantage of our ability to quickly detect differences.

▲ In this poster (right), the designer uses a pictograph to depict the relationship between the source of HIV and humans.

Maziar Zand,
M. Zand Studio, *Iran*

Parallel Processing

The initial visual analysis of preattentive processing is rapid because vast arrays of neurons are working in parallel. We typically detect features with low-level vision at a rate faster than ten milliseconds per item.[3] To better understand the parallel nature of early visual processing, search for the red symbols in this AIDS awareness poster (above, left). Rather than perform a serial search through every single figure in the graphic, our low-level visual system immediately perceives the red figures among the field of black ones. These features tend to pop out and grab our attention.

Serial Processing

In contrast, later vision, which is guided by our selec-tive attention, performs visual operations more slowly through an item-by-item, or serial, search. Trying to detect just the red female symbols in the more com-plex field of this second AIDS awareness poster is a slower, more laborious process (above, right). Because the female symbol shares a color property with two other symbols, red is no longer a unique feature.

In these illustrations of an underwater landslide for Scientific American, *vivid textures enable us to distinguish between land and sea. The dynamic texture of the ocean projects a sense of the oncoming tsunami.*

**David Fierstein,
David Fierstien Illustration,
Animation, & Design,**
United States

Perceptual Organization

The significance of early vision is that it organizes our perceptions and gives structure and coherence to sensory data. Without perceptual organization a picture might appear to be a chaotic set of disconnected dots and lines. During our preconscious visual analysis, we perform two primary types of perceptual organization—discriminating primitive features and grouping visual information into meaningful units.

Primitive features are the unique properties that allow a visual element to pop out of an image during a search, because they are the most salient or prominent. Examples of primitive features are color, motion, orientation, and size. We later merge these features into meaningful objects through the guidance of our focused attention. Primitive features also allow us to discriminate between textures, which we see as regions of similar features on a surface. When we see the discontinuation of a feature, we perceive it as a border or the edge of a surface. This process, known as texture segregation, helps us identify objects and forms and is a related preattentive process.

Whereas the detection and discrimination of primitive features tell us about the properties of an image, the preattentive process of grouping tells us which individual parts go together. Before consciously paying attention, we organize sensory information into groups or perceptual units. This provides information about the relationship of elements to each other and to the whole. A basic perceptual unit can be thought of as any group of marks among which our attention is not divided. A simple example of this concept occurs when we perceive a square. We tend to see the whole shape of the square rather than four straight lines intersecting at right angles. Application of the grouping concept can help a designer ensure that viewers perceive visual information in meaningful units.

Using visual language that speaks to a viewer's preattentive visual processes—discrimination of primitive features and grouping parts into wholes—enables a designer to quickly communicate, grab attention, and provide meaning. This principle can be applied to informational and instructional graphics, promotional materials, warning signs and wayfinding, information visualizations, and technical interfaces.

▶ *This design demonstrates the principle of grouping, in which elements that are close together are seen as one perceptual unit. In an instant, our early perceptual system groups the circles into arrows.*

Veronica Neira Torres,
Nicaragua

▼ *In this identity design for a type foundry in Japan, the overall shape takes precedence over the smaller elements from which it is composed.*

Shinnoske Sugisaki,
Shinnoske Inc., *Japan*

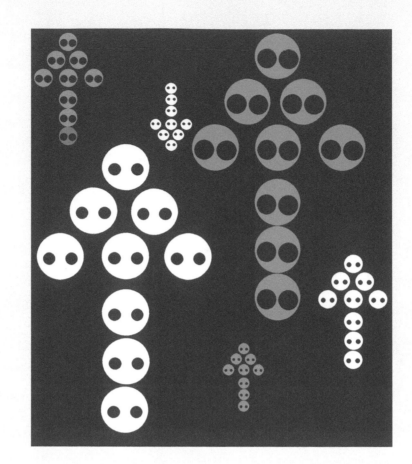

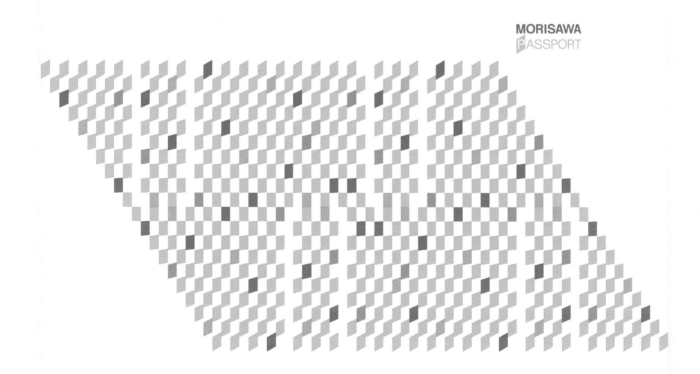

MORISAWA
PASSPORT

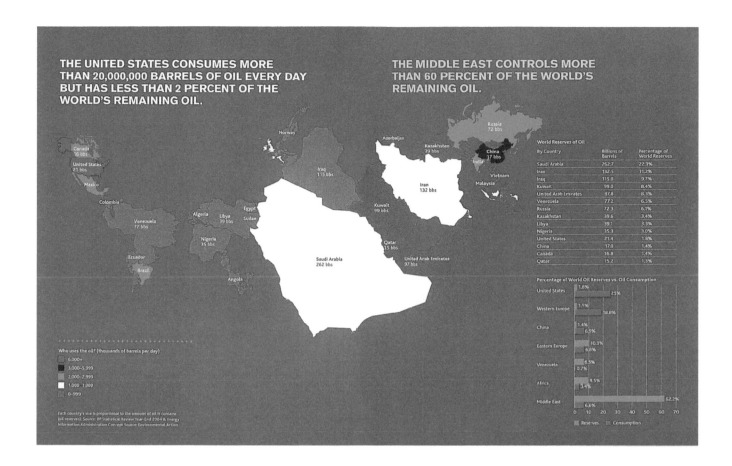

Boosting Cognition

Preattentive processes are initiated when something new appears in our visual field but is outside of our conscious attention. For example, a person may be walking along a city street and perceive the shape of a sculpture in front of a building without consciously paying attention to it. Preattentive processes screen this sensory data so that its meaning is subconsciously recognized. If the person has a particular interest in sculpture, the sensory data is passed on to higher processes so that the sculpture will come under the scrutiny of conscious attention. Sensory data that is not used for further processing simply decays.

Designing the visual structure of a graphic to take advantage of preattentive processes sets the stage for successful comprehension. A graphic's structure can influence how an audience perceives, recognizes, and interprets a picture. As educational psychologist William Winn notes, "Comprehension succeeds or fails to the extent that the information organized by preattentive processes can be assimilated to existing schemata (mental representations), or that schemata can be altered to accommodate that information."[4] This is because the bottom-up flow of information initiated by sensory input quickly influences and interacts with the top-down flow of information guided by our preexisting knowledge and expectations.

For example, emphasizing a primitive feature in a concert promotion poster, such as using bold colors, will quickly attract the audience to the essential message. Accentuating the size of important areas on a map will ensure the audience accurately understands the information. Grouping related information in a graph will help viewers know which data should be compared. Organizing a graphic's structure for early vision can have a domino effect on later vision, reducing the demands placed on working memory, facilitating interpretation, and ultimately enhancing comprehension. This approach to design should also speed information acquisition. When the audience is given a cognitive kick start, the intended message is more likely to be clear at the beginning of the process and there will be fewer opportunities for miscomprehension.

In this map showing oil-consuming nations, high-contrast colors and simplified flat regions enable the viewer to get a sense of the information early in the vision process.

Jennifer Lopardo,
Schwartz Brand Group,
United States

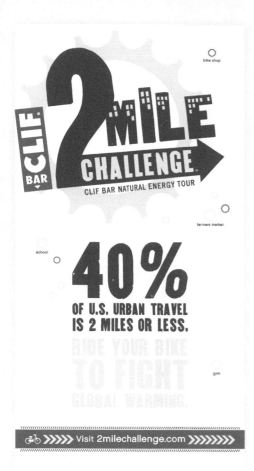

The primitive features of size and color in the title of this 2-mile-challenge poster create immediate emphasis and focus.

**Mark Boediman,
Clif Bar & Company,**
United States

In this three-dimensional visualization of consumer electronics spending for Wired magazine, the individual bars with proximity and similar color form into their own perceptual group. The individual groups form into one whole graph because of proximity and preexisting knowledge of how to read bar graphs.

Arno Ghelfi, l'atelier starno,
United States

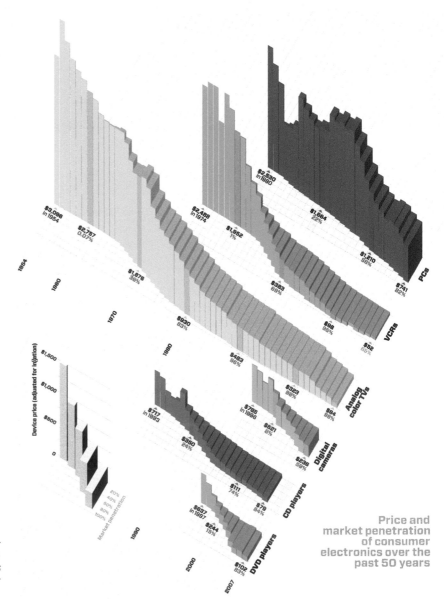

Price and market penetration of consumer electronics over the past 50 years

Applying the Principle

Accommodating our preattentive visual processes through design requires thinking in terms of how the visual information will be detected, organized, and grouped. Fortunately, it is not difficult to predispose the viewer to a well-organized visual structure. The low-level visual system is continuously seeking a stimulus in the environment to provide focus and draw the eyes. When a design calls for quick recognition and response, graphics that emphasize one pronounced primitive feature, such as line orientation or shape, can be placed against a background with few distractors. This primitive feature will be detected during a preattentive rapid scan.

When a project requires an emphasis on aesthetic expression, the designer can take advantage of how early vision segregates features into textures. Using texture as a prominent feature can add visual depth and complexity to a graphic. And because we are adept at detecting texture differences, this can offload some of the processing normally placed on working memory to the perceptual system.

The low-level visual system also seeks to configure parts of a graphic into a whole unit when they are close together or have similar features. One example is how we perceive elements that have a common boundary as one unit. From a compositional perspective, grouping provides opportunities for emphasis, balance, and unity in a design.

By organizing the structure of a design through emphasis of primitive features or through grouping individual elements, viewers will quickly detect the organization of the graphic. Many designers intuitively use these organizing principles, but an awareness of the audience's preattentive capabilities is a way to intentionally improve the communication quality of any informative message.

The way we preattentively organize textures into shapes can be clearly seen in this visualization of apoptosis (cell death).

Drew Berry, Walter and Eliza Hall Institute of Medical Research, *Australia*

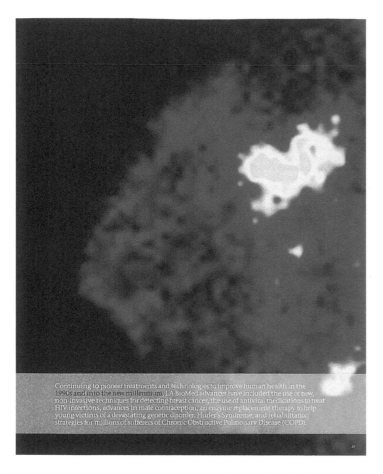

Continuing to pioneer treatments and technologies to improve human health in the 1990s and into the new millennium, LA BioMed advances have included the use of new, non-invasive techniques for detecting breast cancer, the use of antiviral medications to treat HIV infections, advances in male contraception, an enzyme replacement therapy to help young victims of a devastating genetic disorder, Hurler's Syndrome, and rehabilitation strategies for millions of sufferers of Chronic Obstructive Pulmonary Disease (COPD).

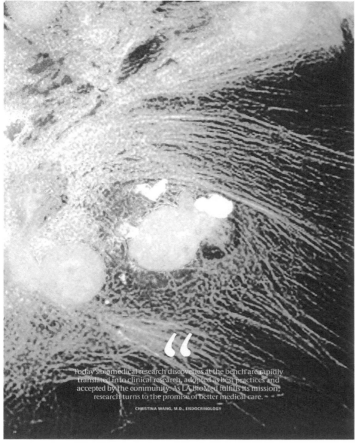

"Today's biomedical research discoveries at the bench are rapidly translated into clinical research, adopted as best practices and accepted by the community. As LA BioMed fulfills its mission, research turns to the promise of better medical care."

CHRISTINA WANG, M.D., ENDOCRINOLOGY

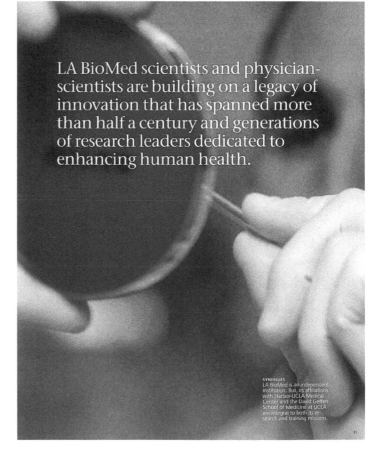

LA BioMed scientists and physician-scientists are building on a legacy of innovation that has spanned more than half a century and generations of research leaders dedicated to enhancing human health.

SYNERGIES
LA BioMed is an independent institution. But, its affiliations with Harbor-UCLA Medical Center and the David Geffen School of Medicine at UCLA are integral to both its research and training missions.

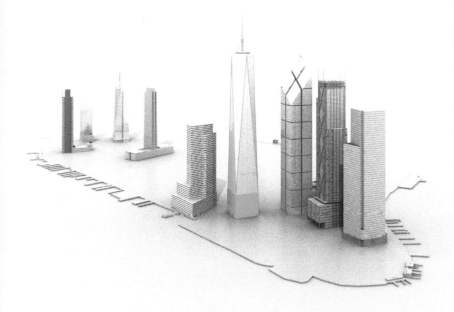

▶ *In this college campus
map, outlined green areas
accentuate regions within
the campus. This helps us
group the buildings within
each region, facilitating the
use of the map.*

David Horton and
Amy Lebow,
Philographica,
United States

◀ *The photographs and imagery in this annual report
use an aesthetic approach
to texture segregation,
communicating a sense
of medical competence
for a biomedical research
institute.*

Jane Lee,
IE Design &
Communications,
United States

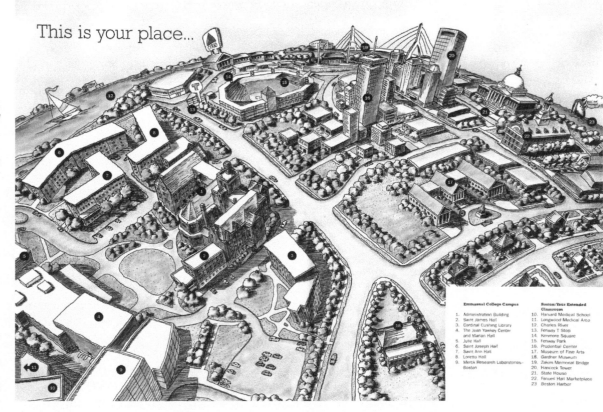

This is your place...

Emmanuel College Campus	Boston: Your Extended Classroom
1. Administration Building	10. Harvard Medical School
2. Saint James Hall	11. Longwood Medical Area
3. Cardinal Cushing Library	12. Charles River
4. The Jean Yawkey Center and Marian Hall	13. Fenway T Stop
5. Julie Hall	14. Kenmore Square
6. Saint Joseph Hall	15. Fenway Park
7. Saint Ann Hall	16. Prudential Center
8. Loretto Hall	17. Museum of Fine Arts
9. Merck Research Laboratories– Boston	18. Gardner Museum
	19. Zakim Memorial Bridge
	20. Hancock Tower
	21. State House
	22. Faneuil Hall Marketplace
	23. Boston Harbor

FEATURES THAT POP OUT

The scientific term *pop out* aptly expresses how we perceive the most unique and conspicuous primitive features in a graphic during early vision. Before consciously paying attention, we rapidly analyze a graphic and register the features that pop out. The purpose is to get an accurate reading of whatever is important in our visual field. After a brief exposure, a feature with prominence or salience is more likely to attract our conscious attention in later vision than an inconspicuous feature.

Primitive features that both pop out and are most likely to control later attention include color, motion, orientation, size, depth, tilt, shape, line terminators (where a line ends), closure (an enclosed space), topological properties (such as a dot inside a circle), and line curvature.[5] Any of these features can be emphasized to establish visual prominence.

To perceive a feature as salient, we must be able to discriminate it from everything else. Through visual discrimination, we determine whether a property is the same as or different from other properties. "Two properties must differ by a large enough proportion or they will not be distinguished," writes professor and researcher Stephen Kosslyn in *Clear and to the Point*. Kosslyn explains that differences between two visual properties are not always detected because a difference is registered as a change in our brain cell activity. If the change in neuronal activity isn't strong, it might be confused with noise in the system, which is a natural occurrence in the brain. To effectively promote visual discrimination, therefore, the differences between two visual properties must be great enough to cause sufficient brain cell activity.

This is particularly relevant during preattentive processing, when discrimination occurs without our conscious awareness. Using two shapes with very different orientations or using two objects of very different sizes will result in effective discrimination. In general, make a primitive feature prominent; don't leave it up to the viewer to make fine or subtle visual discriminations.

▲ *In this poster commemorating the Democratic rebellion in Ecuador, the gestured hands pop out during preattentive processing because of color contrast.*

Antonio Mena,
Antonio Mena Design,
Ecuador

▶ *In these animation frames for the Croatian Architects Association, the letter A appears to pop out because of its contrasting color, shape, orientation, and novelty.*

Boris Ljubicic,
Studio International,
Croatia

اول سلام بعدا کلام ... رنگ پنجم برگزار می‌کند: از ته سوزن رد می‌شه از در دروازه نه . آش کشک خاله‌ته بخوری پایه نخوری پایه . آب از سر چشمه گل آلوده . آتش که گرفت خشک و تر می‌سوزه . آدم پابند کلاه خود را قاضی کند

ضرب‌المثل‌های ایرانی از سیاهی بالاتر، رنگی نیست . آش نخورده و دهن سوخته

سومین نمایشگاه تایپوگرافی ایرانی ۱۳۸۵

۱۸ تا ۳۱ خرداد، گشایش: پنجشنبه ۱۸ خرداد ساعت ۱۶ تا ۲۰

نگارخانه‌ی تهران، خیابان قدس، ضلع شرقی دانشگاه تهران

همزمان در نقش‌خانه‌ی حوزه‌ی هنری اصفهان و نگارخانه‌ی وصال شیراز

... به همراه نمایشگاه گزیده‌ی روی جلدهای بهزاد گلپایگانی.

Iranian Proverbs, the 5th Color's Third Iranian Typography Exhibition 2006 . Tehran Gallery (gallery@ut.ac.ir), East of the University of Tehran, Qods Street . June 8-21, 2006 . Telephone: (021) 61 12 8495 - 44 41 0959. Opening: Thursday, June 8, 4-8 pm. Visiting hours: Saturday to Wednesday 2-8 pm . Thursday & Friday 4-8 pm; Vesal Gallery, Shiraz . with cooperation of The Ministry of Culture in Fars Province and Mushkat Co.; Naqshkhaneh, Isfahan with cooperation of Art Center of Isfahan Province, Markazi Graphics. www.5thcolor.com

◄ *In this elegant array of Iranian proverbs, the designer uses color contrast to ensure that the salient proverbs in white are the most prominent.*

Majid Abassi,
Did Graphics, *Iran*

▶ *This fifth-anniversary advertisement poster for a popular club exploits the primitive feature of depth to create an extreme pop-out effect.*

Sorin Bechira,
X3 Studios, *Romania*

TEXTURE SEGREGATION

One of our first responses to the influx of sensory data is to organize primitive features into segmented regions of texture. In pictures, texture can be thought of as the optical grain of a surface. We unconsciously unify objects into regions that are bound by an abrupt change in texture. We perceive this change as defining where one object, or form, ends and where another begins. Once we segregate a region into textures, we then organize it into shapes or objects that we identify with conscious attention. Our knowledge of texture patterns helps us to identify objects.

Through texture segregation, we also separate foreground from background. When we perceive a difference between two textures, the textured area is typically seen as the figure or dominant shape and the area without texture is typically seen as the ground or neutral form. The relationship between figure and ground is a prerequisite for perceiving shapes and eventually identifying objects. Color and size, also contribute to the figure—ground perception.

Just as primitive features can induce the pop-out effect, so can regions of texture. For instance, when a surface texture is composed of uncomplicated primitive features, such as line orientation or shapes, it's

easy to distinguish the texture from its surroundings. When a form with a complex texture is placed on a busy background, the texture is harder to discriminate and loses its pop-out effect.[6]

Texture perception also presents spatial information by providing cues for depth perception.[7] The texture gradient on a surface contributes to our perception of how near or far an object appears. When the texture's pattern on a surface is perceived as denser and finer, an object appears to recede in the distance; when the pattern is perceived as less dense and coarser, the object appears closer.

Our ability to segregate textures during early vision is key to understanding the meaning of a graphic. An analysis of texture shows that it is constructed from contrast, orientation, and element repetition. Designers can manipulate these individual properties to convey meaning. Texture can be expressive, capturing the essence of an object or mood. Texture can also simulate surface qualities to help us identify and recognize objects. When given appropriate emphasis, texture can become more prominent than shape and line.

▲ *In these three-dimensional displays to promote tourism, the designer used organic textures to express the natural beauty of Croatia. Textures are easily perceived in the early vision process, which makes this example so compelling.*

Boris Ljubicic, Studio International, *Croatia*

▶ *One can almost feel the gooey, melting textures in this poster. The powerful type pops out even against the high-energy colors and shapes because of the contrasts in color and texture.*

Adrian Labos, X3 Studios, *Romania*

◀ This exploded view of a processor setup is a good example of how texture segmentation helps us perceive the figure—ground relationship. The glossy, smooth surfaces of objects in the foreground contrast with the duller receding objects in the background to create this effect.

Christopher Short,
United States

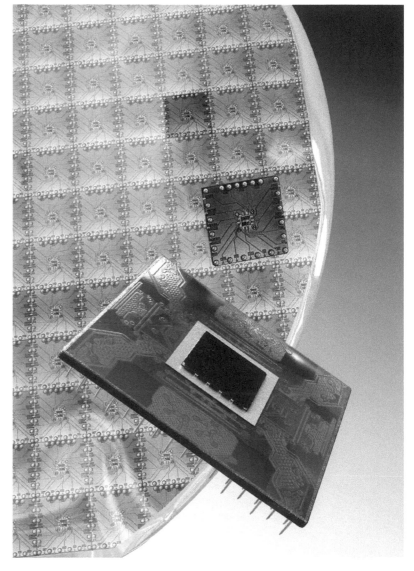

▶ In this rendering of solder-based products, the difference in texture density between the chip in the foreground and those in the background provides cues that help us perceive three-dimensional depth. As an object recedes in space, its texture appears denser.

Christopher Short,
United States

The atmosphere of Tokyo is expressed through the busy textures and buzzing patterns in this poster advertising a café. Even in a dense design, the varied textures make it easy to perceive objects.

Ian Lynam, Ian Lynam Creative Direction & Design, *Japan*

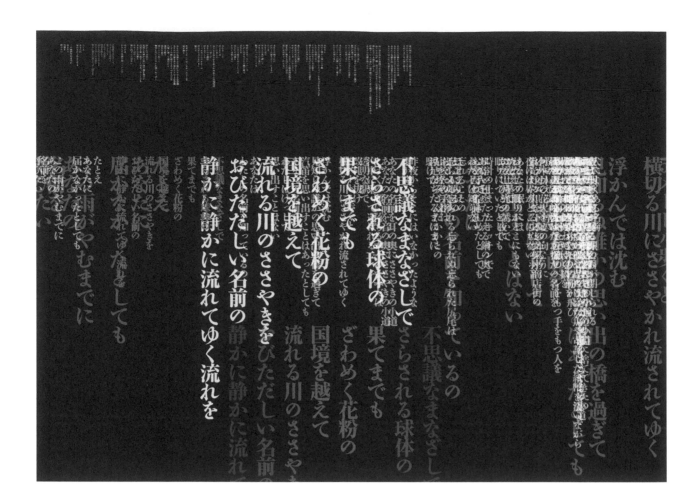

Texture with Text

An appealing way to create texture is through the creative use of type, regardless of whether the type can be read. When type is repeated, varied, layered, or manipulated and altered, it creates an optical grain that conveys meaning. Often, the meaning is expressed on two levels: the words formed by the type communicate a literal message and the texture conveys meaning through design. Using type as texture is particularly appropriate in text-associated themes that relate to books, poetry, and language.

To create textures that are easy to discriminate, use a texture with a simple distinguishing homogenous feature separated from a contrasting region. There should be an easily perceptible difference where two objects or forms meet. Textures that are easy to discriminate might include those with different line orientations, contrasting rhythms of pattern, and regions composed of high-contrast patterns surrounded by regions of low contrast. The phenomenon of texture segregation provides many possibilities for communicating a message early in the perceptual process.

▲ *Thick layers of overlapping type create poetic textures in this work for a collaboration exhibition by a poet and typographers.*

Shinnoske Sugisaki, Shinnoske Inc., *Japan*

▶ *In this poster to commemorate the 200th year of the first reading room in Croatia, type is an appropriate design element for a textured background as it curves and bends through space. The glasses and their shadow emerge from the number 200.*

Boris Ljubicic, Studio International, *Croatia*

ZADAR, 1807. – 2007.
200 GODINA

Pokrovitelj:
Hrvatska akademija znanosti i umjetnosti

Organizatori svečanosti:
Nacionalna i sveučilišna knjižnica u Zagrebu
Gradska knjižnica Zadar

Suorganizatori:
Grad Zadar
Sveučilište u Zadru
Općina Novigrad

Program:
Petak, 29. lipnja 2007.

ZADAR
10.00 sati Gradska loža, Svečanost obilježavanja 200. obljetnice prve hrvatske čitaonice
Predstavu Govorite li hrvatski? izvodi Joško Ševo

11.00 sati Narodni trg, Glazbeno-scenska svečanost
Scenu Perivoj od slave iz Planina Petra Zoranića izvodi Kazalište lutaka Zadar

NOVIGRAD
12.30 sati Otvaranje Knjižnice i čitaonice Novigrad
13.00 sati prigodni program

Obrazloženje:
Uz grad Zadar ove, 2007. godine vezuje se iznimno značajna obljetnica za hrvatsku knjigu i osobito kulturu čitanja u Hrvata. Naime, pred točno dvije stotine godina, odnosno koncem lipnja godine 1807., u Zadru bilježimo važan nadnevak za hrvatsku čitaonicu, jer povijest: u tom je gradu prošlogodišnjim kada se u Zadru obilježila 200. obljetnice prve hrvatske čitaonice Družba od štenja. Ova dva vrijedna... godišnji jubilej u nekom se sp... će povezati s onim prošlogodišnjim kada se u Zadru obilježila 200. obljetnice... novina na ... a ve u našim krajevima, uz ostalo pove... koja se nalazila u ...kulturološka p...tka, prvih iz razdob... je u ... Kraljskog Dalmatina što je izlazio od 1806. do 1810. ... čitaonice i nje... čelu oba projekta... predsjednik. On uprav... Dalmatina Bartolo Renincasa inci... podnesak dalmat... vladi, već idućeg mjeseca, to je u ime gru... nske up... ... naliu 1807., u... na hrva... čitaonica – Družba od šte... vila i... ...ivanje čitaonice u Za... 26. svib... zadarskih intelektualca Vicenzo Dandolo don... luku kojom odobrava... janskom: Gabinetto di le... ra)
Tako je, 30... neralni provid... otvoru na prva ja... ristiti u vrhu promicanja hrvatske knj... će kulture čitanja! Zašto... no – i taj bi va... ipnja 1807., valjalo buduće k... vatska? Jednostavno, njezina je... bila da bude upravo i sa... uprav tu čitao... dnevak valjalo... razna Casina, pa tako i zadarski ... nobile, osnovan godine... 750. čitaonica, a ne nešto drugo... kitili časnim pitetom... užba od štenja i redovito je prim... ostalu recentnu periodi..., i prve Dalje, čitaonica iz 1807. nosila je hr... ko... ika na hrvatskom jeziku tada nije... ba prema tome zadarsk... Družba hrvatske novine Kraljski Dalmatin. Drugih... alo. Ta je ustanova osnovana po... sa slična društva za... micanje od štenja nije mogla nabavljati ono što... Lesegesellschaft, Lekturkabine... su se najprije p... vile u knjige i čitanja (Leseckabinett, Cabinet de... m europskim zemljama. Čita... avilima up... lo na svrhu Engleskoj, zatim u Francuskoj i drugim ra... e, te posebno književna peri... a koju su... nabavljati. društva, a u njima se i navode brojne knjige... je mnoge dobila donaci... nenadmašivu Diderotovu Enciklopediju. Čitaonica je posjedovala i velik broj knjiga... Stipan Štefić darova... gradana. Medu darovateljima posebno je vrijedan doprinos knjižnici čitaonice dao Za... čitanja tu su ve... mnogi korisni razgovori o raznim pitanjima U njoj su se okupljali mnogi hrvatski intelektualci... žba od šte... važno žarište kulturnog i političkog mnijenja svekolikog narodnog života, pa je zasigurno hrvatska... se moglo dobiti na čitanje bili su, uz talijanske i ne samo grada, već i cijele pokrajine. U fondu knjiga č... st. s područja religijske kulture i francuske, i brojni hrvatski naslovi, od kojih i oni tiskani u Zadru početkom XIX. književnosti, politike, prava i poljodjelstva. Čitaonica je bila smještena u sklopu kompleksa samostana sv. Krševana.
Stoga, doista smatram važnim podsjetiti na važan jubilej kojega valja ove godine obilježiti: 200 GODINA PRVE HRVATSKE ČITAONICE, i predložiti da se taj jubilej prigodno obilježi 30. lipnja 2007., na sam dan dvjestote obljetnice, čime će, prigodnim svečanostima i otvaranjem nove knjižnice i čitaonice u Novigradu, ojačiti javna svijest o potrebi jačanja KULTURE ČITANJA I PROMICANJA KNJIGE kao nezaobilaznoj pretpostavki ostvarenja strateškog cilja naše države – da Hrvatska postane "zemlja znanja".

prva
hrvatska
čitaonica
družba
od štenja

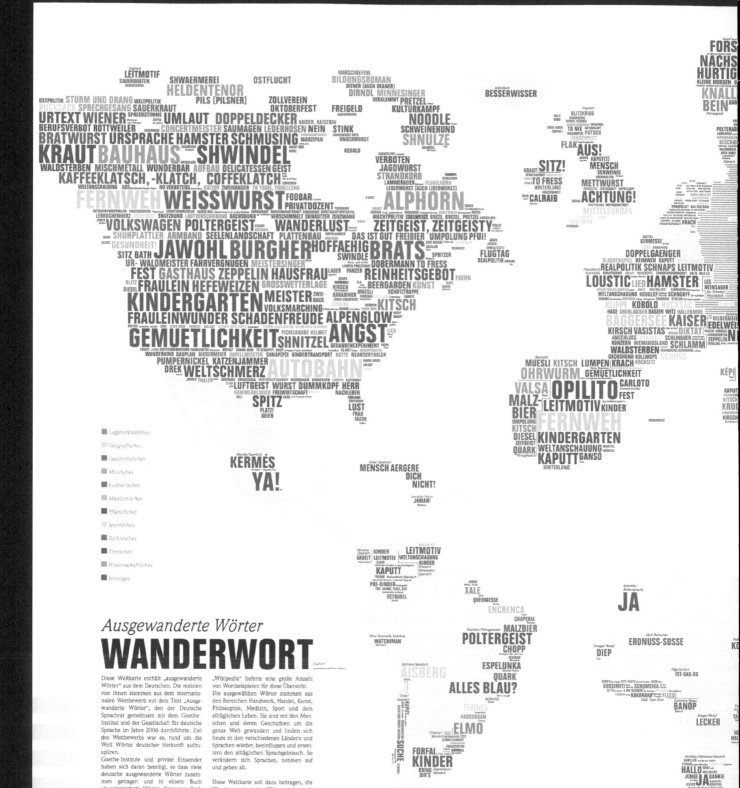

Ausgewanderte Wörter

WANDERWORT

Diese Weltkarte enthält „ausgewanderte Wörter" aus dem Deutschen. Die meisten von ihnen stammen aus dem internationalen Wettbewerb mit dem Titel „Ausgewanderte Wörter", den der Deutsche Sprachrat gemeinsam mit dem Goethe-Institut und der Gesellschaft für deutsche Sprache im Jahre 2006 durchführte. Ziel des Wettbewerbs war es, rund um die Welt Wörter deutscher Herkunft aufzuspüren.

Goethe-Institute und private Einsender haben sich daran beteiligt, so dass viele deutsche ausgewanderte Wörter zusammengetragen und in einem Buch (Ausgewanderte Wörter. Hrsg. von Prof. Dr. Jutta Limbach. Hueber Verlag 2006) veröffentlicht wurden. Jetzt nutzen wir diese Sammlung für eine Weltkarte besonderer Art. Auch die freie Enzyklopädie

„Wikipedia" lieferte eine große Anzahl von Wortbeispielen für diese Übersicht. Die ausgewählten Wörter stammen aus den Bereichen Handwerk, Handel, Kunst, Philosophie, Medizin, Sport und dem alltäglichen Leben. Sie sind mit den Menschen und deren Geschichten um die ganze Welt gewandert und finden sich heute in den verschiedenen Ländern und Sprachen wieder, beeinflussen und erweitern den alltäglichen Sprachgebrauch. So verändern sich Sprachen, nehmen auf und geben ab.

Diese Weltkarte soll dazu beitragen, die Wanderung deutscher Wörter nachzuvollziehen, ihre weltweite Verbreitung zu zeigen und über Veränderungen in ihrer Struktur zu informieren, die sie auf ihrer Reise erfahren haben.

GOETHE-INSTITUT

The repetition of type creates texture and geographical forms in this information graphic depicting German words used around the world.

Jan Schwochow,
Katharina Erfurth, and
Sebastian Piesker,
Golden Section Graphics,
Germany

GROUPING

Understanding where objects are located and how they are arranged in space is essential for moving through the environment. Perhaps that's why spatial organization is a fundamental operation of preattentive perception. The low-level visual system has a tendency to organize elements into coherent groups depending on how they are arranged and where they are located. This preattentive configuration of parts into wholes lets us know that a set of elements in a picture is associated and should be viewed as one unit. During later cognitive processing, the relationship among the perceptual units and their relationship to the whole becomes valuable information that conveys meaning in a graphic.

The perceptual organization of parts into wholes is based on theories promoted by the Gestalt psychologists in the early twentieth century. Their principles demonstrated that under the right conditions, combining parts into wholes takes precedence over seeing the parts themselves. A few of the Gestalt principles that determine whether a whole unit or its parts have visual precedence include proximity, similarity, and symmetry. Elements that exhibit proximity are close to each other in space or time. We perceive elements with proximity as belonging to the same group. We also perceive elements that have similar visual characteristics, such as shape and texture, as one unit. The symmetry principle states that we configure elements into a whole when they form a symmetrical figure rather than an asymmetrical one.

In the past few decades, research in the area of preattentive perception has added to our body of knowledge about the grouping phenomenon. These findings have extended the factors that are thought to influence our natural tendency to group parts into wholes. These newer principles include the concepts of boundary and uniform connectedness. The boundary principle states that if a set of elements is enclosed with a boundary, such as a circle, we group those elements together.[8] Thus, when a boundary encloses a set of items, we perceive this as a unit even though we would perceive the items as separate without the boundary. Connectedness describes our tendency to perceive elements as one unit when they are physically connected by a line or common edge.[9] This is generally how we perceive diagrams.

A design that arranges elements into meaningful units will influence how well the audience organizes, interprets, and comprehends a visual message. Grouping elements enhances the meaning of a graphic, because viewers know that clustered elements are associated. Visual search is speedier as a result of grouping because it is faster to find information that is placed in one location. Grouping elements together can also make new features emerge. For instance, a set of lines radiating from a center point might emerge as a Sun form. Designers can take advantage of the conditions that evoke grouping—proximity, similarity, symmetry, bounding, and connectedness—to facilitate visual communication.

Dining

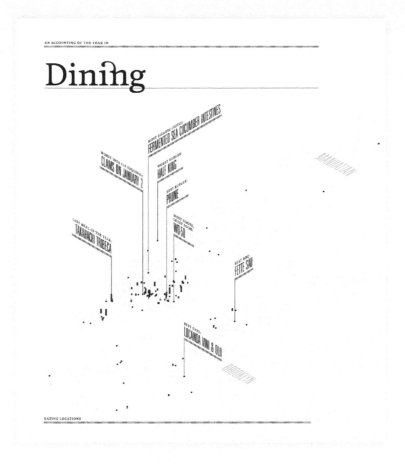

EATING LOCATIONS

Drinking

DRINKING LOCATIONS

In this visualization of dining and drinking data from the Feltron Personal Annual Report, grouping occurs by visual plane—the blue line segments that form the streets create a horizontal group and the street signs form a vertical group.

Nicholas Feltron, Megafone,
United States

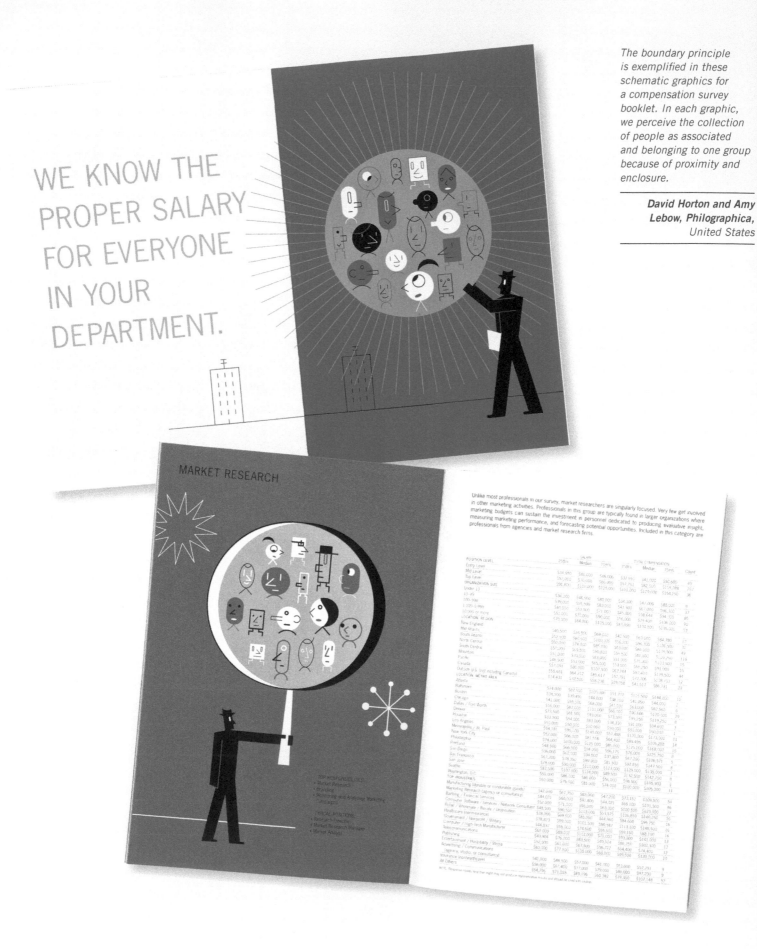

WE KNOW THE
PROPER SALARY
FOR EVERYONE
IN YOUR
DEPARTMENT.

The boundary principle
is exemplified in these
schematic graphics for
a compensation survey
booklet. In each graphic,
we perceive the collection
of people as associated
and belonging to one group
because of proximity and
enclosure.

**David Horton and Amy
Lebow, Philographica,**
United States

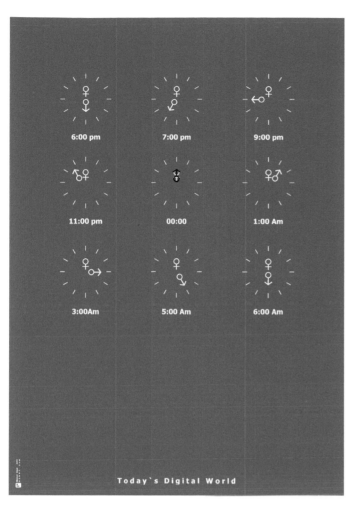

Today's Digital World

In this poster we perceive the circle that forms the clock face as more prominent than the individual lines. Soon after, we perceive the male and female symbols as the hands of the clock.

Maziar Zand,
M. Zand Studio, Iran

This graphic illustrates the concept of setting boundaries for children. Clearly, there is one element per group.

Angela Edwards,
United States

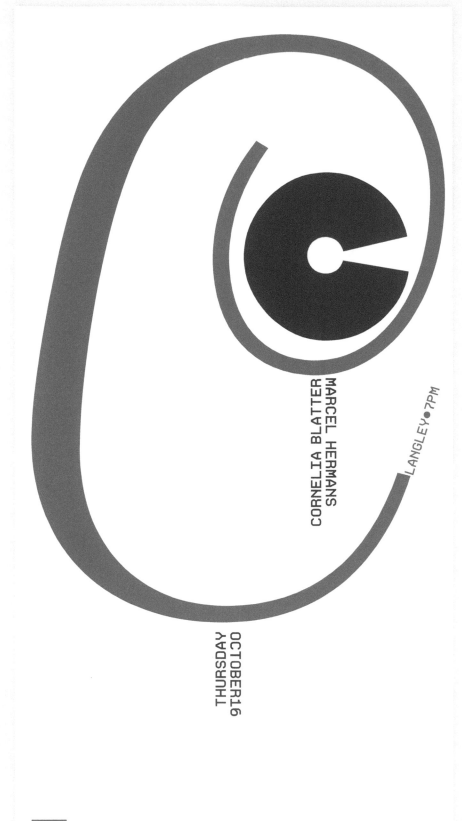

MARCEL HERMANS
CORNELIA BLATTER

LANGLEY●7PM

THURSDAY
OCTOBER16

LYNAM

This poster for a graphic design lecture directs the eyes to the important information along a spiraled path.

Ian Lynam, Ian Lynam Creative Direction & Design, Japan

PRINCIPLE 2 | DIRECT THE EYES

"If the viewer's eyes are permitted to wander at will
 through a work, then the artist has lost control."

JACK FREDERICK MEYERS *The Language of Visual Art*

Although we think of the brain as a system that can process massive amounts of data in parallel, the quantity of input coursing through the optic nerve every second is actually more than the brain can squeeze into conscious awareness. Thus, we shift our visual attention from one location to another in a serial manner to extract the information we want. An interesting feature in the environment may attract our eyes, or an internal goal may direct our attention. Likewise, when viewing a graphic we attend to what is most compelling. Prominent features in a graphic compete for our attention, so if we are not given visual direction we may dwell on the wrong information or become overwhelmed with too much information. To find meaning in what we see, we must selectively attend to what is important. A designer or illustrator can assist this process by purposefully guiding the viewer's eyes through the structure of a graphic. This is one of the more essential techniques visual communicators can employ to ensure that viewers comprehend their intended message.

Directing the eyes serves two principal purposes—to steer the viewer's attention along a path according to the intended ranking order and to draw the viewer's attention to specific elements of importance. When our eyes scan a picture, we do not glance randomly here and there. Rather, our eyes fixate on the areas that are most interesting and informative. We tend to fixate on objects, skipping over the monotonous, empty, and uninformative areas. This is not surprising, since we are continually seeking meaning in what we see. But it does mean that each individual may scan the same picture in his or her unique way depending on what the person considers informative.

Nevertheless, there are common tendencies and biases in how we move our eyes around a picture. The initial scanning process often starts in the upper left corner as the point of entry. We are biased toward left-to-right eye movements and top-to-bottom movements. Diagonal movements of the eye are less frequent. After the first several fixations, we most likely get the "gist" of a picture, and then our eye movements are influenced by the picture's content, its horizontal or vertical orientation, and our own internal influences. It is debatable whether the directional orientation of one's writing and reading system contributes to eye movement preferences.

The eye movements of the viewer are critical to graphic comprehension. Unlike other forms of communication, such as reading, listening to music, or watching a movie, the time spent looking at a graphic can be remarkably brief. Purposefully directing the eyes makes it likely that a viewer will pick up the most relevant information within a limited time frame. The designer can guide the viewer's eyes by using techniques implicit to the composition, such as altering the position of an element or enhancing the sense of movement. The designer can also guide the viewer to specific information by signaling the location with visual cues like arrows, color, and captions. Visual cues do not carry the primary message; their function is to orient, point out, or highlight crucial information.

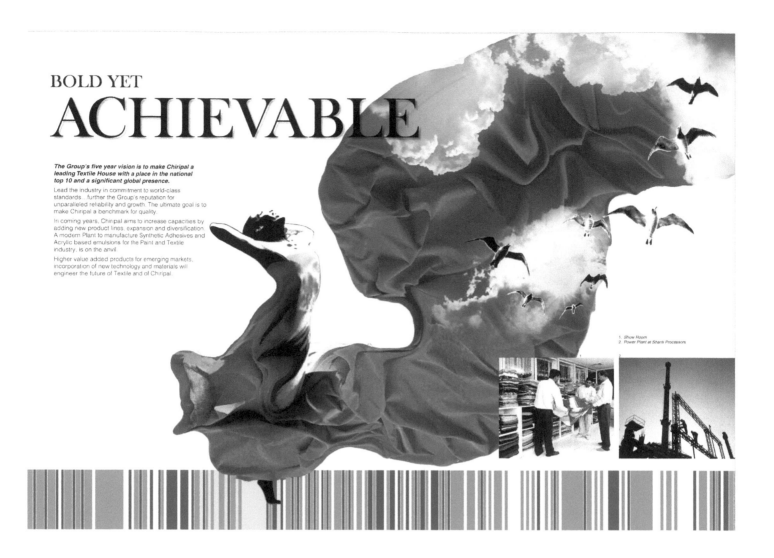

BOLD YET
ACHIEVABLE

The Group's five year vision is to make Chiripal a leading Textile House with a place in the national top 10 and a significant global presence.

Lead the industry in commitment to world-class standards ...further the Group's reputation for unparalleled reliability and growth. The ultimate goal is to make Chiripal a benchmark for quality.

In coming years, Chiripal aims to increase capacities by adding new product lines, expansion and diversification. A modern Plant to manufacture Synthetic Adhesives and Acrylic based emulsions for the Paint and Textile industry, is on the anvil.

Higher value added products for emerging markets, incorporation of new technology and materials will engineer the future of Textile and of Chiripal.

1. Show Room
2. Power Plant at Shanti Processors

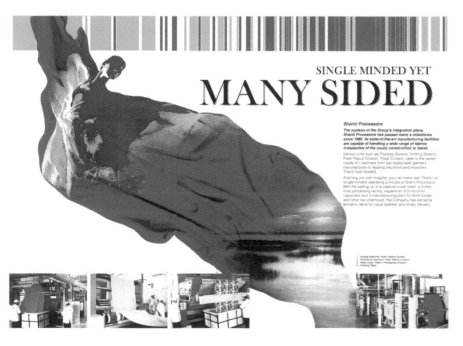

SINGLE MINDED YET
MANY SIDED

Shanti Processors
The nucleus of the Group's integration plans, Shanti Processors has passed many a milestones since 1985. Its state-of-the-art manufacturing facilities are capable of handling a wide range of fabrics irrespective of the count, construction or blend.

Various units such as Process Division, Knitting Division, Polar Fleece Division, Flock Division, cater to the varied needs of customers from top readymade garment manufacturers to leading exporters and importers. That's multi-faceted.

Anything you can imagine, you can make real. That's the single-minded operating principle at Shanti Processors. With the setting up of a captive power plant, a cotton knits processing facility, expansion of production capacities and a manufacturing plant for flock binder and other key chemicals, the Company has earned an enviable name for value addition and timely delivery.

1. Raising Machine, Polar Fleece Division
2. Embossing Machine, Polar Fleece Division
3. Rotary Dryer, Fabric Processing Division
4. Flocking Plant

In these promotional graphics for a textile house, bold fabrics attract attention and guide the eyes to the copy and photographs explaining the company's operations.

Sudarshan Dheer and Ashoomi Dholakia, Graphic Communication Concepts, India

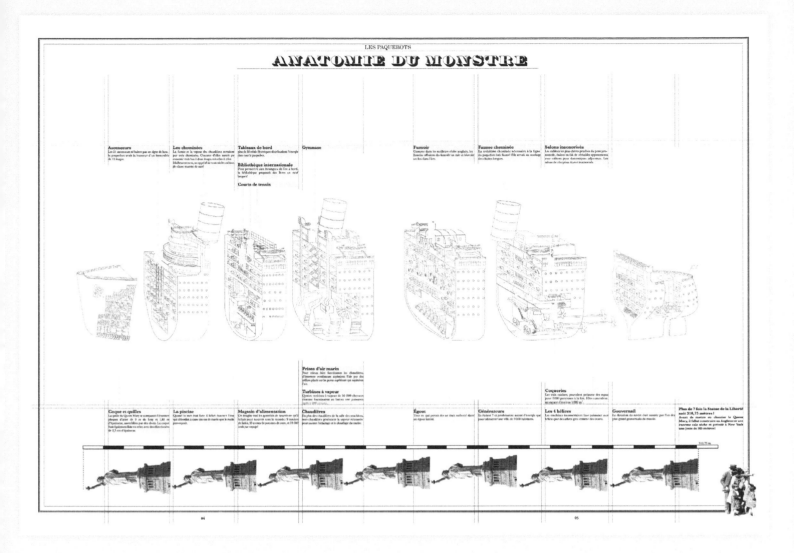

In this visual study of early transatlantic liners created for a student project, the pointing finger is a visual cue styled to fit the early era of transatlantic liners.

Chronopoulou Ekaterini, La Cambre School of Visual Art, Belgium

Both compositional and signaling techniques are effective at guiding the eyes because they make use of prominent features that are picked up early in the perceptual process. Even though eye movements are also controlled by the viewer's expectations and search goals, research shows that using compositional and signaling techniques to direct the eye can be quite effective. In one experiment that gauged eye movement based on compositional techniques, an experienced artist explained to the study authors precisely where he intended observers of his art to look. Observers were then allowed to view the art for thirty seconds while their eye movements were recorded. The scanning paths of the subjects proved to be in "considerable concordance" with what the artist intended.[1]

Signaling the viewer with arrows and color is known to be effective when used in explanatory and informational graphics. Studies show that when an area of a graphic is highlighted as it is being discussed, such as in a multimedia environment, viewers retain more information and are better able to transfer this information than those who did not view the highlighted visuals.[2] Other research has demonstrated that the use of arrows as pointing devices reduces the time it takes to search for specific information in a visual field.[3]

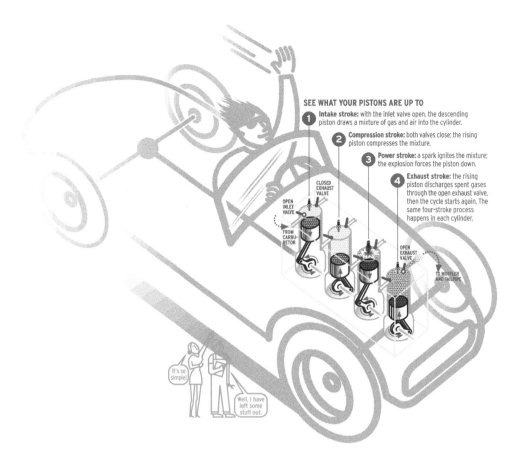

SEE WHAT YOUR PISTONS ARE UP TO

1. **Intake stroke:** with the inlet valve open, the descending piston draws a mixture of gas and air into the cylinder.

2. **Compression stroke:** both valves close; the rising piston compresses the mixture.

3. **Power stroke:** a spark ignites the mixture; the explosion forces the piston down.

4. **Exhaust stroke:** the rising piston discharges spent gases through the open exhaust valve, then the cycle starts again. The same four-stroke process happens in each cylinder.

CLOSED EXHAUST VALVE

OPEN INLET VALVE

FROM CARBU-RETOR

OPEN EXHAUST VALVE

TO MUFFLER AND TAILPIPE

It's so simple!

Well, I have left some stuff out.

Importance of Attention

The cognitive mechanism that underlies eye movement control is selective attention. When we extract sensory data from a picture, it is momentarily registered in our sensory memory in fleeting images. We must detect and then attend to these images through the process of selective attention to transfer visual information into working memory. Through selective attention, we send visual information onward through the visual information–processing system.

Cognitive researchers study eye movements because eye movements reflect mental processes. We typically move our eyes, and sometimes our head and body, to view an object with the fovea—the part of the eye with the sharpest vision. When doing this, our focus of attention usually coincides with what we are seeing. But the relationship between eye movement and attention is not absolute. We can move our attention without moving our eyes, as when we notice something in peripheral vision while looking straight ahead at someone speaking. In this circumstance, the movement of attention precedes the movement of the eyes.[4] Because attention and the eyes can be dissociated, intentionally directing the eye helps to ensure they are aligned.

As discussed in Principle 1 (Organize for Perception), attention can be captured preattentively through the bottom-up processing driven by a stimulus, or it can be captured during conscious attention through top-down processing. Designers can take advantage of either type of processing to direct the viewer's attention. Incorporating contrast or movement into a design will trigger attention through bottom-up processes. Indicating the steps of a sequence through numbers and captions will activate attention through top-down processes.

This information graphic created for Attaché *magazine explains how gasoline engines work, using a sequence of numbers to guide the viewer's attention.*

Nigel Holmes,
United States

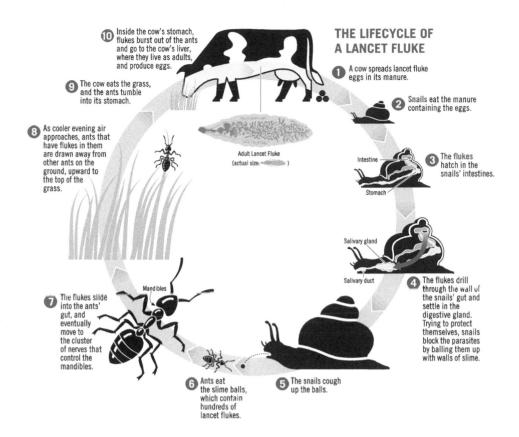

THE LIFECYCLE OF A LANCET FLUKE

1 A cow spreads lancet fluke eggs in its manure.

2 Snails eat the manure containing the eggs.

3 The flukes hatch in the snails' intestines.
Intestine
Stomach

4 The flukes drill through the wall of the snails' gut and settle in the digestive gland. Trying to protect themselves, snails block the parasites by balling them up with walls of slime.
Salivary gland
Salivary duct

5 The snails cough up the balls.

6 Ants eat the slime balls, which contain hundreds of lancet flukes.

7 The flukes slide into the ants' gut, and eventually move to the cluster of nerves that control the mandibles.
Mandibles

8 As cooler evening air approaches, ants that have flukes in them are drawn away from other ants on the ground, upward to the top of the grass.

9 The cow eats the grass, and the ants tumble into its stomach.

10 Inside the cow's stomach, flukes burst out of the ants and go to the cow's liver, where they live as adults, and produce eggs.

Adult Lancet Fluke
(actual size: ~)

Enhancing Cognitive Processes

Promotes speedy perception. When an observer's visual attention shifts to a predetermined location or along a preconceived path, it enhances how the person understands a graphic in many ways. Directing the eyes promotes the efficiency and speed of visual perception, enhances visual information processing, and improves comprehension. Specifically, when a viewer scans a complex graphic, it takes time to get oriented, to determine what is most important, and to extract essential information. Viewers are known to overlook important details in complex illustrations unless they are shown where to attend. When a viewer is directed to a precise location, however, search time is reduced and efficiency is increased.

Improves processing. During preattentive processing, attention is unconsciously directed to features that are most salient. Studies have demonstrated that viewers can be distracted by powerful but irrelevant visual information that captures their attention even against their intentions.[5] Directing the eyes can help ensure that irrelevant information is neither dwelled upon nor processed. Moreover, when a viewer is quickly guided to the essential information, it diminishes the demands placed on working memory that would have been applied to finding important information. More resources are then available for organizing and processing information as well as assimilating new information.[6] This results in better understanding and retention.

Increases comprehension. Directing the eyes can also assist in the comprehension of a picture. The types of visual cues used in informational and instructional graphics, such as arrows and highlights, are more likely to be understood than if instructions were presented in a written form. Comprehension is also aided by visual cues that provide structure, such as adding numeric captions to emphasize the order of a process. Organization is known to improve comprehension because it provides a cognitive framework. Well-organized information helps viewers construct coherent representations in working memory, making it easier to assimilate new information into existing schemas.

This circular format portraying the life cycle of a parasite directs the eyes with a continuous arrow and a number sequence, providing a structure that facilitates comprehension.

Nigel Holmes,
United States

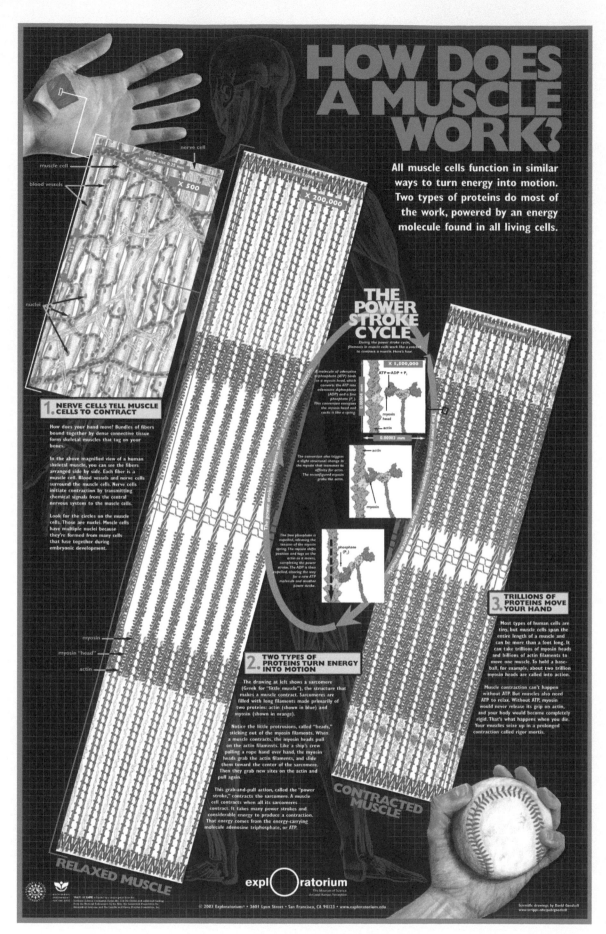

By leading the viewer along a diagonal path from the context graphic in the upper left through masagnified views of muscle fibers to the bottom right, this poster for the Exploratorium reveals how muscles function.

Mark McGowan,
David Goodsell,
Exploratorium,
United States

Trend Meets Technology

Applying The Principle

In the visual arts, the focal point, the magnetic area to which the eyes are drawn, is a principal aspect of a composition. "If a design has no focal point, drawing attention inward, it may seem to fall apart, making it difficult for the viewer to organize what is going on," write Paul Zelanski and Mary Pat Fisher in *Design Principles and Problems*. All of the elements within the frame of a composition have a relationship to one another and to the whole. The focal point can be the largest shape in a graphic or the one with the brightest color; it can be isolated from other elements or placed in a compelling position. We perceive it because our brains are wired to seek and detect differences. To our visual processing system, these differences are informative, causing the eye to pause and extract information. Creating several focal points with varying degrees of weight gives rise to a relative order of importance that guides the viewer's attention and eyes through the flow of information.

Several compositional techniques can be used to direct the eyes. Positioning and emphasis are two powerful ways to achieve this. Positioning refers to the importance associated with an element's location. Emphasis refers to the stress given to an element. In addition to structure, movement also guides the eyes. A picture tends to move and flow according to the directionality and energy of line, shape, and texture. For example, the downward flow of wine pouring from a bottle directs the viewer's eyes along the vertical axis into the wine glass. When the patterns of a texture move in a specific direction, this also guides the eyes. Position, emphasis, and movement provide a visual language for orienting and directing the viewer's vision along an intended path.

In addition, explicit techniques that are overlaid onto a graphic call attention to critical attributes and provide directional information. Explicit cues facilitate attention when used alone or in combination, as long as they are placed correctly and used judiciously. The designer should ensure that the chosen cues are appropriate to the cognitive characteristics of the audience. For example, a younger audience may not know that a dashed line implies directionality. Also, children are not as adept as adults at shifting their attention to important information.

Whether guiding the eyes through a graphic or directing the eyes to a specific location, designers should consider the informative purpose of the graphic, its degree of visual complexity, and the characteristics of the audience when deciding on an approach. Implicit, compositional techniques have an aesthetic dimension that will enhance promotional graphics. For instance, powerful lines that guide the eye are also appealing to the senses. Explicit cueing techniques that indicate location are appropriate in information and instructional graphics and diagrams.

The diagonal lines of this graphic draw the viewer into its kinetic center, as the eyes jump to several focal points derived from contrasts in color, shape, and size.

Shinnoske Sugisaki, *Japan*

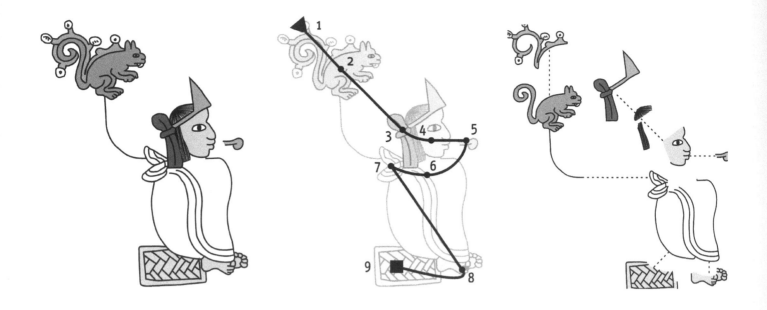

These explanatory line drawings illustrate how ancient Aztec writing is formed. Visual cues include numbers, arrows, and dashed lines, all of which direct the eye.

Lorenzo De Tomasi, Italy

◀ The cover image of this wine merchant's brochure uses a compositional technique to guide the viewer's eyes through the flowing motion of pouring wine.

**Christine Kenney,
IE Design +
Communications,**
United States

K&L WINE MERCHANTS

The directionality of the images and detailed textures direct the eyes in these twenty-fifth-anniversary cards for the Wildlife Rescue Foundation.

H. Michael Karshis,
HMK Archive,
United States

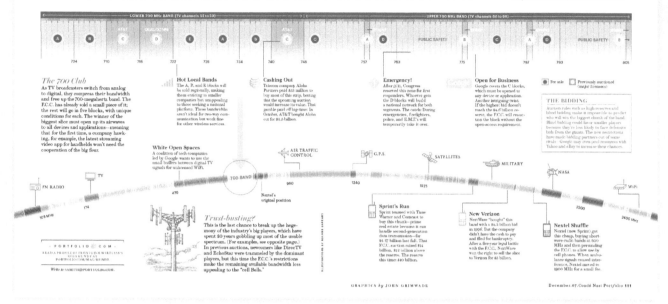

POSITION

The boundaries that define the edges of a graphic, referred to as the frame, have a powerful effect on a composition. Regardless of whether it encloses a post-card, a page, a poster, or a screen, the frame creates meaning for the elements it bounds. Among aesthetic theorists, it is generally accepted that the position of an object within a frame creates a perceptual force or tension that affects the perceived importance of an object and hence where we place our attention.[7]

Through the thoughtful placement of elements, a designer can establish a visual hierarchy to direct the viewer's eyes. The position of each component conveys a progression of relative importance, starting with the element of the highest rank and continuing to those with lesser rank. For example, in a magazine spread, the information graphic might be the most dominant element, followed by a headline and then explanatory text. A standard visual hierarchy consists of three levels—primary, secondary, and equivalent.

Our understanding of positioning in a frame is a metaphor for how we view hierarchies in the world. We speak of people who have important positions as being at the top. Likewise, we have an expectation of this convention in pictures. We anticipate that elements at the top of a page will be the most important.

In fact, research shows that objects in the top half of a picture are considered to be more active, dynamic, and potent. In other words, they have more visual weight.[8] Another study found that viewers spend more time viewing areas appearing on the left and upper half of the field than on areas located on the right and lower half. This appeared to be true in both symmetrical designs and in a double-page spread.[9] Of one thing we can be certain: Varying the position of an object in a frame changes its impact on the observer.

▲ This information graphic for Condé Nast Portfolio establishes an effective visual hierarchy to explain the auction of mobile bandwidths.

John Grimwade and Liana Zamora, Condé Nast Publications, United States

▶ In this poster for a London museum, the designer used a classic approach to positioning by placing the name of the historical exhibition above the fold in an old-timey newspaper design.

Cog Design, United Kingdom

EMPHASIS

A design needs varying degrees of emphasis to capture and guide the viewer's attention. Without emphasis, a graphic feels flat and lifeless, offering a limited sensory experience and diminished possibilities for directing the eye. On the other hand, a design with emphasis is energetic. It attracts the eyes with prominent areas of focus, creating a dominant-subordinate hierarchy by endowing important elements with relative weight and stress. As the observer instinctively moves from the most prominent component to the least, emphasis directs the eyes around a graphic.

Emphasis can be accomplished through techniques that create contrast, which is characterized by a dramatic change in visual information. When we glance at a picture, contrast attracts our attention. We sense that areas of sameness are not as informative as areas of difference. It is through contrast that we discriminate foreground from background and differentiate shapes, textures, and patterns. Through contrast, prominent elements of a graphic emerge and become more visible than their surroundings.

A successful design uses contrast at varying levels so that every element has a place in the hierarchy, avoiding a competition for dominance. An element is most likely to be perceived as a primary focal point when the change is abrupt and the polarity between the element and its surroundings is vivid. The primary focal point must create impact. Secondary and tertiary elements should be progressively toned down.

The options for creating contrast are achieved by juxtaposing elements that differ along one or more dimensions of size, tone, color, texture, and shape. In his book *Art and Visual Perception*, Rudolf Arnheim notes that when all other factors are equal, the visual weight of an element is most dependent on its size. Others suggest that contrast in tonal values has the greatest impact. Regardless of the attribute selected, any contrast between elements should enhance the message, as the audience will interpret a difference as meaningful.

Incongruence can also be used to create emphasis because it provides a focal point. Incongruence refers to the placement of an unexpected object in a familiar context, such as a bathtub in the middle of the desert. It can also be achieved by using an attribute in an unexpected way, such as reversing the size of people so that babies are larger than their parents. Incongruence attracts our attention because we construct schemas of how the world looks, sounds, and works. Incongruence challenges our schemas because what we see is unfamiliar and fails to match our prior knowledge. Our interest is heightened as we attempt to mentally accommodate an unusual juxtaposition or an unconventional attribute.

▲ *The disconnected body parts create incongruence and emphasis in this FIFA World Cup poster.*

**Jonas Banker,
BankerWessel,** *Sweden*

▶ *In this poster promoting a summer club party, the designer uses vivid color contrasts and intricate shapes to provide emphasis.*

Sorin Bechira, X3 Studios, *Romania*

[from here]

[to there]

[from here]

[to there]

◀ Isolation is one way to establish prominence, as shown in these postcards for retail merchandising software.

Luis Jones,
Fusion Advertising,
United States

▲ The unexpected shape of a foot creates emphasis through contrast and surprise in this graphic for the Guardian *newspaper.*

Jean-Manuel Duvivier,
Jean-Manuel Duvivier
Illustration, Belgium

MOVEMENT

When a graphic conveys a dynamic sense of movement, our eyes seem to glide across its surface. Movement can be explained as an energetic force or tension embodied in and between the lines, textures, shapes, and forms of a graphic. Movement is more than the repetition of patterns; rather, it sweeps the viewer's attention through a picture. It is a powerful way for graphic designers to direct the viewer's eye to the important elements in a graphic.

When we perceive movement in a static picture, we perceive its directionality, sensing whether it moves in fits and starts, rounds back onto itself, or takes us off the page. Rudolf Arnheim suggests that the direction of visual forces in a picture is determined by three factors: the attraction exerted from the visual weight of surrounding elements, the shape of objects along their axes, and the visual direction and action of the subject.[10]

That we can perceive directionality and movement in a static two-dimensional picture is a remarkable feat of the eyes and brain. We perceive kinetic information in a still picture because we know the experience of our own physical movement and we understand the motion of objects. In fact, our ability to perceive movement in a static graphic is associated with regions of the brain that we use for observing physical motion. In one study, researchers found that action photographs activated areas of the brain that are sensitive to real motion, whereas photos depicting people in still positions did not activate these areas. According to the study's authors, motion cues in a graphic appear to create the perception that an object is leaping out from its static surroundings.[11] Although this study was based on photographs of people in action, it is likely that our perception of compositional movement is also due to motion-detecting neurons.

In this field hockey equipment catalog, motion shots create the perception of movement and capture the intensity of the sport.

Greg Bennett, Siquis,
United States

Yehudit Sasportas

Graphic designers can exploit the expressive quality of lines and shapes to create movement based on the rhythm of elements. For example, curved lines and undulating shapes create smooth and flowing movement. Jagged lines create tension and make the eyes dart and pause. It is interesting to note that movement that extends in a left-to-right direction is considered easier to perceive. In a survey of art from many cultures, including Chinese, Japanese, Indian, Persian, and Western, this left-to-right asymmetry of emphasis was found to be a common phenomenon.[12] The survey found that across cultures, important elements tended to be located to the left of those that were less important, causing the eyes to flow in a rightward movement. Thus, the left-to-right preference may be neurological rather than cultural.

Designers can also create movement by creating the illusion of three-dimensional perspective, which draws the viewer's eyes into the depth of field. Viewers deduce depth perception in a picture because of their knowledge of how things appear in the physical world. Objects that are larger in size are assumed to be in the foreground. Viewers also perceive the illusion of depth because converging lines create a sense of depth and cooler colors create a sense of distance. Depth perception also creates a visual hierarchy. Most viewers consider objects in the foreground more important than objects in the distance.

This promotional poster for an artist's lecture exemplifies how the visual direction of shapes can create dynamic movement.

**Ian Lynam,
Ian Lynam Creative
Direction & Design,** *Japan*

Three-dimensional perspective effectively directs a viewer's attention further into the depth plane, as illustrated in this cover for SMT magazine.

Christopher Short,
United States

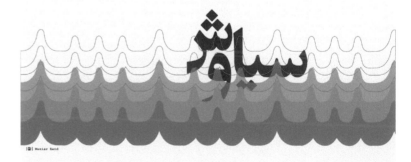

The movement of fire carries the viewer across the page in this typography poster, based on a Persian traditional tale.

Maziar Zand,
M. Zand Studio, Iran

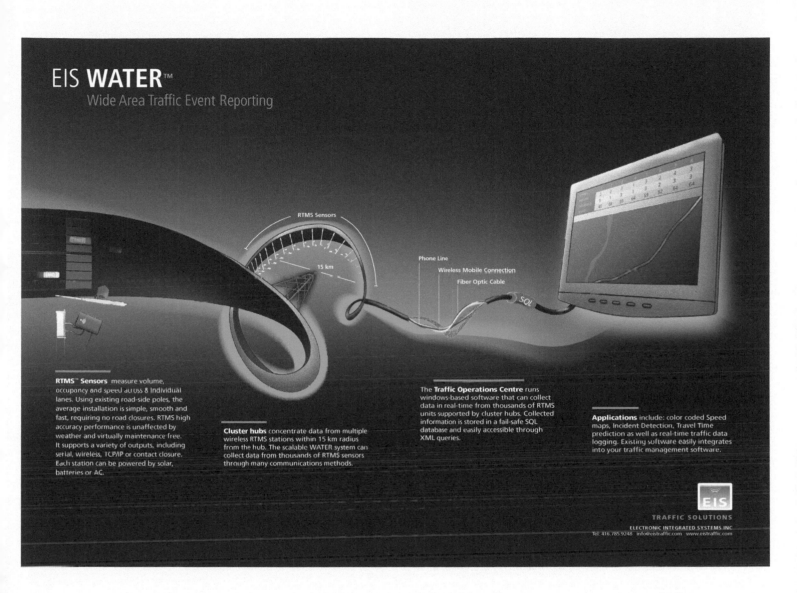

EIS **WATER**™
Wide Area Traffic Event Reporting

RTMS™ **Sensors** measure volume, occupancy and speed across 8 individual lanes. Using existing road-side poles, the average installation is simple, smooth and fast, requiring no road closures. RTMS high accuracy performance is unaffected by weather and virtually maintenance free. It supports a variety of outputs, including serial, wireless, TCP/IP or contact closure. Each station can be powered by solar, batteries or AC.

Cluster hubs concentrate data from multiple wireless RTMS stations within 15 km radius from the hub. The scalable WATER system can collect data from thousands of RTMS sensors through many communications methods.

The **Traffic Operations Centre** runs windows-based software that can collect data in real-time from thousands of RTMS units supported by cluster hubs. Collected information is stored in a fail-safe SQL database and easily accessible through XML queries.

Applications include: color coded Speed maps, Incident Detection, Travel Time prediction as well as real-time traffic data logging. Existing software easily integrates into your traffic management software.

EIS

TRAFFIC SOLUTIONS
ELECTRONIC INTEGRATED SYSTEMS INC
Tel: 416.785.9248   info@eistraffic.com   www.eistraffic.com

The undulating visualization of this traffic event–reporting system guides the viewer through the information flow—from an explanation of the hardware to the software and finally to the end-user advantages.

**Patrick Keenan
and Alan Smith,
The Movement,** Canada

◀ *Shapes and lines create rhythmic movement in this AIGA poster reflecting a 1930s artistic style.*

**Dale Sprague
and Joslynn Anderson,
Canyon Creative,**
United States

▶ *In this information graphic for the* Cleveland Plain Dealer, *the curves in the highway take the viewer along a path to the most important information.*

**Stephen J. Beard,
Plain Dealer,** *United States*

▶ *The curvature of this biological graphic moves the viewer through the mechanisms and processes of gene expression.*

**Daniel Müller,
Haderer & Müller
Biomedical Art,**
United States

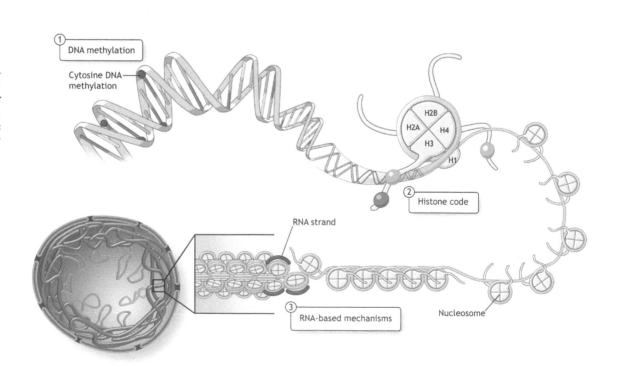

TRAFFIC MYSTERY: THE 'SHOCKWAVE'

Making sense of red lights, construction zones and other roadway phenomena

Why do freeways come to a stop?

It happens to most drivers at least a few times a year. You're sailing along on the freeway when you're forced to come to a stop, or at least a crawl. You can't see why things are slowing around the bend — and when you get there, traffic is moving better.

Traffic planners call this a "shockwave."

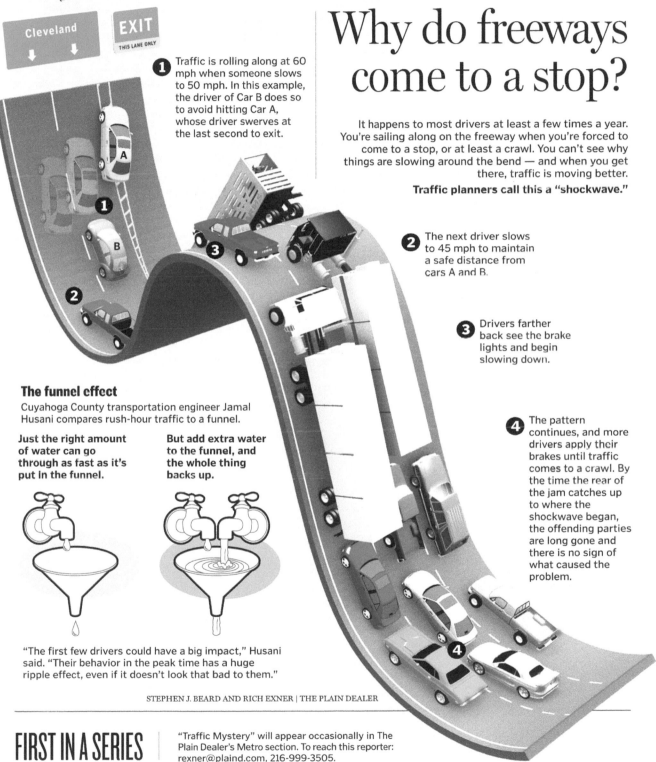

1 Traffic is rolling along at 60 mph when someone slows to 50 mph. In this example, the driver of Car B does so to avoid hitting Car A, whose driver swerves at the last second to exit.

2 The next driver slows to 45 mph to maintain a safe distance from cars A and B.

3 Drivers farther back see the brake lights and begin slowing down.

4 The pattern continues, and more drivers apply their brakes until traffic comes to a crawl. By the time the rear of the jam catches up to where the shockwave began, the offending parties are long gone and there is no sign of what caused the problem.

The funnel effect

Cuyahoga County transportation engineer Jamal Husani compares rush-hour traffic to a funnel.

Just the right amount of water can go through as fast as it's put in the funnel.

But add extra water to the funnel, and the whole thing backs up.

"The first few drivers could have a big impact," Husani said. "Their behavior in the peak time has a huge ripple effect, even if it doesn't look that bad to them."

STEPHEN J. BEARD AND RICH EXNER | THE PLAIN DEALER

FIRST IN A SERIES

"Traffic Mystery" will appear occasionally in The Plain Dealer's Metro section. To reach this reporter: rexner@plaind.com, 216-999-3505.

EYE GAZE

It isn't surprising that we are drawn to pictures of people—our brains appear to have specialized mechanisms for detecting and recognizing human faces. Regardless of whether the face appears as a photograph, a painting, a sketch, or a simple schematic figure, specific neural networks are activated in the brain upon perceiving anything configured as a face.[13] In addition, specialized regions of the brain respond to the recognition of at least one facial feature in isolation—the eyes.[14] We are attuned to detecting faces and eyes because we are communicative beings, and facial expressions convey important emotional and interpersonal information.

A secondary and intriguing characteristic of facial awareness is that we automatically shift our eyes in the direction where someone else is looking. In a long list of studies, eye gaze has been found to orient a viewer's attention.[15] According to researchers Stephen Langton and Vicki Bruce, "Neuropsychological, neurophysiological, and behavioral evidence is emerging in support of the position that there is a functionally specific mechanism devoted to the task of detecting eyes and computing where in the environment eye gaze is directed."[16] Support for this specialized mechanism is found in the fact that infants as young as three months of age can detect the direction of an adult's gaze and will shift their own attention in that direction.[17]

Although it is unclear whether this is innate or learned, gaze perception triggers what is known as joint attention, or shifting our eyes in the direction of someone else's gaze. As a survival mechanism, it is clear that shifting attention to where someone else is looking could prove quite helpful in times of danger. As a social mechanism, joint attention could provide significant information about another person's momentary interest and perhaps their psychological state.

This seemingly automatic ability transfers to pictures. When an observer views a static image of a face, it triggers the viewer's attention to look in the direction of the subject's gaze. Graphic designers can take advantage of this eye gaze reflex to focus attention on a particular graphic by using photographs or illustrations that depict a person gazing in the desired direction.

▲ *Eye gaze is a magnetic attraction for pulling in the viewer.*

Ola Levitsky,
B.I.G. Design, *Israel*

▶ *This poster for an art exhibition features the artist and his wife gazing downward, absorbed in their tasks. Following the direction of their gaze takes the viewer deeper into the graphic.*

Ida Wessel,
BankerWessel, *Sweden*

OTTO 22.9 2007 G.
CARLSUND −6.1 2008

LILJEVALCHS KONSTHALL

The performer's hypnotic stare in this theater program guide makes it difficult to look away.

**Francheska Guerrero,
Unfolding Terrain,**
United States

▼ *In this CD cover for typographer Kurt Weidemann, the designer's eye gaze leads the viewer to the contents of the CD.*

**A. Osterwalder,
P. Bardesono, S. Wagner,
A. Bromer and
M. Drozdowski,
i_d buero,** *Germany*

Illustrated depictions of eye gaze also direct the eyes to crucial areas of a picture.

Jean-Manuel Duvivier,
Jean-Manuel Duvivier
Illustration, Belgium

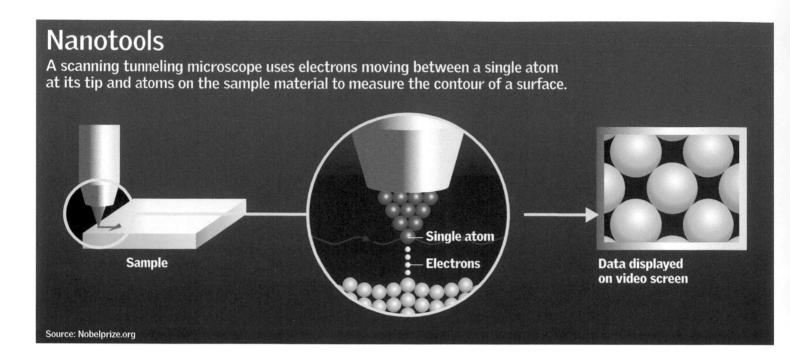

Nanotools

A scanning tunneling microscope uses electrons moving between a single atom at its tip and atoms on the sample material to measure the contour of a surface.

Sample

Single atom

Electrons

Data displayed on video screen

Source: Nobelprize.org

VISUAL CUES

Some of the first tasks a viewer performs when scanning a picture are to search for informative areas, prioritize the information, and select what is most important. The time it takes to locate important information depends on the number of eye fixations that a viewer makes, because the eyes fix on static points much of the time during the search process. Visual complexity makes it more difficult to find important information and increases the number of fixations needed to perform a search.

Designers can facilitate the early tasks of searching, prioritizing, and selecting by signaling the viewer's attention to the location of the most essential information. This involves adding visual cues such as arrows, color, and captions to a graphic. Visual cues optimize the viewing experience by providing a shortcut to relevant information, rendering the need for a visual search unnecessary. Furthermore, visual cues have been shown to improve a person's recall of information.[18] They also enable a viewer to attend to a single area of visual information rather than dividing attention among competing stimuli. There is evidence that when a viewer's attention is divided, the size of the perceived visual field is actually reduced, whereas a visual cue pointing to a target increases the perceived visual area. This speeds up the search for important information.[19]

Bean brew

Making diesel from soy requires three steps.

1. Soybeans are immersed in petroleum derivative hexane to extract crude soybean oil.

2. The crude soybean oil is filtered and piped to a refining tower.

3. Methanol and a catalyst are added at high temperatures, producing diesel fuel.

Sources: Bloomberg, Hedge Fund Research

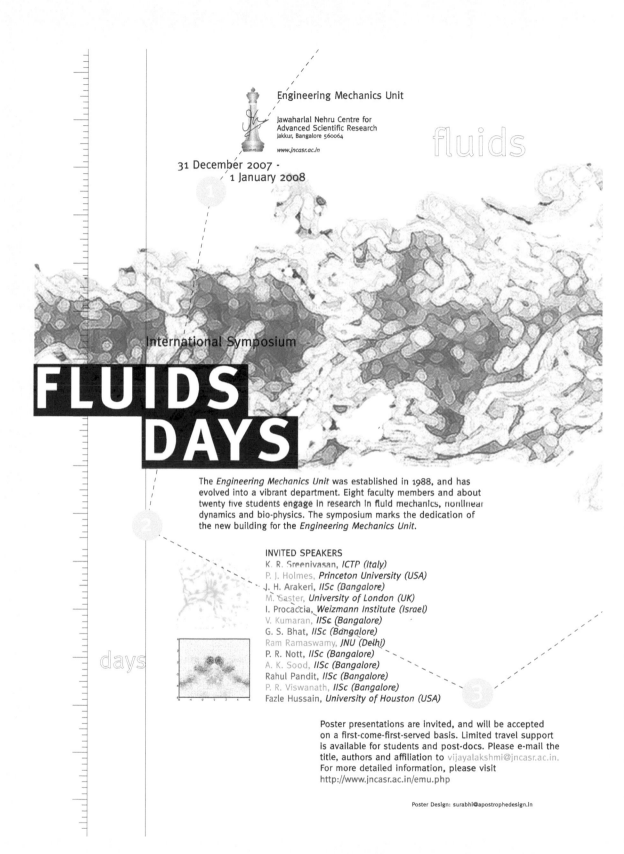

◀ *These information graphics for* Bloomberg Markets *magazine show the value of signaling even for brief visual explanations.*

Eliot Bergman, *Japan*

▶ *In this scientific symposium poster, numbers and dashed lines are visual cues that lead the viewer to the essential information.*

Surabhi Gurukar,
Apostrophe Design, *India*

Engineering Mechanics Unit

Jawaharlal Nehru Centre for
Advanced Scientific Research
Jakkur, Bangalore 560064

www.jncasr.ac.in

31 December 2007 -
1 January 2008

fluids

International Symposium

FLUIDS DAYS

The *Engineering Mechanics Unit* was established in 1988, and has evolved into a vibrant department. Eight faculty members and about twenty five students engage in research in fluid mechanics, nonlinear dynamics and bio-physics. The symposium marks the dedication of the new building for the *Engineering Mechanics Unit.*

INVITED SPEAKERS
K. R. Sreenivasan, *ICTP (Italy)*
P. J. Holmes, *Princeton University (USA)*
J. H. Arakeri, *IISc (Bangalore)*
M. Gaster, *University of London (UK)*
I. Procaccia, *Weizmann Institute (Israel)*
V. Kumaran, *IISc (Bangalore)*
G. S. Bhat, *IISc (Bangalore)*
Ram Ramaswamy, *JNU (Delhi)*
P. R. Nott, *IISc (Bangalore)*
A. K. Sood, *IISc (Bangalore)*
Rahul Pandit, *IISc (Bangalore)*
P. R. Viswanath, *IISc (Bangalore)*
Fazle Hussain, *University of Houston (USA)*

days

Poster presentations are invited, and will be accepted on a first-come-first-served basis. Limited travel support is available for students and post-docs. Please e-mail the title, authors and affiliation to vijayalakshmi@jncasr.ac.in. For more detailed information, please visit
http://www.jncasr.ac.in/emu.php

Poster Design: surabhi@apostrophedesign.in

Bold arrows in this information graphic for Condé Nast Traveler *represent the time it takes to travel from London to Paris by various modes of transport. The arrows are the dominant element that leads the viewer from one piece of essential information to the next.*

John Grimwade,
Condé Nast Publications,
United States

Arrows and the Like

The arrow is an ever-present pictorial device frequently found in explanatory graphics, diagrams, and wayfinding. It is used so often because it is exceedingly effective; the arrow not only directs our attention and our eyes, it guides cognition. Because the arrow is derived from an asymmetric shape—a triangle—it brings a sense of dynamism to a graphic.

The arrow is a symbol, and as such it stands for something else and must be decoded by the viewer. The viewer must recognize the triangular shape of the arrow's head, shaft, and tail as one perceptual unit and associate this shape with one or more "arrow schemas" stored in long-term memory. For those familiar with the arrow symbol, its recognition and meaning are easy and automatic. Upon perceiving a visual cue like an arrow, the viewer rapidly evaluates its directional meaning. Context plays an important part in arrow comprehension. We do not interpret any triangle lying on its side as an arrow, but in the appropriate context, such as in a diagram or when representing a "continue" or "play" button, we interpret a sideways triangle as an arrow.

When the arrow points to a specific location, it helps the viewer filter out extraneous information and focus on the essentials. Cueing the observer's selective attention to important information is the first step in comprehension. When designing the pointer arrow, it must be sufficiently dominant to capture the viewer's attention, but it should not overpower the holistic perception of the graphic.

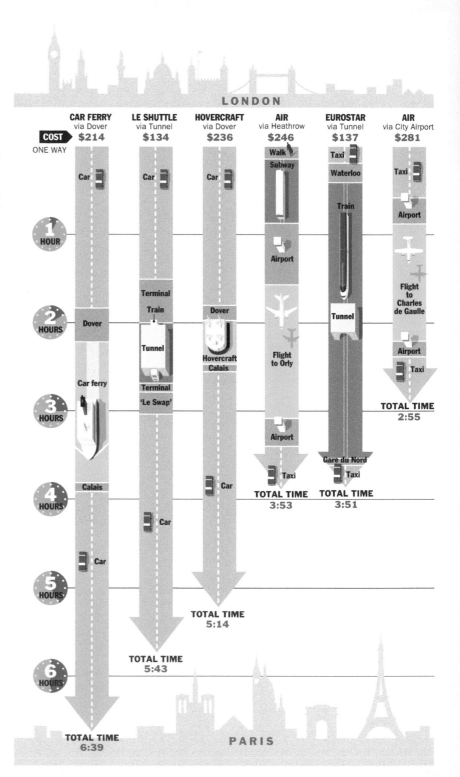

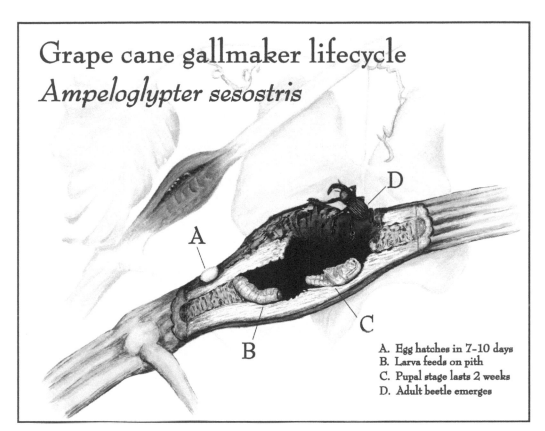

Grape cane gallmaker lifecycle
Ampeloglypter sesostris

A.
B.
C.
D.

A. Egg hatches in 7-10 days
B. Larva feeds on pith
C. Pupal stage lasts 2 weeks
D. Adult beetle emerges

◄ *Unobtrusive lines both point to crucial information and effectively blend with the graphic in this illustration of a beetle's life cycle.*

Melisa Beveridge,
Natural History Illustration,
United States

▶ *These graphics are part of a comprehensive signage program explaining environmental content in a wetlands park. In both signs, arrows are well integrated into each graphic as pointers to associated information.*

Claudine Jaenichen and
Richard Turner,
Jaenichen Studio,
United States

Color Cues

In a rich array of visual information, viewers need a way to filter out what is extraneous in order to attend to the information that is relevant to their task. Time and again, color has proven to be a compelling way to attract attention and prompt the viewer to attend to the most relevant details. As an explicit cueing device, contrast in color—in the form of a circle, a line, or other shape—acts as a signal to direct the eyes. Color is one of the primitive features we detect in preattentive vision, and it can play a dominant role in guiding attention and reinforcing a message.

Color facilitates the interpretation and comprehension of visual information in several ways. In complex visuals, it helps viewers rapidly search through a large quantity of visual information to locate what is most important. Also, viewers have an easier time noticing and distinguishing between objects in a colored graphic as compared to a monochrome one because color often emphasizes figure—ground contrasts. In addition, when a color cue becomes a visual attribute of an object, it helps to make the information memorable.

Color cues are effective in most types of visual communications. During animation sequences, color cues are needed because important information can fly by quickly. In maps and diagrams, color cues are often used to indicate key information. In learning materials, the explicit use of color cues is known to help students comprehend and retain information. There is evidence that color helps us organize and categorize visual information.[20] For information to get noticed quickly, a color cue must vary sufficiently from the background and surrounding objects. Designers should avoid using too many colors.

▶ *Color cues highlight medical device implants in this futuristic super-woman rendered for Wired magazine.*

Bryan Christie,
Bryan Christie Design,
United States

▼ *This informational bro-chure promotes pine forest conservation. The maps use bright colors as visual cues to show the few regions of undeveloped, protected forest where Monterey pines still stand.*

Karen Parry
and Louis Jaffe,
Black Graphics,
United States

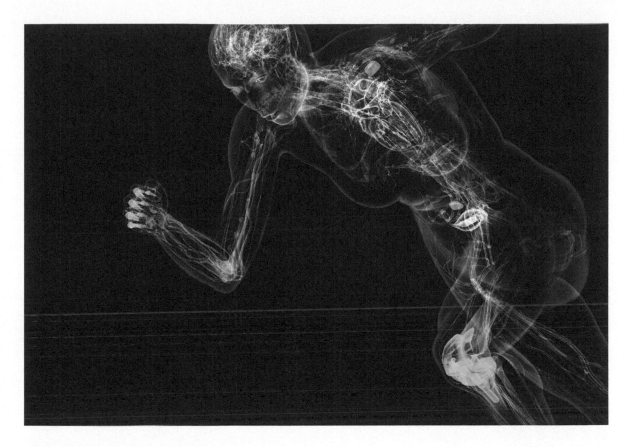

The Monterey Pine Forest:
Vanishing Treasure or Living Forest Legacy?

What's Our Plan?
Create Monterey Pine Forest Conservation Areas

Establishing Monterey Pine Forest Conservation Areas will help conserve outstanding scenic, recreational, economic and biological values in a region rich with distinctive landscapes. The proposed Conservation Areas – Del Monte Forest, Jacks Peak and Point Lobos – contain exceptional examples of native Monterey Pine Forest habitat and unusual Maritime Chaparral, Oak Woodland and Coastal Prairie, that support special status plants and animals. Portions of the Conservation Areas are threatened with incompatible land uses that will degrade the integrity of these unique and irreplaceable areas that help keep our water pure, our air clean, and our natural world healthy and beautiful. Programs could be developed in the Conservation Areas to facilitate long term protection of the native Monterey Pine Forest, including acquisition, restoration, conservation easements, stewardship incentives for private land owners, public lands management plans, and incorporation of conservation policies into County and City planning processes.

Historic Extent of Monterey Pine Forest

Present Extent of Undeveloped Monterey Pine Forest

Protected Monterey Pine Forest Habitat

Jacks Peak County Park

Potential Park Expansion

Non-Monterey Pine Forest Habitat

Source: Base Topography – USGS; Roads – GDT; Geographic Data Technology; Protected Lands – Jones&Stokes Associates; Jacks Peak – Jones&Stokes Associates; Focus Parcels – Jones&Stokes Associates; MPPWF Conservation Areas – MPFW and GFE; Undeveloped Monterey Pine Forest Habitat – MPPW Uncodified from Jones&Stokes data; Public Lands – CA Resources Agency; Urban – HMMF Forestland Mapping and Monitoring Program; Historic extent – Jones&Stokes

What's the Threat?
Our Native Forest is Being Destroyed

Sadly, the native forests in the Monterey region lack a unified conservation plan. Since European colonization began, our forests have become fragmented, diseased and compromised by development, invasive plants and genetic contamination. Half of our native forest has already been removed. Much of the remaining forest is in private hands and subject to development. The long term survival of the remaining forested lands on the Monterey Peninsula is in jeopardy.

Safeguards are Needed Now

Though not a new idea, the conservation of the remaining native Monterey Pine Forest is now of critical importance. The proposed Jacks Peak Conservation Area is the largest tract of unfragmented native Monterey Pine Forest in the world. Conserved lands in the Jacks Peak Conservation Area could span over 3000 contiguous acres to safeguard both the heart of remaining undeveloped native forest, as well as the forest margins that grade into woodland, grassland and scrub. Benefits of conserving land around Jacks Peak include:

- Maintaining open space and establishing the largest protected area of native Monterey Pine Forest in the world.

- Retaining crucial wildlife corridors and connections between the northern Santa Lucia Range, the Carmel River, Fort Ord backcountry and Carmel Valley ridgelands.

- Enhancing property values that strengthen the regional economy and surrounding communities.

- Increasing recreation opportunities near urban centers.

- Lowering fire risk by reducing development in forested lands.

- Enriching the local quality of life by protecting viewsheds and watersheds that help sustain our healthy and inspiring environment now and into the future.

EARLY MORNING ATHLETES

Every morning, thousands of men and women around the country wake up before the crack of dawn and head out to the lake. Their boat, known as **shells**, and their team, called their **crew**, is waiting. Their hands ache for the oar. They long to hear the tiny splash of the **blade** and feel the power of the drive burn in their legs. Rowers are a rare breed that thrive in painful circumstances and revel in early morning practices and long distance sprints.

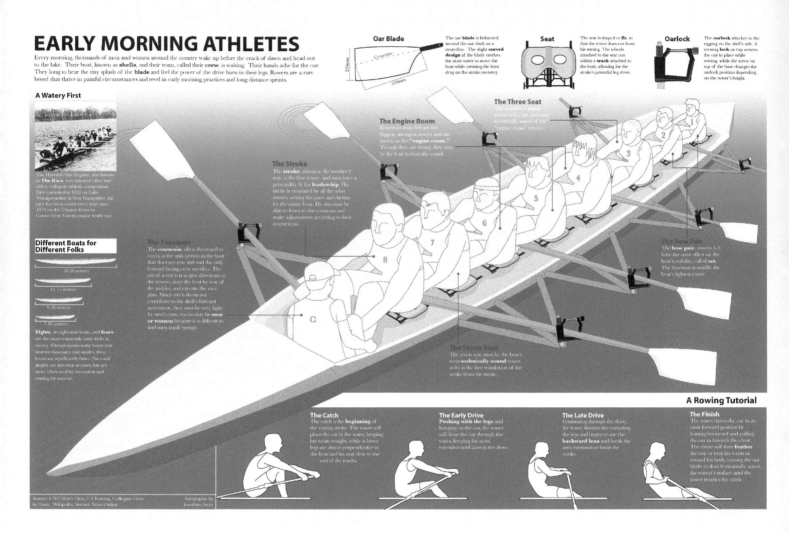

This illustration provides a clear explanation of how a crew team functions. A team member's location in the boat is most significant, so the individuality of each person is de-emphasized so the audience stays focused on the essential information.

Jonathan Avery,
University of North Carolina,
United States

"The simplest way to achieve simplicity
is through thoughtful reduction."

JOHN MAEDA, *The Laws of Simplicity*

There are times when the ideal expression of a message can be achieved through visual shorthand. An effective way to do this is to reduce the realistic qualities embedded in a graphic.

One way to think about realism is in terms of fidelity, or how much an image resembles something recognizable. On a continuum, visuals with the highest fidelity are photographs in full and natural color, and photorealistic 3-D renderings. The high-fidelity visual contains detail, depth, shadow, texture, and nuance of color as close as possible to interpreting what we see in our environment. On the other end of the continuum are visuals with low fidelity, such as line drawings, silhouettes, and iconic images. The low-fidelity image uses fewer visual elements and qualities that resemble a recognizable object. Reducing realism reduces the fidelity of the image.

Low-fidelity graphics are effective when the goal is to focus on essential details, induce a quick response, strengthen the impact of a message, or provide an explanation, particularly to those with nominal knowledge of the content. For example, the designer may consider reducing the realism of graphics in a beginner's cookbook to help a novice understand how to follow the recipes. In contrast, high-fidelity images might work best in a cookbook for experienced chefs.

The communicative intent of the message, the characteristics of the audience, and the appropriateness of the content should influence the degree of image realism used in a design. Images with reduced realism are best suited for general audiences who need to quickly comprehend the message being conveyed, such as wayfinding signage, educational materials, explanatory graphics, and promotional materials.

The spread in this college viewbook smoothly incorporates both high-fidelity (on the left) and low-fidelity imagery (on the right) to suit different purposes.

**Amy Lebow
and Purnima Rao,
Philographica,
United States**

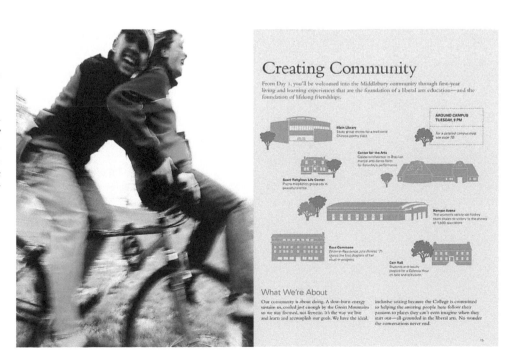

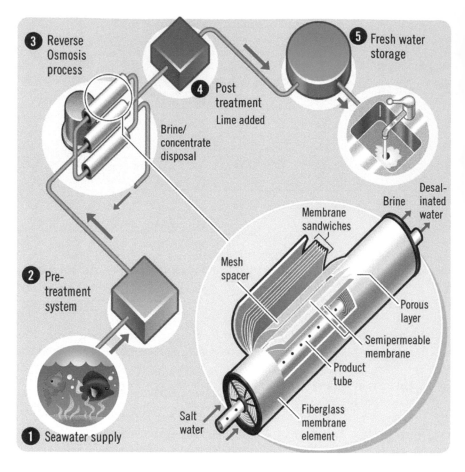

Efficient Visual Information Processing

Designing with a minimalist approach has many advantages when it comes to graphic comprehension. Minimalism makes every phase of the human information-processing system more efficient as we perceive a graphic, hold information in working memory, internally represent information, and interpret it.

When we read an image, we scan it to extract significant information. As our neurons work in parallel, we perceive the primitive features of an image, such as color, shape, and depth. After this initial perception, we extract more complex information that we synthesize into a coherent form. A graphic composed of primitive features, such as a line drawing, will take less time to scan and assimilate compared to one that is more complicated, such as a natural scene in a photograph.

Working memory has a limited capacity and is easily overloaded. When viewing a high-fidelity graphic composed of superfluous elements, the additional information can overload working memory, acting as a barrier to comprehension. Distilling a graphic down to its essential visual elements minimizes the information processing required to understand it.

Low-fidelity graphics require fewer transformations to get them ready for encoding into long-term memory. As the brain processes visual information gleaned from an image, it removes the nonessential sensory input and retains the crucial information, converting it into a bare-bones representation. Some cognitive theorists think we may encode images as "sketchy, cartoon-like representations ... that exaggerate or highlight critical distinctions."[1] Because graphics with reduced realism inherently match how we most likely represent information internally, it takes less effort to recognize them and to prepare them for long-term storage.

The presence of unnecessary elements can distract the viewer from focusing on the key message and potentially cause misunderstandings. Francis Dwyer, professor and researcher of instructional systems, notes that images with highly realistic details are not always successful at communication. "Probably my most surprising finding is the ineffectiveness of realistic images. The very polished, most highly sophisticated visuals don't always work."[2]

▲ *Reduced realism is ideal for explaining a process such as desalination, shown here. The geometric forms, smooth surfaces, and flat areas of color make the components easy to perceive and comprehend.*

Colin Hayes,
Colin Hayes Illustrator,
United States

▶ *Flat areas of color without texture create low-fidelity maps—all the information that is needed for showing the location of this organization's projects.*

Benjamin Thomas,
Bento Graphics, *Japan*

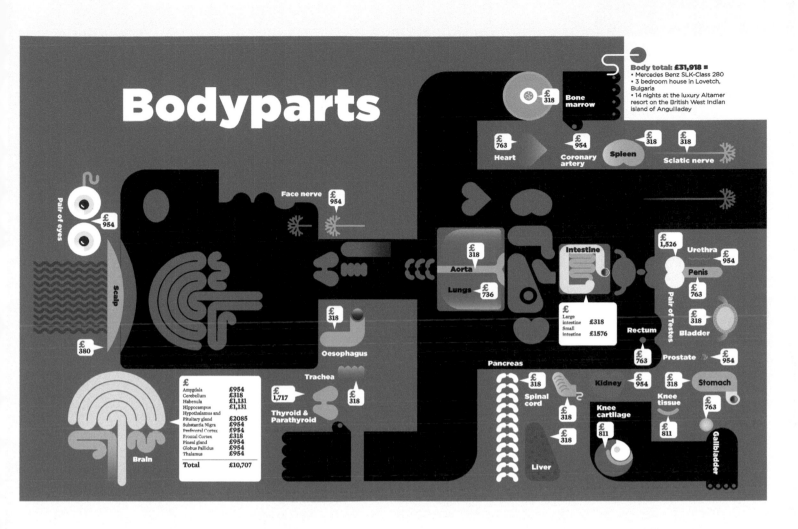

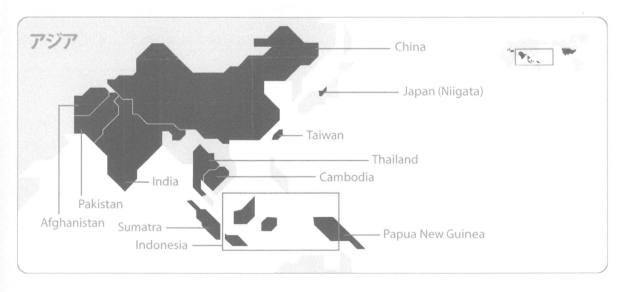

▲ In this graphic for Esquire *magazine, every object is reduced to its essential but recognizable characteristics.*

Peter Grundy, Grundini,
United Kingdom

Applying the Principle

We tend to define a picture as realistic if it appears to be a successful copy of its referent. By definition, however, all pictorial representations deviate to some degree from the objects in our physical environment. Manfredo Massironi explains this in *The Psychology of Graphic Images*. "Any graphic representation is always an interpretation, no matter how faithful to reality it is in proportion and attention to detail. Thus, graphics are always attempts to explain reality." Reduced realism is an attempt to interpret reality through visual abstraction and simplification.

To achieve greater abstraction, the designer needs to reduce the degree of detail and limit the expression of one or more visual dimensions, such as color, depth, or texture. The pictorial dimension that is reduced and the details that are included will affect the meaning of the message and the response of the audience. It takes careful consideration to choose which features to convey, which to ignore, and the degree to which a feature will be emphasized. Most important is to convey the information that is consistent across different views of an object.[3]

According to perception research, several qualities affect how a viewer perceives image realism. A hard shadow is perceived as less realistic than a soft shadow, and a smooth surface is perceived as less realistic than a rough surface.[4] Sharp color and sharp contours are perceived as less realistic, while the appropriate blurring of objects in the distance is more realistic. Designers can implement those qualities that make a graphic seem less realistic.

Another approach to reducing realism is to severely limit the number of elements in a graphic, in contrast to our physical environment, which is overloaded with visual information. This allows the viewer to quickly focus on the crucial element of importance. For example, in a brochure advertising ceramic art, the designer could choose to display an array of photographs showing potters at work or a simple photograph of one ceramic vase. The simplified approach has greater impact.

In their book *Reading Images: The Grammar of Visual Design*, Gunther Kress and Theo van Leeuwen note, "The naturalistic image, whatever it may be about, is always also about detail." Conversely, the image with reduced realism is always about less detail. As a general guideline, designing to reduce realism is a process of selective abstraction with a focus on the essential intent of a message. While a sufficient amount of visual information must remain for the viewer to form an appropriate mental impression, irrelevant information must be eliminated so the viewer perceives the correct information. The end result should be an idealized and processed version of the real thing.

The designer should not be overly concerned that the audience will miss the point when using graphics with reduced realism—viewers can easily fill in missing details based on prior knowledge of familiar objects.[5] Through experience with pictures, viewers have a common knowledge of the way that objects are often depicted. Upon seeing an abstracted version of a familiar object, they easily recognize it as a conventional portrayal. Reducing visual noise, designing with silhouettes or line drawings, using abstracted imagery, and limiting the number of elements are approaches that can reduce the time it takes for a viewer to perceive and comprehend a graphic.

An image with simple shapes and uniform regions of color stands out in a cluttered environment—an essential quality for concert promotion posters.

__Jonas Banker,__
__BankerWessel,__ Sweden

ng LIVE
ckholm
1 MAJ KL. 20.00 OCH 23.00
DR HIGGINS
BUZZCOCKS (UK)
DJ PER SINDING LARSEN
Folk Implosion
Support: Alaska! & Mia Doi Todd
07/5 Copenhagen-Loppen
08/5 Stockholm-Södra Teatern/Kgb
09/5 Oslo-So What
10/5 Malmö-KB
Nytt album "The New Folk Implosion" ute nu!

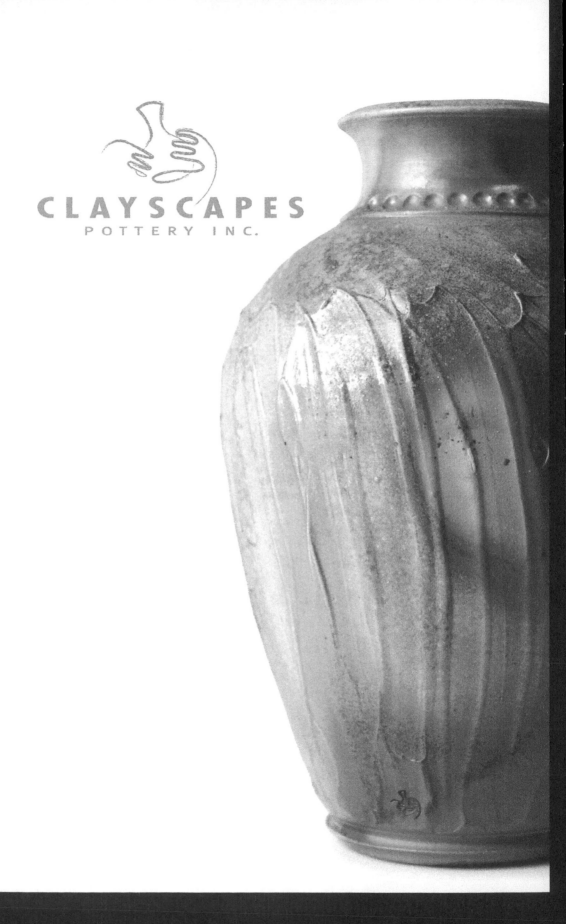

The rich visual qualities of one clay vase capture the essence of pottery with an economy of design in this brochure for a pottery distributor.

Christine Walker,
stressdesign, United States

Minimalism is put to effective use in these frames from an animated exhibit on the circulatory system. When each frame is reduced to its essential details, cognitive operations are more efficient.

**Stephanie Meier,
D. B. Dowd, Taylor Marks,
Sarah Phares,
Sarah Sisterson,
Enrique Von Rohr,
and Amanda Wolff,
Visual Communications
Research Studio-
Washington University,**
United States

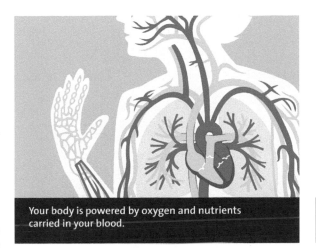

Your body is powered by oxygen and nutrients carried in your blood.

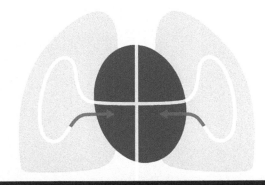

Oxygenated blood, shown as red, goes back to your heart to be pumped out to your body.

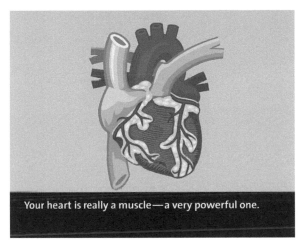

Your heart is really a muscle—a very powerful one.

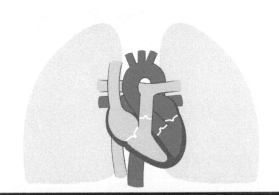

Here's a more detailed look.

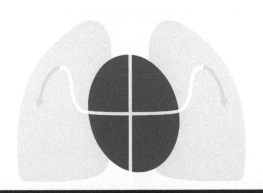

This blood passes through your heart to your lungs, where it picks up oxygen.

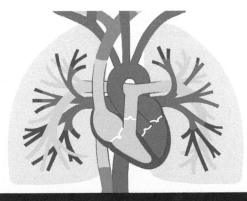

Oxygenated blood (red) enters from the lungs.

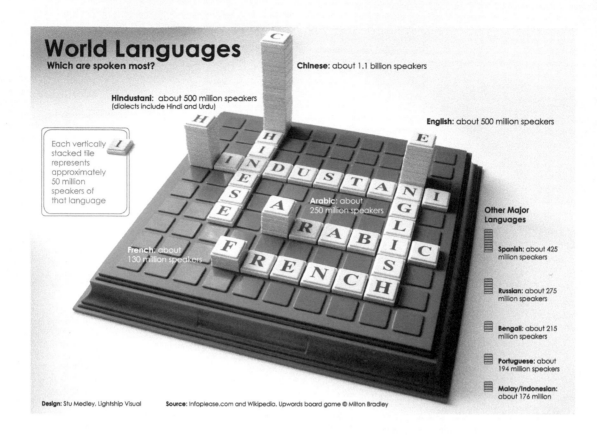

World Languages
Which are spoken most?

Chinese: about 1.1 billion speakers

Hindustani: about 500 million speakers
(dialects include Hindi and Urdu)

English: about 500 million speakers

Each vertically stacked tile represents approximately 50 million speakers of that language

Arabic: about 250 million speakers

Other Major Languages

French: about 130 million speakers

Spanish: about 425 million speakers

Russian: about 275 million speakers

Bengali: about 215 million speakers

Portuguese: about 194 million speakers

Malay/Indonesian: about 176 million

Design: Stu Medley, Lightship Visual   **Source:** Infoplease.com and Wikipedia. Upwords board game © Milton Bradley

VISUAL NOISE

In the context of 3-D graphics, visual noise enhances the perception of realism in imagery. It simulates the rich quality of our physical environment, usually through texture and shading. According to researchers in the field, "A real environment is unlikely to be pristine but will have accumulated dirt, dust, and scratches from everyday use. Although human observers do not perhaps consciously take note of these phenomena, the absence of such features … may indeed affect the viewer's perceived realism of the virtual environment."[6]

Although visual noise adds realism to an image, it can also distract the audience from the real message. The greater the quantity of meaningless information in a communication, the harder it is to decode. For example, because our brains are wired to detect patterns, the viewer may notice and then focus on unintentional patterns found in excessive texture or detail. Minimizing the visual noise in an image is an effective approach to reducing its perceived realism. To do this, the designer can create an environment

that approaches an artificial or pristine world. The graphics shown here demonstrate the hyperreal environment of reduced realism. Lines are extradefined, colored regions are crisp and flat, and surface textures are simplified.

Graphics that are used to support comprehension and learning or as aids to performing a procedure should contain little or no visual noise. The visual information in these types of graphics must be accurately understood. The visual content is often stored in long-term memory and transferred to real-world situations. Visual noise might congest the processing and reduce assimilation of new information.

In both 3-D and 2-D graphics, visual noise can be attributed to high-contrast surface textures, gradated regions of color, the illusion of depth, and detailed or patterned backgrounds. To minimize visual noise, reduce extreme variations in texture, experiment with flat and uniform areas of color, diminish shadows and shading, and lessen background interference.

This comparison of world languages created for Figures *magazine creates an environment with little visual noise. The designer uses sufficient detail to depict the board game metaphor and statistical data, but not enough to overwhelm or distract the viewer.*

Stu Medley,
Lightship Visual, Australia

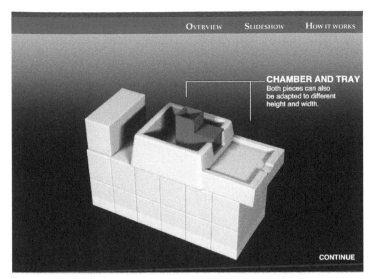

CHAMBER AND TRAY
Both pieces can also
be adapted to different
height and width.

CONTINUE

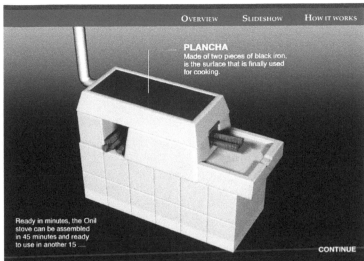

PLANCHA
Made of two pieces of black iron,
is the surface that is finally used
for cooking.

Ready in minutes, the Onil
stove can be assembled
in 45 minutes and ready
to use in another 15 ....

CONTINUE

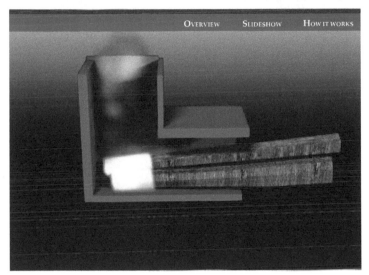

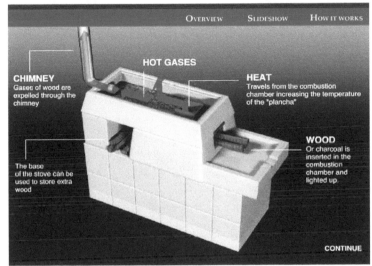

HOT GASES

CHIMNEY
Gases of wood are
expelled through the
chimney

HEAT
Travels from the combustion
chamber increasing the temperature
of the "plancha"

The base
of the stove can be
used to store extra
wood

WOOD
Or charcoal is
inserted in the
combustion
chamber and
lighted up.

CONTINUE

These frames from an
interactive exhibit for the
Houston Chronicle create
a noiseless 3-D world to
explain the workings of
a high-impact, low-tech
stove design. Low-contrast
textures and hard shadows
add enough realism to replicate the stove and burning
wood but do not interfere
with accurate perception
and interpretation of the
animation.

Alberto Cuadra,
Houston Chronicle,
United States

▶ *Viewers often have difficulty perceiving small differences between similar objects. By minimizing the detail on the jets, viewers can focus on the measurements in red.*

Eliot Bergman, Japan

▼ *The illustrations on this medical card show a health care audience how to evaluate the condition of an endoscope (used for looking inside the body). The problems with the three faulty tubes on the right are clearly portrayed through an emphasis on the important features and a lack of extraneous detail.*

Aviad Stark, Graphic Advance, United States

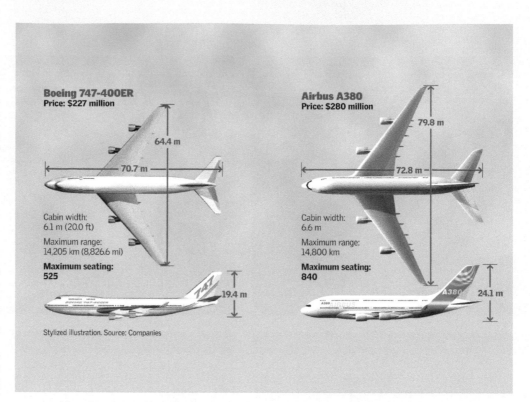

Boeing 747-400ER
Price: $227 million

64.4 m

70.7 m

Cabin width:
6.1 m (20.0 ft)

Maximum range:
14,205 km (8,826.6 mi)

Maximum seating:
525

19.4 m

Stylized illustration. Source: Companies

Airbus A380
Price: $280 million

79.8 m

72.8 m

Cabin width:
6.6 m

Maximum range:
14,800 km

Maximum seating:
840

24.1 m

VISION SCIENCES

FLEXIBLE ENT SCOPE
INSERTION TUBE EVALUATION TEMPLATE

→ Vision Sciences ENT-1000
→ Karl Storz 11101SK1
→ Machida ENT-2L
→ Olympus ENF-XP
→ Pentax FNL-7RP3

→ Vision Sciences ENT-3000
→ Vision Sciences ENT-2000
→ Vision Sciences E-F100
→ Karl Storz 11101RP
→ Karl Storz 11101RP-1
→ Smith & Nephew / Gyrus Duraview OL-1
→ Welch Allyn RL-150
→ Xion EF-NS

→ Machida ENT-3L
→ Machida ENT-30PIII

→ Machida ENT-4L
→ Olympus ENF-V
→ Pentax FNL-13S
→ Pentax VNL-1330
→ Pentax VNL-1130
→ Pentax VNL-1170K

→ Olympus ENF-P4
→ Olympus ENF-P3
→ Olympus ENF-GP

→ Pentax FNL-10P2
→ Pentax FNL-10S
→ Pentax FNL-10RBS
→ Pentax FNL-10RP3

Use this card to evaluate your flexible endoscope prior to using the Slide-On™ ENT Sheath. If your ENT scope shows signs of damage (see below) or will not pass through the size gauge provided, contact the scope manufacturer for repair.

UNDAMAGED

WRINKLED

DENTED

ROLLED OVER

For more information about the Slide-On™ EndoSheath® System, please contact Vision-Sciences, Inc.
Vision-Sciences, Inc. • 9 Strathmore Road • Natick, MA 01760 • T: 800.874.9975 • T: 508.650.9971 • F: 508.650.9976 • www.visionsciences.com

C05164 Rev D

SILHOUETTES

The reduction of an object or scene to its essential profile, as in a silhouette, is an effective technique for minimizing realism. A silhouette typically depicts a form through the outline of its shape, an interior without detail or texture, and a fill of uniform color often within a flat pictorial space. A silhouette evokes recognition by retaining the most important shape information derived from its edge, whether it is a portrait, human form, or object.

A silhouette promotes quick perception and speedy comprehension when it maintains a faithful resemblance to the contours of a real-world form. Although it provides information on the shape dimension alone—without the illusion of depth—human visual perception is remarkably adept at recognizing what it represents.

The silhouette offers many possibilities for expression, depending on its shape, gesture, and context. In its most neutral state, a silhouette is often the visual equivalent of a generalization, conveying the sense that it speaks for all objects in the class it represents. Thus, a silhouette of a man symbolizes Everyman; a silhouette of a mountain symbolizes all mountains.

In a design that evokes emotion, a silhouette can imply anonymity or isolation, as in someone lacking identity. It can quickly convey a sense of mystery, representing a shadowy world devoid of detail. In cartoons, the frame with a silhouette provides a pregnant pause, allowing the audience to step back before the punch line. When a silhouette is given a quantitative value, it becomes a symbol, as in a pictogram. However it is used, a well-designed silhouette is a compact expression of compressed information that can be understood with a minimum of cognitive effort.

Because the silhouette is a closed and featureless form, it can potentially be difficult to perceive. This happens when the shape is ambiguous or cannot be distinguished from its background, causing figure—ground reversal. To avoid perceptual concerns, ensure that the silhouette shape is easy to detect and recognize. Use a formless region for the background and differentiate the figure with a well-defined boundary or color contrast. Do not allow negative space to intrude on the figure. Consider decreasing the size of the foreground objects, as smaller shapes tend to be perceived as the figure rather than the ground.

Expressive silhouettes convey a celebratory theme in this accordion poster for an in-house project. With little effort, we are able to recognize the representations of family and healthy living.

__Janet Giampietro, Langton Cherubino Group,__ United States

The repetition of silhouette shapes provides visual impact in this poster for the Icograda Exhibition in Cuba. Silhouettes provide the base for adding the single distinguishing detail on each form.

Antonio Mena,
Antonio Mena Design,
Ecuador

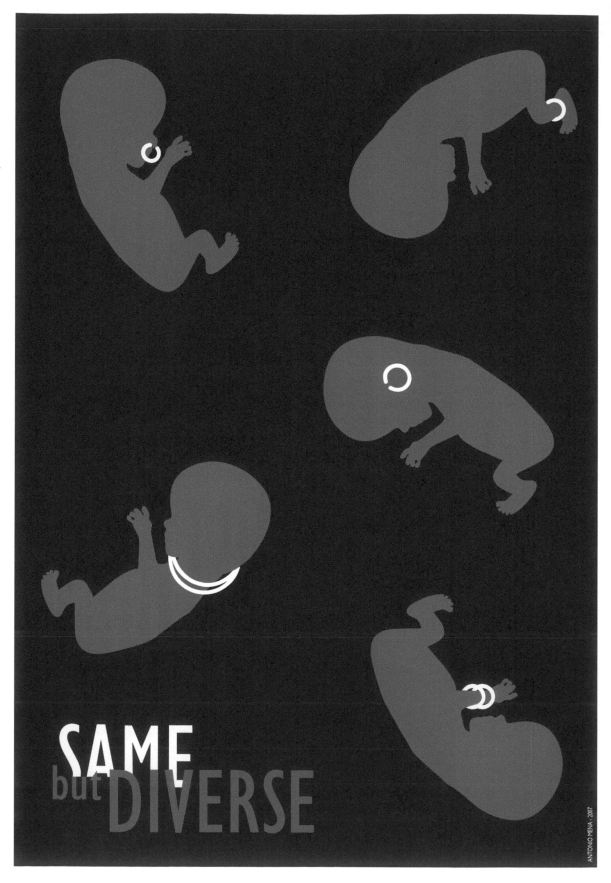

Symbols of music exploding from the hair of this silhouette capture the energy of the festival it advertises. Creative layering makes the silhouette work as both foreground and background.

Cog Design,
United Kingdom

Appealing silhouettes grace the lesson introductions of these science education materials, suggesting the mysteries the books will unravel for young students.

Heather Corcoran, Colleen Conrado, Jennifer Saltzman, and Anna Donovan; Plum Studio and Visual Communications Research Studio, United States

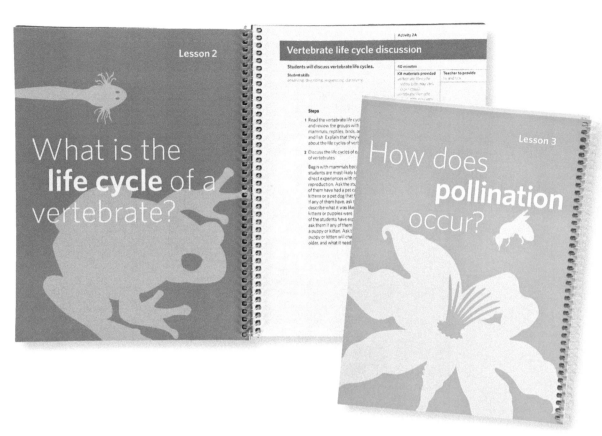

Lesson 2

What is the **life cycle** of a vertebrate?

Vertebrate life cycle discussion

Lesson 3

How does **pollination** occur?

USE YOUR VOICE

In this brochure to raise awareness for children orphaned from AIDS, the silhouette depicts a universal figure, expressing that everyone should take action and get involved.

Jay Smith, Juicebox Designs, United States

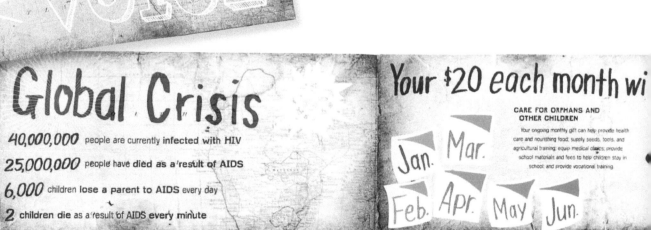

Global Crisis

40,000,000 people are currently infected with HIV

25,000,000 people have died as a result of AIDS

6,000 children lose a parent to AIDS every day

2 children die as a result of AIDS every minute

Your $20 each month wi

CARE FOR ORPHANS AND OTHER CHILDREN

Your ongoing monthly gift can help provide health care and nourishing food; supply seeds, tools, and agricultural training; equip medical clinics; provide school materials and fees to help children stay in school; and provide vocational training.

Jan. Mar.
Feb. Apr. May Jun.

"In 1900, there were 1.5 billion people in the world. Now, there are 6.5 billion. We live together, work together, travel together and, as a result, the potential for spread of disease is high. Global boundaries in the world of infectious disease are functionally disappearing."

JOHN E. EDWARDS, JR., M.D., ADULT INFECTIOUS DISEASES

A New World

Photographic silhouettes reduce individuals to essential shape and posture.

Jane Lee,
IE Design & Communications, United States

EQUIP VOLUNTEER CAREGIVERS FOR ORPHAN FAMILIES

World Vision trains volunteer caregivers to reach out to orphans and vulnerable children in their communities.

Your gifts will support caregivers who help children to be healthy, have enough to eat, attend school and get the love and encouragement they need to thrive.

OFFER HIV-PREVENTION AND ABSTINENCE TRAINING FOR YOUTH

We work with local organizations and churches to provide counseling and training that help HIV-affected children make wise choices for their futures. Your support will help train youth peer educators and form community-based peer support groups. In Uganda, programs like these have helped to reduce the HIV infection rate from 21 percent to 4 percent.

In addition, World Vision is training up community leaders to take the lead in communicating the crucial importance of HIV prevention and ensuring prevention of mother-to-child transmission of HIV.

Jul.
Aug.
Sept.
Oct.
Nov.
Dec.

WHAT DO I DO NEXT?

1. Complete the information on the envelope. Enclose your first monthly gift of $20 or more by debit/credit card, check or cash. Drop off the envelope with a World Vision representative or at the World Vision table.

2. Ask for your special gift, our way of saying thank you for using your debit/credit card. When you sign up for our Automatic Giving Plan, you help save $12 a year in processing and postage costs.

Resemblance Icon

Exemplar Icon

Symbolic Icon

Arbitrary Icon

ICONIC FORMS

The word *icon* has many meanings in art and graphic design. In this book, an iconic form refers to a highly distilled or stylized depiction that captures the essential characteristics of an object or concept. In contrast to the silhouette that communicates through shape alone, the iconic form communicates through an efficient use of shape, line, and color. When an iconic form is a symbol, its meaning is often culturally dependent and must be learned or deduced. Icons embody a quality that cognitive theorists call computational efficiency, meaning they minimize the processing required for an accurate interpretation. Thus, iconic forms are quickly recognized and processed, and their meanings are memorable.

When we think of iconic images, we may picture an abstracted representation of a familiar object, such as the simplified image that indicates a bus stop. Although these types of icons are prolific, iconic forms can also be rendered as simple schematic representations, such as a human face composed of geometric shapes. Though many iconic forms resemble an object in the environment and have a corresponding meaning, others have an associative value and are considered symbols. Context is a strong contributor to the meaning of an iconic form. For example, in one context, an iconic form of concentric curved lines can represent a rainbow, and in another context it can represent wireless service.

Graphic designers may benefit from an icon classification system proposed by professor Yvonne Rogers for user interface design. In her system, icons are categorized by how they depict the concept they represent.[7] This structure provides a way to think about the potential uses of iconic forms. Resemblance icons directly portray the object to which they refer, such as the icon for the ticket counter at the airport. Exemplar icons depict a common example of the class of objects to which they refer, such as a knife and fork to signify restaurant. Symbolic icons convey a concept that is at a higher level of abstraction than the object depicted, as when a cracked wine glass is used to indicate that the contents of a package is fragile. Arbitrary icons have no relationship to an object or concept, and their association must be learned, such as the symbol indicating no entrance.

An iconic classification system adapted from icons by Russell Tate

*__Russell Tate,__
__Russell Tate Illustration,__
Australia*

Playful iconic forms representing exercise and activity decorate the walls of this leisure center in Australia.

Simon Hancock, THERE,
Australia

Iconic forms are appropriate for many uses because they facilitate quick communication. They are effective in signage, maps, technical displays, catalogs, diagrams, and graphs. The iconic form is effective as a memory device or mnemonic, often helpful in training aids and reference materials. Icons can help in the categorization and classification of content, providing meaning to seemingly random information. Icons also succeed as symbols for representing numerical data, as when an icon of a person equals a specific value in a pictograph.

If the goal is to express a message that is direct and immediately understood, the iconic form must be precise and use a simple, effective orientation. Designers may find that the most recognizable version of an object is its side view. When creating an iconic symbol, a corresponding association is more effective than an arbitrary one that must be learned or inferred. Nigel Holmes provides this insight regarding icon design in his book, *Designing Pictorial Symbols*: "It is visually precise; it attempts to get at the essence of an idea— either by being a literal, miniature drawing, or by being a non-literal, visual metaphor. A symbol can give an identity to a subject and, by repeated use, can come to equal it."

These stylized iconic forms for Europe's Thalys train are distilled to their minimum attributes for quick comprehension.

**Jean-Manuel Duvivier,
Jean-Manuel Duvivier
Illustration,** Belgium

◀ *Iconic forms can be expressive, as in these illustrations for a book of urban stories. The figures represent the concepts of monotony, play, inspiration, and urban planting.*

Tamara Ivanova, Germany

▼ *This reference card instructs office employees on how to be a good neighbor. The icons work as a mnemonic device to help people remember the rules of office etiquette.*

Wing Chan, Wing Chan Design, United States

AMERICAN EXPRESS

Good Neighbor Tips | Corporate Affairs and Communications

Heads Up
Avoid popping up in your cubicle to get someone's attention. Speaking over the tops of workstations disrupts your neighbors.

Be BlackBerry and Cell Savvy
Keeping on top of e-mail is important for many of us. But unless you are waiting for an urgent note, you should turn your BlackBerry or other hand-held devices off at group meetings.

Constantly checking your BlackBerry can send the message that you're not interested in what your colleagues have to say.

Good Housekeeping
In shared spaces such as the pantry, conference rooms, copy rooms and break areas, be careful of what you leave behind and try to leave the area clean. Be sure to pick up printed documents,

especially when the information may be confidential. Erase any information written on white boards or flip charts. And, of course, throw away leftover food, empty drink bottles, etc.

Being Punctual Counts
Try to be on time for meetings and gatherings. Allowing yourself an extra five minutes between meetings,

especially when traveling between different floors, is one way to ensure that you're punctual. Being the latecomer can be discourteous and disruptive to others, especially if you're always late for a regularly scheduled meeting.

Turn Down The Volume
When in the open cube environment, remember that sounds carry easily. You may not realize it, but talking loudly can be disruptive to your colleagues, particularly when they're trying to concentrate on a project. In addition, cell phone ringers, palm pilot

notification sounds and radios can be distracting. Remember to keep sounds for these devices turned off or at a very low volume.

Communication Courtesy Suggestions
Having a friendly and productive work environment depends largely on how we communicate with each other. Here are some suggested ways to communicate with your neighbors when it comes office etiquette:

"I'm really sorry to interrupt, but your conversation is distracting and making it difficult for me to focus on my work. Would it be possible for you to move to a conference room or use a quieter tone of voice?"

"I know you may not realize it, but sometimes your voice is a bit loud. I'd really appreciate it if you could lower your voice a bit."

"I know you're really keen on getting your project done. But in the future, if you see I'm on the phone when you come to my cube, I'd appreciate your not trying to interrupt me to talk about something. It would be better to leave me a voicemail, send me an e-mail or stop by later when I'm off the phone."

Saying Hello Goes a Long Way

"I know you're new to the department... Even though we don't work in the same group, I wanted to say hi and introduce myself."

LINE ART

The simple line drawing that focuses on the outline of an object is a graceful way to achieve reduced realism. Often with minimal tonal value or depth, the line drawing describes the shape of an object and its essential details with a few strokes. It is thought that early in the vision process, the brain quickly extracts linear features from a picture or scene. This includes line curvature, line orientation, and the ending point of a line. When we scan an image or an object, most of the visual activity occurs on the edges. Thus, depicting an outline alone is sufficient to convey meaning. Similar to understanding silhouettes, the dimension of shape helps us recognize objects. This may be due to our familiarity with picture conventions. Even though lines do not bind objects in the physical world, we perceive outline drawings "as depicting shapes rather than arrangements of wires."[8]

Our perceptual tendency to organize units into wholes comes into play in line perception. Known as the Gestalt principle of closure, it states that we organize sensory input by closing simple figures to make them whole. In addition, during later stages of vision we transform an image into something that fits with our experience and expectations. For example, we add a third dimension to an image from small depth cues. Although line art appears to be simple, it projects a great deal of information.

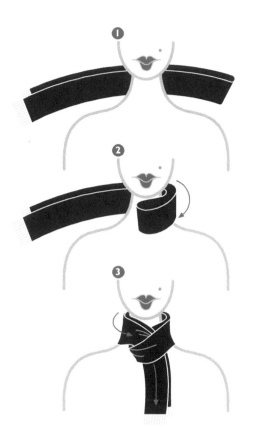

◀ In this lighthearted illustration of how to wear a scarf European style, the instructions are succinctly depicted in line art, providing all the information the viewer needs without a word of text.

Nigel Holmes,
United States

▶ In this information graphic, line art successfully illustrates the history of early thermometers and provides an explanation of how Galileo's version worked.

Diana Litavsky,
Illinois Institute of Art,
United States

In addition to effectively conveying the human figure, line drawings are excellent for technical and explanatory graphics that describe the inner workings of the body or a machine. These drawings typically provide all the necessary detail and omit anything superfluous. Explanatory line drawings are effective as illustrations in documentation and textbooks, as infographics, and for assembly instructions. Surprisingly, people identify the objects in line drawings as easily as the objects in photographs, and line drawings are superior to photographs in terms of making the information conveyed in the picture memorable.[9]

As in other approaches to reducing realism, the line drawing does not need extensive detail, but must capture the contours and prominent features of an object while filtering out irrelevant information. The designer or illustrator must analytically and intuitively seek the few elements that will convey the idea, emotion, or object. Although the drawing and the object will not be equivalent, the visual impression it creates will suffice—the audience will add their knowledge of the world to the interpretation of those few lines.

Evolution of the Thermometer

The Galileo Thermoscope 1592

A Galileo thermometer or thermoscope, which is named after the Italian physicist Galileo Galilei, is a thermometer made of a sealed glass cylinder containing a clear liquid and a series of objects who densities are designed to sink in sequence as liquid is warmed and decreases in density

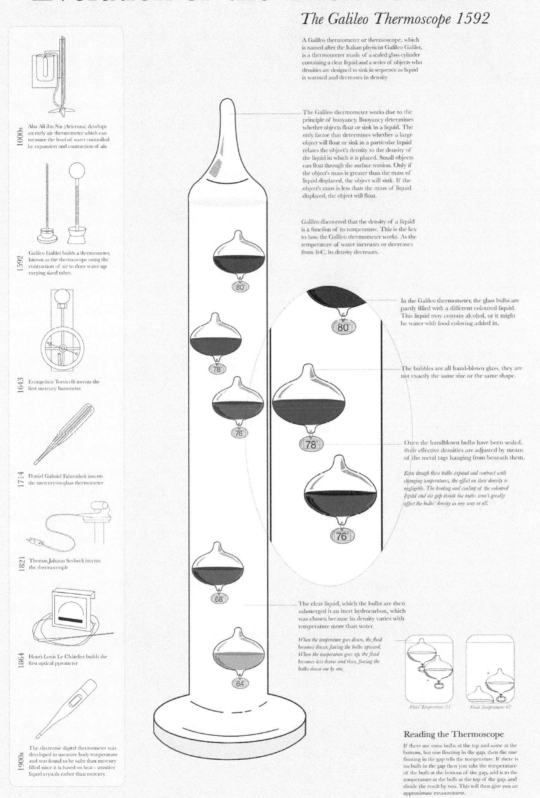

Timeline (left margin)

1000s — Abu Ali Ibn Sin (Avicenna) develops an early air thermometer which can measure the level of water controlled by expansion and contraction of air.

1592 — Galileo Galilei builds a thermometer, known as the thermoscope using the contraction of air to draw water up varying sized tubes.

1643 — Evangelista Torricelli invents the first mercury barometer.

1714 — Daniel Gabriel Fahrenheit invents the mercury-in-glass thermometer

1821 — Thomas Johann Seebeck invents the thermocouple

1864 — Henri-Louis Le Châtelier builds the first optical pyrometer

1900s — The electronic digital thermometer was developed to measure body temperature and was found to be safer than mercury filled since it is based on heat - sensitive liquid crystals rather than mercury

Main article (right column)

The Galileo thermometer works due to the principle of buoyancy. Buoyancy determines whether objects float or sink in a liquid. The only factor that determines whether a large object will float or sink in a particular liquid relates the object's density to the density of the liquid in which it is placed. Small objects can float through the surface tension. Only if the object's mass is greater than the mass of liquid displaced, the object will sink. If the object's mass is less than the mass of liquid displaced, the object will float.

Galileo discovered that the density of a liquid is a function of its temperature. This is the key to how the Galileo thermometer works. As the temperature of water increases or decreases from 4oC, its density decreases.

In the Galileo thermometer, the glass bulbs are partly filled with a different coloured liquid. This liquid may contain alcohol, or it might be water with food coloring added in.

The bubbles are all hand-blown glass, they are not exactly the same size or the same shape.

Once the handblown bulbs have been sealed, their effective densities are adjusted by means of the metal tags hanging from beneath them.

Even though these bulbs expand and contract with changing temperatures, the effect on their density is negligible. The heating and cooling of the coloured liquid and air gap inside the bulbs won't greatly affect the bulbs' density in any way at all.

The clear liquid, which the bulbs are then submerged is an inert hydrocarbon, which was chosen because its density varies with temperature more than water.

When the temperature goes down, the fluid becomes denser, forcing the bulbs upward. When the temperature goes up, the fluid becomes less dense and rises, forcing the bulbs down one by one.

Fluid Temperature 33   Fluid Temperature 67

Reading the Thermoscope

If there are some bulbs at the top and some at the bottom, but one floating in the gap, then the one floating in the gap tells the temperature. If there is no bulb in the gap then you take the temperature of the bulb at the bottom of the gap, add it to the temperature at the bulb at the top of the gap, and divide the result by two. This will then give you an approximate measurement.

NOTICE: Freak-dancing is not permitted at school-sponsored activities

  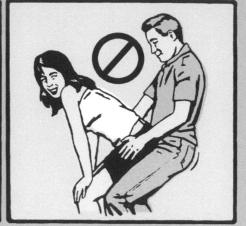

Fig.1 Excellent   *Fig.2* Acceptable   *Fig.3* Prohibited

Line art is used to instruct students on permitted and prohibited school dancing in this humorous illustration for the Seattle Weekly. *Although the illustrations portray the top portion of each figure, our minds complete the missing information as a result of expectations and prior knowledge.*

Eric Larsen, Eric Larsen Artwork, *United States*

Using the low-fidelity imagery of line art, this poster expresses the fun and lightness of Miami's Gallery Walk. Line art may closely match how we store visual information in long-term memory.

Sarah Cazee, Cazee Design, *United States*

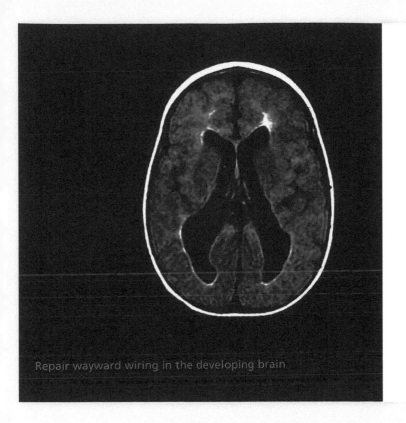

Repair wayward wiring in the developing brain

Swap good genes for bad

QUANTITY

Our natural environment is visually dense and complex. One way to reduce realism is to reverse what we typically see in the environment by strictly limiting the quantity of elements in a design. This allows the viewer to focus on the few essential components needed to understand the intended message. Restricting quantity means limiting the number of images, shapes, lines, and type.

In a quick glance, we can accurately and rapidly perceive a limited number of elements in a visual scene. This capability for quickly judging the number of items without counting is known as *subitizing*. We can automatically subitize up to around four objects.[10] This is similar to the number of elements we can typically hold in visual working memory at one time. By reducing the number of elements, working memory can operate at normal capacity without overload; visual processing is not overwhelmed; and the amount of information to store away is minimal.

Limiting the quantity of elements creates visuals with impact. With this approach, every element has an intentional function, so its message is clear. This approach also makes it easier for designers to rank elements in terms of dominance and subordination. One effective method for reducing the quantity of elements is the subtractive approach, or determining what can be eliminated from a design. Some ways to achieve this are to remove extraneous imagery, shorten text, clean up the background, and cluster items within a border so they are perceived as one unit. The design must continue to work after any element is removed.

To promote the expertise of a children's hospital, this booklet reduces the number of design components on each page as a way of reflecting a childlike artistic simplicity.

Erica Gregg Howe and Amy Lebow, Philographica, United States

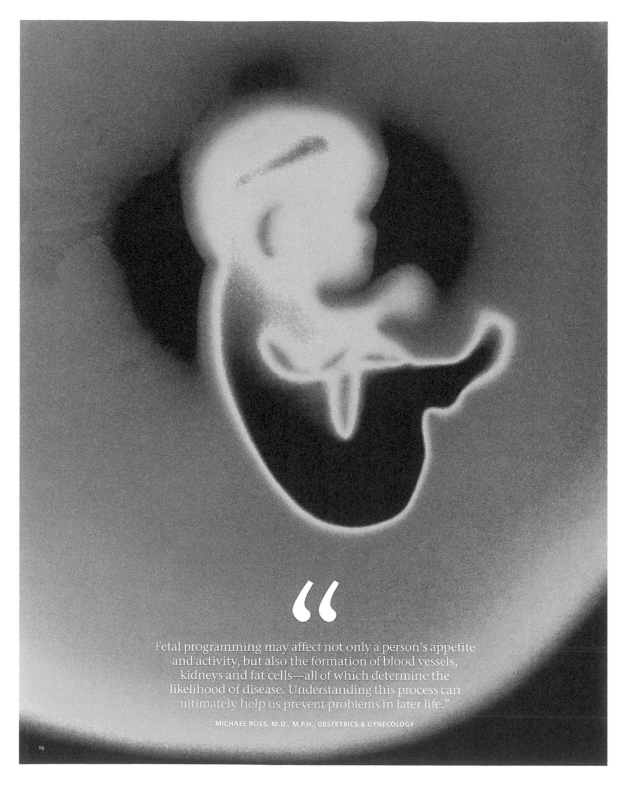

"Fetal programming may affect not only a person's appetite and activity, but also the formation of blood vessels, kidneys and fat cells—all of which determine the likelihood of disease. Understanding this process can ultimately help us prevent problems in later life."

MICHAEL ROSS, M.D., M.P.H., OBSTETRICS & GYNECOLOGY

◄ This design with medical imagery exemplifies re- duced realism—an effective approach for the promo- tional aspect of a medical institute's annual report.

Jane Lee,
IE Design &
Communications,
United States

▶ Limiting the number of elements in this design created for a poets' festival establishes the rich stack of tattered books as the dominant component.

Ira Ginzburg, B.I.G. Design,
Israel

שירה
2006

קריאה, מוסיקה, תיאטרון, שיחות, תערוכות

שלישות

פסטיבל המשוררים
הישראלי ה-9

מטולה, חג השבועות
31.5.06-**3.6**.06
רביעי עד שבת, די-זי סיוון

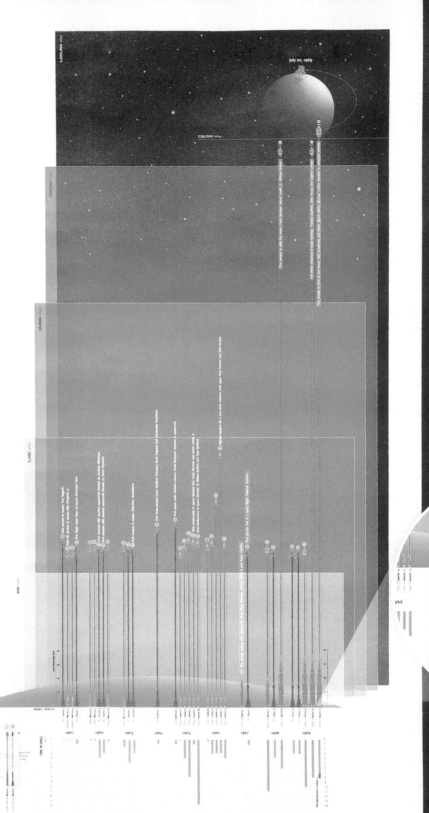

This unique historical time-line depicts the competition between the United States and U.S.S.R. to land the first person on the moon.

**Larry Gormley,
History Shots, and
Dan Greenwald,
White Rhino,** United States

"The progress of civilization can be read in the invention
of visual artifacts, from writing to mathematics, to maps,
to printing, to diagrams, to visual computing."

STUART CARD ET AL. *Readings in Information Visualization*

Visuals help us think. We sketch a map to give directions, draw a diagram to express a complex idea, and read graphs to understand financial data. Visual thinking is an integral aspect of cognition, and the visualizing of abstract concepts helps us understand the world and communicate about it. The contribution that visuals make to our analytical, reasoning, and problem-solving abilities is far reaching. In his book *Things That Make Us Smart*, Donald Norman writes, "The power of the unaided mind is highly overrated. Without external aids, memory, thought, and reasoning are all constrained."

We gain enormous insights from representing information in a visual form. From ancient maps to interactive visualizations, the graphical depiction of data and concepts has created new ways of seeing things and new approaches to solving problems. Two significant examples from the early history of graphs exemplify this point. In 1854, Dr. John Snow visually plotted where deaths were occurring from a cholera epidemic in London. By analyzing his statistical graph, Dr. Snow was able to locate and eliminate the contaminated source of water, which stopped the further spread of cholera. Not too many years later, during the Crimean War, Florence Nightingale invented a new type of statistical chart proving that British soldiers were dying at a much higher rate from preventable diseases than from the wounds of battle. Because Nightingale was able to visually represent the magnitude of preventable disease among soldiers, her petition to improve sanitation conditions was more compelling. Visual portrayals create new forms of knowledge.

Diagrams, charts, graphs, visualizations, maps, and timelines are referred to by many names—abstract, nonrepresentational, logical, and arbitrary graphics. Regardless of their name and form, their purpose is the same—to concretize abstract ideas and concepts. Although abstract graphics were once the domain of statisticians and cartographers, graphic designers and illustrators are frequently called upon to produce them for editorial publications; scientific, technical, and business journals; annual reports; educational and training aids; and promotional materials.

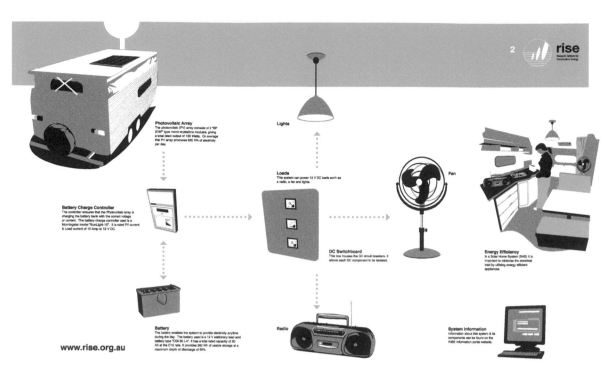

◀ This diagram created for a research institute uses minimalist art and text to explain the practical uses of solar-powered systems. Note how every element in the diagram represents one object or concept.

Stuart Medley, Lightship Visual, Australia

How Abstract Graphics Work

Not only do abstract graphics enhance communication, they also enhance the credibility of a message. There is a sense of objectivity to the nonrepresentational graphic, similar to the way photographs appear to be objective renderings of reality. After all, abstract graphics represent facts and data, concepts, and systems. People expect them to reflect accuracy and precision, believing they are the final word. In truth, however, every abstract graphic is inherently the result of numerous subjective design decisions. The designer must determine such things as what information can fit and what must be excluded; whether the elements should be represented as symbols, icons, or illustrations; which colors and patterns will enhance communicability; and which conventions should be followed and which ignored.

Abstract graphics are unique in that each element has a one-to-one correspondence with what it represents. Each element has only one unambiguous and exclusive meaning.[1] In a map, for example, the icon of a picnic table has a unique meaning—it symbolizes "picnic area." Anyone familiar with maps knows that this symbol has no other interpretations. In a line graph, each point represents a single value, and in a diagram, each component represents one object or concept. This is quite different from pictorial representations like paintings and photographs, where the elements and symbols can have many meanings based on a viewer's subjective interpretation.

Another distinguishing characteristic of abstract graphics is that they depict relationships. Diagrams and charts represent systems and the relationships between the systems' components; graphs represent quantitative relationships; visualizations create patterns that represent complex data relationships; maps represent spatial relationships among geographical locations; and timelines represent the relationships between temporal events. Hybrid graphics that combine two or more forms, such as the combined timeline and graph shown in the NASA infographic (on page 132), represent several levels of relationships.

Abstract graphics are prevalent in technical, scientific, and business publications because they provide a concrete reference for understanding difficult content and facilitate analysis and problem solving. They succeed at depicting intangible concepts that are difficult to express in words. Abstract graphics are also pragmatic, as in the maps we use for navigation and weather information. Many abstract graphics have a powerful aesthetic dimension associated with the rich beauty of information display. They can also serve as vehicles for artistic expression and for making political and social statements.

▶ In this provocative statement against breast augmentation, statistics blend with creative imagery to make a powerful social statement. A breast formation was arranged with 32,000 Barbie dolls, which equals the number of elective breast augmentation surgeries performed monthly in the United States in 2006, according to the artist.

Chris Jordan, United States

These graphics explain the toxic effects of mining and burning coal through many types of abstract graphics. Adding imagery to an abstract graphic, such as this photograph of visible pollution, is a helpful way to quickly communicate a message.

Sean Douglass, University of Washington, United States

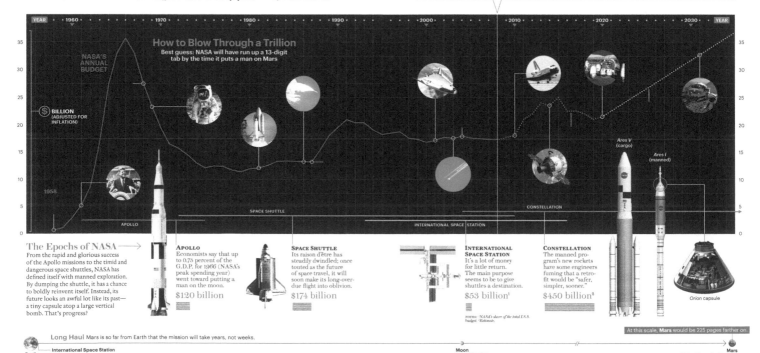

Conquering jet lag with melatonin

Melatonin has been shown in studies to correct the out-of-sync effects of jet lag with dosages of 5 to 10 mg, taken 30 to 90 minutes before bedtime on the day of arrival and for as many nights as symptoms exist. These examples display how jet lag differs on various flights. The red dot on the left globe is your body clock, which remains set to home time. The red dot on the right is your body, which has moved to a new time zone and is now out of sync. The degree of jet lag depends on the minimum number of time zones separating the dots. That is why, regardless of your route from New York to Sydney (east through 15 time zones or west through 9), you will be 9 hours out of sync when you arrive.

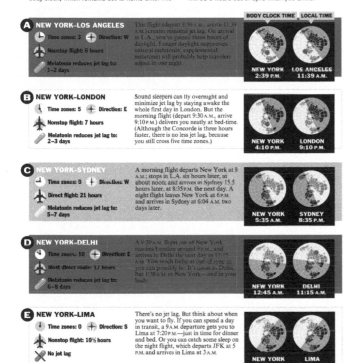

A NEW YORK–LOS ANGELES
🕐 Time zones: 3 ✈ Direction: W
✈ Nonstop flight: 6 hours
💊 Melatonin reduces jet lag to: 1–2 days

BODY CLOCK TIME	LOCAL TIME
NEW YORK 2:39 P.M.	LOS ANGELES 11:39 A.M.

This flight (depart 8:50 A.M., arrive 11:39 A.M.) creates minimal jet lag. On arrival in L.A., you've gained three hours of daylight. Longer daylight suppresses natural melatonin; supplemental melatonin will probably help travelers adjust in one night.

B NEW YORK–LONDON
🕐 Time zones: 5 ✈ Direction: E
✈ Nonstop flight: 7 hours
💊 Melatonin reduces jet lag to: 2–3 days

NEW YORK 4:10 P.M.	LONDON 9:10 P.M.

Sound sleepers can fly overnight and minimize jet lag by staying awake the whole first day in London. But the morning flight (depart 9:30 A.M., arrive 9:10 P.M.) delivers you neatly at bed-time. (Although the Concorde is three hours faster, there is no less jet lag, because you still cross five time zones.)

C NEW YORK–SYDNEY
🕐 Time zones: 0 ✈ Direction: W
✈ Direct flight: 21 hours
💊 Melatonin reduces jet lag to: 5–7 days

NEW YORK 5:35 A.M.	SYDNEY 8:35 P.M.

A morning flight departs New York at 9 A.M.; stops in L.A. six hours later, at about noon; and arrives in Sydney 15.5 hours later, at 8:35 P.M. the next day. A night flight leaves New York at 6 P.M. and arrives in Sydney at 6:04 A.M. two days later.

D NEW YORK–DELHI
🕐 Time zones: 10 ✈ Direction: E
✈ Most direct route: 17 hours
💊 Melatonin reduces jet lag to: 6–8 days

NEW YORK 12:45 A.M.	DELHI 11:15 A.M.

A 9:30 A.M. flight out of New York reaches London around 9 P.M., and arrives in Delhi the next day at 11:15 A.M. You reach India as out of sync as you can possibly be: It's noon in Delhi, but 1:30 A.M. in New York—and in your body.

E NEW YORK–LIMA
🕐 Time zones: 0 ✈ Direction: S
✈ Nonstop flight: 10½ hours
✗ No jet lag

NEW YORK 7:20 P.M.	LIMA 7:20 P.M.

There's no jet lag. But think about when you want to fly. If you can spend a day in transit, a 9 A.M. departure gets you to Lima at 7:20 P.M.—just in time for dinner and bed. Or you can catch some sleep on the night flight, which departs JFK at 5 P.M. and arrives in Lima at 3 A.M.

Jet lag: The arithmetic of travel

Each number represents one (simplified) time zone and one day of jet lag. Imagine yourself in New York at noon, your body in sync with eastern standard time. If you fly to London, five time zones east, your body clock remains set to EST for the first day, and it will slowly catch up—at a rate of about one time zone per day—until your body is in sync with Greenwich Mean Time, about five days after you arrive. Most volunteers who used melatonin after long-haul flights reduced that period of adjustment to three days, or even two. The flights shown here and on the facing page demonstrate the differences encountered in flying east vs. west, flying across latitude vs. longitude, taking short flights vs. long flights, and crossing few time zones vs. many.

◄ This information graphic demonstrates how a great deal of data can be packed into one visual. NASA's annual budget data is depicted as a line graph mapped onto a timeline. Associated images connect to points on the graph, and the length of each era is displayed across the bottom.

John Grimwade
and Liana Zamora,
Condé Nast Publications,
United States

▲ Abstract graphics provide new ways of looking at information. These visualizations demonstrate how jet lag affects the body when flying in various directions.

John Grimwade,
Condé Nast Publications,
United States

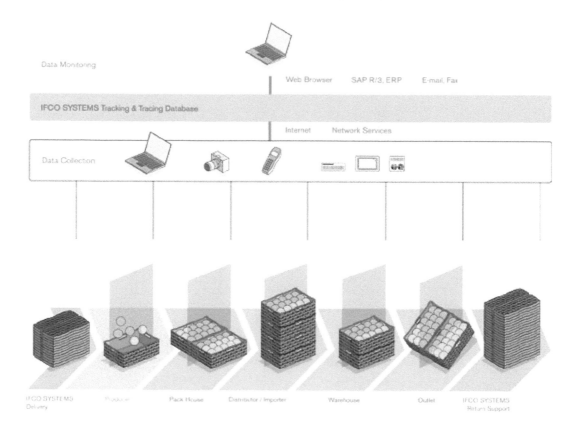

Data Monitoring

Web Browser   SAP R/3, ERP   E-mail, Fax

IFCO SYSTEMS Tracking & Tracing Database

Internet   Network Services

Data Collection

IFCO SYSTEMS Delivery   Producer   Pack House   Distributor / Importer   Warehouse   Outlet   IFCO SYSTEMS Return Support

The Cognitive Aspect

Space conveys meaning. Abstract graphics are often superior to verbal descriptions because of their effect on cognition. We process them more quickly and easily, particularly compared to reading long explanations or performing numeric calculations. Their tangible quality comes from the meaning we find in the spatial relationships among the graphic's components. We easily derive meaning from spatial relationships because of our familiarity and experience with physical space.

In maps, the spatial relationship among elements is analogous to their geographical locations. We know that if a city map oriented to the north shows a building to the west of where we are standing, the building will be to our left because of this analogous relationship. In diagrams, charts, and graphs, the spatial relationships are metaphorical. When elements are displayed in a hierarchical chart, a spatial metaphor helps us understand that the element in the primary position (usually the top or the left) is the most significant or powerful. When a line graph trends toward the top of the page or screen, we use a spatial metaphor to understand that this means an increase in value.

The order, sequence, and distance between elements also communicate meaning. When two events in a timeline are separated by a large interval, we interpret this to mean the events are far apart in time. These interpretations are grounded in our real-world experience and are thought to be "cognitively natural."[2] Because we can easily interpret the spatial metaphors used in abstract graphics, we make fewer mental transformations to understand them than when we read the same information in text. When a visual explanation is used, fewer cognitive resources are needed to get at the meaning.

Reducing cognitive load. Due to our limited-capacity working memory, we quickly reach our limits when we try to integrate numerous pieces of information. Abstract graphics often alleviate this problem because relationships are explicitly illustrated. A line connects related elements in a diagram, related bars are placed in proximity in a bar graph, and a road connects cities on a map. This explicit depiction of relationships helps viewers process information simultaneously rather than sequentially—as when reading text.

Viewers quickly understand the pattern of a diagram to get an initial sense of its meaning. Here, a database system for tracking and collecting product movement is depicted in a hierarchical format, which makes cognitive sense.

Franziska Erdle,
Milch Design, Germany

RIVER BLINDNESS

Onchocerciasis, also known as river blindness, is a parasitic disease caused by tiny worms or "microfilariae" and transmitted by flies. The disease affects an estimated 18 million people worldwide.

World distribution

THE DISEASE CYCLE

① Parasitized
The insect takes a blood meal from a human. A pool of blood is pumped up into the fly, saliva passes into the pool, and infective *Onchocerca* larvae pass from the fly into the host's skin.

② Infection
The larvae enter the host's skin tissue, where they migrate and form nodules, and slowly mature into adult worms

③ Proliferation
New worms form new nodules or find existing nodules and cluster together. Smaller male worms migrate between nodules to mate.

④ Reproduction
After mating, eggs form inside the female worm and develop into microfilariae. A female may produce 1,000 microfilariae per day.

⑤ Transport
When the infected host is bitten by another fly, microfilariae are transferred from the host to the fly.

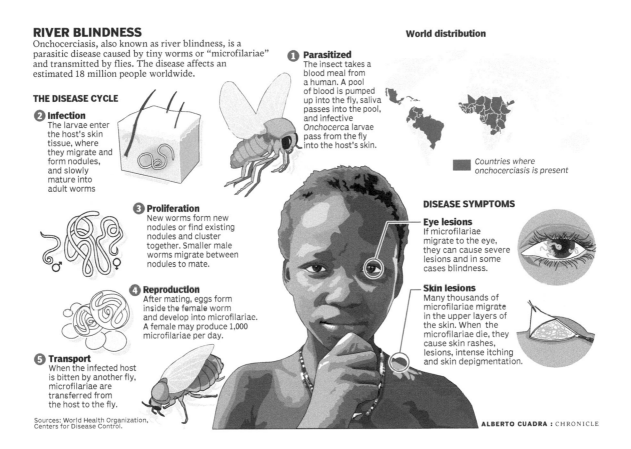

Countries where onchocerciasis is present

DISEASE SYMPTOMS

Eye lesions
If microfilariae migrate to the eye, they can cause severe lesions and in some cases blindness.

Skin lesions
Many thousands of microfilariae migrate in the upper layers of the skin. When the microfilariae die, they cause skin rashes, lesions, intense itching and skin depigmentation.

Sources: World Health Organization, Centers for Disease Control.

ALBERTO CUADRA : CHRONICLE

Upon first looking at this cyclical diagram, the viewer gets the gist of the graphic through the illustrations integrated with the circular arrow. The accompanying text explanation fills in the missing pieces.

Alberto Cuadra,
Houston Chronicle,
United States

Improving search efficiency. When we need to locate information, abstract graphics can often improve the efficiency of the search process compared to reading text. To search through text, we typically start at the beginning, skim through headings and paragraphs, try to remember where important information is located, and then return to each of the various locations. Conversely, abstract graphics are inherently structured so that information is visually linked. When a person searches for and locates the first piece of important information in a diagram, relevant information is typically adjacent to it. This reduces the time and effort involved in acquiring information.[3]

Applying The Principle

The key purpose of a nonrepresentational graphic is to create a visual portrayal that extends the viewer's ability to see, think, and know. To achieve this, the designer can consider which type of mental structure would be most effective to invoke in the viewer. For example, if the goal is to help readers understand how a sequence of actions led to a climactic event, a timeline would facilitate the most effective mental representation. On the other hand, if the intent is to help viewers understand usage patterns on the Internet, then an information visualization that depicts users swarming around Web pages would help the viewer construct the most accurate schemas.

When abstract graphics are complex, designers can enhance them for the automatic processing that occurs in early vision. This shifts more of the cognitive operations to visual perception, reducing the demands on working memory. Based on theories discussed in Principle 1 (Organize for Perception), a graphic can be enhanced for visual perception in several ways. Ensure that similar elements are the same color or shape, so the viewer does not have to unnecessarily discriminate between them. For example, it is easier and quicker to compare the length of bars in a bar graph when they are the same color. When appropriate, cluster similar elements into groups using proximity or bounding lines so the viewer perceives the entities as one unit. Because the size of an object is quickly detected during preattentive vision, use this feature to convey meaning. Make an element half the size of another element if it is of half the value. These techniques will improve the viewer's ability to automatically extract information during early vision.

Each form of abstract graphic has its own unique notation or visual code. We learn these codes through experience and education. For example, we know that a topographical map uses contours to indicate elevation and that line graphs compare two variables. The designer can ensure that the audience understands a particular notational system by following accepted conventions. Viewers infer a great deal from context. Unless the goal is to provide novelty or surprise, remain consistent with what is expected from a notation.

Clarity is an important quality of the abstract graphic, affecting its readability, usefulness, aesthetics, and overall comprehensibility. Take steps to ensure that any visual difference, such as a change in color or texture, is actually intended to convey meaning and remove any unnecessary visual differences. If one arrow in a diagram is larger than the others, for example, this will likely be interpreted as representing an increase in strength or value, even if unintended. Also, avoid ambiguity by making illustrations, icons, and symbols easy to identify and recognize.

Titles, legends, captions, labels, and call-outs add essential information to abstract graphics, making them more substantial and solidifying their meaning. Text often provides redundant information, which creates a second channel for transmitting information. In abstract graphics, ensure that text is legible, brief, and consistent.

These abstract graphics created for a school project effectively use color to convey statistical information about Alzheimer's disease.

Christina Koehn, University of Washington, United States

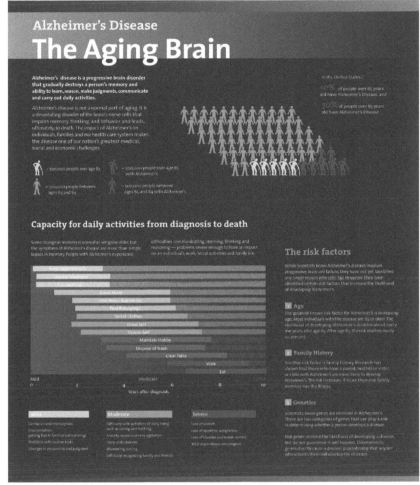

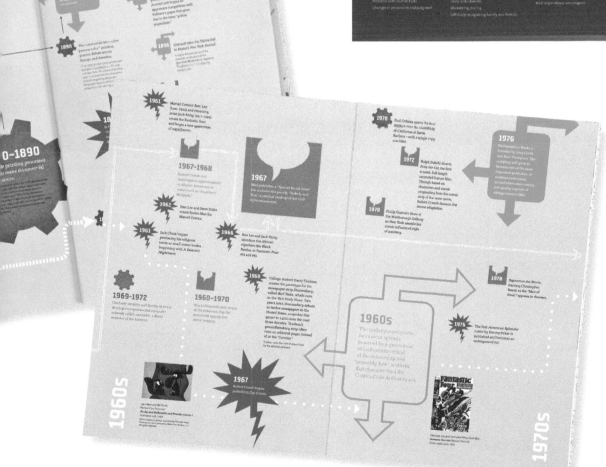

This unusual timeline from the book Strips, Toons, and Bluesies *is a small segment of a multipage, chronology of comics and the graphic arts.*

Heather Corcoran and Diana Scubert, Plum Studio, United States

Color can provide an additional dimension for conveying meaning. We see this in maps when color is used to indicate road types. Color-coding can also indicate that elements are associated, as when color represents different types of data in a statistical map, such as income or political affiliation. The color-coding of elements and data facilitates information retrieval because color is stored in long-term memory along with associated information.

A final design consideration is whether to represent the features of an abstract graphic as icons, illustrations, geometric shapes, or text. The form of the representation can have a significant effect on the meaning of the graphic. For example, to explain how voice over Internet protocol works, an illustrated diagram that portrays signal transmission between two people on phones clarifies the concept more than if boxes and lines are used to explain the system. The choice of how to represent features not only affects meaning, but also affects the graphic's tone and style.

When graphic designers and illustrators—rather than statisticians or cartographers—produce maps, diagrams, and graphs, a new aesthetic naturally emerges. Designers use the context and purpose of the abstract graphic to communicate on an artistic and emotional level. Through techniques such as textured backgrounds, illustrated or photographed imagery, and unique shapes and patterns, designers are able to convey more than the facts, revealing the indefinable feelings and impressions associated with the content of the graphic.

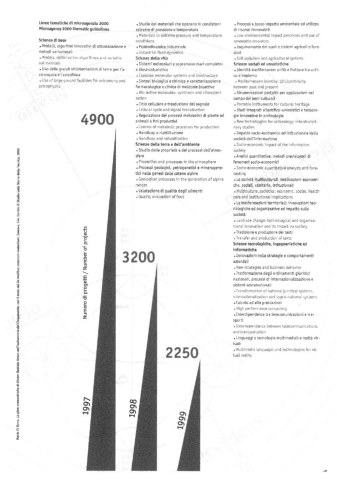

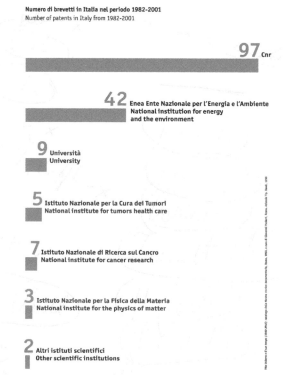

A designer's touch adds a textured and layered look to these graphs created for the National Centre of Research in Italy.

Lorenzo De Tomasi, *Italy*

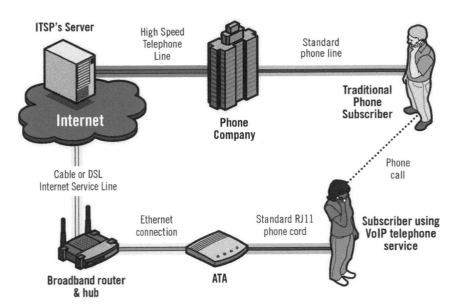

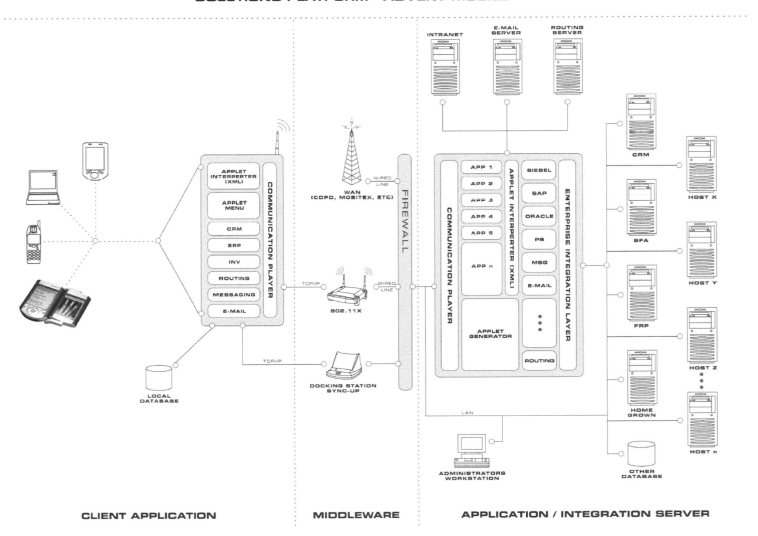

BIG-PICTURE VIEWS

There is no common definition for diagrams among people who use, create, and theorize about them. In this book, diagrams refer to a visual explanation that represents a system rather than statistical data. Diagrams are typically composed of a system's elements and their interrelationships. The elements in a diagram vary in their realism, ranging from a representational illustration to iconic symbols or amorphous shapes.

Even though diagrams use spatial organization to convey meaning, the content they represent is not necessarily spatial. Diagrams depict and help us understand the structure, processes, transformations, cycles, and functions of a system. These facets are expressed through the unique arrangements and positioning of the elements and the lines, arrows, and shapes that connect them. As with other abstract graphics, every element in a diagram has a direct relationship with the object to which it refers. The potentially limitless combination of elements contributes to the rich diversity of diagram types, such as the cyclical diagram that represents a recurring process, the hierarchical diagram that illustrates structure and organization, the tree diagram that dissects categories into fine detail, and the flow diagram that explains a process.

In diagrams, arrows point to important content. When arrows are used as connectors, they link elements together and indicate relationships. Arrows also guide the viewer through the flow of a process or events and show a path that is followed. They are effective in depicting the actions that occur in a system, a movement, or a conversion over time. Adjusting the size, shape, color, and emphasis of an arrow are techniques to control what an arrow represents. To signify movement, the arrow might have a jagged, curved, or twisted shaft. Large, emphasized, or contrasting arrows suggest strength and value. Double-headed arrows depict cyclic or reciprocal relationships.

Using arrows can change the meaning of a diagram. In a study that examined how arrows convey meaning, researchers showed students diagrams of mechanical devices with arrows and diagrams of mechanical devices without arrows. The study's participants interpreted the diagram without arrows as depicting the structure of the mechanical device and interpreted the diagrams with arrows as showing cause and effect and functionality.[4]

Viewers derive meaning from a diagram when they detect and recognize its pattern of elements. The pattern creates the diagram's organizational structure. Research shows that this organizational structure affects how information is mentally represented and encoded.[5] Thus, when viewing a diagram with a cyclical structure, a person will construct an internal representation that encodes the diagram's information in some form of circular fashion. The designer can take advantage of this cognitive process to use the most effective structure for communicating information and facilitating its retention.

A viewer can enter a diagram at the global level and see its overall pattern or enter at the local level and focus on the details. This is significant, because the level of entry is where the viewer begins to search for information.[6] In most cases, global precedence is preferred for diagrams, because much of their initial meaning is obtained from the big-picture view. To help viewers enter a graphic at the global level, the elements must be large enough to easily detect the overall pattern. If the elements are overwhelmingly large, however, the viewer will focus only on the element and its detail first.

▶ This graphic depicting the advantages of a commercial software solution tells two stories. The top portion visualizes a sequence of positive customer events along an arrow-based timeline. The bottom portion uses spatial layout and arrows to diagram how the software synchronizes operations.

Drew Crowley, XPLANE,
United States

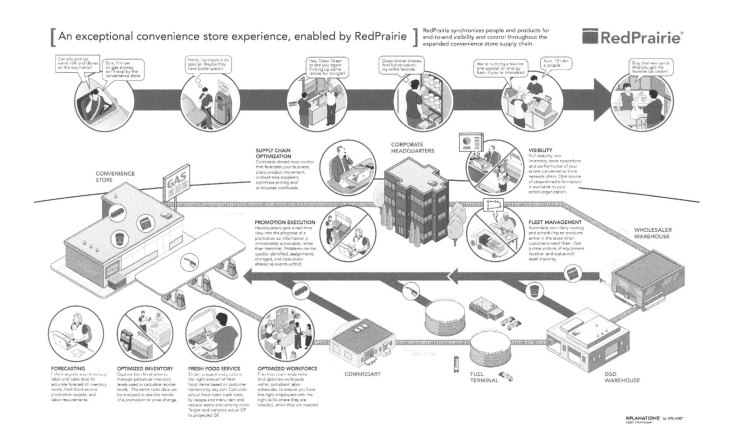

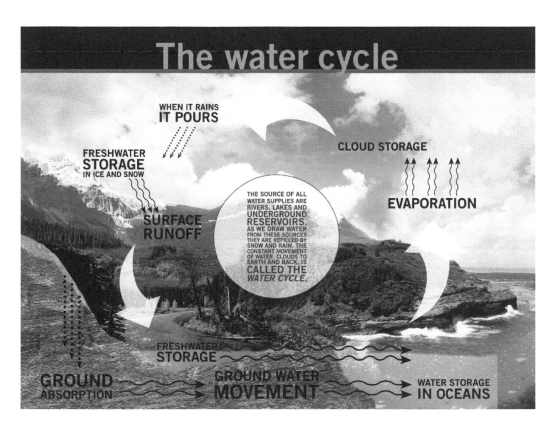

This water cycle diagram for the Chino Creek Wetlands Park uses three different types of arrows to carry much of the information: Large white arrows indicate the cycle's path, dashed arrows represent water, and jagged arrows represent movement.

Claudine Jaenichen and Richard Turner, Jaenichen Studio, United States

▶ Diagrams often provide a holistic view of a system, as depicted in this clever schematic of a bulk email broadcast process portrayed as a circuit board.

Matthew Luckwitz,
Grafport, United States

▼ This tree diagram illustrates the evolution of commercial imagery through two main trunks—illustration and cartooning. The clean design and color-coding make it easy to follow along a single path.

D. B. Dowd, Mike Costelloe,
Sarah Phares, and
Scott Gericke,
Visual Communications
Research Studio—
Washington University,
United States

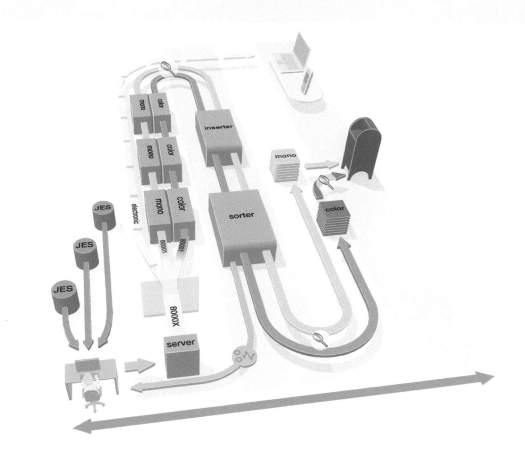

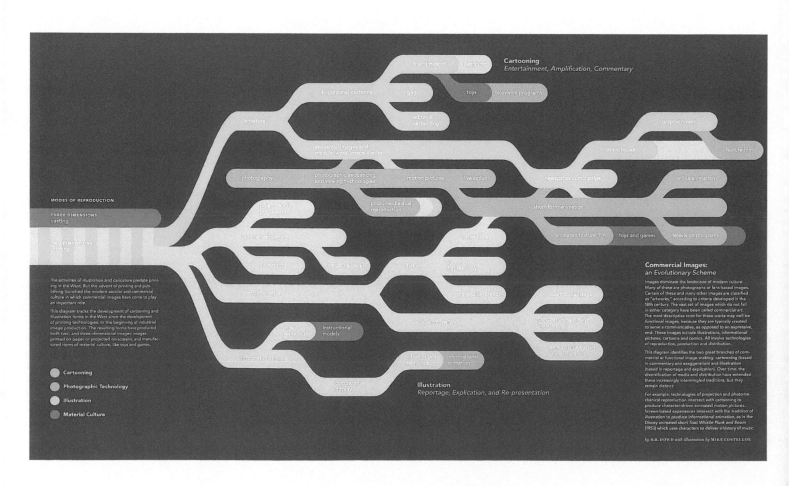

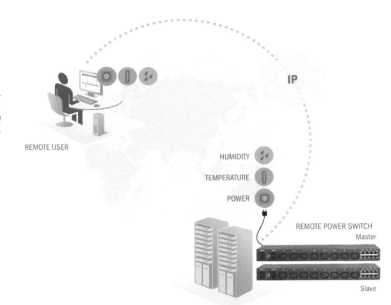

Dashed Lines

In diagrams, the dashed line is often used with or without the arrowhead to signify transactions, connections, and events that cannot be effectively expressed with a solid line. Because the repeated rectangular shape that forms the dashed line conveys a sense of movement, it is often used to represent a form of invisible energy, such as data transmission. Dashed lines often reflect the tentative or provisional quality of an action. When they indicate a relationship between elements, they often mean that the connection is uncertain or not always present. When dashed lines represent a path, it is often a projected or alternative path that will take place in the future.

BROADBAND FOR THE MASSES

The City of Houston is considering two companies to build and maintain a citywide wireless (Wi-Fi) broadband Internet network that will cover up to 600 square miles. How it will work:

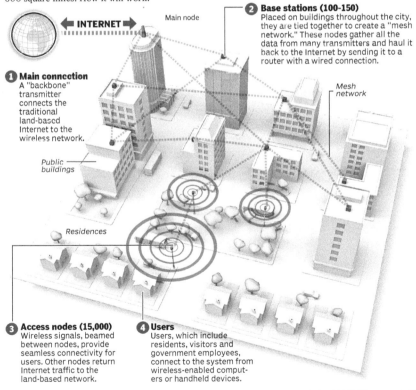

2 Base stations (100-150)
Placed on buildings throughout the city, they are tied together to create a "mesh network." These nodes gather all the data from many transmitters and haul it back to the Internet by sending it to a router with a wired connection.

1 Main connection
A "backbone" transmitter connects the traditional land-based Internet to the wireless network.

3 Access nodes (15,000)
Wireless signals, beamed between nodes, provide seamless connectivity for users. Other nodes return Internet traffic to the land-based network.

4 Users
Users, which include residents, visitors and government employees, connect to the system from wireless-enabled computers or handheld devices.

Sources: EarthLink; howstuffworks.com

ALBERTO CUADRA, JAY CARR : CHRONICLE

DATA DISPLAYS

"A child can tell that one-third of a pie is larger than a fourth long before being able to judge that the fraction ⅓ is greater than ¼," writes statistics professor and author Howard Wainer in *Educational Researcher*. In other words, the visual display of numerical data is easier to understand when we can see it in a concrete form, such as in graphs and tables. Information graphics often use a hybrid approach for displaying data, combining representational art with numeric information.

Data displays, such as graphs, visually communicate the relationships hidden in quantitative information and are probably the most common abstract graphic we find in the popular media. It is difficult to pick up a newspaper or news magazine without seeing some type of graph describing business, technical, or scientific data. The simplest and most common graph framework is configured in an L shape, with a horizontal *x*-axis representing the data being measured and a vertical *y*-axis representing the type of measurement. Of course, there are numerous other types of graphs for expressing value. Pictographs use icons to represent the quantity of a data type, pie charts express data as a percentage of a whole, statistical maps display the distribution of data across a geographic area, and area graphs use the area of a circle or rectangle to indicate value, just to name a few.

Viewers can quickly get a sense of a graph's meaning by understanding how graphs use space to represent values. In a pie chart it is the size of the slice compared to the whole, in a pictograph it is the length of the row of symbols, and in an area graph it is the size of the region. Graphs also convey meaning through spatial positioning, as when data points are plotted and then connected on a line graph. These conventions provide an immediate preunderstanding before activating more involved cognitive processes.

Of all the forms of abstract graphics, people have the most difficulty understanding graphs. Numerous visual and mental processes are invoked upon studying a graph. Early in the process, the viewer rapidly detects geometric shapes, texture, and color.[7] These represent the graph's code for depicting values. The viewer then must call up graph schemas from long-term memory to derive meaning from the graph's notation. This involves reading the labels and captions, determining the graph's scale, glancing back and forth between entities, and comparing relative magnitudes to each other. Using this information and prior knowledge about the data, the viewer makes inferences and constructs relevant concepts. If a person's graph schemas are incomplete, he or she will have difficulties with one or more of these tasks.

Poor design is a major reason why information is misinterpreted in graphs. Although many data displays are technically accurate, they do not accommodate the strengths and limitations of our information-processing system. Twenty years ago, well-known statistician John Tukey wrote that the main purpose of analyzing numerical data is to describe phenomena rather than to simply present the information. He argued that the phenomena derived from the numbers are of most interest to people.[8] For example, if we are viewing a bar graph that illustrates the rising costs of higher education around the world, we probably won't remember the actual cost of tuition in each location. Through an effective graph, however, we will see and remember how rising tuition prices in one's own country compare with others.

As the popularity of graphs in the media increases, a wider variety of formats is used. The circles in this area graph depict sources of greenhouse gas emissions and appear to be released from a factory smokestack.

Arno Ghelfi, l'atelier starno,
United States

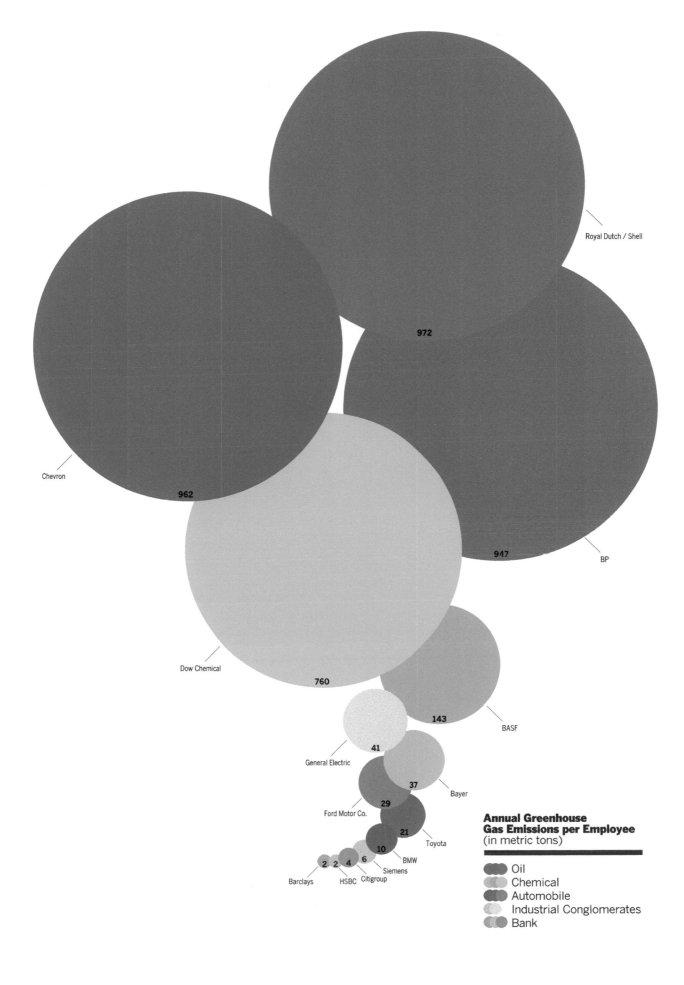

Royal Dutch / Shell
972

Chevron
962

BP
947

Dow Chemical
760

BASF
143

General Electric
41

Bayer
37

Ford Motor Co.
29

Toyota
21

BMW
10

Siemens
6

Citigroup
4

HSBC
2

Barclays
2

**Annual Greenhouse
Gas Emissions per Employee**
(in metric tons)

Oil
Chemical
Automobile
Industrial Conglomerates
Bank

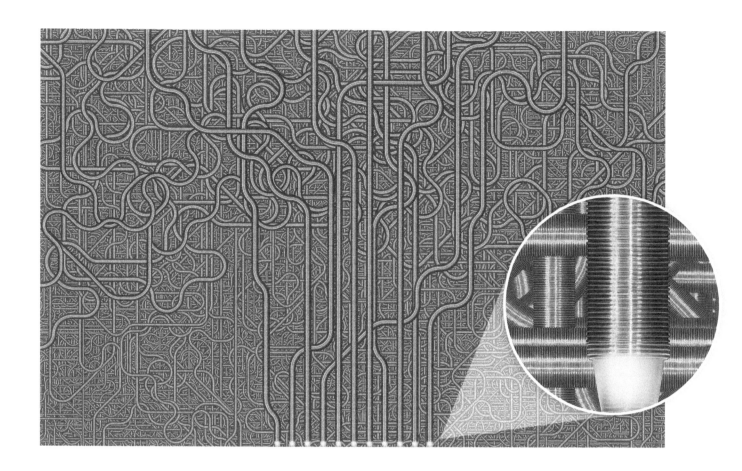

The tasks for which data displays are used—making comparisons, seeing trends, and finding patterns—should ultimately lead to the recognition of phenomena. Tukey emphasized that the foremost quality of an effective graph is to seek impact and immediacy. An effective data display should force the viewer to instantly understand the message. If getting the point is gradual or burdensome, another type of display should be implemented. For instance, if the reader needs to locate individual numerical values, then a table would be more effective than a graph.

In his research on graph design, neuroscientist Stephen Kosslyn expands on several principles of effective data displays to accommodate our visual and cognitive systems. To accommodate the visual system, he notes that all elements in a data display must be large or heavy enough to be detected, and all variations need to be easily discriminated. He also points out the importance of organizing labels and captions so they are grouped with the appropriate visual element. To accommodate the limitations of working memory, Kosslyn recommends restricting displays so there are only four to seven perceptual units. In addition, viewers should not be asked to decompose a display that

is grouped, such as the points on a line. This reverses our automatic tendency to group items that are similar or close together.[9] To meet the expectations and abilities of the audience, provide neither too little nor too much information and consider whether the audience has the appropriate knowledge to understand the display.[10]

A data display is effective if it provides a shortcut to the intended message, promoting visual processing and bypassing the need to make numerical computations. Research has demonstrated that people are better at making comparisons when using bar graphs and better at interpreting trends when using line graphs.[11] When using graphs with an x- and y-axis, minimize numerical computations by using precalculated numbers like percentages and averages for the y-axis rather than raw numerical data.[12] This makes it easier for readers to make quick comparisons. If a designer needs to depict more than two variables, as is common in most graphs in an L framework, use attributes such as color or size to represent the values of additional variables. From a design perspective, imagery can go a long way in conveying the meaning of a graph.

Quantitative depictions can support a social agenda. This display depicts one million plastic cups, which is the number of cups used on airline flights in the United States every six hours.

Chris Jordan, *United States*

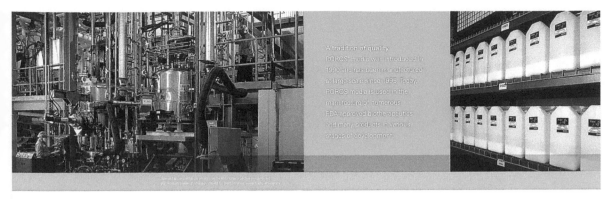

The mix of imagery and graphs helps the viewer see beyond the data in this brochure for a biopharma-ceutical company.

Amy Vest,
Applied Biosystems Brand & Creative Group,
United States

High performance on a large scale

PROTEIN PURIFICATION

High performance on a large scale
Product purification involves several critical steps, each one of which must be designed and optimized during research and early stage development, then scaled up for commercial manufacturing. Ideally, purification procedures developed during the early stages of process development can be optimized and scaled-up directly to manufacturing levels—without sacrificing performance efficiency.

A selection of selectivities
A broad range of POROS® media are available for production-scale, lab-scale, and quality control applications. All 50-micron POROS products are backed by full regulatory support information and Drug Master Files.

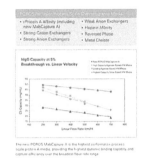

Removing scale-up bottlenecks

PROTEIN PURIFICATION

Applied Biosystems POROS® MabCapture™ A Perfusion Chromatography® Media offer a direct and cost-effective path from lab-scale to production-scale bioseparations. These rigid, robust particles enable high-resolution separations with 2-3X the throughput of conventional fast-flow gels. The unique "throughpore" structure of POROS media is designed to provide unmatched dynamic binding capacities and excellent capture efficiencies at high linear velocities, resulting in smaller column volumes, reduced buffer consumption, and faster processing for higher product throughput. With the recent improvements in cell culture technology resulting in higher expression levels, higher capacity process scale media is needed. Applied Biosystems' newest POROS affinity media, POROS MabCapture A, was specifically designed to address this need.

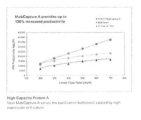

CHARACTERIZE   PURIFY/ANALYZE   QUALITY CONTROL

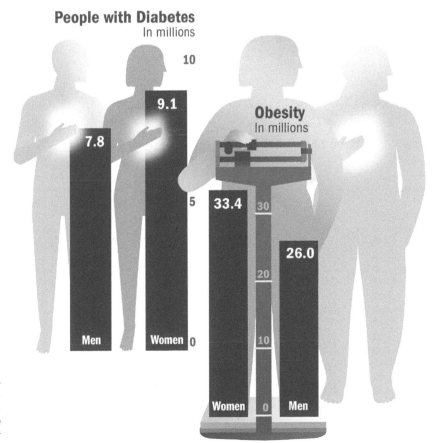

These illustrated bar charts depicting diabetes and obesity statistics appeared in Woman's Day magazine.

Rose Zgodzinski,
Information Graphics,
Canada

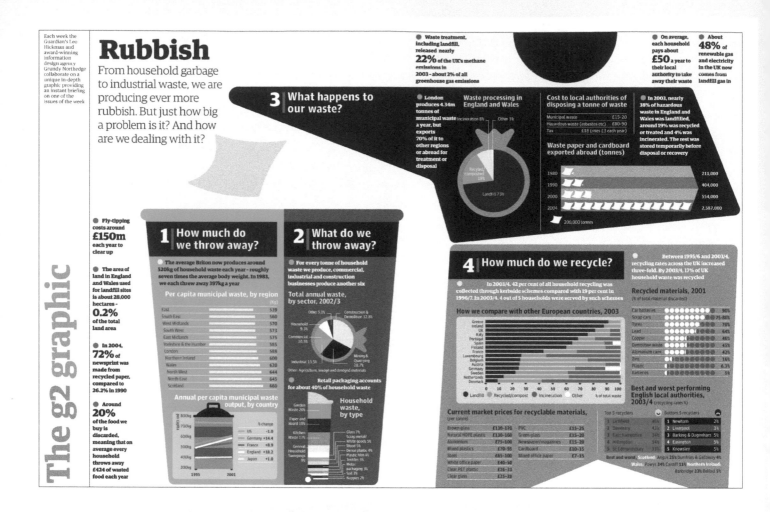

▲ Numerous graph formats depict data regarding trash, recycling, and waste management in the United Kingdom in this information graphic for the Guardian newspapers.

Peter Grundy and Tilly Northedge, United Kingdom

▶ Not all data displays must be in graph form. Here, oversize numbers emphasize academic statistics in this college viewbook.

David Horton and Amy Lebow, Philographica, United States

SO LIEBT DIE WELT

Rosen, Ringe, Poesie

Alles fing damit an, dass ein Mann seinen Kopf verlor. Am 14. Februar 269, so erzählt die Legende, ließ der römische Kaiser Claudius II. den Bischof Valentin von Terni enthaupten. Er hatte Soldaten und deren Freundinnen getraut, obwohl die Krieger nach kaiserlichem Gebot ehelos bleiben mussten. Zur heimlichen Hochzeit gab es für die Paare noch einen Strauß aus dem Bischofsgarten, weshalb Sankt Valentin nicht nur als Schutzpatron der Liebenden, sondern auch der Blumenindustrie gelten kann.

Heute wird der Valentinstag als Tag der Liebe von Milliarden Romantikern auf aller Welt gefeiert. In Frankreich trifft man sich zum Liebesdinner in verschwiegenen Restaurants. In England, wo man den Tag seit dem 15. Jahrhundert begeht, traktiert man sich traditionell mit Gedichten, in Italien stehen kurze Liebesreisen hoch im Kurs. In China schenkt man sich gegenseitig Schönheitsoperationen, und in den USA machen Valentins Jünger am 14. Februar gern ihren Heiratsantrag. Nur in Deutschland halten 67 Prozent den Valentinstag für überflüssig. Doch die Begründung versöhnt: Eigentlich, so die Befragten, solte jeder Tag ein Tag der Liebe sein!

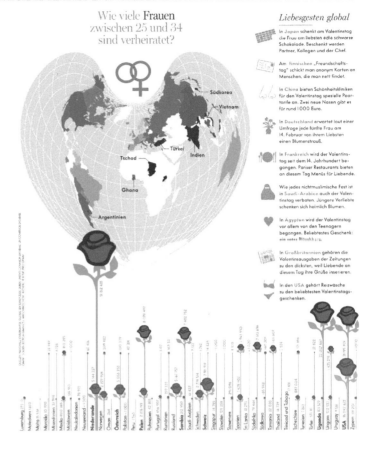

Wie viele **Männer** zwischen 25 und 34 sind verheiratet?

Anteil der Eheleute (in URL von 25 bis 34 Jahren, Angaben in Prozent)

- 85–90
- 80–85
- 75–80
- 70–75
- 65–70
- 60–65
- 55–60
- 50–55
- 45–50
- 40–45
- 35–40
- 30–35
- 25–30
- 20–25
- 15–20
- keine Daten vorhanden

BLÜHENDE LEIDENSCHAFT

Rosen zu kaufen ist der klassische Liebesbeweis – Deutsche, Franzosen und Amerikaner sind demnach die größten Romantiker.

Blütengröße: Volumen des Ein- und Ausfuhren 2005, Angaben in Dollar

EXPORT
IMPORT

Linker Stängel, rosa Blüte: Import
Rechter Stängel, rote Blüte: Export

Wie viele **Frauen** zwischen 25 und 34 sind verheiratet?

Liebesgesten global

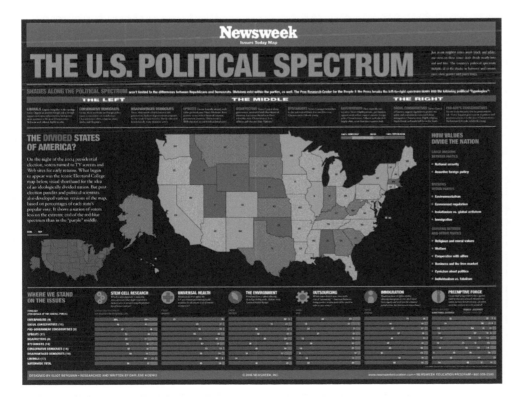

▲ *Stemmed roses become bar charts and the globe is heart shaped in this information graphic about Valentine's Day, love, and roses around the world for* Vanity Fair, *Germany.*

Jan Schwochow,
Golden Section Graphics,
Germany

◄ *Patterns often emerge from statistical maps because data is grouped in new ways across geographical regions. This statistical map of the U.S. political spectrum was produced for the Newsweek Education Program.*

Eliot Bergman, *Japan*

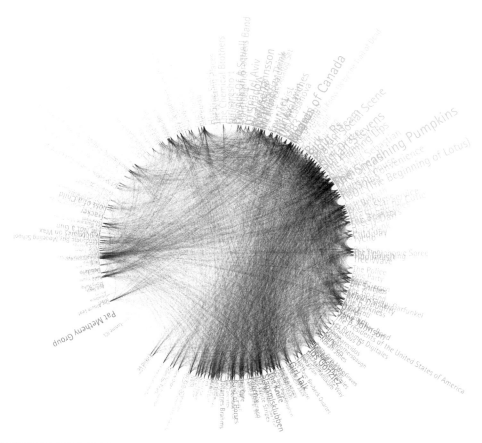

VISUALIZATION OF INFORMATION

In response to the explosion of complex information in many knowledge domains, information visualizations represent and make accessible the structure and intricate relationships found in large sets of data. The information visualization can be thought of as a cognitive tool that expands our ability to comprehend, interpret, and explore data that is too complex for our working memory to manage. It is often a solution for representing information that would otherwise be difficult to comprehend, such as how things change over time or with speed or rotation. Information visualizations are applied to both abstract data and to concrete data about the physical world.[13]

With visualizations, "the important information from more than a million measurements is immediately available. Visualization allows the perception of emergent properties that were not anticipated," notes professor Colin Ware in his book *Information Visualization*. Information visualizations are often generated by a computer and often occur in real time. They provide interactivity and utilize three and often four dimensions. The exploration, rearrangement, and reconstruction of the visualization are a primary means for achieving insight.

Visualizations complement our perceptual and information-processing systems because we are adept at detecting and identifying patterns, we intuitively understand spatial metaphors, and we process information most effectively when it is organized and structured. Most information visualizations use at least two modes of communication: a visual aspect that utilizes space, color, and shape to represent data, and a textual aspect that labels the data.

When computer visualization specialists collaborate with graphic designers, the outcome is more accessible to a wider audience. Perhaps because of this collaboration, the aesthetic dimension of information visualization has become increasingly important. In some visualizations, the beauty of the information and the facility of interaction take precedence over their practical use to create artistic works or promote a political or social agenda.

▲ *This computer-generated visualization depicts the online music-listening history of a user over an eighteen-month period. The frequency of listening is indicated by text size. Color represents the length of listening time periods.*

Lee Byron, *United States*

▶ *Visualizations increase our understanding of data by making it tangible. This computer visualization models the aerodynamic forces of a bat in flight. Designed as a joint effort between engineers at Brown University and MIT.*

Dave Willis,
Mischa Kostandov,
Dan Riskin, Jaime Peraire,
David H. Laidlaw,
Sharon Swartz,
and Kenny Breuer,
Brown University and MIT
United States

Modeling the flight of a bat

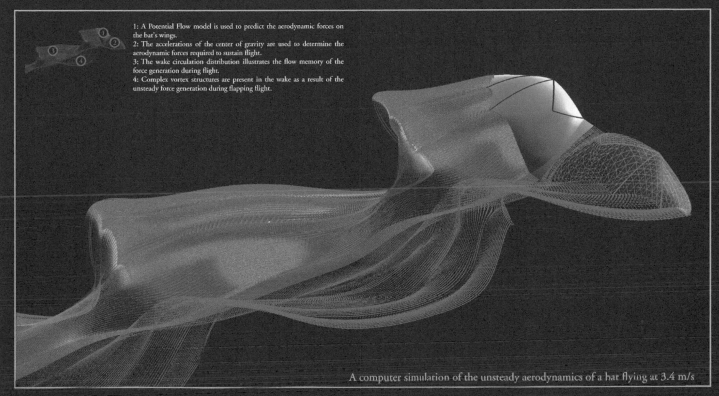

1: A Potential Flow model is used to predict the aerodynamic forces on the bat's wings.
2: The accelerations of the center of gravity are used to determine the aerodynamic forces required to sustain flight.
3: The wake circulation distribution illustrates the flow memory of the force generation during flight.
4: Complex vortex structures are present in the wake as a result of the unsteady force generation during flapping flight.

A computer simulation of the unsteady aerodynamics of a bat flying at 3.4 m/s

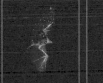

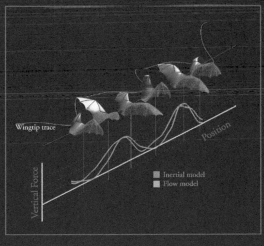

Bats are the only mammals capable of sustained flight. They are highly maneuverable and exploit efficient flight strategies. Today, we are using experiments and computer simulations to understand the details of the invisible air flow around the wings of a flying bat.

To construct a precise time-dependent model of bat flight, state of the art motion capture technology is applied to high speed stereo video of a bat (*Cynopterus brachyotis*) flying in a wind tunnel (above). The three-dimensional positions of the motion capture markers are used to construct the virtual geometry, which is used in the simulations. The surface model is used to compute the aerodynamics forces by applying a boundary element method Potential Flow model as well as a mass distribution inertial model. The vertical forces deduced from the observed accelerations are found to be in good agreement with those predicted by the flow model (right).

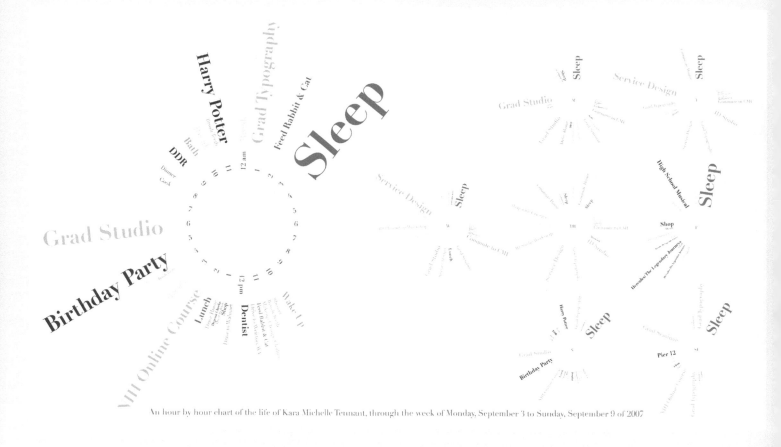

An hour by hour chart of the life of Kara Michelle Tennant, through the week of Monday, September 3 to Sunday, September 9 of 2007

Illustrated Visualization

Coinciding with the popularity of computer-generated visualizations is a genre of illustrated visualizations based on smaller data sets. These range from personal data to an analysis of the words and phrases found in literature. Similar to computer-based versions, these human-generated information visualizations are equally fascinating because they present data in a unique format to promote a fresh analysis and perspective.

Effective visualizations of both varieties have specific qualities. They are relatively easy to perceive and interpret, they find novel ways to structure data and information, they are efficient in the way they communicate comparisons and relationships, their movements and interactions (when available) are intuitive and sensible, and their aesthetic qualities attract and engage the viewer.

▲ *In this illustrated visualization for a school project, the designer mapped her activities throughout one week of graduate school, focusing on time, category, and hierarchy represented by color, size, and positioning of type.*

Kara Tennant, Carnegie Mellon University, *United States*

▶ *This illustrated information visualization represents the complex structure of chapters, paragraphs, sentences, and words in part 1 of Jack Kerouac's* On the Road. *Each thin line represents a word, which is color-coded according to themes, such as "travel, work and survival, and illegal activities and police encounters."*

Stefanie Posavec, *United Kingdom*

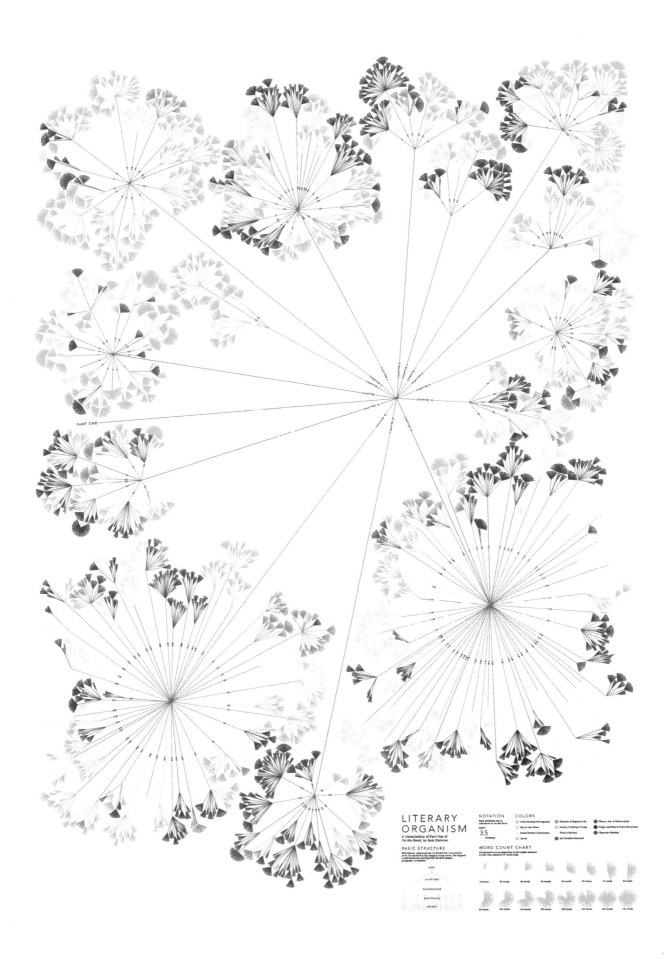

LITERARY ORGANISM

A visualization of Part One of
On the Road, by Jack Kerouac

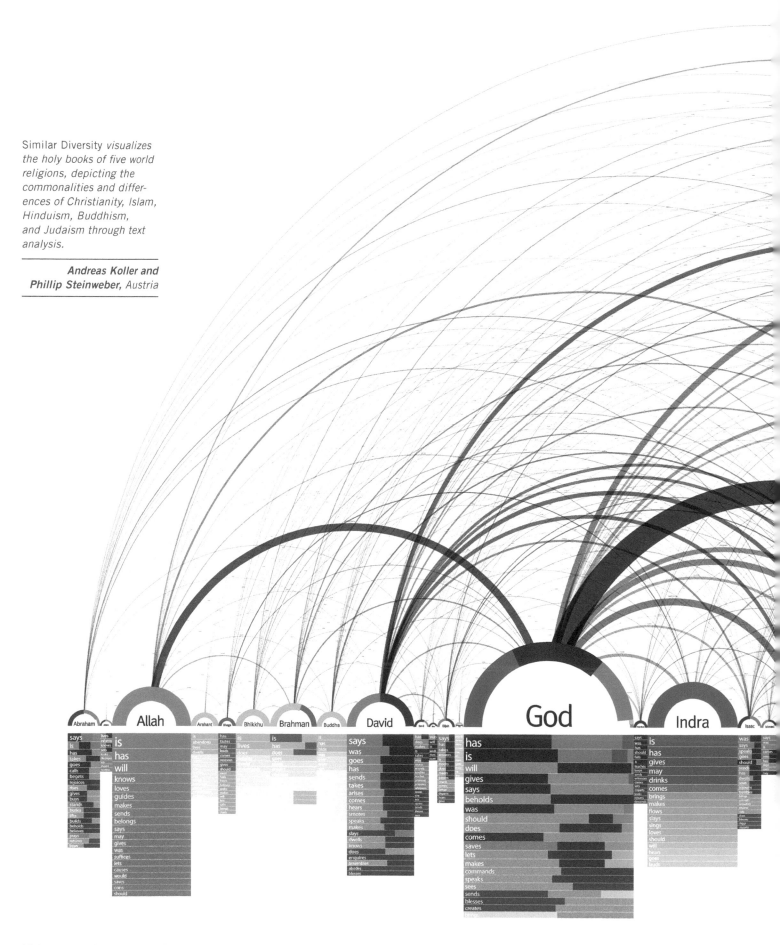

Similar Diversity *visualizes the holy books of five world religions, depicting the commonalities and differences of Christianity, Islam, Hinduism, Buddhism, and Judaism through text analysis.*

Andreas Koller and Phillip Steinweber, *Austria*

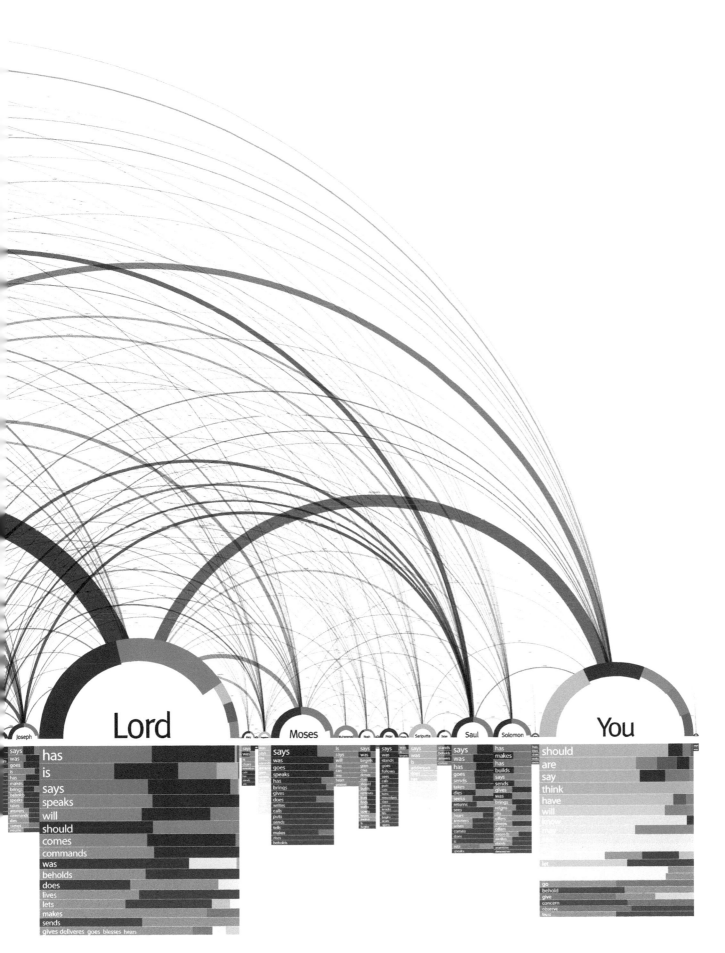

MORE THAN GEOGRAPHY

Maps record and communicate what we know about an environment and serve as reliable wayfinding tools. They provide a basis for the academic study of many subjects, from geography to history to art. Yet maps also possess a mystical dimension. They tug at the imagination, encouraging us to explore and discover landscapes and cities, people and cultures. They allow us to see and consider the impossible—vast stretches of the planet as well as incredible detail of small regions.

Maps are a reduced version of an analogous space and cannot include everything that is in that same physical space. Thus, a map communicates the features that are important to its purpose. To the extent that one understands how maps are affected by purpose, "one is more likely to avoid the mistaken belief that maps are simply miniaturizations (albeit flattened ones) which show some singular 'reality' or 'truth.' Rather there are infinite 'realities' that can be expressed by maps," writes psychology professor Lynn Liben.[14]

If we were to dissect a map, we would find that it is informative on several levels. One level shows feature information, composed of the map's individual symbols, icons, landmarks, and text along with the attributes detected during preattentive vision, such as size, shape, and color. The second level is the structural information relating to the spatial layout of the map. The structure is composed of the distance between the map's features and the distance between a feature and the map's edge. A third level is the structure the viewer mentally projects onto the map. Research has demonstrated that viewers create additional structures, such as drawing imaginary lines between two mountain peaks or between a landmark and the center of

town. The structure and spatial layout of a map is significant, because it is thought that people perceive a map holistically. In other words, a viewer may mentally hold an intact image of a map in working memory.[15] The fourth level is related to the subjective impression and associations a map invokes. The map's designer may add a scenic route, a friendly illustration, or an artistic spatial perspective. The viewer may respond with emotions triggered by memories of places and people once visited and from a longing to visit new lands.

In general, adults are familiar and comfortable with maps; we have a reliable framework for interpreting maps and we know their conventions. The designer must consider these conventions and decide how they can be aesthetically accommodated. The most obvious convention is the assumption that a map's layout corresponds directly to physical space. Another assumption—which is often incorrect—is that a map will be oriented to the north. This convention is so deeply embedded that when a map has a different orientation, most people will rotate the map so north is at the top in order to process the spatial information. Users also rely on legends to explain the symbols and a grid to provide coordinates if needed.

Frida Kahlo's Mexico City *captures the personality and geography of the neighborhoods in this map created for* Attaché *magazine. The illustrator used colors from Kahlo's paintings and iconography from Mexican folklore.*

Poul Hans Lange,
Poul Lange Design,
United States

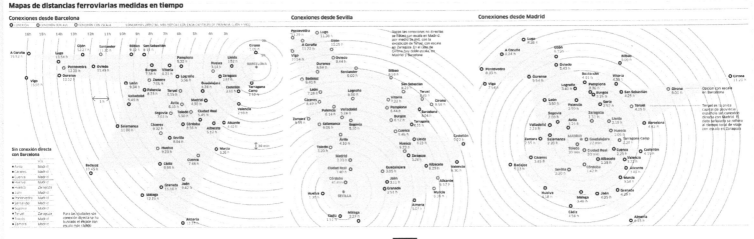

Conexiones desde Barcelona

Conexiones desde Sevilla

Conexiones desde Madrid

Los planes de futuro

Conexiones con Madrid previstas para 2020*

Mapa de alta velocidad

Situación actual   Horizonte 2020

Tiempos de viaje desde Madrid

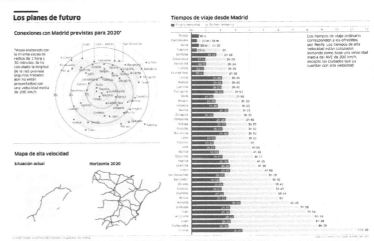

There are an extraordinary number of ways to present map-based information. These travel rail maps, published in the newspaper Público, depict the time it takes to travel to different cities in Spain.

Chiqui Esteban and Álvaro Valiño, Público, Spain

Presenting a bird's-eye view of this farm and garden center's virtual tour helps the viewer immediately understand the layout.

Dermot MacCormack, Patricia McElroy 21xdesign, United States

Make the Abstract Concrete   **157**

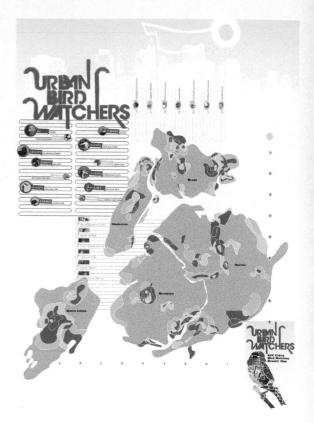

Through experience we know that maps are designed within a context, for different purposes and for different people. Although we expect a road map to be drawn accurately to scale, we may not expect precision of scale in a map showing the location of events at a festival. Interestingly, through convention we also know which notations of a map actually represent a physical feature and which are incidental. In a road map, we know that the curves in a line represent the curves of a road, but the thickness of a line does not represent the width of the road.[16]

Graphic designers and illustrators are typically not cartographers. When they engage in map design, it is to make maps simultaneously functional and aesthetically pleasing. Maps can be made more appealing depending on the vantage point that draws in the viewer and the graphics that represent the terrain and relevant imagery. Typefaces can express the personality of an environment, and color and texture can create a rich visual experience for the map viewer. These aspects of map design provide more than aesthetic appeal; they help users interpret and remember the map's features. When map features are visually distinctive and resemble the real objects they represent—such as illustrated landmarks—viewers can more easily recall a map's features than when only text labels are used.[17] Also, minimizing the number of details and using symbols that are familiar and easy to recognize enhance map comprehension.

Bird densities in the New York City region are depicted through vivid colors and imagery in this map created for a student project.

Eli Carrico, *United States*

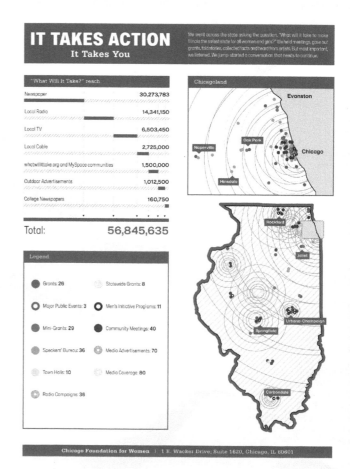

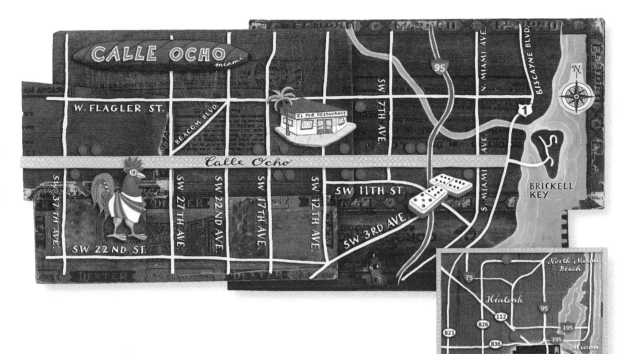

This map of Miami's Cuban neighborhood for Cigar Aficionado *magazine* incorporates wood from old cigar boxes in the background with paint on top.

Poul Hans Lange,
Poul Lange Design,
United States

◀ *Maps are a natural way to display quantitative information. This one shows summary data related to a statewide antiviolence initiative in Illinois.*

Will Miller, Firebelly Design, *United States*

▶ *The illustrated features and clean labels make this ports-of-call map friendly and accessible.*

Russell Tate, Russell Tate Illustration, *Australia*

▶ These maps created for an annual report convey the worldwide locations and network of a logistics service provider. The color of the dots indicates the type of center at each site.

Franzisca Erdle, Milch Design, *Germany*

▶ Maps provide a way to communicate more than geography. This map for an art fair printed in the Indianapolis Star *is also a comprehensive user guide.*

Angela Edwards, *United States*

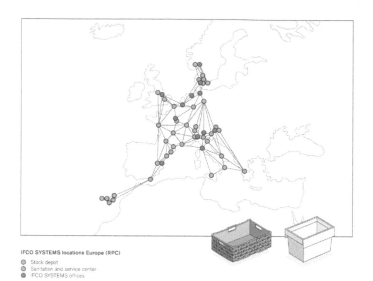

IFCO SYSTEMS locations Europe (RPC)
- Stock depot
- Sanitation and service center
- IFCO SYSTEMS offices

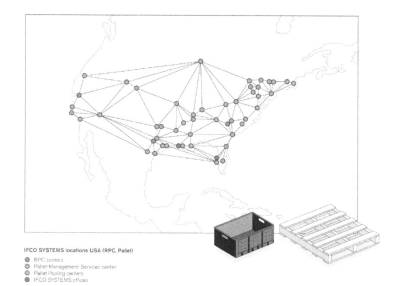

IFCO SYSTEMS locations USA (RPC, Pallet)
- RPC centers
- Pallet-Management-Services center
- Pallet Pooling centers
- IFCO SYSTEMS offices

▼ This portrait of the San Francisco River in Brazil illustrates the culture, people, animals, and plants along the river from its point of origin to its merging with the ocean.

Carlo Giovani, Carlo Giovani Studio, *Brazil*

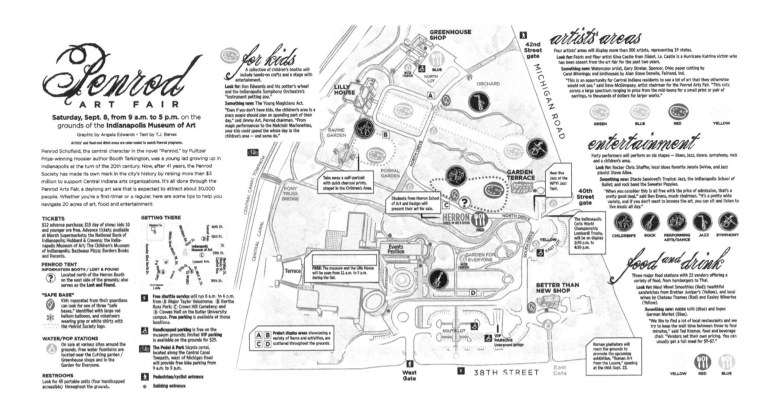

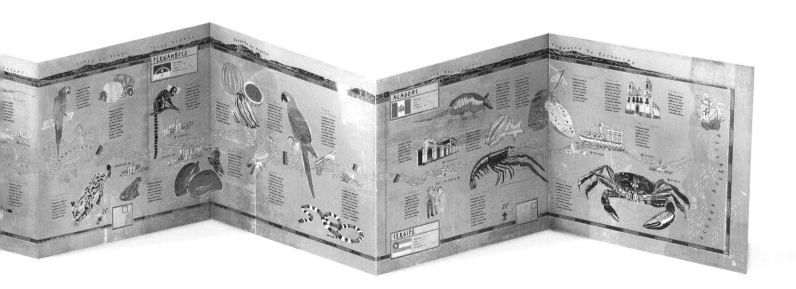

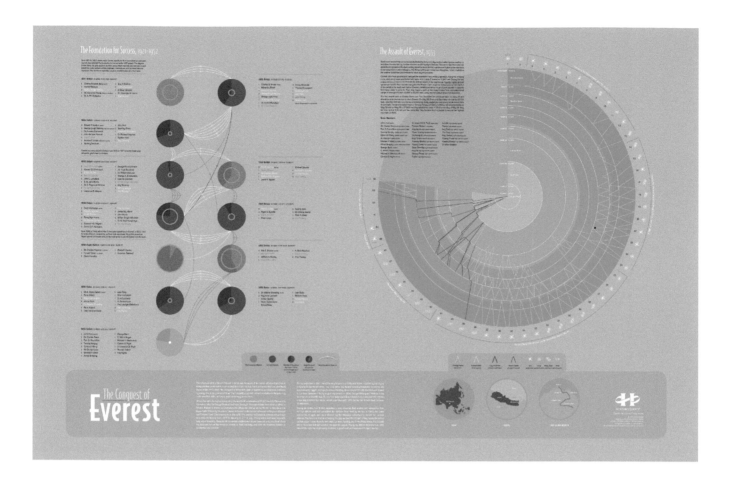

SNAPSHOTS OF TIME

Time has been conceptualized in many ways through history and across different cultures. When we conceive of time, we typically relate it to a spatial metaphor using a horizontal line to move forward. It is also imagined as a cyclical phenomenon that is grounded in natural occurrences, such as the seasons. For some, time is envisioned as a spiral, recurring in the pattern of a helix. In antiquity, scenes were often presented in nonchronological order so that events that were most significant to the artist were placed first. Time is a significant dimension of much information, and it underlies our life experience. Representations of time help us understand relationships and make connections between temporal events.

Of all the graphical forms that depict time, timelines are the most pervasive. Usually, they are depicted in a linear fashion showing time moving forward into the future, perhaps with an arrowhead to indicate direction. It is common to depict an increase in time directionally from left to right or from bottom to top. Timelines are usually structured as a series of fixed temporal events that occur in a chronological sequence. In historical timelines, this may suggest a cause-and-effect relationship between the events.

▲ *This time-based visualization of the 1953 conquest of Mount Everest maps the ascents and descents of the forty-nine-day expedition on the right. On the left, the history of earlier expeditions and their missions and durations are portrayed.*

Larry Gormley, History Shots, and Kimberly Cloutier, White Rhino, *United States*

▶ *In this self-promotional brochure, time is represented in a cyclical zodiac calendar.*

Marlena Buczek-Smith, Ensign Graphics, *United States*

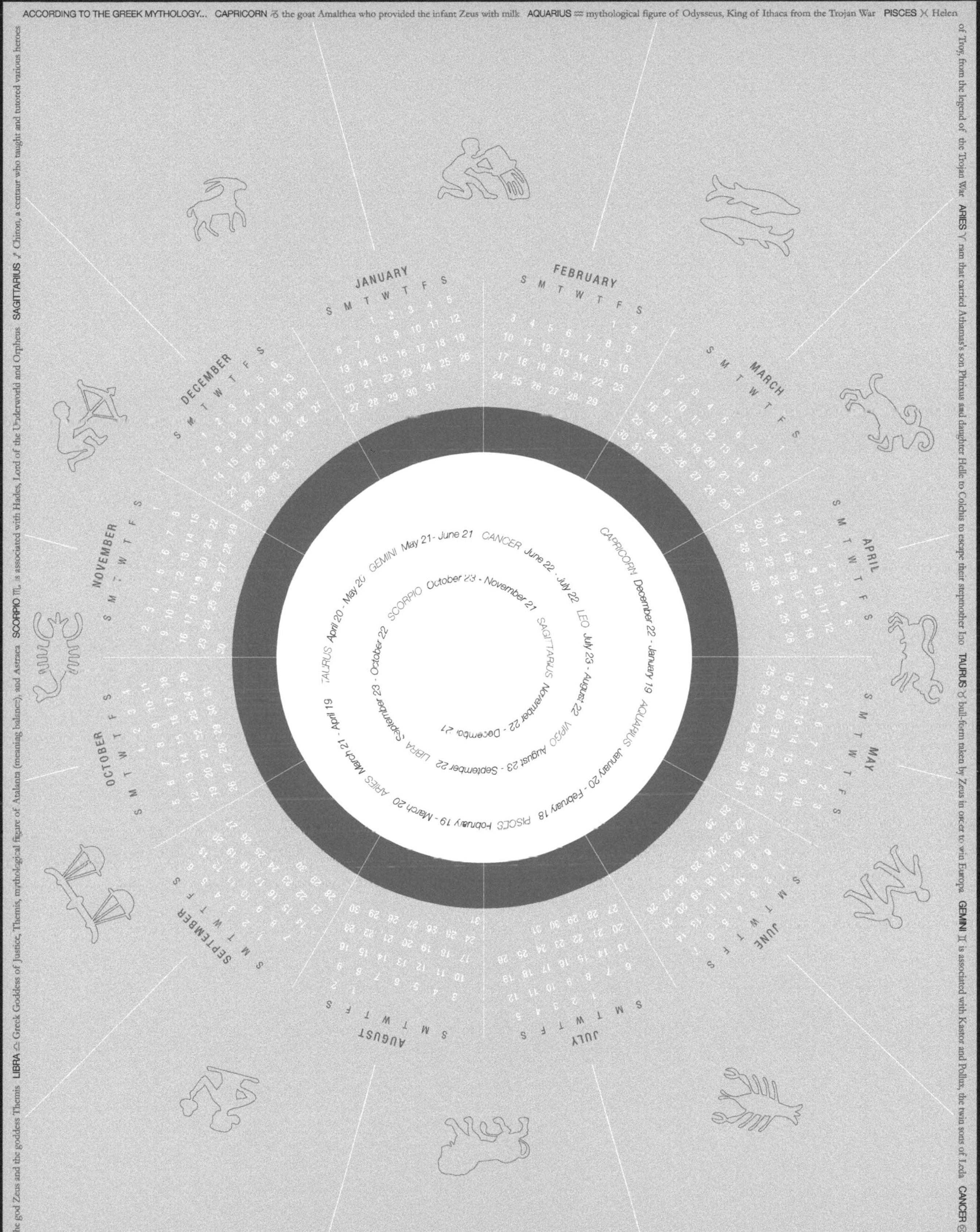
ACCORDING TO THE GREEK MYTHOLOGY... CAPRICORN ♑ the goat Amalthea who provided the infant Zeus with milk AQUARIUS ♒ mythological figure of Odysseus, King of Ithaca from the Trojan War PISCES ♓ Helen of Troy, from the legend of the Trojan War ARIES ♈ ram that carried Athamas's son Phrixus and daughter Helle to Colchis to escape their stepmother Ino TAURUS ♉ bull-form taken by Zeus in order to win Europa GEMINI ♊ is associated with Kastor and Pollux, the twin sons of Leda CANCER ♋ the Lernaean Hydra, one of The Twelve Labours of Herakles and the mythical figure of Perseus LEO ♌ Nemean Lion that was killed by Hercules during one of his twelve labors, and subsequently put into the sky VIRGO ♍ Astraea, the virgin daughter of the god Zeus and the goddess Themis LIBRA ♎ Greek Goddess of Justice, Themis, mythological figure of Atalanta (meaning balance), and Astraea SCORPIO ♏ is associated with Hades, Lord of the Underworld and Orpheus SAGITTARIUS ♐ Chiron, a centaur who taught and tutored various heroes
JANUARY
FEBRUARY
MARCH
APRIL
MAY
JUNE
JULY
AUGUST
SEPTEMBER
OCTOBER
NOVEMBER
DECEMBER
CAPRICORN December 22 - January 19
AQUARIUS January 20 - February 18
PISCES February 19 - March 20
ARIES March 21 - April 19
TAURUS April 20 - May 20
GEMINI May 21 - June 21
CANCER June 22 - July 22
LEO July 23 - August 22
VIRGO August 23 - September 22
LIBRA September 23 - October 22
SCORPIO October 23 - November 21
SAGITTARIUS November 22 - December 21

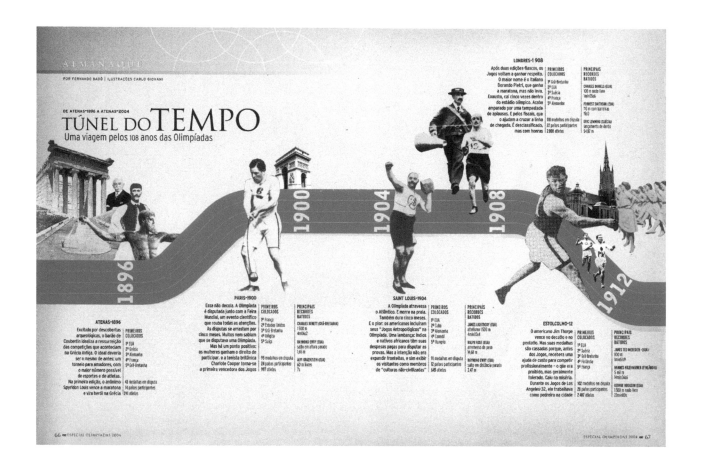

In terms of time span, timelines are quite adaptable. They can potentially represent linear time on any scale, running the gamut from personal or organizational time, which would be represented in days, weeks and years, to historical time represented in centuries or eras, to the deep time of geological events based in millions of years. Visualizing relationships and events through time helps us to make sense of the past and allows us to map out the future.

We can find visual depictions of time in numerous types of media. Organizations often use timelines to tout their accomplishments or to explain their narrative. Newspapers and magazines use them to depict newsworthy events or to show how events might affect the future. Textbooks visually represent time for historical purposes in an effort to make intangible events more concrete. In the sciences, timelines convey transformations and cause and effect. More so than verbal communication, visual language provides a flexible way for exploring and portraying time.

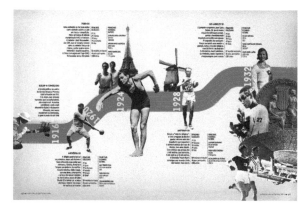

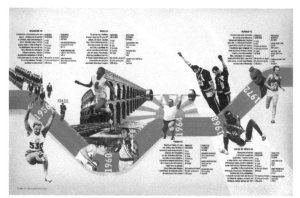

A portion of an extensive Olympic timeline published in Superinteressante *magazine is shown here. The sepia-toned coloring mixed with old photographs expresses the historical aspect of the timeline.*

Juliana Vidigal and Carlo Giovani, Carlo Giovani Studio, *Brazil*

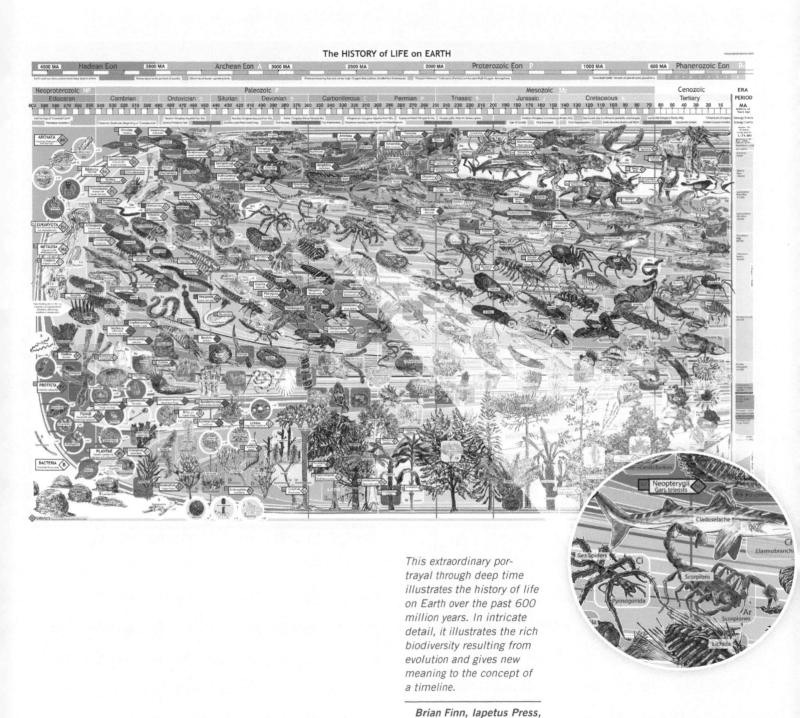

The HISTORY of LIFE on EARTH

This extraordinary portrayal through deep time illustrates the history of life on Earth over the past 600 million years. In intricate detail, it illustrates the rich biodiversity resulting from evolution and gives new meaning to the concept of a timeline.

Brian Finn, Iapetus Press,
United States

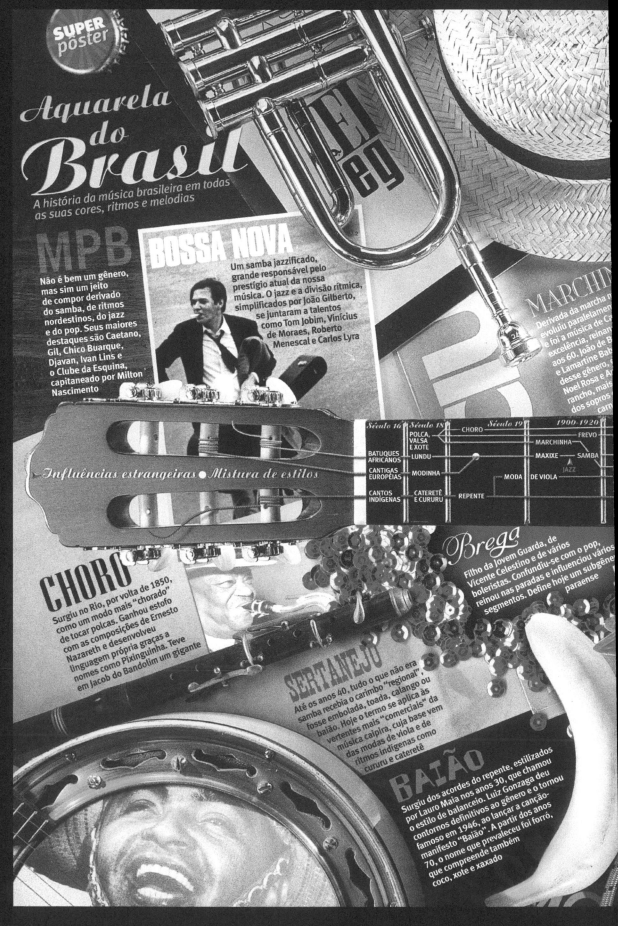

This richly textured time-line about the history of Brazilian popular music is portrayed on the neck of a guitar with the frets indicating years. Each string represents a different musical style.

Rodrigo Maroja and Carlo Giovani, Carlo Giovani Studio, Brazil

SAMBA

O ritmo mais importante do país, adotado como símbolo nacional e difundido com apoio oficial a partir dos anos 30. Nasceu dos batuques africanos e tomou forma no final do século 19, nas casas das "tias" baianas da Praça Onze, no Rio. De lá, levado por Sinhô, chegou aos salões. Pelas mãos de Ismael Silva e outros, subiu os morros. Noel Rosa, Ary Barroso e Ataulfo Alves fizeram o estilo ganhar o mundo e viver sua chamada "época de ouro" na voz de intérpretes como Carmen Miranda e Orlando Silva. Até os anos 50, evoluiu em vertentes como o samba sincopado (de Geraldo Pereira e Wilson Batista), samba-choro, ou samba de gafieira, e o samba-canção, antes de desaguar na bossa nova e nas fusões de Jorge Ben. Nos anos 80, renovou-se em forma de pagode e prestou-se a misturas com o pop, a MPB e a eletrônica

Frevo

Nasceu da marcha-polca e manteve-se basicamente restrito a Pernambuco. Virou tradição no Carnaval baiano com Dodô e Osmar e acabou entrando na receita da axé music

TROPICALISMO

O corte que abriu a cabeça da MPB para influências pop/rock, promovendo também a revisão de gêneros populares como o brega. Respaldada pelo sucesso das obras de Caetano e Gil, a atitude tropicalista funciona como revolução permanente, estejam seus principais artistas no *establishment* ou não

JOVEM GUARDA

O pop/rock internacional mete o pé na porta do mercado brasileiro e, disfarçado de ingênuo modismo adolescente, cai no gosto popular para transformar gerações e gerações. Até hoje!

ROCK

Começou tímido nos anos 50 e foi engolido pela Jovem Guarda e pela Tropicália. Nos anos 70, deu um salto qualitativo com Rita Lee e Raul Seixas. Foi quase deglutido pela MPB a partir de trabalhos como os de Secos & Molhados, Novos Baianos e Alceu Valença. Nos anos 80, ressurgiu com nomes como Lulu Santos, Paralamas, Barão Vermelho, Titãs e Legião Urbana. Desde então, se desenvolve em múltiplos subgêneros

Timeline

...-1945	1946-1960	1961-1970	1971-1980	1981-1990	1991-hoje
				AXÉ	
			FREVO		
			SAMBA		
		MPB	PAGODE		
SAMBA	CANÇÃO — BOSSA NOVA				
				HIP HOP → RAP BRASIL	
SERTANEJO		SERTANEJO		FUNK	
		BREGA		POP	
	ROCK'N'ROLL	JOVEM GUARDA	SOUL BRASIL		
		SOUL MUSIC	BREGA		
			SOUL BRASIL		
	BAIÃO	BREGA	POP		
		POP	ROCK BRASIL		
		ROCK		MÚSICA ELETRÔNICA	
		FORRÓ			

TROPICALISMO

VALSA

© 1. Infográfico Pedro Sô, Rafael Kenski, Carlo Giovanni e Rodrigo Maroja sobre foto de Marcelo Zocchio com produção de Roberta Maroja. Agradecimentos: Antiguidades Minha Avó Tinha, Euro Music e Shopping 1000
© 2 Ag. JB/Rubens Barbosa

© 1

El año de Einstein

un empleado de patentes | 1905: la revolución | tras la relatividad especial

ESCENA I
un empleado de patentes

Pulse Play
para comenzar

Total 02:39/00:00

El año de Einstein

un empleado de patentes | 1905: la revolución | tras la relatividad especial

Total 02:39/01:02

El año de Einstein

un empleado de patentes | 1905: la revolución | tras la relatividad especial

Total 05:04/00:35

El año de Einstein

un empleado de patentes | 1905: la revolución | tras la relatividad especial

ÉTER

Fuente
de luz

Total 06:04/01:00

El año de Einstein

un empleado de patentes | 1905: la revolución | tras la relatividad especial

Espacio ←— Velocidad —→ Tiempo

Observador 1

Observador 2

Total 09:04/02:02

El año de Einstein

un empleado de patentes | 1905: la revolución | tras la relatividad especial

RELATIVIDAD
ESPECIAL

Total 05:04/02:43

El año de Einstein

un empleado de patentes | 1905: la revolución | tras la relatividad especial

Total 05:04/03:28

El año de Einstein

un empleado de patentes | 1905: la revolución | tras la relatividad especial

Masa relativista Velocidad de la luz

$E = mc^2$

Energía

Total 05:04/04:15

El año de Einstein

un empleado de patentes | 1905: la revolución | tras la relatividad especial

Emisión de
energía/radiación

Total 04:50/00:25

El año de Einstein

un empleado de patentes | 1905: la revolución | tras la relatividad especial

Luz como onda

Luz como partículas ("fotones")

Total 04:50/01:08

El año de Einstein

un empleado de patentes | 1905: la revolución | tras la relatividad especial

EFECTO
FOTOELÉCTRICO

Total 04:50/01:32

El año de Einstein

un empleado de patentes | 1905: la revolución | tras la relatividad especial

Total 04:50/02:34

El año de Einstein

un empleado de patentes | 1905: la revolución | tras la relatividad especial

Estructura del
espacio-tiempo

Total 04:50/03:37

El año de Einstein

un empleado de patentes | 1905: la revolución | tras la relatividad especial

Estructura del
espacio-tiempo

Trayectoria
original del rayo

Posición real
de la estrella

Deformación del
espacio-tiempo
por la gravedad

Trayectoria
desviada

Observador

Total 04:50/04:06

El año de Einstein

un empleado de patentes | 1905: la revolución | tras la relatividad especial

RAYO DE LUZ

Estructura del
espacio-tiempo

Trayectoria modificada

Trayectoria original

Total 04:50/04:44

Guión/gráfico Alberto Cairo / Asesoramiento C. Pérez-Castejón, Germán Gómez
Audio Joaquín García (El Mundo TV) / Locución Gemma Santos

CLARIFY COMPLEXITY

"Complexity isn't what it used to be.
It's more—and different."

YVONNE HANSEN, *Information Design*

Visual complexity is a paradox. On the one hand, complexity is a compelling feature known to capture a viewer's attention and stimulate interest. Rather than looking at an entire picture, viewers tend to look at the informative portions, particularly those with intricate detail, patterns, and occlusions. On the other hand, complexity only arouses curiosity up to a point. When a visual is extremely complex, viewers may tend to avoid it altogether.[1]

Although complexity has always surrounded us, the visual depiction of complex objects, systems, and concepts has become increasingly prevalent. Complex subjects are depicted as infographics in newspapers and magazines; as animated segments in newscasts and documentaries; as exhibits in museums; as instructional graphics in textbooks and online courses; as procedural and assembly instructions in product manuals; and as accompaniments to articles in academic journals.

Objective complexity refers to the properties inherent in a system, information, or task. Systems are considered complex when they have many parts or components that interrelate. Information is complex when it is voluminous, dense, and lacking in structure. Tasks become complex when many cognitive operations and strategies are required to complete them.[2] Task complexity also increases when a person's attention is divided while performing simultaneous operations, like using a cell phone while driving. In these situations, both tasks compete for attention, which is limited in capacity.[3]

On the other hand, subjective complexity is based on individual perception and relates to a person's relevant skills, knowledge, and abilities. "What is highly complex to one person may be much less complex to another person. Rather than a feature of the environment, complexity primarily seems to be in the eye of the beholder," write cognitive researchers Jan Elen and Richard Clark.[4]

The complexities of poker are clarified with this deck that includes an on-card explanation of the additional cards needed for the best poker hand.

Drew Davies, Oxide Design, *United States*

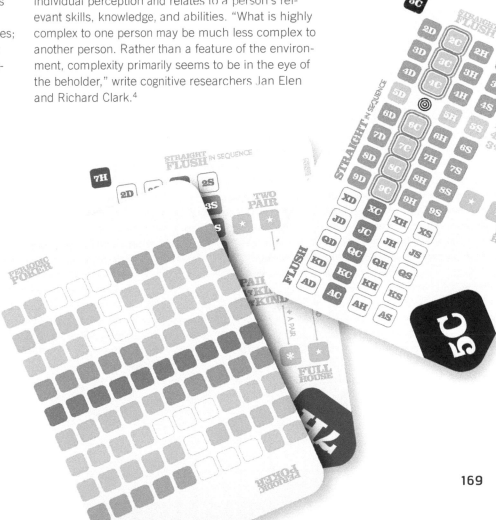

◄ *The frames of this multimedia documentary made for Spain's newspaper* El Mundo *explain Albert Einstein's landmark discoveries from 1905. Breaking complex concepts into small segments can help viewers understand complexity.*

Alberto Cairo, *United States*

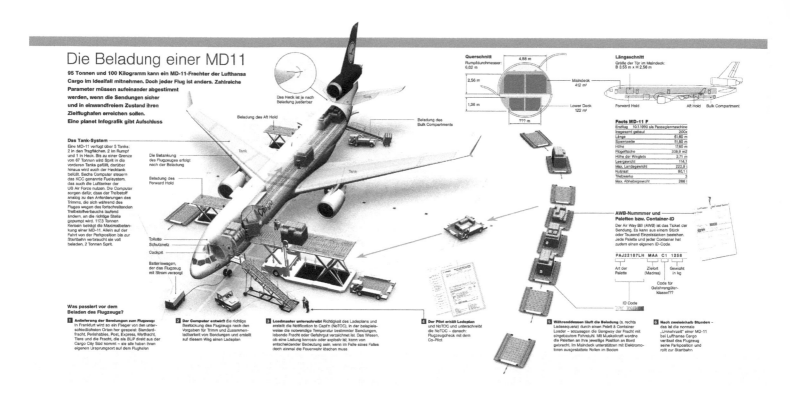

Explaining Complex Concepts

The explanation of complex concepts often results in visually complex graphics. Complex graphics are information rich, conveying meaning through an increased use of detail, patterns, shapes, text, color, density, and diversity of elements. Viewers may have difficulty with these visuals because there are a greater number of pictorial stimuli to discriminate, identify, and process. Also, it takes longer to search through and to locate relevant information when a graphic is complex. One eye-tracking study found that visually complex Web pages produce a more scattered and disordered eye-scanning path than Web pages with fewer elements.[5]

The challenge for visual communicators is to provide a full and complete graphical explanation while accommodating the limits and strengths of human cognitive architecture. It is most effective when designers use techniques to clarify information rather than to simplify it. Although simplification is highly effective for many communication needs, some concepts and systems are too deep and too rich to pare down. As Evelyn Goldsmith writes in her book *Research into Illustration*, "Just as a verbal exposition sometimes needs to consider a number of issues in order to present an argument in its true perspective, so a drawing can lose much of its communicative value if in an attempt at simplicity it is denied an appropriate context."

▲ *A complex explanation requires a visually complex graphic, as shown in these depictions of the import process at Frankfurt Airport for* Planet *magazine.*

Jan Schwochow,
Golden Section Graphics,
Germany

▶ *The features of the high-energy-performance Condé Nast Building are illustrated through call-outs and spot enlargements to make the explanation more effective.*

Mathew Luckwitz, grafPort,
United States

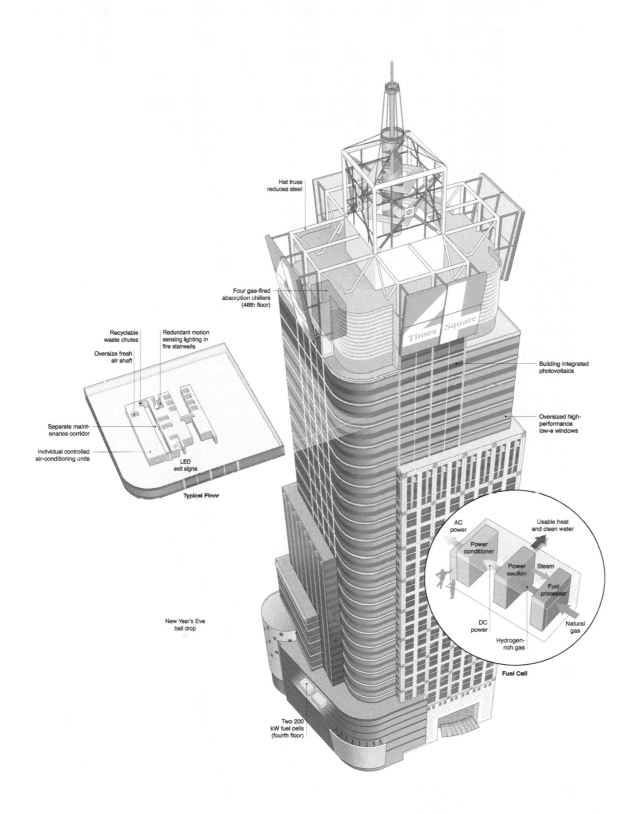

Hat truss
reduces steel

Four gas-fired
absorption chillers
(48th floor)

Recyclable
waste chutes

Oversize fresh
air shaft

Redundant motion
sensing lighting in
fire stairwells

Separate maint-
enance corridor

Individual controlled
air-conditioning units

LED
exit signs

Typical Floor

Building integrated
photovoltaics

Oversized high-
performance
low-e windows

AC
power

Usable heat
and clean water

Power
conditioner

Power
section

Steam

Fuel
processor

DC
power

Hydrogen-
rich gas

Natural
gas

Fuel Cell

New Year's Eve
ball drop

Two 200
kW fuel cells
(fourth floor)

Cognition and Complexity

In a complex world, we are bound to seek all kinds of explanations to better understand it. We rely on previous knowledge, which is structured in mental representations or schemas, to perform cognitive tasks and to assimilate new information. Our schemas are often fuzzy and incomplete. Explanations help us refine them so they are more accurate. Our schemas may have conflicting and illogical concepts. Explanations help dissolve cognitive dissonance.

Regardless of whether it is visual or verbal, a complex explanation places a great demand on working memory. The more the informational components of an explanation interact, the greater the cognitive load. This is because understanding an interdependent system is more difficult than understanding elements in isolation.[6] For example, cognitive load is greater in trying to understand how an entire computer network operates than in trying to understand how one component, such as a router, functions.

Fortunately, our cognitive architecture is equipped to handle complex information. When we come upon something new and complex, it is theorized that we gradually build up schemas into large entities in working memory in order to have more information simultaneously available.[7] This ensures that the limited capacity of working memory will not be strained, as it can only accommodate a few entities at a time.

We also construct mental models to help us understand complex systems. Mental models, which are based on schemas, are broader representations of how different aspects of the world operate. They integrate what is common about a particular type of system or phenomena. For instance, a person who has an accurate mental model of how computer printers work will be able to use this mental model to operate almost any printer. While studying an explanatory graphic, viewers will construct a network of knowledge to understand it and will enhance their mental models with this new information.

Two important contributors to building accurate mental representations are coherency and context. Coherency refers to the consistent logic that makes an explanation meaningful. Coherent explanations might involve understanding cause and effect or the steps of a process. They contain a structure that makes sense. Just as verbal explanations require coherency, so do visual ones. Designers can ensure graphical explanations are coherent by ensuring that the order for viewing information is clear, extraneous information is limited, and the graphic is visually unified and logical.

The context of an explanation is the framework within which new information is assimilated. In picture comprehension, context is a constraining feature that determines what objects to expect and what not to expect in a particular type of visual. As a result, context helps to guide the viewer's attention and influences how a picture is interpreted. It so strongly influences meaning that when something is perceived as out of context, it often does not make sense. Providing context in a complex visual explanation, such as showing the big-picture view and the detail in an inset, goes a long way in helping a viewer understand a concept.

▶ *This visually coherent information graphic explains the causes of obesity in the United States as compared to Japan.*

Alan Lau, *United States*

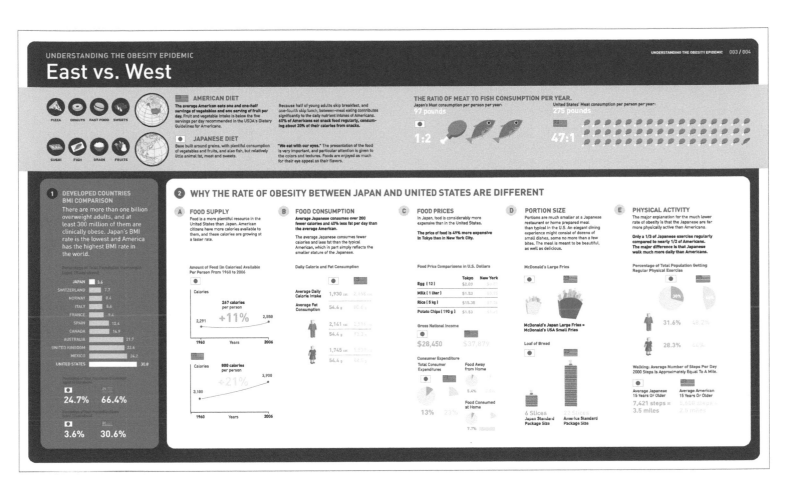

UNDERSTANDING THE OBESITY EPIDEMIC
East vs. West

PIZZA   DONUTS   FAST FOOD   SWEETS

SUSHI   FISH   GRAIN   FRUITS

🇺🇸 AMERICAN DIET
The average American eats one and one-half servings of vegetables and one serving of fruit per day. Fruit and vegetable intake is below the five servings per day recommended in the USDA's Dietary Guidelines for Americans.

🇯🇵 JAPANESE DIET
Base built around grains, with plentiful consumption of vegetables and fruits, and also fish, but relatively little animal fat, meat and sweets.

Because half of young adults skip breakfast, and one-fourth skip lunch, between-meal eating contributes significantly to the daily nutrient intakes of Americans. 60% of Americans eat snack food regularly, consuming about 20% of their calories from snacks.

"We eat with our eyes." The presentation of the food is very important, and particular attention is given to the colors and textures. Foods are enjoyed as much for their eye appeal as their flavors.

THE RATIO OF MEAT TO FISH CONSUMPTION PER YEAR.
Japan's Meat consumption per person per year:
97 pounds
1:2

United States' Meat consumption per person per year:
275 pounds
47:1

1   DEVELOPED COUNTRIES BMI COMPARISON
There are more than one billion overweight adults, and at least 300 million of them are clinically obese. Japan's BMI rate is the lowest and America has the highest BMI rate in the world.

Percentage of Total Population Overweight Aged 15 and older.

JAPAN	3.6
SWITZERLAND	7.7
NORWAY	8.4
ITALY	8.6
FRANCE	9.4
SPAIN	12.4
CANADA	14.9
AUSTRALIA	21.7
UNITED KINGDOM	22.4
MEXICO	24.2
UNITED STATES	30.8

24.7%   66.4%

3.6%   30.6%

2   WHY THE RATE OF OBESITY BETWEEN JAPAN AND UNITED STATES ARE DIFFERENT

A FOOD SUPPLY
Food is a more plentiful resource in the United States than Japan. American citizens have more calories available to them, and these calories are growing at a faster rate.

Amount of Food (in Calories) Available Per Person From 1960 to 2006

Calories
267 calories per person
+11%
2,291 — 2,558
1960 — Years — 2006

Calories
800 calories per person
+21%
3,100 — 3,900
1960 — Years — 2006

B FOOD CONSUMPTION
Average Japanese consumes over 200 fewer calories and 40% less fat per day than the average American.

The average Japanese consumes fewer calories and less fat than the typical American, which in part simply reflects the smaller stature of the Japanese.

Daily Calorie and Fat Consumption

Average Daily Calorie Intake	1,930 cal	2,136 cal
Average Fat Consumption	54.4 g	91.4 g
	2,141 cal	2,516 cal
	54.4 g	92.2 g
	1,745 cal	1,939 cal
	54.4 g	82.5 g

C FOOD PRICES
In Japan, food is considerably more expensive than in the United States.

The price of food is 69% more expensive in Tokyo than in New York City.

Food Price Comparisons in U.S. Dollars

	Tokyo	New York
Egg (12)	$2.03	$xxx
Milk (1 liter)	$1.53	$xxx
Rice (5 kg)	$15.36	$xxx
Potato Chips (190 g)	$1.83	$xxx

Gross National Income
$28,450 $37,879

Consumer Expenditure
Total Consumer Expenditures
Food Away from Home
5.4%
Food Consumed at Home
13%   23%
7.7%

D PORTION SIZE
Portions are much smaller at a Japanese restaurant or home prepared meal than typical in the U.S. An elegant dining experience might consist of dozens of small dishes, some no more than a few bites. The meal is meant to be beautiful, as well as delicious.

McDonald's Large Fries

McDonald's Japan Large Fries = McDonald's USA Small Fries

Loaf of Bread

6 Slices
Japan Standard Package Size

12 Slices
America Standard Package Size

E PHYSICAL ACTIVITY
The major explanation for the much lower rate of obesity is that the Japanese are far more physically active than Americans.

Only a 1/3 of Japanese exercise regularly compared to nearly 1/2 of Americans. The major difference is that Japanese walk much more daily than Americans.

Percentage of Total Population Getting Regular Physical Exercise

31.6%   48.2%

28.3%   42%

Walking: Average Number of Steps Per Day
2000 Steps Is Approximately Equal To A Mile.

Average Japanese 15 Years Or Older
7,421 steps = 3.5 miles

Average American 15 Years Or Older
5,600 steps = 2.5 miles

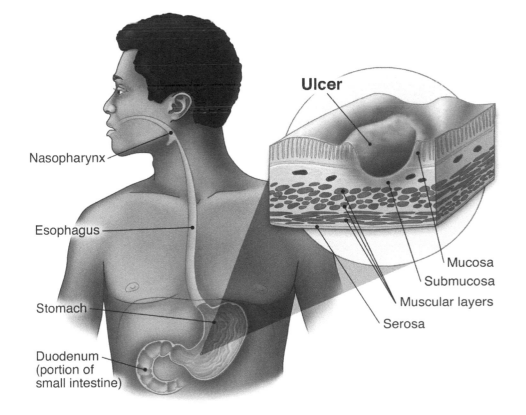

▶ *In this medical illustration for online patient-education materials, presenting the visual context of the stomach provides a reference for the viewer to understand the detail.*

Joanne Haderer Müller,
Haderer & Müller
Biomedical, *United States*

Nasopharynx

Esophagus

Stomach

Duodenum (portion of small intestine)

Ulcer

Mucosa
Submucosa
Muscular layers
Serosa

Lo más parecido a una mano verdadera

La gran ventaja de esta prótesis con respecto a sus antecesoras es la variedad de movimientos que permite y la posibilidad de darle un aspecto casi real

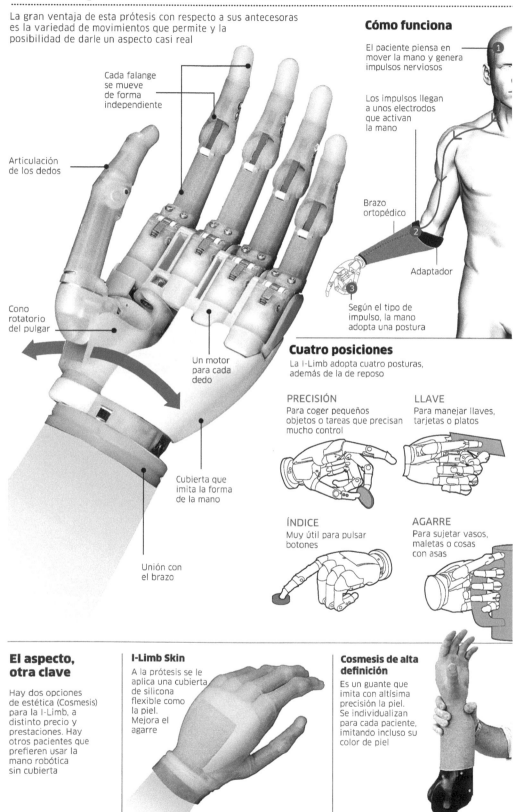

Cada falange se mueve de forma independiente

Articulación de los dedos

Cono rotatorio del pulgar

Un motor para cada dedo

Cubierta que imita la forma de la mano

Unión con el brazo

Cómo funciona

El paciente piensa en mover la mano y genera impulsos nerviosos

Los impulsos llegan a unos electrodos que activan la mano

Brazo ortopédico

Adaptador

Según el tipo de impulso, la mano adopta una postura

Cuatro posiciones

La I-Limb adopta cuatro posturas, además de la de reposo

PRECISIÓN
Para coger pequeños objetos o tareas que precisan mucho control

LLAVE
Para manejar llaves, tarjetas o platos

ÍNDICE
Muy útil para pulsar botones

AGARRE
Para sujetar vasos, maletas o cosas con asas

El aspecto, otra clave

Hay dos opciones de estética (Cosmesis) para la I-Limb, a distinto precio y prestaciones. Hay otros pacientes que prefieren usar la mano robótica sin cubierta

I-Limb Skin

A la prótesis se le aplica una cubierta de silicona flexible como la piel. Mejora el agarre

Cosmesis de alta definición

Es un guante que imita con altísima precisión la piel. Se individualizan para cada paciente, imitando incluso su color de piel

FUENTE: TOUCH BIONICS, DAILY TELEGRAPH Y ELABORACIÓN PROPIA

GRÁFICO: CHIQUI ESTEBAN

In this explanation of how a mechanical hand works for the Público *newspaper, the main illustration with callouts provides the context for the smaller explanatory segments that surround it.*

Chiqui Esteban, Público, *Spain*

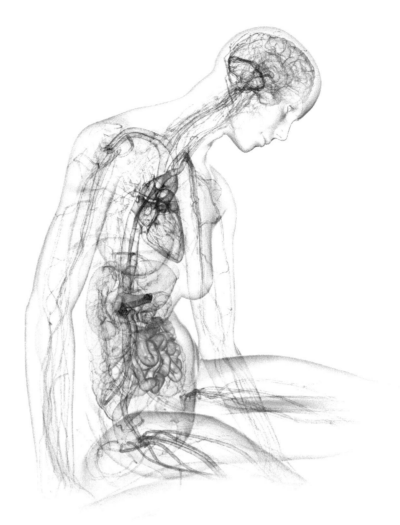

Applying The Principle

It is well known that viewers have an easier time understanding simpler graphics than complex ones. Increased complexity can interfere with the viewer's ability to decode and interpret a visual. Thus, designers must find effective ways to clearly convey meaning without overwhelming the audience. A complex visual explanation does not require extraneous and distracting detail. It does, however, require the detail necessary for providing a coherent explanation.

Several visual approaches can facilitate building accurate schemas and appropriate mental models without overloading the audience. One is to segment complex content into smaller units to minimize the amount of information processed at one time. Organizing information into smaller chunks allows schemas to slowly build up so that content can be gradually understood and ultimately integrated into one whole. Segmenting can take many forms. A designer can present simpler visuals first and then progressively reveal more complex components. Or a complex task can be broken down into simpler steps that form a chronological sequence. Alternately, information can be divided into frames and animated. Any of these approaches can potentially decrease the cognitive demands placed on the viewer.

A second approach to clarifying complexity is to expose parts and components that are normally concealed. This can include a straightforward portrayal of what is normally hidden from sight, creating a variety of interior views, such as cutaways and cross sections or using pictorial devices to show movement. These approaches reveal the inner form of an object or system, conveying new meaning about how things are structured and how they function.

A third technique for clarifying complexity is to reveal the inherent structure of the information, which conveys its organizing principle. Inherent structure is based on an intuitive understanding of how information is ordered. For example, in a calendar, information is structured in months and days. In a graphic about soil, information is structured in layers. This cognitively natural approach provides a somewhat abstract path to facilitating comprehension. When a graphic is visually organized so that it makes conceptual sense, it helps viewers get the message.

The success of creating a complex visual explanation depends on whether the visual techniques meet the goal for which the graphic is created and accommodate the prior knowledge of the viewer. When clarifying complexity, designers and illustrators must balance the cognitive requirement for detail with the knowledge that viewers can become overwhelmed with too much visual information.

In this poignant rendering of a woman with diabetes for the New York Times, a transparent view portrays the organs thought to be associated with the disease.

Bryan Christie,
Bryan Christie Design,
United States

▶ These Christmas Cheat Sheets (one for male and one for female) were created to provide a person's clothing sizes to potential gift givers. The form is organized by the inherent structure of the information.

Simon Cook,
United Kingdom

▼ Text and images in this information graphic are sequenced to pace the information presentation of the ethanol manufacturing process.

Nivedita Ramesh,
University of Washington,
United States

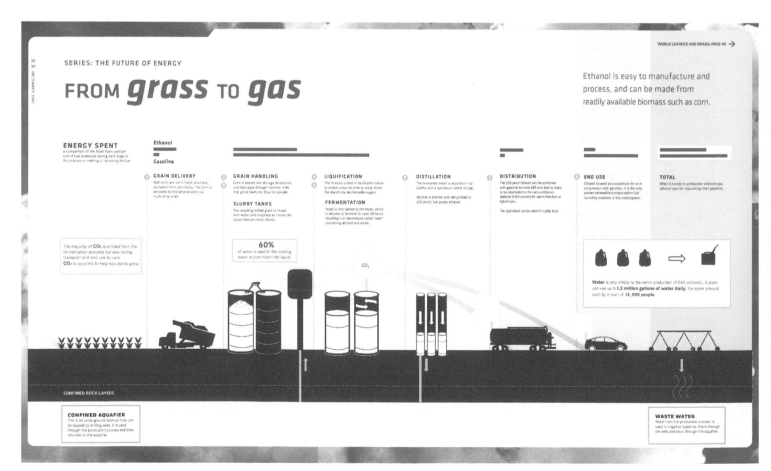

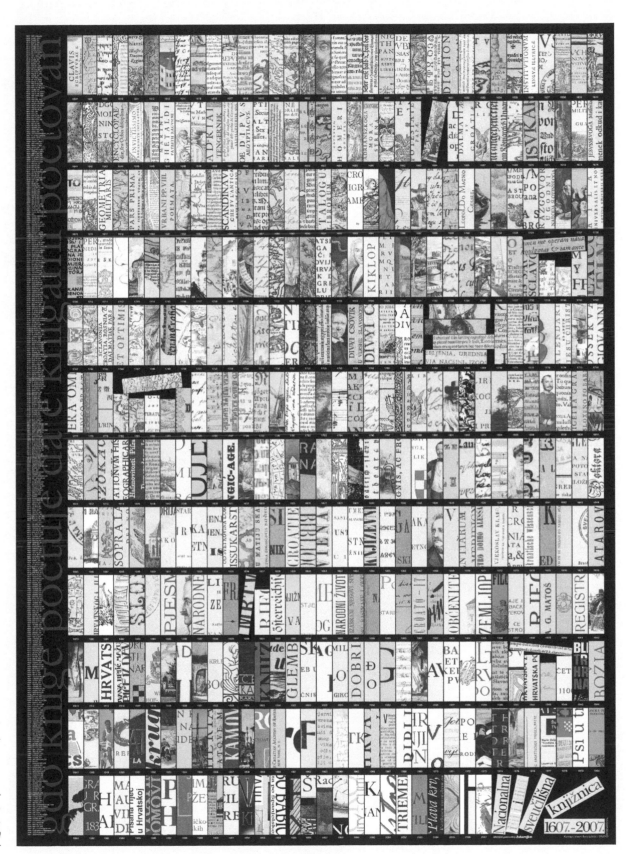

Information has an inherent structure. A poster celebrating a library's 400-year anniversary is structured out of 400 books.

Boris Ljubicic,
Studio International,
Croatia

SEGMENTS AND SEQUENCES

Providing a complex visual explanation in one spatial layout can result in a cluttered composition of disorganized ideas. It takes thoughtful restraint and controlled logic to pace an explanation or to organize it into a sequence with a beginning, middle, and end.

Research has shown that when the entirety of an explanation is presented all at once, people are less likely to comprehend it.[8] In particular, people feel overwhelmed when confronted with complex information for which they have little prior knowledge. Essentially, the amount of processing required to understand the information exceeds what the person can hold in working memory. One effective way designers can avoid creating cognitive overload is to segment information into digestible pieces.

Information segmentation is particularly effective because it is a natural cognitive strategy we use to decompose our world into smaller units. Babies segment sounds when they learn to speak; authors segment books into chapters and topics; designers segment graphics into dominant and subordinate elements; and songwriters segment songs into verse and chorus. We routinely use segments to internally manage our world. As we experience the activities in our life, we naturally parse them into temporal segments and think of them as separate events. We do this because when information is in smaller entities, it is easier to manage in working memory and easier to fit into existing schemas for future storage and retrieval.[9]

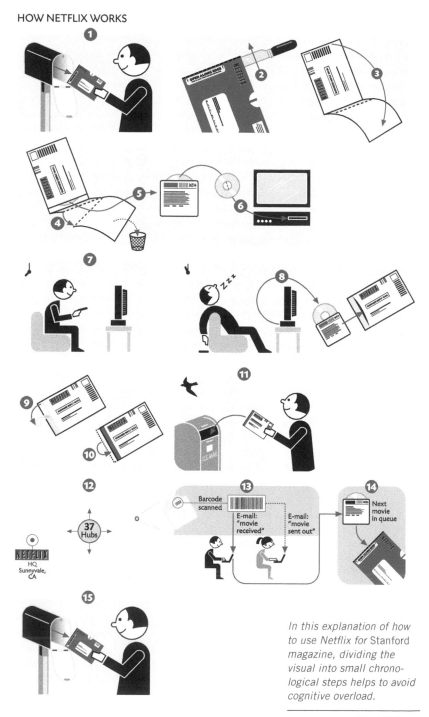

HOW NETFLIX WORKS

In this explanation of how to use Netflix for Stanford *magazine, dividing the visual into small chronological steps helps to avoid cognitive overload.*

Nigel Holmes,
United States

NASA's Cassini-Huygens mission to explore Saturn is a complex online explanation created for El Mundo. *Breaking it into interactive segments controls the pace of the presentation, which helps viewers slowly build their comprehension.*

Alberto Cairo, *United States*

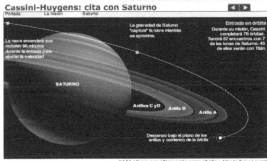

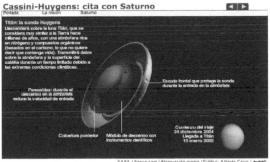

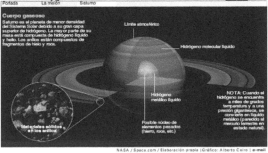

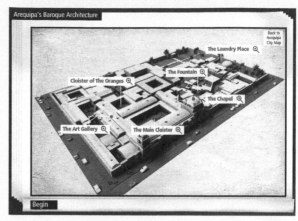

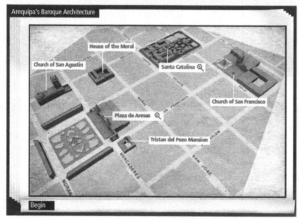

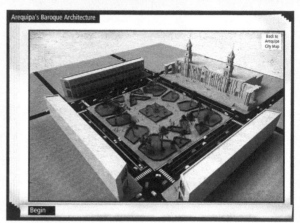

Graphic designers can segment information by dividing a visual into small but meaningful units. Each unit groups conceptually related information. Segmenting slows the pace at which information is introduced, allowing viewers to take the time to process a minimal number of concepts before moving on to the next one. People understand and learn more deeply when information is presented in smaller segments rather than larger ones.

Segmenting is a risk when a viewer cannot combine the individual segments into one coherent mental model. The segment must be maintained in working memory until the person views the next portion of the graphic. Some viewers may be unable to integrate across units of information when a composition is visually fragmented. To avoid this, ensure that the viewer gets the holistic view of a concept or system while studying the smaller segments. This can be achieved in several ways: depicting the big-picture view to provide context; introducing the overriding concept at the start; providing visual continuity to the information; and slowly building on previous concepts. In addition, the designer should ensure that a segmented visual connects elements by directing the viewer's eyes

using the compositional techniques or pictorial devices discussed in Principle 2, Direct the Eyes.

Sequencing is a special type of segmenting that presents information in a chronological order, similar to how it would occur in the real world. This is an effective approach for explaining a procedure, a set of steps, cause and effect, or a complex idea where one principle builds on the next. When creating a sequence, prioritize the information to determine its logical order and display it from left to right or top to bottom. Ensure that the relevant details are displayed for each step, avoiding too much simplification so that information associated with the concept or task does not get lost.

An advantage to sequencing is that it groups important visual information together, often through proximity, a connecting line, or a visual boundary. When items are perceptually organized into a group, they are represented together in visual working memory. This enhances the probability that the information will be encoded as one group into long-term memory.[10] Sequential presentations are also processed faster and tend to increase comprehension.[11]

▲ *Renderings and descriptions of the architecture in Arequipa, Peru, are presented in multiple interactive segments to gradually present the information.*

**Vu Nguyen,
Biofusion Design,**
United States

▶ *In this visualization of how nuclear power is generated, the procedure is clearly sequenced to make a complex process comprehensible.*

**Kimberly Fulton, University
of Washington,**
United States

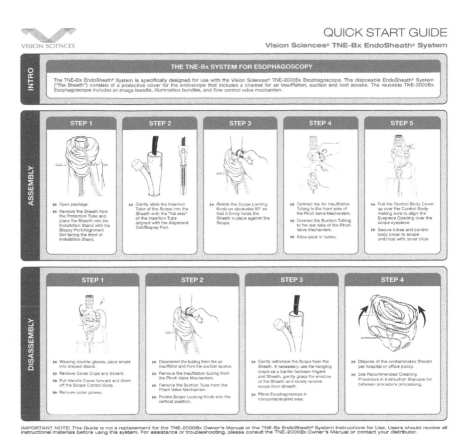

This visual guide breaks down the assembly and disassembly of a medical device into a sequence of clear and discrete steps. This approach facilitates comprehension, allowing working memory to process one step at a time.

Aviad Stark,
Graphic Advance,
United States

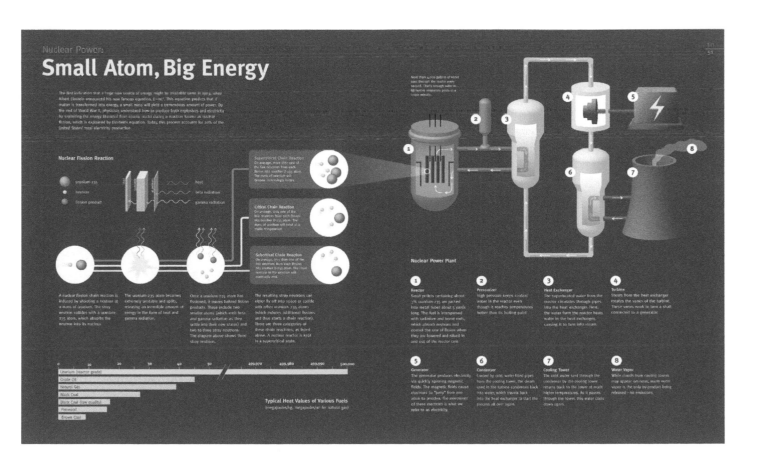

Special Relativity

Special relativity unlocked the secret of the stars and revealed the untold
energy stored deep inside the atom. But the seed of relativity was planted
when Einstein was only 16 years old, when he asked himself a children's
question: what would a beam of light look like if you could race along side?

According to Newton, you could catch up to any speeding object if you
moved fast enough. Catching up to a light wave, it would look like a
wave frozen in time. But even as a child, Einstein knew that no one
had ever seen a frozen wave before.

When Einstein studied Maxwell's theory of light, he found
something that others missed, that the speed of light was
always constant, no matter how fast you moved. He then
boldly formulated the principle of special relativity: the
speed of light is a constant in all inertial frames
(frames which move at constant velocity).

No longer were space and time absolutes,
as Newton thought. Clocks beat at different rates
throughout the universe. This is a profound
departure from the Newtonian world.

Previously, physicists believed
"ether," a mysterious substance
which pervaded the universe
provided the absolute reference
frame for all motions. But the
Michelson-Morely experiment
measured the "ether wind" of
earth as it moved around the s
and it was zero. Either the ear
motionless, or the meter stick
experiment had somehow sho
In desperation to save Newtor
physics, some believed that th
atoms in meter sticks were
mechanically compressed by
force of the ether wind. Einste
showed that the ether theory v
totally unnecessary, that space
contracted and time slowed do
as you moved near the speed
light…

→ 186,282 miles per second.

Imagine a policeman on a motorcycle catching
up to a speeding
motorist.

According to
Newton, the
policeman would
see the driver as if
he were at rest.

But if we watch this
from the sidewalk, we'd see the policeman
and the driver racing
past neck and neck.

Now replace the motorist
with a light beam.

From the sidewalk,
we see the policeman
racing right alongside the
light beam. But later, if you
talked to the policeman,
he would shake his head
and say that no matter
how fast he accelerated,
the light beam raced
ahead at the speed of light,
leaving him in the dust.

But how can the policeman's
story differ so much from
what we just saw from the
sidewalk with our own eyes?
Einstein was stunned when
he found the answer: time
itself had slowed down for
everything on the policeman's
motorcycle.

To Newton, time
was uniform
throughout the
universe. One
second on Mars
was the same
as one second
on earth. One
o'clock on earth
was the same
as one o'clock
on Mars.

But to Einstein,
time beats at
different rates.
The faster you
travel, the
slower time
beats. There is
no such thing
as absolute
time. When you
say that it is
one o'clock on
earth, it's not
necessarily one
o'clock
throughout
the universe.

Critics of relativity point to the "twin paradox."

Imagine putting a twin on a rocket ship which blasts off near the speed of light, while the other twin is on the earth.

Through a telescope, the earth twin sees that the rocket twin is younger.

When the rocket twin comes back to earth, the earth twin has aged, while the rocket twin is much younger.

But from the vantage point of the rocket twin as he took off from earth, it appeared as if he was at rest, and the earth moved away from him. Thus, to him it is the earth twin who has traveled at great speed and become younger while the rocket twin has aged. So who is really younger?

Resolution of the twin paradox
The rocket twin, not the earth twin, reversed directions. Thus, the rocket twin is no longer inertial (traveling with constant velocity), and hence you can tell who is really younger: the rocket twin.

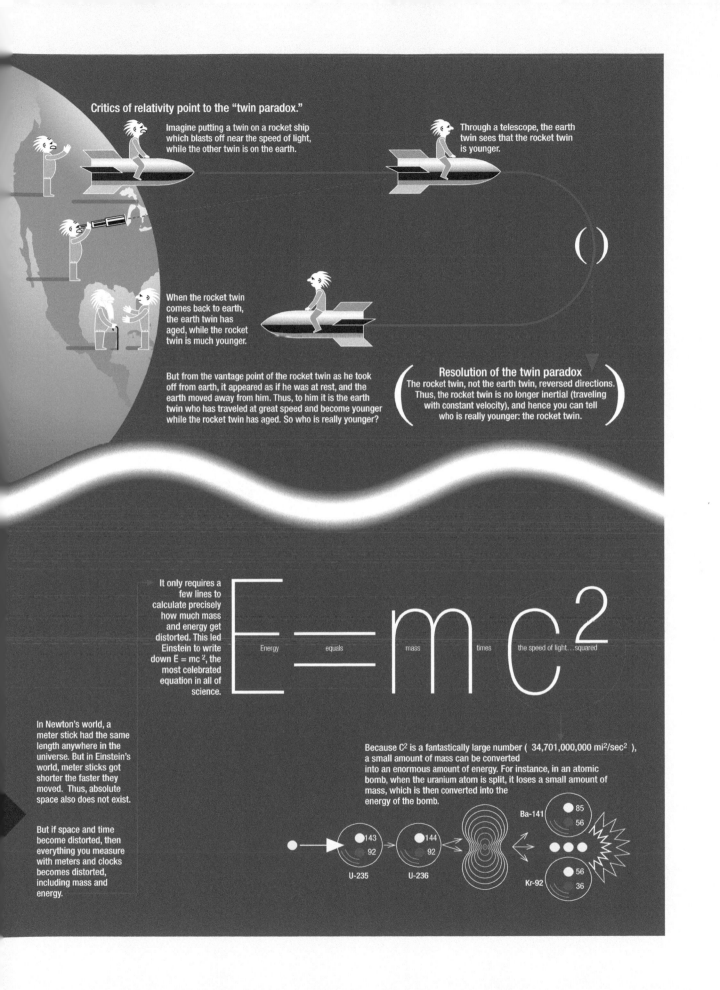

It only requires a few lines to calculate precisely how much mass and energy get distorted. This led Einstein to write down $E = mc^2$, the most celebrated equation in all of science.

$$E = mc^2$$

Energy   equals   mass   times   the speed of light...squared

In Newton's world, a meter stick had the same length anywhere in the universe. But in Einstein's world, meter sticks got shorter the faster they moved. Thus, absolute space also does not exist.

But if space and time become distorted, then everything you measure with meters and clocks becomes distorted, including mass and energy.

Because C^2 is a fantastically large number (34,701,000,000 mi^2/sec^2), a small amount of mass can be converted into an enormous amount of energy. For instance, in an atomic bomb, when the uranium atom is split, it loses a small amount of mass, which is then converted into the energy of the bomb.

143
92
U-235

144
92
U-236

Ba-141
85
56

56
36
Kr-92

SPECIALIZED VIEWS

Although our visual system is remarkably intelligent, it does have its physical limitations. Many structures and mechanisms are invisible to the unaided eye, and many processes can only be seen through their outcomes. Revealing what is physically hidden and depicting unobservable phenomena through special forms of representations and pictorial devices are effective ways to portray complex systems. Cutaways, magnifications, and other interior views work well for depicting structural information. Techniques that depict movement are valuable for communicating functional information.

Specialized views comprise any technique that allows a person to see through the obstructions of the surface and beyond tightly assembled components. These types of graphics are based on the conventions of technical illustration, defined as "a technique used to graphically present complex parts and assemblies so that professional and lay people alike can understand their form and functionality."[12] As graphic designers and generalist illustrators increasingly create explanatory graphics, they find ways to make complex content more accessible and engaging.

To break through the complexity barrier, designers must keep in mind that novices use different cognitive strategies than experts. "Experts are expert not only because they know more but critically because they know differently," write David Evans and Cindy Gadd in *Cognitive Science in Medicine*. When learning about physical systems, the internal representations of a novice focus on the static physical structures with minimal understanding of how things function and operate. Experts have a more integrated model that incorporates the structure, functions, and behaviors of a system.[13]

Contrary to many of the recommendations in this book, increased realism in a graphic may be more effective than highly schematized drawings when viewers will need to apply their knowledge about a physical system to a real system. In this case, highly schematized drawings that omit too much detail can lead to misunderstandings.[14] These findings validate the principle that clarifying rather than simplifying complexity is most effective.

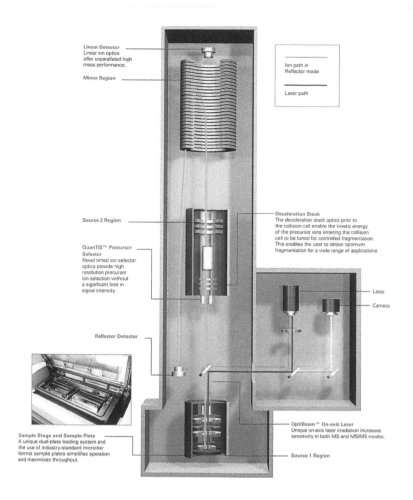

▲ *In promotional materials for a scientific device used for protein analysis, the interior view and call-outs help clarify the optics technology inside.*

Amy Vest,
Applied Biosystems Brand
& Creative Group, *United States*

▶ *The explanations of physical objects and systems often require specialized views because we can often only see the tip of the iceberg, as illustrated here for* Scientific American.

David Fierstein,
David Fierstein Illustration,
Animation & Design,
United States

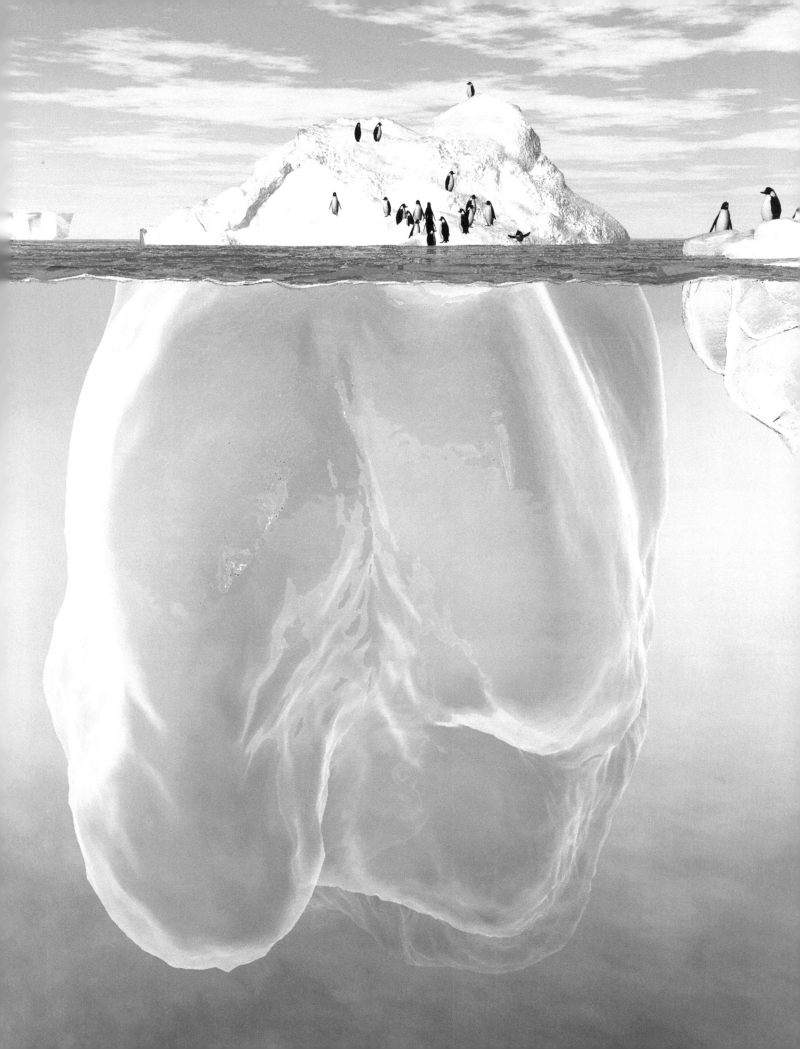

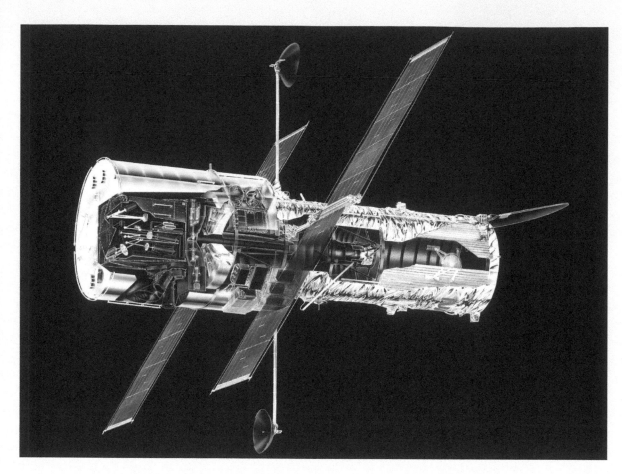

Interior Views

Cutaways, cross sections, and transparent views are established ways of portraying the interior structure of a system. Complex objects and systems are difficult to imagine when their parts are obscured. Cutaways usually remove around one-fourth of the surface so a particular interior region is visible. The view inside is often rendered through a window or tear. As a convention, a jagged or rough edge along the viewing window conveys that a cut has been made, and its inner texture often conveys the quality of the enclosing skin. Interiors are often shown as cross sections, which depict an object cut off at right angles to its axis. Even more revealing are transparent or phantom views that make the exterior surface of an object invisible so the full internal structure is exposed.

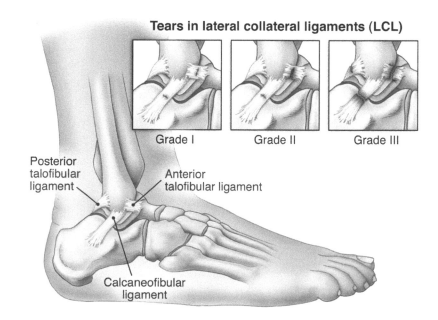

Tears in lateral collateral ligaments (LCL)

Grade I   Grade II   Grade III

Posterior talofibular ligament

Anterior talofibular ligament

Calcaneofibular ligament

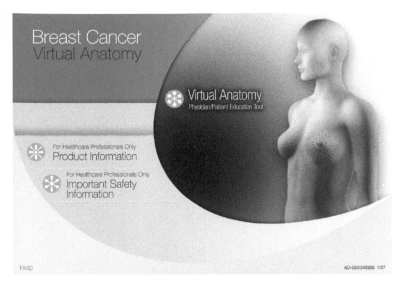

In this virtual anatomy presentation, a transparent view of the human body enables physicians to visually explain the progression of breast cancer to their patients.

Nicola Landucci,
CCGMetamedia,
United States

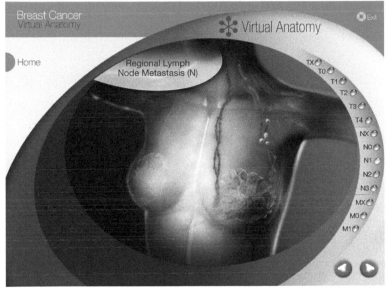

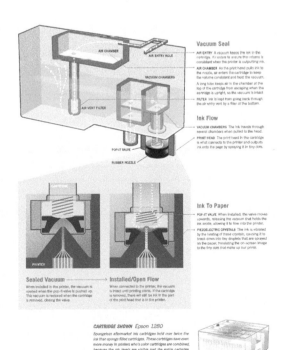

In the Flow INKJET PRINTING A complicated process that takes place in a very small space

This explanation of the inkjet printing process is shown through several specialized views that will help a viewer build a correct mental model. The transparent view portrays the system and how it functions. Cross-sectional views provide details about how a cartridge operates.

Jacob Halton,
Illinois Institute of Art,
United States

Exploded Views

When a machine, architectural structure, or organism has hidden parts that cannot be fully seen with a standard interior view, an exploded version can provide even greater clarification. Exploded views show the components of an object in their correct arrangement, though slightly separated and spread along a common axis, to reveal how they fit together. This is one way to show both the details of the individual parts, their relationships, and the order in which they are assembled.

If the proportions of the exploded pictorial graphic do not fit within the constraints of the layout, the parts may be moved out of alignment. Flow lines can then indicate where the parts fit into the assembly. Call outs are helpful for naming the parts that may be referenced in a verbal explanation. Although exploded views typically convey structure, the drawing can also convey function with the addition of arrows to indicate movement.

Depending on the purpose of the graphic and the qualities of the object, exploded views do not necessarily require a realistic rendering. It is not uncommon for the parts of a device to be portrayed as a line drawing because the components are recognizable by shape. This type of simplification may be helpful when the graphic is used for the purposes of assembly or disassembly. When exploded views are rendered for homes and buildings, increased realistic detail is often appealing. Because exploded views usually eliminate any type of occlusion, viewers get a better understanding of structure.

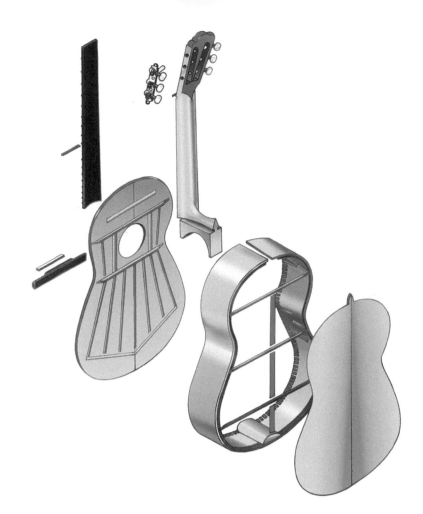

▲ *Pictorial graphics that show how the parts of an object are assembled, as in this exploded view of a classical guitar, provide a greater understanding of a system's structure.*

George Ladas, Base24
Design Systems,
United States

▶ *The exploded view in this information graphic about the mechanical alarm clock clarifies its internal structure and how the gears move.*

MaryClare M. Crabtree,
Illinois Institute of Art,
United States

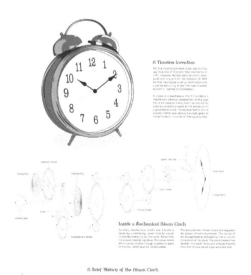

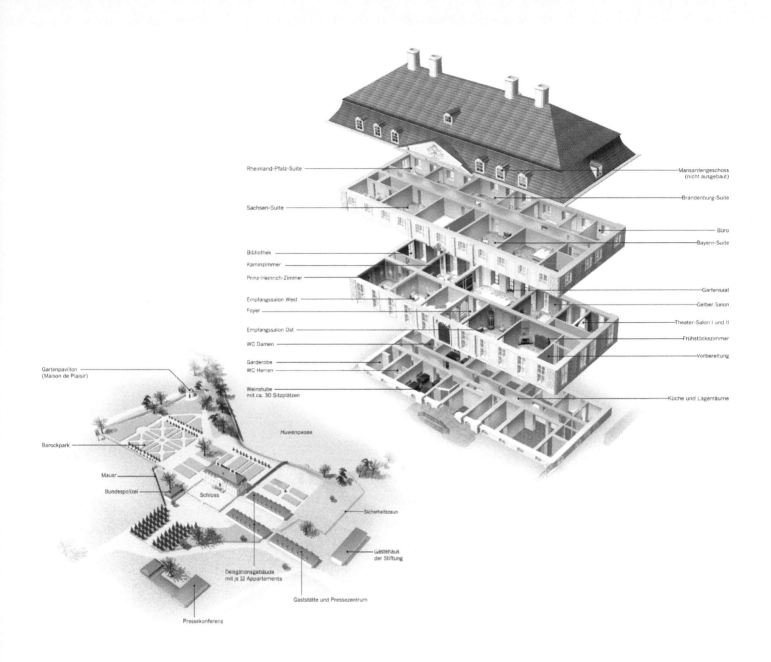

Rheinland-Pfalz-Suite

Sachsen-Suite

Bibliothek
Kaminzimmer
Prinz-Heinrich-Zimmer

Empfangssalon West

Foyer

Empfangssalon Ost

WC Damen

Garderobe
WC Herren

Weinstube
mit ca. 30 Sitzplätzen

Mansardengeschoss
(nicht ausgebaut)

Brandenburg-Suite

Büro
Bayern-Suite

Gartensaal

Gelber Salon

Theater-Salon I und II

Frühstückszimmer

Vorbereitung

Küche und Lagerräume

Gartenpavillon
(Maison de Plaisir)

Barockpark

Mauer

Bundespolizei

Schloss

Huwenowsee

Sicherheitszaun

Gästehaus
der Stiftung

Delegationsgebäude
mit je 12 Appartements

Gaststätte und Pressezentrum

Pressekonferenz

*An exploded view of Castle
Meseburg for the German
Sunday paper* Welt am
Sonntag *allows for an
extremely detailed view
of the interior.*

**Jan Schwochow, Katrin
Lamm, Juliana Köneke,
Jaroslaw K. Kaschtalinski,
Golden Section Graphics,**
Germany

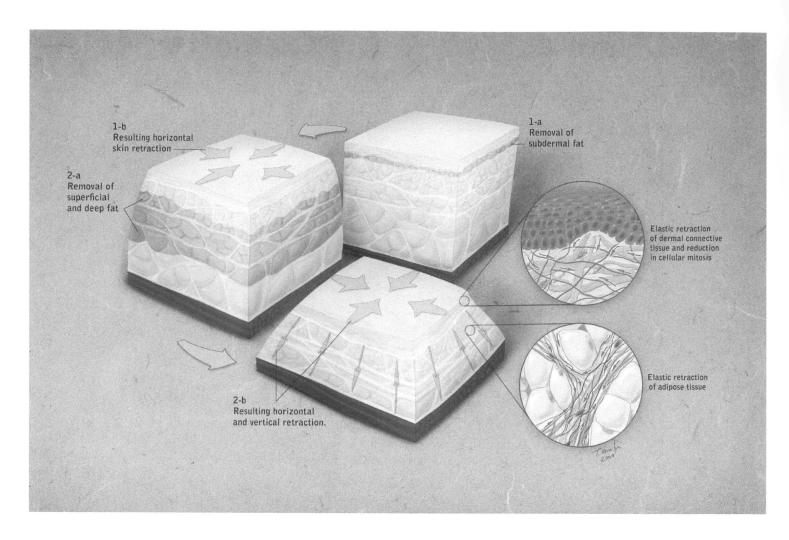

1-b
Resulting horizontal
skin retraction

1-a
Removal of
subdermal fat

2-a
Removal of
superficial
and deep fat

Elastic retraction
of dermal connective
tissue and reduction
in cellular mitosis

2-b
Resulting horizontal
and vertical retraction.

Elastic retraction
of adipose tissue

MAGNIFICATION

Magnification or zoom-ins portray a level of detail that offers a fine-tuned perception of an object. Increasing the level of detail is valuable for focusing on the crucial aspects of a device or system. Usually, the detail is enlarged and arranged as an inset or in a shape of a contrasting color. To highlight the detail, the magnified area can be pulled away from the main illustration but remain connected with lines, arrows, or a zoom effect. An advantage to enlarging individual areas of an object is that the main illustration provides the needed reference for context. This provides a holistic view before the viewer delves into the details.

Detailed areas of skin are magnified to better explain how skin retracts as a result of liposuction.

**Travis Vermilye,
Travis Vermilye Medical &
Biological Illustration,**
United States

This visual explanation of articular cartilage uses a stylized approach to depict the magnified area of the illustration.

Melisa Beveridge,
Natural History Illustration,
United States

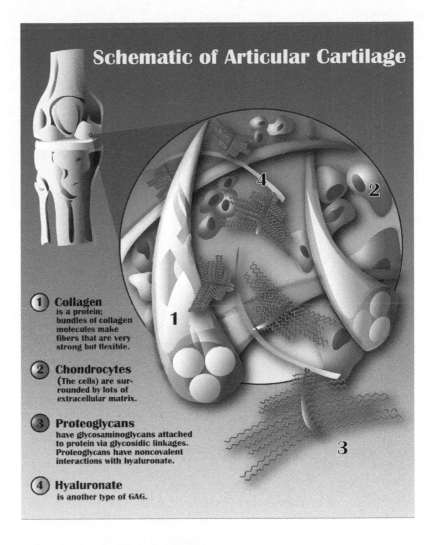

Schematic of Articular Cartilage

(1) Collagen
is a protein; bundles of collagen molecules make fibers that are very strong but flexible.

(2) Chondrocytes
(The cells) are surrounded by lots of extracellular matrix.

(3) Proteoglycans
have glycosaminoglycans attached to protein via glycosidic linkages. Proteoglycans have noncovalent interactions with hyaluronate.

(4) Hyaluronate
is another type of GAG.

In this overview of how a traffic accident is reported for CIO Insight magazine, the significant areas of the graphic are magnified to help the audience understand the explanation.

Colin Hayes, Illustrator,
United States

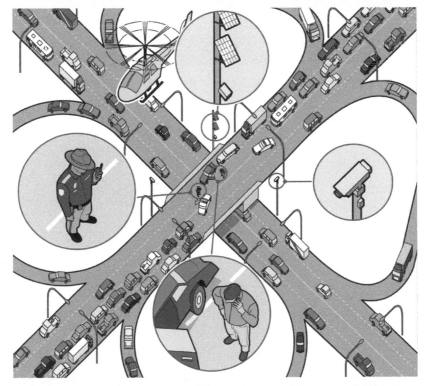

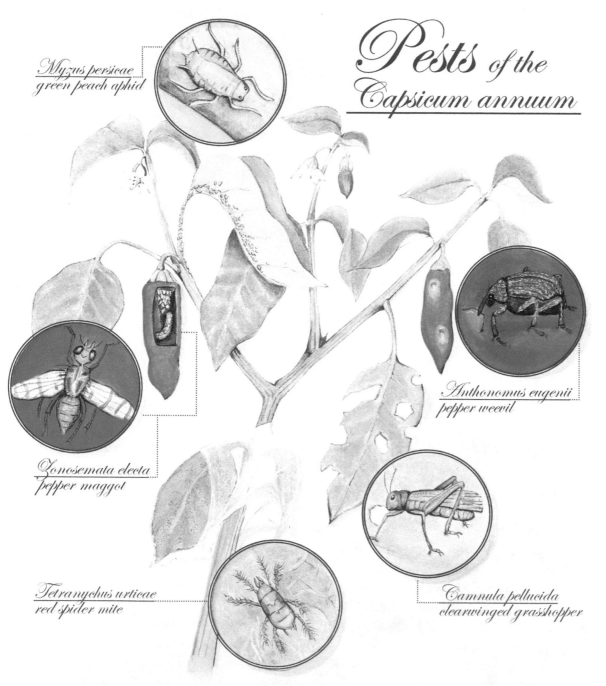

Myzus persicae
green peach aphid

Pests *of the*
Capsicum annuum

Zonosemata electa
pepper maggot

Anthonomus eugenii
pepper weevil

Tetranychus urticae
red spider mite

Camnula pellucida
clearwinged grasshopper

This elegant illustration uses magnification to show the pests of the pepper plant along with the damage they cause.

Melisa Beveridge, Natural History Illustration, United States

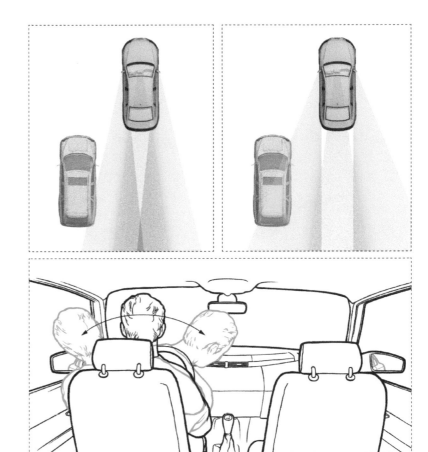

IMPLIED MOTION

Although static interior views are effective at showing structure, they don't clarify the dynamic aspects of a system or concept. Representing motion is important, however, for explaining the workings of a machine, the assembly of a product, human movement, and the dynamics of unseen forces. They clarify the ambiguity that might occur from a structural view and help a viewer to build a dynamic mental model that represents how something moves. Several powerful techniques can create the mental impression of movement. These include motion lines, stroboscopic movement, action arrows, and motion blur.

Motion lines are the set of streaking lines placed behind an object or person to suggest speed. Several studies that examined motion lines found this technique to be quite successful at conveying the impression of quick movement and the direction of motion.[15] Stroboscopic movement, on the other hand, simulates motion by depicting a progression of images that are similar in size and shape but differ in their position or pose. The difference between each image creates the rhythm of the motion. A ghosting technique that creates a transparent object or person makes the transition between images seem even smoother.

A common way to depict motion and its direction in scientific and technical illustrations is with arrows. The arrows are often curved to convey a sense of action. Because the arrow symbol seems to have limitless uses, action arrows often depend on context to be understood. Another technique for showing movement is motion blur. This is often depicted in photographs. A disadvantage to blur is that much of the object's detail can be lost with this approach.

▲ *Arrows convey the correct approach for using side mirrors while passing a car in a graphic for* Popular Mechanics *magazine.*

Jaroslaw Kaschtalinski,
Golden Section Graphics,
Germany

▶ *Arrows demonstrate the ventilation in an eco building—the Pearl River Tower in China.*

Bryan Christie,
Bryan Christie Design,
United States

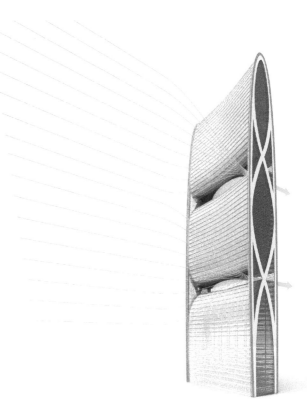

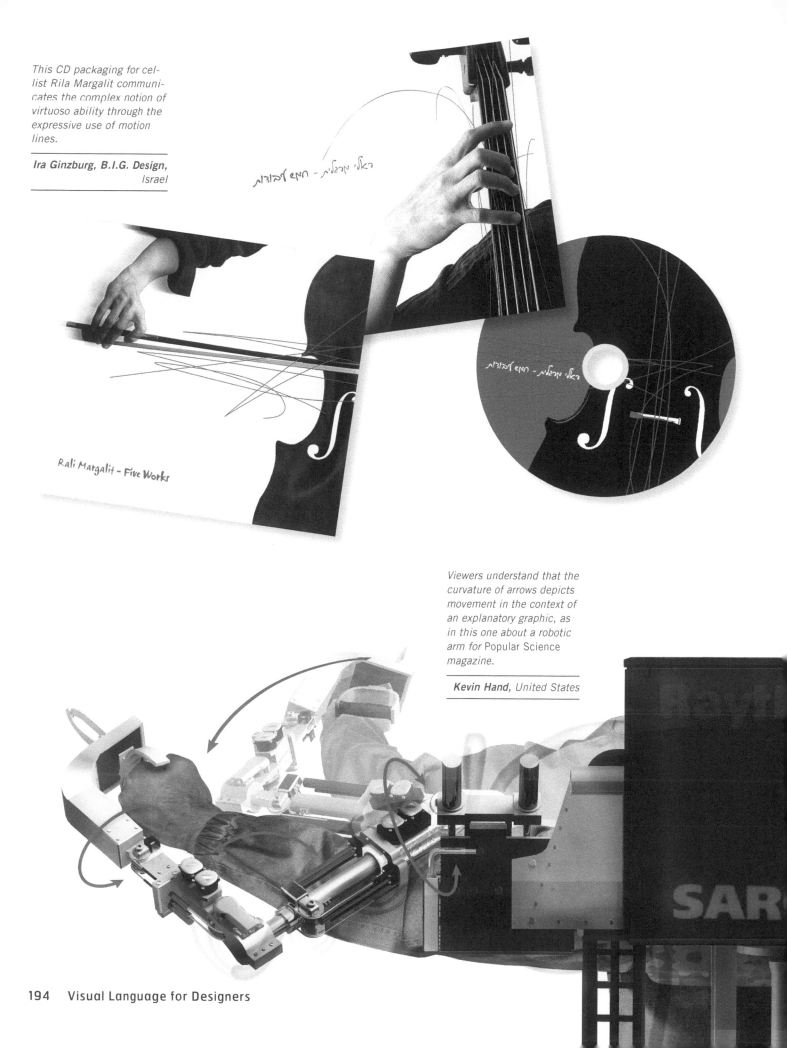

This CD packaging for cellist Rila Margalit communicates the complex notion of virtuoso ability through the expressive use of motion lines.

Ira Ginzburg, B.I.G. Design, *Israel*

Viewers understand that the curvature of arrows depicts movement in the context of an explanatory graphic, as in this one about a robotic arm for Popular Science magazine.

Kevin Hand, *United States*

The use of ghosted stroboscopic movement deftly simulates the action of a snowboard move.

Kevin Hand, *United States*

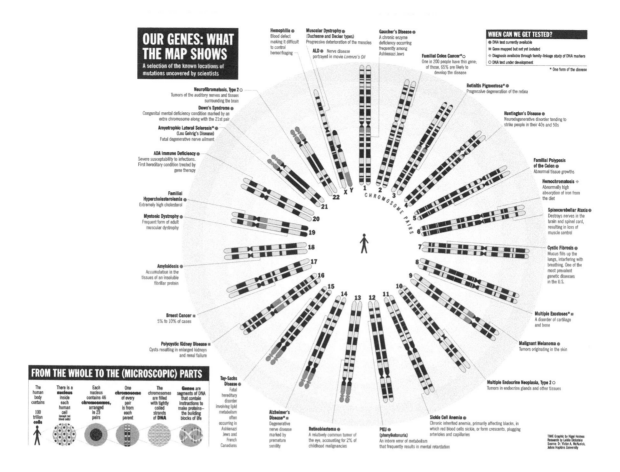

A radial structure, which seems to reflect life itself, is used to map some of the known mutations in the human genome in this information graphic for Time magazine.

Nigel Holmes, United States

INHERENT STRUCTURE

An inherent structure underlies information just as the spokes of an umbrella underlie its covering. Visual communication depends upon structure, and viewers rely on it as a feature that conveys the nature of a graphic. In the radial structure of the genome map shown, the organizing principle transmits a sense of energy, of a biological or mathematical form—a basis for life. The lack of visual hierarchy conveys that all chromosomes have equal importance and are generated from the same source. Thus, the sensory impression of the graphic's structure helps us interpret its meaning.

Our visual and cognitive systems make sense of the world by understanding structure, which is based on the relationships between entities. Phillip Paratore describes this in his book *Art and Design:* "Meaning emerges from relationships. Nothing exists or is perceived in isolation. A design acquires its form and meaning from the relationships on which it is based.

In pictorial design, this is called composition; in music, orchestration; in nature, ecology. The process of developing meaning through the organization of relationships is analogous in all fields, in all media and for all artists."

Memory for content improves whenever information is organized. The theory behind this is that spatial and physical features of the visual structure may be encoded along with the semantic structure of the information. Consequently, when information in memory is well organized, it is thought to be easier to retrieve and to integrate with new information.[16] Researchers have found that memory improves dramatically when people apply hierarchical organization to large amounts of information.[17] This is the basis for the learning strategy known as information mapping, in which people are taught to represent concepts in spatially constructed diagrams to improve their memory of it.

The structures of these exhibit displays, showing the coevolution of butterflies and plants, are based on organic shapes and seemingly random arrangements to emphasize the diversity of nature generated by evolution.

Vivien Chow, Edmund Li, Fang-Pin Lee, Pauline Dolovich, Tony Reich, and Stephen Petri, Reich + Petch, Canada

Evolution Generates Diversity

How could the number and kinds of butterflies and moths change so dramatically?

Over time, as the world changed, some species disappeared. Others endured. And some gave rise to new species through the process of evolution. This process helped to generate the diversity we see today, including the appearance, 50 million years ago of specialized moths that fly by day.

We call them butterflies.

In this exhibit portraying biological evolution for the Smithsonian Institution, the evolutionary relationships of mammals are conveyed by their placement on the double-helix structure of the DNA molecule.

Vivien Chow, Edmund Li, Fang-Pin Lee, Pauline Dolovich, Tony Reich, and Stephen Petri, Reich + Petch, Canada

The layered visual structure of this exhibit signage mirrors the actual structure of the subsurface wetlands that it explains.

Claudine Jaenichen and Richard Turner, Jaenichen Studio, United States

Sub-surface Wetlands

What you can't see beneath the gravel in front of you is a thick mat of plant roots and thousands of tiny organisms swimming through the water located underground. The series below shows what it would look like if you dug a hole down to check it out.

Wetland in early growth stage, Chino, CA

Subsurface wetlands may not look very wet, but beneath their surface there exists a flurry of aquatic activity

Subsurface rocks helps sedimentation

Roots act as screening mechanism

Subsurface wetlands naturally occur when groundwater comes close enough to the surface that aquatic plants can grow their roots down and "tap" into the water supply below. Instead of forming from rainfall or flooding, subsurface wetlands are created by underground water channels.

EAU PROPRE = BONNE SANTÉ

Establishing structure usually involves more than just ordering elements in an aesthetic arrangement. It entails finding the conceptual basis of the graphic's meaning and expressing this through visual language. Visual structures are as varied as there are types of information. For example, the designers of an exhibit that explains mammal evolution and diversity used the structure of the DNA molecule as the organizing principle.

Some information is best organized by physical attributes, when the conceptual purpose is to help viewers discriminate between visual forms, as in field guides. When a set of varied forms are arranged in proximity to one another, the viewer can make comparisons and understand the similarities and differences between objects. It is one way that viewers can build knowledge through inference.

Structuring visual elements according to their organizing principle can have a profound effect on how someone perceives information. In his book *Information Anxiety 2*, Saul Wurman writes, "Each way of organizing permits a different understanding; each lends itself to different kinds of information; and each has certain reassuring limitations that will help make the choices of how the information is presented easier."

Graphic designers may find Wurman's approach to information architecture useful. Known by the acronym LATCH, his recommendation is to order information by location, alphabet, time, category, and hierarchy. Wurman states that this organizational system is the basis for almost all of the structured information we encounter, from telephone directories to entire libraries. Many of these organizational structures are so embedded in our cognitive strategies, we use them without much thought, as when we alphabetize a filing system.

The LATCH system is particularly helpful when considering how to organize large amounts of information. For example, a catalog of retail goods can be sorted by alphabetical order or category of item. A brochure of seasonal performances can be ordered by performance category, season of event, or a hierarchy ranging from the most popular to the least known. For designers, the essence of this approach is to translate the organizing principle into an effective visual form.

In this informational poster about the proper uses of water, the information is arranged in a droplet structure. This enables viewers to quickly get the gist of the visual, promoting a preunderstanding of the message.

Nathanaël Hamon, Slang, and Jaana Davidjants, Wiyumi, Germany

▲ When information is organized into logical categories, as in this paper catalog, it enhances the perception of the products.

Wing Chan, Wing Chan Design, *United States*

▶ This simple arrangement for a poster depicting the leaves of common trees in a St. Louis neighborhood offers a wealth of information by enabling viewers to compare and discriminate the shapes, structures, and textures of leaves.

Heather Corcoran, Plum Studios, *United States*

ough

showcase will

nnovation."

CHARGE IT UP

"The brain states and bodily responses are the fundamental facts of an emotion, and the conscious feelings are the frills that have added icing to the emotional cake."

JOSEPH LEDOUX, *The Emotional Brain*

What raises the voltage level of a graphic and gives it a charge? Why do visuals with that special spark grab attention and sustain interest? Some viewers find the compositional aesthetic compelling. Others may be moved by a poignant image or visual symbolism filled with personal meaning. Some are amused by humorous and entertaining pictures. One thing is certain—good design creates an emotional response.

The common assumption that art evokes emotion is reliably supported through brain research. When viewers look at both pleasant and unpleasant pictures, they consistently demonstrate an emotional reaction indicated by pronounced brain activity that does not occur when they look at neutral pictures. Even with repeated showings of the same affective picture—up to ninety repetitions in one study—viewers continued to elicit a marked emotional response.[1] Viewers also spend more time looking at affective pictures than neutral pictures.

Although by definition emotions are nonverbal, cognitive psychologists have no difficulty finding the words to describe the components of affect. They define emotion as a powerful, usually short-lived experience that is a reaction to a specific stimulus. Emotions result from a rapid appraisal of an object or event's significance in order to prepare us for action. They help us cope with changes in the environment. This is in contrast to feelings, which are the subjective and internal experiences of emotion. Another component of affect is mood, which refers to a longer-lasting, generalized experience that is milder than emotion.

Emotion also has a physical component. Everyone is familiar with the body states associated with emotion, such as the pounding heart, tightened muscles, and sweaty palms that accompany fear or the light-headed, energized sensations of romantic love. On a daily basis, we may not generate particularly powerful emotions, but they do affect us in many ways. For example, emotions often motivate us to pursue goals, like learning a new graphics program or finding a new job.

Viewers have a preference for imagery that evokes emotions. A sensual photograph, such as this one for an arts and culture brochure, will grab a viewer's attention.

GG Lemere, Campbell Fisher Design,
United States

1 OF 4 WEAPONS USED DAILY IN DARFUR

Emotive graphics inform at an immediate, visceral level. Whether they amuse, entertain, sadden, anger, or frighten, emotional graphics arouse an audience. Affective pictures capture attention before the audience processes the content of the message, circumventing many rational and cognitive processes. When this occurs, emotional graphics influence how a message is subsequently perceived and interpreted.

When a potential viewer is distracted, busy, or just plain cynical, aiming at the emotions is a designer's best chance for arousing interest. "Messages which adopt creative, unusual, complex, intense, explicit, unconventional, or fast-paced message strategies can help to overcome boredom and disinterest," writes information design professor Judy Gregory.[2] Grabbing attention gets viewers involved, stimulates interest, and motivates them to decode the rest of the message.

Another reason for emotional appeals is to promote attitude change. This is often the case in social issue promotions, public service announcements, and political campaigns. Some of these appeals use stirring imagery, such as innocent animals in the wild, as a way to trigger emotional responses and persuade

viewers to adopt a particular viewpoint or contribute to a cause. On the other end of the spectrum are the campaigns that evoke fear in order to persuade. In public health promotions, for example, messages based on the fear of harmful consequences from risky behaviors are often used to sway attitudes. In political campaigns, images that evoke fear are used to influence voter opinion. Empirical evidence shows that the experience of fear is effective at persuasion.[3]

Emotion-laden images are a well-known influence on decision making, from voting choices to laundry soap. Advertising specialists provide emotional messages in an effort to bypass cognitive analysis and shorten the decision-making cycle. They often concentrate on positive associations and symbolism to generate a pleasant feeling toward a product or an idea. In her essay "Thinking Positively," communications researcher Jennifer Monahan writes, "The appeal of positive affect for commercial advertisers is simple: Research consistently shows advertisements that arouse positive emotions result in more positive feelings toward the product and greater intent to comply with the message."

This poster is designed with bullet shells to raise awareness that rape is used as a weapon of war in Darfur.

Greg Bennett, Siquis,
United States

▶ Combining the imagery of sugar and slavery in a poster for the Museum of London Docklands creates an emotional reminder of this dark period in the United Kingdom's history.

Cog Design, United Kingdom

▼ Copy and image provide emotional impact for this Native American antismoking campaign.

Dale Sprague, *Canyon Creative*, United States

Emotion and the Information-Processing System

Emotion and cognition. Contrary to the widespread belief that emotion and cognition are opposites, they are now thought to be distinct but inseparable functions. The interplay of emotion and cognition contributes to how we think, feel, and act. Emotion is known to affect mental processes, such as attention, perception, and memory. For example, emotive images can lead to biased perceptions when a persuasive symbol is paired with a neutral object or person. A good example is when news programs consistently pair people of a particular race or religion with images of guns and violence. The negative feelings evoked from the images tend to transfer to individuals of that race or religion.

Emotions also affect how information is processed and encoded into long-term memory. A growing body of research indicates that unpleasant memories fade more quickly than pleasant ones. Furthermore, pleasant phenomena—whether words, images, or events—are processed more efficiently and accurately and recalled more quickly.[4]

Emotions have a powerful impact on our personal life and history. The narrative of our life's experiences is thought to be stored in episodic memory, which is autobiographical. Episodic memory automatically captures the time, place, events, and emotions of our personal story. When we view a picture, autobiographical memories are often triggered by images, symbolism, and compositional elements that convey emotional content. When this connection occurs, the emotional component of a visual message becomes personal and meaningful.

Emotion and attention. Graphics with meaningful emotional content capture attention and interest because they generate a state of arousal, which is a cognitive and biologically energized state. As a general rule, most people find monotony and boredom to be an unpleasant experience and stimulation and activation to be a pleasant experience. Many psychologists theorize that although individuals vary in their need for stimulation, most people want to maintain an optimal state of activation. They seek "newness, change, sensation, or inconsistency" in moderate amounts.[5] Emotional experiences help people achieve and maintain this optimal state of arousal. When a graphic generates a satisfactory level of stimulation, viewers will stay with a message and process it. When a message is considered boring, the viewer will look elsewhere for activation.

The emotional imagery of a dancing skeleton implores viewers to celebrate the Day of the Dead festival.

Lars Lawson, Timber Design Company, *United States*

DAY OF THE DEAD
A FREE CELEBRATION, SATURDAY OCTOBER 27
ALTARS & SHRINES • TRADITIONAL FOOD • DANCE • MUSIC • ART ACTIVITIES
LOVE LIFE
DIA DE LOS MUERTOS
LIFE IS FRAGIL
LOVE IT OR LEAVE IT
3:00~
8:00PM
INDIANAPOLIS ART CENTER
820 EAST 67TH STREET, BROAD RIPPLE

Applying the Principle

Affective visuals generate attention either through an emotional reflex that occurs beneath conscious awareness or through conscious selective attention. In either case, visual language triggers autobiographical memories, arouses curiosity and interest, and enhances the viewer's involvement. Some effective strategies for producing charged graphics are to convey emotional salience, provide a thematic narrative, make use of visual metaphors, and incorporate novelty and humor.

When a graphic has emotional salience, affective appeal is its prominent characteristic. It transmits emotional content in a compelling way. Designers can achieve this by composing with design elements and imagery that have significance for the audience. Graphics with emotional salience take viewers beyond a literal interpretation to one that connects with their feelings.

The visual narrative form also transmits emotion. Narratives are a cognitively and emotionally natural way for people to communicate. Telling a story or tying visuals to a coherent theme draws viewers to the message. Narratives allow designers to create an underlying emotional track that runs through the visual.

The visual metaphor is another effective vehicles for conveying emotion. Metaphors resonate with the non-verbal quality of emotions. Because they result from a synthesis of ideas, visual metaphors are often imaginative and captivating.

A pervasive strategy for evoking emotion is to startle an audience with an innovative and unexpected approach. Not only do viewers enjoy surprise, but novelty arouses curiosity, which sustains audience attention. This includes using humor to shock, entertain, or amuse, as is appropriate with the content of the message.

An important consideration of the emotionally charged graphic is its potential effect on an audience. Emotions are often multifaceted, so a viewer may respond with a mix of conflicting feelings. This can result in an unintended reaction. A good example comes from a study that examined persuasive public service messages to prevent the transmission of AIDS. The research found that when a message evoked fear, the viewer was likely to comply with it. When the message evoked anger along with fear, the persuasive effect of the message was lost.[6] Designers should carefully analyze whether their visual approach will obtain the reaction they desire. For many purposes, a simple emotional response might be the most effective.

▲ *Visual metaphors are a potent way to express emotion, as in this deluge of bits and bytes.*

Erin Cubert, *United States*

▶ *The symbolic image in this poster is effective for a conference on gender and violence in the indigenous communities of Ecuador.*

Antonio Mena,
Antonio Mena Design,
Ecuador

Mujeres Indígenas del Ecuador

ANTONIO MENA - 2007

Seminario género y violencia

3-4 de mayo de 2007 - FLACSO Ecuador - Pradera E7-174 - Quito - PBX: 3238888 (ext.2752) - flacso@flacso.org.ec

EMOTIONAL SALIENCE

The English language has an estimated 400 words to express emotional states, but with visuals the ways are infinite. For a graphic to communicate and evoke emotion, it must be charged with personal meaning and significance. It must appeal to both the eyes and the affect. This motivates a person to attend to and to process a visual message.

Just as salient features such as color and shape pop out from the visual field during preattentive processing, emotional salience stands out against a sea of neutral graphics. People seem to preattentively pick up visual emotional signals, possibly to avoid threatening situations. People also have a tendency to place increased attention on the source of the emotional signal. Emotionally arousing events narrow a person's cognitive focus to concentrate on the causal circumstance. Similarly, emotionally salient graphics almost compel a person to pay attention and engage with the picture.

Moreover, research shows that people prefer emotional pictures to neutral ones. One study that measured emotional responses to advertisements found that successful ads evoke a strong emotional response. "Clearly the level and quality of emotional response is a critical differentiator between the best and the worst advertisements in this sample," concluded the study's author.[7]

Designing for Emotion

Of all the basic design elements, color seems to have the most potential to evoke emotion. This is reflected in English language metaphors, which refer to a veritable rainbow of feelings, such as rose-colored glasses, feeling blue, green with envy, and red with anger. In addition to metaphorical usage, people tend to associate many aspects of color with emotions. These reactions may be influenced by personal experience, indi-

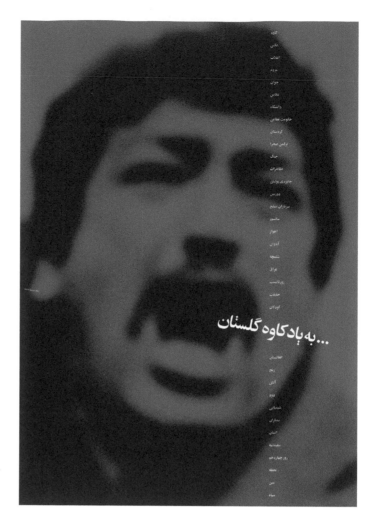

vidual taste, cultural context, and gender. Yet cognitive research has found rather consistent associations between a color and its emotional and physical effects. A group of studies substantiated that cool colors tend to have a sedating effect and warm colors invoke more energetic feelings. Generally, green and blue colors evoke feelings of calmness and decreased anxiety. In contrast, red was found to be exciting, stimulating, and highly emotive. In a continuum from red to yellow, participants associated positive and cheery emotions with the colors that were closer to yellow.[8]

Other aspects of color that can evoke an emotional response are saturation and value. For example, highly saturated colors are more intensely felt than soft, pale, and neutral colors. Lighter colors are associated with more positive feelings and darker colors with more negative feelings.[9] Some researchers claim that saturation and value have a greater effect on emotion than hue. Color combinations with variations of value and saturation are an effective way to communicate emotional content and to convey meaning.

▲ *Through color and pained imagery,* In Memoriam of Kaveh Golestan *expresses the grief felt by the death of the renowned photojournalist killed by a land mine in Iraq.*

Majid Abassi,
Did Graphics, *Iran*

▶ *In this promotional graphic for a poster exhibition, an intriguing, obscured photograph is an effective way to express emotion.*

Majid Abbasi,
Did Graphics, *Iran*

اعلان‌های یک نمایشگاه؛ مجموعه‌ی طراحی پوسترهای مجید عباسی

sters at an Exhibition; A Poster Exhibition by Majid Abbasi

نگارخانه‌ی ویـــژه؛ بیست و نهم آذر تا ششم دی یکهزار و سیصد و هشتاد و شش

Vije Gallery; December 20-27, 2007.

تهران ۱۵۳۳۸۶۴۸۶۱ خیابان خرمشهر، خیابان شهید عربعلی (نوبخت)، کوچه‌ی سوم، شماره‌ی ۱۹   تلفن: ۵ ـ ۸۸۷۳۳۶۷۴

9 Third St. of Nowbakht, Khoramshahr Ave., Tehran 1533864861-Iran

Compositional effects are also powerful ways to express and evoke emotion. To generate a disquieting and disturbing experience, designers can take advantage of the audience's need to resolve tension. Tension can be generated through ambiguity—using shapes and forms that are indistinct, obstructed, and difficult to recognize and identify. Tension may also result from exaggeration, when forms, colors, and textures are obviously overstated. In addition, distortion can arouse emotion because viewers expect objects and people to have a natural or conventional shape. Any effect that prevents cognitive closure can potentially create an unsettling experience.

Powerful imagery increases emotional salience, particularly photographs and drawings of the face. Our brains are especially attuned to appraising facial expressions and following eye gaze. The rapid and efficient detection of facial emotion appears to be another biological mechanism on which designers can rely to increase a message's impact. Incorporating facial gestures that express emotional intensity will capture attention and make a graphic memorable.

Symbolism plays a critical role in visual communication and provides an eloquent way to communicate emotional content to represent abstract and often profound ideas. The diversity of objects and signs that work as visual symbols is enormous, providing designers with a large vocabulary to shape meaning. Through experience, people learn to associate the symbols of their culture with societal values and themes. In this process, many symbols acquire emotional meaning. Religion, nationalism, societal status, oppression, and justice are some of the diverse concepts that can be communicated with symbols.

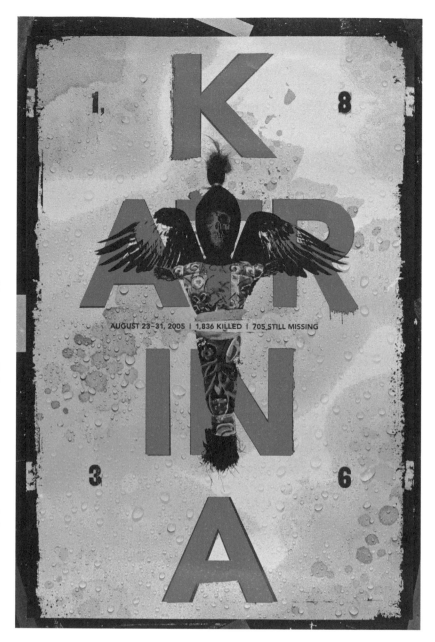

Symbolism associated with New Orleans and the devastation from Hurricane Katrina creates a stirring poster used in a fund-raising effort for victims.

Greg Bennett, Siquis,
United States

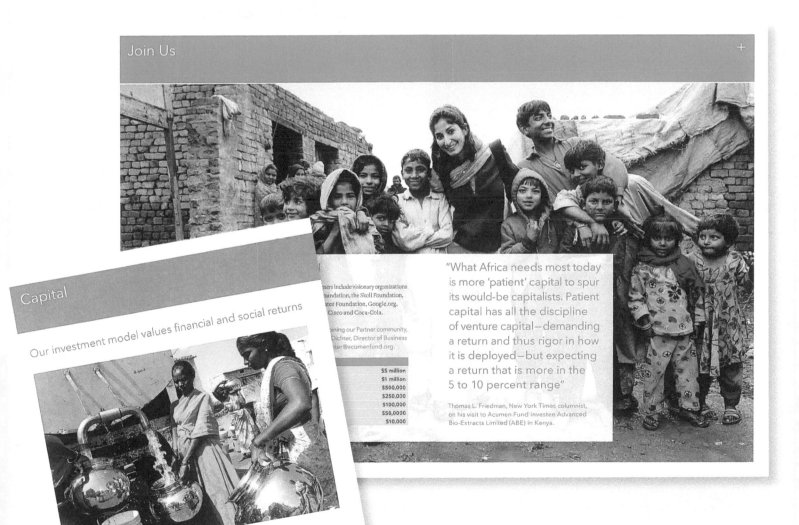

I'M IN CHARGE
of myself and my future. I use condoms.

PLANNED PARENTHOOD
1-800-800-PLAN www.ppnyc.org | **Planning** *is* **Power.**

WE'LL BE PARENTS SOMEDAY
For now we're using condoms.

PLANNED PARENTHOOD
1-800-800-PLAN www.ppnyc.org | **Planning** *is* **Power.**

Join Us

Capital

Our investment model values financial and social returns

"What Africa needs most today is more 'patient' capital to spur its would-be capitalists. Patient capital has all the discipline of venture capital—demanding a return and thus rigor in how it is deployed—but expecting a return that is more in the 5 to 10 percent range"

Thomas L. Friedman, New York Times columnist, on his visit to Acumen Fund investee Advanced Bio-Extracts Limited (ABE) in Kenya.

ners include visionary organizations
oundation, the Skoll Foundation,
tes Foundation, Google.org,
Cisco and Coca-Cola.

ining our Partner community,
Dichter, Director of Business
ter@acumenfund.org.

	$5 million
	$1 million
	$500,000
	$250,000
	$100,000
	$50,0000
	$10,000

The Model
While our model looks a lot like venture capital, our investment criteria are different. We invest in enterprises that can generate a return on our capital, grow by a factor of 10 over the life of our investment, and provide breakthrough insights in the fields of health, water, housing, and energy. ...business models reach consumers in new ways with ...low income people. We invest where there ...and where there

Our mainstay is philanthropic capital – patient capital that provides the flexibility to invest in very difficult environments. We typically invest in companies with a 2-3 year operating history, an established business model, ...enue stream. We give

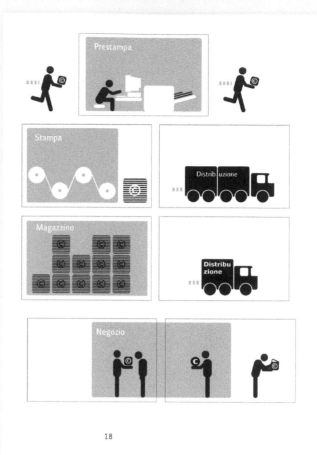

18

NARRATIVES

People are powerfully drawn to stories and use them to naturally organize their own and others' experiences. Through this familiarity and comfort with the structure and emotion of the narrative, people often have a vicarious experience while reading or watching a story. Because of this cognitive and emotional readiness, visual narratives are an excellent way to generate an emotional resonance with the audience.

In books, film, theater, and television, we may find stories with a clever plot to be interesting, but it is their emotional impact that is most attractive. It is not uncommon to continue to watch a show or film with a thin plot and poor acting only to realize it is the magnetism of the emotional drama that sustains our interest. A significant feature of the narrative is that it has the power to captivate an audience regardless of whether it is based on experience or is completely fictional. It is the dramatic and emotional aspect of people's lives—their desires and achievements, their disappointments and sufferings—that is common to a narrative, whether it is fact or fantasy.

The emotional response to narratives has been substantiated in brain research. In a study where subjects listened to a script and were told to imagine their involvement in the scenes, the narratives triggered areas of the brain that emotionally prepared the participants to take physical action.[10] In other words, the brain reacted as though the story was occurring in the physical environment.

Graphic designers can use this natural human affinity for stories in imaginative ways. The crucial point is to create an absorbing visual narrative—a sequence of events and actions tied together with emotional and conceptual continuity. Visual narratives often follow a formal structure with an obvious beginning, middle, and end. Photographic documentaries, animated stories, graphic novels, and comic book formats achieve this because a sequence of images is understood to describe a succession of events. When pictures are placed in a temporal order, viewers will mentally fill in any gaps, such as actions needed to maintain continuity.[11]

In addition to this more structured approach, implicit narratives are also compelling. For example, promotional materials, annual reports, and brochures often embody a narrative that is implied on every page. For some, the narrative might follow the development and history of an organization. Others implicitly suggest a coherent emotional theme through image and type.

▲ A wordless narrative is used here to explain the traditional publishing process. Implementing this as a story adds to its interest.

Lorenzo De Tomasi, Italy

▶ A dramatic story line is illustrated to demonstrate the use of a new device that relays information on the status and location of wounded soldiers.

**Colin Hayes,
Colin Hayes Illustrator,**
United States

Narratives can emerge from timelines. Here, the history of MIT's Urban Studies and Planning Department is described through images and words.

Erica Gregg Howe, Philographica, *United States*

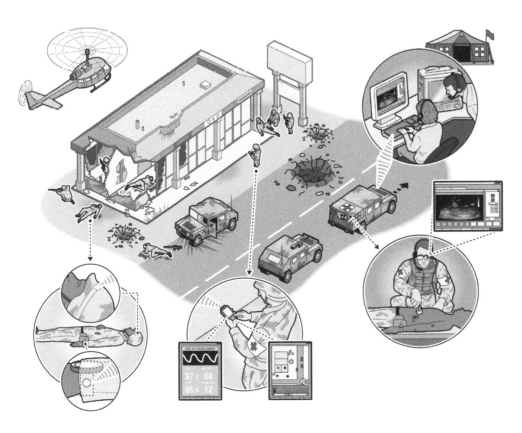

Used as an employee-training tool, these illustrations employ a story-based approach to explain the causes of resistance to coaching and change.

Dixie Albertson and Jeri Bowers, Darning Pixels, United States

▲ The story of movie piracy, from recording to distribution, is effectively described in narrative form for Sound & Vision *magazine.*

Colin Hayes,
Colin Hayes Illustrator,
United States

▼ In this viewbook for a school of engineering, "Listen to our story" presents the advantages of the school in a narrative by its graduates. The narrative is completed through photographs of animated and engaged faculty.

Christine Kenney, IE Design
+ Communications,
United States

Part of this report about careers in the petroleum industry uses an appealing narrative in comic book format to add interest.

Marc Bostian and Cameron Eagle, S Design,
United States

The visual narrative in this college prospectus focuses on a nostalgic photographic journey leading to the present.

David Horton and Ian Koenig, Philographica, United States

We treasure the classic liberal arts tradition

What we do at Kenyon emanates from integrity and a sense of self. We know who we are and what we believe.

We are Kenyon.

"When I wrote my name in the Matriculation Book, I felt connected not only with generations of Kenyon students, but with an unbroken chain of learning that leads back to antiquity. Even as a first-year student, I knew this was serious business."
KATHRYN VANARENDONK, *Class of 2007*

aspirations, and [...] in some ways like us and in other ways [...] And we are always obliged to do so with evidence that is suggestive, fragmentary, and difficult to interpret."
JEFFREY BOWMAN, *McCoy-Bene One Distinguished Teaching Professor and Associate Professor of History*

only thing that can finally save the world is education. ere is nothing we could invest in that will yield more.

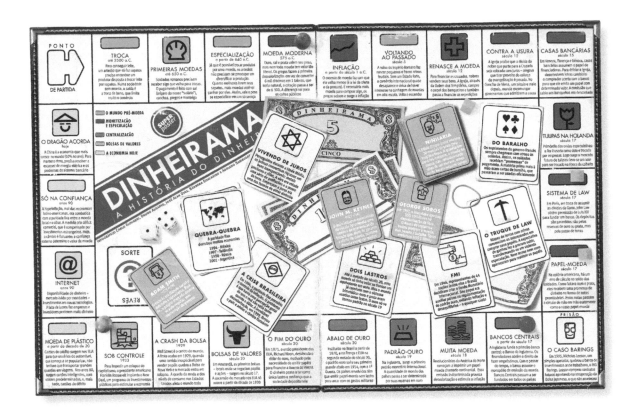

VISUAL METAPHORS

Our cognitive system often relies on metaphors and analogies to think and imagine. It is how we understand things for which we have no specific knowledge. We use metaphors to transfer the properties of one object to another or to conceptualize an idea in terms of another. For example, in her book *Design for Communication*, Elisabeth Resnick describes the metaphor she uses to teach typography. "I describe typography as two-dimensional architecture upon which a foundation of visual communication can be built. Letterforms become the building blocks that create the structure to convey an idea or deliver a message."

We often use metaphors to describe phenomena that are difficult to verbalize, such as emotions. When emotions seem ambiguous and ethereal, metaphors help make them explicit and tangible. Pictorial metaphors can be vivid and imaginative when they compare or combine two previously unconnected objects or ideas. Designers often use emotionally charged imagery in metaphors to create impact. One effective way to bring a metaphor to life is to combine the qualities of two images. An example is a public health advertisement that combines a cooking mushroom with a nuclear mushroom cloud to communicate the potential dangers of food-borne illness.

Another approach is to juxtapose two images in the same graphic, implying that they should be compared; the properties of one image are intended to transfer to the second. Juxtaposing an image of a sleek computer with a racing panther, for example, implies that the computer has fast processing power. Visual metaphors can also stand on their own, as in this information graphic about the history of money explained on a Monopoly board.

When a visual metaphor succeeds, it synthesizes two objects or concepts to reveal a new connection or a deeper meaning. But to understand a metaphor requires knowledge of its cultural context and the ability to make the correct inferences. The viewer must be able to interpret a metaphor's figurative rather than literal meaning. Thus, the metaphor should accommodate the viewer's abilities, using recognizable objects and familiar concepts.

▲ *The history of money is explained in this information graphic for* Superinteressante *magazine that uses a Monopoly board as a metaphor.*

Adriano Sambugaro, Carlo Giovani Studio, *Brazil*

▶ *The clever visual metaphor and clear copy send a straightforward message in this health sanitation campaign.*

Tonatiuh Arturo Gómez, AW Nazca Saatchi & Saatchi, *Venezuela*

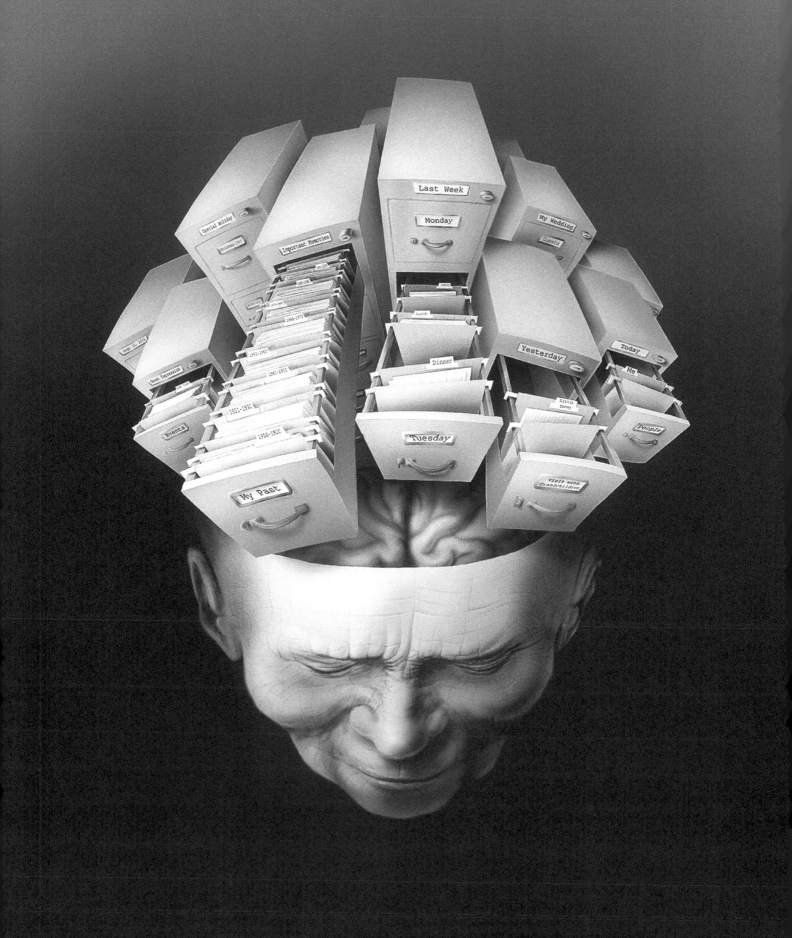

In this future, physicians arrest disease long before it can be seen.

▲ Metaphors can generate an emotional response if they speak to the imagination. This illustration expresses a future promise to arrest disease in an informational brochure about a children's hospital.

Erica Gregg Howe and Amy Lebow, Philographica, United States

◀ This editorial piece on memory loss demonstrates how metaphors emotionally connect with the audience.

Travis Vermilye, Travis Vermilye Medical and Biological Illustration, United States

◀ This metaphor used for the cover graphic of a United Nations report on water and human development aptly demonstrates the coming challenges of the global water crisis.

Peter Grundy and Tilly Northedge, United Kingdom

Human Development Report **2006**

Water and human development
The 21st century challenge

NOVELTY AND HUMOR

In the midst of ubiquitous visual communications, novelty can be riveting. A graphic with an unusual twist invokes an emotional reaction—surprise, astonishment, or possibly, shock. Unusual graphics reliably grab attention and arouse curiosity because they cross into unfamiliar territory, a place that challenges one's visual memory. Novelty tends to be amusing, but it can also tackle serious topics as well. It simply must defy convention and create visual surprise.

Research has found that any novel object triggers an orienting response. Distinctive objects, which are unfamiliar or out of context, create an emotional reaction that triggers attention and heightened interest. Perhaps we think that anything unusual could potentially be threatening, or this reaction may be a natural result of human curiosity. The intensity of the emotional reaction and the significance of the object contribute to the degree of interest that is aroused.

Novelty sustains attention because it doesn't match the associated schemas activated in long-term memory. When there are inconsistencies, such as when something is unexpected or unusual, additional visual attention and processing is required to comprehend the discrepancy.[12] This means that a person spends more time examining a novel graphic to resolve its inconsistencies.

Novelty arises from unusual juxtapositions or from seeing objects in unconventional perspectives. It results when unexpected themes are brought together and when type and image seem to oppose each other. The extent to which a graphic uses novelty affects the audience's emotional reaction. Moderate incongruities seem to generate the most favorable reactions among viewers. Extreme incongruities create confusion.

Humor is another form of novelty that, when properly implemented, evokes amusement and enjoyment. Messages with humor are often considered more interesting than serious messages. Unexpected events and entertaining graphics can generate a positive effect. Humor is usually related to deviating from normal expectations, from incongruity that can be resolved, and from contrasts between the everyday and the unanticipated. People also find humor in surprise and inconsistency. Simply processing and resolving discrepant information can result in humor. As with all forms of novelty, humorous strategies must be implemented with taste. Most people do not find it appropriate to see a light-hearted treatment of a very serious topic. This strategy can reduce the effectiveness of a message.

▲ *Retro graphics and humorous copy appeal to young mobile travelers in this flyer advertising accommodations for backpackers visiting New Zealand.*

Alexander Lloyd, Lloyds Graphic Design,
New Zealand

▶ *Novelty provides a dose of surprise and arises from unexpected and unusual juxtapositions, as in this one-of-a-kind horse.*

George Ladas, Base24 Design Systems, United States

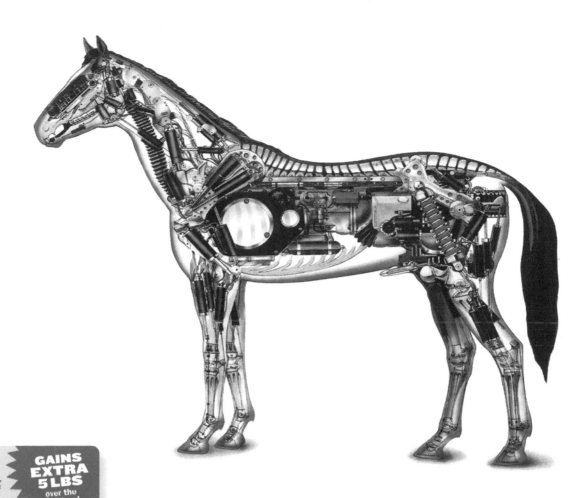

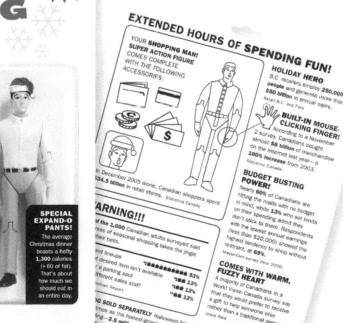

SECRET SCROOGE PERSONALITY!
84% of working Canadians planned to buy Christmas presents, compared to 91% in USA, 90% in France, 89% in Australia and 88% in the UK. 2005 AXA Study

GAINS EXTRA 5 LBS over the holidays!

SUPER ACTION FIGURE
SHOPPING MAN!

CRAZY KUNG-FU SHOPPING ACTION!!

Men are true last-minute shoppers: 21% claimed to start their holiday shopping in the 3rd week of December or later, compared to just 7% of women. MasterCard survey (Nov 2006)

MAGICAL DISAPPEARING CASH!
Canadians spent **$804** each in December 2004, well above the monthly average of **$555** for the rest of the year. Consumers in B.C. were the 4th biggest spenders with an average of **$846**. Statistics Canada

NOW WITH BONUS COP-OUT GIFT!
A recent survey of 11,000 stores in January 2005 showed 68% of retailers now offer gift cards, compared with 53% the year before. Statistics Canada

Every month award-winning advertising and design firm, Rethink, develops the information design to illustrate our featured topic. Vancouver Sun librarian, Kate Bird, compiles all the statistics and information.

PHOTO BY ALASTAIR BIRD PHOTOGRAPHY

SPECIAL EXPAND-O PANTS!
The average Christmas dinner boasts a hefty **1,300** calories (+ 60 of fat). That's about how much we should eat in an entire day.

EXTENDED HOURS OF SPENDING FUN!

YOUR **SHOPPING MAN! SUPER ACTION FIGURE** COMES COMPLETE WITH THE FOLLOWING ACCESSORIES:

HOLIDAY HERO
B.C. retailers employ **250,000** **people** and generate more than **$50 billion** in annual sales. Retail B.C. and 7-eta

BUILT-IN MOUSE-CLICKING FINGER!
According to a November 2 survey, Canadians bought almost **$8 billion** of merchandise on the Internet last year—a **160% increase** from 2003. Statistics Canada

BUDGET BUSTING POWER!
Nearly **60%** of Canadians are hitting the malls with no budget in mind, while **13%** who set limits on their spending admit they don't stick to them. Respondents with the lowest annual earnings (less than $20,000) showed the highest tendency to shop without restraint, at **69%**. MasterCard survey (Nov 2006)

COMES WITH WARM, FUZZY HEART
A majority of Canadians in a World Vision Canada survey say that they would prefer to receive a gift to help someone else rather than a traditional present. Ipsos Reid

In December 2005 alone, Canadian shoppers spent **$34.5 billion** in retail stores. Statistics Canada

[W]ARNING!!!
...of the **1,000** Canadian adults surveyed said ...ress of seasonal shopping takes the jingle ...their bells.

...nd lineups
...r desired item isn't available ▮▮▮▮▮▮▮▮▮▮ 53%
...a parking spot ▮▮▮ 13%
...different sales staff ▮▮▮ 12%
...ndown Report

[DO]G SOLD SEPARATELY ...tmas as the fastest growing holiday for pet ...ing—**2.5 million** more involve their pets than ...s ago. American Pet Products Manufacturers Association

[FA]MILY BONDING NOT GUARANTEED! **70%** of young adults (ages 18-22) and **56%** of parents surveyed say they've made or answered wireless calls during a holiday gathering, and 35% of young adults say they've read or sent an e-mail or text message under the dinner table during a holiday family gathering. T-Mobile survey

HAPPY HOLIDAYS

◀ *The shopping man doll exemplifies how novelty and humor capture attention and interest.*

Nancy Wu, Kim Rigewell, Lisa Nakamura, and Jeff Harrison, Rethink Communications, Canada

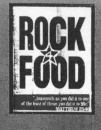

LOGOS
CD PKGS
CORP ID
ANNUAL
REPORTS
POSTERS
CATALOGS
PACKAGING
CALENDARS
WEARABLES
BROCHURES
PRESS KITS
BILLBOARDS
INVITATIONS
ADVERTISING
GREETING AND
HOLIDAY CARDS
HAND LETTERING
AND ILLUSTRATION

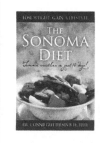

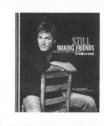

STICK Fly

a play by
Lydia R. Diamond

"...someone fell in love with someone they weren't supposed to..."

Funny and deeply passionate, Chicago writer Lydia R. Diamond's play is a probing family drama and an up-to-the-minute consideration of privilege and perception. When an elite African American family reunites on Martha's Vineyard, incendiary dialogues ignite about race and class, the desire to break free and the need to belong.

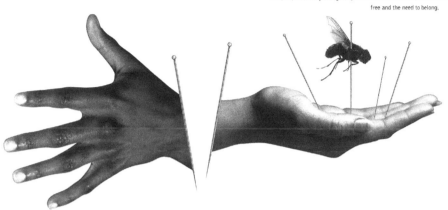

◀ Viewers will spend time reconciling the unusual juxtaposition of objects in this image for a theatrical brochure.

Francheska Guerrero,
Unfolding Terrain,
United States

▼ An unexpected end view of two pigs provides humor for the play *Pig Farm* in a theater festival brochure.

Francheska Guerrero,
Unfolding Terrain,
United States

◀ This amusing idea for a self-promotional poster consists of designs on perforated cards that break apart and fit into a small juice box, which just happens to reflect this company's name.

Jay Smith, Juicebox Designs, *United States*

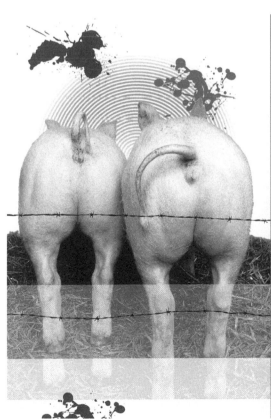

PIG FARM

a play by GREG KOTIS

"You may hate the federal government, Tina. But the federal government loves you. At least, it could. If you'd let it."

From Greg Kotis, Tony-winning writer of the hit musical satire "Urinetown," comes a cliché-skewering comedy about pig farming where men are men, women are women, and pigs are everywhere. The feds want the snouts accurately counted; Tom yearns to farm freely, and his wife just wants a baby. Their love is big as all outdoors — and so is their pig farm.

BIBLIOGRAPHY

Arnheim, Rudolf. Art and Visual Perception (Berkeley: University of California Press, 1974).

Bateson, Gregory. Steps to an Ecology of Mind: Collected Essays in Anthropology, Psychiatry, Evolution, and Epistemology (Chicago: University of Chicago Press, 2000).

Card, Stuart, Jock Mackinlay, and Ben Shneiderman. Readings in Information Visualization: Using Vision to Think (San Francisco: Morgan Kaufman, 1999).

Deregowski, Jan B. Distortion in Art (London: Routledge & Kegan Paul, 1984).

Evans, David, and Cindy Gadd. "Managing Coherence and Context in Medical Problem-Solving Discourse," in Cognitive Science in Medicine, ed. David Evans and Vimla Patel (Cambridge: MIT Press, 1989).

Evelyn Goldsmith, Research into Illustration: An Approach and a Review (Cambridge: Cambridge University Press, 1984).

Holmes, Nigel. Designing Pictorial Symbols (New York: Watson Guptill, 1985).

Kosslyn, Stephen. Clear and to the Point (Oxford: Oxford University Press, 2007).

Kress, Gunther, and Theo van Leeuwen. Reading Images: The Grammar of Visual Design. (London: Routledge, 1996).

Massironi, Manfredo. The Psychology of Graphic Images (Mahwah, NJ: Lawrence Erlbaum, 2001), 70.

Mayer, Richard E., ed., The Cambridge Handbook of Multimedia Learning (New York: Cambridge University Press, 2005).

Monahan, Jennifer. "Thinking Positively," in Designing Health Messages, ed. E. Maibach and R. Parrott (Thousand Oaks, CA: Sage, 1995), 81–98.

Norman, Donald A. Things That Make Us Smart: Defending Human Attributes in the Age of the Machine (London: Perseus Books, 1993), 41.

Paratore, Phillip Carlo. Art and Design (Upper Saddle River, NJ: Prentice Hall, 1985).

Resnick, Elizabeth. Design for Communication: Conceptual Graphic Design Basics (Hoboken, NJ: Wiley, 2003).

Wainer, Howard. "Understanding Graphs and Tables," Educational Researcher 21 (1992).

Ware, Colin. Information Visualization: Perception for Design (San Francisco: Morgan Kaufmann, 2004).

Wurman, Saul. Information Anxiety 2 (Indianapolis: Que, 2001).

Zelanski, Paul, and Mary Pat Fisher. Design Principles and Problems (Fort Worth, Texas: Harcourt Brace College Publishers, 1996).

Bottom-up visual processing: visual awareness that is driven by an external stimulus

Cognitive load: the total amount of mental demand imposed on working memory at a given moment

Cognitive science: the multidisciplinary study of mind and intelligence

Dual coding: the theory that states verbal and visual information are processed through separate channels

Fovea: the region of the retina that gives us sharpness of vision

Long-term memory: a component of memory that provides relatively permanent storage

Mental model: broad conceptualization or representation about how things work in the real world

Schemas: the theoretical underlying structures of memory

Sensory memory: the immediate brief recording of information brought in by the senses that persists after the original stimulus has ceased

Top-down visual processing: visual awareness that is influenced by memories, expectations, and intentions

Working memory: the temporary storage of information while mental work is performed (sometimes known as short-term memory)

SOURCES CITED

INTRODUCTION

1. Michael S. Beauchamp, e-mail message to author, March 19, 2008.

2. Lionel Standing, Jerry Conzeio, and Ralph Norman Haber, "Perception and Memory for Pictures: Single-Trial Learning of 2500 Visual Stimuli," Psychonomic Science 19 (1970): 73–74.

3. Kepes, Gyorgy. Language of Vision (Mineola, NY: Dover, 1995).

4. Dino Karabeg, "Designing Information Design," Information Design Journal 11 (2003): 82–90.

SECTION 1: GETTING GRAPHICS

1. Elizabeth Boling, et al., "Instructional Illustrations: Intended Meanings and Learner Interpretations," Journal of Visual Literacy 24 (2004): 189.

2. Joydeep Bhattacharya and Hellmuth Petsche, "Shadows of Artistry: Cortical Synchrony during Perception and Imagery of Visual Art," Cognitive Brain Research 13 (2002): 170–186.

3. C. F. Noide, P. J. Locher, and E. A. Krupinski, "The Role of Format Art Training on Perception and Aesthetic Judgment of Art Compositions," Leonardo 26 (1993): 219–227.

4. Jorge Frascara, "Graphic Design: Fine Art or Social Science?" in Design Studies: Theory and Research in Graphic Design, ed. Audrey Bennett and Steven Heller (Princeton: Princeton Architectural Press, 2006), 28.

5. Robert Solso, Cognition and the Visual Arts (Cambridge: MIT Press, 1994).

6. Martin Graziano and Mariano Sigman, "The Dynamics of Sensory Buffer: Geometric, Spatial and Experience-Dependent Shaping of Iconic Memory," Journal of Vision 8 (2008): 1–13.

7. Nelson Cowan, "The Magical Number 4 in Short-Term Memory: A Reconsideration of Mental Storage Capacity," Behavioral and Brain Sciences 24 (2000): 87–185.

8. Akira Miyake and Priti Shah, "Models of Working Memory: An Introduction." in Models of Working Memory: Mechanisms of Active Maintenance and Executive Control, ed. Akira Miyake and Priti Shah (Cambridge: Cambridge University Press, 1999), 1–27.

9. Lynn Hasher, Cindy Lustig, and Rose Zacks, "Inhibitory Mechanisms and the Control of Attention," in Variation in Working Memory, ed. Andrew R. A. Conway et al. (New York: Oxford University Press, 2007), 227–249.

10. Milton J. Dehn, Working Memory and Academic Learning: Assessment and Intervention (Hoboken, NJ: Wiley, 2008).

11. John Sweller, "Visualisation and Instructional Design," International Workshop on Dynamic Visualizations and Learning, 2002, www.iwm-kmrc.de/workshops/visualization.

12. Robert A. Bjork and Elizabeth Ligon Bjork, "A New Theory of Disuse and an Old Theory of Stimulus Fluctuation," in From Learning Processes to Cognitive Processes: Essays in Honor of William K. Estes, Volume 2, ed. Alice F. Healy (Mahwah, NJ: Lawrence Erlbaum, 1992), 36.

13. Ibid.

14. Jim Sweller, "Implications of Cognitive Load Theory for Multimedia Learning," in The Cambridge Handbook of Multimedia Learning, ed. Richard E. Mayer (New York: Cambridge University Press, 2005), 19–30.

15. William Winn, "Cognitive Perspectives in Psychology," in Handbook of Research on Educational Communications and Technology, ed. David H. Jonassen and Phillip Harris (Mahwah, NJ: Lawrence Erlbaum, 2003).

16. Joan Peeck, "Increasing Picture Effects in Learning from Illustrated Text," Learning and Instruction 3 (1993): 227–238.

PRINCIPLE 1: ORGANIZE FOR PERCEPTION

1. Anne Treisman, "Preattentive Processing in Vision," Computer Vision, Graphics, and Image Processing 31 (1985): 156.

2. Anne Treisman and Stephen Gormican, "Feature Analysis in Early Vision: Evidence from Search Asymmetries," Psychological Review 95 (1988).

3. Colin Ware, Information Visualization: Perception for Design (San Francisco: Morgan-Kauffman, 2004).

4. William Winn, "Contributions of Perceptual and Cognitive Processes to the Comprehension of Graphics" in Comprehension of Graphics, ed. Wolfgang Schnotz and Raymond W. Kulhavy (Amsterdam: North Holland, 1994), 12.

5. Jeremy M. Wolfe and Todd S. Horowitz, "What Attributes Guide the Deployment of Visual Attention and How Do They Do It?" Nature Reviews Neuroscience 5 (2004): 1–7.

6. Anne Treisman, "Preattentive Processing in Vision," Computer Vision, Graphics, and Image Processing 31 (1985): 156–177.

7. James J. Gibson, The Ecological Approach to Visual Perception (Mahwah, NJ: Lawrence Erlbaum, 1986), 116.

8. Timothy P. McNamara, "Mental Representations of Spatial Relations," Cognitive Psychology 18 (1986): 87–121.

9. Stephen Palmer and Irvin Rock, "Rethinking Perceptual Organization: The Role of Uniform Connectedness," Psychonomic Bulletin & Review 1 (1994): 29–55.

PRINCIPLE 2: DIRECT THE EYES

1. J. P. Hansen and M. Støvring, "Udfordringer er Blikfang," Hrymfaxe 3 (1988): 28–31 in ed. Arne John Glenstrup and Theo Engell-Nielsen, Eye Controlled Media: Present and Future State, University of Copenhagen Institute of Computer Science, 1995, www.diku.dk/~panic/eyegaze/node17.html.

2. Eric Jamet, Monica Gavota, and Christophe Quaireau, "Attention Guiding in Multimedia Learning," Learning and Instruction 18 (2008): 135–145.

3. Jason Tipples, "Eye Gaze Is Not Unique: Automatic Orienting in Response to Uninformative Arrows," Psy-chonomic Bulletin & Review 9 (2002): 314–318.

4. Michael J. Posner, "Orienting of Attention," Quarterly Journal of Experimental Psychology 32 (1980): 3–25.

5. Jan Theeuwes, "Irrelevant Singletons Capture Attention," in Neurobiology of Attention, ed. Laurent Itti, Geraint Rees, and John K. Tsotsos (Burlington, MA: Elsevier Academic Press, 2005), 418–427.

6. Eric Jamet, Monica Gavota, and Christophe Quaireau, "Attention Guiding in Multimedia Learning," Learning and Instruction 18 (2008): 135–145.

7. Walter Niekamp, "An Exploratory Investigation into Factors Affecting Visual Balance," Educational Communications and Technology 29 (1981): 37–48.

8. Ibid.

9. Evelyn Goldsmith, Research into Illustration: An Approach and a Review (Cambridge: Cambridge University Press, 1984).

10. Rudolf Arnheim, Art and Visual Perception (Berkeley: University of California Press, 1974).

11. Jeannette A. M. Lortejie et al., "Delayed Response to Animate Implied Motion in Human Motion Processing Areas," Journal of Cognitive Neuroscience 18 (2006): 158–168.

12. Andrea R. Halpern and Michael H. Kelly, "Memory Biases in Left Versus Right Implied Motion," Journal of Experimental Psychology: Learning, Memory, and Cognition 19 (1993): 471–484.

13. Noam Sagive and Shlomo Bentin, "Structural Encoding of Human and Schematic Faces: Holistic and Part-Based Processes," Journal of Cognitive Neuroscience 13 (2001): 937–951.

14. Shlomo Bentin et al., "Electrophysiological Studies of Face Perception in Humans," Journal of Cognitive Neuroscience 8 (1996): 551–565.

15. Jason Tipples, "Eye Gaze Is Not Unique: Automatic Orienting in Response to Uninformative Arrows," Psychonomic Bulletin & Review 9 (2002): 314–318.

16. Stephen Langton and Vicki Bruce, "You Must See the Point: Automatic Processing of Cues to the Direction of Social Attention," Journal of Experimental Psychology: Human Perception and Performance 26 (2000): 755.

17. Bruce Hood, Douglas Willen, and John Driver, "Adult's Eyes Trigger Shifts of Visual Attention in Human Infants," Psychological Science 9 (1998): 131–134.

18. Patricia D. Mautone and Richard E. Mayer, "Signaling as a Cognitive Guide in Multimedia Learning," Journal of Educational Psychology 93 (2001): 377–389.

19. David E. Irwin, "Fixation Location and Fixation Duration as Indices of Cognitive Processing" in The Interface of Language, Vision, and Action ed. John M. Henderson and Fernanda Ferreira (New York: Psychology Press, 2004), 105–134.

20. Richard J. Lamberski and Francis M. Dwyer, "The Instructional Effect of Coding (Color and Black and White) on Information Acquisition and Retrieval," Educational Communications and Technology Journal 31 (1993): 9–21.

PRINCIPLE 3: REDUCE REALISM

1. Christopher Chabris and Stephen Kosslyn, "Representational Correspondence as a Basic Principle of Diagram Design" in Knowledge and Information Visualization, Searching for Synergies, ed. Sigmar-Olaf Tergan and Tanja Keller (New York: Springer, 2005), 36–57.

2. Joe Savrock, "Visual Aids in Instruction and Their Relationship to Student Achievement" (E-Bridges, Penn State College of Education News), www.ed.psu.edu/.

3. Gary Anglin, Hossein Vaez, and Kathryn Cunningham, "Visual Representations and Learning: the Role of Static and Animated Graphics," in Handbook of Research for Educational Communications and Technology, ed. David H. Jonassen (Mahwah, NJ: Lawrence Erlbaum, 2004).

4. Paul Rademacher et al. "Measuring the Perception of Visual Realism in Images," 2001, http://research.microsoft.com/.

5. Gavriel Solomon, Interaction of Media, Cognition and Learning (Mahwah, NJ: Lawrence Erlbaum, 1994).

6. Peter Longhurst, Patrick Ledda, and Alan Calmers. "Psychophysically Based Artistic Techniques for Increased Perceived Realism of Virtual Environments," in Proceedings of the 2nd International Conference on Computer Graphics, Virtual Reality, Visualisation and Interaction in Africa, February 2003, http://portal.acm.org/.

7. Yvonne Rogers, "Icons at the Interface: Their Usefulness," Interacting with Computers 1 (1989): 105–117.

8. See Note 3: 867.

9. Stephen Doheny-Farina, Effective Documentation: What We Have Learned from Research, (Cambridge: MIT Press, 1988).

10. Janette Atkinson, Fergus Campbell, and Marcus Francis, "The Magic Number 4 ± 0: A New Look at Visual Numerosity Judgments," Perception 5 (1976): 327–334.

PRINCIPLE 4: MAKE THE ABSTRACT CONCRETE

1. Jacques Bertin, Semiology of Graphics (Madison: University of Wisconsin Press, 1984).

2. Barbara Tversky, "Some Ways that Graphics Communicate," in Working with Words and Images, ed. Nancy Allen (New York: Ablex Publishing, 2002).

3. William Winn, "How Readers Search for Information in Diagrams," Contemporary Educational Psychology 18 (1993): 162–185

4. Julie Heiser and Barbara Tversky, "Arrows in Comprehending and Producing Mechanical Diagrams," Cognitive Science 30 (2006): 581–592.

5. William Winn, "Cognitive Perspectives in Psychology," in Handbook of Research on Educational Communications and Technology, ed. David H. Jonassen and Phillip Harris (Mahwah, NJ: Lawrence Erlbaum, 2003).

6. William Winn, "How Readers Search for Information in Diagrams," Contemporary Educational Psychology 18 (1993): 162–185.

7. William S. Cleveland and Robert McGill, "Graphical Perception: The Visual Decoding of Quantitative Information on Graphical Displays of Data," Journal of the Royal Statistical Society 150 (1987): 192–199.

8. John W. Tukey, "Data-Based Graphics: Visual Display in the Decades to Come," Statistical Science 5 (1990): 327–339.

9. Stephen M. Kosslyn, "Understanding Charts and Graphs," Applied Cognitive Psychology 3 (1989): 185–226.

10. Stephen M. Kosslyn, Elements of Graph Design (New York: W. H. Freeman and Company, 1994).

11. Jeff Zacks and Barbara Tversky, "Bars and Lines: A Study of Graphic Communication," Memory and Cognition 27 (1999): 1073–1079.

12. Priti Shah, Richard E. Mayer, and Mary Hegarty, "Graphs as Aids to Knowledge Construction: Signaling Techniques for Guiding the Process of Graph Comprehension," Journal of Educational Psychology 91 (1999): 690–702.

13. Stuart K. Card, Jock D. Mackinlay, and Ben Shneiderman, Readings in Information Visualization: Using Vision to Think (San Francisco: Morgan Kaufmann, 1999), 7.

14. Lynn S. Liben, "Thinking through Maps," in Spatial Schemas and Abstract Thought, Merideth Gattis ed. (Cambridge: Massachusetts Institute of Technology, 2001), 50.

15. Michael P. Verdi and Raymond W. Kulhavey, "Learning with Maps and Texts: An Overview," Educational Psychology Review 14 (2002): 27–46.

16. Lynn S. Liben, "Thinking through Maps," in Spatial Schemas and Abstract Thought, ed. Merideth Gattis (Cambridge: Massachusetts Institute of Technology, 2001) 45–78.

17. William A. Kealy and James M. Webb, "Contextual Influences of Maps and Diagrams on Learning," Contemporary Educational Psychology 20 (1995): 340–358.

PRINCIPLE 5: CLARIFY COMPLEXITY

1. Larry Nesbit, "Relationship between Eye Movement, Learning, and Picture Complexity," Educational Communications and Technology Journal, 29 (1981): 109–116.

2. Richard Clark, Keith Howard, and Sean Early, "Motivational Challenges Experienced in Highly Complex Learning Environments," in Handling Complexity in Learning Environments, ed. Jan Elen, Richard Clark, and Joost Lowcyck (Oxford: Elsevier, 2006), 27–42.

3. David Strayer and Frank Drews, "Attention," in Handbook of Applied Cognition, ed. Francis Durso (Hoboken, NJ: Wiley & Sons, 2007), 29–54.

4. Jan Elen and Richard E. Clark, "Setting the Scene: Complexity and Learning Environments," in Handling Complexity in Learning Environments: Theory and Research (Oxford: Elsevier, 2006), 2.

5. Eleni Michailidou, "ViCRAM: Visual Complexity Rankings and Accessibility Metrics," Accessibility and Computing 86 (2006).

6. John Sweller, "How the Human Cognitive System Deals with Complexity," in Handling Complexity in Learning Environments: Theory and Research, ed. Jan Elen and Richard E. Clark (Oxford: Elsevier, 2006), 13–25.

7. Ibid.

8. E. Pollick, P. Chandler, and J. Sweller, "Assimilating Complex Information," Learning and Instruction 12 (2002): 61–86.

9. Christopher Kurby and Jeffrey Zacks, "Segmentation in the Perception and Memory of Events," Trends in Cognitive Sciences 12 (2007): 72–79.

10. Woodman et al., "Perceptual Organization Influences Visual Working Memory," Psychonomic Bulletin & Review 10 (2003): 80–87.

11. Eric Jamet, Monica Gavota, and Chrisophe Quaireau, "Attention Guiding in Multimedia Learning," Learning and Instruction 18 (2008): 135–145.

12. Gary Bertoline et al., Technical Graphics Communication (Boston: McGraw-Hill, 1997), 995.

13. Cindy Hmelo-Silver and Merav Pfeffer, "Comparing Expert and Novice Understanding of a Complex System," Cognitive Science 28 (2004): 127–138.

14. Mary Hegarty, "Multimedia Learning about Physical Systems," in Cambridge Handbook of Multimedia Learning, ed. Richard E. Mayer (New York: Cambridge University Press, 2005), 447–466.

15. Takahiro Kawabe and Kayo Miura, "New Motion Illusion Caused by Pictorial Motion Lines," Experimental Psychology 55 (2008): 228–234.

16. William Winn, "Cognitive Perspectives in Psychology," in Handbook of Research on Educational Communications and Technology, ed. David H. Jonassen and Phillip Harris (Mahwah, NJ: Lawrence Erlbaum, 2003).

17. Lawrence W. Barsalou, Cognitive Psychology: An Overview for Cognitive Scientists, (Mahwah, NJ: Lawrence Erlbaum, 1992).

PRINCIPLE 6: CHARGE IT UP

1. Maurizio Codispoti, Vera Ferrari, and Margaret M. Bradley, "Repetition and Event-Related Potentials," Journal of Cognitive Neuroscience 19 (2007): 577–586.

2. Judy Gregory, "Social Issues Infotainment," Information Design Journal 11 (2003): 67–81.

3. Dillard et al., "The Multiple Affective Outcome of AIDS PSAs," Communication Research 23 (1996): 44–72.

4. Margaret Matlin, Cognition (Hoboken, NJ: John Wiley and Sons, 2005).

5. Lewis Donohes, Philip Palmgreen, and Jack Duncan, "An Activation Model of Exposure," Communication Monographs 47 (1980): 295–303.

6. Dillard et al., "The Multiple Affective Outcome of AIDS PSAs," Communication Research 23 (1996): 44–72.

7. Bruce F. Hall, "On Measuring the Power of Communications," Journal of Advertising Research 44 (2004): 181–187.

8. Tom Clarke and Alan Costall, "The Emotional Connotations of Color: A Qualitative Investigation," COLOR Research and Application 33 (2008): 406–410.

9. Ibid.

10. Dean Sabatinelli et al., "The Neural Basis of Narrative Imagery: Emotion and Action," Progress in Brain Research 156 (2006): 93–103.

11. Patricia Baggett, "Memory for Explicit and Implicit Information in Picture Stories," Journal of Verbal Learning and Verbal Behavior 14 (1975): 538–548.

12. G. R. Loftus and N. H. Mackworth, "Cognitive Determinants of Fixation Location during Picture Viewing," Journal of Experimental Psychology: Human Perception and Performance 4 (1978): 565–572.

Majid Abbasi
Did Graphics, Inc.
Tehran, Iran
didgraphics.com
Page 56, 210, 211

Dixie Albertson and Jeri Bowers
Darning Pixels, Inc.
Waterloo, IA USA
darningpixels.com
Page 216

Jonathan Avery
University of North Carolina
Morganton, NC USA
averyj@email.unc.edu
Page 102

Jonas Banker and Ida Wessel
BankerWessel
Stockholm, Sweden
bankerwessel.com
Page 82, 93, 106

Stephen J. Beard
Stephen J. Beard Infographics
Fishers, IN USA
stephenjbeard.com
Page 91

Sorin Bechira
X3 Studios
Timisoara, Romania
x3studios.com
Page 57, 82

Greg Bennett
Siquis
Baltimore, MD USA
siquis.com
Page 86, 204, 212

Eliot Bergman
Shinjuku-ku, Tokyo Japan
ebergman.com
Page 28, 96, 112, 149

Drew Berry
The Walter and Eliza Hall Institute of
Medical Research
Parkville, Victoria Australia
wehi.edu.au
Page 51

Melisa Beveridge
Natural History Illustration
Brooklyn, NY USA
naturalhistoryillustration.com
Page 99, 191, 192

Annie Bissett
Northampton, MA USA
anniebisset.com
Page 25

Rhonald Blommestijn
Amersfoort, Netherlands
blommestijn.com
Page 18, 29, 34

Mark Boediman
Clif Bar & Company
Berkeley, CA USA
clifbar.com
Page 50

Marc Bostian and Cameron Eagle
s design, inc.
Oklahoma City, OK USA
sdesigninc.com
Page 218

Marlena Buczek-Smith
Ensign Graphics
Wallington, NJ USA
ensigngraphics.net
Page 163

Lee Byron
Pittsburgh, PA USA
lee@megamu.com
leebyron.com
Page 150

Alberto Cairo
University of North Carolina
Chapel Hill, NC USA
albertocairo.com
Page 168, 179

Eli Carrico
Los Angeles, CA USA
modulate.net
Page 158

Ninian Carter
ninian.net
Page 39

Sarah Cazee
Miami, FL USA
iamsarahcazee.com
Page 124

Wing Chan
Wing Chan Design, Inc.
New York, NY USA
wingchandesign.com
Page 121, 201

Vivien Chow, Edmund Li, Fang-Pin Lee,
Pauline Dolovich, Tony Reich, and
Stephen Petri
Reich + Petch
Toronto, ON Canada
reich-petch.com
Page 197, 198

Bryan Christie
Bryan Christie Design
Maplewood, NJ USA
bryanchristiedesign.com
Page 53, 101, 175, 193

Gordon Cieplak
Schwartz Brand Group
New York, NY USA
ms-ds.com
Page 32

Kristin Clute
University of Washington
Seattle, WA USA
kristinclute@gmail.com
Page 38

Cog Design
London, UK
cogdesign.com
Page 80, 115, 205

Simon Cook
London, UK
made-in-england.org
Page 176

Heather Corcoran
Plum Studio
St. Louis, MO USA
sweetplum.com
Page 201

Heather Corcoran and Diana Scubert
Plum Studio
St. Louis, MO USA
sweetplum.com
Page 137

Heather Corcoran, Colleen Conrado,
Jennifer Saltzman, and Anna Donovan
Plum Studio and Visual Communications
Research Studio
St. Louis, MO USA
sweetplum.com
Page 116

Mike Costelloe and D.B. Dowd
Visual Communications Research Studio
(VCRS) at Washington University
St. Louis, MO USA
Page 142

MaryClare M. Crabtree
Illinois Institute of Art
Chicago, IL USA
crabtreemc@gmail.com
Page 188

Drew Crowley
XPLANE
St.Louis, MO USA
xplane.com
Page 141

Alberto Cuadra
The Houston Chronicle
Richmond, TX USA
acuadra.com
Page 111, 135, 143

Erin Cubert
Nashville, TN USA
erincubert@gmail.com
Page 208

Jaana Davidjants
Wiyumi
Berlin, Germany
wiyumi.com
Page 200

Drew Davies
Oxide Design Co.
Omaha, NE USA
oxidedesign.com
cherubino.com
Page 169

Lorenzo De Tomasi
Sesto Calende, VA Italy
isotype.org
Page 78, 138, 214

Sudarshan Dheer and Ashoomi Dholakia
Graphic Communication Concepts
Mumbai, India
gccgrd.com
Page 72

Greg Dietzenbach
McCullough Creative
Dubuque, IA USA
shootforthemoon.com
Page 37

Sean Douglass
Sammamish, WA USA
colossalhand.com
Page 132

Jean-Manuel Duvivier
Jean-Manuel Duvivier Illustration
Brussels, Belgium
jmduvivier.com
Page 6, 42, 85, 95, 120

Angela Edwards
Indianapolis, IN USA
angelaedwards.com
Page 69, 161

Chronopoulou Ekaterini
La Cambre School of Visual Art
Brussels, Belgium
catcontact@gmail.com
Page 73

Franziska Erdle
Milch Design
Munich, Germany
milch-design.de
Page 134, 160

Chiqui Esteban
Público
Madrid, Spain
infografistas.com
Page 174

Chiqui Esteban and Álvaro Valiño
Público
Madrid, Spain
infografistas.com
Page 157

Nicholas Felton
Megafone
New York, NY USA
feltron.com
Page 67

David Fierstein
David Fierstein Illustration, Animation
& Design
Felton, CA USA
davidiad.com
Page 47, 185

Brian Finn
Iaepetus Press
Bend, OR USA
iapetuspress.com
Page 165

Kimberly Fulton
University of Washington
Kirkland, WA USA
kjfulton@washington.edu
Page 181

Arno Ghelfi
l'atelier starno
San Francisco, CA USA
starno.com
Page 13, 50, 145

Arno Ghelfi and Katie Kleinsasser
Public Media Center
San Francisco, CA USA
publicmediacenter.org
Page 213

Janet Giampietro
Langton Cherubino Group
New York, NY USA
Langton
Page 113

Tonatiuh Arturo Gómez
AW Nazca Saatchi & Saatchi, Venezuela
Caracas, Miranda Venezuela
Page 221

Larry Gormley
History Shots
Westford, MA USA
historyshots.com
Page 128

Larry Gormley
History Shots
Westford, MA USA
historyshots.com
Page 162

Dan Greenwald and Kimberley Cloutier
White Rhino
Burlington, MA USA
Whiterhino.com
Page 128, 162

John Grimwade
Condé Nast Publications
New York, NY USA
johngrimwade.com
Page 98, 133

John Grimwade, Liana Zamora,
and Christine Picavet
Condé Nast Publications
New York, NY USA
johngrimwade.com
Page 80, 132

Peter Grundy and Tilly Northedge
Grundini
Middlesex, UK
grundini.com
Page 11, 105, 148, 223

Francheska Guerrero
Unfolding Terrain
Hagerstown, MD USA
unfoldingterrain.com
Page 94, 100, 227

Surabhi Gurukar
Apostrophe Design
Bangalore, Karnataka India
apostrophedesign.in
Page 97

Lane Hall
Wauwatosa, WI USA
lanehall@uwm.edu
Page 35

Jacob Halton
The Illinois Institute of Art
Chicago, IL USA
jacobhalton@gmail.com
jacobhalton.com
Page 187

Nathanaël Hamon
Slang
Berlin, Germany
slanginternational.org
Page 200

Simon Hancock
There
Sydney, Australia
there.com.au
Page 119

Kevin Hand
Jersey City, NJ USA
kevinhand.com
Page 20, 40, 194, 195

Colin Hayes
Colin Hayes Illustrator, Inc.
Everett, WA USA
colinhayes.com
Page 104, 139, 191, 215, 217

Bruce W. Herr II, Todd M. Holloway,
and Katy Borner
Bloomington, IN USA
scimaps.org/maps/wikipedia
Page 16–17

Nigel Holmes
Westport, CT USA
nigelholmes.com
Page 11, 30, 74. 75, 122, 178, 182-183

David Horton and Ian Koenig
Philographica, Inc.
Brookline, MA USA
philographica.com
Page 219

David Horton and Amy Lebow
Philographica, Inc.
Brookline, MA USA
philographica.com
Page 68

Erica Gregg Howe
Philographica, Inc.
philographica.com
Brookline, MA USA
Page 215

Erica Gregg Howe and Amy Lebow
Philographica, Inc.
Brookline, MA USA
philographica.com
Page 125, 223

Information Design Studio
Amsterdam, Netherlands
theworldasflatland.net
Page 134

Tamara Ivanova
Berlin, Germany
itamara.com
Page 121

Claudine Jaenichen and Richard Turner
Jaenichen Studio
Pasadena, CA USA
jaenichenstudio.com
Page 99, 199

Luis Jones
Fusion Advertising
Dallas, TX USA
fusionista.com
Page 85

Chris Jordan
Seattle, WA USA
chrisjordan.com
Page 131, 146

H. Michael Karshis
HMK Archive
San Antonio, TX USA
sharkthang.com
Page 79

Jaroslaw Kaschtalinski
Golden Section Graphics GmbH
Berlin, Germany
golden-section-graphics.com
Page 193

Patrick Keenan and Alan Smith
The Movement
themovement.info
Page 89

Christine Kenney
IE Design + Communications
Hermosa Beach, CA USA
iedesign.com
Page 78

Christina Koehn
Seattle, WA USA
christinakoehn.com
Page 137

Andreas Koller and Phillip Steinweber
Strukt
Vienna, Austria
similardiversity.net
Page 154–155

Adrian Labos
X3 Studios
Timisoara, Romania
x3studios.com
Page 41

George Ladas
Base24 Design Systems
Roselle, NJ USA
base24.com
Page 186, 188, 225

Nicola Landucci
CCG Metamedia
New York, NY USA
ccgmetamedia.com
Page 187

Poul Hans Lange
Poul Lange Design
New York, NY USA
poulhanslange.com
Page 156, 159

Eric Larsen
Eric Larsen Artwork
Portland, OR USA
eric_larsen_art.home.comcast.net
Page 124

Allen Lau
Redmond, WA USA
allenylau.com
Page 173

Lars Lawson
Timber Design Company, Inc.
Indianapolis, IN USA
timberdesignco.com
Page 207

Amy Lebow and Purnima Rao
Philographica, Inc.
Brookline, MA USA
philographica.com
Page 103

Jane Lee
IE Design + Communications
Hermosa Beach, CA USA
iedesign.com
Page 52, 117, 126

GG LeMere
Campbell Fisher Design
Phoenix, AZ USA
thinkcfd.com
Page 202

Ira Ginzburg,
Ola Levitsky
B.I.G. Design
Jerusalem, Israel
bigdesign.co.il
Page 92, 127, 143, 194

Diana Litavsky
Illinois Institute of Art
Chicago, IL USA
dianalitavsky@yahoo.com
Page 123

Boris Ljubicic
Studio International
Zagreb, Croatia
studio-international.com
Page 44, 55, 58, 63, 177

Alexander Lloyd
Lloyds Graphic Design Ltd.
Blenheim, New Zealand
Page 224

Jennifer Lopardo
Schwartz Brand Group
New York, NY USA
ms-ds.com
Page 49

Matthew Luckwitz
grafPort, Inc.
Denver, CO USA
grafport.com
Page 142, 171

Ian Lynam
Ian Lynam Creative Direction & Design
Tokyo, Japan
ianlynam.com
Page 61, 70, 87

Dermot MacCormack, Patricia McElroy
21xdesign
Broomall, PA USA
21xdesign.com
Page 157

Taylor Marks
XPLANE
St. Louis, MO USA
xplane.com
Page 12

Taylor Marks, Stephanie Meier, D. B.
Dowd, Sarah Phares, Sarah Sisterson,
Enrique VonRohr, and Amanda Wolff
Visual Communications Research Studio
(VCRS) at Washington University
St. Louis, MO USA
Page 109

Rodrigo Maroja and Carlo Giovani
Carlo Giovani Studio
São Paulo, Brazil
carlogiovani.com
Page 166-167

Mark McGowan and David Goodsell
Exploratorium
San Francisco, CA USA
exploratorium.edu
Page 76

Stuart Medley
Lightship Visual
Duncraig, Australia
lightshipvisual.com
Page 110

Antonio Mena
Antonio Mena Design
Quito, Ecuador
Page 54, 114, 209

Will Miller
Firebelly Design
Chicago, IL USA
firebellydesign.com
Page 158

Daniel Müller and Joanne Haderer Müller
Haderer & Müller Biomedical Art, LLC
Melrose, MA USA
haderermuller.com
Page 10, 31, 90, 173, 186

Vu Nguyen
Biofusion Design
Seattle, WA USA
biofusiondesign.com
Page 180

Niall O'Kelly
Schwartz Brand Group
New York, NY USA
ms-ds.com
Page 213

A. Osterwalder, P. Bardesono, S. Wagner,
A. Bromer and M. Drozdowski
i_dbuero.de
Stuttgart, Germany
Page 94

Karen Parry and Louis Jaffe
Black Graphics
San Francisco, CA USA
blackgraphics.com
Page 101

Stefanie Posavec
London, UK
stefpos@gmail.com
Page 153

Nivedita Ramesh
University of Washington
Seattle, WA USA
nivi@u.washington.edu
Page 176

Emmi Salonen
Emmi
London, UK
emmi.co.uk
Page 120

Adriano Sambugaro
Carlo Giovani Studio
São Paulo, Brazil
carlogiovani.com
Page 220

Jan Schwochow, Katharina Erfurth,
Sebastian Piesker, Katrin Lamm, Juliana
Köneke, Jaroslaw Kaschtalinski
Golden Section Graphics GmbH
Berlin, Germany
golden-section-graphics.com
Page 64–65, 149, 170, 189

Christopher Short
Christopher B. Short, LLC
Stroudsburg, PA USA
chrisshort.com
Page 60, 88

Jay Smith
Juicebox Designs
Nashville, TN USA
juiceboxdesigns.com
Page 116, 226

Dale Sprague, Joslynn Anderson
Canyon Creative
Las Vegas, NV USA
canyoncreative.com
Page 90, 205

Aviad Stark
Graphic Advance
Palisades Park, NJ USA
graphicadvance.com
Page 112, 139, 181

Shinnoske Sugisaki
Shinnoske, Inc.
Osaka, Japan
shinn.co.jp
Page 48, 62, 77

Russell Tate
Clovelly, Australia
russelltate.com
Page 118, 159

Kara Tennant
Carnegie Mellon University
Pittsburgh, PA USA
karatennant@gmail.com
karatennant.com
Page 152

Benjamin Thomas
Bento Graphics
Tokyo, Japan
bentographics.com
Page 105

Veronica Neira Torres
Granada, Nicaragua
ariesbeginner.deviantart.com
vero_nt88@hotmail.com
Page 48

David Van Essen, Charles Anderson,
Daniel Felleman
Produced with permission from *Science*
magazine
Page 24

Travis Vermilye
Travis Vermilye Medical & Biological
Illustration
Denver, CO USA
tvermilye.com
Page 190, 222

Amy Vest
Applied Biosystems Brand &
Creative Group
Foster City, CA USA
Page 147, 184

Juliana Vidigal, Reneta Steffen,
and Carlo Giovani
Carlo Giovani Studio
São Paulo, Brazil
carlogiovani.com
Page 21, 160–161, 164

Christine Walker
stressdesign
Syracuse, NY USA
stressdesign.com
Page 108

Dave Willis, Mischa Kostandov,
Dan Riskin, Jaime Peraire,
David H. Laidlaw, Sharon Swartz,
and Kenny Breuer
Engineers from Brown University and MIT
Providence, RI USA
fluids.engin.brown.edu
Page 151

Nancy Wu, Kim Rigewell, Lisa Nakamura
and Jeff Harrison
Rethink Communications
Vancouver, British Columbia Canada
rethinkcommunications.com
Page 225

Maziar Zand
M. Zand Studio
Tehran, Iran
mzand.com
Page 8, 46, 69, 88

Rose Zgodzinski
Information Graphics
Toronto, Ontario Canada
chartsmapsanddiagrams.com
Page 147

CPSIA information can be obtained
at www.ICGtesting.com
Printed in the USA
LVHW01s1034050817
543851LV00010B/11/P

Essential Case Studies in Public Health: Putting Public Health into Practice

Katherine L. Hunting, PhD, MPH

Professor
Environmental and Occupational Health & Epidemiology and Biostatistics
The George Washington University
School of Public Health and Health Services
Washington, DC

Brenda L. Gleason, MA, MPH

President
M2 Health Care Consulting
Professorial Lecturer
The George Washington University
School of Public Health and Health Services
Washington, DC

JONES & BARTLETT
LEARNING

World Headquarters

Jones & Bartlett Learning
5 Wall Street
Burlington, MA 01803
978-443-5000
info@jblearning.com
www.jblearning.com

Jones & Bartlett Learning Canada
6339 Ormindale Way
Mississauga, Ontario L5V 1J2
Canada

Jones & Bartlett Learning International
Barb House, Barb Mews
London W6 7PA
United Kingdom

Jones & Bartlett Learning books and products are available through most bookstores and online booksellers. To contact Jones & Bartlett Learning directly, call 800-832-0034, fax 978-443-8000, or visit our website, www.jblearning.com.

Production Credits
Publisher: Michael Brown
Associate Editor: Maro Gartside
Editorial Assistant: Teresa Reilly
Editorial Assistant: Chloe Falivene
Associate Production Editor: Cindie Bryan
Senior Marketing Manager: Sophie Fleck
Manufacturing and Inventory Control Supervisor: Amy Bacus
Composition: Publishers' Design and Production Services, Inc.
Cover Design: Kristin E. Parker
Cover Image: © Mariasats/Dreamstime.com
Image Credits: © Andy Piatt/ShutterStock, Inc., © Ailin/Fotolia.com, © Simone van den Berg/ShutterStock, Inc., © Attila Németh/Dreamstime.com, © Photos.com
Printing and Binding: Malloy, Inc.
Cover Printing: Malloy, Inc.

Library of Congress Cataloging-in-Publication Data
Hunting, Katherine.
    Essential case studies in public health : putting public health into practice / Katherine Hunting, Brenda Gleason.
        p. ; cm.
    ISBN-13: 978-0-7637-6131-8 (pbk.)
    ISBN-10: 0-7637-6131-1 (pbk.)
    1. Public health—Case studies.   I. Gleason, Brenda L.   II. Title.
    [DNLM: 1. Public Health Practice. WA 100]
    RA427.H86 2012
    362.1—dc22
        2011006566

6048

Printed in the United States of America
15   14   13   12   11   10   9   8   7   6   5   4   3   2   1

Contents

About the Editors   vii

Prologue   ix
Richard Riegelman

Contributors   xi

Introduction   xv

PART I   Assessment Cases: Overview   1

Case 1   The Toronto Severe Acute Respiratory Syndrome II Experience   5
           Larissa May and Richard Schabas

Case 2   A Feasibility Study of Routine Screening for HIV in an Urban
           Emergency Department   15
           Katherine L. Hunting and Jeremy Brown

Case 3   Male Circumcision and HIV: An Evidence-Based Public Health
           Approach   23
           Richard Riegelman

Case 4   Research Synthesis: Systematic Review and Meta-Analysis of Vioxx®
           and Cardiovascular Events   33
           Michelle D. Althuis

PART II Policy Development Cases: Overview   45

Case 5 The Heart Truth®: A Social Marketing Approach to Increase
Awareness about Heart Disease in Women   49
*Ann M. Taubenheim, Sally McDonough, Terry Long,
Jennifer Wayman, and Sarah Temple*

Case 6 An Outbreak of Yellow Fever in Paraguay: Health Risk
Communication in a Crisis   59
Jon K. Andrus, Tilly Gurman, Brenda L. Gleason, and Barbara Jauregui

Case 7 Challenges with Implementing a Community-Based Potable
Water System in a Rural Honduras Community   69
Elizabeth L. Andrade and Kathryn Zoerhoff

Case 8 Building on Strengths: A School-Based Mental Health Program   81
Olga Acosta Price, Jodie Fishman, and Mimi V. Chapman

Case 9 Building Trust in Communities: The Narragansett Indian Tribe
and the State of Rhode Island   89
E. Blaine Parrish

Case 10 The Strategies to Overcome and Prevent Obesity Alliance   95
*Erica Breese, Casey Langwith, Christine Ferguson,
GinaMarie Mangiaracina, and Allison May Rosen*

Case 11 Should HPV Vaccine Be Required for School Entry?   103
Alexandra M. Stewart and Marisa A. Cox

Case 12 Plan B Emergency Contraception: Caught in a Web of Science,
Regulation, and Politics—What's a Woman to Do?   113
Susan F. Wood and Alison M. Miller

Case 13 Implementing Policy Changes to Decrease Racial and Ethnic
Disparities in Pediatric Asthma Outcomes   123
Anne Rossier Markus and Shavon Artis

Case 14 Coal Ash: Disasters and Opportunities   131
Rebecca Parkin and Elizabeth Holman

Case 15   The Diethylstilbestrol Story: An Investigation into the Evolving Public
           Health Policy for Pharmaceutical Products   145
           Margaret Ann Miller, Emily Blecker, and Meghal Patel

PART III Assurance Cases: Overview   153

Case 16   Beyond Measurement? Evaluating Environmental Public Health:
           Assessing the Effectiveness of Food Safety Programs   157
           Lindsey Realmuto and Surili Sutaria

Case 17   Cardiac Rehabilitation for the Elderly: A Public Health Perspective   165
           Larry F. Hamm

Case 18   The X-Pack Smoking Cessation Kit: A Social Marketing Case Study   171
           Lorien Abroms, Brenda L. Gleason, Katelin Lucariello, and Allison Mobley

Case 19   Mumps Epidemic in Iowa: Lessons Learned from the Front Line
           of Testing   179
           Michael A. Pentella

Case 20   Big Brother is Watching: Using Clinical Decision Support as a Tool
           to Limit Adverse Drug Events   187
           Aaron Roberts

Case 21   The 2009–2010 H1N1 Influenza Pandemic: When You Make
           Mistakes, Don't Miss the Lessons   195
           Pietro D. Marghella

           Index   203

About the Editors

KATHERINE L. HUNTING, PHD, MPH

Kathy Hunting is professor of environmental and occupational health and of epidemiology and biostatistics at The George Washington University School of Public Health and Health Services. She is an expert in epidemiologic study design and injury epidemiology, particularly as they pertain to studies of workers. Her connection to real-world issues is demonstrated not only by her teaching, research, and community service activities, but by the fact that she is conversant in the jargon of the construction trade—and even owns her own hard hat.

Professor Hunting joined The George Washington University in 1988 as a research scientist, and was a founding faculty member of the School of Public Health and Health Services. She is vice chair for educational activities in the environmental and occupational health department and also directs the master of public health (MPH) program in environmental health science and policy. She served in the dean's office from 2004 to 2010, first as associate dean for student and faculty development and subsequently as associate dean for academic affairs.

Professor Hunting teaches environmental health to undergraduates and principles of epidemiology, environmental and occupational epidemiology, and injury epidemiology to master's students. She is a passionate teacher and brings to life even potentially dry topics such as research methods. Professor Hunting has twice been selected by School of Public Health and Health Services students for the Excellence in Teaching award, and she was also honored to receive the Public Health Student Association award for Dedication and Excellence.

Professor Hunting earned both her MPH and PhD in epidemiology at the Johns Hopkins University School of Hygiene and Public Health. Her BS in environmental science is from the University of California at Riverside.

BRENDA L. GLEASON, MA, MPH

Brenda Gleason is the president and founder of M2 Health Care Consulting, a strategic policy and communications consulting firm providing services to Fortune 100 companies, multinational professional services companies, and private equity firms, in addition to nonprofit health associations. Professor Gleason brings a unique perspective to analysis, problem solving, and communications because of her broad-ranging, health-related experience in government, publishing, and business.

Professor Gleason began her career in health policy at the Massachusetts Department of Public Health. She has served as the editor of several healthcare publications, including *Community Health Funding Report* and the *Medicaid Pharmacy Bulletin*, and worked on policy and strategy issues for Pfizer, Inc. and for the contract research organization PAREXEL International. Prior to starting M2 in 2005, Professor Gleason was the vice president of Healthcare Markets for Informed Decisions, LLC, a provider of innovative health information technology solutions for government and commercial providers. Informed Decisions created the award-winning eMPOWERx platform—the first point-of-care e-prescribing program used by a state Medicaid agency.

Frequently quoted as a health policy expert, Professor Gleason has been featured in publications such as the *Wall*

Street Journal, Bloomberg, Los Angeles Times, Crain's New York Business, Managed Healthcare Executive, Pharmaceutical Executive, Healthcare Finance News, Journal of Oncology Practice, Washington Business Journal, and *Pharmawire* (part of the *Financial Time*s Group). She is also the author of *What We Don't Want to Hear About Health Care: It's All Our Fault—8 Things We Can Do to Fix the System.*

Professor Gleason holds a lecturer title at The George Washington University School of Public Health and Health Services. She earned an MA from Boston College and an MPH from Boston University.

Prologue

Editors Katherine Hunting and Brenda Gleason have done a remarkable job of bringing together and tying together *Essential Case Studies in Public Health: Putting Public Health into Practice*. The collection of cases is organized around the 10 essential public health services and the three IOM core public health functions. Each case addresses one or more of these essential services. Together, the cases engage students and practitioners in the process of thinking through problems inherent in implementing the 10 essential services and the three core functions. Understanding these 10 essential public health services is key since they now serve as the framework for accreditation of state and local health departments.

The editors and authors have worked closely together to ensure that the cases follow the standard format recommended by the North American Case Research Association. Each case is based on an actual public health problem that has come to local, national, and/or global attention in recent years. Most cases begin with interesting and compelling vignettes reflecting the circumstances of case protagonists—"the hook"—as it is called in the language of case studies. The case summaries read like detective stories waiting for public health professionals to untangle and solve the problem using evidence, experience, and public health expertise.

Many of the cases go on to lead the reader though a series of questions demanding thoughtful responses drawing on the disciplines of public health, from social and behavioral sciences, to epidemiology and biostatistics, to environmental health, to management and policy. The question format requires students and practitioners to build upon what they have learned in the case study and recommend what to do next. The cases require the users to draw their own conclusions using evidence and public health judgment and to reflect on the lessons learned and the challenges ahead.

An extensive faculty website accompanies the cases. It includes facilitator guides for each case, providing detailed suggested answers to the study questions. The facilitator guides go beyond providing answers; they provide case learning objectives, summaries of the cases, tips on teaching the materials, and an epilogue recounting what happened in the weeks and years that followed the case. In addition, information is provided to connect each case with the Association of Schools of Public Health master of public health core and cross-cutting competencies that form the basis for the public health certifying examination. Some cases include supplementary web-based materials for student use that expand on and deepen students' understanding of the case.

Essential Case Studies in Public Health: Putting Public Health into Practice is a key component of the *Essential Public Health* series. In many ways, it is the capstone or synthesis book for the series because it draws on and can be used with many of the other books in the series. In addition, the book is ideal for continuing education for public health practitioners whose daily work challenges them to apply the 10 essential services and the three core functions.

Katherine Hunting and Brenda Gleason have engaged this process with their time, teaching expertise, and editing skills. As experienced and empathic teachers, they understand the need of students and practitioners and have ensured that each case study speaks to the users. As experienced teachers used to teaching courses with multiple faculty, they provided clear and frequent guidance on the development of the cases. As skilled editors, they provided repeated feedback designed to ensure consistency and quality of the case studies. As an author of a case, I can vouch for their commitment to reviewing, providing important feedback, and rereading multiple versions of the cases.

Whether you are an undergraduate student using this book as part of a capstone or synthesis course, a graduate student using the text to master the discipline based and cross-cutting competencies of public health, or a public health practitioner using the cases to build upon your fundamental skills, you will find that these case studies bring public health to life in a way that helps you learn.

Richard Riegelman, MD, MPH, PhD
Series Editor, *Essential Public Health* series

Contributors

Lorien Abroms, ScD, MA
Assistant Professor of Prevention and Community Health
The George Washington University School of Public Health
and Health Services

Michelle D. Althuis, PhD, MA
Founder and Principal Epidemiology Consultant
Lincoln Greystone, LLC

Elizabeth L. Andrade, MPH
Research Scientist and DrPH Candidate
Department of Prevention and Community Health
The George Washington University School of Public Health
and Health Services

Jon K. Andrus, MD
Deputy Director
Pan American Health Organization

Shavon Artis, MPH
Public Health Analyst
Eunice Kennedy Shriver National Institute of Child Health
and Human Development

Emily Blecker
Undergraduate Student in Sociology (concentrating in
Health and Medicine)
University of Pennsylvania

Erica Breese, BS
Research Program Coordinator
Department of Health Policy
The George Washington University School of Public Health
and Health Services

Jeremy Brown, MD
Associate Professor and Director of Clinical Research
Department of Emergency Medicine
The George Washington University School of Medicine and
Health Sciences

Mimi V. Chapman, MSW, PhD
Associate Professor
University of North Carolina at Chapel Hill School of Social
Work

Marisa A. Cox, MA
Senior Research Associate
Department of Health Policy
The George Washington University School of Public Health
and Health Services

Christine Ferguson, JD
Professor of Health Policy
The George Washington University School of Public Health
and Health Services

Jodie Fishman, MPH
Senior Account Executive
Hagar Sharp, Inc.

Brenda L. Gleason, MA, MPH
President and Founder
M2 Health Care Consulting
Lecturer
Department of Health Policy
The George Washington University School of Public Health
and Health Services

Tilly Gurman, DrPH
Assistant Professor of Global Health
The George Washington University School of Public Health and Health Services

Larry F. Hamm, PhD
Professor of Exercise Science
The George Washington University School of Public Health and Health Services

Elizabeth Holman, MS, EdM
Physical Scientist
Office of Pesticide Programs, U.S. Environmental Protection Agency
DrPH Candidate
Department of Environmental and Occupational Health
The George Washington University School of Public Health and Health Services

Katherine L. Hunting, PhD, MPH
Professor of Environmental and Occupational Health and of Epidemiology and Biostatistics
The George Washington University School of Public Health and Health Services

Barbara Jauregui, MD, MSc
Manager, ProVac Initiative
Comprehensive Family Immunization Project
Pan American Health Organization

Casey Langwith, BA
Research Program Coordinator
Department of Health Policy
The George Washington University School of Public Health and Health Services

Terry Long, BA
Consultant in Health Communications
Former Communications Director
National Heart, Lung, and Blood Institute

Katelin Lucariello, MPH
Senior Consultant
M2 Health Care Consulting

GinaMarie Mangiaracina, BA
Team Lead
Strategies to Overcome and Prevent (STOP) Obesity Alliance
Chandler Chicco Agency

Pietro D. Marghella, DHSc(c), MSc, MA, CEM, FACCP
President/CEO, Medical Planning Resources, Inc.

Lecturer
Department of Health Services Management and Leadership
The George Washington University School of Public Health and Health Services

Anne Rossier Markus, JD, PhD, MHS
Associate Professor of Health Policy
The George Washington University School of Public Health and Health Services

Larissa May, MD
Assistant Professor of Emergency Medicine and of Microbiology, Immunology and Tropical Medicine
The George Washington University School of Medicine and Health Sciences
Assistant Professor of Epidemiology and Biostatistics
The George Washington University School of Public Health and Health Services

Sally McDonough, BA
Director, Office of Communications
National Heart, Lung, and Blood Institute

Alison M. Miller, MPH
Research Assistant
Department of Health Policy
The George Washington University School of Public Health and Health Services

Margaret Ann Miller, PhD, MS
Associate Director of Regulatory Activities
National Center for Toxicological Research
U.S. Food and Drug Administration
Professorial Lecturer
Department of Environmental and Occupational Health
The George Washington University School of Public Health and Health Services

Allison Mobley, MHS
Director
Behavior Works

Rebecca Parkin, PhD, MPH
Professorial Lecturer
Department of Environmental and Occupational Health
The George Washington University School of Public Health and Health Services

E. Blaine Parrish, PhD, MA
Assistant Professor of Health Policy and of Prevention and Community Health, Associate Dean for Student Affairs

The George Washington University School of Public Health
and Health Services

Meghal Patel, MPH
ORISE Fellow
National Center for Toxicological Research
U.S. Food and Drug Administration

Michael A. Pentella, PhD, SM(ASCP), CIC, D(ABMM)
Associate Director for Infectious Disease
University of Iowa Hygienic Laboratory
Clinical Associate Professor
University of Iowa College of Public Health

Olga Acosta Price, PhD
Associate Professor of Prevention and Community Health
Director, Center for Health and Health Care in Schools
The George Washington University School of Public Health
and Health Services

Lindsey Realmuto, MPH
Environmental Health Analyst
Association of State and Territorial Health Officials

Richard Riegelman, MD, MPH, PhD
Professor of Epidemiology and Biostatistics and of Health
Policy, Founding Dean
The George Washington University School of Public Health
and Health Services
Professor of Medicine
The George Washington University School of Medicine and
Health Sciences

Aaron Roberts, BS
Research Assistant
Brown University

Allison May Rosen, BS
Global Leadership Council
Chandler Chicco Companies
Lecturer, Department of Health Policy
The George Washington University School of Public Health
and Health Services

Richard Schabas, MD, FRCPC
Medical Officer of Health
Hastings and Prince Edward Counties Health Unit,
Ontario, Canada
Adjunct Associate Professor
Queen's University School of Medicine

Alexandra M. Stewart, JD
Assistant Professor of Health Policy
The George Washington University School of Public Health
and Health Services

Surili Sutaria, MS
Senior Environmental Health Analyst
Association of State and Territorial Health Officials

Ann M. Taubenheim, PhD, MSN
Chief
Health Campaigns and Consumer Services Branch
Office of Communications
National Heart, Lung, and Blood Institute

Sarah Temple, BA
Senior Vice President
Ogilvy Public Relations Worldwide

Jennifer Wayman, MHS
Executive Vice President
Ogilvy Public Relations Worldwide

Susan F. Wood, PhD
Associate Professor of Health Policy
Executive Director, Jacobs Institute of Women's Health
The George Washington University School of Public Health
and Health Services

Kathryn Zoerhoff, MPH, MA
Monitoring and Evaluation Associate
Neglected Tropical Disease Control Program
RTI International

Introduction

Welcome to *Essential Case Studies in Public Health: Putting Public Health into Practice*, a collection of 21 teaching and learning cases. Each case is based on real events and problems. The case authors include over 40 public health faculty members, graduate students, and practitioners—most writing from their own experiences. These cases vividly illustrate how professionals across various disciplines tackle public health challenges. The topical areas run the gamut from cardiovascular disease to clean water, from obesity to asthma, from vaccination to mental health, from pharmaceutical policy to environmental regulation. In learning through these cases, students apply a wide range of knowledge and skills relevant to public health outbreak investigation, policy analysis, regulatory decision making, ethics, program development, program evaluation, research synthesis, screening programs, working with stakeholders, social marketing, health risk communication, laboratory management, emergency preparedness, and more.

Each case in this book has been developed with specific learning objectives in mind; these focus on concepts and issues that comprise the heart of public health undergraduate and graduate education and are key to practitioners of public health. The Association of Schools of Public Health master of public health degree core disciplinary competencies in biostatistics, environmental health, epidemiology, health policy management, and social and behavioral sciences are covered in detail in these cases. Case-based learning may be an even more effective approach for developing competency in highly applied cross-cutting domains such as communication, informatics, diversity and culture, leadership, professionalism, program planning, public health biology, and systems thinking. This book's cases have been explicitly developed to help students and practitioners develop competencies in the Association of Schools of Public Health disciplinary core and cross-cutting domains.[1] In addition, the cases provide opportunities to analyze current health issues from an arts and sciences perspective focused on "promoting and protecting population health, safety, and well-being at local and global levels"[2(Project Background)] as well as "eliminating health and social disparities worldwide,"[2(Project Background)] as called for in the Association of Schools of Public Health Undergraduate Learning Outcomes Development Project. The learning objectives are embedded in the cases but are also explicitly laid out in the facilitator guides available to instructors.

These cases are not merely stories that relate compelling public health issues, problems, or accomplishments, and then sum up the lessons learned. Rather, they are carefully constructed narratives, most of which put learners in the seat of a protagonist who has a problem to solve. While these decision cases present contextual information, they don't provide the answers; evaluation of possible solutions and approaches is left to students. A few of the cases (for example, "The Heart Truth®," "Mumps Epidemic in Iowa," and "The Strategies to Overcome and Prevent Obesity Alliance") do not explicitly ask learners to make decisions, but instead, provide opportunities for students to actively analyze what made a program stumble or succeed, or to identify the lessons learned and then transfer them from historical to present-day context.

The subtitle of this text, *Putting Public Health into Practice*, bears comment. A theme running through all 21 cases is how evidence is utilized to frame and drive decision making about public health programs, policy initiatives, or interventions. The cases illustrate how front-line activities of public health practitioners are informed and enhanced by active research from the disciplines, and why protecting public health requires continuous process improvement and systems-level thinking. Whether told from the point of view of researchers; local, state, or federal officials; clinicians; consultants; or advocates, these cases illustrate public health in action. The intent is to take you behind the scenes, to let you glimpse the challenges and pitfalls, the strategies and successes, of the job of protecting the public's health. As a learner, these cases place you in communities, organizations, government agencies, and public health and healthcare systems—and encourage you to think about what you might do. These cases can help prepare you for the day you may find yourself on the front lines, for real.

THE 10 ESSENTIAL PUBLIC HEALTH SERVICES

The 10 essential public health services linked to the three core functions (see Box 1) provide the organizing framework for this case book. It's worth understanding something of their history. In 1988, the Institute of Medicine published a landmark report entitled, *The Future of Public Health*. This report resulted from a study undertaken to "address a growing perception … that this nation has lost sight of its public health goals and has allowed the system of public health activities to fall into disarray."[3(p 1)] Seeking to provide direction for public health to effectively fulfill its mission, the Institute of Medicine identified assessment, policy development, and assurance as the core functions common to local, state, and federal public health agencies.[3] In 1994, the Core Public Health Functions steering committee (comprised of diverse public health stakeholders) further elaborated these functions as part of a vision for healthy people in healthy communities and a mission to "promote physical and mental health and prevent disease, injury, and disability."[4] In doing so, the committee outlined the 10 essential public health services shown in Box 1.

As illustrated in Figure 1, the assessment function involves monitoring trends in disease and injury and analyzing risk and protective factors through further investigation. The development of effective policies and practices rests upon effective communication and education approaches as well as broad involvement from all public health stakeholders. The assurance function entails enforcement of laws and statutes, provision of health services, and evaluation of programs and services. Public health workforce competency, though labeled an assurance function, is necessary for all public health functions. Finally, research provides the evolving evidence base that continually informs and enhances public health practice across all essential functions and services.

BOX 1 The 10 Essential Public Health Services

1. Monitor health status to identify community health problems
2. Diagnose and investigate health problems and health hazards in the community
3. Inform, educate, and empower people about health issues
4. Mobilize community partnerships to identify and solve health problems
5. Develop policies and plans that support individual and community health efforts
6. Enforce laws and regulations that protect health and ensure safety
7. Link people to needed personal health services and assure the provision of health care when otherwise unavailable
8. Assure a competent public health and personal healthcare workforce
9. Evaluate effectiveness, accessibility, and quality of personal and population-based health services
10. Research for new insights and innovative solutions to health problems

Source: U.S. Department of Health and Human Services. Public health in America—essential public health services. http://www.health.gov/phfunctions/public.htm. Accessed November 28, 2010.

Recently, the National Public Health Performance Standards Program has brought increased visibility to the 10 essential public health services. The National Public Health Performance Standards Program is a collaborative effort to establish national performance standards for U.S. state and local public health systems, defined as "all public, private, and voluntary entities that contribute to public health activities within a given area."[5(p 2)] The National Public Health Performance Standards Program has adopted the 10 essential services as its framework for describing and examining the "breadth of public health practice, performance, and infrastructure capability …"[5(p 2)] and informing a process of quality improvement.[5]

FIGURE 1 The 10 essential public health services.

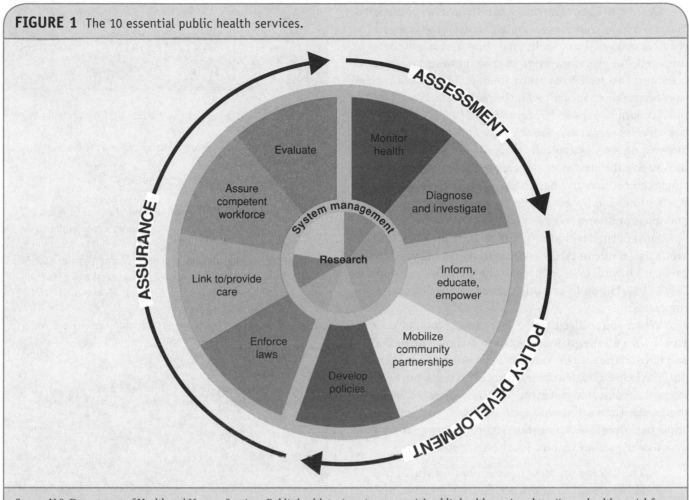

Source: U.S. Department of Health and Human Services. Public health in America—essential public health services. http://www.health.gov/phfunctions/public.htm. Accessed November 28, 2010.

THE CASE METHOD: A NOTE TO LEARNERS

As every learner knows, opportunities to apply theories and concepts enhance your ability to understand them. Even the best lecturers, who pepper engaging and well-organized presentations with lots of interesting and relevant examples, can merely transfer information. You appreciate full well that the best teachers follow their lectures with opportunities to *apply* concepts, knowledge, and skills—whether through problem sets, critical analysis of research articles or current issues, class discussions, role plays, research projects, or case studies.

The case study approach is very effective for solidifying concepts and developing critical thinking skills. When you learn through case studies, you engage actively with the material, analyzing and synthesizing information. According to Dr.

Lew Brown of the University of North Carolina at Greensboro and associate editor of the *Case Research Journal*, case-based learning will give you practice defining problems, identifying appropriate information, organizing what is known and what is not, developing options, evaluating alternatives, generating action plans, and effectively communicating your insights.[6] According to another case study proponent:

> If reading, arguing, and challenging are hallmarks of critical thinking, then case studies are the poster children for the process. Most of them are discipline specific, certainly. But they all grapple with the essence of critical thinking—asking for evidence—developing a habit of mind that should permeate everyday life.[7(p 65)]

In order to learn from case studies, you must be prepared. You must have *read* the case, *thought about* the case, and be *ready to discuss* the case. In analyzing a case, you must be prepared, "to give it meaning in relation to its key issues or questions that have been asked about it. The goal is to come to conclusions congruent with the reality of the case, taking into account its gaps and uncertainties."[8(p 6)] Although some questions in some cases are objective and actually have right answers, this is not typically the situation. Mostly—as with life outside the classroom—there are shades of gray with no single correct answer. Thus, to learn effectively through cases, you will need to become more comfortable with ambiguity and uncertainty.

Most of the cases in this book involve protagonists who are facing a dilemma. To prepare to discuss these decision cases, it's helpful to keep in mind the questions presented in Box 2, in addition to any other specific questions raised by the case.

When you're discussing a case, do not look to your instructor for all the answers. Listen to your classmates' ideas, and have confidence in your own. The instructor is there as a guide to help facilitate your learning experience, but he or she is also learning alongside you. The classroom is a safe place to practice the analysis and synthesis skills you will need to apply in the professional world. According to an experienced case teacher at the Harvard Business School:

> The discussion process itself requires students to become profoundly and actively involved in their own learning, to discover for themselves rather than accept verbal or written pronouncements. ... Such creative activity cannot be ordered or imposed upon the unwilling. Teachers can police attendance and monitor the memorization of theory and fact by tests. But we cannot order our students to be committed to learning and willing to risk experimentation, error, and the uncertainty of exploration.[9(p 24)]

Indeed, that commitment to learning is up to you as you develop and hone foundations for professional practice. May you enjoy learning as you experience public health problems coming alive through these cases!

BOX 2 Questions to Consider as You Prepare to Discuss a Decision Case

- What is the problem to be resolved or decision to be made?
- Who are the decision makers, and what is motivating each of them?
- Who are the other stakeholders? What are their objectives?
- What questions must be addressed or issues must be resolved in order to solve the problem or come to a decision?
- What contextual issues might affect the decision? These may include health issues, social and political environment, technical barriers, or any other constraints and opportunities.
- What are the upsides and downsides associated with alternative actions?
- What would you do? Why?

Source: Data from Lynn LE. Welcome to the case method! The electronic hallway. http://www.hallway.org. Accessed November 28, 2010.

REFERENCES

1. Education Committee, Association of Schools of Public Health. Master's degree in public health core competency model, version 2.3. August 2006. http://www.asph.org/userfiles/version2.3.pdf. Accessed December 5, 2010.

2. Association of Schools of Public Health. Undergraduate public health learning outcomes development project. http://www.asph.org/document.cfm?page=1085. Accessed December 5, 2010.

3. Institute of Medicine. *The Future of Public Health*. Washington, DC: National Academies Press; 1988.

4. U.S. Department of Health and Human Services. Public health in America—essential public health services. http://www.health.gov/phfunctions/public.htm. Accessed November 28, 2010.

5. Centers for Disease Control and Prevention. National Public Health Performance Standards Program—frequently asked questions. http://www.cdc.gov/nphpsp/PDF/FAQ.pdf. Accessed April 15, 2011.

6. Brown L. Developing field-researched public health cases. Presentation at Workshop on Writing Teaching Cases, George Washington University School of Public Health and Health Services; June 22, 2009; Washington, DC.

7. Herreid CF. Can case studies be used to teach critical thinking? In: Herreid CF, ed. *Start With a Story: The Case Study Method of Teaching College Science*. Arlington, VA: National Science Teachers Association Press; 2007:62–66.

8. Ellet W. *The Case Study Handbook: How to Read, Discuss, and Write Persuasively about Cases*. Boston, MA: Harvard Business School Press; 2007.

9. Christensen CR. Premises and practices of discussion teaching. In: Barnes LB, Christensen CR, Hansen AJ. *Teaching and the Case Method: Text, Cases, and Readings*. 3rd ed. Boston, MA: Harvard Business School Press; 1994:23–33.

PART I

Assessment Cases: Overview

Assessment is the foundation of public health. Before decisions can be made, before policies can be determined, before programs can be planned, public health professionals must assess the situation at hand. Two of the 10 essential public health services fall into the category of assessment:

- Monitoring health status to identify community health problems.
- Diagnosing and investigating health problems and health hazards in the community.

Additionally, as with all of the services categories, research is an integral component. Thus, assessment also includes the 10th essential public health service: research for new insights and innovative solutions to health problems.

The assessment section includes four case studies that can be used to examine issues related to assessing health status and community health problems. The cases are:

1. The Toronto Severe Acute Respiratory Syndrome II Experience
2. A Feasibility Study of Routine Screening for HIV in an Urban Emergency Department
3. Male Circumcision and HIV: An Evidence-Based Public Health Approach
4. Research Synthesis: Systematic Review and Meta-Analysis of Vioxx and Cardiovascular Events

In March of 2003, the World Health Organization (WHO) declared a global health alert for severe acute respiratory syndrome (SARS). An acute respiratory illness, SARS was first mistaken for atypical pneumonia when patients presented to hospitals in Hong Kong and China. The case study, *Toronto Severe Acute Respiratory Syndrome II Experience*, takes place after SARS was identified as a new and deadly illness and presents the events as they unfolded in Canada after the first reported infections and deaths occurred in other countries.

The Toronto case examines how public health officials in the Ontario province of Canada grappled with the challenges of detecting and diagnosing a new disease, SARS, in 2003. As WHO and countries affected by SARS reacted and responded to the transmission of the disease, people were advised against traveling to infected regions, including Toronto. Over the course of 10 weeks in 2003, Toronto moved back and forth on worldwide travel advisories. This case considers lessons Toronto might have learned between its first outbreak and the second wave of cases that hit the city.

At the core of the Toronto SARS II case, as with the others in this section, is the use of epidemiology as an analytical process used to assess infection, risk, and response. All of the cases in this section can be used to help learners better under-

stand what epidemiologic measures are relevant, depending on the circumstances at hand. Learners will also have opportunities to practice calculations and to use the results to make recommendations for next steps.

Two cases in this section address the human immunodeficiency virus (HIV), but in very different circumstances. *A Feasibility Study of Routine Screening for HIV in an Urban Emergency Department* examines whether to institute a routine screening program for HIV in a Washington, DC, hospital. The District's AIDS incidence rate was higher than any other major metropolitan area in the United States in 2006. Further, national estimates indicated more than 1 million U.S. residents were infected with the human immunodeficiency virus, and approximately one-quarter of these individuals were unaware they were infected.[1]

In order to assess whether to begin a routine screening program, public health experts needed to consider who would be screened, estimate how many people would need to be screened, and estimate how many people screened would need counseling or other support. The concepts of prevalence, predictive value positive and predictive value negative are considered, along with exercises to calculate each. The case also pays close attention to the ethical and logistical issues a screening program would create for the hospital, health providers, patients, and the public health in general if executed.

Male Circumcision and HIV: An Evidence-Based Public Health Approach considers HIV from the perspective of public health experts making recommendations to countries around the world as they determine whether and how to create male circumcision interventions as a mechanism to decrease the transmission of HIV. The case begins by putting learners in the shoes of experts tasked with defining the problem and assessing the evidence for efficacy as to whether male circumcision works under the conditions in which it had been studied.

Again, epidemiologic methods lie at the heart of the case. Students are asked to assess evidence from randomized clinical trials on male circumcision as an intervention. The case study steps through the process by which such an analysis might be undertaken. Concepts such as relative risk, attributable risk percentage, and transmission rate are covered along with exercises to calculate each.

Both of the HIV cases address not just the analytical methods used to determine epidemiologic results, but also how to use this information in real-world circumstances. Data calculated in the abstract can be difficult to apply in populations involving actual human beings in complex societal settings! Sensitivity to cultural issues, the need for transparent and continued communication, and health systems issues are all key components of these cases.

To close the assessment section, *Research Synthesis: Systematic Review and Meta-Analysis of Vioxx and Cardiovascular Events* presents students with basic information on how to review, assess, and evaluate studies in order to summarize and interpret epidemiologic evidence on human health effects. The case explains the procedures used for conducting systematic reviews and meta-analyses.

After students become familiar with the methods, the case presents information from two systematic reviews and meta-analyses published by scientists scrutinizing adverse cardiovascular outcomes among patients using the drug rofecoxib (Vioxx®). Learners are encouraged to assess data and to interpret and draw conclusions about the information presented to them from the two published meta-analyses.

Assessment is the first step in a cycle of activities to support the public's health. The collected cases emphasize the use of evidence to drive solutions and policies. Just as importantly, these cases help provide key insights from real-world examples that move from the theoretical to the practical when deriving public health solutions.

REFERENCES

1. Branson BM, Handsfield HH, Lampe MA, et al. Revised recommendations for HIV testing of adults, adolescents, and pregnant women in healthcare settings. *MMWR Recomm Rep.* 2006;55(RR-14):1–17. http://www.cdc.gov/mmwr/PDF/rr/rr5514.pdf. Accessed September 25, 2009.

The Toronto Severe Acute Respiratory Syndrome II Experience

LARISSA MAY AND RICHARD SCHABAS

"SARS I was not avoidable. We were struck by lightning. Everything after that was [avoidable]."
—Dr. Richard Schabas, chief of staff, York Central Hospital

INTRODUCTION: SEVERE ACUTE RESPIRATORY SYNDROME II IN TORONTO: AN AVOIDABLE EPIDEMIC?[i]

In late April 2003, Toronto began to take a collective sigh of relief as severe acute respiratory syndrome (SARS) faded away. Toronto had been one of a handful of cities hit by SARS and the only one outside of East Asia. The hospital and public health sectors had operated in crisis mode since March. There had been a total of 140 probable SARS cases, 178 suspect cases, and 24 deaths in a metropolitan area of 4.5 million people.[1]

A provincial emergency had been declared on March 26. In an effort to decrease SARS transmission, strict infection control measures had been imposed on all area hospitals, and two hospitals had been shut down entirely to new admissions. About 20,000 people, possibly exposed to SARS, had been told to go into voluntary quarantine for 10 days.[1]

On April 23, the World Health Organization (WHO) had issued a travel advisory about Toronto—recommending against nonessential travel.[2] Toronto was the focus of unwel-

come global media attention. The city's reputation and its economy were suffering. The entire population was on edge.

And then SARS was gone, almost as suddenly as it had arrived. Public health authorities announced that there had been no new cases of SARS for 20 days—two full incubation periods. A delegation of dignitaries led by the provincial minister of health, an elected politician, had gone to WHO's headquarters in Geneva to plead Toronto's case that travelers were never at risk and the outbreak was over in any case. WHO officials seemed to be receptive to Toronto's message. On April 29, WHO lifted its Toronto travel advisory on the assumption that the SARS outbreak there was over.[3]

Cautious optimism began to replace the pervasive sense of gloom in Toronto.

However, Dr. Bill Osler, chief of staff at the North Toronto General Hospital (NTGH) was not so sanguine. He was aware of some troubling cases of pneumonia among staff and patients at NTGH over the course of a few weeks. None of these cases met the definition of SARS (see Box 1-1) because none of the staff or patients had direct contact with SARS patients.

Dr. Osler knew that pneumonia was not a rare disease, especially among hospitalized patients. SARS pneumonia is clinically and radiologically indistinguishable from pneumonia caused by dozens of other bacteria and viruses. Serologic tests for antibodies to the novel coronavirus that causes SARS were in their infancy and were still unreliable. There was no diagnostic test for SARS.

Dr. Osler was still concerned. NTGH did care for some SARS patients, although this was in a special isolation unit. Three of the five patients with hospital-acquired pneumo-

---

[i] This case study is based on the SARS II outbreak in Toronto in April to May 2003. However, many of the facts have been altered and the persons portrayed are fictional and not meant to represent any real persons.

nia were from the psychiatric ward—not a typical high-risk group. An NTGH nurse admitted to another hospital with a diagnosis of pneumonia did have direct exposure to an elderly orthopedic patient with hospital-acquired pneumonia. Typical hospital-acquired pneumonia is not contagious.

Dr. Osler shared his concerns on the biweekly teleconference of Toronto area hospitals and with public health officials. No one seemed interested. "SARS is over," was the attitude. Time to move on.

In early May, Dr. Osler and NTGH faced a crucial decision. Toronto was approaching 30 days—three maximum incubation periods—without a new reported case of SARS. Ontario and Toronto public health authorities were preparing to declare the outbreak over. This had already happened with the SARS outbreaks in Hanoi and Singapore. WHO had lifted Toronto's travel advisory.

More directly relevant to NTGH, the Ontario Ministry of Health announced that the strict infection control protocols—routine screening of staff, patients, and visitors; gowns, gloves, and respirator masks for all staff all of the time—imposed in March would be lifted on May 6. SARS was gone, the logic ran, so these precautions were no longer necessary.

However, Dr. Osler received some disquieting information. Several patients who had recently been discharged from the orthopedic ward at NTGH had developed pneumonia while at a nearby convalescent hospital. Postoperative pneumonia in elderly patients is not uncommon. Still, Dr. Osler

was concerned that NTGII had seen more than its share in the previous few weeks. The weight of circumstantial evidence was mounting that something unusual was afoot. Was this just a run of bad luck or could this have been SARS?

Dr. Osler was also aware of a commentary in the most recent edition of the *Canadian Medical Association Journal* (CMAJ) warning that Toronto hospitals needed to continue strict isolation procedures (see Box 1-2) for SARS.[4]

There would be substantial consequences—for NTGH, for the Toronto healthcare institutions, for public health, and for the provincial government—if this was declared a possible SARS outbreak. On the other hand, lifting the infection control measures and allowing SARS to spread unhindered would be too terrible to contemplate.

Dr. Osler looked back . . .

LIGHTNING STRIKES—SARS I

In November 2002, new cases of atypical pneumonia (subsequently determined to be caused by a novel coronavirus) began to appear in Guangdong Province in China.[5,6] Because atypical pneumonia is not unusual (the *atypical* refers to the causative organism and not any usual presentation) and the cases did not appear related, these early SARS cases were not recognized as a new disease.[7] On February 14, 2003, the World Health Organization reported more than 300 cases of atypical pneumonia in Guangdong, along with 5 deaths, since November 2002. Of particular concern was that more than 30% of cases occurred in healthcare workers—a very unusual pattern.

There was controversy about the causative agent. The Ministry of Health of China initially declared the illnesses were caused by *Chlamydia pneumoniae*—a common cause of atypical pneumonia. However, ProMED-mail, a global electronic reporting system for outbreaks of emerging infectious diseases, alerted its electronic mailing list subscribers that based on lack of autopsy confirmation, the illnesses might not be caused by *Chlamydia*.[1,8]

A physician from Guangdong, who had treated some of the cases of atypical pneumonia, arrived in Hong Kong to attend a family member's wedding and stayed at the Metropole Hotel on February 21.[1] Displaying signs of an illness that was later determined to be a new disease, termed severe acute respiratory syndrome (SARS), he subsequently infected at least a dozen hotel guests and travelers from several countries. On February 23, Mrs. K returned to Toronto from Hong Kong after a 10-day stay where she had been unknowingly exposed to the infected Chinese doctor. On her return home, she fell ill. After several days of fever, muscle aches, and a cough, Mrs. K died at home on March 5, 2003. No autopsy was performed, and her cause of death was attributed to a cardiac arrest.

On March 7, Mrs. K's son, Mr. T, who had not traveled to Hong Kong, became ill with a fever, cough, and worsening shortness of breath. He presented with these symptoms to Scarborough Grace Hospital's Emergency Department. Due to hospital overcrowding, he waited more than 18 hours in the emergency department for inpatient admission. During his emergency department stay, he received nebulized[ii,8] medications and had contact with many staff, patients, and outside visitors. Upon admission to a hospital ward, however, he was isolated due to concerns about tuberculosis. A public health investigation and contact tracing ensued as per routine public health guidelines. None of the physicians caring for Mrs. K or Mr. T were aware of the unusual respiratory infection that had started in Guangdong, China, spread to Hong Kong, and—at that point—Toronto.[1] (While Mr. T undoubtedly had SARS and was the critical case in triggering the Toronto outbreak, he did not meet the case definition for SARS because he had no history of either travel to China or contact with a person known to have SARS.)

Another early case in Toronto's first SARS outbreak (SARS I) was Mr. P, who had been in the emergency department bed next to Mr. T's at Scarborough Grace Hospital. He became ill about 1 week later. He was later admitted to the ICU, where he died 5 days later. His wife and several other family members were infected.

Mr. D was another Scarborough Grace patient infected in the emergency department. He became ill at home and was admitted back into Scarborough Grace Hospital in mid-March with acute shortness of breath. This symptom was ascribed to congestive heart failure. Since Mr. D had kidney failure, he was transferred to a regional dialysis center—York Central Hospital—without any warnings about the advisability of respiratory precautions. Mr. D proceeded to trigger the second large hospital outbreak of SARS I.[1]

Meanwhile, on the other side of Canada, a separate index patient who had traveled from Hong Kong arrived at the Vancouver general hospital with respiratory symptoms. The Vancouver hospital had been alerted to the danger of SARS, and this patient, unlike Toronto's Mr. K, met the case definition because he had traveled to China. This man was placed in strict respiratory isolation immediately and no secondary cases developed.[1]

THE PUBLIC HEALTH RESPONSE TO SARS I

On March 12, WHO declared a global health alert for a new disease being called severe acute respiratory syndrome (SARS).[9] SARS was predominantly occurring among healthcare workers in Hanoi and Hong Kong. Local, provincial, and national public health agencies failed to alert Toronto's hospital physicians about the new threat. Rather, clinicians discovered the WHO alert on their own and on March 13 reported the Toronto cluster to Health Canada. The following day, Health Canada began a coordinated public health response and information-sharing campaign.[1]

Ultimately, about 80% of the SARS cases in Toronto were hospital acquired by staff and patients.[10] Virtually all of the other Toronto SARS cases were from household contact with a person who had become infected in a hospital. This was truly a hospital-driven outbreak.

Mr. K's visit to Scarborough Grace Hospital Emergency Department was the lightning strike. Since Mr. K didn't even meet the SARS case definition, it was hard to see how the outbreak could have been prevented entirely. But, if a public health announcement had gone out earlier or if communications between hospitals and public health had been more robust, SARS I in Toronto would have been much less severe.

On March 23, the Ontario Ministry of Health closed Scarborough Grace Hospital to all new admissions after more than 50 SARS cases were linked to that institution. On March 26, a provincial emergency was declared and the Ministry of Health assumed a more direct role in managing Toronto's 26 acute care hospitals. On March 29, York Central Hospital was also closed when a new cluster of SARS cases appeared there.[1]

[ii] Procedures that were high risk for aerosolization of the SARS coronavirus, including intubation and nebulization, were thought to have contributed to SARS transmission in the healthcare setting and especially among healthcare workers.

Strict new infection control measures were mandated for all Toronto hospitals. Everyone entering a Toronto hospital—staff, visitors, and patients alike—was screened for respiratory illness. (Ironically, hospitals were the only places with active disease. People should have been screened on the way out, not on the way in.) All hospital staff wore full protective gear—gowns, respirator N95 masks, and gloves. Most outpatient services were cancelled, as was elective surgery. Public health officials ordered about 20,000 people—mostly staff, patients, and visitors from Scarborough Grace and York Central Hospitals—into quarantine. All hospitals were mandated to develop specialized SARS units.[1] After an investigation of the initial outbreak in Toronto, a press conference was held.

Toronto public health was overwhelmed by the sheer effort of trying to track tens of thousands of potentially exposed people. Epidemiologic information systems were also overwhelmed, not by the number of cases (which was never very large) but by the volume of alleged contacts. Ultimately, only a small fraction of people directed into quarantine were compliant. Jurisdictional and personality conflicts added to an overall sense of crisis and confusion.

Second-, third-, and fourth-generation cases appeared. All were directly linked to Mr. K by direct contact with SARS patients. Despite fears and numerous false alarms, there was little or no community (i.e., nonhospital) spread beyond the household contacts of hospital-acquired cases.

As the Easter and Passover holidays approached, Toronto braced itself for the anticipated explosion of cases. But then, like the morning dew, the crisis evaporated. It seemed that SARS was gone as quickly as it had come. In addition, the SARS outbreaks in Hanoi and Singapore seemed to be over, too, and the news from Hong Kong, with the largest outbreak, was encouraging.

COULD SARS II HAVE BEEN PREVENTED BY THE LESSONS LEARNED FROM SARS I?

On May 5, Dr. Osler organized a roundtable meeting for key stakeholders; they brought with them the evidence assembled to date. Meeting attendees included:

1. Dr. Bill Osler, who represented NTGH. NTGH had a major stake in the decision. If a SARS outbreak were declared, NTGH would be put into virtual lockdown for at least 20 days. Thousands of staff, inpatients, outpatients, and visitors would be ordered into quarantine. The hospital's reputation would be seriously damaged. On the other hand, if this were SARS and nothing were done, then everyone associated with NTGH would have been in grave peril.

Question 1 What were the options available to NTGH? Did NTGH need to be closed? Did the risks of not declaring a SARS outbreak outweigh the immediate penalties?

2. Dr. Norm Bethune, who represented Toronto Public Health, the local public health agency in the forefront of the response to SARS. The efforts required to quarantine 20,000 people had exhausted public health staff. Although a recent CMAJ commentary[4] questioned the value of quarantine in SARS control, Toronto Public Health was committed to quarantine strategy. Furthermore, public health limited the designation of SARS to pneumonia cases with a direct contact with a probable SARS case—all tracing back to the Toronto index case in February. The NTGH cases lacked this crucial "epi link." Designating these cases as SARS would have thrown into question the whole definition of the outbreak, as well as its apparent control. Declaring a SARS outbreak at NTGH would plunge Toronto Public Health back into crisis.

Question 2 Was the demand for an epi link too rigid? Did the case definition need to be broadened? Was mass quarantine a necessary response to an NTGH outbreak? Were less draconian responses available? Did the risks of an underresponse outweigh the penalties of an overresponse?

3. Dr. Chuck Best, an infectious disease consultant who had become the recognized SARS expert. He was the principal medical advisor to Toronto Public Health and the Ministry of Health and a prominent media "talking head." Dr. Best had reviewed the NTGH cases and concluded that they were not SARS. This was based on his clinical review of the cases, the absence of an "epi link," and negative serology. Dr. Best's laboratory had done the serology testing of these patients and he thought the testing was reliable, both sensitive and specific. A negative test meant no SARS. Dr. Best didn't think the cases of hospital-acquired pneumonia at NTGH were so unusual. He had seen thousands in his long career.

Question 3 The reliability of clinical and laboratory diagnosis of SARS is uncertain. Should it be used as the basis for public health decision making? What are the differences between public health case definitions and clinical diagnostic criteria? What was the appropriate application of both in this context? Did Dr. Best really know the reasonable background rate of hospital-acquired pneumonia?

4. Edie Cavell, who was the chief nurse at NTGH. She had insisted that Dr. Osler invite her to the roundtable. Cavell

had only one real issue—worker safety. There had already been more than 30 cases of SARS among healthcare workers in Toronto, and three victims—two nurses and a doctor—had died. She was stridently opposed to lifting the respiratory precautions at NTGH until there were no more cases of pneumonia.

Question 4 Was her position reasonable? Were respiratory precautions for all staff, all of the time really necessary, or would stringent surveillance and strict isolation and precautions for those actually ill with pneumonia suffice? Are there occupational hazards associated with full precautions all of the time?

5. Dr. Fred Banting, who represented the provincial Ministry of Health. Dr. Banting was a nonpartisan civil servant, but he was aware of the political and economic ramifications of the issues. Declaring a SARS outbreak at NTGH would plunge Toronto back into the figurative SARS doghouse. WHO might reinstate its travel advisory and Toronto's protests would have very little credibility in the future. The economy would suffer, particularly the lucrative summer tourist trade. The minister's personal involvement meant that any backtracking would have a political impact. A provincial election was pending. Declaring a SARS outbreak at NTGH could bring down the government.

Question 5 Are nonhealth issues economic, political, and public confidence—valid considerations? How do we weigh the relative costs and benefits of these competing interests? Should these concerns even be on the table at all? What would be the economic and political costs of missing a SARS outbreak?

EPILOGUE

Box 1-3 describes the time line of the SARS outbreak, which ultimately led to over 8,000 cases, including 1,700 cases in healthcare workers. The case fatality rate among probable SARS cases varied from 4% (China)[iii] to 18% (Toronto). Up to 30% of patients required critical care.[11–13] SARS led to worldwide panic and a rapid response to the outbreak, including travel restrictions, quarantine measures, and collaborative research leading to the discovery of the new virus.[14] WHO announced in July 2003 the outbreak had been contained.

Ultimately, there were 250 confirmed SARS cases in Ontario, and 44 SARS deaths spread over almost 4 months, all

in the Toronto area. Ontario's response to the first SARS wave, SARS I, was guided by implementation of the provincial emergency and the mandated decrease in elective and ambulatory hospital activity, the creation of SARS isolation units, implementation of personal protective measures for staff, and strict infection control measures in hospitals.[1] The real burden of SARS I was felt in a handful of hospitals, primarily Scarborough Grace and York Central, accounting for almost all of the cases.[1]

The Scientific Advisory Committee, comprised of Toronto physicians and public health experts, developed voluntary quarantine and isolation guidelines. Unfortunately, the participation of these individuals on the committee limited their provision of direct care, in part due to concerns that placing them at risk of contracting the virus would compromise the entire committee.[1]

Barriers to infection control included the lack of staffing and the inability to compare baseline rates for respiratory infections due to the paucity of epidemiologic data. In late April and early May, officials at North Toronto General Hospital and Toronto Public Health investigated multiple cases of pneumonia, including those on the orthopedic ward, and determined those cases to be due to postoperative infection.[1] On May 23, about 1 week after the WHO declaration that Toronto was SARS free, health officials declared a second SARS outbreak in Toronto (SARS II), despite the unclear epidemiologic link.

In the postincident evaluation, Dr. Richard Schabas, chief of staff of York Central Hospital, declared "SARS I was not avoidable. We were struck by lightning. Everything after that was [avoidable]."[1]

SARS II was more explosive than SARS I, with almost as many cases. SARS had been allowed to spread virtually unchecked in North Toronto General Hospital and St. John's Convalescent Hospital for several weeks. However, once announced, the second outbreak was controlled quickly. There were only a few new infections contracted after May 23—all in household contacts—and the last Toronto SARS case was probably infected around June 5. Then it was over. Really.

SARS was controlled quickly and relatively easily by identifying and isolating suspected cases and using strict infection control in their care. Mass quarantine of suspected SARS contacts was used more aggressively in Toronto than in other SARS outbreaks. Ultimately, more than 30,000 people were ordered into quarantine. Evidence subsequently confirmed that SARS was not infective during its incubation period—the target of quarantine—and quarantine is now discouraged for SARS control by WHO.[15]

Ultimately, SARS was controlled because it was only significantly infective to very close contacts of very ill people.

---

iii Advocates for traditional Chinese medicine were disappointed to learn that the lower mortality in China was a reflection of the younger, healthier demographics of the population affected there.

BOX 1-3 SARS Time Line

November 16, 2002	The first case of an atypical pneumonia is reported in the Guangdong province in southern China.
February 26, 2003	First cases of unusual pneumonia are reported in Hanoi, Vietnam.
February 28, 2003	World Health Organization officer Carlo Urbani, MD, examines an American businessman with an unknown form of pneumonia in a French hospital in Hanoi, Vietnam.
March 10, 2003	Urbani reports an unusual outbreak of illness, which he calls sudden acute respiratory syndrome or SARS, to the main office of the WHO. He notes that the disease has affected an unusually high number of healthcare workers (22) at the hospital.
March 11, 2003	A similar outbreak of a mysterious respiratory disease is reported among healthcare workers in Hong Kong.
March 12, 2003	WHO issues a global alert about a new infectious disease of unknown origin in both Vietnam and Hong Kong.
March 15, 2003	WHO issues a heightened global health alert about the mysterious pneumonia with a case definition of SARS after cases in Singapore and Canada are also identified. The alert includes a rare emergency travel advisory to international travelers, healthcare professionals and health authorities. CDC issues a travel advisory stating that persons consider postponing travel to the affected areas in Asia (Hong Kong, Singapore, Vietnam, and China).
March 17, 2003	An international network of 11 leading laboratories is established to determine the cause of SARS and develop potential treatments. CDC holds its first briefing on SARS and says the first 14 suspected SARS cases are being investigated in the U.S.
March 24, 2003	CDC officials present the first evidence that a new strain of a virus most frequently associated with upper respiratory infections and the common cold in humans called the coronavirus might be likely cause of SARS.
March 29, 2003	Carlo Urbani, who identified the first cases of SARS, dies as a result of the disease. Researchers later suggest naming the agent that causes the disease after the infectious disease expert.
April 2, 2003	WHO issues its first travel warning recommending that all non-essential travel to Hong Kong and Guangdong province be postponed.
April 3, 2003	WHO-sponsored team of international infectious disease experts arrives in Guangdong province to investigate the outbreak.
April 4, 2003	President George W. Bush adds SARS to the list of quarantinable diseases, which gives the CDC the authority to isolate persons who might have been exposed to the disease.
April 9, 2003	WHO investigative team gives initial report on Guangdong outbreak. The team found evidence of "super spreaders" who were capable of infecting as many as 100 persons.
April 12, 2003	Canadian researchers announce they have completed the first successful sequencing of the genome of the coronavirus believed to cause SARS.
April 14, 2003	CDC officials announce their laboratories have sequenced a nearly identical strain of the SARS-related coronavirus. The CDC version includes an additional 15 nucleotides, which provides the important beginning of the sequence.
April 16, 2003	A new form of a coronavirus never before seen in humans is confirmed as the cause of SARS according to Koch's postulates, which are four specific conditions that must be met for a pathogen to be confirmed as a causal agent of disease.
April 22, 2003	The CDC issues a health alert for travelers to Toronto, which is the epicenter of the Canadian outbreak of SARS. CDC director Julie Gerberding says the health alert alone is not a reason for potential travelers to avoid travel to the U.S. neighbor to the north, but it is part of the agency's effort to give travelers practical information to protect themselves from the global threat of SARS.

BOX 1-3   SARS Time Line (Continued)

April 23, 2003	The World Health Organization adds Toronto, Beijing, and the Shanxi province of China to the list of regions travelers should avoid to reduce the risk of becoming infected with SARS and taking the deadly disease back home with them. WHO officials say the travel advisory will remain in effect for at least the next three weeks.
April 28, 2003	WHO removes Vietnam from list of SARS affected areas, making it the first country to contain SARS successfully. WHO also lifts travel advisory to Hanoi, Vietnam.
April 29, 2003	The WHO lifts its warning against nonessential travel to Toronto, Canada, citing local measures to stop the spread of SARS. The affected area had not reported new cases in the preceding 20 days.
May 6, 2003	The CDC lifts its travel advisory for Singapore because no new cases of SARS had been reported in 20 days.
May 15, 2003	The CDC removes its travel alert for Hanoi, Vietnam because more than 30 days have elapsed since the last SARS symptoms were reported.
May 17, 2003	WHO extends its travel warning to include Hebei Province, China. A similar warning to postpone all non-essential travel is in effect for Hong Kong, Taipei, Taiwan, and several other areas of mainland China, including Beijing, Guangdong, Inner Mongolia, Shanxi, and Tianjin.
May 20, 2003	The CDC lifts its travel alert for Toronto, Canada, because more than 30 days have elapsed since the last case of SARS was reported there.
May 23, 2003	The WHO lifts its advisory against all but essential travel to Hong Kong and the Guangdong province of China saying the SARS situation in those areas has improved significantly.
May 26, 2003	The WHO changes the status of Toronto, Canada, listing it as an area where SARS has recently been transmitted locally after Canadian health officials report new clusters of 26 suspect and eight probable SARS cases linked to four Toronto hospitals.
May 31, 2003	The WHO removes Singapore from the list of areas where SARS has been transmitted locally. It has been 20 days after the last locally transmitted case was reported.
June 13, 2003	WHO lifts its travel warning against nonessential travel to several provinces in China, including Hebei, Inner Mongolia, Shanxi, and Tianjin.
June 17, 2003	WHO lifts its travel warning against nonessential travel to Taiwan. CDC downgrades its travel warning for mainland China to a travel alert, although a travel warning from both the CDC and WHO remains in effect for Beijing.
June 23, 2003	WHO removes Hong Kong from its list of areas with recent local SARS transmission after 20 days passed since the last SARS case was reported and isolated, which breaks the chain of human-to-human transmission and eliminates the risk of infection for both local residents and travelers.
June 24, 2003	WHO removes its last remaining SARS travel warning for Beijing, China. The city was also removed from the WHO's list of areas with recent SARS transmission after 20 days passed since the last new SARS case was isolated.
June 25, 2003	CDC downgrades its travel SARS travel advice for Beijing, China and Taiwan from "advisory" to "alert" status, which does not advise against travel to the regions but informs travelers of a SARS health concern and advises them to take precautions.
July 2, 2003	WHO removes Toronto, Canada from its list of areas with recent local SARS transmission after 20 days passed since the last SARS case was reported and isolated.
July 8, 2003	CDC lifts its SARS travel alert for Toronto, Canada after more than 30 days had elapsed since the date of onset of symptoms for the last SARS case.
July 9, 2003	CDC lifts its SARS travel alert for Hong Kong retroactively to July 1 because the last SARS case there was reported on May 31.

Source: Data from WebMD Health News, SARS: Timeline of an Outbreak. http://www.webmd.com/lung/news/20030411/sars-timeline-of-outbreak. Published 2003. Accessed March 1, 2011.

This explained the heavy concentration of cases in hospital staff and patients. SARS could spread efficiently in an unsuspecting acute care hospital, but it could not support sustained spread in the community. Once hospitals responded to the danger, SARS died out. SARS is best described as an animal (zoonotic) infection with limited capacity for human-to-human spread rather than a true human infection. Given its known infectivity and virulence, SARS was likely never a true pandemic threat.

Although it is difficult to estimate, SARS had a great economic impact—up to 2% of gross domestic product of the six affected cities. Hong Kong and Singapore were hardest hit economically, largely due to their high level of consumer trade and retail activity.[7] In Ontario's provincial election in October 2003, the progressive conservative government was defeated, in part because of its perceived mismanagement of SARS.

About the Authors

Larissa May, MD, is assistant professor of emergency medicine, epidemiology and biostatistics, and microbiology and tropical medicine at The George Washington University in Washington, DC. Dr. May completed her MD and residency training and her MSPH at The George Washington University. She is a member of The George Washington Hospital's Infection Control and Emergency Management committees. Formerly codirector of the master of science in public health microbiology and emerging infectious diseases, Dr. May has experience developing curricula in emerging infectious diseases and disease surveillance for undergraduate, medical, and graduate students, as well as clinicians and public health practitioners. Dr. May is chair of the Education and Training committee of the International Society for Disease Surveillance. Her principal academic interests are in emerging infectious diseases, syndromic surveillance, emergency preparedness, and novel educational methods.

Richard Schabas, MD, FRCPC, is an internal medicine and public health physician. Dr. Schabas was Ontario's chief medical officer of health from 1987 to 1997. He was chief of staff at York Central Hospital during the 2003 SARS outbreak. He is currently medical officer of health for the Hastings and Prince Edward Counties Health Unit in Ontario, Canada, consultant internist at Campbellford Memorial Hospital, and an adjunct associate professor at Queen's University School of Medicine.

REFERENCES

1. Health Canada. Learning from SARS. Renewal of Public Health in Canada. Available from: http://www.phac-aspc.gc.ca/publicat/sars-sras/naylor. Published October 2003. Accessed November 15, 2010.

2. World Health Organization. Global Alert and Response Network. Update 37—WHO extends its SARS-related travel advice to Beijing and Shanxi Province in China and to Toronto Canada. http://www.who.int/csr/sars/archive/2003_04_23/en/index.html. Published April 23, 2003. Accessed November 15, 2010.

3. World Health Organization. Global Alert and Response Network. Update 42—Travel advice for Toronto, situation in China. http://www.who.int/csr/sars/archive/2003_04_29/en/index.html. Published April 29, 2003. Accessed November 15, 2010.

4. Schabas R. SARS: prudence not panic. *CMAJ.* May 2003;168:1432–1434.

5. Xu R, He J, Evans M, et al. Epidemiologic clues to SARS origin in China. *Emerg Infect Dis.* 2004;10(6):1030–1037.

6. Rosling L, Rosling M. Pneumonia causes panic in Guangdong Province. *BMJ.* 2003;326(7386):416.

7. United States General Accounting Office. Report to the Chairman, Subcommittee on Asia and the Pacific, Committee on International Relations, House of Representatives. *Emerging infectious diseases. Asian SARS outbreak challenged international and national responses*; 2004. Washington, DC, United States General Accounting Office.

8. ProMED Mail. PRO/EDR> Pneumonia—China (Guangdong) (06). http://www.promedmail.org/pls/otn/f?p=2400:1202:254157255849534 1::NO::F2400_P1202_CHECK_DISPLAY,F2400_P1202_PUB_MAIL_ID:X,20756. Published February 20, 2003. Accessed November 15, 2010.

9. Scto WH, Tsang D, Yung RW, et al., and Advisors of Expert SARS Group of Hospital Authority. Effectiveness of precautions against droplets and contact in prevention of nosocomial transmission of severe acute respiratory syndrome (SARS). *Lancet.* 2003;361:1519–1520.

10. World Health Organization. Global Outbreak and Response Network. WHO issues a global alert about cases of atypical pneumonia. Cases of severe respiratory illness may spread to hospital staff. http://www.who.int/csr/sars/archive/2003_03_12/en/index.html. March 12, 2003 press release. Accessed November 15, 2010.

11. Booth CM, Matukas LM, Tomlinson GA, et al. Clinical features and short-term outcomes of 144 patients with SARS in the Greater Toronto area. *JAMA.* June 4, 2003;289(21):1–9. http://jama.ama-assn.org/cgi/reprint/289.21.JOC30885v1.pdf. Accessed November 15, 2010.

12. Ksiazek T, Erdman D, Goldsmith C, et al. A novel coronavirus associated with severe acute respiratory syndrome. *N Engl J Med.* 2003;348(20):1953–1966.

13. Poon L, Guan Y, Nicholls J, et al. The aetiology, origins, and diagnosis of severe acute respiratory syndrome. *Lancet Infect Dis.* 2004;4(11):663–671.

14. Phua GC, Govert J. Mechanical ventilation in an airborne epidemic. *Clin Chest Med.* 2008;29(2):323–328.

15. Peiris J, Yuen K, Osterhaus A, et al. The severe acute respiratory syndrome. *N Engl J Med.* 2003;349(25):2431–2441.

16. Heymann DL, ed. *Control of communicable diseases in man.* 19th ed. APHA; 2008:555. Washington, DC.

A Feasibility Study of Routine Screening for HIV in an Urban Emergency Department

KATHERINE L. HUNTING AND JEREMY BROWN

A BOLD UNDERTAKING

It was spring 2006. The Centers for Disease Control and Prevention (CDC) estimated more than 1 million U.S. residents were infected with the human immunodeficiency virus (HIV), and approximately one-quarter of these individuals were unaware they were infected. In 2004, 39% of people diagnosed with AIDS had first tested positive for HIV infection less than 1 year prior to their AIDS diagnosis; a large majority of these individuals were already symptomatic by the time they learned that they were HIV infected.[1] These two statistics illustrated vividly that HIV screening programs—directed at early detection among pregnant women, persons at high risk, and healthcare settings with high HIV prevalence—were not adequately reaching infected individuals.

A team of physicians and epidemiologists from the George Washington University (GW) Medical Center in Washington, DC, was focusing closer to home. Every day, their work reminded them that Washington's AIDS incidence rate was higher than any other major metropolitan area in the United States. They were familiar with numerous studies demonstrating that individuals who know their HIV status and are able to receive counseling and treatment not only live longer (a personal health benefit), but also change their behavior, thereby reducing the likelihood of infecting others (a population health benefit).[2,3]

Because of the severe impact of HIV/AIDS in the District of Columbia, this team, led by Dr. Jeremy Brown, was contemplating a bold new undertaking—a project to test the feasibility of implementing near-universal opt-out HIV screening at the emergency department (ED) of The George Washington University Hospital. As safety net providers, emergency departments are the most likely source of medical services for low-income and indigent people[4] who are also among those most at risk of acquiring HIV infection. The GW ED provided care to a diverse population of 60,000 patients annually, and many of its patients might not otherwise have a regular source of medical care where they could be screened for HIV.

Dr. Brown and his team members knew they faced numerous challenges if they were to get the proposed program off the ground in the fall of 2006, including:

- Convincing hospital administrators they should screen everyone, rather than just individuals who fit a high-risk profile
- Estimating the number of people who would assent to be screened
- Estimating the number that would screen positive, and of those, the number that would and would not be infected with HIV
- Deciding whether to conduct confirmatory testing in the ED or to refer people who screened positive to other providers for confirmatory testing
- Deciding whether they were comfortable with the ethical and civil liberties implications associated with omitting substantial pretest counseling and written informed consent from the HIV screening process
- Anticipating other challenges that might be encountered during the pilot project

A BRIEF HISTORY OF HIV

Researchers believe HIV-1 (the predominant strain of HIV in the developed world) originated in chimpanzees native to west equatorial Africa, and the virus entered humans in the mid-1900s via hunters exposed to infected blood. HIV first emerged in the United States between 1979 and 1981 among men who had sex with other men. The term *acquired immunodeficiency syndrome* (AIDS) was coined in 1982 to denote the spectrum of illnesses associated with advanced HIV infection; U.S. surveillance of AIDS cases began the same year.[5] HIV testing first became available in 1985; the incidence of HIV in the United States also peaked around that time. There was no effective treatment, but in 1987, the U.S. Public Health Service began to promote HIV counseling and testing as a means of preventing spread of the disease. Since 2000, the number of new cases per year in the United States has been relatively stable at 55,000 to 58,500.[6]

In 1996, with the advent of antiretroviral therapy, the progression of HIV infections to AIDS decreased markedly in the United States and other countries where antiretroviral therapies were available. With these new medications, HIV went from being a fatal disease to a chronic disease. Screening to identify HIV infection in asymptomatic individuals now enables a true delay in symptoms and improved survival.[1]

HIV SCREENING POLICY: THE NATIONAL AND LOCAL LANDSCAPE

Since 2001, CDC guidelines called for HIV screening among pregnant women, persons at high risk, and in healthcare settings with high HIV prevalence (defined as HIV seroprevalence rates of > 1% or AIDS diagnosis rates of > 1 per 1,000 discharges). Recommendations to screen pregnant women as a routine part of prenatal care had, for the 5 years leading up to the 2001 policy, incorporated streamlined pretest counseling and informed consent processes to reduce barriers for providers. However, screening in high-risk populations required more extensive pretest counseling and written informed consent. Because it can be difficult to identify high-prevalence healthcare settings and because of resource constraints, many healthcare providers did not introduce HIV screening programs as called for in the CDC guidelines.[1]

The CDC recognized that the effectiveness of risk-based HIV screening was limited, and throughout 2005 it engaged in a comprehensive evaluation of strategies to expand HIV testing. This process included broad input from healthcare providers, public health agencies, community organizations, people living with HIV, researchers, and clinicians. Dr. Brown and his GW colleagues were aware that the CDC was pre-paring to recommend, later in 2006, a major change in HIV screening policy—opt-out HIV screening for almost all patients in virtually all healthcare settings.[1]

Specifically, the CDC was planning to recommend routine opt-out screening for all patients aged 13–64 years, unless the "prevalence of undiagnosed HIV infection in their patients has been documented to be < 0.1%."[1(p 7)] Opt-out screening meant "performing HIV screening after notifying the patient that 1) the test will be performed and 2) the patient may elect to decline or defer testing. Assent is inferred unless the patient declines testing."[1(p 4)] The CDC was further planning to specify that:

- "Separate written consent for HIV testing should not be required; general consent for medical care should be considered sufficient to encompass consent for HIV testing."[1(p 3)]
- "Prevention counseling should not be required with HIV diagnostic testing or as part of HIV screening programs in healthcare settings."[1(p 3)]

Meanwhile, the District of Columbia Department of Health was also aware of the upcoming changes in the CDC's recommendations for HIV screening in healthcare settings. Because of the severe impact of HIV/AIDS in the District of Columbia, the DC Department of Health was planning to adopt a groundbreaking initiative that went even further: to encourage HIV screening for every District resident between the ages of 14 and 84 and to immediately refer those who test positive for counseling, medical care, and treatment. The Department of Health was working to launch its new program, "Come Together DC—Get Screened for HIV," on June 27, 2006, National HIV Testing Day.[7]

So, in the spring of 2006, with HIV screening policy changes on the horizon at both the national and local levels, healthcare providers were weighing their options. On the one hand, universal HIV screening seemed like a positive public health move. On the other hand, many administrators grumbled that the upcoming policy changes constituted an unfunded mandate—yet another procedure requiring materials and personnel time without the promise of full cost recovery. This strain would be particularly evident in hospital emergency departments, whose primary mission was to care for urgently ill or injured patients—*not* to conduct public health programs.

HIV SCREENING TESTS

In March 2004, the U.S. Food and Drug Administration approved the OraQuick Advance HIV1/2 Antibody Test (also called the "HIV rapid test," "rapid HIV test," "rapid oral swab test," and "rapid test") for use in screening both oral fluid and plasma for HIV antibodies.[8] Previously, a whole blood specimen from either a finger stick or tube of blood was needed for testing.

With the HIV rapid test, the oral fluid specimen is collected via a gum swab and produces a result in 20 to 40 minutes. Interpretation is visual and no instrumentation is required.

The GW ED could obtain screening test kits at no cost from the DC Department of Health.

A reactive (positive) rapid test result means that HIV-1 or HIV-2 antibodies have been detected in the specimen. Clinical studies by the manufacturer demonstrated a sensitivity of 99.3% and a specificity of 99.8%.[8] Like other antibody tests for HIV, the rapid test is not able to detect recent infections; false negative results may occur within a window period of up to 3 months following infection with HIV. This is why CDC recommended that any individual who tests negative but who has had known or suspected exposure to HIV within 3 months should be instructed to obtain repeat screening 3 months after the exposure.[9]

Although they are extremely accurate, rapid test results are not definitive; therefore confirmatory testing using either Western blot or immunofluorescent assay methods is necessary for all positive rapid HIV test results. The Western blot assay, more expensive and technically more difficult to perform than screening tests, is the gold standard, considered to be 100% accurate. It generally takes several days to obtain Western blot results.

NAILING DOWN THE DETAILS: WHAT TO EXPECT?

The GW Hospital is a tertiary care hospital serving a diverse group of patients, including residents of Washington, DC and nearby Maryland and Virginia, as well as tourists and visiting dignitaries. About 60,000 patients are treated annually in the ED, which is a level I trauma center.

Surveillance data from 2004 (the latest year with complete data) indicated at least 3% of Washington, DC residents had been diagnosed with HIV infection.[7,10] However, Dr. Brown and his team did not know the prevalence of undiagnosed HIV infection among the GW ED patient population. They were also uncertain as to whether those who opted out of the routine screening program would have a different prevalence of infection from those who agreed to be tested.

In addition to not screening patients who already knew they were HIV-positive or had been given an HIV test in the previous 3 months, the research team made some up-front decisions about what, for this pilot study, they would exclude from screening. The exclusions included:

- Patients who did not speak English or Spanish (because the patient needed to give informed verbal consent)
- Patients who had an altered mental status (because they could not give informed consent)
- Patients who required urgent medical intervention (because their urgent medical needs took priority)

They also questioned the utility of screening older patients. Because of disproportionately low HIV prevalence among older adults, the CDC had called for screening through age 64 years.[11,12] But the DC Department of Health, which was providing the HIV test kits free of charge, wanted to expand testing to persons up to age 84.

To inform their pilot program, the research team found it useful to model screening program results under varying scenarios. They enlisted their research assistant, a public health student named Priya who had recently completed her first epidemiology course. Eager to get some practical experience, Priya agreed to help with some calculations. For ease of comparing results, they asked her to base calculations on three scenarios, each involving 10,000 GW ED patients who would meet screening criteria and agree to be tested using the HIV rapid test (sensitivity 99.3%; specificity 99.8%).

Scenario 1: Ages 65 to 84
Assumption: Actual prevalence of undiagnosed HIV infection in screening population = 0.1%

Scenario 2: Ages 13 to 64—low estimate
Assumption: Actual prevalence of undiagnosed HIV infection in screening population = 1.0%

Scenario 3: Ages 13 to 64—high estimate
Assumption: Actual prevalence of undiagnosed HIV infection in screening population = 3.0%

Priya learned in her epidemiology class what to do next, so she got out her calculator and got to work. Follow Priya's process to come up with projected screening program results under these three scenarios and present them to Dr. Brown. The formulas in Box 2-1 will be helpful for those who need a review of screening statistics.

Question 1

For each of the three scenarios, Priya constructed a two-by-two table to show the distribution of screening results. Dr. Brown reminded her to be sure to round all cell values to whole numbers.

Then, for each scenario, she calculated the predictive value positive (PVP) and the predictive value negative (PVN). She found that one decimal place was fine for PVP

BOX 2-1 Review of Screening Statistics— Applied to HIV Rapid Test Screening

	HIV Infection		
Rapid Test	**Yes**	**No**	**Total**
Positive	True positive (A)	False positive (B)	Total test + (A + B)
Negative	False negative (C)	True negative (D)	Total test − (C + D)
Total	Total with HIV infection (A + C)	Total without HIV (B + D)	Total screened

Sensitivity: the percent probability that the HIV rapid test result will be positive when administered to persons who are actually infected with HIV.

Sensitivity
$= [A / (A + C)] \times 100$

Specificity: the percent probability that the HIV rapid test result will be negative when administered to persons who are not infected with HIV.

Specificity
$= [D / (B + D)] \times 100$

Predictive Value Positive: the percent probability that a person with a positive HIV rapid test is actually infected with HIV.

$PVP = [A / (A+B)] \times 100$

Predictive Value Negative: the percent probability that a person with a negative HIV rapid test is not infected with HIV.

$PVN = [D / (C+D)] \times 100$

If you are given HIV prevalence, test sensitivity, and test specificity, and asked to fill in a two-by-two table for a given screening population size, here are the steps:

1. First fill in the total screened. For example, in scenarios 1, 2, and 3, the total screened is N = 10,000.
2. Multiply N by the prevalence to calculate the marginal value for the number of people with HIV infection.
3. Subtract to fill in the number of people without HIV infection.
4. Use your sensitivity and specificity values to fill in the internal cells of the table. Round all cell values to whole numbers.

---

but she needed to use two decimal places to distinguish differences in PVN. Construct Priya's three tables, and for each one, calculate PVP and PVN.

Question 2 Priya met with Dr. Brown to summarize the key findings from the three sets of calculations. What would her important points have been?

Question 3 Dr. Brown asked Priya to specifically detail the pros and cons for including individuals age 65 and over in this screening program. What pros and cons would she have likely identified?

OPERATIONALIZING PILOT STUDY LOGISTICS

Impressed by Priya's ability to calculate and interpret screening statistics, Dr. Brown and his team invited her to also help develop the study's operations manual. One section of the manual included scripts for communicating various test re-

sults to patients. The purpose of these scripts was for healthcare providers to describe in lay terms what the screening results meant for prototypical patients. In language that the average person can understand, the scripts were to explain what the test values indicate about the possibility of HIV infection and what the patient should do next.

Question 4 In one script, Priya was to assume that HIV prevalence in the screened population was 3.0%, as in scenario 3. If an asymptomatic 23-year-old woman had a reactive (positive) HIV rapid test, what should the healthcare worker have told her?

Question 5 Another script was based on scenario 1, with an HIV prevalence of 0.1%. If an asymptomatic 68-year-old man had a positive HIV rapid test, how should the script have been different for communicating his results?

Question 6 Finally, Priya assumed that the HIV prevalence was 1% as in scenario 2. A 31-year-old woman was being treated in the ED for symptoms of a sexually transmitted disease. How should the script have read for describing the results of her *negative* HIV rapid test?

A positive test result will ultimately lead to in-depth counseling. However, the GW ED protocol for patients who screened negative indicated they would only be given written materials about preventing HIV infection, regardless of whether a patient was in a high-risk group. This represented the loss of a potentially teachable moment, where some type of intervention may have prevented disease transmission. In fact, since 1994, CDC has recommended client-centered counseling for individuals with high-risk behaviors, focusing on the development of individualized prevention goals and strategies.[1] Some states even have detailed legal requirements for counseling. (See, for example, www.nccc.ucsf.edu/StateLaws/Index.html.)

Priya was aware that CDC's upcoming recommendations[1] would not recommend required prevention counseling as part of HIV screening programs in healthcare settings. This was a radical change from the way things had been done in the past, but she was particularly troubled that pretest counseling would not be required for someone like the 31-year-old woman with a possible sexually transmitted disease, and she questioned the ethics of this policy stance. (Requirements for pretest and posttest counseling vary widely from state to state. The District of Columbia had no legal requirements in 2006, nor do they as of 2011, although, of course, physicians use their discretion about the need for counseling.)

Question 7 This resulted in a vigorous debate among the project staff about whether the public health benefit of omitting pretest counseling outweighs the harms. Briefly outline the pros and cons the staff would likely have discussed.

TO CONFIRM OR NOT TO CONFIRM?

As mentioned previously, confirmatory testing would be necessary for any individual with a positive HIV rapid screening test. The ED did not have an infrastructure to support confirmatory Western blot testing and follow-up, although the hospital's lab would be able to run the test if blood was drawn in the ED. The hospital's division of infectious diseases did have the capacity to support confirmatory testing, as did local free clinics. As they planned the pilot study, Dr. Brown and his team debated whether to draw blood in the ED for confirmatory Western blot testing or to refer people who screened positive to other providers for confirmatory testing.

Question 8 It takes several days to get results back from confirmatory HIV testing, but the ED is organized for acute care. Dr. Brown asked Priya to think through the new process the team would need to put in place if they decided to conduct confirmatory testing in the ED as part of the pilot program. If you were Priya, what process would you recommend?

Question 9 Briefly describe key arguments that Dr. Brown's team might have made *for* and *against* conducting confirmatory testing in the ED as part of this pilot study.

The research team concluded it was not feasible to conduct confirmatory Western blot testing in the ED, at least not for the pilot study. Given that the rapid testing program would produce some false positives and it would be useful to reduce these false positives before the patients left the ED, another idea was to screen all individuals whose first rapid test result was positive with a second test. The second test under consideration was the OraQuick Advance HIV1/2 Antibody Test utilizing a whole blood specimen from either a finger stick or venipuncture.

Dr. Brown asked Priya to work up the numbers for what the second round testing would look like using the OraQuick whole blood test. This test was reported to have a sensitivity of 99.6% and a specificity of 100%.[13] For this projection, Priya went back to her highest risk assumption—scenario 3, which assumed an actual prevalence of 3% HIV infection in the screened population of 10,000. Further, she assumed all individuals with a reactive (positive) rapid test result would consent to be given a confirmatory Western blot test.

Priya was a little rusty on serial screening statistics, so she needed to review her epidemiology notes. "Ah yes," she thought. "I need to start with the two-by-two table I created for the first round of testing." [Question 1, scenario 3.] "Then, to complete the second two-by-two table for projecting serial screening results, I need to take my *entire* positive row from round 1 and bring it down intact to form my *total* row for round 2."

Question 10 What did Priya's second-round two-by-two table look like? Calculate the positive predictive value for the second-round test.

Question 11 What is the actual prevalence of HIV infection in the group who would receive the second-round screening test?

Question 12 What is the net sensitivity of this serial testing program? The net specificity? (Refer to Box 2-2 for a primer on these definitions.)

BOX 2-2 Net Sensitivity and Net Specificity for Serial Screening

Net Sensitivity: The number of people who correctly screen positive on both tests (that is, the individuals in the TP cell for the second test) as a percent of all people with HIV infection.

Net Specificity: The number of people who correctly screen negative on the first test, plus people who correctly screen negative on the second test, as a percent of all people without HIV infection.

THE PILOT PROGRAM LAUNCHES

The GW ED launched a 3-month pilot HIV screening program on September 12, 2006, 10 days before the CDC's revised recommendations were published. All English- and Spanish-speaking patients aged 13–64 were eligible to be offered an HIV test. Patients with altered mental status, who needed urgent medical treatment, or who knew they were HIV positive were excluded. The triage nurse determined whether patients met screening criteria and informed those who did that free HIV screening was available and provided them with written materials about HIV disease and the importance of HIV testing.[14]

At an appropriate time during their ED evaluations, eligible patients were approached by specially trained screeners; the screeners were available in the ED between 8:00 AM and midnight every day. The HIV screener explained that the ED was routinely offering HIV screening to everyone, and that the patient could opt out if he or she wanted to.[14]

During the 3-month pilot study, nearly 15,000 patients were treated in the GW ED—4,151 of whom met screening criteria and were offered rapid HIV screening. Of these, 2,476 (59.6%) accepted the test, and a rapid oral swab test was conducted. Twenty-six individuals tested positive, which was 1.1% of those tested. The proportion of patients testing positive differed significantly by sex (with males testing positive more often than females), and by race (with blacks testing positive more often than whites); no differences were seen by age.[14]

Of the 26 individuals with positive screening results, nine were confirmed by Western blot to be infected with HIV, and all but one of these individuals were linked to long-term care. Four individuals were confirmed to not have HIV. The remaining 50% of those who screened positive were lost to follow-up despite vigorous efforts to contact them.[14]

Question 13 As the pilot project drew to an end, Dr. Brown and his team decided to extend the program. However, given the results described, they felt they could improve their screening program. Identify some key issues they were likely grappling with, and suggest possible solutions.

Early detection and treatment of HIV results in substantial increases in survival. In the CDC recommendations, Branson and colleagues concluded, "Even if only a limited fraction of patients who receive HIV-positive results are linked to care, the survival benefits per dollar spent on screening represent good comparative value."[1(p 8)] Altogether, the 3-month pilot program at the GW ED cost approximately $44,000. Thus, each preliminary positive test result cost approximately $1700, while each confirmed case of HIV infection cost approximately $4900. Dr. Brown and his colleagues were happy to add more evidence relating to the cost-effectiveness of HIV screening, and stated, "This program is the first to demonstrate that compared with other methods of early detection, routine opt-out screening in the ED is also cost-effective."[14(p 400)]

PRIYA MOVES ON . . .

Fast-forward 2 years. Priya received her public health degree and secured a research coordinator position with a major healthcare provider in her hometown. This healthcare provider had not previously implemented universal HIV screening, but was considering doing so. Knowing of her previous experience, Priya's supervisor has asked her to think back on some lessons learned from the GW pilot program and to do some preliminary research to inform program design. Priya thought back to one of the first challenges confronting Dr. Brown's team—how important it was to estimate the prevalence of undiagnosed HIV infection in the population that would be screened. Priya could see that any healthcare organization would want to characterize HIV/AIDS in its community before launching a screening program.

For insight into this, Priya could have looked at HIV/AIDS incidence, prevalence, or mortality data for her hometown, or she could have looked for surveillance data about demographic or behavioral risk factors for HIV/AIDS.

Question 14 Reproduce Priya's investigation for your own hometown or any other location that interests you by choosing any health indicator relevant to population risk for HIV. Utilize a primary *government* source of surveillance data to characterize this health indicator for the population living in the town or region you specify. [Note that while there are many reputable sources of health status information, typically information from federal, state, or local government data sources would be considered most trustworthy.] If you prefer, you can zero in on a high-risk subgroup of interest rather than looking at population-wide characteristics. Summarize what you find, describing the following:

- Surveillance methods (Who do data represent? What was measured? When were the data collected? How were they collected?)
- What do the results show?
- Where you obtained the data (website reference, etc.)

The principles of good public health screening programs proposed by Wilson and Jungner in 1968 (see Box 2-3) are still used today to guide screening policy and practice. Priya's supervisor asked her to consider these principles as she reviewed the surveillance data for their community, as well as all she knew about HIV screening in general.

Question 15 Choose any six of these principles and evaluate healthcare-based HIV screening in your chosen setting against those principles. Base your evaluation on what you know from the *MMWR* article[1] and this case. How does HIV screening stack up against these principles?

About the Authors

Katherine L. Hunting, PhD, MPH, is professor of environmental and occupational health and of epidemiology and biostatistics at The George Washington (GW) University School of Public Health and Health Services. A GW faculty member for more than 2 decades, she directs the Master of Public Health program in Environmental Health Science and Policy and has served as associate dean for academic affairs and also as associate dean for student and faculty development. Dr. Hunting is an occupational epidemiologist whose research has focused primarily on occupational injury and ergonomics. She teaches courses on environmental and occupational epidemiology, injury epidemiology, introductory epidemiology, and introductory environmental health.

Jeremy Brown, MD, is the director of clinical research and an associate professor of emergency medicine at The George Washington University Medical Center. He is a practicing emergency physician and the founding director of the ED HIV screening program. This program, which began in 2006 in response to the revised recommendations from the CDC, has screened over 30,000 patients in the ED at GW for HIV.

BOX 2-3 Principles of Good Public Health Screening Programs

1. The condition being sought is an important health problem for the individual and the community.
2. The natural history of the condition, including its development from latent to recognized disease, is adequately understood.
3. There is a recognizable latent or early symptomatic stage.
4. There is a suitable screening test or examination for detecting the disease at the latent or early symptomatic stage, and this test is acceptable to the population.
5. There is an acceptable form of treatment for patients with recognizable disease.
6. Treatment at the presymptomatic, borderline stage of a disease favorably influences its course and prognosis.
7. The facilities required for diagnosis and treatment of patients revealed by the screening program are available.
8. There is an agreed policy on whom to treat as patients.
9. Case finding is a continuous process, and not a once and for all project.
10. The cost of the screening program (which would include the cost of diagnosis and treatment) is economically balanced in relation to possible expenditure on medical care as a whole.

Note: For Wilson & Jungner's elaboration of these principles, see http://whqlibdoc.who.int/php/WHO_PHP_34.pdf, pp 26–39.

Source: Adapted from Wilson JMG, Jungner G. *Principles and Practice of Screening for Disease.* Geneva, Switzerland: World Health Organization; 1968:26–39. http://whqlibdoc.who.int/php/WHO_PHP_34.pdf. Accessed June 22, 2010.

The clinical program has generated several research papers and presentations, which have been published in *JAIDS, Annals of Emergency Medicine, Academic Emergency Medicine, Public Health Reports*, and *The New York Times*. The program has also been highlighted in *American Medical News* and the *ADAP Report*, which described the GW program as a model for emergency room testing.

RECOMMENDED PREPARATORY READING

Branson BM, Handsfield HH, Lampe MA, et al. Revised recommendations for HIV testing of adults, adolescents, and pregnant women in health-care settings. *MMWR Recomm Rep.* 2006;55(RR-14):1–17. http://www.cdc.gov/mmwr/PDF/rr/rr5514.pdf.

CDC HIV/AIDS website: http://www.cdc.gov/hiv/

REFERENCES

1. Branson BM, Handsfield HH, Lampe MA, et al. Revised recommendations for HIV testing of adults, adolescents, and pregnant women in health-care settings. *MMWR Recomm Rep.* 2006;55(RR-14):1–17. http://www.cdc.gov/mmwr/PDF/rr/rr5514.pdf. Accessed September 25, 2009.

2. Institute of Medicine Committee on HIV Prevention Strategies in the United States. No time to lose: getting more from HIV prevention. Washington, DC: National Academy Press. http://www.nap.edu/openbook.php?isbn=0309071372. Published 2001. Accessed September 25, 2009.

3. Marks G, Crepaz N, Senterfitt JW, Janssen RS. Meta-analysis of high-risk sexual behavior in persons aware and unaware they are infected with HIV in the United States: implications for HIV prevention programs. *J Acquir Immune Defic Syndr.* 2005;39(4):446–453.

4. Burt CW, Arispe IE. Characteristics of emergency departments serving high volumes of safety net patients: United States, 2000. *Vital Health Stat 13.* 2004;155:1–16.

5. Centers for Disease Control and Prevention. HIV/AIDS basics. http://www.cdc.gov/hiv/resources/qa/definitions.htm. Modified November 6, 2006. Accessed July 5, 2010.

6. Centers for Disease Control and Prevention. Estimates of new HIV infections in the United States, August 2008. http://www.cdc.gov/hiv/top-ics/surveillance/resources/factsheets/incidence.htm. Modified August 3, 2008. Accessed July 5, 2010.

7. District of Columbia Department of Health. Come together DC—get screened for HIV. http://doh.dc.gov/doh/lib/doh/services/administration_offices/hiv_aids/pdf/june_27_flyer.pdf. Accessed September 12, 2009.

8. Centers for Disease Control and Prevention. OraQuick rapid HIV test for oral fluid—frequently asked questions. http://www.cdc.gov/hiv/topics/testing/resources/qa/oralfluidqandafin.htm. Modified October 19, 2006. Accessed September 12, 2009.

9. Centers for Disease Control and Prevention. Revised guidelines for HIV counseling, testing, and referral. *MMWR.* 2001;50(RR-19):1–57. http://www.cdc.gov/mmwr/preview/mmwrhtml/rr5019a1.htm. Accessed September 19, 2009.

10. DC Department of Health, Administration for HIV Policy & Programs. Executive summary and epidemiologic profile. In: *Comprehensive Plan for HIV Health and Support Services, 2006–2008.* Washington, DC: Author; n.d.:1–12. http://doh.dc.gov/doh/frames.asp?doc=/doh/lib/doh/services/administration_offices/hiv_aids/pdf/2006-2008_comprehensive_plan_hiv.pdf. Accessed September 12, 2009.

11. Centers for Disease Control and Prevention. *HIV/AIDS Surveillance Report, 2004.* Vol 16. Atlanta, GA: US Department of Health and Human Services; 2005:Tables 1 and 8. http://www.cdc.gov/hiv/surveillance/resources/reports/2004report/ Accessed September 19, 2009.

12. Interim projections of the population by selected age groups for the United States and states: April 1, 2000 to July 1, 2030. http://www.census.gov/population/projections/SummaryTabB1.pdf. Accessed September 19, 2009.

13. Centers for Disease Control and Prevention. FDA-approved rapid HIV antibody screening tests. http://www.cdc.gov/hiv/topics/testing/rapid/rt-comparison.htm. Modified February 15, 2008. Accessed September 26, 2009.

14. Brown J, Shesser R, Simon G, et al. Routine HIV screening in the emergency department using the new US Centers for Disease Control and Prevention guidelines: results from a high-prevalence area. *J Acquir Immune Defic Syndr.* 2007;46(4):395–401.

Male Circumcision and HIV:

An Evidence-Based Public Health Approach

RICHARD RIEGELMAN

"Male circumcision protects men from HIV," read the headlines in Ralph Hong's local newspaper in early 2007. Ralph was not surprised since he was an expert in HIV/AIDS, though he had not been involved in any of three recently completed randomized clinical trials in Africa that concluded that male circumcision protects against HIV in males. Ralph was, however, a bit surprised when he received a call from the World Health Organization, asking him to chair an expert panel to decide what these results meant and what the countries of the world should do in response. Ralph's panel of experts from all over the world had their work cut out for them.

The expert panel was asked to spend a week in Geneva developing a World Health Organization recommendations document that could be used by a range of countries to help decide whether to implement male circumcision programs, and if they did, how to implement the programs. In addition, the recommendations could be used by international funding agencies such as the U.S. President's Emergency Plan for AIDS Relief initiative to decide whether to fund male circumcision programs in areas of limited resources.

The expert panel was asked to use an evidence-based public health approach to the question of male circumcision: defining the problem and assessing the evidence for efficacy as to whether male circumcision works under the conditions in which it had been studied. If it found that male circumcision had efficacy, the expert panel was asked to address its application to African countries with a high prevalence of HIV and low rates of male circumcision. In addition, the members were asked to address its future application to African countries with lower prevalence of HIV and already-high rates of

male circumcision. If they recommended male circumcision in either of these settings, they were asked to take a systems approach to address how male circumcision could be combined with other current interventions for control of HIV/AIDS. Finally, they were asked to address the use of male circumcision in other countries, for example, India and the United States.

The thick briefing manual the World Health Organization provided to the expert panel included the following summary of male circumcision, which it asked the panel to integrate into its recommendations.[1]

Male circumcision is considered the oldest surgical procedure. Egyptian tomb art from before 2000 BC depicts adult males undergoing circumcision. Approximately 30% of males are circumcised globally with approximately two-thirds of these being from among the Muslim population of over 1 billion. Circumcision rates vary worldwide; for example, the practice is uncommon among Hindu and Chinese populations. In India, the Hindu religion is neutral on male circumcision. However, circumcision may be the only visual difference between Hindu and Muslim men; thus, Hindu men are often reluctant to undergo circumcision. Jews have traditionally performed circumcision as a religious ceremony 8 days after birth. Christian populations have varied widely in their use of circumcision. Male circumcision is relatively uncommon in Latin American countries and among Hispanics in the United States.[1]

Neonatal circumcision is the general practice among Jews, Christians, and many, but not all, Muslims. Adolescent and young adult circumcision is the rule in Africa and selected areas of Asia such as the Republic of Korea. In the Philippines, neonatal and adolescent and young adult circumcision are each widely practiced.[1]

Circumcision may slightly reduce tactile sensation in the glans penis, but males do not generally report reduced sexual satisfaction. In contrast, in some populations, a perception of increased sexual pleasure is a motivator for undergoing circumcision. Penile hygiene is widely reported as an important advantage of male circumcision.[1]

Male circumcision must be distinguished from female circumcision, often called "female genital mutilation." There is no standard medical indication for female circumcision. It can cause severe health problems and may alter female sexual pleasure.[2]

PROBLEM DESCRIPTION

In the evidence-based public health approach, the description of a health problem begins by considering the basic epidemiology, including characterization of disease occurrence by person, place, and time. The HIV epidemic began in sub-Saharan Africa, and that continent has been severely affected. By the mid-1980s, the epidemic was affecting millions of Africans and grew exponentially over the following 2 decades. In Af-

rica, HIV is transmitted primarily by heterosexual intercourse and affects both males and females.

The expert panel began by looking at the origin of the hypothesis that male circumcision protects against HIV infection. The heart of the HIV epidemic lies in central and southern Africa. Studies beginning in the mid-1980s indicated most men in this region were uncircumcised. Figure 3-1 indicates how closely lower rates of circumcision correlate with higher rates of HIV.[3] From these data, a hypothesis was generated that male circumcision was protective against heterosexually acquired HIV.

The data suggested the existence of a geographic zone of southern African countries, including Zambia, with male circumcision prevalence of less than 20% and high prevalence of HIV. In contrast, areas of east Africa and equatorial Africa, including Senegal, had high male circumcision rates and lower prevalence of HIV infection.

Question 1 Can you conclude from this evidence that there is a causal relationship between absence of circumcision and HIV infection? Why or why not?

During the 1990s and the early years of the 21st century, a large number of case-control and cohort studies investigated

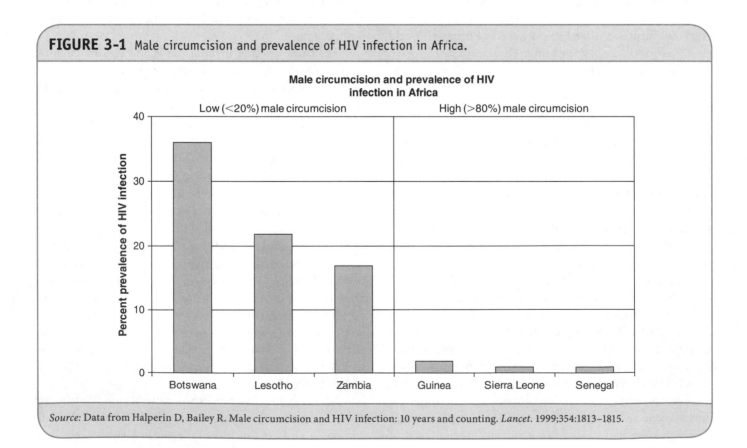

FIGURE 3-1 Male circumcision and prevalence of HIV infection in Africa.

Source: Data from Halperin D, Bailey R. Male circumcision and HIV infection: 10 years and counting. *Lancet.* 1999;354:1813–1815.

the relationship between male circumcision and HIV at the individual level. These studies were later combined as a meta-analysis that suggested 50% or more of the African population's risk of HIV infection was associated with the absence of male circumcision.[4]

Despite the exponential growth of the epidemic in much of Africa and growing evidence that male circumcision is associated with reduced HIV transmission, there was until recently no organized international effort to promote or fund male circumcision as a means to prevent HIV infection.

Among the possible reasons for this delay were the following:

- Western donors were hesitant to recommend an invasive personal intervention in countries with a history of colonialism.
- The major focus of HIV prevention research was on development of a vaccine.
- There was no widely accepted mechanism of action for the claimed efficacy of male circumcision. That is, biological plausibility was not established.

Another major explanation was that the investigations conducted up to that point were observational. That is, they were case-control studies and cohort studies that observed the course of events. There were no large, well-conducted, randomized clinical trials—experimental studies to determine whether male circumcision altered the probability of acquiring HIV infection. Randomized clinical trials are the gold standard for establishing the efficacy of an intervention. By the early years of the 21st century, it was clear that randomized clinical trials were needed to establish the efficacy of male circumcision for prevention of HIV, at least among males.

ETIOLOGY/EFFICACY—MALE CIRCUMCISION AND HIV

In an evidence-based public health approach, establishing that an intervention has efficacy (works under research conditions) requires evidence that the intervention alters the outcome when investigated in a well-defined population, ideally using randomized clinical trials.

The World Health Organization, the National Institutes of Health, the Centers for Disease Control and Prevention, and the Gates Foundation collaborated on three large, well-conducted, randomized clinical trials in Africa to study the impact of male circumcision among predominately heterosexual males.[5] In order to increase the statistical power, or the chances of demonstrating statistical significance of the results, all studies were conducted in areas with high incidence rates of new HIV infections per year. To provide a large population of

adolescent and young men potentially interested in circumcision, the investigations were conducted in areas with relatively high rates of HIV, low prevalence of circumcision, and high expressed willingness to undergo circumcision.

In all three randomized controlled trials, HIV-free heterosexual volunteers were randomized to one of two groups. The intervention group was offered medically supervised cost-free circumcision as well as extensive HIV education, including warnings to abstain for 6 weeks after the procedure until an examination confirmed complete healing. Those randomized to the comparison group received extensive HIV education and were offered free circumcision after the completion of the trial. The data in Table 3-1 describe the randomized controlled trial study populations.[5]

Since the results of the three studies were very similar, the expert panel decided to present an example utilizing the Orange Farm, South Africa study results. The Orange Farm, South Africa study, followed participants for up to 18 months before the investigation was stopped early because of the impressive results. In this study, there were 20 cases of HIV among the 1862 men randomized to the circumcision group and 49 cases among a nearly equal number randomized to

TABLE 3-1 Descriptive Data for Three Randomized Controlled Trials of Male Circumcision for the Prevention of HIV[5]

	Orange Farm South Africa	Rakai Uganda	Kisumu Kenya
Population	Semiurban	Rural	Urban
Circumcision %	20%	16%	10%
HIV yearly incidence	1.6%	1.3%	1.8%
Age range	18–24 yrs	15–49 yrs	18–24 yrs
Sample size (total)	3,724	4,996	2,784
Completion	April 2005	December 2006	December 2006

Source: Data from Siegfried M, Muller N, Deeks JJ, Volmink J. Male circumcision for prevention of heterosexual acquisition of HIV in men. *The Cochrane Database of Systematic Reviews.* Issue 2, Art. No. CD003362. DOI: 10.1002/14651858.CD003362.pub2. http://www.mrw. interscience.wiley.com/cochrane/clsysrev/articles/CD003362/frame. html. Accessed April 17, 2010.

the comparison group. The incidence of new HIV infection was 0.85 per 100 person years of follow-up in the circumcision study group compared to 2.1 per 100 person years of follow-up in the comparison group.

These data reflect the generally accepted method of analysis called intention-to-treat analysis in which the data are analyzed based upon the group to which each participant is randomized. Thus, incidence among the circumcised group is calculated for all those assigned to the circumcision group even if they did not subsequently undergo the procedure. Incidence among the noncircumcised group is calculated for all those assigned to the comparison group, even if they underwent circumcision outside the study protocol during the study period.

The results of all three studies were statistically significant. Investigators controlled (adjusted) for differences between the intervention and comparison groups in behavioral factors, including condom use, health-seeking behavior, and risky sexual behavior. Adjusting for these potential confounding variables had little impact on the results.

The analysis of the results also helps researchers estimate the potential magnitude of the impact of male circumcision. In making these calculations, it is important to recognize the studies were designed to determine whether male circumcision protected heterosexual males from HIV. They were not designed to address the questions of direct protection of women or males who have sex with males from contracting HIV.

The first measure of the magnitude of the impact of male circumcision is the relative risk. The relative risk can be calculated as the probability of developing HIV in the noncircumcised comparison group compared to the probability of developing HIV in the circumcised study group.

Question 2 In the Orange Farm study, what is the relative risk among those randomized to the noncircumcision comparison group compared to those in the circumcision study group? How do you interpret this relative risk?

The relative risk also allows us to calculate the percent efficacy or the attributable risk percentage. That is the percentage of HIV infection that can potentially be prevented among men without circumcision by performing male circumcision. When the relative risk is more than one (i.e., the factor that increases the risk is in the numerator of the relative risk equation), the formula for percent efficacy is:

$$\left[\frac{(\text{relative risk} - 1)}{(\text{relative risk})} \right] \times 100\%$$

When the relative risk is less than 1, the percent efficacy is calculated as follows:

$$(1 - \text{relative risk}) \times 100\%$$

Question 3 In the Orange Farm study, what is the percent efficacy (i.e., the attributable risk percentage among those without circumcision)? How do you interpret this result?

Before concluding that male circumcision has efficacy for the prevention of HIV in heterosexual males, the expert panel looked for evidence of biological plausibility. That is, it looked for evidence of a biological mechanism that could explain the evidence for efficacy.

In recent years, a number of potential explanations of the biological advantages of male circumcision have been put forth. It is generally accepted now that the inner lining of the foreskin contains large numbers of HIV target cells—white cells in close proximity to the surface. The mucosal inner surface of the foreskin is also considered to be more susceptible to abrasions and tears than the glans penis. Finally, research has shown that ulcerative lesions (more common in uncircumcised males) also increase the probability of acquiring HIV infection.[1]

Based on all the evidence, the expert panel concluded male circumcision has efficacy for the prevention of HIV in males. This was a key step in their report, but it was only the beginning. Taking an evidence-based public health approach, the expert panel then needed to address the question of whether to recommend male circumcision.

RECOMMENDATIONS

The question facing the expert panel was whether to recommend male circumcision for the communities studied or for similar populations. To do this, the panel needed to consider not only whether male circumcision has efficacy, but also whether it has effectiveness (that is, it works under the conditions of real-world clinical or public health practice). In addition, the panel needed to assess the potential harms or safety of male circumcision. Thus, recommendations should be based upon the net benefits, that is, the benefits minus the harms as they occur in practice.

Benefits

In addition to the results of the intention-to-treat analysis, an additional analysis known as as-treated or per-protocol analysis compared HIV incidence among those who actually underwent circumcision versus those who remained uncircumcised. For those actually undergoing circumcision, the percent efficacy or protective effect was over 60%. This higher protective effect for males who actually underwent circumcision suggests that successful circumcision may have an effectiveness of even greater than 60% when actually used in practice.

Harms

Harms or adverse events are especially important when considering a preventive intervention. Only a small percentage of those who receive a preventive intervention can be expected to experience the benefits. However, all those who receive the intervention are at risk of the harm. In addition, it is not always possible to identify those who benefit from the intervention, but those who are harmed will often be visible and vocal. Thus, it is important to understand the potential harms and to monitor their occurrence not only in research investigations, but in practice as well.

Male circumcision performed under unhygienic conditions can cause infection, penile damage, and a range of other complications. There is general agreement that adolescent and adult male circumcision should be conducted under medical supervision to help ensure hygienic and technically competent implementation. Complications are possible in both neonatal and adolescent/young adult circumcision, though the procedure is simpler, safer, and the healing more rapid when performed soon after birth.

During the approximately 6-week healing period for adolescent and young adult circumcision, it is generally agreed that the risk of acquiring HIV is increased. Transmission of HIV by HIV-positive males is increased during this 6-week period due to the greater potential for partners to be exposed to infected blood. Consequently, abstinence during this period is strongly encouraged.

In the randomized clinical trials, under well-supervised surgical conditions, the chance of complications totaled 3–4%. The complications were mostly minor and short lived; however, there was a greater than 1% chance of infection, a serious complication, in one of the study centers.

The randomized clinical trials conducted in Africa also established that male circumcision reduced the prevalence of herpes genitalis and HPV viruses, both common infections in the United States and other developed countries.[5]

Question 4 Based upon the information provided, what key finding or evidence would you take into account to draw conclusions about the net benefits of male circumcision in the communities studied in these investigations?

The expert panel was faced with the question of whether male circumcision was likely to work as well in Zambia and in Sen-

egal. The expert panel had chosen Zambia as an example of an African country with a high incidence rate of HIV and a low prevalence of male circumcision. Senegal was chosen as an example of an African country with a lower incidence rate of HIV and a higher prevalence of male circumcision. The expert panel assumed that 20% of males were circumcised in Zambia and 80% were circumcised in Senegal.

To estimate the impact of a successful program of male circumcision in Zambia, the expert panel calculated the population attributable risk percentage. The population attributable risk percentage estimates the percentage of the disease in the entire population (HIV in males) that can potentially be prevented. The population attributable risk percentage is calculated using the following formula:

$$\frac{\left(\begin{array}{c}\text{proportion with the}\\\text{risk factor}\end{array}\right)\left(\begin{array}{c}\text{relative risk if risk}\\\text{factor present} -1\end{array}\right)}{\left(\begin{array}{c}\text{proportion with the}\\\text{risk factor}\end{array}\right)\left(\begin{array}{c}\text{relative risk if risk}\\\text{factor present} -1\end{array}\right)+1}$$

This formula is appropriate when the relative risk is greater than 1. That is, the risk factor, absence of circumcision, is in the numerator of the relative risk equation.

For male circumcision, the formula would be:

$$\frac{\left(\begin{array}{c}\text{proportion males}\\\text{without circumcision}\end{array}\right)\left(\begin{array}{c}\text{relative risk if}\\\text{no circumcision} -1\end{array}\right)}{\left(\begin{array}{c}\text{proportion males}\\\text{without circumcision}\end{array}\right)\left(\begin{array}{c}\text{relative risk if}\\\text{no circumcision} -1\end{array}\right)+1} \times 100\%$$

In making this calculation, the expert panel assumed that the relative risk was 2.5 for uncircumcised adult males compared to circumcised adult males.

Question 5 What is the population attributable risk percentage in Zambia? What does this tell us about the likely impact on HIV incidence of a successful male circumcision program in Zambia?

The situation in Senegal is quite different since 80% of the adult males are already circumcised. Thus only 20% are at risk due to being uncircumcised. Thus for Senegal, the expert panel calculated the population attributable risk percentage assuming that the relative risk was 2.5 and the probability of being uncircumcised was 0.2.

Question 6 What is the population attributable risk percentage in Senegal? How would you interpret this population attributable risk percentage? What else would you consider in evaluating the impact of male circumcision in Senegal besides the population attributable risk percentage?

The expert panel's final step in making general recommendations on male circumcision was to address the questions of cost effectiveness.

The World Bank had concluded that an increase in the prevalence of male circumcision from approximately 20% to approximately 80% had the potential to reduce the overall prevalence of HIV by 50% over a 10-year period.[6] This was based on the assumption that circumcision is only effective in preventing transmission to the circumcised males themselves. However, HIV infection is known to be transmitted more readily from males to females than from females to males. Thus even if male circumcision does not directly protect females, the reduced prevalence of HIV among males will, over time, reduce female exposure to HIV and subsequent spread of the infection. Nonetheless, it is important to recognize women are actually at increased risk of HIV if they have intercourse with males who have recently been circumcised.

The World Bank estimated the cost of medically supervised adolescent and young adult male circumcision to be $25 per procedure in African countries. This surprisingly low cost is largely due to the dramatically lower local labor costs. The World Bank estimated that 15 to 60 circumcisions needed to be performed to prevent one additional case of HIV infection. This is known as the number needed to treat. From this the World Bank calculated the cost of preventing one case of HIV in high-prevalence countries through use of circumcision to be in the range of $375 to $1500. The World Bank concluded that even at the high end, this cost was far below the lifetime cost of providing HIV drug treatment.[6]

> **Question 7** In concluding that circumcision is cost effective, identify the standard or existing intervention against which the new approach—circumcision—is being compared. Is there another intervention against which circumcision should be compared? How might this change the results of the cost-effectiveness analysis?

Based on all of this evidence on benefits, harms, and costs, Ralph's expert panel made the general recommendation that male circumcision had net effectiveness. In addition, it concluded that male circumcision was cost effective, at least under the circumstances in which it had been studied in Africa.

IMPLEMENTATION

When considering implementation of a program, it is important to consider *who* should be offered the service, *when* it should be offered, and *how* it should be provided. Ralph's expert panel called this the "who, when, and how" approach to implementation.

Who

The randomized clinical trials did not provide evidence that male circumcision reduces the transmission of HIV to females, though these investigations were not designed to be large enough or long enough to detect a small or delayed effect. Thus, if male circumcision turns out to have a direct impact on heterosexual transmission, this will be an added benefit. In addition, there is no consistent evidence that male circumcision protects against male homosexual transmission through rectal intercourse. Thus, when considering implementation, only the direct impact on heterosexual males should be considered.

If male circumcision is performed on HIV-positive males, there is an increased frequency of transmission if unprotected intercourse is performed during the 6-week healing period. Thus, it is generally accepted that male circumcision should be targeted at HIV-negative heterosexual males.

When

Neonatal circumcision has not been the typical practice in Africa. Circumcision as traditionally practiced in Africa has often been a ritual associated with entry into adulthood for preadolescent and adolescent males. Neonatal circumcision is estimated to cost only 10% as much as adolescent and young adult circumcision. In terms of addressing the HIV epidemic in Africa, however, the use of neonatal circumcision would represent a major cultural change and would result in a delay of decades before its impact would be fully felt. Thus, in the short run, adolescent and young adult circumcision is likely the most effective HIV intervention in Africa. However, neonatal circumcision programs might also be considered in addition to adolescent and young adult programs.

How

When considering how to implement an intervention, the acceptability of the intervention and its cost must be determined. Additionally, experts must account for the barriers to successful implementation and the potential changes in behavior that may occur as a result of the intervention.

The potential to rapidly increase the prevalence of male circumcision based upon adolescent and young adult circumcision is illustrated by the Republic of Korea, where male circumcision was virtually unknown before 1945. Male circumcision in the Republic of Korea among 20-year-olds was approximately 20% in 1980, but increased to approximately 90% by 2000.[1]

In African regions where male circumcision is not traditionally practiced, the majority of males report a willingness to undergo circumcision if it can be done under safe conditions and at minimum cost. It is important that males undergoing circumcision be informed that condom use is still necessary and that circumcision is not being used as a substitute for condom use. Studies of barriers to adolescent and young adult circumcision identified fear of pain, concerns for safety, and the cost of the procedure as the three most important barriers to undergoing the procedure in African countries in which circumcision is not commonly practiced.[7]

Factors to consider when implementing a male circumcision program include:

- The cultural, religious, and economic barriers to increasing the prevalence of circumcision including those that favor or discourage neonatal vs. adolescent and young adult male circumcision.
- The extent to which recently circumcised males can be convinced to remain abstinent for 6 weeks or refrain from high-risk sexual contact during that period.

EVALUATION

Ralph's expert panel chose Zambia as an example of a high-risk country for HIV. Before recommending extending the service to the entire country, they decided to encourage a demonstration project to evaluate the impacts of a male circumcision program in a regional area of Zambia with a high rate of HIV.

The panel considered methods for evaluating the success of the demonstration program. As a first measure, it suggested using the rate of new HIV infections among young males in this targeted region before and after the introduction of the circumcision program. In addition, the expert panel recommended evaluating how well the male circumcision demonstration project addressed the associated social, cultural, and healthcare issues.

> **Question 8** In addition to the rate of new HIV infections in males in this region of Zambia, what other social, cultural, and healthcare issues should be addressed as part of the evaluation of the demonstration project?

SYSTEMS THINKING

Ralph Hong's expert panel was also asked to use a systems thinking approach to evaluate the use of male circumcision as part of a comprehensive HIV control program in African countries. Again, the experts decided to use Zambia as an example of a high-risk African country and Senegal as an example of a lower risk African country.

Their systems thinking approach began by outlining the factors and interventions that were part of the existing strategy. The expert panel assumed African countries were already utilizing the following intervention strategies as part of their national HIV control programs:

- Male condom use was advocated as a cornerstone of prevention, and free condoms were widely available. Cultural resistance, especially among males, and to a lesser extent religious objection, both limited the effectiveness of this strategy.
- Widespread HIV testing and treatment was advocated as a way of recognizing high-risk individuals and reducing their infectivity (as well as improving their prognosis) through drug treatment. This strategy was limited by the fact that the greatest period of infectivity was during the first few weeks of infection, when standard HIV testing usually produces false negative results.[8]
- Educational programs encouraged serial monogamy rather than multiple simultaneous partners. In models of the HIV epidemic, serial monogamy appeared to slow down the spread of the disease in the population as a whole since fewer partners had contact with HIV-positive individuals, especially during the periods of high infectivity.[9] The approach was limited by a culture in which males frequently have multiple simultaneous sexual partners.

Ralph's expert panel was asked to consider the short-term and long-term role male circumcision could play in HIV control programs already utilizing the aforementioned approaches. A systems thinking approach considered the factors that were believed to influence the outcome of interest, that is, the incidence of HIV.

The next step in systems thinking is to compare the strength of each of these interventions to draw conclusions about potential advantages of each. Male circumcision was likely the most effective of these interventions in terms of prevention of HIV in heterosexual males assuming that use of condoms has not gained widespread acceptance.

The third step in systems thinking is to ask questions about how the potential interventions work together.

Questions to assist in the analysis include:

- Do the interventions reach different populations?
- Would widespread application of more than one of the interventions multiply the protection against HIV

infection; i.e., are there any synergies between the interventions?

- Would widespread use of any one of the interventions interfere with the success of any of the other interventions?

There is one piece of evidence from the randomized clinical trials that bears on these interactions. The issue known as risk compensation, or disinhibition, must be considered in the implementation of a program of male circumcision. Risk compensation, or disinhibition, addresses the extent to which male circumcision provides unrealistic perceptions of protection and leads to high-risk behavior. High-risk sexual behavior may include a greater number of simultaneous sexual partners, failure to use condoms, and/or failure to take HIV medications.

Data from randomized clinical trials in Kenya were studied extensively to look for the existence of risk compensation. No evidence of this—such as an increase in the number of sexual partners among those undergoing circumcision—was found.[10]

Systems thinking also requires considering the dynamic changes that are likely to occur with the introduction of a new intervention such as male circumcision. For instance, would there be bottlenecks that slowed down or even prevented the success of implementation? For example, would there be enough healthcare personnel to successfully implement hygienic circumcision or would men turn to other practitioners? If so, would the adverse effects be frequent enough to discourage large-scale acceptance of male circumcision?

Question 9 What are your thoughts on how male circumcision might affect the success of other interventions if it were introduced into a comprehensive HIV control program in Zambia? How well do you think a male circumcision program would fit into a comprehensive HIV control program for Zambia?

APPLICATION TO OTHER COUNTRIES

Having made recommendations for implementation in countries in Africa, Ralph's expert panel next needed to address the implications of the evidence for other countries including India and the United States.

The expert panel assumed that India had an HIV prevalence of 0.3–0.4%, largely due to heterosexual transmission. In India, Hindu males are rarely circumcised while Muslim males are routinely circumcised, most often neonatally, resulting in an overall circumcision prevalence in the Indian population of less than 20%.

The HIV epidemic in India had increased from its beginning among sex workers. The disease was primarily concentrated among heterosexuals and among Hindus, who do not generally practice male circumcision. The prevalence of HIV was still relatively low but was gradually increasing.

Question 10 What recommendations would you make for utilizing male circumcision among Hindus in India?

As of 2006, the United States had an HIV prevalence of approximately 0.4%.[11] The HIV epidemic in the United States began as a homosexually transmitted disease, as well as a disease transmitted by blood transfusions and intravenous drug use. Today, the epidemic is rapidly expanding among the heterosexual population—especially among African Americans and to a lesser degree among Hispanics. The rate of new HIV infections among African American men is approximately six times the incidence rate among whites.[12]

It has been assumed, but not proven, that circumcision is effective in partially protecting males from heterosexual transmission of HIV in the United States despite the fact the HIV subtype most common in the United States differs from the subtype circulating in Africa.

Neonatal male circumcision is the predominant method of circumcision in the United States. In 2006, 56% of newborns were circumcised, compared to approximately 65% in 1980. This gradual overall reduction reflects of a complex pattern of changes by region, race, and ethnicity. Circumcision rates in the western United States decreased substantially during this period; this is believed to reflect the increased proportion of births to Hispanic parents and the greater choice provided to parents to make healthcare decisions. The proportion of African American males who are circumcised at birth has increased from 1980 to 2005 and is now comparable to the white population.[13,14]

Public policy has also had a hand in the declining circumcision rates in the United States. Many Medicaid programs have reduced or eliminated coverage of male circumcision. In addition, the American Academy of Pediatrics has taken a neutral stance, neither encouraging nor discouraging neonatal male circumcision.[15]

Question 11 Using the who, when, and how approach, what issues does Ralph's expert panel need to consider in making recommendations for male circumcision in the United States?

ACKNOWLEDGMENTS

A number of people made important contributions to conceptualizing and implementing this case study. Douglas Huber,

MD, MSc, a reproductive health consultant with many years of experience with male circumcision and HIV, provided a helpful review of an early draft. Alan Greenberg, MD, MPH, chair of the Department of Epidemiology and Biostatistics at The George Washington University School of Public Health and Health Services, provided important leads and encouragement in the development of the case. Katherine L. Hunting, PhD, MPH, and Brenda L. Gleason, MA, MPH, reviewed drafts, and their extensive feedback was incorporated into the final case.

About the Author

Richard Riegelman, MD, MPH, PhD, is professor of epidemiology and biostatistics and of health policy at The George Washington University School of Public Health and Health Services. He is the founding dean of the School of Public Health and Health Services. Dr. Riegelman is the series editor for the Essential Public Health series published by Jones & Bartlett Learning and is the author of a book in that series, *Public Health 101: Healthy People-Healthy Populations*. Richard Riegelman has been a national leader in efforts to develop undergraduate public health education.

REFERENCES

1. World Health Organization/UNAIDS. Male circumcision: global trends and determinants of prevalence, safety and acceptability. http://www.who.int/hiv/pub/malecircumcision/globaltrends/en/index.html. Published December 14, 2007. Accessed July 13, 2010.

2. World Health Organization. Female genital mutilation. http://www.who.int/mediacentre/factsheets/fs241/en/. Published February 2010. Accessed July 13, 2010.

3. Halperin D, Bailey R. Male circumcision and HIV infections: 10 years and counting. *Lancet*. 1999;354:1813–1815.

4. O'Farrell N, Egger M. Circumcision in men and the prevention of HIV infection: a "meta-analysis" revisited. *Int J Std AIDS*. 2000;11(3):13742.

5. Siegfried M, Muller N, Deeks JJ, Volmink J. Male circumcision for prevention of heterosexual acquisition of HIV in men. *The Cochrane Database of Systematic Reviews*. Issue 2, Art. No. CD003362. DOI: 10.1002/14651858. CD003362.pub2. http://www.mrw.interscience.wiley.com/cochrane/clsysrev/articles/CD003362/frame.html. Accessed April 17, 2010.

6. Wilson D, de Beyer J. World Bank global HIV/AIDS program. Male circumcision: evidence and implications. http://siteresources.worldbank.org/INTHIVAIDS/Resources/375798-1132695455908/M&EGR_MaleCircumcision_Mar31.pdf. Published 2006. Accessed July 13, 2010.

7. United States Agency for International Development. Issue brief: Male circumcision and HIV prevention. http://www.usaid.gov/our_work/global_health/aids/TechAreas/research/mcfactsheet.html. Accessed March 24, 2011.

8. Vignoles M, Bibini M, Sorrentino A, Sanchez Puch S, Gomez Carrillo M, Salomon H. False-negative results in HIV-1/2 antibodies screening tests. *Antivir Ther*. 2003;8 (Suppl.1):abstract no. 1229. http://gateway.nlm.nih.gov/MeetingAbstracts/ma?f=102263501.html. Accessed November 13, 2010.

9. Gray RH, Wawer MJ, Brookmeyer R, et al. Probability of HIV-1 transmission per coital act in monogamous, heterosexual, HIV-1-discordant couples in Rakai, Uganda. *Lancet*. 2001;357:1149–1153.

10. Mattson CL, Campbell RT, Bailey RC, et al. Risk compensation is not associated with male circumcision in Kisumu, Kenya: a multi-faceted assessment of men enrolled in a randomized controlled trial. *PLoS ONE*. 2008;3(6):e2443. doi:10.1371/journal.pone.0002443.

11. Campsmith ML, Rhodes P, Hall HI, Green T. HIV prevalence estimates—United States, 2006. MMWR. 2008;57(39):1073–1076. http://www.cdc.gov/mmwr/preview/mmwrhtml/mm5739a2.htm. Accessed March 13, 2011.

12. Centers for Disease Control and Prevention. HIV among African Americans. http://www.cdc.gov/hiv/topics/aa/. Modified September 9, 2010. Accessed November 13, 2010.

13. Centers for Disease Control and Prevention. Male Circumcision and Risk of HIV Transmission and Other Health Conditions: Implications for the United States. Available at: http://www.cdc.gov/hiv/resources/factsheets/circumcision.htm. Accessed July 13, 2010.

14. Circumcision Reference Library. United States Circumcision Incidence. Available at http://www.cirp.org/library/statistics/USA/. Accessed March 22, 2011.

15. American Academy of Pediatrics Task Force on Circumcision. Circumcision Policy Statement. *Pediatrics*. 1999;103(3):686–693.

Research Synthesis:

Systematic Review and Meta-Analysis of Vioxx® and Cardiovascular Events

MICHELLE D. ALTHUIS

VIOXX® AND CARDIOVASCULAR EVENTS

On September 30, 2004, the Food and Drug Administration (FDA) issued a public health advisory announcing Merck & Co., Inc. voluntarily withdrew its blockbuster pain drug from the U.S. market because of life-threatening side effects.[1] Vioxx® (rofecoxib) is a COX-2 selective, nonsteroidal anti-inflammatory drug that was approved in May of 1999 for the management of osteoarthritis and acute pain in adults. Also approved for the treatment of menstrual symptoms and rheumatoid arthritis in adults and children, Vioxx® was a widely used prescription medication. In nearly 5.5 years on the U.S. market, more than 100 million Vioxx® prescriptions had been filled.[2]

The FDA announcement read, in part:

> The Agency was informed by Merck & Co., Inc. on September 27, 2004, that the Data Safety Monitoring Board for an ongoing long-term study of Vioxx® (APPROVe) had recommended that the study be stopped early for safety reasons. The study was being conducted in patients at risk for developing recurrent colon polyps. The study showed an increased risk of cardiovascular events (including heart attack and stroke) in patients on Vioxx® compared to placebo, particularly those who had been taking the drug for longer than 18 months. Based on this new safety information, Merck and FDA officials met the next day, September 28, 2004, and during that meeting FDA was informed that Merck was voluntarily withdrawing Vioxx® from the marketplace.
>
> The risk that an individual patient taking Vioxx® will suffer a heart attack or stroke related to the drug is very small. Patients who are currently taking Vioxx® should contact their physician for guidance regarding discontinuation and alternative therapies.[1(p)]

Epidemiologists, clinicians, and regulators were keen to understand if they could have better detected the earliest signs of serious adverse events. The sentiment among scientists today is that potentially unacceptable risks associated with Vioxx® were initially suggested in the Vioxx® Gastrointestinal Outcomes Research Study (VIGOR), which was completed in 2000. The VIGOR trial found that patients randomized to rofecoxib (Vioxx®) had 4 times as many myocardial infarctions as those receiving the comparative therapy naproxen.[3] At the time, Bombardier and coauthors interpreted this excess as the result of cardioprotective effects of naproxen as opposed to toxicity of rofecoxib.

Some scientists believe an extensive review of the trials completed by 2001 may have led to an earlier withdrawal of rofecoxib. Other investigators felt the review of observational studies might have clarified whether the suggested cardioprotective effects of naproxen were likely to be real.

The primary purpose of this case study is to provide students with experience interpreting reviews that synthesize research data from multiple epidemiologic studies, using the issues that surrounded the highly publicized market withdrawal of Vioxx® as context. To this end, the following pages ask students to examine two reviews of the relationship between Vioxx® (rofecoxib) and cardiovascular events. In 2004, *Lancet* published a cumulative meta-analysis of myocardial infarction in randomized clinical trials (RCTs) of rofecoxib among patients with musculoskeletal disorders.[i,4] A meta-analysis of controlled observational studies, published in 2006 by *JAMA*, compared cardiovascular events between users and nonusers of rofecoxib.[5] See Appendix I for abstracts of these two papers.

BRIEF INTRODUCTION TO SYSTEMATIC REVIEWS AND META-ANALYSIS IN EPIDEMIOLOGY

Systematic reviews and meta-analyses are now the preferred methodological approaches for summarizing and interpreting epidemiologic evidence on human health effects. Over the past 2 decades, these methods have been increasingly used as a first step in assessing causation in evidence-based medicine. Systematic reviews and meta-analyses provide a way for scientists, regulators, and litigators to stay abreast of rapid advances in scientific progress. Whether used for causal assessments or for keeping pace with science, systematic reviews and meta-analyses aim to be transparent and are reliable methods for identifying, summarizing, and interpreting the results of scientific studies.

The quality of reviews in the published literature can be highly variable. It is important to note that until recently many researchers had published narrative style reviews, which are written to support the view of the authors and rely on a nonsystematic selection of papers. Surprisingly, narrative-type research summaries are still published today, although to a lesser extent. In contrast, a systematic review is ideally designed to assess all research on a topic, with the ultimate goal of an unbiased summary of the question at hand.

A meta-analysis is the quantitative summary of data across epidemiologic studies (observational or clinical). Sometimes a systematic review will include this component, earning the title, "systematic review and meta-analysis."

Systematic Reviews

A high-quality systematic review is a summary of carefully selected scientific studies to which qualitative (and sometimes quantitative) methods of interpretation have been applied. An example of a quantitative method is meta-analysis. Important elements of an effective review are summarized in Box 4-1.

Meta-Analysis

Meta-analysis is a two-step quantitative method for integrating summary data from individual studies to produce an overall measure of an effect or relationship across all studies examined. Extracting or calculating the appropriate summary statistic—for example, the odds ratio or relative risk (RR)—for each of a set of studies is the first step. The second step involves combining these statistics into an appropriate weighted average that represents an overall summary measure relating the exposure to the outcome.

Meta-analysis can be particularly powerful for combining findings from RCTs. RCTs are ideally designed to provide an unbiased estimate of the effect of an experimental treatment. For a group of sensibly selected and combined trials, the variability of the results between the studies is theoretically attributable to random variation. Thus, the overall effect calculated from a meta-analysis of well-conducted RCTs is essentially an unbiased estimate of the treatment effect, with better precision than any one trial alone. More practically speaking, meta-analysis improves the precision of estimates of treatment effects, reducing the probability of false-negative results and potentially leading to timely introduction of effective treatments or identification of adverse events.

BOX 4-1 Important Elements of a High-Quality Systematic Review

- A detailed protocol that states a clear purpose
- Methods of searching the literature
- A clear description of the studies included (and excluded) for further interpretation
- Use of a data abstraction instrument
- A description of the study quality considerations
- Techniques for summarizing the data from the studies selected for inclusion
- Methods for interpreting the summarized data (e.g., criteria-based methods)
- A presentation of clear claims and/or recommendations, depending upon the stated purpose of the review

---

[i] The Juni et al. study included two sets of analysis. This case study focuses on the first analyses, which examined randomized controlled trials of the association between myocardial infarctions and rofecoxib. Juni et al. also evaluated both RCTs and observational studies to examine whether naproxen was cardioprotective; this analysis is not touched upon in this case study.

PROTOCOL FOR A SYSTEMATIC REVIEW AND META-ANALYSIS

The following sections provide a basic summary of the procedures used for conducting a systematic review and meta-analysis. Every protocol will differ depending on the goals of the review or the meta-analysis. Nonetheless the following paragraphs provide a flavor of the detail and attention needed for a quality systematic review and meta-analysis.

Detailed Protocol

Systematic reviews are planned in a manner consistent with any other research project; that is, a detailed protocol is written in advance. The investigator formulates the review question and, a priori, defines the criteria for including and excluding studies. Usually, a brief description of the protocol can be found in the methods section of the publication.

Selecting Studies/Trials

Details of the search strategy will also be provided in the methods section of a well-executed systematic review. Usually this includes a description of the key word search and the databases used. In striving to identify an unbiased collection of all eligible studies, investigators generally cast a broad net, preferring to be more inclusive in looking for potentially eligible studies. Databases routinely searched for systematic reviews include Medline and EMBASE (a biomedical and pharmacologic bibliographic database). Other sources also frequently include The Cochrane Controlled Trials Register, conference proceedings, reference lists, and sources of ongoing and/or unpublished studies. The investigator must weigh the importance of exclusion criteria such as year of publication, publication status, or language. Including unpublished studies, while time consuming, may help to reduce publication bias inherent in reviews of the published literatures. Sources used for unpublished studies include the British Library Index to Conference Proceedings, The Cochrane Register of Trial Registers, Clinical Trials.gov, and the Glaxo Wellcome register of clinical trials.

A flowchart tracing the study selection process is considered essential in a high-quality systematic review. A flowchart explicitly documents exclusion and inclusion criteria used to select studies for review. Tracking studies via a trial flowchart that includes details on the selection of potentially relevant studies, those included and excluded, studies that have usable information, and those withdrawn and reasons for their withdrawal often provides the clearest picture of the study design.

Figure 4-1 is an example flowchart based on the McGettigan (2006) study.[5] The investigators of this review searched electronic databases for relevant documents from January 1985 to January 2006 using a broad search strategy. Search terms included names of individual drugs, cardiovascular and cerebrovascular outcomes, and study design, yielding 7086 potentially relevant titles. Figure 4-1 details the process of review, and the included and excluded studies. The vast majority of studies were excluded after review of the title or abstract, simply because they were the wrong study design, therapy, or cardiovascular outcome. As shown at the bottom of the figure, only 23 studies were included in the final analysis.

Data Abstraction

A data abstraction instrument should be used to systematically and objectively collect qualitative and quantitative data from each study. The gold standard is to conduct data abstraction in duplicate, with the reviewers blinded to the authors and the journal of publication. The importance of unbiased data abstraction is underscored by inclusion of the method in the 2006 *JAMA* abstract.[5] McGettigan and coworkers specify that two people independently abstracted data from every included study.

Data abstraction forms usually include qualitative information about the study and its participants, including study design, patient characteristics (age, gender, disease severity), details of the intervention (dose or escalation regimens), and outcome definitions. Because inadequate quality of studies may distort the results from meta-analysis and systematic reviews, data may also be collected on study methods and execution.

This form should also be designed to abstract relevant quantitative information, either simply for summarizing or for statistical integration. Quantitative information often includes measures of effect (means, proportions, odds ratios, or relative risks), variance, loss to follow-up, and handling of missing data.

Question 1 Using information in the abstract, concisely describe the purpose of the systematic review and meta-analysis published by Juni et al.[4] Limit your answer to the purpose as it pertains to experimental studies of rofecoxib.

Question 2 Juni and coworkers[4] conducted a search of the literature for all randomized clinical trials that compared rofecoxib with another nonsteroidal anti-inflammatory drug or placebo. The investigators reviewed 383 reports in order to identify 18 RCTs they considered eligible for their analysis. Can you suggest four possible reasons for exclusion of reports from the final analysis?

Question 3 In total for the rofecoxib trials,[4] 52 myocardial infarctions (MIs) were observed among patients

FIGURE 4-1 Results of searches and screening of potentially relevant studies.

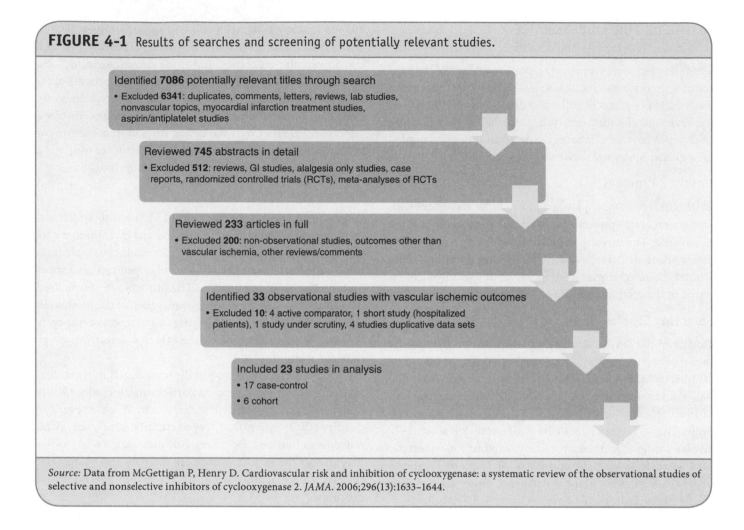

Identified **7086** potentially relevant titles through search
- Excluded **6341**: duplicates, comments, letters, reviews, lab studies, nonvascular topics, myocardial infarction treatment studies, aspirin/antiplatelet studies

Reviewed **745** abstracts in detail
- Excluded **512**: reviews, GI studies, alalgesia only studies, case reports, randomized controlled trials (RCTs), meta-analyses of RCTs

Reviewed **233** articles in full
- Excluded **200**: non-observational studies, outcomes other than vascular ischemia, other reviews/comments

Identified **33** observational studies with vascular ischemic outcomes
- Excluded **10**: 4 active comparator, 1 short study (hospitalized patients), 1 study under scrutiny, 4 studies duplicative data sets

Included **23** studies in analysis
- 17 case-control
- 6 cohort

Source: Data from McGettigan P, Henry D. Cardiovascular risk and inhibition of cyclooxygenase: a systematic review of the observational studies of selective and nonselective inhibitors of cyclooxygenase 2. *JAMA.* 2006;296(13):1633–1644.

randomized to the rofecoxib groups, while 12 MIs were observed in the comparison groups. What conclusions can you draw from the data on events? Are data on events alone adequate to establish an association? If not, what additional information would be useful?

ANALYZING DATA FROM META-ANALYSES: EXAMPLE FROM JUNI AND COLLEAGUES

The first step in a meta-analysis of RCTs is to present simple summary results for each treatment group in each trial. Data are summarized using descriptive statistics such as two-by-two tables of counts, proportions, or means, and standard deviations. Results from each study are frequently displayed graphically. At minimum, a useful meta-analysis generates a forest plot to provide a visual assessment of the study results and heterogeneity. (Heterogeneity is the degree of variation between individual study results.)

Figure 4-2 is a forest plot from the Juni meta-analysis[4] that graphically depicts the relationship between rofecoxib group assignment and myocardial infarction. Findings for each RCT are summarized on the right-hand side, on the same line as the reference. The box represents the point estimate (relative risk) and the horizontal line, the 95% confidence interval (CI); results are presented on a log scale. The size of the box corresponds to the relative size of the study. For example, the Ehrich study (2001)[6] was a relatively small study with wide confidence intervals. Risk of MI was slightly less among patients assigned to rofecoxib than among those assigned to the control group; however, the relationship was not statistically significant and the RR was very close to the null.

The diamond at the bottom of the forest plot is centered on the combined relative risk (2.24 in this case); the width of the diamond is the 95% CI of the combined RR. Note when describing results of a meta-analysis, it is important to use

FIGURE 4-2 Meta-analysis of randomized trials comparing rofecoxib with a control.

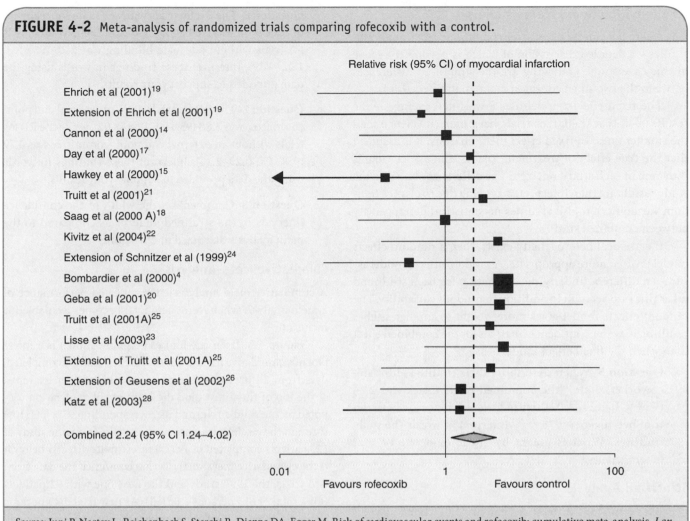

Source: Juni P, Nartey L, Reichenbach S, Sterchi R, Dieppe DA, Egger M. Risk of cardiovascular events and rofecoxib: cumulative meta-analysis. *Lancet.* 2004;364(9450):2021–2029.

language such as "combined risk" or "estimate from all trials combined."

> **Question 4** Examine Figure 4-2 and interpret findings of the two trials denoted by Bombardier et al.[3] and Extension of Truitt et al.[7]

Heterogeneity

An important step in a systematic review is the thoughtful consideration of whether it is appropriate to combine all of the studies in a meta-analysis. A statistic is frequently used to investigate the degree of variation between individual study results, which is called statistical heterogeneity. Where heterogeneity is considerable, the authors may investigate reasons for the differences between trial results. Clinical heterogeneity may be revealed by conducting analyses within strata of clinical features of the study subjects. Heterogeneity as a consequence of bias can be assessed by sensitivity analyses that examine whether study results differ by measures of methodological quality. Some basic examples that may lead to statistical heterogeneity include combining studies of different populations such as adults with children or combining data from patients suffering from different levels of disease severity such as those with metabolic syndrome and diabetes. It is important to note that statistical heterogeneity can also be a consequence of differences in study design and, for example, may be a result of combining cohort and case-control studies or clinical trials using disparate methods to adjudicate the outcome.

Fixed and Random Effects Models

Several analytic methods exist for combining data from health studies—a detailed discussion of which is beyond the scope of this case study. Following are the simplified differences between the two most common meta-analytic methods.

The fixed effects model uses a weighted average of the results such that the larger trials have more influence than the smaller ones. In fixed effect meta-analysis, it is assumed that the true effect of treatment, that is, the association, is the same in each study, or fixed. The differences between the study results are then interpreted as being due to chance (random variability). It also assumes no statistical heterogeneity between combined studies.

If statistical heterogeneity exists, then a random effects model is often more appropriate. A random effects model assumes a different underlying association for each study and takes this into account in addition to random variability. The random effects model gives more weight to smaller studies resulting in wider confidence intervals for the combined effect than when the fixed effect model is used.

Question 5 When describing their findings, Juni and coworkers state, "the combined relative risk was 2.24 (95% CI, 1.24–4.02), with little evidence of between trial heterogeneity."[4(p 2024)] Interpret in words the study findings. What is meant by "little evidence of trial heterogeneity?"

Stratified Analysis

Because significant differences can arise by chance (type I error), caution is advised when interpreting comparisons between subgroups. Where multiple possible sources of heterogeneity are investigated, the chance that one will be statistically significant increases. Thus, the number of factors considered should be limited, and if possible, determined prior to beginning the data analysis.

Juni and coworkers[4] collected data on two components of trial quality:

1. Concealment of allocation of patients to treatment groups—that is, whether there was adequate evidence of blinding.
2. External review of the end point, MI—that is, whether there was independent review and verification of the cardiovascular diagnoses contained in the medical records of study subjects.

They found only four trials described adequate concealment of allocation and that cardiovascular events were only externally reviewed in eight trials. The publication summarizes stratified analyses of the relative risk relationships between rofecoxib and MI.

Question 6 The RR for trials with adequate concealment of allocation was 2.04 (95% CI, 0.32–12.93), while the RR for trials without adequate blinding was 2.26 (95% CI, 1.22–4.19). Interpret these findings in words using the data provided to support your results.

Question 7 The RR for trials with an external end point committee was 3.88 (95% CI, 1.88–8.02), while the RR for trials without an external end point committee was 0.79 (95% CI, 0.29–2.13). Interpret these findings in words using the data provided to support your results.

Question 8 Comment on the width of the confidence intervals in the stratified analysis as compared to the main analysis discussed in Question 5.

Cumulative Meta-Analysis

A cumulative meta-analysis is the repeated performance of a meta-analysis whenever a new trial becomes available for inclusion.

Figure 4-3 (from the Juni et al. publication[4]) is a forest plot of a cumulative meta-analysis. As each study is completed, data from all previous studies are combined. For example, at the top of the forest plot, the estimate of association (denoted by the solid circle) and its corresponding 95% CIs (line through the circle) summarizes the results from one study of 523 patients completed in 1997. The estimate directly below it is the cumulative meta-analysis that combined the data from two trials, the 1997 study and the next one with 92 patients (for a total of 615 persons studied). As new trial data became available, it was added chronologically, such that each circle represents all trial data combined using meta-analytic methods up to that point in time.

In the discussion, the authors conclude: "Our cumulative meta-analysis of randomized controlled trials indicates that an increased risk of myocardial infarction was evident from 2000 onwards. At the end of 2000, the effect was both substantial and unlikely to be a chance finding."[4(pp 2024–2025)]

Question 9 Refer to the forest plot in Figure 4-3[ii] presenting results from the cumulative meta-analysis by Juni et al.[4] and describe what happened in 2000 to lead to the authors' stated conclusion.

[ii] Readers may note in examining Figures 4-2 and 4-3 that they both present results from 16 studies. Yet Figure 4-2 references 4 studies with publication dates after 2001, while Figure 4-3 references 16 studies adding evidence before the end of 2001. This apparent discrepancy is explained by the following information from Juni et al.: "In cumulative meta-analysis, cardiovascular safety data were included the year they first became available—i.e., the earliest of: submission of data to the FDA, presentation at a major conference, or publication in a journal."[4(p 2022)]

FIGURE 4-3 Cumulative meta-analysis of randomized trials comparing rofecoxib with a control.

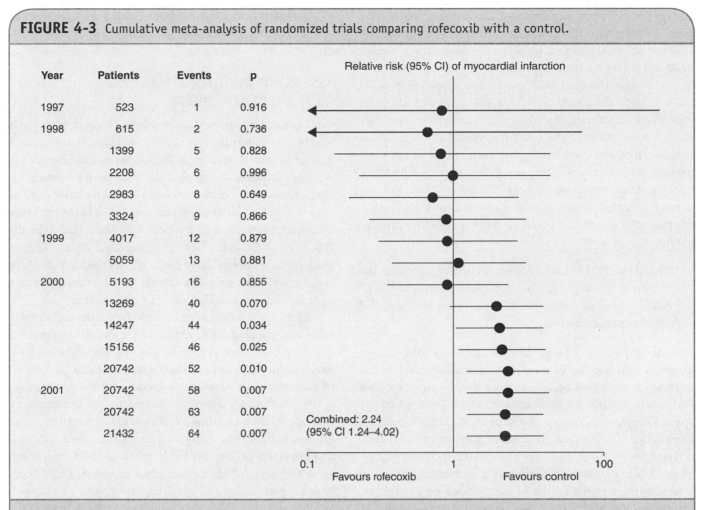

Year	Patients	Events	p
1997	523	1	0.916
1998	615	2	0.736
	1399	5	0.828
	2208	6	0.996
	2983	8	0.649
	3324	9	0.866
1999	4017	12	0.879
	5059	13	0.881
2000	5193	16	0.855
	13269	40	0.070
	14247	44	0.034
	15156	46	0.025
	20742	52	0.010
2001	20742	58	0.007
	20742	63	0.007
	21432	64	0.007

Relative risk (95% CI) of myocardial infarction

Combined: 2.24
(95% CI 1.24–4.02)

0.1   1   100
Favours rofecoxib   Favours control

Source: Juni P, Nartey L, Reichenbach S, Sterchi R, Dieppe DA, Egger M. Risk of cardiovascular events and rofecoxib: cumulative meta-analysis. *Lancet.* 2004;364(9450):2021–2029.

Question 10 The Juni et al.[4] meta-analysis was restricted to patients with chronic musculoskeletal disorders. Recall that in addition to management of osteoarthritis and acute pain in adults, rofecoxib was also approved for the treatment of menstrual symptoms and rheumatoid arthritis in adults and children. Comment on how generalizable the findings are from the Juni et al. meta-analysis. To whom can these data be extrapolated?

META-ANALYSIS OF OBSERVATIONAL EPIDEMIOLOGIC STUDIES: EXAMPLE FROM MCGETTIGAN AND HENRY

Today, systematic reviews and meta-analysis of observational epidemiologic studies are nearly as common as for clinical trials. The evidence available through clinical trials rarely answers all the important questions about the medical effectiveness of an intervention. Most clinical trials are designed to control bias when assessing the effectiveness of an intervention in a select population and clinical setting. Hence, patients enrolled in RCTs are often different from the average patient who might be taking a medication. Additionally RCTs are designed to detect treatment effects and do not usually include a large enough population to identify less common adverse events. Case-control and cohort studies add essential data about different populations and adverse events, and, in particular, those occurring later or after long-term use of an intervention.

There are indeed hypotheses that cannot be tested ethically using an RCT, such as environmental exposure to a potential carcinogen. Thus, in these situations, the best available data will come from observational studies. Therefore, systematic review and meta-analysis are increasingly important for summarizing the state of the science and generating the best available summary measure of effect for observational studies designed to test etiologic hypotheses.

Although the analytical methods are the same as described for RCTs, meta-analysis of case-control and cohort studies are complicated by additional biases that may distort study results. For example, when treatments or interventions are chosen by study subjects rather than randomly assigned, the people exposed to these interventions may have healthier lifestyles than unexposed people. Therefore it is important to recognize that meta-analysis of observational studies has the potential to produce precise but biased overall estimates of effects.

Question 11 Review the abstract and clearly state the purpose of the publication by McGettigan & Henry.[5] State specifically what the authors mean by controlled observational studies.

McGettigan and Henry[5] report findings from a large number of diverse study participants. Seventeen case-control analyses contributed 86,193 cases of cardiovascular events and nearly 530,000 control subjects. The 6 included cohort studies summarized about 75,000 users of COX-2 inhibitors, more than 375,000 users of nonselective nonsteroidal anti-inflammatory drugs, and nearly 600,000 unexposed participants. Study participants varied on a number of important confounding variables such as age, gender, geographic location, comorbidities, and concomitant drug use (such as aspirin). The outcome, serious cardiovascular events, was defined broadly, but in actuality was comprised mostly of two types of events: acute myocardial infarction and sudden cardiac death.

Question 12 Randomized clinical trials are considered the gold standard for assessing causality. When you think specifically about the case of Vioxx®, what additional information can you glean from a meta-analysis of observational studies of the relationship between rofecoxib and cardiovascular events?

Question 13 What is the primary outcome for the McGettigan study?[5] How does it differ from the primary outcome in the analysis completed by Juni et al.?[4] Comment on whether the outcome definition is broader or more specific. What are the implications of these differences when comparing these two meta-analyses?

Question 14 McGettigan and coworkers comment that "As with any systematic review, the limitations reflect those of the individual studies."[5(p 1642)] Discuss three

potential limitations of conducting a meta-analysis of observational epidemiologic studies.

ASSESSING WHETHER AN ASSOCIATION IS CAUSAL

One of the most important questions for the epidemiologist is how to determine causality; that is, whether a factor causes a disease. Sir Austin Bradford Hill, a British medical statistician, is known for his early appreciation of the need for a methodologic approach to causal inference. His criteria-based method appeared in 1965 (after a 5–6 year discussion in the literature on causal inference in chronic diseases and 1 year after the U.S. Surgeon General's Committee on Smoking and Cancer used a similar criteria-based method in its assessment). Hill's criteria (and more generally, criteria-based methods) remain a cornerstone of causal inference in epidemiology.[8]

The large numbers of epidemiologic studies and variable study designs used today can make the causal assessment a daunting task. Thus systematic reviews and meta-analyses have become important tools as one step in assessing causality. Meta-analyses are particularly important for assessing consistency of findings across studies and providing a summary estimate of effect. Question 15 asks you to interpret four causal criteria: temporality, strength of association, dose-response, and consistency. These are only a subset of Hill's criteria and are not enough to deem an association causal. At a minimum, biologic plausibility and specificity must also be assessed. While a detailed discussion of Hill's criteria is beyond the scope of this case, additional readings are listed at the end of the case. Synthesizing research data (e.g., systematic reviews and meta-analysis) is a useful tool and necessary step to determine causality. Assessing causality is a much broader question than the synthesis of study findings and requires the subsequent application of criterion-based methods.

Question 15 Now that you have reviewed evidence from Juni et al.[4] and McGettigan and Henry,[5] do you think that rofecoxib causes an excess risk of cardiovascular events? Describe evidence or lack of evidence contributed by each study for the following four causal criteria:

1. Temporality requires that the causal factor precedes its effect. Discuss the type of study designs and include specifics from the two meta-analyses as to how they do or do not establish temporality.
2. Strength of association refers to the magnitude of the relative risk estimates. Usually the larger the relative risk, the more likely the observed association is causal. *Interpret* estimates of effect from both papers.

3. Dose-response refers to the extent to which the relative risk estimates increase in magnitude as the dose increases. Using the following information, *interpret* estimates of effect of rofecoxib at different dose levels (don't forget to include 95% CIs).

    a. Juni et al.[4] report risk associated with low (12.5 mg/day), medium (25 mg/day), and high (50 mg/day) doses of rofecoxib corresponded to combined RRs of 2.71 (95% CI, 0.99–7.44), 1.37 (95% CI, 0.52–3.61), and 2.83 (95% CI, 1.24–6.43) respectively. Among trials with duration of 6 months or more, rofecoxib was associated with a 2.17 fold (95% CI, 1.03–4.59) increased risk of MI relative to the control group. Among trials with duration less than 6 months, the risk of MI associated with rofecoxib was similar, combined RR = 2.33 (95% CI, 0.90–6.03).

    b. McGettigan and Henry[5] report the combined RR for persons who took higher doses of rofecoxib (> 25 mg/day) was 2.19 (95% CI, 1.64–2.91) compared with those who took less than 25 mg/day, combined RR = 1.33 (95% CI, 1.00–1.79).

4. Consistency refers to the extent to which scientific results are similar across studies, that is with different populations, using different study designs, or within the same study design but conducted by different investigators. Generally, the more consistent the results, the more likely the observed association is causal. *Interpret* the consistency of findings across studies of rofecoxib and cardiovascular events.

CONCLUSION

One of the most important roles of the epidemiologist is to be able to objectively synthesize findings from multiple studies. For public health epidemiologists, the expertise to interpret combined findings from randomized clinical trials, cohort, and case-control studies is an integral tool in assessing health risk.

ACKNOWLEDGMENT

Thanks to Dr. Douglas L. Weed for his careful review and thoughtful insights on this chapter.

About the Author

Michelle Althuis, PhD, is an epidemiologist in private practice. Dr. Althuis helps clients to understand current research and epidemiology methods, and to use them to elucidate potentially causal relationships in evidence-based medicine. Dr. Althuis has more than 10 years of experience in epidemiological methods and research, as well as experience as an organic chemist. She has worked in private, public, and academic sectors, and, in each, maintained a strong focus on epidemiologic methodology, including but not limited to systematic reviews, weight of evidence methods, and assessment of causality. Dr. Althuis holds an academic appointment at the University of Maryland Baltimore, School of Medicine and has cotaught courses in epidemiologic methods at The George Washington University, School of Public Health and Health Services.

RECOMMENDED READINGS ON SYSTEMATIC REVIEWS, META-ANALYSIS, AND CAUSAL INFERENCE

Breslow RA, Ross SA, Weed DL. Quality of reviews in epidemiology. *Am J Public Health*. 1998;88(3):475–477.

Egger M, Smith GD, Altman DG, eds. *Systematic Reviews in Health Care, Meta-analysis in Context*. London, England: BMJ Publishing Group; 2001.

Perel P, Roberts I, Sena E, et al. Comparison of treatment effects between animal experiments and clinical trials: systematic review. *BMJ*. 2000;334(7586):197.

Petitti DB. *Meta-analysis, Decision Analysis, and Cost-effectiveness Analysis: Methods for Quantitative Synthesis in Medicine*. 2nd ed. New York, NY: Oxford University Press; 2000.

Stroup DF, Berlin JA, Morton SC, et al. Meta-analysis of observational studies in epidemiology: a proposal for reporting. *JAMA*. 2000;283(15):2008–2012.

Sutton AJ, Abrams KR, Jones DR, Sheldon TA, Song F. *Methods for meta-analysis in medical research*. Chichester, UK: John Wiley & Sons, Ltd; 2000.

Weed DL. Methodologic guidelines for review papers. *J Natl Cancer Inst*. 1997;89(1):6–7.

Weed DL, Gorelic LS. The practice of causal inference in cancer epidemiology. *Cancer Epidemiol Biomarkers Prev*. 1996;5(4):303–311.

REFERENCES

1. FDA. FDA Public health advisory: safety of Vioxx®. http://www.fda.gov/Drugs/DrugSafety/PostmarketDrugSafetyInformationforPatientsandProviders/ucm106274.htm. Updated September 30, 2004. Accessed December 10, 2010.

2. Graham DJ, Campen D, Hui R, et al. Risk of acute myocardial infarction and sudden cardiac death in patients treated with cyclo-oxygenase 2 selective and non-selective non-steroidal anti-inflammatory drugs: nested case-control study. *Lancet*. 2005;365(9458):475–481.

3. Bombardier C, Laine L, Reicin A, et al. Comparison of upper gastrointestinal toxicity of rofecoxib and naproxen in patients with rheumatoid arthritis. *N Engl J Med*. 2000;343(21):1520–1528.

4. Juni P, Nartey L, Reichenbach S, Sterchi R, Dieppe DA, Egger M. Risk of cardiovascular events and rofecoxib: cumulative meta-analysis. *Lancet*. 2004;364(9450):2021–2029.

5. McGettigan P, Henry D. Cardiovascular risk and inhibition of cyclooxygenase: a systematic review of the observational studies of selective and non-selective inhibitors of cyclooxygenase 2. *JAMA*. 2006;296(13):1633–1644.

6. Ehrich EW, Bolognese JA, Watson DJ, Kong SX. Effect of rofecoxib therapy on measures of health-related quality of life in patients with osteoarthritis. *Am J Manag Care*. 2001;7:609–616.

7. Truitt KE, Lee M, DeTora LM, Anderson M, Zhao Rahway PL. Results of a pivotal (Phase III) placebo and active comparator controlled efficacy trial of rofecoxib 12·5 and 25 mg in adult patients with rheumatoid arthritis (RA). *Arthritis Rheum*. 2001;44:S369.

8. Hill AB. The environment and disease: association or causation? *Proc Roy Soc Med*. 1965;58:295–300.

Appendix

Abstract for Juni et al. 2004.[4]

Background: The cyclo-oxygenase 2 inhibitor rofecoxib was recently withdrawn because of cardiovascular adverse effects. An increased risk of myocardial infarction had been observed in 2000 in the Vioxx® Gastrointestinal Outcomes Research study (VIGOR), but was attributed to cardioprotection of naproxen rather than a cardiotoxic effect of rofecoxib. We used standard and cumulative random-effects meta-analyses of randomized controlled trials and observational studies to establish whether robust evidence on the adverse effects of rofecoxib was available before September, 2004.

Methods: We searched bibliographic databases and relevant files of the US Food and Drug Administration. We included all randomized controlled trials in patients with chronic musculoskeletal disorders that compared rofecoxib with other non-steroidal anti-inflammatory drugs (NSAIDs) or placebo, and cohort and case-control studies of cardiovascular risk and naproxen. Myocardial infarction was the primary endpoint.

Findings: We identified 18 randomized controlled trials and 11 observational studies. By the end of 2000 (52 myocardial infarctions, 20, 742 patients) the relative risk from randomized controlled trials was $2 \cdot 30$ (95% CI $1 \cdot 22 – 4 \cdot 33$, p = $0 \cdot 010$), and one year later (64 events, 21 432 patients) it was $2 \cdot 24$ ($1 \cdot 24 – 4 \cdot 02$, p = $0 \cdot 007$). There was little evidence that the relative risk differed depending on the control group (placebo, non-naproxen NSAID, or naproxen; p = $0 \cdot 41$) or trial duration (p = $0 \cdot 82$). In observational studies, the cardioprotective effect of naproxen was small (combined estimate $0 \cdot 86$ [95% CI $0 \cdot 75 – 0 \cdot 99$]) and could not have explained the findings of the VIGOR trial.

Interpretation: Our findings indicate that rofecoxib should have been withdrawn several years earlier. The reasons why manufacturer and drug licensing authorities did not continuously monitor and summarize the accumulating evidence need to be clarified.

Abstract for McGettigan & Henry, 2006.[5]

Context: Evidence that rofecoxib increases the risk of myocardial infarction has led to scrutiny of other nonsteroidal anti-inflammatory drugs (NSAIDs). Regulatory agencies have provided variable advice regarding the cardiovascular risks with older nonselective NSAIDs.

Objective: To undertake a systematic review and meta-analysis of controlled observational studies to compare the risks of serious cardiovascular events with individual NSAIDs and cyclooxygenase 2 inhibitors.

Data Sources: Searches were conducted of electronic databases (1985–2006), scientific meeting proceedings, epidemiological research websites, and bibliographies of eligible studies.

Study Selection: Eligible studies were of case-control or cohort design, reported on cardiovascular events (predominantly myocardial infarction) with cyclooxygenase 2 inhibitor, NSAID use, or both with nonuse/remote use of the drugs as the reference exposure. Of 7,086 potentially eligible titles, 17 case-control and six cohort studies were included. Thirteen studies reported on cyclooxygenase 2 inhibitors, 23 on NSAIDs, and 13 on both groups of drugs.

Data Extraction: Two people independently extracted data and assessed study quality with disagreements resolved by consensus.

Data Synthesis: Data were combined using a random-effects model. A dose-related risk was evident with rofecoxib, summary relative risk with 25 mg/d or less, 1.33 (95% confidence interval [CI], 1.00–1.79) and 2.19 (95% CI, 1.64–2.91) with more than 25 mg/d. The risk was elevated during the first month of treatment. Celecoxib was not associated with an elevated risk of vascular occlusion, summary relative risk 1.06 (95% CI, 0.91–1.23). Among older nonselective drugs, diclofenac had the highest risk with a summary relative risk of 1.40 (95% CI, 1.16–1.70). The other drugs had summary relative risks close to 1: naproxen, 0.97 (95% CI, 0.87–1.07); piroxicam, 1.06 (95% CI, 0.70–1.59); and ibuprofen, 1.07 (95% CI, 0.97–1.18).

Conclusions: This review confirms the findings from randomized trials regarding the risk of cardiovascular events with rofecoxib and suggests that celecoxib in commonly used doses may not increase the risk, contradicts claims of a protective effect of naproxen, and raises serious questions about the safety of diclofenac, an older drug.

PART II

Policy Development Cases: Overview

Policy development is the process of making decisions as to how to address societal problems. Assessment and research provide the evidence base for the development of policies that determine which practices to support, how resources should be allocated, and how efforts should be mobilized to achieve the defined policy goals.

In addition to research, which underlies all other essential services, 3 of the 10 essential public health services fall into the category of policy development. They include:

- Informing, educating, and empowering people about health issues.
- Mobilizing community partnerships to identify and solve health problems.
- Developing policies and plans that support individual and community health efforts.

The policy development section includes 11 case studies. The cases are:

5. The Heart Truth® Campaign—A Social Marketing Approach to Increase Awareness about Heart Disease in Women
6. An Outbreak of Yellow Fever in Paraguay: Health Risk Communication in a Crisis
7. Challenges with Implementing a Community-Based Potable Water System Project in a Rural Honduran Community
8. Building on Strengths: A School-Based Mental Health Program
9. Building Trust in Communities: The Narragansett Indian Tribe and the State of Rhode Island
10. The Strategies to Overcome and Prevent (STOP) Obesity Alliance
11. Should HPV Vaccine Be Required for School Entry?
12. Plan B Emergency Contraception: Caught in a Web of Science, Regulation, and Politics—What's a Woman to Do?
13. Implementing Policy Changes to Decrease Racial and Ethnic Disparities in Pediatric Asthma Outcomes
14. Coal Ash: Disasters and Opportunities
15. The Diethylstilbestrol (DES) Story: An Investigation into the Evolving Public Health Policy for Pharmaceutical Products

Three cases in this section address the function of informing, educating, and empowering people about health issues, which is an essential precursor to informed policy development and implementation. The Heart Truth® campaign is the first U.S. government-sponsored campaign aimed at increasing awareness among women about their risk of heart disease.

The Heart Truth—A Social Marketing Approach to Increase Awareness about Heart Disease in Women describes the social marketing techniques the campaign used to dramatically increase women's understanding. In 2000, only 34% of U.S. women knew heart disease was their leading cause of death; by 2009, 54% were aware.

An Outbreak of Yellow Fever in Paraguay: Health Risk Communication in a Crisis helps learners think through a different aspect of communications, that of informing the public when a disease outbreak occurs. The case considers the difficulties government officials face when balancing the need to inform without creating undue fear in a community at risk. The last case addressing communications, *Challenges with Implementing a Community-Based Potable Water System Project in a Rural Honduran Community,* is about the role public health professionals can play in empowering people whose voices are underrepresented or even sometimes ignored in the policy-making process. Using a participatory approach, this case provides insight into the following questions: How should policy makers incorporate stakeholders in their decision processes? How can policies that best address the people they are most likely to affect be formed?

Mobilizing community partnerships is the next essential public health service covered in the volume. Three cases present learners with opportunities to examine the processes—including their associated trials and tribulations—of forming and mobilizing partnerships for the betterment of communities. *Building on Strengths: A School-Based Mental Health Program* addresses how to maintain a successful partnership between a school district, 2 local public schools, a university school of social work, and a community mental health center. The partnership helps students in a bilingual and bicultural region in Mississippi, but struggles to overcome community biases and faces budgetary pressures in the ongoing economic crisis. *Building Trust in Communities: The Narragansett Indian Tribe and the State of Rhode Island* also considers the public health needs of minorities. The interrelated issues of trust, history, and cultural relations are examined, and learners are encouraged to think about the different ways bridges can be built between fragmented concerns.

Addressing different types of constituencies, the STOP Obesity Alliance acts as a bridge between the private and public sector to promote solutions to the complex challenges of obesity. Bringing together representatives from for-profit companies, government agencies, academia, patients, healthcare providers and healthcare payers, *The Strategies to Overcome and Prevent (STOP) Obesity Alliance* provides real-life nuts and bolts information on how divergent interests can come together to address public health problems.

Perhaps the most well-known aspect of policy development is the creation of policies and plans. This volume presents 5 cases that consider different aspects of the essence of policy development: addressing conflicting views about how resources should be allocated and what course of action should be pursued. The first 2 of these cases present deliberations between government decision makers and specific constituent groups. *Should HPV Vaccine Be Required for School Entry?* discusses how a community makes a decision about whether to require girls to receive the HPV vaccine before they can enroll in school. Parents, religious leaders, government officials, and public health experts weigh in on the pros and cons of such a requirement.

Similarly, *Plan B Emergency Contraception: Caught in a Web of Science, Regulation, and Politics—What's a Woman to Do?* shows how a government regulatory process supposedly driven by science can also be influenced by the political,

ethical, and moral concerns of a broad range of interested parties. In the case, *Implementing Policy Changes to Decrease Racial and Ethnic Disparities in Pediatric Asthma Outcomes*, the authors describe yet an additional hurdle health policy makers face: overcoming infrastructure barriers to access to preventive and healthcare services, especially for disadvantaged populations.

The policy development section is rounded out with two cases illustrating that policy formation is ever evolving. *Coal Ash: Disasters and Opportunities* and *The Diethylstilbestrol (DES) Story: An Investigation into the Evolving Public Health Policy for Pharmaceutical Products* examine the role of U.S. federal government agencies as writers and implementers of public health policy. Both cases present learners with a retrospective view of how policies, once made, need to be revisited, assessed for effectiveness, and changed, if necessary, to continue to assure the public's health is protected.

The Heart Truth®

A Social Marketing Approach to Increase Awareness about Heart Disease in Women

ANN M. TAUBENHEIM, SALLY MCDONOUGH, TERRY LONG, JENNIFER WAYMAN, AND SARAH TEMPLE

Inspire. Engage. Empower. These three words express the aspirations of The Heart Truth®, the first federally sponsored campaign aimed at increasing awareness among women about their risk of heart disease. The campaign, launched in September 2002, is sponsored by the National Heart, Lung, and Blood Institute (NHLBI), part of the U.S. National Institutes of Health. It aims to raise women's awareness that heart disease is their No. 1 killer and motivate them to take action to reduce their risk.

BACKGROUND AND CONTEXT: HEART DISEASE—WOMEN'S HEALTH ISSUE

In 2000, only 34% of U.S. women knew that heart disease was their leading cause of death.[1] Yet, at that time, one in three deaths in U.S. women was due to heart disease, and even today the condition kills more women than all forms of cancer combined.[2] Consumer research showed that women perceived heart disease as a condition that overwhelmingly affects men, and they often failed to take their own risk seriously or personally.[3]

Women's heart disease risk starts to rise dramatically in middle age. Although many women underestimate their

---

The Heart Truth, The Red Dress, and Heart Disease Doesn't Care What You Wear—It's the #1 Killer of Women are registered trademarks of the U.S. Department of Health and Human Services.

National Wear Red Day is a registered trademark of the U.S. Department of Health and Human Services and American Heart Association.

personal risk of developing heart disease, fully 80% of midlife women have one or more of the modifiable factors that increase heart disease risk—high blood pressure, high cholesterol, overweight/obesity, physical inactivity, diabetes, and smoking. Women are developing risk factors at younger ages than ever before. Of women ages 20–39, 60% have one or more of the risk factors, and more than 2 million women ages 25–44 already have heart disease.[4] Furthermore, compared with other groups, African American and Hispanic women have higher rates of some of the heart disease risk factors, and although awareness of heart disease risk has increased in these groups, they are still significantly less likely to be aware than white women.[5] Having one or more of the risk factors dramatically increases a woman's chance of developing heart disease. Just one risk factor doubles the risk. Having two risk factors—for example, being overweight and having high blood pressure—increases risk fourfold, and having three or more risk factors increases risk more than tenfold.[6]

Recognizing the seriousness of the problem, the NHLBI convened a strategy development workshop in March 2001 to gain advice from women's health leaders and other experts on an action plan to help reduce heart disease risk in women. The group unanimously recommended that the NHLBI undertake a national campaign to raise women's awareness about their risk of heart disease and how to lower it. Later that year, the NHLBI awarded a contract to Ogilvy Public Relations Worldwide to plan and implement such a campaign. After about a year of consumer research and analysis, materials development and testing, and partnership building, the NHLBI launched The Heart Truth® in September 2002. The campaign was designed as a social marketing initiative that integrated a strong branding strategy. The launch of the campaign included the introduction of what proved to be a powerful new brand for women's heart disease—The Red Dress®.

CAMPAIGN PLANNING AND DEVELOPMENT

To guide development and implementation, the campaign used the social marketing process described in *Making Health Communication Programs Work*[7] and in Box 5-1. The campaign also drew on relevant constructs from behavior and social change theories and models that support the development of effective strategies for influencing attitudes and behavior, including theories focused on determinants of behavior (Health Belief Model, Theory of Reasoned Action/Planned Behavior, and Social Learning Theory) and the Transtheoretical Model of stages of individual behavior change.

Formative Research and Planning Process

As the federal government's first national campaign on women and heart disease, The Heart Truth® had a golden opportunity at the outset to build a campaign based on strong formative research. The initial research process included the following:

- A comprehensive analysis of midlife women, including demographics and psychographics, geographic and socioeconomic factors, heart health knowledge, attitudes and behaviors, and media preferences
- A literature review of 200+ research articles on cardiovascular health and women
- Eight focus groups in four cities across the country to test creative concepts and messages
- Materials review by the campaign's core government and community organization partners

This research influenced a range of elements in the planning process, including defining the target audience and objectives, message and materials development, channel and activity selection, and partner recruitment. Updated research continues to inform the campaign implementation and overall direction, including refining the target audience selection, new messages and materials, and decisions about partnership and event opportunities and media strategy.

Audience and Objectives

The primary audience for the campaign was women ages 40–60 (a time when women's risk rises dramatically), especially those who have at least one risk factor for heart disease and were not taking action. A secondary audience was women

of all ages, since heart disease develops over time and can start as early as the teen years, and it is never too late for women to take action to lower their heart disease risk. Another secondary audience, physicians and other health professionals, was addressed mainly by campaign partners.

The campaign objectives were:

- Increase awareness among women that heart disease is their No. 1 killer
- Increase awareness of the risk factors that can lead to heart disease, disability, and death
- Encourage women to talk to their doctors, learn their personal risk factors, and take action to prevent or control their risk

Research-Based Insights and Creative Platform

The formative research revealed that women were (1) generally aware of the risk factors, (2) not making the personal connection between their risk factors and their own personal risk of heart disease, (3) surprised to learn that heart disease was their No. 1 killer, (4) shocked to learn that it kills significantly more women than breast cancer, and (5) of the belief that heart disease is a man's disease and not a woman's issue.

The research also showed that the campaign should include specific message elements. It should state clearly that heart disease is women's leading killer. It should "put a face" on heart disease to show that it could happen to them. Furthermore, the research showed that women responded well to a hard-hitting approach that clearly showed the consequences of heart disease. This finding led the planners to take a significant departure from the messages then in use to communicate to women about heart disease. These were generally softer wellness-oriented educational efforts that did not focus on how heart disease can lead to disability and even death. The research also showed that to balance the negative approach, the message should include a sense of hope that women can lower their risk, and it should give a clear call to action, although still coupled with a sense of urgency.

Testing of several potential creative executions showed that women were engaged by concepts featuring women like themselves (e.g., real women) and receptive to the analogy of caring for both their outer (appearance) *and* inner (health) selves. It also showed women's receptivity to a strong wake-up call about the dangers of heart disease.

From this research, a creative platform emerged as the backbone of the entire campaign: **"Heart Disease Doesn't Care What You Wear—It's the #1 Killer of Women.®"** The platform was paired with the newly created brand for women and heart disease—The Red Dress®. At the time the campaign began, use of branding was increasing in the public health arena as more social marketers began to understand that branding principles were not only applicable to products and services, but also to health behaviors, attitudes, and beliefs. By integrating a strong branding strategy into a traditional social marketing approach, the campaign sought to give a unique identity to the women's heart disease issue and create a strong emotional connection with women. In testing, the brand proved to appeal to a wide diversity of women. It made the emotional connection that was needed . . . the "red alert" for women to care about their inner selves and change the way they think about heart disease. Based on women's attraction to the brand and its potential for enhancing virtually every phase of implementation, the campaign proceeded to introduce the Red Dress® as the national symbol for women and heart disease awareness. The brand has become the central driving force of the campaign, attracting corporate and media partners, creating a focal point for national and local campaign events and media coverage, and providing consistent imagery across the campaign materials, as well as in partner-sponsored advertising and promotions.

CAMPAIGN IMPLEMENTATION

Since its launch, The Heart Truth® has employed three broad tracks of activity: partnership development, media relations, and community programming.

Partnership Development: Since the beginning, the campaign was envisioned to be a partnership-based initiative in order to provide an element that social marketing programs often lack—a distribution and promotion infrastructure, as well as monetary and in-kind resources. An aggressive strategy has been used to engage partners in the corporate, media, and nonprofit sectors that count women among their core target audience and support national promotional programming and outreach. In the corporate sector, partnerships span women-oriented areas such as fashion, cosmetics, nutrition, and retail. Media partners have included major national broadcast, print, and online outlets. The focus for nonprofit partners has been on organizations that offer useful infrastructures—for example, local affiliates or chapters—that are capable of reaching women at the national and/or local levels.

Media Relations: National earned media (that is, publicity gained through promotional efforts other than advertising/paid media) and social media outreach has sought to position the NHLBI as a leader of the women's heart disease awareness movement by capitalizing on the campaign's national platforms and leveraging regional and local activities.

Community Programming: Relationships with national nonprofit organizations are reinforced with programming sponsored directly by the campaign that reaches women at the local level.

The campaign's brand-driven social marketing mix of national and local programming includes both high-visibility national signature programs and community-level interventions. Within the three broad tracks of activities previously noted, the campaign's main implementation venues include signature programs and activities, community partnerships and programs, corporate partnerships and programs, media relations, media partnerships, and social media marketing.

Signature Programs and Activities

Seeking to mobilize an industry intrinsically tied to women to help advance the Red Dress® symbol, the campaign forged a groundbreaking collaboration between the federal government and the fashion industry. This partnership, along with the campaign's media and community outreach strategies, served as the foundation for a number of signature national programs and activities, including:

- The Red Dress Collection® fashion show held each February since 2003 at New York's Fashion Week, featuring more than 150 designs from top fashion designers modeled by a diverse roster of celebrity women, such as Sheryl Crow, Kelly Ripa, Heidi Klum, Venus Williams, Angela Bassett, Rachael Ray, Christie Brinkley, Vanessa Williams, Rita Moreno, Billie Jean King, Sarah Ferguson, Ana Ortiz, Cicely Tyson, Christina Milian, Fergie, Eartha Kitt, and Liza Minnelli.
- Support from former First Lady Laura Bush as the campaign's founding ambassador. Mrs. Bush participated in more than a dozen national and local events across the country and hosted two White House events, including a February 2008 reception to salute the fashion industry's support of The Heart Truth® and the campaign's fifth anniversary.
- More than 500 The Heart Truth® local events through initiatives such as The Heart Truth® Road Show, a traveling educational exhibit that featured free educational materials and heart health screenings; and Single-City events, where partners in local communities hosted events featuring a selection of dresses from the Red Dress Collection®, alongside campaign messages.
- Creation of National Wear Red Day® in partnership with several national organizations and corporations. On National Wear Red Day—observed on the first Friday in February—partners and the public were asked to wear red and conduct educational activities in support of women and heart disease awareness.
- Implementation of The Heart Truth® Champions Program to train and equip health educators and women's health advocates as The Heart Truth® Champions in their local communities. These champions, in turn, conducted a wide range of heart health education activities and events.

Community Partnerships and Programs

Examples of community partnerships and programs include:

- Ongoing relationships and outreach programs with more than 25 national and local community organizations, including WomenHeart: the National Coalition for Women with Heart Disease, the General Federation of Women's Clubs, and Hadassah.
- Women of color and faith-based initiatives with organizations such as The Links, Inc., National Black Nurses Association, Association of Black Cardiologists, National Coalition of Pastors' Spouses, National Latina Health Network, and the Black Women's Health Imperative.
- Development of health provider education tools and continuing medical education programs in partnership with the U.S. Department of Health and Human Services' Office on Women's Health. These efforts were promoted to providers through partnerships with the American College of Cardiology and The Heart Truth® health provider exhibit at 25 professional conferences reaching more than 275,000 health professionals.

Corporate Partnerships and Programs

Examples of corporate partnerships and programs include:

- Establishment of partnerships with more than 50 corporations, including IMG Fashion, Diet Coke, Johnson & Johnson, General Mills, TimeWarner, Swarovski, Celestial Seasonings, Albertsons, and American Express, among others.
- Ongoing promotional programming that reached millions of women, including on-pack and in-store promotions and advertising with Diet Coke, Cheerios, Swarovski, and Bobbi Brown Cosmetics.

Media Relations, Media Partnerships, and Social Media Marketing

The campaign has focused on targeted outreach to print, broadcast, and online media outlets, especially health, lifestyle, fashion, entertainment, and women's media. Media relations plans were implemented for the campaign's major recurring signature events that take place during February—National Wear Red Day® and the Red Dress® fashion shows—as well as other related observances and events throughout the year, such as Mother's Day. Media impressions increased each year as the campaign gained experience and the signature events became better recognized by entertainment and fashion media outlets.

Social media marketing has been defined as "a way of using the Internet to instantly collaborate, share information, and have a conversation about ideas or causes we care about."[8](slide 15) The term is sometimes confused with social marketing, a process that is several decades old that aims to bring about social change. The campaign's marketing efforts using social media platforms such as Facebook, Flickr, and YouTube began with a pilot project in 2007 and increased as the campaign matured and the online world evolved. The campaign team measured results each year and adjusted tactics accordingly. The various social media and Internet marketing tactics have provided a combined impact of many millions of additional audience impressions at a relatively low cost. Highlights of media relations and social media include the following:

- Aggressive implementation of media relations at the national level, especially for the campaign signature events, which resulted in extensive coverage in top-tier media outlets. Community-based activities such as road shows and appearances by former First Lady Laura Bush also generated substantial coverage in local markets throughout the year.
- Partnerships with numerous media outlets, including *Newsweek*, *Glamour*, Lifetime TV, *Essence*, *Hispanic*, *Woman's Day*, and Time Inc. Women's Group, which generated substantial editorial coverage, advertorials, and public service announcement placement.
- Outreach to influential bloggers within the women's, health, news, and fashion communities. Selected bloggers were invited to the Red Dress fashion show and were given additional information about the campaign to include in their blogs.
- Topical public service advertising banners with campaign imagery and messaging that garnered placements on major media websites, such as AOL.com, USAToday.com, and MSN.com.
- The federal government's first consumer-focused widget (interactive virtual tool that provides a service). First launched in 2008, The Heart Truth National Wear Red Day® countdown widget was made free for anyone to download to a website, Facebook page, or blog. The application streamed images from The Heart Truth® Flickr gallery and helped supporters count down to National Wear Red Day®. The tool was promoted through influencer outreach, blog postings, message boards, and social networks.
- The Heart Truth® Facebook Fan page, which launched in 2008, created a social forum for the campaign to directly connect with consumers and provided a quick and cost-effective way to deliver campaign updates and heart health information to "fans" of the campaign.
- In 2010, The Heart Truth® launched a Twitter handle (@TheHeartTruth) and hosted its first ever Twitter party on National Wear Red Day®, gathering supporters online during a specified time period to share stories about heart health. The campaign team offered a free Twitter training to The Heart Truth® community partners to encourage supporters to spread campaign messages through this platform during American Heart Month (February) and year-round.

MATERIALS DEVELOPMENT

During its 8 years, the campaign continued to develop and update research-based educational materials in various formats for use by the public and partners. Based on formative research and testing, the materials were built around compelling photos and stories of real women's struggles with heart disease. These served to put a face on women's heart disease and provided consistent branding across various types of materials. Materials include:

- Creation of a comprehensive suite of educational and marketing materials, including a Red Dress® pin; wallet card with space to record blood pressure levels and other personal risk factor data; a 100-page risk-reduction action guide, the *Healthy Heart Handbook for Women*; a "talk in a box" speaker's kit with 10-minute video and PowerPoint presentation; fact sheets for women of color and other audiences; real women posters; and print and broadcast public service announcements.
- Launch and maintenance of the campaign's web pages (www.HeartTruth.gov), which include campaign materials and resources, a Spanish-language subsite, a National Wear Red Day® online tool kit providing ideas and resources for educational activities, and an activity registry to encourage individuals and organizations nationwide to share information about The Heart Truth® and the Red Dress® activities they have implemented.

RESULTS

The Heart Truth® ignited a powerful awareness movement, rallying the women's health community, major corporations, local and regional community groups, and the national media toward a common goal of greater awareness and better heart health for all women. The campaign had a limited budget for measuring results and sought to stretch its evaluation resources by collecting some data in house and using outside sources when possible. In general, campaign resources were used to collect data on process measures such as audience impressions (number of people estimated to have seen a message), partner contributions, and social media and other media coverage. In measuring campaign impact (which can be more expensive), the team used surveys and studies already being conducted by the American Heart Association to assess progress in raising women's awareness and motivating behavior change. In addition, corporate and media partners provided process information such as the extent of brand promotions on product packaging and also funded some audience surveys to measure impact. This combination of in-house and outside resources helped provide a cost-effective picture of the campaign's results. Highlights included process measures and impact and outcome measures, among others.

Process Measures

- Corporate partners produced billions of audience impressions (that is, the number of people estimated to have seen the image or message) on product packaging and in print and broadcast advertising, including Diet Coke-sponsored ads during the 2008, 2009, and 2010 Oscars telecasts and the 2010 Winter Olympics.
- By March 2010, the campaign brand promotion on cereal, beverage, and other product packaging totaled more than 15 billion.
- In-kind promotional support, including from the fashion and celebrity industries, is conservatively valued at more than $100 million. Corporate sponsors made it possible to execute the campaign's seven Red Dress Collection® fashion shows and multiple road show events.
- A media audit showed that coverage of the women and heart disease issue increased 70% in the year following the launch of the Red Dress®.
- Media impressions (the combined total of viewers/ listeners/readers of the media outlets that carried the story) increased each year since the campaign's launch. Broadcast, newspaper, magazine, and online placements all contributed to nearly 3 billion audience impressions by 2009. Coverage has included high-circulation lifestyle, entertainment, fashion, and women's media.
- Overall, in 2009, social media have contributed an estimated 64 million unique monthly visitors from postings generated by social media outlets and users, both organically and through outreach by the campaign team.
- Corporate partners such as Diet Coke and Johnson & Johnson also contributed to the online impact. Their many online offerings such as advertisements, e-newsletters, microsites, web banners, and blogs, highlighted the campaign and resulted in millions of additional audience impressions.

Impact and Outcome Measures

- Awareness among women that heart disease is their leading cause of death has increased substantially. In 2000, only 34% of women knew that heart disease is the No. 1 killer of women. In 2009, 54% were aware.[9]
- Rising awareness about risk has done more than just inform women; it is leading them to take action. Recent research shows that women who are aware of the threat

of heart disease are 35% more likely to be physically active and 47% more likely to report weight loss than women who are less aware.[10]

- The awareness gap among younger women has narrowed. In 1997, only 16% of women women ages 25–34 were aware that heart disease is women's No. 1 killer. In 2009, 50% were aware.[11]
- The Red Dress® has been adopted as the national symbol for women and heart disease awareness across the country. The symbol has also been recognized and adopted internationally. In 2010, about 60% of women recognized the Red Dress® as the symbol for women and heart disease, up from 25% in 2005. The symbol clearly resonates with women; those who have seen, heard, or read about the Red Dress® were more likely to know that heart disease is their leading killer than women who were not familiar with the symbol. The women familiar with the symbol were also substantially more likely than other women to take at least one risk-reducing action as a result—up from 35% in 2008 to 57% in 2010.[12]
- A crucial first step toward reducing heart disease risk is finding out about one's personal risk, and more women are doing this. A recent survey shows that 48% of women reported discussing heart disease with their doctors in 2009, up from 30% in 1997.[13]
- In addition to increases in awareness and associated preventive action, there has also been progress in reducing heart disease deaths in women. In 2003, of the women who died in America, one in three died of heart disease. This has shifted to one in four women.[14] Although the decline in mortality is mostly associated with factors such as improved treatment, the increase in awareness and actions to reduce risk that are associated with The Heart Truth® and other campaigns also have likely played a role.

Other Measures

- The Heart Truth® campaign won all major health communications and PR industry awards in its class for its creativity and success in marketing heart health awareness to women across America.
- In 2010, *The Holmes Report* named The Heart Truth® as one of the five most successful campaigns of the decade.
- *Social Marketing Quarterly*, Fall 2008 (Vol. XIV, No. 3) featured a special section on The Heart Truth®, including a main article on the campaign development and results, and additional articles on aspects of the

campaign—formative research, branding, social media, and partnership building. Another brief article shared the campaign team's 10 top insights into what makes a campaign successful.

FUTURE DIRECTIONS

The Heart Truth® continues to seek ways to build on past success and create a vibrant future for the women and heart disease movement. The campaign team believes that a key to future success is to continue the emphasis on thoughtful and strategic brand-driven social marketing approaches that strengthen existing programs and infuse the campaign with new ideas. In the current phase of the campaign, these approaches include the following:

- Expand the message and strategies of the campaign to focus more heavily on motivations and barriers to heart healthy behaviors, while at the same time continuing to build awareness of heart disease as women's leading cause of death.
- Enhance existing strategies and activities that reach younger women since women are developing risk factors at younger ages than ever before, and 60% of women ages 20–39 have one or more of the risk factors.
- Continue the national focus of the campaign as a means of sparking excitement and visibility and sustaining awareness, while also ensuring the availability of programs at the local level that help women move from awareness to action.
- Continue to focus on women of color, who have lower levels of awareness and higher prevalence of some heart disease risk factors, through specialized outreach and tailored messages.
- As the Red Dress® brand becomes mature, refine the way it is presented and promoted in order to keep it fresh and appealing to women. Continue to emphasize programs, media strategies, and mechanisms that advance the visibility of the Red Dress® and enhance its ability to accelerate the campaign's momentum.
- Continue to cultivate partners across the corporate, media, and nonprofit sectors, using strategies that sustain existing partnerships and reveal new ones that will complement the campaign's directions.

To achieve effective, meaningful follow-up to the approaches described in this case study, the campaign will need to sustain the momentum it has helped to build and seek to produce results that lead to lasting change in the lives of women.

CONCLUSION

In the 8 years since its launch, The Heart Truth® has sparked a national movement to reach women across America about their risk of heart disease. To do so, the campaign reached out to and involved the women's health community, major corporations, local and regional community groups, and national, local, and social media. The driving force of The Heart Truth® is its powerful brand, the Red Dress®, which has contributed substantially to the campaign's progress toward its stated objectives: to *inspire* women to become more aware about heart disease risk, *engage* them in finding out their personal risk, and *empower* them in communities nationwide to take action to reduce their risk. More information is available on the campaign's website, www.hearttruth.gov.

About the Authors

Ann M. Taubenheim, PhD, MSN, is the chief of the Health Campaigns and Consumer Services Branch, Office of Communications at the National Heart, Lung, and Blood Institute (NHLBI) of the U.S. National Institutes of Health. She serves as project director for The Heart Truth® campaign, overseeing strategic program planning and development, implementation, and evaluation. She also serves as the project officer for the NHLBI Health Information Center and leads the center's work in developing new technologies for responding to public inquiries and marketing and promoting the Institute's health information to patients, health professionals, and the public.

Sally McDonough, BA, is the director of the Office of Communications for the National Heart, Lung, and Blood Institute. She leads the Institute on communications strategy and the execution of all public affairs and media activities and oversees the Institute's Health Information Center and its public health campaigns. Prior to joining the NHLBI, Ms. McDonough served as special assistant to the President and director of communications and press secretary to First Lady Laura Bush and as vice president and director of cause-related programming at Ogilvy Public Relations Worldwide, where she managed a broad portfolio of accounts.

Terry Long, BA, served as the communications director of the National Heart, Lung, and Blood Institute, where she directed media relations, education campaigns, and product marketing for NHLBI's research and education programs. She was the senior manager of The Heart Truth®, NHLBI's national campaign to increase awareness about women and heart disease. Before joining NHLBI, she managed media relations, campaigns, and prevention programs for other agencies of the U.S. Department of Health and Human Services. She retired from the National Institutes of Health in 2007 and is now a consultant in health communications.

Jennifer Wayman, MHS, is an executive vice president with Ogilvy Public Relations Worldwide and codirector of Ogilvy's Social Marketing Practice in Washington, DC. She specializes in the strategic development, implementation, and evaluation of national social marketing and health communications campaigns, with an emphasis on women's health. Currently, Jennifer serves as corporate monitor for Ogilvy's work on the National Heart, Lung, and Blood Institute's The Heart Truth® campaign, after serving as the project director for the campaign's first 5 years.

Sarah Temple, BA, is a senior vice president with Ogilvy Public Relations Worldwide, where she specializes in strategic health communications planning, public/private partnership development, and corporate social responsibility programming. Currently, Sarah serves as the project director for Ogilvy's work on the National Heart, Lung, and Blood Institute's The Heart Truth® campaign, and she also serves as partnership director for the campaign, guiding outreach and engagement of all partners in the corporate, media, and nonprofit sectors.

REFERENCES

1. Christian AH, Rosamond W, White A, Mosca L. Nine-year trends and racial and ethnic disparities in women's awareness of heart disease and stroke: an American Heart Association national study. *J Womens Health.* 2007;16:68–81.

2. National Center for Health Statistics, Health Data Interactive. *Underlying Cause of Death, 1981 to 2006.* http://205.207.175.93/hdi/ReportFolders/ReportFolders.aspx?IF_ActivePath=P,21. Accessed August 1, 2010.

3. Long T, Taubenheim AM, Wayman J, Temple ST, Ruoff BA. The Heart Truth: using the power of branding and social marketing to increase awareness of heart disease in women. *Soc Marketing Q.* 2008;XIV(3):3–29.

4. National Heart, Lung, and Blood Institute. The Heart Truth campaign statistics. Unpublished tabulation of prevalence estimates from the National Health and Nutrition Examination Survey, 1999–2004. National Center for Health Statistics; 2009.

5. Mosca L, Mochari-Greenberger H, Dolor RJ, Newby LK, Robb KJ. Twelve-year follow-up of American women's awareness of cardiovascular disease risk and barriers to heart health. *Circ Cardiovasc Quality Outcomes.* 2010. doi: 10.1161/CIRCOUTCOMES.109.915538.

6. National Heart, Lung, and Blood Institute. The Heart Truth campaign statistics. Unpublished tabulation of prevalence estimates from the National Health and Nutrition Examination Survey, 2005–2008. National Center for Health Statistics; 2009.

7. National Cancer Institute. *Making Health Communications Programs Work: A Planner's Guide.* Bethesda, MD: U.S. Department of Health and Human Services. National Institutes of Health; 2002.

8. Wilcox D, Kanter B. Demystifying web 2.0 for volcom groups: blogs, rss, tagging, wikis and beyond. Slide set for Lasa UK Circuit Rider Conference, January 15, 2007; Birmingham, England. http://socialmedia.wikispaces.com/presentation. Accessed August 1, 2010.

9. Mosca L et al. 2010.

10. Mosca L, Mochari H, Christian K, et al. National study of women's awareness, preventive action, and barriers to cardiovascular health. *Circulation.* 2006;113:524–534.

11. Mosca L et al. 2010.

12. National Heart, Lung, and Blood Institute. The Heart Truth tracking study: top-line findings. Unpublished report; 2010.

13. Mosca L et al. 2010.

14. Heron M, Hoyert DL, Murphey SL, Xu J, Kochaneck KD, Tejada-Vera B. Deaths: final data for 2006. *National Vital Statistics Reports.* 2009;57(14). National Center for Health Statistics. Retrieved from http://www.cdc.gov/nchs/data/nvsr/nvsr57/nvsr57_14.pdf. Accessed August 1, 2010.

An Outbreak of Yellow Fever in Paraguay:

Health Risk Communication in a Crisis

JON K. ANDRUS, TILLY GURMAN, BRENDA L. GLEASON, AND BARBARA JAUREGUI

It was February 15, 2008.[i] Paraguay was experiencing what appeared to be its first outbreak of yellow fever (YF) in decades and had declared a national state of emergency in order to attempt to control the outbreak.

The Pan American Health Organization (PAHO) had just deployed several experts to Paraguay to assist with the crisis, including an epidemiologist, a clinician/virologist, a risk communicator, immunization advisers, and emergency management experts. Within a few days, a Brazilian laboratory scientist was expected to join Paraguay's national public health laboratory.[1]

The reemergence of YF in Paraguay induced widespread panic throughout the country. Where vaccines were available, people waited in line for hours to get their dose. As the outbreak intensified, so, too, did community tension, especially since the nationwide demand for vaccines outpaced the available supply. As a result, anxious and angry crowds of Paraguayans started picketing the presidential palace in Asunción, near the outbreak's epicenter.

Newspapers ran front-page stories every day about the latest mortality and morbidity numbers, the continued vaccine shortage, and the government's response to the outbreak. Television broadcasts also provided intense daily updates of the situation. Between the vaccine shortage and the public outcry, the government was portrayed by the mass media as being on the brink of collapse.

The minister of health (MOH) sat at her desk watching the latest television news report on the YF outbreak. Hundreds of people were shown in lines waiting for vaccines. A woman who reported having waited in line for 2 hours commented that she just heard an announcement that there are no more vaccines. Expressing her frustration at the government's response, she looked directly into the camera and said:

> The government does not care for us. They keep telling us that we need to use repellants and wear protective clothing. But what are they doing for us? Not only are they keeping vaccines from us, but I am not sure they care that Paraguayans are dying more and more each day. I fear for tomorrow.

The MOH turned off the television and sighed when she realized the two seemingly insurmountable tasks that lay ahead. It was clear that, until the government could make the YF vaccine readily available, the public outcry would only keep getting louder. As a result, the MOH knew she must somehow figure out a way to secure sufficient vaccines for the current outbreak. In addition, her team had to determine how to better communicate the government's response to the public.

---

[i] This case study draws limited information from publicly available reports and news sources. Even though the Paraguayan outbreak was a real event, the dialogs and descriptions of events described are fictitious and do not represent what actually occurred in Paraguay, and therefore the identities of the real persons involved in the outbreak are not revealed. Any resemblance to persons involved in the events of yellow fever outbreak in Paraguay in 2008 are coincidental and unintentional.

ABOUT YELLOW FEVER

Yellow fever (YF) virus causes approximately 200,000 cases of YF each year and 30,000 fatalities in Latin America and Africa, where it is endemic. Most affected people recover within 3–4 days from symptoms that include fever, muscle pain with prominent backache, headache, shivers, loss of appetite, and nausea or vomiting. However, some patients develop more severe disease, which can involve hemorrhage, as well as liver and kidney failure. Diagnosis is often difficult, as YF symptoms can be confused with those of many other diseases, especially during the early stages. Within Latin America, Bolivia, Brazil, Colombia, Ecuador, and Peru are considered at greatest risk for YF outbreaks because the disease is enzootic there—that is, it consistently presents in monkeys.[2,3]

Two patterns of vector-borne YF transmission exist—jungle YF and urban YF.[3] Jungle YF is found in tropical rain forests where the wild mosquitoes, *Haemagogus*, can infect monkeys with YF virus. Monkeys serve as the reservoir for the virus. Infected mosquitoes can transmit the virus to humans who enter the rain forest. Human victims of jungle YF infection are typically young males who work or hunt in the rain forest. Urban YF, on the other hand, occurs when *Aedes aegypti* mosquitoes transmit the virus between humans. Urban YF transmission does not require monkeys. The epidemiology of urban YF involves high case fatality rates, both sexes, a wider age distribution, and more explosive outbreak presentations than the more sporadic jungle YF. Depending upon the quality of surveillance, case fatality rates can be as high as 40%.

According to the World Health Organization (WHO), YF vaccine is affordable and safe for most population subgroups, with few serious side effects. Within 1 week of vaccination, 95% of individuals will develop effective immunity. One dose protects against YF for at least 30 years.[3]

Prior to 2008, the last case of urban YF in Paraguay was in 1904, while the last case of jungle YF in Paraguay was in 1974.[4] The last urban YF case in the American continent occurred in 1942.[5] Despite the elapsed time since the last YF outbreak, Paraguay started routine vaccination against YF along border areas within close proximity to enzootic areas in neighboring countries, Brazil and Bolivia, in 2001. By 2006, YF vaccine was fully integrated into the routine national childhood immunization program. In 2007, the routine YF vaccination coverage for Paraguay's general population was 24%, while along the border areas it was around 60%.[6] Paraguay also made improvements to its national YF surveillance program.

An Outbreak in Paraguay

A YF outbreak occurred in Paraguay between January and May 2008 with 28 confirmed YF cases. Eleven people died, for a case fatality rate of 39%,[6] which is the percentage of people who get the disease and subsequently die. The outbreak consisted of both jungle and urban YF, and four clusters were identified.

The first cluster began January 13, 2008, in San Estanislao, San Pedro Department,[ii] and consisted of seven YF cases. Five were in hunters with a recent travel history to a nearby jungle, one patient resided next to the hunters, and the last person who was afflicted worked in their neighborhood. Because the hunters traveled to an enzootic area within the same region, this cluster was classified as jungle YF transmission.[7]

The second cluster was identified on February 27, 2008, in the Santa Domingo and Santa Lucia areas of San Pedro Department. This cluster consisted of seven cases, which resulted in three deaths—a case fatality rate of 43%. Most of the patients became infected when they traveled to attend the funeral of another YF victim. Approximately half of the victims were female. Wild *Haemagogus* mosquitoes, indicative of jungle YF transmission, as well as *Aedes aegypti*–infected mosquitoes, characteristic of urban YF transmission, were collected from sources of standing water around victims' homes. Therefore, it was not possible to identify the mode of transmission for this second YF cluster with certainty.

The third cluster began in early February in the Laurelty neighborhood of the San Lorenzo district of the Central Department. This cluster consisted of 10 cases—five in females—and three people died. *Aedes aegypti*–infected mosquitoes were identified but no *Haemagogus* wild mosquitoes were found, indicating urban YF transmission.[iii]

PAHO reported on the YF outbreak as follows:

> The reports of suspected cases from San Lorenzo, a suburb of the capital, Asunción, precipitated an overwhelming demand for vaccinations which soon outstripped supply at the vaccination centers and prompted public outcry. A team of PAHO/WHO advisors arrived in Paraguay on 16 February to assist the Ministry of Health in organizing vaccination campaigns and procuring vaccines from neighboring countries . . . The

---

[ii] Paraguay consists of 17 departments and 1 capital district.
[iii] The fourth cluster occurred after the date in which this case is set, in late February through early March 2008 in the Caaguazu Department. It consisted of four cases and had a case fatality rate of 100%. Mosquitoes were collected at only two of the sites, and both urban and jungle YF transmitting mosquitoes were found to be infected with the YF virus. As a result, it was not possible to conclude the mode of transmission with certainty.[6]

mass vaccination strategy continues with priority given to areas with confirmed cases.[8(p 1)]

YELLOW FEVER VACCINATION STRATEGY

As YF reemerged in Africa and Central and South America in the 1980s, a more concerted effort was made by international public health experts to determine which populations were most at risk for contracting yellow fever. A meeting of experts in 2006 concluded with the creation of a model pointing to six risk indicators as follows:

Exposure Related

1. Environmental risk—ecological risk zone (15° N–10° S, wet savannah or dry forest)
2. Geographic area has reported a confirmed case since 1960
3. Geographic area has reported a suspected case and then established surveillance of cases
4. Number of years in which a case was reported after 1960
5. Geographic area close to a geographic area with notified cases

Susceptibility Related

6. Proportion of people in the population who are not immunized[9]

Based on the six exposure and susceptibility-related risks identified by the model, a targeted vaccination effort was in order in Paraguay because the 2008 YF outbreak seemed to meet the geographic area exposure-related risk indicators, as well as the susceptibility-related risk indicator—a low percentage of the population immunized against YF. However, the success of this massive initiative was contingent upon readily accessible YF vaccines.

When the 2008 outbreak began, Paraguay assessed its vaccine resources—a stockpile of 300,000 YF vaccine doses available nationally and an additional 50,000 vaccine doses already distributed to peripheral vaccination centers. For each emerging cluster of YF cases, the immediate rapid response included establishing rings of vaccination around the sites where infection was suspected to have happened. The first ring had an 800-meter diameter and the subsequent concentric rings were 2,400 meters in diameter.[7] In ring vaccination, health officials aim to vaccinate every susceptible individual in the ring, controlling transmission by creating a buffer of immune individuals.

In addition to these targeted vaccination efforts, Paraguay's Ministry of Health decided to expand the vaccination response to include other susceptible people in the Asunción[iv] metropolitan area, which included approximately 1.5 million individuals between the ages of 1 and 59 years.[6] Eventually, Paraguay would need to determine whether to expand its vaccination response to a nationwide campaign targeting all susceptible individuals aged 1 to 59 years who had never received the YF vaccine. In addition to offering vaccinations at fixed sites, the campaign also included nationwide door-to-door outreach tactics.

> **Question 1** Once the minister of health, along with other decision makers in the Paraguayan government, have declared a state of emergency, and determined, along with assistance from experts in the region and from PAHO, that mass emergency vaccination will be needed in Asunción, how should the health officials proceed in order to obtain the necessary vaccines?

ENSURING AVAILABILITY OF VACCINES

WHO and the United Nations Children's Fund jointly collaborate on The Yellow Fever Initiative, a strategic approach to eliminating yellow fever that recommends including the vaccine in childhood immunization regimens, mass vaccinations in high-risk areas, providing surveillance and outbreak response and working to increase vaccine production to meet worldwide demand. The initiative includes partners such as the Agence de Médecine Préventive, the Centers for Disease Control and Prevention (United States), the International Federation of Red Cross and Red Crescent Societies, the Institut Pasteur in Dakar, Médecins sans Frontières, the Robert Koch Institute (Berlin), vaccine manufacturers, and others.[10]

Funded primarily by the country-level partners and the GAVI Alliance (formerly the Global Alliance for Vaccines and Immunisation), the initiative provides 6 million doses of emergency vaccines annually in a global emergency stockpile. The global YF vaccine stockpile that exists in Geneva usually contains about 6 million doses for emergencies. The stockpile is managed by the Yellow Fever-International Coordinating Group, which includes representatives from the United Nations Children's Fund, Médecins sans Frontières, the International Federation of Red Cross, and WHO, acting as secretariat. Emergency vaccines are allocated by the YF-International Coordinating Group based on criteria set forth originally for other epidemic responses. The basic requirements are evidence of an ongoing outbreak, a mass vaccination plan, and availability of relevant materials and storage facilities.[11] Further, countries must be able to pay for the vaccines and accompanying shipping costs.

[iv] Asunción is Paraguay's capital, as well as its largest city.

The 350,000 YF vaccine doses available in Paraguay fell far short of the target population of 1.5 million people to be included in the outbreak vaccination response. As soon as the shortage was made known, there was widespread panic throughout the country. The mass media only fueled the panic, exaggerating and highlighting the risk for the population. Where vaccines were available, people waited for hours to get their dose. As community tension increased, the demand for vaccines also increased nationwide. Newspapers provided front-page stories every day. Television broadcasts also provided intense daily updates of the situation.

While the global yellow fever vaccine stockpile usually has 6 million doses, at the onset of the Paraguay urban YF outbreak, there were only 2 million YF vaccine doses available because two of the three vaccine producers had prioritized their stockpiles to the recurrent outbreaks in Brazil.[12]

In the initial days of the outbreak, officials from PAHO met several times per day with the MOH and her staff in response to her request for technical support and expert consultancy. The MOH was increasingly feeling the pressure of media reports and the community at large as they expressed frustration and anger at the government's response to the YF outbreak. Recognizing this pressure, PAHO activated an accelerated communication response, which included partners managing the global stockpile. Given the worldwide shortage, PAHO and the MOH also initiated contacts with other countries in the region. They hoped that engaging in global health diplomacy (see Box 6-1) would free up vaccines for use in Paraguay from other nations' stockpiles.

The government of Paraguay and the MOH were also faced with an ethical problem. The limited number of YF vaccines meant only some people could be vaccinated as part of an emergency response effort. The minister was familiar with the general ethical issues surrounding vaccines. Public health experts and bioethicists often used seven principles to guide mass vaccination programs. Most of the principles seemed like common sense, for example, programs should target serious public health diseases, vaccines should be safe and effective, and vaccination should generally not be compulsory.

Experts also recommend the just distribution of benefits and burdens in vaccination programs.[16] Treating people justly would mean explaining why some people would receive vaccination and others would not. The trade-off between treating people justly and treating them equally was at the forefront of the MOH's consideration of how to communicate what decisions the government was making regarding the YF outbreak.

Considering the situation before her, the MOH knew it would be just to protect those who were most susceptible and

---

BOX 6-1 What is Global Health Diplomacy?

Global health diplomacy is a relatively new concept describing the interaction between health and foreign policy goals. One definition of global health diplomacy is "the processes by which state and non-state actors engage to position health issues more prominently in foreign policy decision-making."[13(p 1)]

Another definition of the concept of global health diplomacy is the "multi-level and multi-actor negotiation processes that shape and manage the global policy environment for health."[14(p 230)]

Still "other conceptions of health diplomacy de-emphasize both negotiations and the primary role of global health, instead describing efforts to improve health within the larger context of supporting state interests."[15(p 1)]

Global health diplomacy, public health experts argue, includes at least six overlapping, and sometimes competing concepts, which are: "security, development, global public goods, trade, human rights and ethical/moral reasoning."[13(p. 1)]

---

most likely to be exposed to YF, anticipating that vaccinating that portion of the population would protect the broader public's health. She was making the just choice, but also the utilitarian one, that is, deciding the greatest good for the greatest number of people would come from selective vaccination.

Question 2 What is the role of global health diplomacy in a situation of disease outbreak and response?

Question 3 What is the responsibility of other nations to supply Paraguay with vaccines? Do countries in the region have more responsibility?

COMMUNICATING IN A HEALTH CRISIS

The MOH and her communication team needed to make some quick decisions. They needed to come up with a strategy to address the vaccine shortage as quickly as possible and then figure out the best way to communicate their response to the public.

They knew that during a disease outbreak, whether at the epidemic or pandemic level, effective communication with the public would be imperative. This outbreak was no different. During a crisis, people often simplify the information that they hear, cling to current beliefs and attitudes related to illness and disease, and remember most clearly what they see or hear first. Because of the need to simplify information and rely on what they already knew or believed, residents of Asunción demonstrated limited capacity to uptake new or complex information about YF. As a result, misinformation about YF continued to circulate. In this crisis, it was important to communicate clear messages about the vaccine shortage and the government's response to help assuage public fears and uncertainty.

The MOH understood that once the decision on how to address the vaccine shortage was made, it would be critical to "communicate with the public in ways that build, maintain, or restore trust."[17(p 5)] When trust is lost or credibility of the message or messenger is questioned, the result can be catastrophic for the communication efforts.[16,18] The MOH had already experienced a loss of credibility as the public's anxiety increased over time. Taking these considerations into account,

the MOH looked for guidance on how her team could better communicate the government's response to the YF outbreak. What she found was a set of well-established guidelines, first introduced by the U.S. Environmental Protection Agency,[19] for effective communication of risk to the public. These seven cardinal rules of risk communication[19] are to:

1. Accept and involve the public as a partner.
2. Plan carefully and evaluate your efforts.
3. Listen to the public's specific concerns.
4. Be honest, frank, and open.
5. Work with other credible sources.
6. Meet the needs of the media.
7. Speak clearly and with compassion.

Box 6-2 presents the Environmental Protection Agency's associated practical tips for communicating risk during a crisis.

The MOH felt that time was of the essence and that she needed to be more proactive. In an attempt to try to regain credibility with the public, she convened a meeting with her

---

BOX 6-2 U.S. Environmental Protection Agency Guidelines for Health Risk Communication

1. **Accept and involve the public as a partner.**
   Tips:
   - Involve community stakeholders as early as possible in the decision-making process.
   - Develop communication materials with a focus on creating an informed public that can be actively involved in the response efforts.
2. **Plan carefully and evaluate your efforts.**
   Tips:
   - Develop clear objectives about what your efforts hope to achieve.
   - Create risk communication materials and messages with a particular audience in mind. For example, parents, policy makers, and first responders will have different interests, responsibilities, and priorities.
   - Recruit and train spokespeople who are appropriate for and able to interact with the intended audience.
   - Pretest risk communication materials with the intended audience in order to ensure that the messages you are developing are appropriate and interpreted correctly.
   - Evaluate your communication efforts, identifying both what worked well and what needs to be improved.
3. **Listen to the public's specific concerns.**
   Tips:
   - Find out what your intended audience thinks, knows, and feels about the specific situation at hand.
   - Conduct research, including interviews, focus group discussions, and surveys, to identify the public's concerns.
   - Recognize that people are often more interested in trust, credibility, competency, fairness, and compassion than in detailed (and often changing) mortality and morbidity statistics.

BOX 6-2 U.S. Environmental Protection Agency Guidelines for Health Risk Communication *(Continued)*

4. **Be honest, frank, and open.**
   Tips:
   - Do not expect the public to view you as a credible source of information based on your credentials alone. In other words, you must work to establish and maintain the public's trust.
   - Disclose accurate, science-based information about the specific crisis or risk in a timely manner, especially given the multimedia universe in which we currently live. Credibility and trust also hinge on the ability to communicate, react, and respond early.
   - Present an accurate current level of risk based on the best available information. Do not minimize or exaggerate risk.
   - Say what you know as well as what you do not know. In other words, it is important to not overly reassure the public, speculate, or lie. Instead, transparency is key in both acknowledging uncertainty and disseminating accurate information.
   - Create channels for disseminating accurate and timely information, such as hotlines and websites.

5. **Work with other credible sources.**
   Tips:
   - Establish relationships with other organizations, agencies, etc. that have shared interests. Involve these entities in the planning process of a crisis communication strategy.
   - Identify other trustworthy individuals (i.e., university professors, physicians, local officials) who may serve as credible media spokespeople.
   - Coordinate communication efforts (both the development and release of risk information) with your collaborative partners. Such coordination is critical to ensure consistent messaging and continued trust by the public. Opposing messages will undermine trust, raise fear, and increase confusion held by the public.

6. **Meet the needs of the media.**
   Tips:
   - Establish relationships with specific reporters and media outlets.
   - Be accessible to reporters.
   - Tailor risk communication information to the specific media channel. For example, clear and simple charts and graphs may be helpful for print media.

7. **Speak clearly and with compassion.**
   Tips:
   - Use simple, nontechnical language. In particular, make sure to avoid the use of jargon.
   - Be consistent in your messaging. For example, if you are going to have more than one spokesperson, they should be trained to adhere to the same messages. Inconsistent messaging will lead to a loss of credibility with the intended audience and may increase their level of fear, anxiety, and uncertainty.
   - Write material to a fourth-grade reading level. The reading level of written materials can be assessed using readability formulas such as the SMOG formula. http://www.harrymclaughlin.com/SMOG.htm.
   - Address misinformation, stigmatization, and rumors promptly.
   - Include specific action steps that community members can take to protect themselves and their families.
   - Come across as open and empathetic to the public.

Source: From Covello VT, Allen F. *Seven Cardinal Rules of Risk Communication.* Washington, DC: U.S. Environmental Protection Agency. Policy Document OPA-87-020; 1988.

communication team to develop a stronger communication strategy. The lead communication strategist stressed that the MOH needed to be prepared to answer questions about the global vaccine stockpile, in order to better clarify the difficult decisions that Paraguay had to make. The MOH agreed. By the end of the meeting, the team had identified a set of possible questions that might be asked—either by an inquisitive media or by an anxious public. The list included the following questions:

- Why has the government been so slow to respond to this crisis?
- Why isn't everyone being provided with a vaccine?
- What has been Paraguay's attempt at obtaining vaccines either from neighboring countries or from global partners?
- If there is a stockpile available for global emergencies, why has Paraguay not been successful in obtaining vaccines?
- What warrants support from global partners? Are not the deaths of innocent Paraguayans enough of an emergency?

In response to each of these questions, the team came up with a list of talking points. In addition, they identified the sensitive nature of their response and the potential implications for global health diplomacy. For example, the MOH knew that their initial request for vaccines from the global stockpile had been denied. She feared, however, that if she placed blame, the chance of ever getting vaccines from the stockpile might be forever compromised. After creating the responses, she and her team also came up with a pros and cons list to each communication message decision they developed to assess and choose the best message points.

Health Risk Communication Strategy

A risk communication strategy can be divided into three components, corresponding to the time line of the specific incident at hand. The first is the response period, during which all of the preparation elements to a crisis are put into action. During this period, communication strategies focus on preventing the particular situation from worsening, providing recommendations to people via mass media communication channels, and informing health personnel and first responders about their roles and responsibilities. The communication efforts implemented during this phase tend to be visible, since the public witnesses the initial response to the crisis first hand. As a result, the communication efforts during this period have the potential to become what the public associates with the response to the particular situation in the long term.

After the initial response to the epidemic has occurred, the next phase is the recovery period, during which the intent is to make sure the crisis has been resolved in order to start rebuilding a sense of normalcy. The third phase is the revision period, which takes place once the crisis has been resolved. During this period, the public evaluates the overall response, assessing how well the crisis situation was managed, including the communication and resolution. Because much of what the public associates with the response to the crisis occurs during the response period, good preparation and planning before a crisis actually occurs is essential.

Question 4 Once the vaccine strategy has been decided, how should the MOH communicate the government's response to the public?

Question 5 What should the MOH do to regain the public's trust, given its current level of panic, fear, and overall distrust? Suggest a timeline for disseminating information and identify communication priorities.

Hearing the noise of chattering reporters outside her office door, the MOH looked around the table at her team and took a deep breath. She felt ready to go answer the questions from the media, and from the people of Paraguay about the YF outbreak and the government's response.

"Let's go!" she said. "We have work to do," as she opened the door to her office to go out and communicate about the crisis.

About the Authors

Jon Kim Andrus, MD, a public health expert with 25 years of experience working in the field of vaccines, immunization, and primary care in developing countries, is the deputy director of the Pan American Health Organization, Regional Office for the Americas of the World Health Organization (PAHO/WHO). In his capacity as deputy director, Dr. Andrus is responsible for overseeing PAHO's areas of work covering governing body processes, emergency response and preparedness, knowledge management and communication, resource mobilization, program budget management and evaluation, and ethics. Previous to his deputy director appointment, Dr. Andrus served as lead senior technical advisor for PAHO's immunization program and also as professor of global health at The George Washington University School of Public Health and Health Services. Earlier in his career, Dr. Andrus worked in key positions with the CDC and WHO on polio eradication in Latin America, Southeast Asia, and Africa. Dr. Andrus earned his MD degree from the University of California at Davis School of Medicine.

Tilly Gurman, DrPH, serves as an assistant professor in the Department of Global Health at The George Washington University School of Public Health and Health Services. Bringing more than 15 years experience in global health settings, she is an expert in health communication, with interest in adolescent health, reproductive health, cultural competency, mass media communication, and patient–provider communication. A Venezuelan native, Dr. Gurman has worked in a variety of countries, including Guatemala, El Salvador, Mexico, and Swaziland. Moreover, Dr. Gurman is dedicated to combining qualitative and quantitative research methods to inform public health practice.

Brenda L. Gleason, MA, MPH, is the president and founder of M2 Health Care Consulting, a strategic policy and communications consulting firm with offices in Denver and Washington, DC. Beginning her career in health policy at the Massachusetts Department of Public Health, she has worked on issues at the intersection of business and policy for a range of industries for more than 15 years. She is a professorial lecturer at The George Washington University School of Public Health and Health Services. She earned an MA from Boston College and an MPH from Boston University.

Barbara Jauregui, MD, MSc, is an Argentinean native with 8 years of experience in program development/management and applied research, in both governmental and nonprofit organizations. Dr. Jauregui is especially skilled at using quantitative tools for analyzing and improving systems and processes to promote equity in health. She has been working for PAHO's immunization unit since the beginning of 2008. Under direct supervision of the principal investigator, Dr. Jon Andrus, she is currently managing the ProVac Initiative in Latin America and the Caribbean countries, providing training and technical collaboration in the generation of cost-effectiveness analysis regarding new vaccine introduction.

REFERENCES

1. World Health Organization. News report: Yellow fever in Paraguay. http://www.who.int/csr/don/2008_02_20a/en/index.html. February 20, 2008. Accessed March 15, 2011.

2. Monath T. Yellow fever vaccines. *Expert Rev Vaccines.* 2005;4(4):689–693.

3. World Health Organization. Yellow fever fact sheet number 100. http://www.who.int/mediacentre/factsheets/fs100/en/. January 2011. Accessed March 15, 2011.

4. Pan American Health Organization. PAHO Group of Experts. Yellow Fever in Paraguay. 22 May 2008. Report to the Minister of Health of Paraguay.

5. Vainio J, Cutts F. Yellow Fever. World Health Organization, Geneva, 1998. http://www.who.int/vaccines-documents/DocsPDF/www9842.pdf. Accessed March 15, 2011.

6. Pan American Health Organization. Emerging and reemerging infectious diseases, region of the Americas. *Epidemiol Bull.* 2008;5(5).

7. Novotny T, Hannah L, Adams V, Kickbusch I. Health diplomacy: A literature review. UCSF/IGCC Project on Health Diplomacy; 2008. San Francisco, CA.

8. Pan American Health Organization. PAHO special report: Yellow fever in Paraguay. http://www.reliefweb.int/rw/RWFiles2008.nsf/FilesBy-RWDocUnidFilename/EDIS-7CGT7P-full_report.pdf/$File/full_report. pdf. Published March 3, 2008. Accessed March 18, 2011.

9. WHO. Assessment of yellow fever epidemic risk—a decision-making tool for preventive immunization campaigns. *Wkly Epidemiol Rec.* 2007;82(18):153–160. http://www.who.int/wer/2007/wer8218.pdf. Accessed March 18, 2011.

10. UNICEF, WHO. Yellow Fever Initiative: Providing an opportunity of a lifetime. http://www.who.int/csr/disease/yellowfev/YFIbrochure.pdf. Published 2010. Accessed March 18, 2011.

11. UNICEF, WHO. International Coordinating Group on Vaccine Provision for Epidemic Meningitis Control (ICG) guidelines for applying to the emergency stockpile. http://www.who.int/csr/disease/meningococcal/ICG_guidelines_2008_02_09.pdf. Published 2008. Accessed March 19, 2011.

12. World Health Organization. Epidemic and pandemic alert and response. Yellow fever in Brazil. http://www.who.int/csr/don/2008_02_07/en/index.html. Published 5, 2008. Accessed March 3, 2009.

13. Labonté R, Gagnon ML. Framing health and foreign policy: lessons for global health diplomacy. *Global Health.* 2010;6:14.

14. Kickbusch I, Silberschmidt G, Buss P. Global health diplomacy: the need for new perspectives, strategic approaches and skills in global health. *Bull World Health Organ.* 2007;85(3):230–232.

15. Feldbaum H, Michaud J. Health diplomacy and the enduring relevance of foreign policy interests. *PLoS Med.* 2010;7(4):e1000226.

16. Verweij M, Dawson A. Ethical principles for collective immunisation programmes. *Vaccine.* 2004;22:3122–3126.

17. World Health Organization. WHO outbreak communication guidelines. http://www.who.int/infectious-disease news/IDdocs/whocds200528/whocds200528en.pdf. Published 2005. Accessed August 30, 2010.

18. Glik DC. Risk communication for public health emergencies. *Annu Rev Public Health.* 2007;28:33–54. https://www.annualreviews.org/doi/pdf/10.1146/annurev.publhealth.28.021406.144123. Accessed August 30, 2010.

19. Covello VT, Allen F. *Seven Cardinal Rules of Risk Communication.* Washington, DC: U.S. Environmental Protection Agency. Policy Document OPA-87-020; 1988.

Challenges with Implementing a Community-Based Potable Water System Project in a Rural Honduran Community

ELIZABETH L. ANDRADE AND KATHRYN L. ZOERHOFF

A MORNING WITHOUT MUCH WATER

Miguel's eyes flickered like candles in his dark one-room house in San Gabriel, Honduras. He heard the roosters crowing from his neighbors' yards and the radio streaming from houses in the distant hills, as he customarily did every morning at dawn. As he lay there in his hammock, he heard the noises of the countryside swelling to a humming chorus, and daylight lit the cracks in the tile roof. The hens were coming down from their roost, the men were starting to till cornfields in the distance, and the wooden wheel from the water well creaked and whistled as his wife starting pulling up water for the day. As he swung his feet over the side of the hammock and placed them on the packed, smooth dirt floor, a twinge in his stomach reminded him he had felt ill for days due to an intestinal infection—from the well water, he suspected. Nevertheless, today was an important day. He knew he couldn't miss the community meeting where the community development association (asociación de desarrollo comunitario [ADC]) would be discussing construction progress of the community's potable water system. Virginia and Cassandra, U.S. volunteers from Travelers University (TU) in Springfield, were visiting to provide updates about the project. His family had hoped to tie into the water system because during the dry season, there was always a shortage of water, and during the rainy season, he often missed work and his children missed school because of diarrheal disease and parasitism. It also took a significant amount of time to pull water up from the well, and when they boiled water for the baby, a large amount of

firewood was required, depleting the brush and trees in the surrounding areas.

In San Gabriel, 60% of households use their home's well water, 20% use their neighbor's well, 15% have piped water in their home, and 5% use their neighbor's piped water. The primary collectors of water in 90% of homes are women. The wells are highly contaminated with fecal coliform.

Lowering his head, Miguel stepped outside of his house, a precarious adobe frame with no windows, a leaky roof, and a pit latrine around back. As he emerged, he felt the dry, hot air warm his face and his feet kicked through the dust in the yard. His daughter was on the patio in their makeshift kitchen forming tortillas in her wet hands and slapping them onto the firewood griddle.

Homes in San Gabriel, in many cases, are precarious and relatively unstable. About 60% of homes have dirt floors and most have no sealed windows. Many of the homes (40%) have walls made of brick, 35% of adobe, 14% of cement, 6% of mud and 5% of *baharenque* (mud and wood). Roofing of homes is made of ceramic tiles (80%) and metal laminate (20%). Most households (75%) have electricity.

"Luisa!" Miguel called to his wife. "Can you bring me some water?"

"I'm not getting much water from the well, Miguel," she answered from the side of the house where the well wheel was located. "What I've pulled up is just enough for cooking and to boil for the baby to drink. You'll have to see if one of the neighbors with a deeper well has any water. The dry season has been long this year."

"What about brushing my teeth? I'm so thirsty . . ." he grumbled.

He was interrupted by the TU volunteers, Virginia and Cassandra, who were staying with his family. When they emerged from behind the house, they were carrying clothes they had pulled from the clothesline.

"We couldn't wash any clothes, Miguel," said Virginia, "so we'll have to wear the clothes we worked in yesterday. Here are your clothes from yesterday. I just hung them on the clothesline to air out."

"Have you checked the rain catchment container on the roof?" asked Miguel.

"Nothing," Cassandra sighed heavily. "You know we haven't had rain for days."

San Gabriel is located in one of the driest and hottest regions of Honduras, and on average, receives approximately 1,500–1,700 mm/year of precipitation. During the dry season, the land is parched and water is scarce, except when drawn from extremely deep wells or piped water systems.

"Don't worry. We'll see what we can find out at today's meeting," he said.

"Yes, at today's meeting, we plan on giving updates on the project's progress, and we're going to tell everyone it shouldn't be much longer to finish the construction of the water system," offered Cassandra.

"We've been saying the same thing for so long to the community, and the economy is getting worse every day," he responded. "I'm tired of being sick, and we can't afford any more doctor's bills or pills for parasitism. I can't even afford enough rice and milk. I've brought my son, Marco, to the doctor three times in the past 2 months. He's only 1 year old, and he's been so dehydrated and had a few close calls. A lot of other kids get severe diarrhea too. I think it's the most dangerous for children. You said it's because of contaminated water *and* poor hygiene. We've made progress with hygiene, but we still need water, so I'm getting impatient to move forward on this water project."

With nearly one in five child deaths due to diarrhea, it is the second most common cause of death for children under 5 years of age worldwide,[1] second only to pneumonia. The death toll is greater than that caused by AIDS, malaria, and measles combined.[2] Most people who die from diarrhea actually die from dehydration and severe fluid loss. Children are at greater risk of life-threatening dehydration because water constitutes a greater proportion of a child's body weight, and excessive water loss can take a heavy toll on a child. Children are also at greater risk for exposure to higher levels of contaminants in water because they drink more water per day than adults due to higher metabolic rates.[2]

"Here," responded Cassandra. "Here are some pills I picked up at the pharmacy yesterday. Instead of waiting until we feel sick, we have to work towards preventing illness. The whole community needs to move in the direction of prevention. I know it's a different way of thinking for everyone, and many people don't know about the causes of illness. There are still problems of poor hygiene and inadequate sanitation, but you're right, we're making progress," she assured him. "Disease transmission is very complicated. We'll have to improve hygiene, sanitation, and water quality to reduce disease as much as possible."

According to the World Health Organization (WHO) and the United Nations Children's Fund (UNICEF),[2] diarrheal disease is usually a symptom of gastrointestinal infection caused by a variety of bacterial, viral (primarily rotavirus) and parasitic organisms that are transmitted through the fecal-oral pathway, which is a complex set of interdependent pathways through which microorganisms spread in contaminated food and drinking water or from person to person as a result of poor hygiene.[2] More than 80% of the cases of diarrhea worldwide are produced by fecal-oral contamination.[3-6] These pathways are represented in the F-diagram,[7] which classifies contamination as mediated through food, fingers, fomites and flies.[8,9] The purpose of diarrhea prevention strategies, such as improvement of water supply and quality, provision of sanitary facilities, and hygiene education programs, is to block these transmission routes. Disease transmission pathways are important to take into consideration when making decisions related to educational interventions or the type of structural interventions that might be selected (for example, communal versus household water access, and household point-of-use water treatment versus piped water system chlorination).

Cassandra continued, "The volunteers from Potable Water for All have constructed a lot of the water system, and they say it shouldn't take too long to raise the rest of the needed funds and finish construction. That way, everyone will be hooked up instead of only some houses."

"Maybe this new funding opportunity we heard about from Engineers, Ltd. to the municipality will give us what we need to make it happen soon," Miguel said hopefully. "Are you ready to go to the meeting?"

"I'm ready, but we're waiting for Ramón," Cassandra said, and then added, "Here he comes."

Ramón, a community health promoter, let out a sharp whistle to get their attention as he approached up the steep, rocky road. Miguel grabbed his notebook, kicked off his sandals, and slipped on the shoes he had polished the night before. He knew the roads were dusty this time of year, but he always wanted to look his best at ADC meetings, since he was the president.

"Buenos días," Ramón called out, as he passed the house's entrance. Miguel, Virginia, and Cassandra hurried to catch up to him on the road, and they set out quickly on their way.

A HISTORY OF CONTROVERSY OVER THE WATER PROJECT

"So what have you heard about the new funding from Engineers, Ltd.?" Ramón asked the others.

"I don't know much yet, just that a representative from the municipality will be at the meeting and they say that this funding might help us to finish the construction of the water system immediately. But, they are proposing that the funding go through the municipality," replied Miguel. "It sounds promising, but you know that anything coming from the chief commissioner will be controversial. I have my doubts about him because there have been concerns about accountability with some of his projects. To make it more complicated, half of the residents of San Gabriel belong to his political party and half to another, which will make it even more difficult to convince the second half to accept any project he proposes," he added.

"Yeah, I hear there's been a lack of transparency with water projects in this region," offered Virginia. "So, you're saying half of the community favors the chief commissioner and half doesn't trust him?" she asked.

"That's right," said Miguel. "We've tried to do a water project so many times with the chief commissioner and we've come close. If we let go of our differences with him, maybe this time it will work out. I still have my doubts, though."

"As long as the funds cover the health promoter hygiene promotion program and a gray water disposal mechanism, I'll support it," said Ramón. "Otherwise it won't go over well with my counterparts in the Ministry of Health. Water is really important, but so is hygiene improvement. Without education from the health promoters, things won't change and it won't matter if there's water or not," he said.

Hygiene promotion projects have shown a reduction in diarrhea disease of 33%, and hand-washing interventions specifically have reduced diarrhea by 43%.[10]

Ramón continued, "They are predicting an outbreak of dengue fever this rainy season, and excess gray water from the water system would only make the problem worse."

Gray water comes from washing, cooking, bathing, and other similar activities. If left as standing water in a yard for a long period of time, it will become malodorous and contain bacteria similar to sewage. Gray water can be used for agriculture or disposed of through subsurface irrigation.[11]

Gray water is a significant problem in San Gabriel, an endemic region for dengue fever. Combined with standing water from rainfall, agriculture, and watering of animals, gray water provides increased opportunity for mosquito breeding. As of 2009, almost 40% of households employed ineffective methods for eliminating standing water from their yards; a third of the community does not take any measure to prevent standing water; 6% let it flow freely from the yard; 3% of homes dig a passage for the water to flow away above ground, and small numbers of homes sweep the water puddles.

"Whatever happens, don't forget what we've talked about," Virginia reminded them. "The water system should be community owned and operated, and it should be equitable to all households. This way, you can make your own decisions about the system, ensuring that the system is well maintained and that the water is adequately chlorinated. If the system fees also pay the health promoters' salaries, San Gabriel can maintain a community-run health program that can respond to the specific needs of the community. By empowering community members to be the decision makers, it minimizes reliance on outside resources, which may be scarce, inconsistent, and not always in touch with our community's perspective."[12-26]

"All I know is that people in San Gabriel are getting restless," said Miguel. "They come to me and that's all I hear about. Our attempts to get a water system have been unsuccessful for over 10 years, and we've tried to collaborate with the chief commissioner, with in-country nonprofit organizations and with engineering firms. We just don't know how to navigate these relationships and people take advantage of us. It is good that Potable Water for All is helping us to learn more about this for future community projects. The community's losing faith in ADC, and we have to keep them organized and motivated," he added.

"I agree," responded Virginia. "Community capacity building and empowerment will be the key to moving the community forward. You can see the success that we've had with the health promoter program; we have people in the community who are trained, respected leaders, and they are an important asset. They unify the people to work for the community's well-being, and since they are from the community, people listen to them. We can be sure they have the community's best interest at heart," she added.[27-35]

A review of 121 rural water supply projects indicated that beneficiary participation was the most critical factor in the effectiveness of water projects, significantly determining both the overall quality of implementation and the quality of operation and maintenance.[36]

Cassandra chimed in, "They are losing faith because they can't see the physical evidence of water in their taps. We know the project is moving forward with fund-raising in Springfield, but it's hard to see on this end. Sure, we built the storage tank and chlorination system and the hygiene promotion project has been going now for 2 years, but that doesn't put water in their taps. It is hard to encourage people about the project, and we've been disappointed with so many previous attempts. Without community support, we won't have manual labor to dig ditches for the pipeline, we won't have contributions to buy land that the pipes pass through, and we won't be able to borrow equipment for digging or leveling the land. Community approval will be the deciding factor in anything. For any decisions that will be made as a result of this meeting, the community's impatience and doubts will certainly be influential factors."

In 2006, the community of San Gabriel reached out to Virginia and Travelers University School of Public Health about how to improve the health of the village. After an initial assessment, the public health team and community leaders concluded that improving the water supply and improving key hygiene behaviors would provide the greatest benefit to the community.

Next, the public health team approached the recently formed Potable Water For All (PWFA) chapter in Springfield, which agreed to take on the project and design a water distribution system. Since then, PWFA had been working with the residents of San Gabriel to develop a potable water system to serve 5,000 residents. The system design included a central water tank, pump, chlorination system, and a main water line extending throughout the community to which individual households could connect, and gray water pits for safe water disposal at each household. In addition, PWFA hired and trained five health promoters from the community who deliver household- and school-based hygiene promotion.

Phase I of the water system construction had already been completed. However, construction was stalled due to the withdrawal of a key funder. Phase I included the installation of a pump in a 100-meter-deep tube well, pipeline up to an elevated storage tank, the construction of the storage tank and chlorination system, and part of the distribution network to the main school and a limited number of households. Phase II was to include the expansion of the distribution network to include every home in the community that still lacked piped water.

As they continued on, Virginia thought once again about her worries for the project. It would be a challenge to keep all of the partners successfully engaged in the project because they all had different interests, but each partner had an important role. She wasn't sure how she fit in, and didn't want to involve herself inappropriately. She also worried that consensus regarding project decision making would be a challenge. Had they done a good job of clearly communicating partnership dynamics and negotiations with community members? Virginia reflected on how challenging it can be to make information accessible to community members, especially when there are language and/or cultural barriers or when the educational/literacy levels of community members limit them from fully understanding the details and implications of all aspects of the project. Virginia felt that it would be very difficult to connect community members and other partners all at the same level for planning, negotiating, and decision making.

Of the household heads in San Gabriel, 30% do not have any education, and another 30% have not completed primary school. Almost two thirds (65%) of the heads of household cannot both read and write.

THE PARTNERS AND THEIR PRIORITIES

The partnership seemed promising. The project had been community- and evidence-based and included partners from multiple disciplines. The project also responded to local development priorities. A relationship between partners had been cultivated since 2006, and all partners had been key in the identification of community development priority issues; assessment of needs and assets; conceptualization of project plans and timelines; and the implementation of engineering (potable water), public health (hygiene promotion), and community training project components.

Project partners included:

- **ADC** was the driving force behind the project, from the initial stages of conceptualization to the implementation stage. The members were elected and represented the community in their ownership of the resultant water and hygiene project. ADC's priorities were for the water system to be community owned and managed, equitable, and delivered to households.
- Volunteers from **Travelers University (TU)**. These volunteers initiated the relationship with the community in 2006 by conducting a needs/assets assessment and assembled the partnership. TU volunteers were another guiding force in developing the project, conducting formative assessments, and serving as community liaisons. TU provided training and oversight of the hygiene program. Volunteers from TU supported the community in their efforts to secure a community-owned system and especially to ensure the success and

sustainability of the hygiene program for improved health outcomes.

- **PWFA**, which was the lead volunteer technical group working on technical assessment, design, and implementation of the water system construction, as well as fund-raising. All of the project costs were financed by charitable donations. PWFA volunteers were concerned with constructing a high-quality, sustainable system to meet the needs of households. PWFA was under pressure to raise the rest of the money needed to finish the water system.
- **Alianza de Sistemas de Agua Rural (ASAR)**, a Honduran nonprofit organization providing technical assistance to communities and their water systems. It offered community training in the areas of operation and maintenance of the water system; administration, like transparent bookkeeping, income/expense reports, and development of user fees; general and state laws governing potable water systems; protection and conservation of the water source; community empowerment and leadership as owners of the system; and participatory, democratic decision making. ASAR was interested in promoting the rights and best interests of communities constructing rural water systems and sought to protect communities in their partnerships with government and other agencies. In addition, ASAR received $0.08 for every dollar of collected water fees for each system. This fee supported its organization and services provided to communities. It wanted to have San Gabriel be part of its association, rather than having the water system managed by the municipality.
- The **local municipal government**, which provided tools, financial, and political support/influence for the project. The municipal government was interested in having ownership of the resultant water system, having control over its administration, and determining fees for users.
- The **Honduran Ministry of Health (MOH)**. The MOH assisted with initial assessments, water testing, and additional training for the health promoters. An MOH health promoter serviced San Gabriel and oversaw the hygiene promotion project. The MOH was interested in having the household water fees finance the health promoter positions, since the MOH had limited resources and could only allocate one government-funded health promoter for each canton. Its main interest was the health of San Gabriel and health services provision.
- **Engineers, Ltd.**, a Honduran for-profit engineering firm. The firm specialized in rural water systems and worked regularly with municipalities for the construction and management planning of these systems. Engineers, Ltd. approached the chief commissioner of San Gabriel and offered funds to start a water project in San Gabriel immediately. The approach that Engineers, Ltd. proposed resembled a consulting model, where the municipality would contract Engineers, Ltd. to build the system, which would be owned and operated by the municipality. It was interested in the municipality setting user fees and in acquiring more business contracts.
- **Institution International**, the primary funding agency for the project. It was interested in moving forward with the current plan of the household water delivery system. It had an intricate approval process for the disbursement of funds, and the project was being delayed because of this process. It had additional funds to donate, but these funds would only partially cover the completion of phase II of the project.

THE COMMUNITY MEETING

Community members stood, waiting under a Guanacaste tree to shield themselves from the oppressive sun. Men were wearing their cowboy hats with machetes strapped on their belts, and women wore their finest skirts and traditional aprons. Being foreigners, Virginia and Cassandra were easy to identify in the crowd. Virginia was mulling over what she would say to community members during the meeting. She was nervous and since the volunteers only visited a couple times a year, everyone showed up to the meetings to hear what they had to say. In terms of updates on progress of the project, she had many good things to report, but also had some news that might not be well received. She loved this community and did not want to disappoint them. Her thoughts were interrupted by Miguel calling the meeting to order.

After his regular, ceremonial introduction, he said, "We are all here today to discuss the water system and we have *licenciada* Virginia and *licenciada* Cassandra here from Springfield to tell us about the project's progress. Also with us are Luís from the chief commissioner's office, Jorge from ASAR, and Ana from the MOH."

He announced that Virginia would speak first, and she stood in front of the crowd near a flip chart that she used to help explain the setup and process.

"Thank you, Miguel. I appreciate everyone being here and I have good news to report," Virginia began. "As you know, TU has been working closely with ADC and PWFA in assessing the community's needs and priorities, evaluating the resources we have available to us, monitoring the community's health, and advising on decisions about this project. For 2 years, the health promoters have done an excellent job of educating homes and schoolchildren about hygiene and disease prevention. The community's practices and health have improved significantly. Based on the data that we have collected, we have decided to continue the program. As you know, to have good hygiene, you need enough water, so we have been working hard on the water project," she began.

Ana echoed Virginia's comments, "It's true. We've had less people coming to the clinic with diarrheal disease and parasitism. We're very happy with the program so far."

Virginia continued, "We have successfully finished phase I of the water project including the pump, tank, and chlorinator. We are ready to move to phase II of running the distribution network through the community and connecting homes. As decided by ADC, the current plan for the future of the system is as follows: operation, maintenance, chlorination, collection of fees, and administration will be managed by ADC. Each household will have a mandatory gray water soak pit to prevent standing water and will be responsible for the connection of the home to the main pipeline as well as the installation of the gray water soak pit. Each household will need to pay for the soak pit and the household connection. Service will cost $8 per household monthly. PWFA has worked with ADC to create a business plan so that the user fees will pay for system maintenance and salaries of the health promoters. Any extra money will be saved for future community development projects. In addition, eight cents on the dollar will pay the fee to ASAR, which will provide ongoing technical support and training, low-cost replacement parts, and electrical subsidies."

She paused while the crowd stirred and people nodded in approval.

Virginia continued, "The only thing we're waiting for is the processing of the additional funds from Institution International so we can start with phase II. Institution International manages its online donations by earmarking them for different projects. If the project is not specified by donors, the board of directors invests that undesignated money, waits for a return on the investment, and then uses it to support other projects. Since the economy has slowed, Institution International has not received much return on its investments, so it has to make tough decisions about what projects to support."

Online? Earmarking? Board of directors? Investment? Virginia cringed after she heard herself explain all of this. She doubted community members would understand the ins and outs of Institution International's funding scheme, the recession, or interest rates. Virginia looked out at the crowd and noted the confused looks on the community members' faces. She wanted to be transparent about what was happening with the funding, but she couldn't figure out a simpler way to explain it. She continued, trying to rephrase her explanation.

"Since the economy has entered a recession, things are getting expensive and people aren't donating as much money."

Community members nodded in agreement. One woman spoke up, "Yeah, corn is the most expensive I've ever seen it, and I can't afford to buy meat any more at these prices."

Although she felt conflicted about it, at this point, Virginia didn't dare mention that although they had some funds promised for phase II, they didn't have the full amount. They only had funds to complete part of phase II, and she felt discouraged about raising more funds during a recession. Since it had become increasingly difficult to acquire the rest of the funds, she didn't want to promise any projected dates for system completion to avoid disappointment and mistrust.

"When will the project be finished?" a woman called out from the back of the group. This was exactly what Virginia feared. Prior to the meeting, Virginia had been informed by Miguel about the community's restlessness and impatience to finish the project and avoid any more water shortages in the dry season and high levels of diarrheal disease in the wet season.

As Virginia started to answer, she was interrupted by another woman, "When you say we're close to starting phase II, what do you mean?" Virginia had no way of knowing that answer either.

She responded, "We're waiting for processing of the funds through Institution International, and they don't know an exact date, but it should be soon. The phase costs $50,000, and it takes time to raise that much money," responded Virginia.

People in the crowd started to grumble in protest, and one woman called out, "I knew it! It's not going to happen. What about all of the manual labor we've done so far? Doesn't that help to pay for it?"

Another woman spoke up. "I don't know how much longer we can wait," she exclaimed. "I lost a son last year to diarrhea. I can't lose another child."

Ramón stepped forward next to Virginia to respond to the mother's concern. "I've been working with TU to collect data about sickness and hygiene in the community. There are a lot of unhygienic practices among households, and if we improve these practices, we can significantly reduce disease while we are waiting for the water system to be constructed. It will also be important when we have the water system to keep our water clean. We've made a lot of progress on improving hygiene so far, but we can still do better." He deferred to Cassandra to continue with the specifics of program outcomes.

"Ramón is right," Cassandra said in broken Spanish. "Before the health promoter program started, the annual mortality rate was 4 per 1,000 children under the age of 5, and 3 per 1,000 children between ages 6 and 12. Our recent data show that the rate has been reduced to 1 per 1,000 children in both age categories, a decrease from the baseline rate. There has also been a 15% reduction in days missed from school and a 25% reduction in the purchase of antiparasite pills at the pharmacy. In addition, before the program, 50% of the community knew that diarrhea could be caused by contaminated food, 20% by dirty hands, and 10% by microbes. After 1 year of hygiene promotion through local health promoters, these figures increased to 75%, 50%, and 50%, respectively. . . ."

As Cassandra rambled on, excited about the drastic improvements in hygiene behavior, she noticed that community members didn't share her enthusiasm. She wondered if they weren't listening, if it was her halting Spanish, or if maybe they didn't understand. She decided to move on from the statistics, and spoke more simply.

"Fewer children are dying, and more people understand what is causing them to get sick and how to prevent it from happening. This is promising news, and while we are waiting for the water system, the health promoters can continue to help you improve personal, domestic, and food hygiene, as well as proper waste disposal for disease control. We can boil water, wash hands, and keep our latrines covered and clean, but we need cooperation from everyone, and that means changing the way you do some things."

Meeting attendees looked unimpressed. "I don't know what all of that has to do with children dying or getting water. I sweep my home clean and cook good food," one woman called out.

Cassandra knew that behavior change for domestic hygiene and environmental sanitation had always been difficult in San Gabriel due to the challenging physical environment, especially in the dry season. It didn't matter if a household wanted to keep its water jugs and dishes clean when the family lived in an environment full of dust and there was little water to wash it away. Behavior change is difficult even in the best environments and with ample resources. She knew that good hygiene was vital to reduction in diarrhea and parasitism, but that changing behaviors to break the fecal-oral pathway was daunting.

There have been significant challenges in achieving sustainable diarrheal disease reduction. It is increasingly recognized that successful diarrhea prevention is reliant on changes in hygiene behavior. More and more, hygiene behaviors are recognized as clusters, or domains of behaviors, including food, domestic, and personal hygiene as well as sanitation and water management behavior. The hygiene cluster approach is rooted in the transmission of disease through the various fecal-oral pathways previously described. Improved hygiene practices within multiple domains reduce the incidence of disease[10,37] relative to narrowly targeted interventions (such as hand washing). Behavior changes in each cluster may affect the likelihood that pathogens will be transmitted, directly correlating with reductions in disease prevalence.[7]

There was widespread understanding in the community of disease *treatment*, but less familiarity among residents about disease *prevention*.

That was evident when one woman asked, "Well, will you be dispensing pills? Because we have to have pills to avoid sickness."

Ramón responded, "We can reduce the number of people getting diseases by preventing the diseases before they happen. You see, those pills don't prevent illness . . ." Ramón paused. "On behalf of the team of health promoters, you have my commitment that we will do our best to help." Attendees stood quietly, and most of them had their heads down.

"There's still the difficulty of pulling water up from the wells or transporting it on oxen-pulled carts from the neighbor every day," added a young woman. "I spend 3 hours a day pulling up water."

"Don't people in Springfield know our situation?" asked a man in the back.

Virginia and Cassandra exchanged glances with Miguel and Ramón. They weren't sure how to respond.

Virginia responded, "Of course they do, but it's not a question of . . ."

One man interrupted, "What about the funding from Engineers, Ltd.? I heard the chief commissioner was offered funding for the water project. Is that true?"

Everyone fixed their eyes on the chief commissioner's representative, Luís, who came to speak about this possible funding.

"I would be delighted to respond," said Luís, as he stepped forward from the crowd of community members with a smile on his face. "Yes, as some of you know, Engineers, Ltd. has offered funding to the municipality for the water project in San Gabriel. The chief commissioner is grateful for this exceptional opportunity. Engineers, Ltd. has offered $50,000 to dig four boreholes at central locations in San Gabriel that would be fitted with state-of-the-art pumps. This way, water is available to all of the households that want to access the pumps. The municipality would assist the community by removing the burden to ADC of managing the collection of water fees and other administration. The chief commissioner's office can manage the finances and with those funds, help to plan projects for other development needs, like improvement of roads or addition of classrooms to schools. The fees for each household would be only $4 per month for unlimited water. We can talk to the MOH about hiring the health promoters, and we may be able to work things out."

Some community members nodded their heads in approval, while others weren't convinced. There was a long pause before anyone responded. Ana of the MOH was the first to speak up. "According to my calculations, that's still about 75 houses per tap, not including the houses in the central neighborhood covered by the current water system. I'm worried about the hygiene of the tap, and what if there's not enough water from any given tap? Who is going to chlorinate the water? Will you conduct regular tests for quality? We have to worry about quantity and quality of the water, especially for those homes with children under 5 years of age."

Nobody mentioned the cost estimate of the project. Cassandra did some calculations in her head, and suspected this proposed project would only cost approximately $20,000 to dig the boreholes and set up the pumps, but what about the rest of the project? She knew that the reason the MOH didn't already allocate more than one health promoter was because it didn't have adequate funds. She wondered if this would affect support for the current additional promoters. She kept quiet because she didn't feel comfortable getting involved with local politics or accusing anyone of unethical proposals. She wasn't sure if that was her role.

"One benefit is with fewer points of use, as opposed to taps at every home, it is more likely that standing water could be minimized. This helps to reduce dengue fever. Still, I'm not sure these communal pumps would be easy to use for everyone, particularly the elderly," added Ramón. "People will still have to transport water, introducing more opportunities for the water to become contaminated."

Jorge from ASAR looked nervous. The plan was for him to provide technical assistance to the community, for which ASAR would receive a fee. This new option might eliminate him from the picture.

As attendees continued to call out questions, the atmosphere became confused. With his hands raised to quiet the crowd, Miguel announced, "We will have to stop the meeting now because we will meet with ADC to get more details on all of the options. We can reconvene to make a decision once we have more information. We will send out invitations to the next meeting. Thank you for all coming, and you can see any ADC member afterwards to voice your concerns." Community members dispersed and formed into groups, chatting about the meeting.

DECISION MAKING AND CONSIDERATIONS

The community meeting was followed by a closed-door ADC meeting that included Virginia and Cassandra. With the input from these volunteers, ADC was tasked with making the decision between a cheaper project that would have an immediate, known timeline for a communal water system or a larger, more expensive project that would have an undefined timeline and didn't have all of the funds raised, but would

service every household. Sustainability of the water system, water quality, water access equity, potential increase in cost per household, and system maintenance were some factors to be considered for each decision. A heated debate ensued and they reviewed all of the risks, benefits, and drawbacks of each choice. Some members brought up concerns that were not raised at the community meeting.

ADC and the community were divided between factions, primarily in line with political tendencies, but also guided by personal priorities and those of partners they favored. Those members who belonged to the chief commissioner's political party trusted the chief commissioner to manage the system and wanted the party to have publicity from doing good community work. They had faith that future projects would be supported with the collected system fees, and the funds wouldn't go to projects in the other two cantons in the municipality. They also believed that system maintenance and chlorination would meet their needs. Those siding with the other political party wanted the control to be in the hands of the community to ensure transparency and responsiveness to community priorities.

The discussion centered around considerations for the PWFA system and those for Engineers, Ltd. system.

Considerations for the PWFA System

It was unknown how long it would take to raise the funds for phase II. User fees would be more expensive per household than the communal water taps, and the community would have control over setting the fees. The system would have a comprehensive gray water component, but families would have to pay for materials to install gray water disposal pits as well as their water connection to the main line. The project would include a hygiene promotion component, which would be subsidized by user fees. Water would be delivered to each household, making it more equitable since each home did not have to travel for water, and also more likely that proper water hygiene and handling could be possible.

Administration of the system and the hygiene program would be the responsibility of the community; however, ADC had less administrative infrastructure and fewer support services and resources than the municipality. Although there were fewer administrative processes in place, the project would be managed by democratically elected ADC members, who were more likely to be trusted by community members. The system would be community owned. The members of the community would decide about future projects instead of these decisions being made for them by the municipality. In the meantime, while the system was being built, more children could die if practices were not changed. It was possible child mortality could be reduced through behavior change, which can be too difficult to achieve in the short term. TU conducted multiple community assessments, identifying community priorities, needs, assets, educational levels, and living conditions that might affect household water management and hygiene.

This choice had the potential of building the capacity of the community, but it also had the potential to be a disaster if not properly executed. This option would present a challenge for future sustainability in the sense that ADC would need ongoing technical training for system management, where the relationship between ASAR and ADC would be crucial. Although ASAR seemed to be a reliable organization, it was uncertain whether it would measure up to its promises of technical assistance. Other communities that were members of ASAR had both positive and negative experiences with ASAR and its responsiveness to water system needs.

Considerations for the Engineers, Ltd. System

The timeline for initiation of construction was known and it was promised construction could start immediately, making it more likely to reduce child mortality in the wet season and water shortages in the next dry season. However, there was no guarantee the project would be completed in the timeline promised. An agreement had already been made that all of the funds have been guaranteed to complete the project. User fees would be cheaper than the PWFA system, but it was unknown and out of community control whether fees would ever be increased. The system included communal pumps, but not delivery to each household. The system had a gray water component at the communal pumps. It was possible the existing hygiene promotion program could be supported by the MOH, but there was no guarantee at that point. Administration and chlorination of the system would be managed by the municipality. The system would be owned by the municipality. There was no indication about ongoing technical assistance or community education/training around the water system.

The profit of this system would go to the municipality but would be earmarked for future San Gabriel projects, provided there was not a change of office when the projects are decided. The municipality would decide how the funds were spent and would be accountable for expenditures. The municipality consists of three other cantons besides San Gabriel (the total municipal population was approximately 12,000), all of which had development project needs. It was possible that if the funds were not used by San Gabriel, they could go to San Julián, another canton in the municipality that was also lacking potable water. The scope of the project (communal water taps) would not respond to the requests of the community (delivery to each household), and it would not be equitable for all households due to the variation in distances that residents would have to travel to collect water. Engineers, Ltd. had not conducted any formal community as-

sessments and knew nothing about the community's priorities, needs, assets, educational levels, or living conditions that might affect water hygiene. The Engineers, Ltd. system would not allow PWFA to review the system technical design plans, review the scope, or cost out the materials.

Trust was a major factor in both choices, regardless of the details of each option. There was no guarantee for either option as to how quickly the system would be finished, and the quality of the resultant systems was an unknown factor.

Which Way is the Best Way?

ADC adjourned the meeting and agreed that the final decision regarding next steps would be made the following day. Miguel, Ramón, Virginia, and Cassandra started their walk back home before the hottest part of the day.

"Well, what do you think?" asked Virginia.

"It's a difficult decision. We've been working towards this for so many years that it makes you want to start immediately. My family is pushing me to choose the Engineers, Ltd. system, but they don't understand all of the other factors involved in making this decision," replied Miguel.

"Do we really have the capacity to manage such a large system?" asked Ramón.

"You don't think we can?" Miguel asked, and then explained his thoughts on the subject. "ASAR provides training for this, and we'll have to build our capacity. But we also have to consider the possibility that our relationship with ASAR would change. What if we're not happy with their service—who would we go to for technical assistance, and could we afford it?"

"I'm in favor of the PWFA system because there would be less water contamination since it wouldn't have to be transported. But I will have to work hard to get households to prevent standing water and to handle the water hygienically. I may need more training for this," responded Ramón.

"I think it will be best to have a unanimous decision. A vote would be the next best alternative. Ultimately, I am just a visitor and it will be the community's decision. I think the most important thing to keep in mind is the long-term well-being of the community," added Cassandra.

They continued down the dusty road, greeting neighbors on their way. They arrived at Miguel's front entrance by the road. Virginia, Cassandra, and Miguel stopped, and Ramón kept walking, letting out a whistle and *¡Que le vaya bien!* ("Take care!") As the group opened the wooden gate and walked up to the house, they heard the babbling of children in the yard and the sounds of cooking.

"Alooo," Cassandra called out to the children. Luisa approached Miguel and asked, "What happened?"

Miguel slowly responded, "You'll have your water one way or another, darling. The question is: which way is the best way?"

About the Authors

Elizabeth L. Andrade, MPH, is a research scientist at The George Washington University School of Public Health and Health Services (GWU SPHHS) in the Department of Prevention and Community Health. She is also the principal investigator of the intervention study, Evaluating the Efficacy of a Community-Based Hygiene Promotion Intervention in Santa Clara, El Salvador, done in collaboration with the GWU SPHHS and Engineers without Borders. Ms. Andrade has extensive experience working with Latino immigrant/refugee populations in the Washington, DC, metropolitan area in both programmatic and research capacities. Internationally, she has consulted for UNICEF, Save the Children, and the Virginia Hospital Center Medical Brigade. Ms. Andrade has extensive experience in conducting community assessments and in program design, implementation, and evaluation. She earned her master of public health degree from the GWU SPHHS in 2004, and is currently a doctor of public health candidate in health behavior. Her work in the areas of community-based participatory monitoring and evaluation, multidisciplinary partnering, community-based capacity building, and program evaluation inspired this case study.

Kathryn Zoerhoff, MPH, MA is the monitoring and evaluation associate for the Neglected Tropical Disease Control Program at RTI International. Ms. Zoerhoff is responsible for planning and implementing monitoring and evaluation activities for the Neglected Tropical Disease Control Program, a United States Agency for International Development-funded program that currently operates in 13 countries in Africa, Asia, and the Caribbean. Ms. Zoerhoff has also carried out monitoring and evaluation activities with White Ribbon Alliance for Safe Motherhood in Tanzania, International Medical Corps, and Engineers without Borders in El Salvador. She earned an MPH in global public health and an MA in international development studies from The George Washington University in 2009. Ms. Zoerhoff's professional interests and experience include monitoring and evaluation, women's health issues, training/capacity building, and community-based development.

REFERENCES

1. Bryce J, Boschi-Pinto C, Shibuya K, Black RE, WHO Child Health Epidemiology Reference Group. WHO estimates of the causes of death in children. *Lancet.* 2005;365(9465):1147–1152.

2. World Health Organization-United Nations Children's Fund. *Diarrhoea: Why Children Are Still Dying and What Can Be Done.* http://whqlibdoc.who.int/publications/2009/9789241598415_eng.pdf. Published 2009. Accessed November 15, 2010.

3. Curtis V, Cairncross S. Effect of washing hands on diarrhoea risk in the community. *Lancet Infect Dis.* 2003;3:275–281.

4. Clasen T, Cairncross S. Household water management: refining the dominant paradigm. *Trop Med Int Health.* 2004;9(2):187–191.

5. Huttly SRA, Morris SS, Pisani V. Prevention of diarrhea in young children in developing countries. *Bull World Health Org.* 1997;75(2):163–174.

6. Bateman OM, Jahan RA, Brahman S, Zeitlin S, Laston SL. *Prevention of Diarrhea through Improving Hygiene Behaviors.* Washington, DC: EHP-CARE-ICDDR/B, EHP Joint Publication No. 4; 2002.

7. Wagner JM, Lanoix JN. Excreta disposal for rural areas and small communities. *WHO Monograph series No 39.* Geneva, Switzerland: WHO; 1958.

8. Curtis V, Caimcross S, Yonii R. Domestic hygiene and diarrhea—pinpointing the problem. *Trop Med Int Health.* 2000;5:22–32.

9. Huttly SR, Lanata CF. Feces, flies, and fetor: findings from a Peruvian shantytown. *Rev Panam Salud Publica.* 1998;4:75–79.

10. Fewtrell L, Kaufmann RB, Way D, et al. Water, sanitation, and hygiene interventions to reduce diarrhea in less developed countries: a systematic review and meta-analysis. *Lancet Infect Dis.* 2005;5:42–52.

11. Morel A, Diener S. *Greywater Management in Low and Middle-Income Countries: Review of Different Treatment Systems for Households or Neighborhoods.* Sandec report; No. 16/06. Dübendorf, Switzerland: Sandec Water and Sanitation in Developing Countries; 2006.

12. Minkler M, Wallerstein NB. Improving health through community organization and community building. In Glanz K, Rimer BK, Lewis FM, eds. *Health Behavior and Health Education.* San Francisco, CA: Jossey-Bass; 2002.

13. Rappaport J. Studies in empowerment: introduction to the issue. *Prev Hum Serv.* 1984;3(2, 3):1–7.

14. Nyswander DB. Education for health: some principles and their application. *Health Educ Monogr.* 1956;14:65–70.

15. Bandura A. Exercise of personal and collective efficacy. In Bandura A, ed. *Self-Efficacy in Changing Societies.* New York, NY: Cambridge University Press; 1995.

16. Wandersman A, Florin P. Citizen participation and community organizing. In Rappaport J, Seidman E, eds. *Handbook of Community Psychology.* New York, NY: Kluwer Academic/Plenum Publishers; 2000.

17. Eng E, Briscoe J, Cunningham A. The effect of participation in state projects on immunization. *Soc Sci Med.* 1990;30(12):1349–1358.

18. Katz R. Empowerment and synergy: expanding the community's healing resources. *Prev Hum Serv.* 1984;3:201–226.

19. Braithwaite RL, Murphy F, Lythcott N, Blumenthal DS. Community organization and development for health promotion within an urban black community: a conceptual model. *Health Educ.* 1989;2(5):56–60.

20. Cottrell LS Jr. The competent community. In Watten R, Lyon L, eds. *New Perspectives on the American Community.* Homewood, IL: The Dorsey Press; 1983.

21. Bernstein E, Wallerstein N, Braithwaite R, Gutierrez L, Labonte R, Zimmerman M. Empowerment forum: a dialogue between guest editorial board members. *Health Educ Q.* 1994;21(3): 281–294.

22. Israel B, Checkoway B, Schulz A, Zimmerman M. Health education and community empowerment: conceptualizing and measuring perceptions of individual, organizational, and community control. *Health Educ Q.* 1994;21(2):149–170.

23. Purdey A, Adhikari G, Robinson S, Cox P. Participatory health development in rural Nepal: clarifying the process of community empowerment. *Health Educ Q.* 1994;21(3):329–344.

24. Goodman RM, Speers MA, McLeroy K, et al. Identifying and defining the dimensions of community capacity to provide a basis for measurement. *Health Educ Behav.* 1998;25(3):258–278.

25. Fawcett SB, Francisco VT, Schultz JA, Berkowitz B, Wolff TJ, Nagy G. The community tool box: a web-based resource for building healthier communities. *Public Health Rep.* 2000;113(2, 3):274–278.

26. Kieffer C. Citizen empowerment: a developmental perspective. Studies in empowerment: steps toward understanding and action. *Prev Hum Serv.* 1984;3(2, 3):9–36.

27. Witmer A. Community health workers: integral members of the health care work force. *Am J Public Health.* 1995;85:1055–1058.

28. Wilson K, Brownstein JN, Blanton C. Community health advisor use: insights from a national survey. In US Department of Health and Human Services, Centers for Disease Control. *Community Health Advisors/Community Health Workers: Selected Annotations and Programs in the United States.* Vol 3. Atlanta, GA; June 1998.

29. DiClemente RJ, Crosby RA, Kegler MC. *Emerging Theories in Health Promotion Practice and Research.* San Francisco, CA: Jossey-Bass; 2002.

30. Israel B. Social networks and social support: implications for natural helper and community level interventions. *Health Educ Q.* 1985;12:65–80.

31. Beam N, Tessaro I. The lay health advisor model in theory and practice: an example of an agency-based program. *Fam Community Health.* 1994;17:70–79.

32. Love MB, Gardner K, Legion V. Community health workers: who they are and what they do. *Health Educ Behav.* 199;724:510–522.

33. Satterfield DW, Burd C, Valdez L, Hosey G, Eagle Shield J. The "in-between" people: participation of community health representatives in diabetes prevention and care in American Indian and Alaskan Native communities. *Health Promot Pract.* 2002;3(2):166–175.

34. Basch PF. *Textbook of International Health.* New York, NY: Oxford University Press; 1990:200–212.

35. Rogers EM. *Diffusion of Innovations.* New York, NY: The Free Press; 1962.

36. Narayan D. The contribution of people's participation: evidence from 121 rural water supply projects. *Environmentally Sustainable Development Occasional Paper Series,* No 1. Washington, DC: World Bank; 1995.

37. Esrey SA, Potash JB, Roberts L, Shiff C. Effects of improved water supply and sanitation on ascariasis, diarrhoea, dracunculiasis, hookworm infection, schistosomiasis, and trachoma. *Bull World Health Organ.* 1991;69:609–621.

Building on Strengths: A School-Based Mental Health Program

OLGA ACOSTA PRICE, JODIE FISHMAN, AND MIMI V. CHAPMAN

A TROUBLED STUDENT WITH A TROUBLED PAST

Juanita, a 12-year-old seventh-grader in middle school in New City, Mississippi, was once again in in-school suspension (ISS) for being disruptive in class, fighting with other students, and refusing to follow instructions. School administrators and staff admitted frustration at Juanita's behavior, and her classroom teacher was overheard saying, "There are rules in place and she just has to learn to follow them, period."

By design, the ISS classroom had an open section and a section with cubicles where students were restricted from seeing those around them to help students concentrate on schoolwork they were supposed to be doing while in the ISS classroom. This particular setting, however, was triggering potentially traumatic memories for Juanita.

Juanita frequently mumbled, "I hate it here. I wish everyone would leave me alone."

Juanita and her mother came to the United States in June of 2009 from a small, poverty-stricken town outside of Mexico City, Mexico. Juanita's mother wanted to give Juanita a better life, and even a low-wage job in the United States would provide a much better standard of living than they were used to in Mexico. Juanita's mother had a first cousin living in New City, Mississippi. She heard there was a large community of Mexican immigrants already living there and work was plentiful.

The lure of a better life convinced Juanita's mother to use a coyote to smuggle her and her daughter illegally across the border from Mexico to the United States. While making this journey, Juanita and her mother were subjected to living in tiny spaces, fed only rice and water once a day. They saw several fellow illegal immigrants die of dehydration. Juanita was left alone more than once in the small confinement and when her mother was returned to the space by the coyotes, she did not talk about what happened; Juanita felt a huge distance from her mother.

Having spent all their money on the coyote, when Juanita and her mother reached New City in June, they moved into a small apartment with cousins. Juanita slept on the floor next to the couch where her mother slept. Juanita's mother worked at the local chicken processing plant, but rumors abounded that the plant would close any day. Juanita attended school, but she had a rough adjustment; she had no friends there and struggled to understand the expectations of her new teachers. She was lonely, frustrated, and angry that she had to leave everything familiar to her.

A PROBLEM STUDENT, OR STUDENT WITH A PROBLEM?

As part of an externally funded, school-based program called Building on Strengths, a school-family liaison, a Latina immigrant, was able to help Juanita. The liaison talked with Juanita about school and the ISS classroom in which she often found herself. Juanita explained being in the cubicle in ISS brought back painful memories of being in the confined space during her "importation" to New City.

"I start to remember that time when my mother and I were with the coyotes and I can't get those thoughts out of my head," Juanita complained.

"Why didn't you mention this to anyone before?" the liaison asked.

"I don't think the teachers care," said Juanita, "and they don't speak Spanish anyway, so it is hard for me to explain it. I just don't feel comfortable talking with them."

School staff members admitted they often did not know what their students and their families had been through and were not always aware of the symbolism of their own actions. The school-family liaison spoke first to the school principal, explaining Juanita was likely expressing retraumatization. Although she was not experiencing a true flashback, the ISS experience was triggering potentially traumatic memories. The principal agreed in-school suspension was not productive for Juanita.

The Building on Strengths program allowed the school-family liaison to help change the ISS, as well as work with Juanita and her mother to further address the traumatic experiences in their past. The liaison completed an intake with Juanita and her mother to better assess their mental health needs, and they were referred to *Nuestra Comunidad*, a community mental health clinic in their area to facilitate their adjustment to New City. Juanita's mother was connected to county-funded social services to assist her with learning English and to explore other employment opportunities. She also indicated she was willing to participate in a parent night event after learning that she would meet other parents in similar circumstances.

BUILDING ON STRENGTHS

The Building on Strengths program represented a partnership of the school district, two local public schools, the State University of Mississippi School of Social Work, and *Nuestra Comunidad*, a bilingual and bicultural community mental health center. The 3-year program started in 2007 and was funded through a private foundation for $100,000 per year. The first year focused on launching the program, while the second and third years were dedicated to program implementation.

The goals of Building on Strengths were to create a system of care with an emphasis on early identification of emotional and behavioral problems through the use of a liaison or cultural broker[i] and to improve services for immigrant Latino children and their families by reducing barriers to access. The program plan included diversity and cultural competence training for school staff, training for parents about youth mental health issues, and training to enhance mental health knowledge for teachers and staff. The program conducted a number of parent night events every year, attracting an average of 30 Latino parents at each meeting, a significant increase over previous attempts to bring parents together at the school.

_____

[i] An individual who engages in the act of bridging, linking, or mediating between groups or persons of differing cultural backgrounds for the purpose of reducing conflict or producing change.[1]

The meetings included information on school processes and expectations, resources available to parents and their children, and preliminary discussions of typical stresses children face adjusting to life at a new school. Postmeeting feedback indicated parents were satisfied with these events and found the information useful to their lives.

Building on Strengths offered school-based mental health services at James Middle School and Larson High School, two schools in New City with a high percentage of Latino students. A Latina school-family liaison was hired and assigned to the two schools to serve as a cultural broker and to provide limited direct clinical services as well as referrals to other agencies for specialized services. Building on Strengths' grant funding fully supported the liaison's salary, although she was employed by *Nuestra Comunidad* and supervised by its staff. The liaison was a qualified mental health provider who was well liked by the community and earned credibility among parents and educators alike. She provided consultation to teachers and school staff on issues that were interfering with student academic progress, identified students with signs of mental health problems, engaged families in creating solutions and action plans for their children, and advocated for students and families, especially those who were Spanish-speaking and unfamiliar with the American public school or mental health systems. Individual students were assessed to determine the extent of their emotional or behavioral needs, and referrals were made to *Nuestra Comunidad* for youth with significant mental health conditions. A 16-week evidence-based counseling group was started in the third year of the program in both schools to try to improve the skills necessary for regulating emotions and behavior among 12- to 18-year-old girls. The group demonstrated positive behavioral outcomes among its participants.

NUESTRA COMUNIDAD: MEETING MENTAL HEALTH NEEDS THROUGH COMMUNITY

A coalition of psychiatry residents, members of social service agencies serving Latinos, and primary care clinicians founded *Nuestra Comunidad*, which is Spanish for *our community*. This group united around a mutual concern about the unmet needs of Latinos with behavioral health problems. *Nuestra Comunidad* incorporated in November 2004, received its first grant in the spring of 2005, and saw its first clients in November 2005. The organization had a staff of six employees and four trainees, all of them bilingual. *Nuestra Comunidad* described its mission as providing, in collaboration with consumers, university partners, and local, state, and national agencies, best practice mental health and substance abuse treatment and resources for the under-served Latino-Hispanic population of Mississippi in collaboration with consumers and local, university, state and national agencies.

Based in Carter, Mississippi, *Nuestra Comunidad* opened a second office in New City in July 2006. Approximately 78% of *Nuestra Comunidad* clients had incomes below the federal poverty level; 65% of clients were uninsured, and another 28% were insured by government programs such as Medicaid and Mississippi's Child Health Insurance Program. The agency was able to seek reimbursement through Medicaid for the clinical services offered (i.e., individual, group, and family therapy) but public funding did not support the outreach and early intervention services provided by the liaison, so those efforts were supported via a private grant. Although *Nuestra Comunidad* was committed to the prevention and early intervention goals of the Building on Strengths program, its staff were concerned about how to support these activities after the private grant ended.

RISK FACTORS FACING LATINO YOUTH IN THE UNITED STATES

Although local data on Latino youth are scarce, national research on young Latinos indicates cause for worry. Latino youth are engaged in behaviors and situations that put them at increased risk for mental health difficulties or may be symptomatic of existing, untreated mental illness. Information from the Youth Risk Behavior Survey[2] shows higher percentages of Latino youth report carrying weapons to school, and a higher prevalence of drug and alcohol use than other youth their age; over 11% of Latino students report they did not go to school at least once in the last 30 days because they felt unsafe, a proportion higher than any other ethnic group. Other studies have found Latinos experience higher rates of physical and sexual abuse than either black or white[ii] adolescents.[3] Further, Latina girls have the highest incidence of suicide attempts compared to girls from other groups.[4] To complicate the picture, about 35% of Latino adolescents nationally report being sexually active, yet they are less likely than their white or black counterparts to use condoms or birth control to prevent pregnancy or sexually transmitted diseases.[6]

These risk factors have been associated with poorer academic and economic outcomes. Latino youth are less likely to complete high school, are more likely to drop out of school, and fare worse on educational achievement tests than their

white counterparts.[7] These phenomena also hold true for students enrolled in the New City public schools. Local estimates are that more than half of the 1,500 self-identified Latino students enrolled in school (of the 7,400 students in the school system) have some type of mental health need, but only 3–5% are accessing services in the community. The stigma associated with receiving mental health care is one barrier, with public sentiments of being "crazy" hindering efforts to seek professional help. In addition, service utilization data from the local public mental health agency show that three times more whites and five times more African American residents are served in community mental health agencies in New City than Latino residents, even though the mental health needs are thought to be as significant, if not more so, for Latino immigrants. Focus groups conducted with local Latino adolescents found that the majority of participants reported incidents of discrimination and that, although they would welcome support to address their family's mental health needs, they do not know where to go or whom to trust.

MIGRATION TO NEW CITY, MISSISSIPPI

The rapid influx of immigrants to New City[iii] meant Juanita was not the only Latino student in the school identified with behavioral and academic problems. In the decade between 1990 and 2000, the Latino population of Mississippi grew 394%,[8] primarily due to booming construction and the proliferation of low-wage jobs. Since the 1990s, New City had seen an influx of Spanish-speaking immigrants due to an abundance of jobs in the chicken-processing industry, with the majority of the new residents being undocumented immigrants. According to 2000 census data, Hispanics of any nationality comprised 39% of the population in New City, a small, rural, and high-poverty community in Mississippi. The median income for a household in New City in 2000 was $33,651.

New City is not an isolated case. Southeastern states have some of the fastest-growing populations of Latino immigrants in the United States. Educators in particular have been caught by surprise at the demographic changes in their classrooms, with the proportion of Latino K-12 students in the South increasing from 5 to 17% from 1972 to 2004 and the rate of English language learners in the state skyrocketing by more than 300%.[7] The rapid growth and the lack of empirical data about these new arrivals have left schools and other youth-serving organizations to create interventions in an ad-hoc

---

[ii] White refers to an individual who identifies as a member of the white race and is not Hispanic or Latino. Hispanic or Latino is a term used by a person of Cuban, Mexican, Puerto Rican, Cuban, South or Central American descent, or other Spanish culture or origin, regardless of race.[5]

[iii] Statistics provided are for a state within the United States but are not necessarily reflective of the demographics of Mississippi.

fashion. In particular, there is a significant lack of cohesive information about the social, behavioral, and academic needs of Latino immigrant youth ages 12 to 18 years, most of whom are U.S. citizens but whose parents are not. The burgeoning Latino population has created additional challenges around service delivery, including the poor provision of mental health and social services due in large part to the limited number of bilingual or bicultural providers. Agencies in and around New City, such as county social services, juvenile justice, and child welfare agencies, have tried to adjust to the changing demographics but these institutions have very specific criteria for inclusion in their services and were able to engage only a small segment of the population given their restricted mandates. Additional groups, such as other community mental health providers, psychiatric service professionals, and mental health advocacy groups, remain limited in their ability to respond to the increase in service needs due to the lack of qualified bilingual staff available to work with Latino families. The board of commissioners and the merchants association are also supportive of efforts to expand services but have little ability to shepherd resources toward this needy population.

Latino immigrants in the New City area face a number of barriers to successful acculturation, especially the significant number who are undocumented. New City can be described as moderate politically, but the surrounding counties are socially and economically conservative. The poverty and unemployment rate in and around New City contributed to a growing schism between those who believed dwindling public resources should only be available to citizens of the United States and those who felt that helping all in need ultimately benefits the entire community. Although significant coethnic communities have been developing, the native population is ambivalent about new Latino immigrants. Some communities reached out to the newcomers, welcomed their business, and hired them for previously abundant low-wage jobs, while other factions reacted with open hostility and aggression about the unfair burden on public institutions and the overuse of social services by illegal residents. Their anger was fueled by the growing number of non-Latino families unable to identify qualified mental health providers who could see their own children. This was due, in large part, to the statewide mental health reform that included privatization of the mental health system. Privatization created some efficiencies but also made accessing mental health care much more difficult for many people, both citizens and noncitizens.

When the migration to New City began in the mid-1990s, national anti-immigrant speakers were brought in to rally residents to protest their presence. Across the state, there was continuing debate around higher education opportunities for immigrant youth who were undocumented but educated in the state's public schools and whether they should be eligible to attend the state's 4-year and community colleges. Outspoken advocates for new immigrants received death threats and some required FBI protection. Anti-immigrant sentiment in the community and across the state complicated advocacy efforts to create seamless networks of support for vulnerable families. Media stories highlighted accounts of local raids that resulted in detention and deportation of many adults, leaving parents fearful of venturing from their homes and students anxious that they would not see their parents upon returning from school. In addition, service providers, ranging from public schools to mental health agencies, struggled to find teachers, therapists, and other professionals who were able to simply communicate in Spanish, much less provide culturally appropriate services.

A number of community advocates suggested that a public awareness or social marketing campaign highlighting the benefits of population-based prevention strategies would do wonders to help shift public opinion. Such a strategy had been used with some success in this region around other social and health issues, such as the prevention of HIV/AIDS, teen pregnancy, and domestic violence. Yet, sentiments towards the growing immigrant population were particularly charged, and everyone in New City was aware of the ever-increasing community divide. Local business owners warned that if law enforcement officials continued to deport undocumented immigrants, their businesses would suffer and New City itself would be economically devastated. But other realities led program leaders to be cautious. The fight over dwindling mental health resources added to the tension. Accordingly, publicity about programs that provided mental health services to new immigrants were thought to be particularly ill advised. The general sentiment among residents, advocates, and legislators of New City was that assistance to immigrants, especially undocumented immigrants, was successful only when provided "under the radar." The demise of any helpful policy or program would be assured when brought into public view and scrutiny, resulting in widespread controversy. The exception was the advocacy conducted by a few pastors or other religious leaders who were respected by the community at large and unlikely to be vilified for their support of the disadvantaged.

ADDRESSING CULTURAL COMPETENCY

James Middle School and Larson High School both employed only one school counselor and one school social worker, neither of whom spoke Spanish. Thus, a substantial responsibility rested on the shoulders of the school-family liaison funded by

Building on Strengths. How could one liaison reach all of the vulnerable Latino students? Should she even try to identify every student's needs knowing qualified mental health care might not be consistently available?

Thus, another Building on Strengths initiative centered around classroom-based consultation and skills training offered to teachers. Program staff believed this might prevent the constant flow of students exhibiting behavioral problems and being referred to ISS.

Like many school systems, the New City school system participated in numerous cultural competency initiatives in the past with the goal of creating a climate that welcomed diverse student populations. However, many of these programs focused on specific instructional techniques or descriptions of particular groups that inadvertently reinforced stereotypes or the notion that members of certain groups were completely defined by their cultural background. Expected changes in teacher and staff attitudes were, therefore, not realized. The school system invested heavily in improving language access for Latino students and families. As a result, the number of English-as-a-second-language teachers increased across the school district (from 3 to 28), more interpreters were hired, and bilingual hotlines were created. Yet, school leaders acknowledged that the majority of school staff could use ongoing cultural competence training to adequately address the education and health needs of Latino families and children.

Building on Strengths program staff conducted cultural competency training for 20 teachers, staff members, principals, and district-level administrators in August of 2007. The innovative curriculum was more intensive and contributed to the development of insights about personal biases and discrimination that affected participants in a deeply personal way. Participants were vocal about the impact of the training and their newfound investment in initiating changes that would improve the climate of their schools. The challenge was to keep that initial work moving and spreading throughout the two target schools and the larger school system. The main barriers were scheduling and funding. The 4 teacher training days per year were largely scheduled to conduct mandatory activities, leaving little room for additional training or dissemination of nonacademic information. After-school times were problematic because teachers and staff are involved with sports teams or school clubs and union mandates required overtime pay for activities falling outside of regular school hours.

STORIES OF CHANGE

As the program was implemented, the James Middle School principal expressed some ambivalence about the program and the services offered. His concerns grew about how much time students might spend out of the classroom and away from academic instruction, whether teachers would be asked to take on new roles or responsibilities, and how much flexibility the liaison would request around the interpretation of mandatory school policies and procedures. The principal's reluctance to embrace the program caused worry among program leaders who knew that school leadership support would be critical to the success of this school-based mental health program.[9] Teachers were unsure at first whether referring students to the liaison would prove beneficial, but, after several months, decreases in classroom disruptions and increases in time spent on academic instruction confirmed the value of the liaison's support. After hearing the positive anecdotes from the teachers, the principal conceded that allowing the liaison to see students individually and having his staff participate in cultural competence training would likely benefit his staff and help keep students out of ISS. He became convinced that gaining a better understanding of the differences in learning and communication among immigrant children and the impact of trauma and loss on classroom behavior would likely improve teachers' patience, empathy, and effectiveness.

Accordingly, the principal let the Building on Strengths project director know that he was ready to expand programming. However, he also had some barriers to overcome. When past school budgets provided more plentiful resources, principals and the school board had been willing to help subsidize programs for students and families and to fund nonacademic skill development for teachers and staff. Unfortunately, the school budget no longer allowed for that level of generosity. An additional challenge remained about how to identify days and times that school staff could participate in this training since professional development days were already committed for the year.

LIMITED DATA AND ORGANIZATIONAL CHALLENGES

Building on Strengths was entering its last 6 months of funding. Additional organizations (social service agencies, community groups, churches, mental health providers, and advocates) were interested in the physical and mental health needs of newly arriving Latinos and had a brief history of providing services to this growing population. Despite this interest, program leaders had a difficult time forming an advisory committee for the project, and time constraints and political concerns had limited strategic efforts to increase program visibility among potential partners. Although some efforts were made from the beginning of the funding period, existing partners were unable to secure commitments internally to continue services beyond the grant due to the fiscal instability within most organizations. Yet, all agreed that continuing to build broader community and system-wide connections to the program would be beneficial.

There were some university-based resources and supports available to collect and analyze data for the program, but early data collection efforts were problematic, and information collected was unreliable. There was an underdeveloped evaluation plan guiding program evaluation efforts, and no information technology system was available to improve the quality of data collection. The private funding acquired to support the program was not sufficient to invest in a more rigorous evaluation of the main program components. Advisors to the program strongly recommended that additional attention to monitoring the impact of program activities was necessary to successfully secure future funding. Yet, given the day-to-day pressures facing program leaders, resources and time allocated to evaluation were almost nonexistent.

The lack of comprehensive data about positive outcomes associated with the program put willing supporters at a disadvantage. The two school principals in particular, who were beginning to see the changes at the classroom and school-wide levels, were interested in advocating for funding to the school board and the superintendent's office, but the ever-increasing demand for accountability and results made them reluctant to champion a cause with little evaluation information. Stories of change were accumulating, but teachers were nervous about sharing them for fear of political retaliation in their community, and parents were frightened their testimonials would bring them to the attention of immigration and law enforcement officials.

Juanita's mother had a powerful story to tell about the help she and her daughter received through the program and the impact it had made in their lives in New City, but her fear of deportation forced her silence.

On the heels of learning that the school principal was finally interested in taking full advantage of the various components of the program, the project director of Building on Strengths received disheartening news that funds for the project were running low and decisions needed to be made about which aspects of the program could be retained. The sustainability of the program's hard-won accomplishments was at risk.

AT A CROSSROADS—THE CASE SCENARIO

After working in the school system for 2.5 years, Building on Strengths acquired a quiet, but loyal, following of supporters. The program made progress toward its goals, but the project director, whose time was not fully funded through

this project, was often conflicted about what to prioritize and how to build public support for what some considered a controversial program. Long-term sustainability plans for the program seemed to rest on the leaders' ability to explore opportunities among private and public (as well as local and national) funding sources, but program implementation and management took precedence.

The economic recession, which had an impact on the entire country, hit New City particularly hard in 2009. The chicken processing plant was scheduled to close entirely within months, which created a great deal of anxiety among workers and community leaders, as well as elected officials. Latino students and their families faced the likelihood of increased hardship with few places to turn for reliable support. *Nuestra Comunidad* was not spared the blow of the economic downturn. The agency relied on public financing for its operations, and those dollars were drying up, so the director of the community mental health agency decided to cut programming and release core mental health staff. The tension felt in the community and within homes fueled anxiety among children and youth who had no control over the social and economic circumstances affecting them. These stressors contributed to an increase in the number of behavioral and academic difficulties demonstrated by students across a number of classrooms.

Building on Strengths was forced to reduce its third-year financial commitment to *Nuestra Comunidad* so that only 40% of the liaison's time was covered by project funds. The majority of the budget supported staff—the cultural liaison in particular, as well as a small percentage of time for her supervisors at *Nuestra Comunidad* and for the project director overseeing the entire project. Moving forward, the liaison would need to supplement her salary by billing Medicaid for clinic-based treatment services outside of her responsibilities in the schools. The project director was informed by the project's accounting office that $25,000 was available for the remaining 6 months of the grant, half of what was expected at that point in the budget cycle. Building on Strengths leadership needed to decide how to meet program objectives, cover expenses, and prioritize limited time and scarce resources. With the end of the school year looming and the grant ending, time was of the essence.

Key Questions

1. What aspects of the Building on Strengths program are most important to preserve in light of impending funding cuts (i.e., training parents, cultural competence training for teachers, providing direct services, improving data collection and evaluation, focusing on partnership development, engaging in antistigma campaigns, etc.?). What is the rationale for this choice? What critical stakeholders should be involved in the planning, implementation, and

evaluation of these program components? What additional information does the project director need in order to make this decision?

2. What other sources of funding or strategic actions could the project director engage in to help sustain this school-based mental health project beyond the grant? What program elements are most important to continue, especially given the absence of a strong organizational infrastructure? What cultural and political challenges influence the existence and expansion of such a program?

3. What other partners or advocates should the project director enlist for help? How could Building on Strengths utilize parents and community members more in the development and sustainability of its program? What barriers to engaging immigrant parents (both documented and undocumented) might they encounter, and how can they address these challenges?

About the Authors

Olga Acosta Price, PhD, is director of the Center for Health and Health Care in Schools, a national resource and policy center committed to building effective school health programs. Dr. Price is currently managing a Robert Wood Johnson Foundation-funded program that addresses the mental health needs of children and youth from immigrant and refugee families. She is an associate professor at the School of Public Health and Health Services at The George Washington University in the Department of Prevention and Community Health.

Jodie Fishman, MPH, helped develop this case study as a culminating project for her master's of public health degree, which she received from The George Washington University in May 2009 in maternal and child health. Mrs. Fishman currently lives in Seoul, Korea, where she runs a *Chlamydia* education, screening, and surveillance program on an army base for the U.S. Defense Department.

Mimi V. Chapman, MSW, PhD, is an associate professor at the University of North Carolina at Chapel Hill School of Social Work. Her research and teaching focuses on child and adolescent mental health, in particular the needs of new immigrant youth and youth involved with child welfare.

REFERENCES

1. Jezewski MA, Sotnik P. (2001). *The Rehabilitation Service Provider as Culture Broker: Providing Culturally Competent Services to Foreign-Born Persons.* Buffalo, NY: Center for International Rehabilitation Research Information and Exchange. http://cirrie.buffalo.edu/monographs/cb.php. Accessed October 9, 2009.

2. Centers for Disease Control and Prevention. YRBSS: Comparisons between state or district and national results, 2009. http://www.cdc.gov/HealthyYouth/yrbs/state_district_comparisons.htm. Modified June 7, 2010. Accessed March 29, 2011.

3. Tienda M, Kleykamp M. *Physical and Mental Health Status of Hispanic Adolescent Girls: A Comparative Perspective.* Princeton, NJ: Office of Population Research, Princeton University; 2000.

4. Zayas LH, Pilat AM. Suicidal behavior in Latinas: explanatory cultural factors and implications for intervention. *Suicide Life Threat Behav.* 2008;38:334–342.

5. Office of Management and Budget (OMB). Revisions to the standards for the classification of federal data on race and ethnicity. http://www.census.gov/population/www/socdemo/race/Ombdir15.html. Published 2003. Accessed November 4, 2010.

6. Abma JC, Martinez GM, Mosher WD, Dawson BS. Teenagers in the United States: Sexual activity, contraceptive use, and childbearing, 2002. National Center for Health Statistics. *Vital Health Stat 23* (24). http://cdc.gov/NCHS/data/series/sr_23/sr23_024FactSheet.pdf. Published 2004. Accessed March 3, 2010.

7. Kohler AD, Lazarin M. *Hispanic Education in the United States.* Washington, DC: National Council of La Raza. http://www.nclr.org/content/publications/download/43582. Published 2007. Accessed October 13, 2009.

8. U.S. Census Bureau. Estimated national demographic components of change: April 1, 2000 to July 1, 2001. http://www.census.gov/popest/archives/2000s/vintage_2001/US-2001EST-02.html. Published 2001. Accessed June 10, 2009.

9. Acosta OM, Tashman NA, Prodente C, Proescher E. Establishing successful school mental health programs: guidelines and recommendations. In: Ghuman HS, Weist MD, Sarles RM (eds). *Providing Mental Health Services to Youth Where They Are: School and Community-Based Approaches.* New York, NY: Brunner-Routledge; 2002: 57–74.

Although this case is based on a real project, the names of individuals, schools, and locations have been changed to protect the confidentiality of those involved. In addition, some of the issues facing the project have been added for teaching purposes.

Building Trust in Communities:

The Narragansett Indian Tribe and the State of Rhode Island

E. BLAINE PARRISH

ABOUT THE NARRAGANSETT INDIANS

The Narragansett Indians are descendants of the aboriginal people of the State of Rhode Island, where they have existed for more than 30,000 years.[1] According to the 2005–2007 American Community Survey estimates, the state of Rhode Island was home to more than 3,900 Native Americans, about 0.4% of the total population. While Native Americans living in Rhode Island report belonging to dozens of tribes, the Narragansett Indian Tribe, with more than 2,000 members, represents the largest tribe in the state.[2]

The Narragansett people have had long-standing disputes with the State of Rhode Island. In 1975, the tribe filed suit against the state and individual landowners in order to reclaim land the tribe asserted rightfully belonged to them. An out-of-court settlement in 1978 concluded with the return of 1,800 acres of land, where the tribe established its reservation. Finally, in 1983, the tribe was given federal recognition of its sovereignty and has participated in federal programs funded by the Bureau of Indian Affairs and the Department of Indian Health Services.

> Through the Federally funded programs the tribe is able to service many of its Tribal Body members in all aspects of life. The mission of the Tribe is to continue to promote and develop awareness among Tribal members [of] the importance of education, culture, and family life within their own tribal community.[3](Nationhood section)

Public Health Issues for Native Americans Living in Rhode Island

A number of public health issues face the Narragansett people. The median age for the Native American population is 26 years, whereas the overall state median is 38 years. Over 92% of the Native American population is age 65 or younger, while 86.2% of the overall state population is age 65 or younger.[2]

Socioeconomic Indicators: The percentage of Native Americans living below poverty is over three times higher than the overall state population, and almost five times higher than the white population. The median household income for Native Americans is $22,800; this is $31,300 less than the state median and $35,400 less than that of the white population. A lower percentage of Native Americans graduate from high school compared to the overall state and the white populations. A greater percentage of Native Americans is unemployed compared to the overall state population and the white population.[4]

Behavioral Risk Factors: Native Americans have a higher percentage of both overweight and obese adults compared to the white and the overall state populations. This is especially pronounced for obesity—28.0% of Native American adults are obese, compared to 20.8% for Rhode Island as a whole. The percentage of Native Americans who smoke cigarettes (35.5%) is nearly two times higher than that of the white (19.5%) and the overall state (19.4%) populations.[4]

Maternal and Child Health: The overall state and the white populations have more favorable maternal and child health outcome indicators than the Native American population in Rhode Island. Native Americans are about twice as likely to receive delayed prenatal care as are the white or the overall state populations. The percentage of Native American teens (ages 15–19) who give birth is more than four times greater than it is for the overall state or the white populations. Over 13% of Native American infants are low birth weight, compared to approximately 8% for white infants and for infants across all racial and ethnic groups.[4]

Access to Health Care: Most samples are too small to draw reliable conclusions regarding Native Americans and access to health care. One-third of Native American adults said there was a time in the past year when they could not afford to see a doctor; a statistic over three times that of the overall state population and over four times that of the white population. The percentage of Native Americans having no health insurance is more than double that of the overall state population and nearly four times that of the white population.[4]

Environmental Concerns: A number of environmental issues are being addressed by the tribe, including surface and groundwater pollution; "incremental non-point source pollution from surrounding residential development and Tribal development;"[5](Environmental Concerns section) air pollution; hazardous waste; highway run-off; illegal dumping; lead paint; radon; and "biological and chemical contamination of drinking water."[6](Environmental Concerns section)

RHODE ISLAND PLAN FOR MINORITY CARE

In order to address the public health needs of minorities, the Rhode Island State Department of Health facilitated the development of a community action plan, which was informed by a community assessment and feedback process begun in 1998. This was followed by an internal assessment conducted in 1998 and three state breakout sessions of the New England Region Conference for the Elimination of Health Disparities that took place in 1999, 2001 and 2003.[7](para 1)

The vision from the action plan was to allow for all racial and ethnic minorities in Rhode Island to have an equal opportunity "to live safe and healthy lives in safe and healthy communities."[7](para 2) The minority community set as its mission to reduce health risks and improve health outcomes by disseminating health education materials and engaging the community in healthier behaviors.[7]

To support this mission, minority communities in Rhode Island were asked to participate in the development of policies, plans, and tracking systems to ensure that their community's needs are integrated and addressed within all state health department programs. Specific goals of the plan were: (1) racial and ethnic health disparities would be eliminated by 2010; and (2) racial and ethnic minority populations would "have equal access to high quality health services."[7](para 4)

In order to achieve these outcomes, six goals/priorities were identified; the plan was to implement them within a 3-year period:

1. "All HEALTH [Rhode Island Department of Health] programs meet the needs of racial and ethnic minority populations.
2. Establish uniform guidelines and procedures regarding the collection, use, analysis and dissemination of data on racial and ethnic populations.
3. Establish policies and procedures ensuring meaningful and productive minority community involvement and participation in all planning, monitoring and evaluation of health activities.
4. Improve work force diversity within HEALTH and promote the need for diversity in all health care institutions.
4a. Ensure that all LEP [limited-English-proficiency] individuals receive the same quality health services (Title VI of the Civil Rights Act).
5. Build community capacity to provide health education, health promotion, and disease prevention activities that are aligned with HEALTH overall priorities targeting racial and ethnic minority populations.
6. Facilitate and develop public/private partnerships at the state, regional and national level to eliminate racial and ethnic health disparities."[7](Introduction)

While not specifically developed for the Narragansett people, the tribe has used the plan as a blueprint for addressing and evaluating its own process for improving health outcomes for its people. This action follows a trend among Native American tribes to take more control over their own healthcare planning and implementation. Ongoing studies suggest that various models are available for Native American tribes to use to either enhance or in some cases replace care provided through the Indian Health Services. While the federal government is responsible, through law and agreements, to provide care to Native Americans, many Native American tribes elect to run their own programs with funding from the federal government.[8] One model includes development of an independent public health department, which would function as the public healthcare leader in the tribal community. The Gila River Indian Community has already implemented this model and other Native American tribes are following their lead.[9] Currently, their programs are limited to providing health education materials, referrals, and training, but they also include specific educational interventions for diabetes, since American Indians and Alaskan Natives are more than twice as likely as non-Hispanic whites to have type 2 diabetes.

Even with plans, either independent of the Indian Health Services or in collaboration with it, Native American tribes have competing interests with some public health issues, in this instance tobacco use and sales.

A STUDY OF TRUST, HISTORY, AND CULTURAL RELATIONS

In July of 2003, the Narragansett Indian Tribe, a federally recognized tribe that maintains a government-to-government relationship with the United States of America, began selling cigarettes from a shop on tribal lands to promote economic development. The state and tribe have disagreed on certain rights on the reservation. The sale of cigarettes without the state-required tax took place over the objections of Rhode Island Governor Donald L. Carcieri, who did not believe the tribe could legally sell cigarettes without charging state taxes. On July 14, 2003, the Governor Donald Carcieri ordered a raid on the tribe's tax-free smoke shop, which devolved into a physical confrontation between Rhode Island state troopers and Narragansett tribal members, including several members of the tribal leadership. Following the conflict, seven tribal members were charged with misdemeanors, including simple assault, disorderly conduct, and resisting arrest. The tribal leadership contended that their sovereignty was under attack and demanded that state troopers be held responsible for the force used during the conflict. However, no state troopers were charged as a result of their behavior in the raid. After the raid, Chief Sachem Matthew Thomas of the Narragansett Indian Tribe and Governor Carcieri issued statements.

Thomas said, "The Narragansett Tribe did what it's always done; it stood to protect its land. … It's unfortunate [we had to do this] because it's 2003."[10(para 4)]

Carcieri supported the state by saying, "Today's actions were precipitated by the Narragansett Indians and their flagrant violation of state law."[11(para 4)]

In 2005, a three-judge panel of the U.S. First Circuit Court of Appeals declared the raid a violation of the tribe's sovereignty, but reversed the decision during a hearing by the full court. The decision held that the raid was not a violation of the tribe's sovereignty because of an agreement signed by the Narragansett tribe that agreed the tribe would adhere to state laws, even on its own land.[12]

In a separate federal civil rights lawsuit, the tribe charged the police with the use of excessive force during the 2003 raid on the smoke shop. The jury was asked to decide if Trooper Kenneth Jones used excessive force when he broke the ankle of the plaintiff Adam Jennings. Police contend that Jennings resisted arrest, however Jennings testified that he did not resist arrest and that when the officer attempted to handcuff him, he complied.[13]

On April 4, 2008, a Superior Court jury found Chief Thomas and two other elected tribal members guilty of misdemeanor charges while clearing four others. Upon his conviction, Chief Thomas stated, "I didn't expect anything really different. I was waiting to get it over."[14(para 11)]

While acquitted of all the charges against her, Ms. Bella Noka, a former tribal councilor and wife of Randy Noka, first councilor, was quoted as saying, "We are reminders of their awful past and we are constant reminders of everything they've done and they won't stop until we no longer exist."[15(para 4)]

Meanwhile, Governor Carcieri's spokesperson issued the following statement, "With the conclusion of this trial, Governor Carcieri hopes that the Narragansett Indian Tribe and the State of Rhode Island can put the smoke-shop incident behind us and move forward into a more cooperative future."[16(para 20)]

CHALLENGES MOVING FORWARD

Moving forward would be difficult for members of the Narragansett tribe. Abuse at the hands of government agents, government entities, and even those working to improve the lives and health of Native Americans was still a real fear for many tribal members. These abuses were not just about sovereignty, land rights, and cultural identity, but also about questionable studies conducted on Native Americans under the guise of health research.

For many Native Americans, experiences with public health researchers, governmental or institutional, have been negative, and as a result, have severely impacted trust. Mistrust was not limited solely to those institution(s) conducting the research; it affected the individuals conducting the research as well. "Too often, research has been conducted 'on' rather than 'with' American Indian communities, resulting in their being stigmatized or stereotyped."[17(p 1399)]

Research activities such as those on Navajo flu, the Barrow alcohol study, and the collection of blood samples, consented for one study but then used for other studies without consent, are but a few of the unethical behaviors by researchers that caused deep mistrust in the Native American community.[18] Other minorities have similar issues of mistrust based on past public health initiatives; African Americans experienced similar health research deception in the Tuskegee syphilis study,[19] and stories have been passed down from times of slavery regarding experiments being conducted on their ancestors and the sale of their bodies for medical experiments following their death.[20] Today, one third of African Americans believe that HIV/AIDS was introduced into their community by the federal government. Other recent scandals have generally undermined the general public's trust in community organizations, businesses, and public figures, including the Clinton-Lewinsky scandal, the Enron bankruptcy scandal, and the legal troubles for American icon Martha Stewart.[21]

Signs of distrust can be found in each of these situations. Broken promises, leaders acting in their own best interest, individual rights sacrificed for expediency or lack of compassion, and the desire to advance research at any cost illustrate the need for more accountability.[22] But accountability alone cannot build public trust. There must be transparency of action and decision making; a consensus-building process that includes community members; dissemination of materials and information that provide for informed consent; a reason for the community to participate; and finally, incentives to facilitate participation.[23]

BUILDING TRUST IN A COMMUNITY TO FURTHER PUBLIC HEALTH—WHAT NOW?

Following graduation from her public health training, Jennifer moved to the state of Rhode Island to begin working as a public health analyst at the Rhode Island Department of Health (a state-affiliated agency). Jennifer was asked to head a prevention and community health team that would design a comprehensive health program to address medical, behavioral, and preventive care needs of the Narragansett people, including prevention of heart disease, diabetes, and cancer. In addition, she would need to specifically address tobacco and alcohol use among the Narragansett people. Jennifer's activities would include researching public health issues within the minority communities of Rhode Island, iden-

tifying programs that work in these communities for possible use with the Narragansett Indian Tribe, designing prevention and primary care programs that consider the culture of the Narragansett people, developing a health promotion campaign in collaboration with the community, and reviewing currently available evaluation tools to assess the effectiveness of current initiatives and the possible use of these tools in her program design.

As a first step, Jennifer and her team were asked to meet with the Narragansett tribal leadership to gauge their interest, ask for their ideas, get buy-in for the collaboration, and identify their counterparts in the tribe. Jennifer and her team had less than a month to develop an agenda, including detailed information about each agenda item, prepare for the meeting, and run their ideas past the department's senior management.

About the Author

Blaine Parrish, PhD, is the associate dean for student affairs and an assistant professor in the Departments of Health Policy and Prevention and Community Health at The George Washington University School of Public Health and Health Services. An expert in the field of leadership, organization, and management, Dr. Parrish's scholarly interests focus on community-based organizations that provide public health services to vulnerable and underserved populations. His current research includes a 4-year, $4 million dollar research project to study the feasibility and effectiveness of implementing an evidence-based childhood asthma management intervention in community health centers, evaluations of two physical activity wellness programs, and an evaluation of teen pregnancy prevention programs in the Greater Washington, DC, area. In earlier positions, Dr. Parrish served as a public health analyst in the HIV/AIDS Bureau at the Health Resources and Services Administration, and has also been executive director of AIDS Resources of Rural Texas, the largest rural-based AIDS service organization in the United States. He has a BA in education from the University of Central Oklahoma, an MA in humanities from the University of Texas (Arlington) and a PhD in organization and management from Cappella University School of Business.

REFERENCES

1. Historical perspective of the Narragansett Indian Tribe. http://www.narragansett-tribe.org/history.html. Accessed August 18, 2009.

2. Rhode Island Office of Minority Health. Minority health facts: Major health indicators in the racial and ethnic minority population of Rhode Island. The Rhode Island Department of Health. http://www.health.ri.gov/publications/factsheets/minorityhealthfacts/Summary.pdf. Published 2010. Accessed April 14, 2011.

3. Historical perspective of the Narragansett Indian Tribe. http://www.narragansett-tribe.org/history.html. Accessed August 18, 2009.

4. Rhode Island Office of Minority Health. Minority health facts: Native Americans in Rhode Island. The Rhode Island Department of Health. http://www.health.ri.gov/publications/factsheets/minorityhealthfacts/NativeAmericans.pdf. Published 2010. Accessed April 14, 2011.

5. Narragansett Indian Tribe. FY03 fact sheet. Sixth Annual New England Tribal Environmental Training Conference; May 12–15, 2003; Presque Isle, Maine. http://www.micmac-epa.us/html/body_tribal_fact_sheets.html. Accessed August 18, 2009.

6. Ibid.

7. Excerpts from the Rhode Island Department of Health minority plan for action: introduction. http://www.health.ri.gov/publications/actionplans/2004MinorityHealth.pdf. Published 2004. Accessed March 23, 2011.

8. Robert Wood Johnson Foundation. Native American tribes in Wisconsin improve health care delivery. http://www.rwjf.org/reports/grr/033190.html. Published January 2007. Accessed November 18, 2010.

9. Allison M, Rivers P, Fottler M. Future public health delivery models for Native American tribes. *Public Health*, 2007;121(4):296–307.

10. Chief: Tribe was protecting its sovereignty. *Providence Journal*. July 14, 2003. http://www.projo.com/news/content/projo_20030716_chief16.bfccd.html. Accessed April 1, 2011.

11. Carcieri: Raid was regrettable but necessary. *Providence Journal*. July 14, 2003. http://www.projo.com/news/content/projo_20030716_gov16.c0565.html, accessed April 1, 2011.

12. *Narragansett Indian Tribe of Rhode Island v. State of Rhode Island and Providence Plantations*. (3d Cir 1975). http://www.ca1.uscourts.gov/pdf.opinions/04-1155-01A.pdf. Accessed August 18, 2009.

13. Staff and wire reports. Judge overturns verdict against state trooper in smoke-shop case. *Providence Journal*. August 24, 2005. http://www.projo.com/digitalbulletin/content/projo-20050824-overturned.a6a7602e.html. Accessed April 1, 2011.

14. Bakst CM. Reflections on the verdicts in the Narragansett Indian smoke-shop trial. http://www.projo.com/news/mcharlesbakst/BAKST_COLUMN_05_04-05-08_IE9LFBJ_v13.35849d4.html. Published April 5, 2008. Accessed August 18, 2009.

15. Ibid.

16. McKinney MP. Verdict mixed in Narragansett Indian smoke-shop raid-case. *Providence Journal*. April 5, 2008. http://www.projo.com/extra/2003/smokeshop/content/projo_20080404_smokeshop_verdict.302f9f22.html. Accessed August 18, 2009.

17. Christopher S, Watts V, McCormick AKHG, Young S. Building and maintaining trust in a community-based participatory research partnership. *Am J Public Health*, 2008;98(8):1398–1406.

18. Ibid.

19. Freimuth V, Quinn S, Thomas S, Col G, Zook E, Duncan T. African Americans' views on research and the Tuskegee syphilis study. *Soc Sci Med*. 2001;52(5):797–808.

20. Whetten K, Leserman J, Whetten R, et al. Exploring lack of trust in care providers and the government as a barrier to health service use. *Am J Public Health*. 2006;96(4):716–721.

21. Dwyer R, Beauvais C. Building and maintaining trust: the essential ingredient for organizational success. *Revue-e-J*. 2006;(1)1–12. http://web.ustpaul.ca/Philosophy/revue/pdf/2006_dwyer.pdf. Accessed April 1, 2011.

22. Gilson L, Erasmus E. *Trust and accountability in health service delivery in South Africa*. Technical report. Johannesburg, South Africa: Centre for Health Policy; 2006.

23. Quah SR, ed. On trust and health consensus-building in the governance of epidemics. In: *Crisis Preparedness: Asia and the Global Governance of Epidemics*. Stanford, CA: Stanford University APARC;2007:113–133.

The Strategies to Overcome and Prevent Obesity Alliance

ERICA BREESE, CASEY LANGWITH, CHRISTINE FERGUSON, GINAMARIE MANGIARACINA, AND ALLISON MAY ROSEN

A WEIGHTY ISSUE

Imagine a disease that affected two thirds of adults in the United States, with a prevalence that had doubled in the last 25 years and showed no sign of stopping its upward trend. One would expect any disease this widespread would receive national attention both in the media and policy arena. Policy makers would demand insurance coverage for treatment and prevention. The public would actively protect themselves and their families from contracting the disease or seek treatment if they contracted it. Physicians would screen for the disease regularly and have straightforward conversations with those who contracted the disease. The American public health and medical systems would be geared toward treating and preventing further spread of this disease.

Surprisingly, there is a disease that currently affects two thirds of the U.S. population, yet has not received the expected response. In 2009, 66.4% of the adult population in the United States was overweight or obese (body mass index ≥ 25),[i] which is more than twice the prevalence rate from 3 decades before.[1,2] Adults are not the only ones affected; childhood obesity rates have also tripled in the last 30 years.[3] Additionally, if the existing rates of increase continue, 86.3% of U.S. adults will be overweight and 51.1% will be obese by 2030.[4] These are staggering numbers for any health condition,

but especially one that is related to a multitude of chronic diseases, such as diabetes, hypertension, high cholesterol, stroke, heart disease, certain cancers, and arthritis.[5] Beyond the individual health risks, overweight and obesity also contribute to increased health costs, both nationally and for individuals. For example, in 2008, medical spending attributable to obesity was estimated to have been $147 billion, accounting for 9.1% of annual medical spending.[6]

These statistics show obesity plays a major role in the U.S. healthcare system and affects the lives of millions of Americans. However, despite the extreme prevalence of obesity, the disease often does not receive adequate attention in the healthcare community. In 2010, First Lady Michelle Obama launched her *Let's Move* campaign, which aims to reduce childhood obesity within a generation, helping to bring the issue of childhood obesity to the forefront. In contrast, adult obesity continues to garner little interest. Some groups, however, are focusing on this often overlooked area because they believe real change can be made. The Strategies to Overcome and Prevent (STOP) Obesity Alliance is a collaboration of consumer, provider, government, labor, business, health insurance, and quality-of-care organizations united to drive innovative and practical strategies that combat obesity. The alliance's history is unique, demonstrating how partnerships among public relations teams, public health researchers, business and labor leaders, advocates, and the private sector can work together to make important changes.

---

[i] The body mass index is defined as an individual's body weight (in kg) divided by the square of his or her height (in meters). A body mass index of 25.0 to 29.9 is considered overweight while a body mass index of 30 or more is considered obese.

EARLY STAGES

In 2006, the France-based pharmaceutical company sanofi-aventis issued a request for proposals for public relations firms to help promote and improve coverage for an obesity drug in their pipeline. Chandler Chicco Agency (CCA) responded, pitching the idea of pulling together major health advocacy organizations to form a coalition focused on the issue of cardiometabolic risk. A key element of CCA's proposal was to create an administrative home for the coalition at an academic institution, which would take the lead on generating policy research related to cardiometabolic risk. After securing the contract, the project lead at CCA, Allison May Rosen, identified The George Washington University Department of Health Policy (DHP) as a potential academic home for the coalition. CCA approached DHP professor Christine Ferguson, JD, to become program director, because of her unusual experience working in both federal and state government.

CCA believed a partnership between a healthcare public relations firm and an academic institution, such as The George Washington University, would be ideal for both the creation and maintenance of the coalition it envisioned. CCA and DHP worked collaboratively to develop the idea. CCA brought public relations expertise and knowledge of how to structure and orient the coalition to get the attention of policy makers. CCA was assisted by Mehlman Vogel Castagnetti Inc, a seasoned government affairs firm in Washington, DC. On the other hand, the team at DHP brought academic expertise and an understanding of policy making in the public and private sectors, as well as research and publishing capabilities unavailable to CCA. The strong teamwork and equality between CCA and DHP was exceptional—the groups used one another's skills and resources to create something stronger than either could achieve individually.

Conversations between CCA and DHP initially focused on how to develop the project to address public and private policy makers' needs, recruit member organizations, and achieve the goals outlined for the project. Cognizant of the way policy makers think about public health issues, Ferguson maintained that while *cardiometabolic risk* was the accurate term to describe the condition, the phrase would not resonate with policy makers or the general public. Instead, she suggested obesity was truly at the heart of the equation, and was a significant public health problem that had long been ignored by policy makers. After significant discussion, the group adopted obesity and its comorbidities, such as diabetes and heart disease, as the main focus for the coalition. They chose to name the new group Strategies to Overcome and Prevent (STOP) Obesity Alliance. Surgeon General Dr. Richard

Carmona was recruited as the health and wellness chairman of the alliance to provide high-level public health visibility to the alliance leadership and steering committee members. Ferguson served as the director. The next step was to recruit representatives of influential health-focused organizations to serve as a steering committee to help direct the work.

Recruiting the organizations from a cross-section of disciplines to serve on the steering committee was a months-long process that involved identifying the organizations, setting up initial discussions, and securing official sign-offs for the organizations to join the alliance. These conversations were important to ensure the organizations understood and agreed with the overall goals of the alliance. As seen in Figure 10-1, the resulting steering committee was comprised of medical, patient, government, labor, business, health insurance, and quality-of-care organizations dedicated to changing the way policy makers think about and approach obesity. The steering committee drew members from diverse groups with an interest in obesity, including the American Diabetes Association, the American Heart Association, America's Health Insurance Plans, the American Medical Group Association, the Canyon Ranch Institute, the Centers for Disease Control and Prevention's Division of Nutrition, Physical Activity and Obesity, DMAA: The Care Continuum Alliance, the National Business Group on Health, the National Committee for Quality Assurance, the National Quality Forum, the Service Employees International Union, and Trust for America's Health.

> **Question 1** The steering committee organizations represented groups from across the policy spectrum. What views did the various steering committee organizations bring to the alliance, and can you identify any possible conflicts between the organizations?

ESTABLISHING THE STOP OBESITY ALLIANCE

The first steering committee meeting was held in July 2007. Representatives from each of the steering committee organizations came to a daylong meeting to discuss the state of obesity efforts and barriers to addressing obesity. Unexpectedly, many of the steering committee representatives shared stories of their personal struggles with weight.

At the meeting, DHP researchers presented data from existing obesity research, focusing on three major barriers they identified. First, patients, physicians and even weight loss researchers often used unrealistic definitions for successful weight loss based more on physical appearance than health. In 1998, the National Heart, Lung and Blood Institute issued guidelines recommending obese individuals attempt to lose 10% of body weight over a 6-month period and then evalu-

FIGURE 10-1 STOP Obesity Alliance steering committee members (as of July 2010).

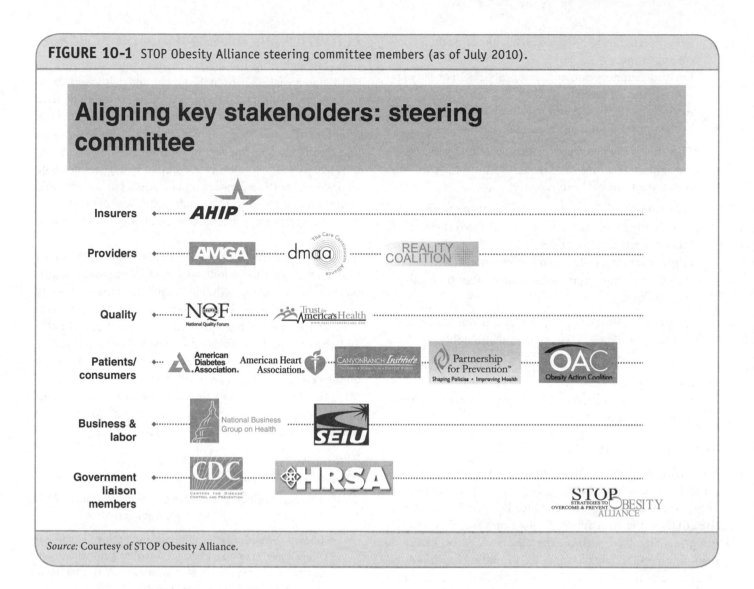

Source: Courtesy of STOP Obesity Alliance.

ate whether additional weight loss was needed.[7] The alliance referred to medical research, which showed many health benefits of weight loss can be achieved after a sustained 5–10% weight loss.[ii,8] Despite these results, a group of The George Washington University researchers found evidence suggesting many patients would consider this amount of weight loss a failure.[9,10]

The second major barrier was that although medical interventions for obesity exist, there is a widespread perception that weight loss treatments do not work.[11] In addition, some view medical treatments for obesity, especially bariatric sur-

gery, as an easy way out. This attitude prevents people from seeking and receiving appropriate medical interventions. Finally, stigma toward the obese was an overwhelming driver in the way the public and policy makers thought about the problem of obesity.[12] Most saw obesity as rooted in a failure of willpower and personal responsibility. The belief was that because the obese had brought the condition upon themselves, they did not deserve to receive treatment, and especially insurance coverage, for their obesity. In the meeting, steering committee representatives talked about how they saw these barriers reflected in their own areas of expertise and brainstormed ways their organizations, both individually and as part of the alliance, could work to overcome the barriers.

Out of these discussions, the steering committee came to agreement on the following principles to guide the work of the new alliance:

ii In addition to the cited reference, see also Lavie CJ, Milani RV, Artham SM, Patel DA, Ventura HO. The obesity paradox, weight loss, and coronary disease. *Am J Med*. 2009;122(12):1106–1114. http://www.amjmed.com/article/S0002-9343%2809%2900500-2/abstract.

1. Redefine success to be based on health rather than physical appearances
2. Encourage innovation and best practices in obesity prevention and treatment
3. Address and reduce stigma as a barrier to treatment
4. Broaden the research agenda on obesity

The alliance issued these principles publicly in 2008 as policy recommendations and have since used the principles to direct the actions of the alliance.

> **Question 2** While these recommendations were created specifically for obesity policy, they are also applicable to other diseases and health conditions. What other diseases might warrant similar recommendations? Are some of the recommendations more transferable than others? Which ones?

> **Question 3** What is the role of stigma in other conditions? Think of examples (HIV, mental health, tobacco).

> **Question 4** Do you think people who feel they have a connection to obesity—either personally or in their families—are more likely to be interested in the issue and accept its complexities?

ACTING AS AN ALLIANCE

The cornerstone idea in the founding of the alliance was the creation of a coalition that would operate through consensus. While the CCA-DHP team managed the daily activities of the alliance, the steering committee met monthly and was integrally involved with all the alliance's work, including helping direct the research agenda, providing expert advice, and supporting alliance initiatives. Beyond this guiding role, steering committee members also reviewed and agreed to all publications issued under the alliance's name. Achieving consensus among steering committee members took time but ensured the work of the alliance represented all members and did not create conflicts for any individual organization. This consensus approach strengthened the message of the alliance from the beginning. Any policy recommendation from the alliance was backed by its diverse membership body, many of whom found themselves on opposite sides of policy debates. While this variety was a significant asset for the alliance, it also forced the alliance to remain neutral on issues where consensus could not be reached.

> **Question 5** The alliance specifically chose a consensus governance model for its strengths, but there are weaknesses. What are the strengths and weaknesses? What other public health problems could benefit from the alliance's model?

ACTIVITIES AND OBJECTIVES OF THE ALLIANCE

From the beginning, the alliance mainly targeted its work towards policy makers in both the private and public sectors. In order to reach this specific audience, the alliance conducted a range of research and activities about obesity. One of the key functions of the alliance was to bring together policy makers and influential stakeholders to discuss and brainstorm innovative solutions to obesity prevention and treatment. The alliance was not an advocacy organization, but instead used education and research to provide policy makers with tools to create effective approaches toward obesity and its related conditions.

During the first 3 years, the alliance hosted numerous roundtables and discussions on various topics, such as primary care, body image in the media, and the impact of obesity on women, to highlight current research and innovative practices. The diversity of research topics and activities of the alliance represented its broad membership base and message. The alliance continually stressed that all decisions must be based on the existing obesity research and evidence and worked to bring this information to policy makers. In addition, the alliance engaged in its own primary research activities in order to expand the evidence available to decision makers.

Highlights from the Alliance's Research and Activities

To advance its goals, the alliance engaged in a number of key research, communication, and advocacy activities.

*   **Obesity GPS (Guide for Program and Policy Solutions):** The alliance created a navigation tool to guide the development and assessment of policies aimed at addressing overweight and obesity. The Obesity GPS offers questions to consider when designing legislative or private sector initiatives focused on health, research, and clinical issues. The tool is intended to help policy makers create programs that reflect the four policy principles of the alliance. The tool was publicly released at an event at the U.S. Capitol in December 2008.
*   **Health Decision Makers Survey:** The alliance commissioned a survey on employer and employee attitudes toward obesity. The results were published in the January/February 2009 issue of *Health Affairs*. The article was one of the 20 most viewed articles on the journal's website in 2009, indicating growing interest in obesity.
*   **STOP Obesity Alliance E-Newsletter:** The monthly newsletter provided commentary and news on alliance and member activities. In addition to the website, the newsletter was the primary way for people outside of the alliance to receive information about alliance updates. As of mid-2010, the newsletter had over 2,000 subscribers, including mem-

bers of Congress and staff, federal agency representatives, healthcare advocacy groups, physicians, and academics.

- **Has America Reached Its Tipping Point on Obesity? Forum:** Although alliance member organizations were on opposite sides of many issues within the national health reform debate, in September 2009, the alliance reached consensus on four recommendations that should be included to address obesity within health reform. These four recommendations were: (1) standardized and effective clinical interventions; (2) enhanced use of clinical preventive services; (3) effective, evidence-based community programs and policies; and (4) coordinated research efforts. At the forum to release the recommendations, former Surgeons General Dr. David Satcher and Dr. Richard Carmona spoke about the urgent need to address obesity. The event and simultaneous webcast were attended by over 100 policy makers and health advocates. The release garnered significant media attention, including ranking as the No. 1 most e-mailed story on *Yahoo! News*.
- **Improving Obesity Management in Primary Care Roundtable and Paper:** Recognizing the significant role primary care physicians could play in addressing obesity, the alliance convened a roundtable of physicians and stakeholders in August 2009 to discuss strategies for improving the prevention and treatment of obesity in primary care. The DHP research team translated the key ideas from the roundtable into a white paper, *Improving Obesity Management in Primary Care*. The paper was released in March 2010 along with preliminary results from a Harris Interactive survey commissioned by the alliance on primary care physician and patient attitudes toward obesity.
- **Weighty Matters:** Working in partnership with the National Eating Disorders Association, the alliance convened an expert media panel in April 2010 on the depiction of weight issues in the media. The panel emphasized the impact of media on body image, the importance of portraying realistic images and weight loss stories, and the need to focus on health rather than appearance. This unprecedented collaboration was attended by nearly 100 attendees and attracted high-level media interest.
- **Task Force on Women:** In 2010, the alliance created a task force on women to call attention to the significant and disproportionate impact obesity has on women's health. Comprised of 18 advocacy and research organizations, the task force identified the following four ways in which women are uniquely affected by obesity: (1) physiological, psychological, cultural, and socioeconomic factors; (2) pervasive racial and ethnic disparities in obesity prevalence and health outcomes; (3) systemic, gender-based biases portrayed in the media and encountered in educational, workplace, social, and healthcare environments; and (4) the role of women as caretakers for their families.

Question 6 These activities showcase the broad range of research topics and event types that the alliance engaged in during the first 3 years. Which do you think was the most effective based on the goals of the alliance? How might these activities differ if the alliance was targeted at the public instead of policy makers?

MEASURING THE IMPACT

Expanding the Alliance: Associate and Government Liaison Members

Since its founding, the alliance grew immensely; each year, more groups expressed interest in partnering with the alliance or becoming involved with its work. As a way to broaden its reach by engaging additional groups while thoughtfully managing growth, the alliance created an associate member category. Associate members are organizations that partner with the alliance, but do not serve on the steering committee. As of mid-2010, there were over 30 associate members. Because of the significant racial and ethnic disparities in obesity prevalence, one focus area for associate membership has been groups with ties to minority communities, including the Black Women's Health Imperative, the National Hispanic Medical Association, and the National Indian Health Board.

Alliance leadership also saw the need for another membership category that reflected the unique position of government agencies. Called government liaison members, these members participate in steering committee meetings but do not comment on or endorse certain alliance activities, such as commenting on obesity-related legislation.

Question 7 Why were these new membership categories needed? What did the associate and government liaison members bring to the alliance?

Forming Strategic Partnerships

In addition, the alliance partnered with or supported many obesity-related initiatives, including:

- Virgin HealthMiles' National Employee Wellness Month, 2009 and 2010
- Obesity policy forum at the Obesity Society annual scientific meetings in 2009 and 2010
- World Health Congress 2009 and 2010 obesity congresses

Media Attention

Beyond growth of the group, the alliance gained national media coverage for its research and sponsored events. For example, the release of the alliance's policy paper, *Has America Reached Its Tipping Point?*, based on the steering committee consensus-driven recommendations for health reform legislation, received significant attention, including an op-ed piece by former Surgeons General Satcher and Carmona in *The Atlanta Journal Constitution*. An article on the recommendations and the event also became the most e-mailed news story on *Yahoo! News*. Similarly, the release of primary care survey research by the alliance garnered coverage in national news media, including *The New York Times*, *USA Today*, and *The Washington Post*.

As obesity gained more prominence nationally, federal policy makers included suggestions supporting the alliance's recommendations, shifting the use of some of the work of the alliance. In 2009, the Government Accountability Office recommended the federal government provide guidance to states for the coverage of obesity-related services, such as screening and counseling, for children enrolled in Medicaid, as well as consider similar guidance for coverage of Medicaid-enrolled adults.[13] Additionally, federal health reform efforts began with little support or mention of obesity, but the Patient Protection and Affordable Care Act passed on March 23, 2010, included many obesity-specific provisions, which supported alliance recommendations.

These successes demonstrated the strength of the alliance's research. Many of the alliance's continued achievements can be attributed to the strong partnership between CCA and DHP. Since the inception of the alliance, CCA and DHP worked as equal partners in the day-to-day maintenance of the group. Both groups participated in all planning, messaging, and research, but brought their own expertise to each decision. Loosely, CCA handled the logistical planning and messaging for the alliance; specifically, it managed press contacts, organized events, and monitored the media presence of the alliance. Conversely, DHP was the research arm of the team. DHP staff monitored research on obesity, both in policy and clinically, and engaged in and analyzed primary research. DHP brought quick and responsive research capabilities to the alliance, but also added an academic legitimacy. Despite these dual roles, all projects involved the efforts of both CCA and DHP staff. This close working relationship between CCA and DHP helped ensure that the work of the alliance was communicated clearly and effectively.

Question 8 Both CCA and DHP played important roles in the creation and maintenance of the alliance. Why were both roles necessary and how might the alliance have differed without one or the other?

EPILOGUE

When reflecting on the events that have occurred since the founding of the alliance, the leadership of the alliance identified the beginning of three fundamental shifts in the way policy makers and the public think about obesity. First, the conversation about obesity has shifted from portraying obesity as mainly an appearance issue to acknowledging its serious health consequences. Beyond the impact on health, the increasing recognition of the impact of chronic diseases on the U.S. health system has also raised the profile of obesity. Second, policy makers and the public began to realize that fighting obesity is not just about personal responsibility—it's about creating a society where good personal choices are possible. These trends were reflected in alliance decision-maker surveys, in which many employers and primary care physicians agreed that they have a role to play in addressing obesity. Third, many started to recognize that beating obesity goes beyond simply losing weight; in fact, sustaining the weight loss may be the hardest part. This recognition is especially relevant when promoting the creation of healthy communities that support individual success for weight loss.

As obesity begins to gain more traction as a prominent health issue, the alliance hopes to help bridge the gap between the public health and health services communities. Rather than viewing obesity as a problem requiring a single approach or having a silver bullet solution, the alliance believes policy makers should focus on creating environments that support healthy choices that are easy to make, while also providing access to medical treatment for obesity.

In the future, the alliance hopes to expand its influence into state health policy by identifying barriers policy makers face when trying to address obesity at the state level. Many important public health decisions are made at the state level, so making sure policy makers understand the complexities of obesity is essential. Additionally, with the passage of the Patient Protection and Affordable Care Act, there is increased emphasis on the prevention and treatment of obesity and other chronic diseases. Alliance leadership hopes that as the federal government implements the health reform law, it will use the research findings and recommendations of the alliance to further create communities and solutions that support healthy choices for obesity prevention and treatment.

About the Authors

Erica Breese, BS, is a research program coordinator in The George Washington University Department of Health Policy in the School of Public Health and Health Services. Erica primarily provides project management support for multiple projects with the Department of Health Policy, including the STOP Obesity Alliance. In addition to project management, Erica's work with the alliance focuses on community health centers and state-level obesity initiatives. She graduated with a bachelor of science degree in neuroscience and behavioral biology from Emory University in 2008.

Casey Langwith, BA, is a research assistant in the Department of Health Policy within The George Washington University's School of Public Health and Health Services. Casey primarily works on the STOP Obesity Alliance, drafting research papers and conducting project management. Most recently, she has focused on developing materials, including memoranda and summary tables, highlighting the public health and prevention provisions in the Patient Protection and Affordable Care Act. Casey also works on obesity management in primary care, the economic costs of obesity, and state-level obesity initiatives, including coverage issues. Casey graduated magna cum laude with a bachelor of arts degree in sociology and history from Rice University in 2009.

Christine Ferguson, JD, is a professor in The George Washington University School of Public Health and Health Care Services in the Department of Health Policy. She has served at the highest levels of federal and state government. Her areas of research include Medicaid, state health policy and financing, federal health reform implementation, and obesity. Prior to joining the School of Public Health and Health Services in 2006, she served as commissioner of the Department of Public Health in Massachusetts; the director of the Rhode Island Department of Human Services, and counsel and deputy chief of staff to then-U.S. Senator John H. Chafee. Her accomplishments as an influential health policy maker have been recognized by Faulkner & Gray[14] and by *National Law Journal*, which named her one of the nation's 100 most influential lawyers. Ms. Ferguson was also named one of the top 25 most influential working mothers by *Working Mothers* magazine. She is a sought-after speaker and commentator and has appeared on *Good Morning America*, NPR Marketplace, in *USA Today*, *The Wall Street Journal*, *The Washington Post*, *The New York Times*, and various other regional news outlets and trade publications.

GinaMarie Mangiaracina, BA, has worked in healthcare public relations for more than 10 years. She joined the Chandler Chicco Agency in 2006 and is currently the team lead for the Strategies to Overcome and Prevent (STOP) Obesity Alliance. Past work at CCA has included playing leadership roles in public relations and public affairs efforts for the not-for-profit hospital alliance, VHA Inc., and the VHA Foundation.

Allison May Rosen, BS, serves on the Global Leadership Council for the Chandler Chicco Companies from its Washington, DC, office, where she provides strategic communications counsel, coalition management, and editorial services and media training for clients trying to build support for an issue, influence public opinion, or launch a brand or service. Her planning, issue framing, messaging, and advocacy development skills have been put to work for clients including the Strategies to Overcome and Prevent (STOP) Obesity Alliance; the Robert Wood Johnson Foundation Commission to Build a Healthier America; VHA, the national not-for-profit hospital alliance; and other major consumer brands and disease-specific campaigns. Previously, Allison was press secretary for the U.S. Overseas Private Investment Corporation, worked for Texas Governor Ann Richards in Washington, DC, and was an aide on Capitol Hill. Allison served as lecturer for The George Washington University Department of Health Policy chair's seminar and regularly speaks to industry associations on communications and the media. She received her BS from the S.I. Newhouse School of Public Communications at Syracuse University.

REFERENCES

1. National Center for Chronic Disease Prevention and Health Promotion. Behavioral risk factor surveillance system. http://apps.nccd.cdc.gov/brfss/list.asp?cat=OB&yr=2009&qkey=4409&state=All. Published 2009. Accessed 11/1/2010.

2. National Center for Health Statistics. Chartbook on Trends in the Health of Americans. Hyattsville, MD: Centers for Disease Control and Prevention; 2008.

3. Ibid.

4. Wang Y., et al. Will all Americans become overweight or obese? Estimating the progression and cost of the US obesity epidemic. *Obesity.* 2008;16(10): 2323–2330.

5. Malnick SD, Knobler H. The medical complications of obesity. *QJM.* 2006;99(9):565–579.

6. Finkelstein EA, Trogdon JG, Cohen JW, Dietz W. Annual medical spending attributable to obesity: payer- and service-specific estimates. *Health Affairs.* 2009;28:w822–w831.

7. National Heart, Lung and Blood Institute. *Clinical Guidelines on the Identification, Evaluation and Treatment of Overweight and Obesity in Adults: The Evidence Report.* Bethesda, MD: National Institutes of Health; 1998.

8. Aucott L, Rothnie H, McIntyre L, Thapa M, Waweru C, Gray D. Long-term weight loss from lifestyle intervention benefits blood pressure? A systematic review. *Hypertension.* 2009. doi:10.1161/HYPERTENSIONAHA.109.135178.

9. Jain A, Ferguson C, Mauery DR, Pervez F, Gooding M. *Re-visioning Success: How Stigma, Perceptions of Treatment, and Definitions of Success Impact Obesity and Weight Management in America.* Washington, DC: The George Washington University School of Public Health and Health Services, Department of Health Policy; 2007.http://www.stopobesityalliance.org/wp-content/assets/2009/06/report_re-visioning_success.pdf. Published November 2007. Accessed 11/1/2010.

10. Linne Y, Hemmingsson E, Adolfsson B, Ramsten J, Rossner S. Patient expectations of obesity treatment-the experience from a day-care unit. *Int J Obes Relat Metab Disord.* 2002;26(5):739–741.

11. Jain et al., 2007.

12. Ibid.

13. Government Accountability Office. *Medicaid Preventive Services: Concerted Effort Needed to Ensure Beneficiaries Receive Services.* Washington, DC: GAO-09-578; 2009.

14. Healthcare Information Center. *Health Care 500: A Complete Guide to the Most Influential Health Policy Makers in the U.S.* Washington, DC: Faulkner & Gray; 1992.

Should HPV Vaccine Be Required for School Entry?

ALEXANDRA M. STEWART AND MARISA A. COX

The Pattersons pulled into the visitor parking lot of the State House. "Wow, look at the size of the crowd! What are all these people doing here?" Mrs. Patterson wondered.

As she put on her glasses to read the signs they carried, the crowd approached the car and began chanting, "My daughter, my choice! My daughter, my choice!"

"Let's just turn around and go home . . ." Mr. Patterson's voice trailed off.

"Absolutely not! We've already talked about this. We've already agreed. We must participate. We have to tell our story!" Mrs. Patterson insisted.

With that they pulled into the last available parking space, exited their car and slowly began to wade through the thick crowd. The state police had erected barricades around the main entrance, but it was useless; most of those gathered had broken through. After passing through security, the Pattersons made their way to a large, crowded room. Some people were sitting quietly alone, while others talked excitedly in groups, and still others waved the same signs as those seen outside. The crisp morning air was frigid, but it was warm inside, and the Pattersons found two seats in the back. They sat down to wait for events to unfold.

Meanwhile, shielded from the audience by a partition, Senator Angela Jenson watched the gathering crowd. As a senior member of the committee, the senator was not a stranger to large, opinionated groups. It seemed that everyone was always trying to lobby her about one thing or the other. As she scrutinized the audience, she got the sense that today was going to be different. Her staff had received more calls from constituents regarding this topic than any other and the media attention was overwhelming. Nevertheless, she was surprised by the turnout for this hearing, and the growing groups of protesters and media representatives gather-

ing in front of the tall windows. She knew that in order to ensure that things would not get out of hand she would have to set firm ground rules for conducting the session and anticipate possible outbursts from an emotional audience. She approached the podium to call the hearing to order. The audience fell silent; the chanting from the protesters outside drifted into the room.

"Good morning and welcome to the Committee on Health and Human Services' first legislative session of 2006–2007. I am Senator Angela Jenson, chair of the committee. Our first order of business is to decide whether we should require girls entering the sixth grade to be vaccinated with the new human papillomavirus vaccine—HPV vaccine for short. The purpose of today's hearing is to learn from the invited witnesses who will educate the committee regarding several issues surrounding the vaccine. Their testimony will help us make our decision. We have a full roster of witnesses today: a healthcare provider, a vaccine policy expert, and members of the public. Each witness will have 5 minutes to deliver his or her presentation. Following each presentation, we ask the witness to remain standing for any questions.

"I apologize if anyone had a hard time getting in, but there has been unprecedented interest in the subject of today's hearing. In fact, I understand that many state legislatures are considering the same question at this very moment.[i] Finally, let me say that the committee recognizes that this is

---

[i] The legislatures included those in California, Colorado, Connecticut, the District of Columbia, Florida, Georgia, Illinois, Indiana, Kansas, Kentucky, Maine, Massachusetts, Michigan, Minnesota, Mississippi, Missouri, New Jersey, New Mexico, New York, Ohio, Oklahoma, South Carolina, Texas, Vermont, Virginia, West Virginia, and Wisconsin.

an intensely emotional topic involving our children. However, the committee and I request that all audience members refrain from displaying any banners or signs. Of course, verbal outbursts or other disruptions of any kind will not be permitted. Anyone who does not follow these instructions will be removed. The meeting is now called to order.

"Our first witness is Dr. Michael Jenner, a pediatrician who practices at Metropolitan Hospital."

WITNESS 1

Dr. Jenner walked behind the podium. "Thank you, Ms. Chairperson and committee, for allowing me to discuss how children can benefit from one of the greatest achievements of public health."

Although many in the crowd were unaware of it, Dr. Jenner was alluding to a Centers for Disease Control and Prevention list of 10 great public health achievements, which included vaccination.[1]

"I first must tell the committee that the history of vaccines and recommended immunizations is long and has been profoundly productive."

Dr. Jenner went on to explain that vaccines have saved more lives than any surgical technique or any medication ever invented, including antibiotics.[1] He reminded those in attendance that population-wide vaccination has eradicated smallpox across the globe, and the incidence of diphtheria, polio, congenital rubella syndrome, and influenza type b have decreased by almost 100% in the United States.[2] He added that large-scale immunization programs have reduced U.S. infant mortality rates from 20% a century ago to only 1% today.[3] Because of the contributions vaccines have made to human health throughout history, he noted, most governments have developed policies that support comprehensive population-wide immunization programs.[4]

"But what do all of these achievements in the science of immunization have to do with why we are here today? I have a brief presentation that I hope will help the committee to understand the importance of immunization against HPV and the consequences of rejecting a mandate for sixth-grade girls."

Dr. Jenner nodded to someone near the light switch, and the lights dimmed as Dr. Jenner began clicking through his slide show.

The first slide explained that HPV is the most common sexually transmitted infection in the United States; it included the following statistics. Over 20 million individuals are infected. Half of these individuals are young adults between the ages of 15 and 24, and 6.2 million additional persons will become newly infected this year. Of these newly infected individuals, 4.2 million will be between the ages of 15 and 24. The infection usually develops shortly after the onset of sexual activity. More than 80% of all sexually active women will have acquired genital HPV infection by age 50 years.[5]

"These figures should illustrate just how relevant this threat is to our daughters," Dr. Jenner said.

He clicked to go to the next slide.

"Slide No. 2 shows us that there are over 100 strains of HPV, and that two types, 16 and 18, are associated with 70% of cervical cancer cases in the United States."[ii]

Slide No. 2 also showed that an estimated 11,150 women are diagnosed with cervical cancer and 3,700 die of it each year.[6] Additionally, HPV strains 6 and 11 cause 90% of genital warts, recurrent respiratory papillomatosis,[iii] and low-grade cervical abnormalities.[5]

"I know that some of you are thinking that HPV will never affect your daughter, because she is not sexually active and will refrain from sexual activity until marriage, and her husband will do the same. Some of you are even thinking that I have no right to tell you how to raise your families, and that the government certainly has no right to force parents to submit their children for any particular medical treatment. But, I ask you to reconsider.

"As the next slide shows, the age of sexual debut will vary, and there are alternative methods that can reduce the rate of infection, including abstinence, monogamy, limitation of the number of sex partners, and consistent and correct use of condoms."

Dr. Jenner used his laser pointer to emphasize two key points: that no single HPV prevention method is 100% effective;[7] and that research about the average age of sexual debut in the United States indicated that children as young as 11 could benefit from the vaccine.[8]

"This is why receiving three doses of the recently recommended vaccine, Gardasil, produced by Merck and Co., Inc., is so important. Further, the vaccine is most effective if administered *before* exposure to the virus."

Dr. Jenner's next slide indicated that the human papillomavirus vaccine (Gardasil) will protect against HPV strains 6, 11, 16, and 18. The vaccine is almost 100% effective and the protection it offers will last for at least 5 years.[5] The

---

[ii] Strains 16 and 18 also cause cervical abnormalities, anal and anogenital cancers, and are present in approximately one third of head and neck cancers. Approximately 35,000 head and neck cancers occur each year in the United States, accounting for 5% of all cancer; they are more common in men. Incidence of vulvar cancer is rising among young American women. HPV 16 and 18 are involved in approximately 70% of vulvar and vaginal cancers. *See generally*, American Cancer Society.

[iii] Approximately 20,000 cases of recurrent respiratory papillomatosis develop per year in the United States. It affects males and females. It is a rare, debilitating, and recurrent disease that causes obstructive papillomas (noncancerous tumors or warts) to grow in the respiratory tract. It is most common in juveniles and is believed to be maternally transmitted during birth. The median number of surgeries to remove the growths and maintain an open airway is 13, with a range of 2 to 179. *See MMWR*, 2007:56(No. RR-2) at 7.

Food and Drug Administration approved Gardasil for sale in the United States in June 2006. Dr. Jenner asserted that it is safe and effective, and is recommended by the Advisory Committee on Immunization Practices (see Box 11-1).

"ACIP has recommended the HPV vaccine for girls and women ages 9 through 26."

The next slide indicated the recommendations:

1. Girls ages 9 and 10 may be vaccinated at the discretion of their parents or guardians and physician.
2. Girls ages 11 or 12 are to be routinely vaccinated.
3. Females ages 13 through 26 should be vaccinated as a catch-up if they have not already received the vaccine.[9]

"As you can see from the recommendations, sixth-grade girls typically fall in the 11- or 12-year-old age category and should receive the vaccine as part of their routine pediatric visits.

"You may have also heard this vaccine is very expensive and many families who want the vaccine have even decided that their budgets will be unable to stretch to cover it. Let me reassure you. Insurance coverage or alternate funding is available."

He clicked to the next slide.

"This slide describes the public and private programs that are available to help families afford the vaccine. Thus far, my patients who are covered by private health insurance have spotty coverage for the vaccine. This is not unusual, because insurers take a period of time before covering any newly recommended vaccines and I expect that those of you who are privately insured will see the coverage catching up soon."

Dr. Jenner added that Medicaid covers all vaccines as soon as they are recommended.[10] He further explained that those who do not have health insurance coverage of any type would be eligible for vaccines free of charge through a federal program called the Vaccines for Children program (VFC). The VFC program purchases almost half of the vaccines administered in the United States and distributes them to eligible providers.[11]

"I am a registered VFC provider," he said. "Thus, all of my eligible patients will receive all three doses of the vaccine free of charge."

He described another federal program, called the 317 program, that may provide free or reduced vaccines to children,[12] and he added that, depending on their budgets, state and local programs might provide the vaccine to children who do not qualify for 317 or VFC.

As the lights came back on, Dr. Jenner concluded his speech. "I appreciate the opportunity you have given me to speak with you this morning and look forward to working with my patients and their families to ensure that HPV does not affect them in the future. I will stand for any questions."

Senator Jenson responded, "Thank you Dr. Jenner. Are there any questions or brief comments?"

A gentleman sitting in the middle of the room stood and asked, "Dr. Jenner, my son is about to start sixth grade. If preventing HPV is such an important part of health care, why is the vaccine only for girls?"

Dr. Jenner commented that many others had asked him the same question, and explained that the vaccine is recommended for females only because no boys or men were included in the clinical trials or tests that studied the vaccine.[13] But further research that focuses on males was under way.[iv,5]

"When the trials are concluded, and if they show that the vaccine is safe and effective for boys, I expect that a recommendation for males will be forthcoming. By the way, this is anecdotal evidence, but some of my colleagues have already administered the vaccine to their sons. I anticipate that use in both boys and girls will be common once the studies are completed and a recommendation is made. Until then, please remember that males can contract and pass the infection and also experience adverse health effects of their own if they become infected. That is why the same discussions

BOX 11-1 The Advisory Committee on Immunization Practices

The Advisory Committee on Immunization Practices (ACIP) is made up of experts in fields associated with immunization who have been selected by the secretary of the U.S. Department of Health and Human Services. The committee's only job is to provide advice and guidance to the secretary, the assistant secretary for health, and the Centers for Disease Control and Prevention. ACIP drafts and issues written recommendations for the routine administration of vaccines to children and adults in the civilian population. The recommendations are based on research that identifies the appropriate age, dosage, precautions, and contraindications for each vaccine.[6] A contraindication is a condition that makes administering the immunization inadvisable.[7]

[iv] On October 21, 2009, ACIP issued recommendations for the permissive use of Gardasil in males aged 9 through 26 to reduce the likelihood of acquiring genital warts. However, ACIP did not recommend the vaccine for routine use in males.

that are taking place with and about our daughters must also include our sons."

A woman in the front of the room stood and asked, "If my daughter is not sexually active, why must she receive the vaccine now? I would prefer that she wait and make the decision for herself when she becomes an adult."

"Another excellent question. The simple answer is that the vaccine will not be as effective because most adults will already have been exposed to at least one strain of the virus. As a result, the recommendation is for 11- and 12-year-old girls. The virus is transmitted via sexual contact. Remember, the age of sexual debut varies for each individual, and it is best to administer the vaccine earlier rather than later in order to provide protection before exposure. You can think about it like any other vaccine. We do not always know when we will be exposed to a disease, but we are vaccinated to ensure that we are protected *just in case* we are exposed. This does not mean that the exposure will occur, only that we are protected. For example, we routinely receive immunizations for tetanus but never really expect to step on a rusty nail. The HPV vaccine is no different. Prevention is always better than treatment. The goal is to vaccinate girls so that they will not have to endure the medical interventions required to treat cervical cancer and other HPV-related diseases. Thank you for your question."

After a pause during which no one else stood or raised a hand, Senator Jenson approached the podium. "As there are no further questions, our next witness is Ms. Angela P. Vincent, a professor from State University."

WITNESS 2

Ms. Vincent took her place and greeted those in attendance. "Good morning Chairwoman Jenson and committee members. I am pleased to participate in this important discussion regarding whether to require HPV vaccine for school entry. This debate will provide the committee the opportunity to consider the scientific, legal, ethical, and financial issues surrounding compulsory vaccination. I will discuss how school entry requirements impact our nation's health and how vaccines are financed through public and private payment systems.

"One of the first questions I am asked, no matter the audience, is 'how is it possible that the government can force me to submit my child to unwanted medical treatment?' In fact, mandating immunizations is deeply embedded in the United States legal system. The Tenth Amendment of the Constitution grants states the right to pass laws that require the vaccination of children for school entry, and all states have done so. The validity of these laws has withstood multiple challenges in state and federal courts."

Ms. Vincent then explained that the laws outline the specific immunizations that are required and also allow children to be excused from the requirements for one of the following three reasons:

1. Exemption may be granted for medical reasons in all 50 states.
2. Exemption may be granted for religious reasons in 48 states.
3. Exemption may be granted because of the parent's personal beliefs in 20 states.[14]

However, despite the availability of exemptions, over 95% of all school-age children ultimately receive mandated immunizations.[15] For example, in 2006, an estimated 23% of children aged 19–35 months had not received all the recommended immunizations. By age 5 years, 95% of children were up to date. The increase in coverage rates is directly associated with school immunization requirements. The laws have proven to be the most effective mechanism ever devised to vaccinate children.[15]

"Because of these mandates," Ms. Vincent continued, "the use of all recommended vaccines has increased, the incidence of vaccine-preventable diseases has decreased, and diseases that were once common have all but disappeared. Disparities in vaccine coverage have been dramatically reduced. Children who have low-income families or whose families have been unable to establish a medical home receive vaccinations because of school requirements. Finally, the laws increase public funding for vaccines.

"Based on the facts, we can safely assume that a state law requiring HPV immunization is a good public policy decision because it will achieve more widespread protection against cervical cancer than if we were to rely on other policy reforms such as parental education and persuasion.

"It is essential that every community vaccinates enough of its citizens to achieve herd immunity, which is the resistance to a disease that develops in the community when a sufficient number of individuals are vaccinated."[v]

Ms. Vincent stressed that in order to ensure that immunization rates remain high, public and private stakeholders including government, academia, vaccine manufacturers, healthcare providers and consumers must continue to work together.[15]

"The existing framework for financing vaccines is designed to accommodate newly recommended vaccines. HPV vaccine will be distributed through this mechanism, which has already been implemented. The public funding streams for vaccines include Medicaid and the State Children's Health Insurance Program. These programs are intended for children who live in families with low income," Ms. Vincent said.

---

[v] Herd immunity protects those few individuals who are unable to receive vaccinations due to age or health status. Each vaccine-preventable disease requires a different percentage of coverage before herd immunity is achieved; this necessary coverage ranges from 75% for mumps to 94% for pertussis.

She reiterated what Dr. Jenner indicated, that the VFC program provides free vaccines to children through age 18 who are Medicaid eligible, uninsured, or who have private insurance that does not provide coverage for the HPV vaccine, or who are Native American or Alaska Native.[16] Also, federally qualified health centers and rural health clinics may charge for vaccines on a sliding scale.

Ms. Vincent went on, "The private funding streams for vaccines include employer-based or individually purchased medical insurance. Many insurers will reimburse enrollees and providers for the cost of HPV vaccine according to their current cost-sharing and payment standards. Every healthcare service is assigned a current procedural terminology code that determines the amount of reimbursement a provider will receive from an insurer. A current procedural terminology code has already been established for HPV vaccine, an indication that it is already considered standard medical practice.

"As the committee reviews the many questions surrounding an HPV vaccine mandate, I hope my comments have informed this discussion. I will be happy to answer any questions. Thank you."

Senator Clark raised his hand with a question. "Thank you Professor Vincent. Can you tell me how much the vaccine will cost? I understand that it is the most expensive vaccine to date. I am concerned a school entry requirement will break the state's budget and that families will not be able to pay for a mandatory vaccine."

"There is no single answer to that question," Ms. Vincent began. "The price of the vaccine is dependent on the purchaser. Many people have heard that each dose costs $120, making the three-dose series a whopping $360. However, that price is reserved for only those few individuals who will purchase the vaccine privately, without health insurance or access to government support. As Dr. Jenner and I explained, most Americans do not pay the full retail price for vaccines out of pocket.

"If the purchaser has private insurance, the vaccine will be subject to the plan's usual cost-sharing arrangements. If the purchaser is a Medicaid or SCHIP beneficiary, has private insurance that does not cover the vaccine, or is Native American or Alaskan Native, the vaccine will be free through the Vaccines for Children program.[16] Let me remind you that since VFC vaccines are financed by the federal government, there is no fiscal impact on the state.

"If our Department of Health wishes to purchase vaccines for those who do not otherwise qualify for different programs, the department may take advantage of a predetermined federal discount rate. The purchase, of course, will be made with state funds. So you can see that very few individuals will pay full retail price, and the state will never pay full price."

"Thank you Professor Vincent, I think I understand now," Senator Clark commented.

Senator Jenson stood and said, "Thank you, Professor Vincent, for your helpful testimony today. If there are no further questions, I now recognize the next witness, Mrs. Elizabeth Ellsworth."

WITNESS 3

Mrs. Ellsworth spoke loudly and clearly. "Thank you for allowing me to voice my absolute outrage over this unacceptable and inappropriate intrusion of my family values. I do not believe that the government should be able to interfere with my rights, as a parent, to make medical decisions for my children! Forced vaccination is un-American enough, but now you tell me that my 11-year-old daughter is going to contract a sexual disease while sitting in her classroom! It's just too much! HPV is not spread by casual contact; there is no reason to require vaccination for school attendance.

"I am afraid that if my daughter receives this vaccine, that she will think that she is protected from all diseases and that it is a green light for her to have sex! I believe that the school system should work *with* families to deliver the same message to our children about early and inappropriate sexual activity. And that message should be abstinence only! We should support the federal programs that teach abstinence until marriage as the sole strategy for preventing early sexual activity and sexually transmitted infections among adolescents. Indiscriminate administration of the HPV vaccine to young children does not do that. I hope that the committee rejects the attempt to displace my authority over my children and to legislate family values. In order to protect our way of life, every member of this committee must vote against this bill. If this measure is adopted, I will certainly not be voting to reelect any member of the committee come the next election."

An agitated audience member rose and exclaimed, "Girls deserve protection! We all believe our daughters are not sexually active, but the truth of the matter is that they engage in sex very frequently! If there were a vaccine for a predominantly male cancer, there would be no debate . . . we would readily accept a mandate. We want to save our children, and there is no point in making this a political debate, it is a life or death situation, and I believe we owe it to our daughters to protect them!"

Hoping to calm the crowd, Senator Jenson returned to the microphone, saying, "Mrs. Ellsworth, thank you for your comments." As security guards swiftly escorted the heckler from the room, Senator Jenson asked for questions.

A woman stood and asked, "If this measure is implemented, will the school distribute any information about it to our girls? I am concerned that any information given to our children may be too graphic and explain more than they are equipped to handle at this age."

Senator Jenson once again approached the podium. "Thank you for the question. I can assure you that we have no plans to distribute any additional material to the students. I anticipate that parents will receive an explanation of the requirement as well as information regarding HPV infection, the vaccine, the connection between HPV and cervical cancer, and how the requirement can be satisfied. The materials will be approved by both federal health authorities and each school district. You may also wish to call our curriculum coordinator to request a copy of the sexual education materials that will be used in health classes this year."

Senator Jenson introduced the fourth witness, Mr. Jason Samuels.

WITNESS 4

"Thank you, Senator Jenson and the committee. I have two children, a boy, 8 years old and a girl, 14. I am here to warn the committee about the dangers and certain harm that will result if this vaccine is required for our daughters. I have information that the government is keeping from the public. Did you know that the Food and Drug Administration approved Gardasil on an expedited basis?"

Gardasil was approved after only 6 months of review.[17]

"This process is highly unusual—what's the rush? I think that the government favors big business over the health and safety of our children. Did you know that Merck—the company that makes Gardasil—produced Vioxx®, the drug that is responsible for several heart attacks and deaths? Merck wants Gardasil to be mandated because they want to recover profits that were lost to several Vioxx® lawsuits. Additionally, there are recent reports that three girls died shortly after taking Gardasil. How many more deaths are we going to allow while supporting drug manufacturers? I do not want my daughter to be a subject in a mass government experiment. Trying to force Gardasil on us is just like the abuse that African American men suffered during the Tuskegee experiments. Did the government ever apologize? Did the government ever compensate their families for their loss?

"In closing, I want the committee to stand for *our* children and *not* the drug companies. My daughter, my choice!"

Senator Jenson rose, looked hesitantly into the audience, and asked for questions. A woman sitting near the front of the room rose. "I have a daughter about the same age as yours. You speak of several deaths that may have been associated with the vaccine. What about the young women who die of cervical cancer each year?"

Mr. Samuels looked at the woman and replied "I feel sad for the families who have lost loved ones to cervical cancer, but with proper screening, these tragedies can be prevented. I am more uncomfortable exposing my healthy daughter to a medical intervention when effective, tested, and long-term detection and treatment methods are already in place. I hope that you will not put your healthy daughter in harm's way when all you have to do is ensure that she gets all appropriate screenings."

A man stood and said, "Mr. Samuels indicated that the vaccine may be dangerous and he seemed to say that the government can't be counted on to compensate victims for their pain. I don't understand why we're even talking about compensation. Shouldn't we be talking about avoiding harm? If the vaccine isn't required, we don't have to worry about risk and compensation."

Senator Jenson approached the podium. "Thank you for your comments. Perhaps Professor Vincent can help us understand how the government addresses vaccine injuries. Professor Vincent?"

Professor Vincent returned to the podium. "Thank you Senator Jenson. While in a perfect world, vaccines would never cause harm to those who receive them; unfortunately, this is not a perfect world. We must realize that all medical interventions come with some amount of risk. The U.S. government acknowledges this fact and has established a program called the Vaccine Injury Compensation Program—VICP. The VICP provides a system—the vaccine court—for individuals who have been injured by vaccines to receive compensation."

Box 11-2 describes the VICP and vaccine court.

"The vaccine court program is funded through a tax on each dose of vaccine administered. While some of you might think that this system is just another mechanism to shield manufacturers, it is important to remember that vaccines are vital to public health, are costly to develop and manufacture, and that the government buys most of the doses administered in the United States at a lower, negotiated rate. If manufac-

BOX 11-2 The Vaccine Injury Compensation Program and the Vaccine Court

The Vaccine Injury Compensation Program's vaccine court is an alternative to the traditional legal system. Persons who believe that they have been injured by a vaccination file claims before the U.S. Court of Federal Claims, instead of a state court. The claims are heard by a special master instead of a judge. Claims may be filed if the injury has lasted for more than 6 months after the administration of the vaccine or resulted in a hospital stay and surgery or resulted in death.[18] Injured parties may be represented by a lawyer, but this is not required.[19]

turers were to be exposed to the high cost of litigation from various lawsuits in different state courts, there would be little incentive to remain in the market and we would all suffer the consequences of reduced supply, lack of innovation, and an increase in cases of vaccine-preventable diseases.

"Claims for injuries associated with the HPV vaccine may be brought to the VICP. While this is not directly related to a decision to mandate the vaccine, the committee should note that the VICP provides another safeguard to ensure that the vaccine is administered responsibly. Thank you for this important question."

Senator Jenson said, "Thank you Mr. Samuels and Professor Vincent. We appreciate your taking the time to come here today and will consider your comments as we deliberate. If there are no further questions, our next witness is Ms. Roberta Espinoza."

WITNESS 5

Ms. Espinoza made her way to the podium and began. "Thank you for the opportunity to speak with you this afternoon. I have two daughters, one who will be starting sixth grade at Parkland Middle School in the fall. When I heard that there was a shot to prevent my girls from developing cancer, I couldn't help but think how times have changed, how medical science has advanced, and how promising the future looks for my kids. When I was growing up, we didn't know much about cancer, and there was limited opportunity to prevent it. This is why I am so excited about Gardasil. We now have the means to protect our children from developing cervical cancer. I did some research on my own about HPV infection and the numbers of people who are infected, how it is spread, Gardasil and its connection to cervical cancer, and the importance of early preventive measures. I believe that Gardasil is a very good thing and that girls should be vaccinated.

"I understand that some parents may believe that allowing young girls to be vaccinated may send a different message about their personal conduct than what we teach them at home. I understand that some may be worried that any deviation from an abstinence-only message will encourage early sexual activity. But I also understand that if my daughters do not receive the vaccine, I am putting them at risk unnecessarily. As their mother, my job is to protect my children from all potential threats. I am not willing to take the chance that they could develop cervical cancer simply because I am uncomfortable talking to them about their bodies. I owe them more than that."

Ms. Espinoza took aim at abstinence-only programs. She asserted that the programs have failed and that research evaluations by Congress have showed that abstinence-only education makes no difference at all.[7]

"They do not prevent early sexual conduct," she said. "I learned that students involved in these programs have the same rates of sexually transmitted infections and unintended pregnancies as anybody else. While the abstinence message may reflect the values and aspirations of many parents, clearly, it is not a reality for millions of teenagers.

"I also understand that some of you may still be concerned that if we begin to teach our children about safe sex, that they will think that it is okay to start having sex at a young age. However, I have done some research on the topic."

While doing her research Ms. Espinoza discovered that studies show the following:

1. Adolescents did not change reported rates of sexual activity or increase the frequency of unprotected intercourse when they were educated about the availability of emergency contraception.
2. The percentage of adolescents who had ever had sex did not change when condoms were available or in schools with condom availability programs.[7]

"In light of this evidence, I do not think that introducing HPV vaccine to our girls will encourage early sexual activity.

"If it were up to me, I would add HPV vaccine to the required list of vaccines. I want my daughters to be vaccinated. I want all girls to be vaccinated early. I want my children to receive comprehensive sexual education that includes a full discussion of ways to protect themselves from all the negative consequences of unprotected sex. I want you to have the courage to take advantage of the opportunities for a healthy future that the vaccine promises. I thank you, Senator Jenson, and I thank the committee."

Once again, Senator Jenson rose and asked for questions. A woman seated in the back of the room rose and asked: "I thought that at the very least, as an American citizen, I had the right to make decisions about my family's religious and moral upbringing. The school has no place teaching my children about sex when I have chosen an abstinence-only message for them. That is what our religion requires. Mandating this vaccine will force the issues upon us and result in conversations that should not be had with children, especially at school. School is a place for reading, writing and arithmetic, not sex education. This committee has no right to violate my religious beliefs. How can I stop the school from dictating how I raise my family?"

Senator Jenson asked, "May I take this question Ms. Espinoza?"

Ms. Espinoza nodded, and Senator Jenson reminded the crowd that many school mandates include three types of exemptions, including those for medical contraindications[vi,20] and those for religious and philosophical beliefs.

[vi] Contraindication—A characteristic or attribute of an individual that may be temporary or permanent that prohibits the administration of a drug, vaccine, or other therapeutic intervention.

"I can assure you that any requirement will include, at a minimum, an exemption for medical contraindication. The committee will also consider additional exemptions to accommodate philosophical and religious beliefs. I can assure you further, that your comments will be considered and that we will have the conversations necessary to ensure that we have balanced the interests of religious expression with our obligation to protect the public's health. Thank you for your thoughtful comments.

"Our final witness is Mrs. Emily Patterson."

WITNESS 6

It was finally Mrs. Patterson's turn. She slowly made her way through the aisle to the podium. After she adjusted the microphone, she reached into her tote bag and pulled out an 8×10 picture of an attractive young woman in a silver frame. She took a deep breath and looked around the room.

"Good afternoon, Senator Jenson, committee members and guests. I am grateful to be able to talk with you all today. I'd like to introduce you to Tracy. Isn't she lovely? We always thought so. She loved to swim and bake. In early 2001, she began having stomach pains and unusual bleeding that went on for several months.[21] She never said anything to me or her father about it. She finally went to a doctor when her pain was so severe, she could not stand up. When her cervical cancer was diagnosed, it was already at stage IIB."

After diagnosis, cancer is identified by stages from zero to IV.[vii,22] Mrs. Patterson told the crowd that her daughter was 25 years old when she was diagnosed, which is younger than the usual victim.[viii,23]

"She did not visit a doctor earlier because she was trying to save money. You see, Tracy's job provided health insurance, but she always said that because she was just beginning her career straight out of college, she could not afford the premiums for something that she never used. After paying her student loans, rent, and buying fancy coffee, there was nothing left, so she took a chance. She missed her recommended Pap exams that most likely would have detected the disease early enough to save her life. What's the harm? She had always been so healthy and so athletic. We didn't press her. We should have.

"During the next 2 years, my daughter Tracy was forced to move back in with us and suffered through multiple rounds of brutal internal and external radiation, chemotherapy, surgeries, hair loss, weight loss, and unrelenting nausea, pain, and fatigue. Her uterus, cervix, most of her vagina, ovaries, fallopian tubes, colon, and rectum were removed. Then she tried experimental treatments at the National Institutes of Health outside Washington, DC. Through it all, we never gave up. We thought we were lucky because we could afford the expensive care.

"Tracy knew she would heal. Her hair would grow back, she would adopt children, her scars would be hidden, she would find another job, and she would rebuild everything. Tracy wanted to live. Of course, the end came too soon, and Tracy died when the cancer spread throughout her body. She was 27. Our only child is buried next to her grandparents and we visit her often.

"Tracy's father is with me today. We implore the committee to make the HPV vaccine a requirement for girls going to school. I have carefully listened to the other witnesses' concerns as they have been expressed here today."

Mrs. Patterson asserted that more than 4,000 women like Tracy would die that year.[24]

"Each one will be someone's daughter, someone's mother, someone's sister, someone's friend. And you will miss them. Isn't prevention better than all the latest treatments? Your honors, I believe that I have gone past my allotted time to speak, but don't you think our children are worth it?"

The room was silent as Mrs. Patterson placed Tracy's picture back in her tote bag. As she turned, Mr. Patterson was there to help her back through the room, through the chanting crowd outside, through the parking lot, and back to their car.

CONCLUSION

As the Pattersons made their way out, Senator Jenson gathered herself and approached the microphone, "Mrs. Patterson, I'm sure I speak not only for myself, but for the entire committee and our guests, when I thank you most sincerely for your moving testimony. We thank all the witnesses for their contributions today and of course our audience for their patience and cooperation. We will consider all comments carefully and intend to make our decision with the best interests of our children in mind."

About the Authors

Alexandra M. Stewart, JD, is an assistant professor in the Department of Health Policy at The George Washington University School of Public Health and Health Services. Professor Stewart has over 10 years' experience examining how state and federal laws impact U.S. vaccine policy and practice. She has completed analyses of the 2010 health reform initiatives to determine how changes will impact all areas of immuni-

---

[vii] Stage IIB = The cancer has spread beyond the cervix to the upper two thirds of the vagina and to the tissues around the uterus.
[viii] From 2002 to 2006, the average age of a woman diagnosed with cervical cancer was 48. Very few cervical cancer diagnoses (0.2%) are in women under age 20; 14.9% occur between ages 20 and 34; 26.2% between ages 35 and 44; 23.5% between ages 45 and 54; 15.8% between ages 55 and 64; 10.4% between ages 65 and 74; 6.6% between ages 75 and 84; and 2.5% ages 85 and over.[23]

zation policy, as well as how other laws influence immunization access. She directs Epidemiology of U.S. Immunization Law, a Centers for Disease Control and Prevention-supported initiative that conducts research and provides technical assistance to improve standards for immunization coverage and performance in children and adults. This project produced the largest single legal analysis of immunization policy ever undertaken and contributed to the development of essential tools for public health practice and policy. It has explored access to immunizations under Medicaid, the federal employee health benefit programs, and state insurance law, produced reports detailing immunization requirements for staff and residents of long-term care facilities, and reviewed state laws as they relate to the use of standing orders to deliver immunization services. Professor Stewart is also lead instructor of a graduate level course focusing on U.S. vaccine policy. She earned her law degree from The George Washington University Law School.

Marisa A. Cox, MA, MPH is a research scientist at the Department of Health Policy at The George Washington University School of Public Health and Health Services. Ms. Cox has been a researcher on the Centers for Disease Control and Prevention-funded Epidemiology of U.S. Immunization Law project since its inception in 2003 and has researched issues such as mandatory vaccination of healthcare workers, health reform and immunization, HPV vaccine and school entry requirements, and Medicaid coverage and adult immunization. Ms. Cox also serves as the teaching assistant for Professor Stewart's vaccine policy course. Ms. Cox earned a master of arts degree in philosophy and social policy and an MPH in health policy, both at The George Washington University.

REFERENCES

1. Centers for Disease Control and Prevention. Ten great public health achievements—United States 1900–1999. *MMWR.* 1999;48(12):241–243. http://www.cdc.gov/mmwr/preview/mmwrhtml/00056796.htm. Accessed September 14, 2010.

2. Centers for Disease Control and Prevention. What would happen if we stopped vaccinations? http://www.cdc.gov/vaccines/vac-gen/whatifstop.htm. Modified August 27, 2010. Accessed September 14, 2010.

3. Houppert K. The unlikely antivaccine alliance. *CBS News.* March 11, 2007. http://www.cbsnews.com/stories/2007/03/09/opinion/main2555357.shtml. Accessed September 14, 2010.

4. Stern AM, Markel H. The history of vaccines and immunization: familiar patterns, new challenges. *Health Affairs.* 2005;24:611, 614, citing Barquet N, Domingo P. Smallpox: the triumph over the most terrible of the ministers of death. *Ann Intern Med.* 1997;127:635.

5. Centers for Disease Control and Prevention. Quadrivalent human papillomavirus vaccine recommendations of the Advisory Committee on Immunization Practices (ACIP). *MMWR.* 2007;56(No. RR-2).

6. National Cancer Institute, U.S. National Institutes of Health. Surveillance, epidemiology, and end results (SEER) cancer statistics review, 1975–2007, cervix uteri. http://seer.cancer.gov/csr/1975_2007/results_merged/sect_05_cervix_uteri.pdf. Accessed September 14, 2010.

7. The George Washington University, School of Public Health and Health Services. Risky sexual behavior among American adolescents: how can unintended pregnancies and sexually transmitted infections be lessened? GW School of Public Health and Health Services, Rapid Public Health Policy Response Project. Washington, DC: September 2008.

8. Markowitz L, Dunne EF, Saraiya M, et al. Quadrivalent human papillomavirus vaccine: recommendations of the Advisory Committee on Immunization Practices (ACIP). MMWR. 2007;56(early release):1–24. http://www.cdc.gov/mmwr/preview/mmwrhtml/rr56e312a1.htm. Accessed September 14, 2010.

9. Centers for Disease Control and Prevention, Office of Enterprise Communication. CDC's advisory committee recommends human papillomavirus virus vaccination [press release]. June 29, 2006. http://www.cdc.gov/media/pressrel/r060629.htm. Accessed September 14, 2010.

10. The Henry J. Kaiser Family Foundation. HPV vaccine: implementation and financing policy in the U.S. [women's health policy fact sheet]. February 2008. www.kff.org/womenshealth/upload/7602_02.pdf. Accessed September 14, 2010.

11. Birkhead GS, Orenstein WA, Almquist JR. Reducing financial barriers to vaccination in the United States: call to action. *Pediatrics.* 2009;124;S451–S454.

12. Centers for Disease Control and Prevention. Immunization grant program (Section 317): what is the public health issue? www.cdc.gov/NCIRD/progbriefs/downloads/grant-317.pdf. Published February 2007. Accessed September 14, 2010.

13. U.S. Food and Drug Administration. Gardasil (human papillomavirus vaccine) questions and answers. June 8, 2006. http://www.fda.gov/BiologicsBloodVaccines/Vaccines/QuestionsaboutVaccines/ucm096052.htm. Updated June 21, 2010. Accessed September 14, 2010.

14. The National Conference of State Legislatures (NCSL). States with religious and philosophical exemptions from school immunization requirements: school immunization exemption state laws. http://www.ncsl.org/default.aspx?tabid=14376. October 2010. Accessed March 27, 2011.

15. Orenstein WA, Hinman AR. The immunization system in the United States—the role of school immunization laws. *Vaccine.* 1999;17(Suppl 3):S19–S24.

16. Centers for Disease Control and Prevention. VFC: for parents. www.cdc.gov/vaccines/programs/vfc/parents/default.htm#eligible. Modified February 22, 2011. Accessed March 27, 2011.

17. U.S. Food and Drug Administration. FDA licenses new vaccine for prevention of cervical cancer and other diseases in females caused by human papillomavirus: rapid approval marks major advancement in public health. www.fda.gov/NewsEvents/Newsroom/PressAnnouncements/2006/ucm108666.htm. Published June 8, 2006. Accessed September 14, 2010.

18. U.S. Department of Health and Human Services, Health Resources and Services Administration. National vaccine injury compensation program (VICP): persons eligible to file a claim. www.hrsa.gov/Vaccinecompensation/persons_eligible.htm. Accessed September 14, 2010.

19. U.S. Department of Health and Human Services, Health Resources and Services Administration. National vaccine injury compensation program (VICP): filing a claim with the VICP. www.hrsa.gov/Vaccinecompensation/filing_claim.htm. Accessed September 14, 2010.

20. Centers for Disease Control and Prevention. Definitions of terms. *Manual for the Surveillance of Vaccine-Preventable Diseases.* 4th ed. Atlanta, GA: Author; 2008.

21. National Cancer Institute, U.S. National Institutes of Health. What you need to know about cervical cancer: symptoms. http://www.cancer.gov/cancertopics/wyntk/cervix/page5. Accessed March 27, 2011.

22. National Cancer Institute, U.S. National Institutes of Health. Stages of cervical cancer. http://www.cancer.gov/cancertopics/pdq/treatment/cervical/Patient/page2. Accessed September 14, 2010.

23. National Cancer Institute. SEER stat fact sheets: cancer: cervix uteri. http://seer.cancer.gov/statfacts/html/cervix.html. Accessed September 14, 2010.

24. American Cancer Society. Detailed guide: cervical cancer: what are the key statistics about cervical cancer? http://www.cancer.org/Cancer/CervicalCancer/DetailedGuide/cervical-cancer-key-statistics. Modified December 23, 2010. Accessed March 27, 2011.

Plan B Emergency Contraception:

Caught in a Web of Science, Regulation, and Politics—What's a Woman to Do?

SUSAN F. WOOD AND ALISON M. MILLER

THE DOG DAYS OF SUMMER IN WASHINGTON, DC

It was late August, 2005. A woman was sitting on her bed wondering what to do. While walking home to her apartment the previous night, she was raped. She did not want to go to the hospital or call the police until she had time to think about it. While this is perhaps not the best choice, it is a common one. Worried she would have an unintended pregnancy, she wondered if she could prevent it. Her only option was to find a healthcare provider willing to prescribe Plan B, which could be particularly hard considering it was a Sunday.

As the director of the Office of Women's Health at the U.S. Food and Drug Administration (FDA), Susan Wood was monitoring the application process for changing Plan B emergency contraception from a prescription drug to an over-the-counter drug. She knew of several scientific and health reasons why the drug should go over the counter. But the compelling personal stories she heard and read brought home the importance of the issue.

The decision to make Plan B available over the counter (OTC) had not been like other drug approval processes. Plan B had been deemed safe for OTC use by a scientific review panel and recommended for approval by FDA's scientific and medical staff. The FDA had been expected to make a decision in February 2004, but had so far refused to make Plan B available OTC. There were multiple delays through August 2005, when FDA leadership announced it was initiating a new regulatory process to review the ability of the FDA to keep Plan B as a prescription drug for younger teenagers but OTC for older teens and adult women. This clearly contradicted standard procedures at the FDA. Dr. Wood's frustration with the exceptional processes regarding Plan B and the needs of consumers were forcing a decision as to how she would proceed as the director of the Office of Women's Health at the FDA.

WHAT IS PLAN B?

Plan B is emergency contraception that can be taken if another form of contraception fails. It is high-dose progestin (levonorgestrel), the same compound found in many regular birth control pills. There is a clear need for emergency contraception to be available to women who may be at risk for unintended pregnancy. The statistics of unintended pregnancy in the United States illustrate this need.

In 2001 (the latest information at the time of the levonorgestrel decision, and still true as of publication of this book), nearly half of the pregnancies in the United States were unplanned (Figure 12-1).[1] Notably, only 5% of unintended pregnancies result with consistent contraceptive use (Figure 12-2).[2] The rate of unintended pregnancy in 2001 was substantially above average among women aged 18–24, unmarried (particularly cohabiting) women, low-income women, women who had not completed high school, and minority women.[3] Of the 6.4 million pregnancies in the United States in 2001, 62.5% resulted in births, 20% in abortions, and 17% in fetal losses. Of the 3.1 million unintended pregnancies, 44% ended in births, 42% in abortions and 14% in fetal losses (Figure 12-1).[1] Also, 48% of these unintended pregnancies occurred among women who were using contraception (Figure 12-2).[2] In 2005, the highest percentages of reported abortions were for women who were known to be unmarried (81%), white (53%), and aged younger than 25 years (50%).[3]

FIGURE 12-1 Percentage distribution of pregnancies, by intent and outcome, 2001 (N = 6.4 million pregnancies).

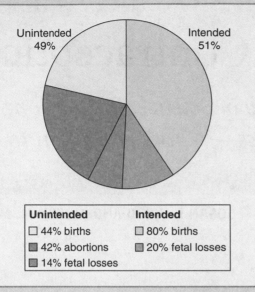

Unintended	**Intended**
☐ 44% births	☐ 80% births
▨ 42% abortions	▨ 20% fetal losses
▨ 14% fetal losses	

Source: Finer LB, Henshaw SK. Disparities in Rates of Unintended Pregnancy in the United States, 1994 and 2001. *Perspect Sex Reprod Health.* 2006;38(2):90–96, Figure 1. Copyright The Alan Guttmacher Institute June 2006.

FIGURE 12-2 Unintended pregnancies by consistency of contraceptive use during month of conception, 2001 (N = 2.1 million unintended pregnancies).

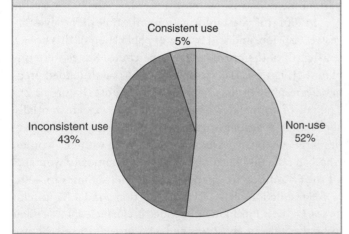

Source: Gold RB, Sonfield A, Richards CL, Frost JJ. *Next Steps for America's Family Planning Program: Leveraging the Potential of Medicaid and Title X in an Evolving Health Care System.* New York, NY: Guttmacher Institute; 2009, Figure 1.2 (b). www.guttmacher.org/pubs/NextSteps.pdf. Accessed November 1, 2010.

FIGURE 12-3 Birth rates (live births) per 1,000 women aged 15–19 years, with total percent change, 2005–2007.

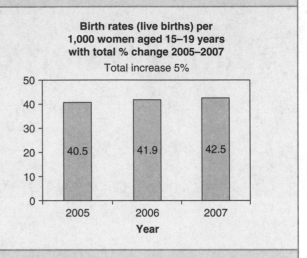

Source: CDC (2010) Teen birth rates rose again in 2007, declined in 2008. http://www.cdc.gov/Features/dsTeenPregnancy/. Updated May 5, 2010. Accessed November 1, 2010.

For teens, the numbers are higher. Nearly half of all 15–19-year-olds are sexually active by the time they graduate high school, and roughly 80% of teen pregnancies are unintended.[1,4] As shown in Figure 12-3, the birthrate of pregnancies among women aged 15–19 increased 5% between 2005 and 2007.[5]

Though there are currently many contraceptive options available (Figure 12-4), new methods need to be made available to address the differing needs of women and couples. Emergency contraception is one method that can help reduce the risk of unintended pregnancy when other contraceptive methods fail or are not used, or in the case of rape. But emergency contraception needs to be utilized quickly after unprotected sex in order to have maximum effectiveness. This is a key reason to have such a product available without a prescription.

HOW EMERGENCY CONTRACEPTION WORKS

Plan B is emergency contraception that attempts to prevent pregnancy in the prefertilization stages. Emergency contraceptive pills (ECPs) provide higher doses of the same hormones found in regular birth control pills and prevent pregnancy by keeping the egg from leaving the ovary (ovulation) or keeping the sperm from joining the egg (fertilization). In fact, in multiple doses, many regular birth control pills also can be used as ECPs.[6] While it is possible ECPs will work by keeping

FIGURE 12-4 Birth control guide.

Medicines to help you

Birth control guide

	Methods	Number of pregnancies expected per 100 women	How to use it	Some risks
Most effective ↑	Sterilization surgery for women	1	One-time procedure; nothing to do or remember	• Pain • Bleeding • Infection or other complications after surgery • Ectopic (tubal) pregnancy
	Surgical sterilization Implant for women	1	One-time procedure; nothing to do or remember	• Mild to moderate pain after insertion • Ectopic (tubal) pregnancy
	Sterilization surgery for men	1	One-time procedure; nothing to do or remember	• Pain • Bleeding • Infection
	Implantable rod	1	One-time procedure; nothing to do or remember	• Acne • Hair loss • Weight gain • Headache • Cysts of the ovaries • Upset stomach • Mood swings • Dizziness • Depression • Sore breasts
	IUD	1	One-time procedure; nothing to do or remember	• Cramps • Lower interest in • Bleeding sexual activity • Pelvic inflammatory disease • Changes in your • Infertility periods • Tear or hole in the uterus
	Shot/injection	1	Need a shot every 3 months	• Bone loss • Bleeding between periods • Weight gain • Breast tenderness • Headaches
	Oral contraceptives (combined pill) "The Pill"	5	Must swallow a pill every day	• Dizziness • High blood pressure • Nausea • Blood clots • Changes in your cycle (period) • Heart attack • Changes in mood • Strokes • Weight gain
	Oral contraceptives (progestin-only) "The Pill"	5	Must swallow a pill every day	• Irregular bleeding • Weight gain • Breast tenderness
	Oral contraceptives extended/continuous use "The Pill"	5	Must swallow a pill every day	• Risks are similar to other oral contraceptives • Bleeding • Spotting between periods
	Patch	5	Change the patch once a week for three weeks. During the fourth week, you do not wear a patch.	• Exposure to higher average levels of estrogen than most oral contraceptives
	Vaginal contraceptive Ring	5	Must leave ring in every day for 3 weeks. On the 4th week, you don't use a ring.	• Vaginal discharge • Swelling of the vagina • Irritation • Similar to oral contraceptives
	Male condom	11–16	Must use every time you have sex; requires partner's cooperation. Except for abstinence, latex condoms are the best protection against HIV/AIDS and other STIs.	• Allergic reactions
	Diaphragm with spermicide	15	Must use every time you have sex	• Irritation • Allergic reactions • Urinary tract infection • Toxic shock
	Sponge with spermicide	16–32	Must use every time you have sex	• Irritation • Allergic reactions • Hard time removing • Toxic shock
	Cervical cap with spermicide	17–23	Must use every time you have sex	• Irritation • Allergic reactions • Abnormal Pap test • Toxic shock
	Female condom	20	Must use every time you have sex. May give some protection against STIs.	• Irritation • Allergic reactions
Least effective	Spermicide	30	Must use every time you have sex	• Irritation • Allergic reactions • Urinary tract infection
Emergency contraceptive — if your primary method of birth control fails				
	Emergency contraceptives "The morning after pill"	15	Must use within 72 hours of unprotected sex. It should not be used as a regular form of birth control.	• Nausea • Vomiting • Abdominal pain • Fatigue • Headache

Source: FDA Office of Women's Health. http://www.fda.gov/downloads/ForConsumers/ByAudience/ForWomen/FreePublications/UCM132770.pdf. Accessed November 1, 2010.

a fertilized egg from attaching to the uterus, the most up-to-date research suggests ECPs do not function as such.[7,8]

By 2005 in the United States, there was only one FDA-approved pill specifically manufactured and marketed to be used as an ECP: Plan B, a progestin-only (levonorgestrel) formulation. Research suggests a levonorgestrel-only hormone regimen, such as Plan B, can reduce the risk of pregnancy by 89% if taken within 72 hours after intercourse, becoming less effective over time.[9]

CONTRACEPTION: A PHILOSOPHICAL AND POLITICAL ISSUE

Emergency contraception and other products related to reproduction are embroiled in controversy. Public discussion of the use of such a product without the need for prescription has sometimes focused on medical data or public health need. Other times, however, discussion has been driven by misinformation that such products cause abortion or would promote promiscuity, particularly among teens. Reviews of this product by the FDA's medical and scientific staff documented their support for approval of this product as an over-the-counter drug for all females of child-bearing potential. The staff concluded that evidence strongly supported its safety and efficacy, and there was no data suggesting it changed sexual behavior.[10]

However, FDA leadership, including the FDA commissioner (a political appointee), apparently was under pressure to avoid approving Plan B as an over-the-counter product. At the same time, Senator Patty Murray (D–WA) and then-Senator Hillary Clinton (D–NY) raised questions at various points about the ongoing delays, including attempting to block confirmation of the FDA commissioner.[11]

In order to have more public discussion of the evidence and to get input from outside experts, the FDA convened an advisory committee meeting on December 16, 2003, to discuss the approval of the over-the-counter status of Plan B. This meeting provided experts and FDA staff the opportunity to review the data on Plan B in a public setting and to hear public comments at the meeting about many of the common reasons people either oppose or are proponents of Plan B being available over the counter and without age restrictions.

A Range of Issues for Opponents

The transcripts from the December 16, 2003, meeting[12] provided insights into the varied views about whether the FDA should approve the availability of Plan B over the counter. Views include those from the general public, doctors, and an elected official.

Dr. Hanna Klaus, an ob-gyn with extensive experience in natural family planning, believed that because "the

Chlamydia and gonorrhea rates have risen nearly 20% in the past 4 years, concomitant to the high profile advertising of the morning after pill, which intended or not, promote the notion that taking Plan B will make up for lack of sexual responsibility."[12(pp 182–184)] She also stated that "conception can occur in six days in the cycle, making the pills unnecessary for at least 24 days out of each cycle." [12(pp 182–184)] She believed that women should be taught their fertility cycle "so they know when to say yes and when to say no."[12(pp 182–184)]

Judie Brown, the president of American Life League, said she believed "Emergency contraception . . . is not contraception. So-called emergency contraception can by definition abort a child before it implants. A human being begins at conception, not at implantation."[12(pp 212–213)]

Jill Stanek, from Concerned Women for America, said she believed "making EC's available would be a welcome tool for adult sexual predators who molest family members, children of friends, or students. They could keep a stash in their bedroom drawer or their pocket to give their victims after committing each rape."[12(pp 226–227)]

Jennifer Taylor, director of communications for Human Life International, stated she is "30 years old and I have been married for two and a half years. I don't believe in contraception, and I don't use it, and I've never been pregnant, and my husband and I don't abstain as much as people might want to make you believe they do when it comes to NFP [natural family planning]."[12(pp 238–239)]

Robert Marshall, a state legislator from Virginia, stated that "Playboys, adolescent adult males are going to be the primary beneficiaries of this. I will suggest to you they may be the major purchasers of this, who in turn will sell it to high school kids that we're going to have to deal with the appropriations from the State of Virginia."[12(pp 162–164)] He also highlighted that he believed "this drug was never proven safe in the first place. . . . The FDA did not rely on any independent test conducted for safety or efficacy."[12(pp 162–164)] Speaking about doctors, he stated that "Perhaps this causes abortion and perhaps [some] of them have a conscience about this and don't want to be forced into this like they will be. . . . You all are doing a disservice, and you will disrespect the rights of women to be informed patients . . ."[12(pp 162–164)]

A Range of Issues for Proponents of Over-the-Counter Status and for Use without Age Restriction

Numerous stakeholders also spoke in support of levonorgestrel being available over the counter at the December 2003 meeting.[12]

Proponents unrelated to the FDA made the following points: Dr. Gretchen Stuart, on behalf of the National Family Planning and Reproductive Health Association, stated that because many clinics are closed nights and weekends, it makes it hard for people to get access to emergency contraception if it is not sold over the counter. She also reiterated the fact stated previously that "80% of all teen pregnancies are unintended and nearly 50% of teens are sexually active by the time they graduate high school."[12(pp 160–161)] She mentioned the "economic and social cost of unintended teen pregnancies are devastating: less than one-third finish high school leaving them unprepared for the job market and are likely to raise their kids in poverty."[12(pp 160–161)]

The American Medical Association stated that it would "work with the American College of Obstetricians and Gynecologists, Physicians for Reproductive Choice and Health, local and state medical societies, and other interested organizations to continue its efforts to increase access to emergency contraception, including further lobbying of the FDA and Congress to make emergency contraception available over-the-counter."[13(p2)]

The American Academy of Pediatrics press statement read that it "continues to support improved availability of emergency contraception to teens and young adults, including over-the-counter access and limiting the barriers to access placed by some healthcare providers and venues."[14(p 1032)]

The American Congress of Obstetricians and Gynecologists was among the organizations estimating that greater access to emergency contraceptives could reduce the U.S. unintended pregnancy and abortion rates. It also stated that "research released . . . supports the contention that the leadership of the federal Food and Drug Administration (FDA) shortchanged and underestimated women last year by failing to approve over-the-counter (OTC) status for the emergency contraceptive Plan B.[15(para1)]

The Advisory Committee Weighs In

The FDA advisory committee took a series of votes on questions posed by the FDA and voted unanimously that it is safe for emergency contraception to be available over the counter. Members also noted that Plan B has no potential for overdose or addiction. The committee also voted that Plan B met the requirements for over-the-counter use. In a vote recommending making a switch from prescription to OTC, the joint advisory committee supported this by a vote of 23–4.

FDA REGULATION AND PUBLIC HEALTH

Before discussing further specifics of what happened with Plan B, it is important to understand the role and usual processes for drug approval at the FDA.

The FDA works to oversee the safety of food, drugs, blood supply, vaccines, and medical devices and has a very broad public health mission to use its regulatory authority to protect the public's health. The standard review processes for approving a new prescription drug and for changing a drug from prescription status to over-the-counter status are outlined in Box 12-1.

It is important to note that typically, decisions are made by reviewers within the appropriate center at the FDA—in this case, the Center for Drug Evaluation and Research. Generally, neither the center director nor the commissioner of the FDA intervenes. Unless there is significant conflict based on scientific or medical issues that needs to be resolved at higher levels within the FDA, the authority to approve a switch to

BOX 12-1 FDA's Approval Process for a New Prescription Drug

1. Preclinical (animal) testing.
2. An investigational new drug application outlines what the sponsor of a new drug proposes for human testing in clinical trials.
3. Phase 1 studies (typically involve 20–80 people).
4. Phase 2 studies (typically involve a few dozen to about 300 people).
5. Phase 3 studies (typically involve several hundred to about 3,000 people).
6. The pre–new-drug-application period, just before a new drug application is submitted. This is a common time for the FDA and drug sponsors to meet.
7. Submission of a new drug application is the formal step asking the FDA to consider a drug for marketing approval.
8. The FDA reviews information that goes on a drug's professional labeling (information on how to use the drug) and how it can be marketed.
9. The FDA inspects the facilities where the drug will be manufactured as part of the approval process.
10. FDA reviewers will issue a decision.

Source: Food and Drug Administration. The FDA's drug review process: ensuring drugs are safe and effective. http://www.fda.gov/drugs/resourcesforyou/consumers/ucm143534.htm. Updated February 2010. Accessed November 1, 2010.

OTC status routinely rests with midlevel career scientific and medical FDA staff.

The FDA will authorize a prescription-to-OTC switch only after it is determined that the drug in question has met the certain FDA criteria outlined in Box 12-2.

The Role and Nature of the Advisory Committee

Advisory committees play a key role in making recommendations for actions to be taken by the FDA. A critical aspect of FDA advisory committees is that the meetings take place in an open and public forum. There are 48 committees and panels established by the FDA to obtain independent expert advice on a range of scientific, technical, and policy matters. They can be convened at the discretion of the FDA.

The FDA is charged with recruiting qualified experts with minimal conflicts of interest who are interested in serving on FDA advisory committees for fixed terms or as one-time consultants. Although the FDA is not bound to follow advisory committees' recommendations, it usually does. This is particularly true if FDA professional staff is in agreement with the advisory committee recommendations.

Role of the FDA's Office of Women's Health

The FDA Office of Women's Health mission statement is to "Protect and advance the health of women through policy, science, and outreach and to advocate for the participation of women in clinical trials and for sex, gender, and subpopulation analyses."[16] Within the organizational structure of FDA, the Office of Women's Health is within the Office of the Commissioner and not part of the review and formal decision process. However, as the face of women's health for FDA, the office and its director must explain and defend FDA actions to the public and to the medical and scientific communities. The situation that developed around approving Plan B as an OTC product created a profound challenge for the Office of Women's Health.

A SLOW REGULATORY PROCESS FOR PLAN B

In 2003, Plan B started the formal process to change its status from a prescription drug to being available over the counter. The approval process was long and took far more time than other drugs being considered for the same switch. Following is a time line of Plan B's nonapproval/partial approval through August 2005. Figure 12-5 shows the usual process for approval of an OTC switch and the Plan B actions taken by the FDA at different levels between 2003 and 2005.

Timeline of Events[17,18]

July 28, 1999: The FDA approved Plan B, an emergency contraceptive pill, for prescription use.

February 14, 2001: A citizens' petition was filed with the FDA on behalf of over 70 medical and public health organizations to make Plan B available over the counter.

April 21, 2003: Women's Capital Corporation (the product sponsor) filed an application with the FDA to make Plan B available without a prescription (OTC).

December 16, 2003: Members of the joint advisory committee voted 23–4 to recommend making a switch from prescription to OTC.

Late December 2003/January 2004: After a panel of FDA experts recommended approval of the Plan B application, Dr. Steven Galson, acting center director, informed his staff that the FDA's regular procedures would not be followed regarding Plan B's application to switch to OTC status, and the FDA joint advisory committee would not make the final decision. The decision would instead be made by the acting center director.[19]

May 6, 2004: The acting director of FDA's Center for Drug Evaluation and Research rejected the recommendations

---

BOX 12-2 FDA's Process to Switch a Prescription Drug to Over-the-Counter Status

1. It has an acceptable safety profile based on prescription use and experience.
2. It has a low potential to be abused.
3. It has an appropriate safety and therapeutic index.
4. It has a positive benefit-risk assessment.
5. It is needed for a condition or illness that is self-recognizable, self-limiting, and requires minimal intervention by a healthcare practitioner for treatment.

Source: Government Accountability Office, Food and Drug Administration. Decision process to deny initial application for over-the-counter marketing of the emergency contraceptive drug Plan B was unusual. GAO-06-109. http://www.gao.gov/new.items/d06109.pdf. Published November 2005. Accessed November 1, 2010.

FIGURE 12-5 Flow of an OTC switch application through the decision process within CDER for first-in-a-class drug.

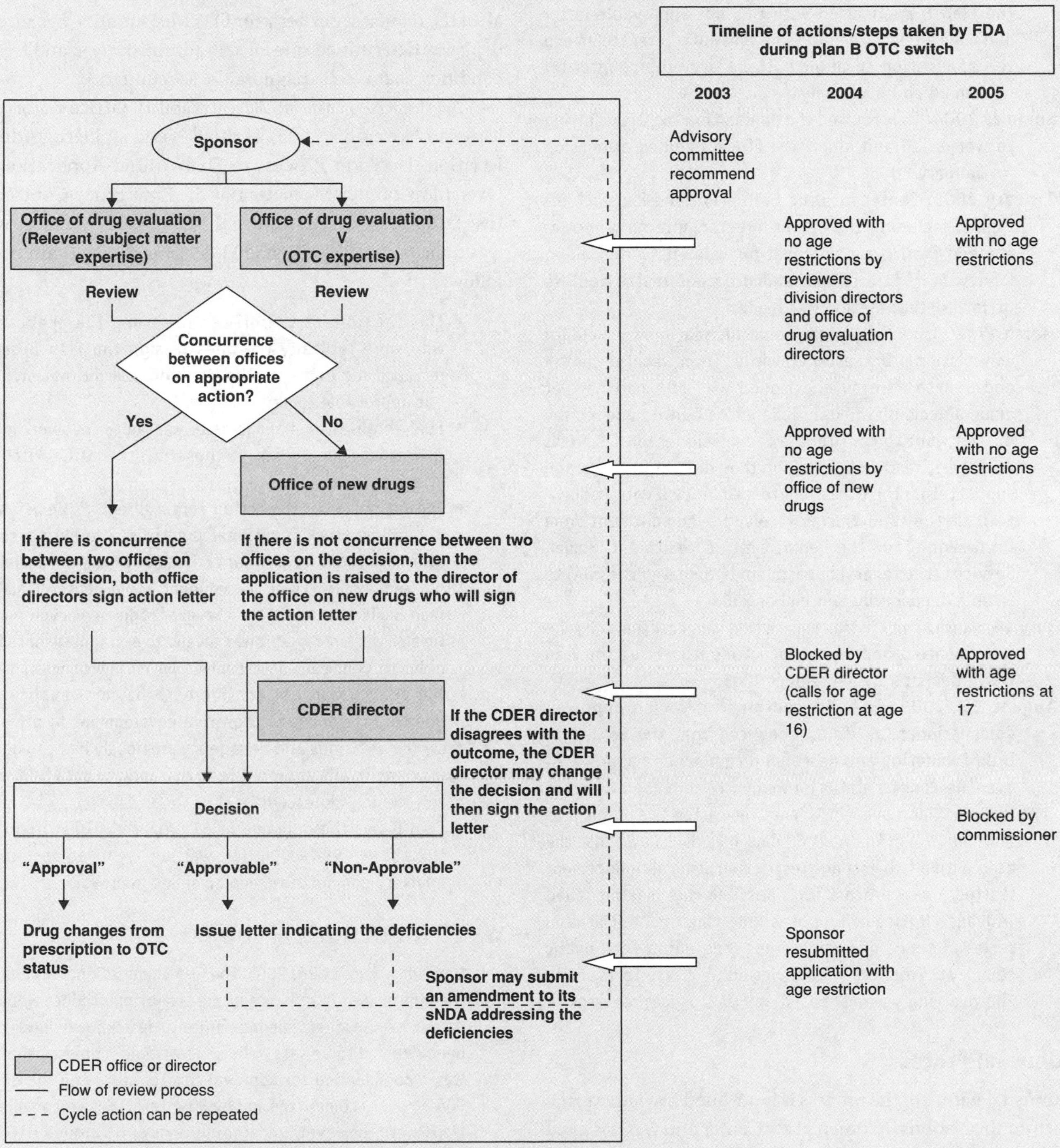

Timeline of actions/steps taken by FDA during plan B OTC switch

	2003	2004	2005
	Advisory committee recommend approval	Approved with no age restrictions by reviewers division directors and office of drug evaluation directors	Approved with no age restrictions
		Approved with no age restrictions by office of new drugs	Approved with no age restrictions
		Blocked by CDER director (calls for age restriction at age 16)	Approved with age restrictions at 17
			Blocked by commissioner
		Sponsor resubmitted application with age restriction	

Flowchart elements:

- **Sponsor**
- **Office of drug evaluation (Relevant subject matter expertise)** — Review
- **Office of drug evaluation V (OTC expertise)** — Review
- **Concurrence between offices on appropriate action?** — Yes / No
- **Office of new drugs**
- If there is concurrence between two offices on the decision, both office directors sign action letter
- If there is not concurrence between two offices on the decision, then the application is raised to the director of the office on new drugs who will sign the action letter
- **CDER director** — If the CDER director disagrees with the outcome, the CDER director may change the decision and will then sign the action letter
- **Decision** — "Approval" / "Approvable" / "Non-Approvable"
- Drug changes from prescription to OTC status
- Issue letter indicating the deficiencies
- Sponsor may submit an amendment to its sNDA addressing the deficiencies

Legend:
- CDER office or director
- Flow of review process
- Cycle action can be repeated

Source: Government Accountability Office, Food and Drug Administration. Decision process to deny initial application for over-the-counter marketing of the emergency contraceptive drug Plan B was unusual. GAO-06-109. November 2005. http://www.gao.gov/new.items/d06109.pdf. Published November 2005. Accessed November 1, 2010

of the joint advisory committee and lower ranking FDA review officials by signing the not-approvable letter for the Plan B OTC switch application.[20,21] The FDA denied the Plan B application with this not-approvable letter and advised Barr, the drug's new manufacturer,[i] to amend the application to allow it to be over the counter for women 16 and older only.

Summer 2004: Barr revised the application for OTC applying to women 16 and older; the FDA scheduled a decision for January 2005.

January 2005: Center for Drug Evaluation and Research officials, including the center director, internally recommended Plan B for approval for women 17 and older. Review staff still recommended no age restriction. No official determination was made.

March 17, 2005: A Senate confirmation hearing was held for Commissioner Dr. Lester Crawford. Then-Senator Clinton and Senator Murray questioned why FDA had not yet made a decision on Plan B. Senators Clinton and Murray did not want to confirm the commissioner until Plan B's status was resolved. Although they did not have enough support from the other senators to block a vote (filibuster), Clinton and Murray received a commitment from Dr. Crawford and the Department of Health and Human Services (the federal department overseeing the FDA) to issue a decision by September 2005.

July 18, 2005: Commissioner Crawford was confirmed by the U.S. Senate based on his commitment to issue the Plan B OTC decision by September 2005.

August 26, 2005: The FDA continued delaying approval. Commissioner Crawford announced that the Center for Drug Evaluation and Research recommended approval of over-the-counter status for women 17 and older. However, in a peculiar move, the agency requested the public provide input over the next 60 days on how to dispense the drug with a two-tier age restriction. This announcement started a new process for a possible rule making called "Advance Notice of Proposed Rule Making," initiating a series of time-consuming steps, beginning with public comment. This was widely viewed as a way to avoid an approval and was not based on FDA's usual processes.

An Unusual Process

The unusual nature of the process was outlined in a letter to the FDA from the National Women's Law Center and was cosigned by former FDA general counsels, who were quite familiar with the legal authority of the FDA and what was considered standard procedure. The letter discussed how the FDA routinely

changed the status of drugs from prescription to OTC without requiring a formal rule-making process (which was the case in this instance). The letter also noted the fact that Plan B met all of the regulatory criteria for OTC dispensation because the drug was determined safe for self-administration and treats a condition that is self-diagnosable, as required.[22]

A later Government Accountability Office report (released in November 2005), entitled "Food and Drug Administration: Decision Process to Deny Initial Application for Over-the-Counter Marketing of the Emergency Contraceptive Drug Plan B Was Unusual," discussed at length what was unusual in the earlier 2004 decision.[20] The main points follow:

- The directors of the offices reviewing the application, who were typically the ones to sign the Plan B action letter, disagreed with the decision and did not sign the not-approvable letter.
- FDA's high-level management was more involved in the review of Plan B than in those of other OTC switch applications.
- The rationale for the acting center director's decision did not follow FDA's traditional practices. The acting center director stated he was concerned about the potential behavioral implications for younger adolescents of making Plan B OTC because of their level of cognitive development. He also declared that it was invalid to extrapolate data from older to younger adolescents. FDA review officials noted the agency had not considered behavioral implications due to differences in cognitive development in prior OTC switch decisions and the agency previously had considered it scientifically appropriate to extrapolate data from older to younger adolescents.
- Plan B was the only one of 67 proposed OTC switch decisions from 1994–2004 that was not approved despite the advisory committee's recommended approval.

WHAT SHOULD DR. WOOD DO?

On Friday, August 26, 2005, the FDA commissioner announced the approval of Plan B as a nonprescription product would be delayed again, this time indefinitely. He acknowledged it had been deemed to be safe to be used without a prescription and was recommended for approval for OTC status by the expert FDA advisory committee and by FDA staff. These recommendations were, however, undergoing review. He argued OTC Plan B was a unique situation since the same product would be available by prescription only for some consumers (women under 17), and without prescription for all other women, and that this tiered approval approach required a new process of review. Meanwhile, no one would have access to Plan B without a prescription.

---

[i] Barr purchased Plan B from Women's Capital Corporation in February 2004.

Dr. Susan Wood, the director of the FDA's Office of Women's Health, has been faced with a product that clearly benefits women being blocked indefinitely from over-the-counter access due to unusual FDA processes. Plan B approval has been repeatedly denied by the FDA to go to over-the-counter status in contradiction of the medical evidence and the typical FDA process and to the detriment of women's health. The Office of Women's Health has not been directly involved in the review and approval process, nor in the discussions or decision making of the FDA leadership, yet it has closely monitored the progress of the Plan B review. Dr. Wood believes that FDA has acted against the scientific evidence, and she must decide what to do.

Questions to Consider

1. Should the FDA be able to make exceptions to the standard drug-approval process? If so, what issues should the FDA consider in deciding whether an exception should be made?

2. How do you think the public would be affected if drugs with safety concerns—for example, acetaminophen—were available only with a prescription?

3. Should additional data be required for young teenage girls (of reproductive potential) for this or other over-the-counter products? Should emergency contraception be considered different from other contraceptive products or other over-the-counter products generally?

4. What should the director of the Office of Women's Health do in this situation?

About the Authors

Dr. Susan F. Wood is Associate Professor of Health Policy and of Environmental and Occupational Health at The George Washington University School of Public Health and Health Services. She is also the Executive Director of the Jacobs Institute of Women's Health and works with the School's Project on Scientific Knowledge and Public Policy. Professor Wood has dedicated her career to applying scientific evidence to health policy decision making. She joined the School from the FDA, where she was Assistant Commissioner for Women's Health and Director of the Office of Women's Health until 2005, when she resigned on principle over the continued delay in approving emergency over-the-counter contraception. A long-time champion of women's health, Dr. Wood previously served as Director for Policy and Program Development at the U.S. Department of Health and Human Services' Office on Women's Health. Prior to joining DHHS, Dr. Wood was Science Advisor and then Deputy Director of the Congressional Caucus for Women's Issues. In that capacity, she was directly involved with policy initiatives and legislative proposals designed to advance biomedical research, women's health, family planning and health care reform. Professor Wood has been honored with the FDA Commissioner's Special Citation (2204), the DHHS Secretary's Distinguished Service Award (2003) and the Keystone Award in Women's Health Research (2000), among other awards. She is also Adjunct Associate Professor in American University's School of Public Affairs, where she teaches women's health policy.

Alison M. Miller received her Master of Public Health with a concentration in health policy from The George Washington University School of Public Health and Health Services in 2009. She has worked with the Jacobs Institute of Women's Health since 2008 and enjoys working on women's health issues. Alison's other passion is children's health. She interned with Maternal and Child Health Bureau at the Health Resources and Services Administration in 2009. Prior to coming to The George Washington University, she worked as the public policy associate at Girls Inc.

REFERENCES

1. Finer LB, Henshaw SK. Disparities in rates of unintended pregnancy in the United States, 1994 and 2001. *Perspect Sex Reprod Health.* 2006;38(2):90–96.

2. Gold RB, Sonfield A, Richards CL, Frost JJ. *Next Steps for America's Family Planning Program: Leveraging the Potential of Medicaid and Title X in an Evolving Health Care System.* New York, NY: Guttmacher Institute; 2009. www.guttmacher.org/pubs/NextSteps.pdf. Accessed November 1, 2010.

3. Centers for Disease Control and Prevention. Abortion surveillance—United States, 2005. *MMWR Surveill Summ.* 2008;57(SS13):1–32. http://www.cdc.gov/mmwr/preview/mmwrhtml/ss5713a1.htm?s_cid=ss5713a1_e. Accessed November 1, 2010.

4. Abma JC, Martinez GM, Mosher WD, Dawson BS. Teenagers in the United States: Sexual activity, contraceptive use, and childbearing. *Vital Health Stat.* 2004;23(24).

5. Centers for Disease Control and Prevention. Teen birth rates rose again in 2007, declined in 2008. http://www.cdc.gov/Features/dsTeenPregnancy/. Updated May 5, 2010. Accessed November 1, 2010.

6. Trussell J, Stewart F, Guest F, Hatcher R. Emergency contraceptive pills: a simple proposal to reduce unintended pregnancies. *Fam Plann Perspect.* 1992;24(6):269.

7. *HHS, Office on Women's Health.* Emergency contraception (emergency birth control); frequently asked questions. http://www.womenshealth.gov/faq/emergency-contraception.cfm. Updated 2009. Accessed November 1, 2010.

8. Davidoff F, Trussell J. Plan B and the politics of doubt. *JAMA.* 2006;296(14):1775–1778.

9. Boonstra H. Emergency Contraception: The Need to Increase Public Awareness. The Guttmacher Report on Public Policy, 2002, 5(4):3–6. http://www.guttmacher.org/pubs/tgr/05/4/gr050403.html. Accessed March 27, 2011.

10. Moreau C, Bajos N, Trussell J. The impact of pharmacy access to emergency contraceptive pills in France. *Contraception.* 2006;73:602–608.

11. Murray, Clinton declare victory in fight over Plan B: decision on over-the-counter sales of emergency contraceptives will be made by September 1 [news release]. Washington, DC: U.S. Senator Patty Murray; July 15, 2005. http://murray.senate.gov/public/index.cfm?p=NewsReleases&ContentRecord_id=6cb57b61-b7d8-47ef-ad83-99e277dd64e4&ContentType_id=0b98dc1b-dd08-4df2-adac-21f6ae03beed&Group_id=97a054dd-8a74-4cd0-8771-fbc3be733874&YearDisplay=2005. Accessed November 1, 2010.

12. United States of America Food and Drug Administration Center for Drug Evaluation and Research. Nonprescription Drugs Advisory Committee (NDAC) in joint session with the Advisory Committee for Reproductive Health Drugs (ARCHD). [meeting transcript]. Gaithersburg, MD; December 16, 2003. www.fda.gov/ohrms/dockets/ac/03/transcripts/4015T1.htm. Accessed November 1, 2010.

13. American Medical Association House of Delegates. Resolution 443: FDA rejection of over-the-counter status for emergency contraception pills [memo to Reference Committee D]. www.ama-assn.org/ama1/pub/upload/mm/15/res_hod443_a04.doc. Accessed November 1, 2010.

14. American Academy of Pediatrics. Policy statement: organizational principles to guide and define the child health care system and/or improve the health of all children; Committee on Adolescence; Emergency Contraception. *Pediatrics.* 2005;116(4):1026–1035.

15. Statement of Vivian M. Dickerson, MD, President on *JAMA* Emergency Contraception study [news release]. Washington, DC: The American College of Obstetricians and Gynecologists; January 5, 2005. http://www.acog.org/from_home/publications/press_releases/nr01-05-05.cfm. Accessed November 1, 2010.

16. Food and Drug Administration. About FDA: Office of Women's Health. http://www.fda.gov/AboutFDA/CentersOffices/OC/OfficeofWomensHealth/default.htm. Updated April 2010. Accessed November 1, 2010.

17. Center for Reproductive Rights. Emergency contraception timeline—the fight for emergency contraception: every second counts. http://reproductiverights.org/en/emergency-contraception-timeline. Accessed November 1, 2010.

18. Wood SF. Women's health and the FDA. *N Engl J Med.* 2005;353(16):1650–1651.

19. *Tummino et al. v. von Eschenbach* [John Jenkins deposition]; June 2006. U.S. District Court, Eastern District of New York. Retrieved from http://reproductiverights.org/sites/crr.civicactions.net/files/documents/JenkinsFullDeposition6.21.pdf. Accessed November 1, 2010.

20. Government Accountability Office, Food and Drug Administration. Decision process to deny initial application for over-the-counter marketing of the emergency contraceptive drug Plan B was unusual. GAO-06-109. http://www.gao.gov/new.items/d06109.pdf. Published November 2005. Accessed November 1, 2010.

21. Department of Health and Human Services. Non-approval letter NDA 21-045/S-011 to Barr Research Inc.; May 6, 2004. www.fda.gov/downloads/Drugs/DrugSafety/.../ucm109793.pdf. Accessed November 1, 2010.

22. FDA Dockets Management. National Women's Law Center Comment on Docket No. 2005N-0345; October 2005. http://www.fda.gov/ohrms/dockets/dockets/05n0345/05n-0345-c000383-vol27.pdf. Accessed March 28, 2011.

Implementing Policy Changes to Decrease Racial and Ethnic Disparities in Pediatric Asthma Outcomes

ANNE ROSSIER MARKUS AND SHAVON ARTIS

Alex, a 12-year-old from Englewood, Chicago, Illinois, has asthma. His mother, Michelle, has spent the last decade looking for answers to keep her son's asthma attacks at bay. Alex's hacking cough has triggered multiple asthma attacks that have sent Michelle rushing to the emergency room with Alex six times over a recent 12-month period. These hospital runs meant many missed classes and school days; Alex has been falling behind. Michelle has shuttled him back and forth to multiple doctors, followed their orders, and agreed to have her son try multiple treatment regimens. Yet, asthma flare-ups have remained frequent. Michelle has often felt alone, overwhelmed, and filled with unanswered questions.

One day in Fall 2010, the cell phone rang while Michelle was at work, 45 minutes away from where Alex went to school. On the other end of the line was an emergency medical technician who told her, "Alex has been admitted to the hospital after being revived with CPR; he just had a life-threatening asthma attack."

Rushing to the hospital, dreadful thoughts rushed into Michelle's mind. But once she arrived at the hospital and found Alex recovering, the terrifying experience became a learning opportunity, leading Michelle and Alex to an innovative asthma program. The program, a hospital-community partnership, takes a comprehensive approach to managing asthma, including home health assessments, tailored education, and goal setting.

African Americans have the highest rates of asthma death in the United States, and Illinois has the nation's highest African American asthma death rate. Within Chicago, the asthma-related hospitalizations in the nearly 100% African American Englewood neighborhood are double the city's average. When an entire community is shouldering such a heavy burden of a complex, chronic disease like asthma, it takes more than educating families about asthma to conquer the disease; it must be a collaborative effort.

IMPROVING CHILDHOOD ASTHMA OUTCOMES: POLICY RECOMMENDATIONS UNHEEDED

Alex's aunt is the senior policy analyst for the President's Task Force on Environmental Health Risks and Safety Risks to Children. The task force was originally established in April 1997 under President Clinton by Executive Order 13045, renewed twice during President Bush's administration until 2005, and just revived in 2010 under President Obama, following the release of an evidence-based policy report entitled, *Changing pO₂licy: The Elements for Improving Childhood Asthma Outcomes.*[1] This policy report recommended, among other things, the creation of a Department of Health and Human Services–led, cross-agency, administration-wide national plan for changing childhood asthma outcomes and coordinating existing and new programs and policies that directly affect children with asthma. The task force, a collaborative effort, is cochaired by the secretary of the Department of Health and Human Services and the administrator of the Environmental Protection Agency and includes representatives from 16 departments and White House offices (see Box 13-1).

BOX 13-1 Members of the President's Task Force on Environmental Health Risks and Safety Risks to Children

- Secretary of education
- Secretary of labor
- Attorney general
- Secretary of energy
- Secretary of housing and urban development
- Secretary of agriculture
- Secretary of transportation
- Director of the Office of Management and Budget
- Chair of the Council on Environmental Quality
- Chair of the Consumer Product Safety Commission
- Assistant to the president for economic policy
- Assistant to the president for domestic policy
- Assistant to the president and director of the Office of Science and Technology Policy
- Chair of the Council of Economic Advisers
- Other officials of executive departments and agencies as the president may, from time to time, designate

The task force initially identified asthma as one of four priority areas for immediate attention. In 1999, the task force wrote *Asthma and the Environment—A Strategy to Protect Children* to further understand how environmental factors relate to the onset of asthma and triggers of asthma attacks.[2] In this strategic document, it recommended the:

- Strengthening and acceleration of focused research into the environmental factors that cause or worsen childhood asthma.
- Implementation of public health programs that improve the use of scientific knowledge to prevent and reduce the severity of asthma symptoms by reducing environmental exposures.
- Establishment of a coordinated nationwide asthma surveillance system for collecting, analyzing, and disseminating health outcome and risk factor data at the state, regional, and local levels.
- Identification of the reasons for and elimination of the disproportionate burden of asthma among dif-

ferent racial and ethnic groups and those living in poverty.

Eleven years later, the *Changing pO$_2$licy* report found the majority of the task force's recommendations had yet to be implemented. As a result, the administration set the task force in motion again and established a subcommittee on asthma disparities to consider the recommendations of the evidence-based policy report, particularly which ones to follow and how best to implement them. In addition, the task force considered the context set by health reform legislation passed by Congress and signed by President Obama. Enacted on March 23, 2010, the Patient Protection and Affordable Care Act called for the restructuring of health insurance markets, significant expansions of insurance coverage, and reform in provider payment and service delivery systems, and it established a number of new national pilot programs to improve performance of the health system. Many provisions of the new law had implications for the coverage of children with asthma and the performance of the system in providing high-quality care to these children, which was also raised in the report.[1]

Since much had changed since 1999, the task force had to map out a new strategy. To begin, members set out to answer the following questions framed around three essential areas—describing the health problem, describing possible solutions, and laying out recommendations:

- What are the key risk factors that trigger asthma and hinder proper management of the condition?
- What are the existing programs and policies that can be leveraged to improve childhood asthma treatment and management?
- What are the existing programs and policies that can be amended to improve childhood asthma treatment and management?
- What will be the impact of comprehensive health reform on existing strategies for improving childhood asthma treatment and management? What are the new opportunities presented by health reform?
- What recommendations can be made to reduce the overall burden of asthma and racial and ethnic disparities, and in particular, disparities in access to effective treatment and health outcomes?

ASTHMA IS PREVALENT AND COSTLY, YET MANY ADVERSE OUTCOMES CAN BE PREVENTED AND UNNECESSARY COSTS AVOIDED

Asthma is a chronic lung disease that affects people of all ages, but often begins in childhood. It can impose serious limitations on the normal activities of childhood and can lead to death if not treated and managed properly. However, appropriate treatment and management can control symptoms and allow those with the disease to be able to continue to enjoy healthy, active lives. According to data drawn from the National Health Interview Survey and the Medical Expenditures Panel Survey, asthma is the most common chronic condition among children. In 2008, 1 in every 7 (10.2 million) U.S. children had lifetime asthma and 1 in 11 children (6.95 million) had current asthma.[3]

Asthma is not only common among children, but it is costly. Asthma adds about 50 cents to every healthcare dollar spent on children with asthma compared to children without asthma. In 2006, the average total healthcare expenditures for children with asthma were $1,906 compared to $1,263 for children who were not diagnosed with asthma.[4]

Unfortunately, the presence of asthma is growing. The percentage of children ever being diagnosed with asthma increased from 11.4% in 1997 to 13.5% in 2006.[5]

Asthma appears to be equally prevalent in children living in rural and urban areas. However, low-income and minority children bear the heaviest burden of asthma and its consequences. One in three children living with asthma is poor, and 60% have family incomes below twice the federal poverty level.[1,6] African American and Hispanic children receive about half as much outpatient care and medication management as white children.[4] Death from asthma is nearly seven times higher among African American children compared to white children. Minority children have more missed days of school or work, higher rates of hospitalizations, emergency room visits, and elevated risks for mortality.[7]

An estimated 9% of all the children living with asthma remain completely uninsured.[5,6] The evidence shows that uninsured children with asthma receive fewer office and outpatient visits, prescriptions, and preventive checkups than publicly insured children.[5,6] Even where access exists, care may be clinically incomplete and inadequate. It has been estimated that fewer than 50% of children with asthma receive quality care.[8]

Asthma Risk: A Constellation of Factors

Asthma is the result of many factors, some of which can be controlled, some of which cannot be. Among children, certain immutable characteristics, such as gender and genetic predisposition, seem to be predictors of asthma. A history of allergies also appears to be a predictor. For children with these risk factors, paying attention to controllable risks may be especially important.

A major body of research into the effective management and treatment of asthma underscored four major risk factors that can be controlled or changed through intervention. They are:

1. Inadequate access to appropriate, high-quality health care and case management
2. A failure to address the indoor air environment and other indoor asthma triggers and outdoor environmental triggers that affect communities in which children live and grow
3. The absence of a means for monitoring asthma prevalence and treatment in order to effectively deploy resources at the local level
4. A coordinated research strategy

Inadequate Access and Case Management

Experts from the National Heart, Lung, and Blood Institute/National Asthma Education and Prevention Program presented comprehensive recommendations on clinical practice standards that built on the best evidence. But the current national system performance standards failed to capture many of these recommended clinical standards (see Table 13-1), particularly asthma education, case management, and environmental remediation. Neither the National Heart, Lung, and Blood Institute/National Asthma Education and Prevention Program clinical practice guidelines nor the system performance measures captured providers' ability to use health information technology in practice, to exchange data with other clinical providers and healthcare entities, to exchange data with school systems and other community programs serving children with asthma, or to report treatment and management data to payers or public health agencies. None of the available measures could assess the effectiveness of reporting from ambulatory care settings into a public health registry or the effectiveness of reporting between a public health registry and payers.

A Failure to Address the Environment and Asthma Triggers

The data showed exposure to cigarette smoke, other irritants (such as strong odors and nitrogen dioxide), and certain indoor allergens (dust mites, pets, cockroaches) increase children's risk of developing or losing control of asthma.

The Absence of a Means for Monitoring Asthma Prevalence and Treatment

An effective system has never existed for monitoring the prevalence of asthma at the national, state, and community levels and for gauging the availability of effectiveness of treatment and its outcome on child health. A systematic approach

TABLE 13-1 Recommended Clinical Standards Compared to Performance Measures for Asthma[1]

Asthma Categories	Clinical Standards	Performance Measures	
	NAEPP EPR3 Guidelines for the Diagnosis & Management of Asthma	National Quality Forum Measures	CHIPRA Children's Health Quality Core Measures, AHRQ
Asthma Measurement	Yes	Yes[1]	No
Asthma Management: Asthma Education	Yes	No	No
Written Action Plans	Yes	Yes[2,3]	Yes[4,5]
Case Management	Yes	No	No
Management of Co-morbid Conditions	Yes	No	Yes[6]
Environmental Remediation	Yes	No	No
Appropriate Medication	Yes	Yes[7–10]	Yes[11–13]
Hospitalizations & Use of ED	No	Yes[14]	Yes[15,16]

[1] Asthma Assessment—Percentage of patients who were evaluated during at least one office visit for the frequency (numeric) of daytime and nocturnal asthma symptoms

[2] Management plan for people with asthma—Percentage of patients for whom there is documentation that a written management plan was provided either to the patient or the patient's caregiver or at a minimum, specific written instructions on under what conditions the patient's doctor should be contacted or the patient should go to the emergency room

[3] Home Management Plan of Care Document Given to Patient/Caregiver—Documentation exists that the Home Management Plan of Care (HMPC) as a separate document, specific to the patient, was given to the patient/caregiver, prior to or upon discharge.

[4] From 3rd round of measures that did not meet thresholds for Delphi II scoring, CHIPRA Children's Healthcare Quality Measures, AHRQ: Percentage of patients for whom there is documentation of a written asthma action management plan was provided either to the patient or the patient's caregiver OR, at a minimum, specific written instructions on under what conditions the patient's doctor should be contacted or the patient should go to the emergency room

[5] AHRQ, Joint Commission only measure: Children's asthma care: percent of pediatric asthma inpatients with documentation that they or their caregivers were given a Home Management Plan of Care (HMPC) document

[6] From 2nd round of measures that passed Delphi II but not recommended, CHIPRA Children's Healthcare Quality Measures, AHRQ: Annual influenza vaccination (all children and adolescents diagnosed with asthma)

[7] Suboptimal Asthma Control (SAC) and Absence of Controller Therapy (ACT)—Rate 1: The percentage of patients with persistent asthma who were dispensed more than 5 canisters of a short-acting beta2 agonist inhaler during the same three-month period. Rate 2: The percentage of patients with persistent asthma during the measurement year who were dispensed more than five canisters of short-acting beta2 agonist inhalers over a 90 day period and who did not receive controller therapy during the same 90-day period.

[8] Use of Appropriate Medications for People with Asthma—Percent of patients who were identified as having persistent asthma during the measurement year and the year prior to the measurement year and who were dispensed a prescription for either an inhaled corticosteroid or acceptable alternative medication during the measurement year

[9] Asthma Pharmacologic Therapy—Percent of all patients with mild, moderate, or severe persistent asthma who were prescribed either the preferred long-term control medication (inhaled corticosteroid) or an acceptable alternative

[10] Use of Systemic Corticosteroids for Inpatient Asthma—Percentage of pediatric asthma inpatients (age 2–17 years) who were discharged with principle diagnosis of asthma who received systemic corticosteroids for inpatient asthma.

[11] From 2nd round of measures that passed Delphi II but not recommended, CHIPRA Children's Healthcare Quality Measures, AHRQ: Use of appropriate medications for people 5–20 years of age with Asthma-Average number of member controller months

[12] AHRQ, Joint Commission only measure: Children's asthma care: percent of pediatric inpatients who receive systemic corticosteroids during hospitalizations

[13] AHRQ, Joint Commission only measure: Children's asthma care: percent of pediatric asthma inpatients who received relievers during hospitalization

[14] Use of Relievers for Inpatient Asthma—Percentage of pediatric asthma inpatients, age 2–17, who were discharged with a principal diagnosis of asthma who received relievers for inpatient asthma

[15] Annual number of asthma patients (> 1 year old) with > 1 asthma-related ER visit

[16] From 2nd round of measures that passed Delphi II but not recommended, CHIPRA Children's Healthcare Quality Measures, AHRQ: Annual number of asthma patients (> 1 year old) with > 1 asthma-related hospitalization

Source: Markus A, Lyon M, Rosenbaum S. *Changing pO₂licy: The Elements for Improving Childhood Asthma Outcomes.* Washington, DC: The George Washington University School of Public Health and Health Services. http://www.mcanonline.org/policy_issues/index.html. Revised March 10, 2010. Accessed November 1, 2010.

to asthma monitoring that captured asthma prevalence information was also absent.

A Coordinated Research Strategy

Despite the disproportionately large number of funded asthma studies and numerous agencies involved in asthma research, there was no single unified research agenda, though, as of 2010, research and policy initiatives that address childhood asthma existed at Health and Human Services, Department of Housing and Urban Development (HUD), Environmental Protection Agency, and the Department of Education.

Childhood asthma is a serious and chronic health issue that affects many U.S. children like Alex and their families, compromising their health and quality of life and placing a heavy financial burden on families as well as an enormous strain on the healthcare system. Treating, managing, and ultimately preventing and reducing the burden of asthma represents a critical test of the ability of the U.S. health system—health insurers, clinical care providers, and public health agencies—to work together.

TURNING KNOWLEDGE INTO STRATEGY

From the evidence base of in-depth research into the effective management and treatment of asthma, the task force knew the factors that could be controlled or changed through intervention.

At a minimum, elements for improving childhood asthma outcomes included the following:

- Stable and continuous health insurance
- High-quality clinical care, case management, and asthma education available for all children, including those who remain ineligible for insurance coverage
- Ability to continuously exchange information and monitor progress, using as much health information technology as possible
- Reduction of asthma triggers in homes and communities
- Learning what works and increasing knowledge

Since asthma is disproportionately concentrated among lower income children, Medicaid and the Children's Health Insurance Program were particularly key. As of 2009, 29 million children were enrolled in Medicaid and 7 million in the Children's Health Insurance Program. The Children's Health Insurance Program Reauthorization Act of 2009 provided enhanced funding to permit coverage of children in families with incomes up to 300% of the federal poverty level, while providing federal assistance at regular Medicaid matching rates in states that elect to extend coverage still further. Of this number, an estimated 180,000 would be previously uninsured children with asthma. The Children's Health Insurance Program Reauthorization Act allowed states to reach all financially eligible, legally resident children during the first 5 years of their U.S. residency. The Children's Health Insurance Program Reauthorization Act further simplified citizenship documentation requirements and provided bonus payments to states whose enrollment and retention efforts produced enrollment levels that exceeded their target rates. Full implementation of these reforms could help reach the nearly 600,000 children with asthma who were eligible for coverage in 2010 but remained unenrolled. The reauthorization also provided $100 million in outreach funds, established a multiyear clinical quality improvement initiative, and contained demonstration funding to improve the use of health information technology.[9]

The quality of the clinical care available to children with asthma is critical. In Fall 2010, the elements of recommended clinical practice in the case of pediatric asthma based on the latest National Heart, Lung, and Blood Institute/National Asthma Education and Prevention Program guidelines boiled down to a key imperative: a medical home with skilled and knowledgeable healthcare professionals who, acting as a team, continuously monitored a child's health status over time and managed the medications crucial to improved long-term lung function (not merely episodic management of attacks).[10,11] Furthermore, healthcare professionals had to be able to effectively communicate to children and families at an appropriate literacy level (including having easily comprehensible health education materials and written asthma action plans), so that families were armed with the knowledge and information they need to reduce risks and manage their children's condition. In addition to effective communication with families, health professionals had to be able to communicate with each other in the treatment and management of asthma, through the appropriate and efficient use of health information technology.

Some families whose children had asthma were able to put knowledge into practice on their own. Other families, whose children might be at the highest risk, also faced added barriers of poverty, family stress, and other factors that could limit their ability to turn knowledge into action. For these families, the healthcare system needed to be able to support them outside of the office practice and in community settings through home visits and case management supports.

Knowing which communities experience a particularly great burden of asthma and the number of children receiving effective treatment, tracking serious incidents, such as the hospitalization or death of a child from asthma, and having the information needed to deploy community prevention resources are the hallmarks of an effective and engaged public health system. An additional critical role for public health is translating evidence into information regarding asthma's prevalence and impact in order to provide the evidence base for community-wide interventions aimed at reducing environmental risks, such as vehicle emissions (including idling around schools), pesticide control, environmental tobacco smoke, and pest management for housing units. With nationwide adoption of such a registry system would come far better knowledge about the prevalence of asthma and the quality of treatment.

Because asthma can be initially triggered or retriggered by many environmental factors, their removal from a child's home environment is essential.[12] Seminal National Institutes of Health–funded, multisite, randomized, controlled, intervention research studies published in the late 1990s and early 2000s[13–20] yielded important insight into the role of integrated pest management and other cleaning strategies to reduce triggers and control asthma symptoms in the home. A growing body of evidence suggested that interventions designed to improve the environments where children played and lived could help decrease asthma morbidity.[13–20]

UPDATING THE NATIONAL STRATEGY

With this information in hand, task force members were faced with updating their strategy. The senior policy analyst on the task force reflected on how effective her nephew's comprehensive hospital-community asthma management program was in helping him to gain and keep control of his asthma. She was able to describe to the members that the program consisted of the following:

- Case management (by nurses) for children with excessive absences and/or emergency department use; children are linked with asthma care provider either through free clinic or asthma-mobile
- Children in case management assisted in enrolling in state insurance program
- Collaboration with partners to deliver provider education
- Enforcement of self-management skills for children and improvement of knowledge amongst school staff
- Work to promote asthma management activities in other school districts
- Pilot age-appropriate asthma curricula aligned with health education standards for the state in elementary/middle/high schools
- Implementation of tools for schools and education about the state's integrated pest management service
- Participation and attendance at local asthma coalition meetings and events and presentations and dissemination of educational materials at local health fairs

- In-home assessments, education and environmental mitigation by nurse case managers, distribution of mattress/pillow covers and referrals for other services (smoking cessation, low interest home improvement loans)
- Collaborations with community and government agencies to educate about safe indoor air quality
- Establishment of a case-management tracking system that captures ethnic and socioeconomic status information and other data such as emergency room visits and days of school missed
- Identification of culturally and linguistically appropriate asthma materials

In order to produce their strategic document, task force members needed to answer the following key questions:

- What are the key risk factors that trigger asthma and hinder proper management of the condition today?
- What are the existing programs that can be used or amended to improve childhood asthma treatment and management?
- What policies can be developed to facilitate the implementation of these existing programs?
- What has been the impact of comprehensive health reform so far on existing strategies for improving childhood asthma treatment and management, and what are new opportunities presented by other recent reforms?
- What recommendations can be made to reduce the overall burden of asthma and racial and ethnic disparities—in particular, pertaining to access to effective treatment and health outcomes?

About the Authors

Anne Rossier Markus, JD, PhD, MHS, is associate professor in the Department of Health Policy at The George Washington University School of Public Health and Health Services, where she teaches and researches topics related to the financing and organization of health care and access to quality care, with a particular emphasis on health reform, managed care, Medicaid/Children's Health Insurance Program, health centers, and how they address the needs of women and children, including those with special needs. Prior to joining the department, she was a research associate at the university's Intergovernmental Health Policy Project, where she tracked, researched, and analyzed healthcare legislation and issues on healthcare reform, managed care, access to care, and bioethics. Previously, she worked for the Washington (National) Business Group on Health, a national organization of Fortune 500 employers that has worked to restructure healthcare financing and delivery since 1974. Dr. Markus holds a law degree from the University of Lausanne School of Law in Switzerland, a master's degree in health policy from the Johns Hopkins University School of Hygiene and Public Health, and a PhD in public policy from The George Washington University Columbian College and Graduate School of Arts and Sciences. Dr. Markus was the lead author of the evidence-based policy report entitled, *Changing pO$_2$licy: The Elements for Improving Childhood Asthma Outcomes.*

Shavon Artis, MPH, is a doctor of public health candidate in the Department of Health Policy at The George Washington University. She has 10 years of experience in developing and implementing health promotion/disease prevention programs. She has developed and conducted health programs to improve the health of women, children, and minority communities, developed culturally tailored health education materials for national health promotion programs, developed and conducted training workshops for communities and health professionals, and has produced health policy reports for senior government health officials. In her current position as a public health analyst at the Eunice Kennedy Shriver National Institute of Child Health and Human Development at the National Institutes of Health in Bethesda, Maryland, she oversees and directs the Back to Sleep campaign, a national outreach effort to reduce infant deaths from sudden infant death syndrome. She is responsible for carrying out a plan for building strategic partnerships and conducting focused outreach to promote the campaign and other health initiatives across the country.

REFERENCES

1. Markus A, Lyon M, Rosenbaum S. *Changing pO₂licy: The Elements for Improving Childhood Asthma Outcomes*. Washington, DC: George Washington University School of Public Health and Health Services. Available at: http://www.mcanonline.org/policy_issues/index.html. Revised March 10, 2010. Accessed November 1, 2010.

2. President's Task Force on Environmental Health Risks and Safety Risks to Children. Asthma and the environment: a strategy to protect children. January 28, 1999. www.aspe.hhs.gov/sp/asthma/appxd.pdf. Revised May 2000. Accessed November 1, 2010.

3. Bloom B, Cohen RA, Freeman G. Summary health statistics for US children: National Health Interview Survey, 2008. *Vital Health Stat.* 2009;10(244). www.cdc.gov/nchs/data/series/sr_10/sr10_244.pdf. Accessed November 1, 2010.

4. Dor A, Richard P, Tan E. Analysis of 2008 MEPS data. In: Markus, A., Lyon, M., Rosenbaum S, ed. *Changing pO₂licy: The Elements for Improving Childhood Asthma Outcomes*. Washington, DC: George Washington University School of Public Health and Health Services; 2010. http://www.mcanonline.org/policy_issues/index.html. Accessed November 1, 2010.

5. Centers for Disease Control and Prevention. Asthma: data and surveillance—National Health Interview Survey (NHIS) data, lifetime and current asthma, 2006. http://www.cdc.gov/asthma/nhis/06/data.htm. Accessed March 27, 2011.

6. Kim H, Kieckhefer GM, Greek AA, Joesch JM, Baydar N. Health care utilization by children with asthma. *Prev Chronic Dis.* 2009;6(1). http://www.cdc.gov/pcd/issues/2009/jan/07_0199.htm. Accessed November 1, 2010.

7. Leiu TA, Lozano P, Finkelstein JA, et al. Racial/ethnic variation in asthma status and management practices among children in managed Medicaid. *Pediatrics.* 2002;109:857–865. http://pediatrics.aappublications.org/cgi/content/abstract/109/5/857. Accessed November 1, 2010.

8. Mangione-Smith R, DeCristofaro A, Setodji C, et al. The quality of ambulatory care delivered to children in the United States. *N Engl J Med.* 2007;357(15):1515–1523.

9. Kaiser Family Foundation. *Children's Health Insurance Program Reauthorization Act of 2009 (CHIPRA) Fact Sheet*. Washington, DC: Author; February 2009. http://www.kff.org/medicaid/upload/7863.pdf. Accessed November 1, 2010.

10. U.S. Department of Health and Human Services. Expert panel report 3 summary report 2007: guidelines for the diagnosis and management of asthma. http://www.nhlbi.nih.gov/guidelines/asthma/asthgdln.htm. Accessed November 1, 2010.

11. U.S. Department of Health and Human Services. Expert panel report 3 full report 2007: guidelines for the diagnosis and management of asthma http://www.nhlbi.nih.gov/guidelines/asthma/asthgdln.htm. Accessed November 1, 2010.

12. Institute of Medicine. *Clearing the Air: Asthma and Indoor Exposures*. Washington, DC: National Academy Press; 2000. http://books.nap.edu/openbook.php?record_id=9610. Accessed November 1, 2010.

13. Kattan M, Mitchell H, Eggleston P, et al. Characteristics of inner-city children with asthma: the National Cooperative Inner-City Asthma Study. *Pediatr Pulmonol.* 1997;24(4):253–262.

14. Evans R 3rd, Gergen PJ, Mitchell H, et al. A randomized clinical trial to reduce asthma morbidity among inner-city children: results of the National Cooperative Inner-City Asthma Study. *J Pediatr.* 1999;135(3):332–338.

15. Crain EF, Walter M, O'Connor GT, et al. Home and allergic characteristics of children with asthma in seven U.S. urban communities and design of an environmental intervention: the Inner-City Asthma Study. *Environ Health Perspect.* 2002;110(9):939–945.

16. Krieger JK, Takaro TK, Allen C, Song L, Weaver M, Chai S, Dickey P. The Seattle-King County healthy homes project: implementation of a comprehensive approach to improving indoor environmental quality for low-income children with asthma. *Environ Health Perspect.* 2002;110(Suppl 2):311–322.

17. Morgan WJ, Crain EF, Gruchalla RS, et al. Results of a home-based environmental intervention among urban children with asthma. *N Engl J Med.* 2004;351:1068–1180.

18. Krieger J, Takaro T. Housing and asthma: interventions and strategies from Seattle. Presented at the American Public Health Association annual meeting. November 9, 2004; Washington, DC.

19. Brugge D, Hyde J, Weinbach BH, Levy JI, Steinbach S. Economic benefits of including environmental issues as a component of comprehensive asthma care: a managed care perspective. *Dis Manage Health Outcomes.* 2004;12(4):259–272.

20. Sandel M, Phelan K, Wright R, Hynes HP, Lanphear BP. The effects of housing interventions on child health. *Pediatr Ann.* 2004;33(7):474–481.

Coal Ash: Disasters and Opportunities

REBECCA PARKIN AND ELIZABETH HOLMAN[i]

A DISASTER OF MASSIVE PROPORTIONS

On December 15, 2008, President-Elect Obama nominated Lisa P. Jackson, former commissioner of the New Jersey Department of Environmental Protection, to become the administrator of the United States Environmental Protection Agency (EPA). About a week later, 1.1 billion gallons of coal fly ash slurry (enough to fill almost 1700 Olympic-sized swimming pools[ii]) surged out of a containment pond in Kingston, Tennessee. This waste was generated by the nearby coal-fired power plant operated by the Tennessee Valley Authority. In a few hours, this massive wave of contaminated muck covered 300 acres, destroyed 3 homes and damaged 42 more, smothered farmlands and roads, uprooted trees, ruptured a gas line and a water line, spilled metal and other contaminants into the Clinch and Emory Rivers, killed hundreds of fish, derailed a train, and created a 2-mile long wall of waste from 2' to 25' high (Figures 14-1 and 14-2).

The impacts of this catastrophic failure on December 22 were even more devastating because this area was already strained by the nationally depressed economy, and this all happened just before the start of the holiday season.

One resident mourned: "The most we could hope for is TVA [Tennessee Valley Authority] buying our property. It's ruined. We don't even have the money to relocate."[1(para 2)]

An affected farmer observed, "There are a couple of places that I don't think will ever be back to normal."[2(para 17)] It will take many years to understand what cleanup is possible and what public health harms have occurred or will occur.

In early January 2009, Senator Barbara Boxer (D-CA) said that the Kingston spill "must be a wakeup message to the TVA and to the US EPA that the current situation is unacceptable."[1(para 6)]

Three weeks after the spill, Sen. Boxer confronted EPA nominee Jackson at her congressional hearing, saying, "It seems to a lot of us that there are disasters waiting to happen out there. We just need very quick action. You're not going to fix it in a day. But we need to get it fixed."[3(para 11)]

Rep. Nick Rahall (D-WV) declared, "The disaster at the Kingston, TN, facility . . . was a clarion call for action. Now is the time to take that action before any lives are lost to a similar disaster."[3(para 14)]

Nominee Jackson testified, "I think the EPA needs to first and foremost assess the current state of what's out there . . . that's only the beginning. . . . I think it's time to . . . re-look at the state of regulations."[3(para 4)]

The die was cast; nominee Jackson would have to act on coal combustion waste (CCW)[iii] issues very soon after her January 26th swearing in. She would be held accountable for addressing the long-standing lack of federal regulations for these wastes.

---

[i] The views expressed in this case study are those of the authors and do not necessarily reflect the views or policies of the U.S. Environmental Protection Agency.

[ii] One report states that this amount is 100 times larger than the oil spilled from the *Exxon Valdez* in Alaska in March 1989. See Source-Watch. Kingston Fossil Plant. http://www.sourcewatch.org/index.php?title=Kingston_Fossil_Plant.

[iii] Collectively, these materials go by many names including, fly ash, coal combustion waste [CCW], coal combustion product, coal combustion ash, fossil fuel combustion waste, coal combustion material, coal combustion by-product, and coal combustion residue. For this case study, we will use the simplest term, *coal ash*.

FIGURE 14-1A Aerial image before Kingston ash slide.

Source: Tennessee Valley Authority. Aerial image of Kingston ash slide pre-event 2008. http://www.tva.gov/kingston/photo_gallery/KIF_webMaps_PhotosOnly_8-5x11_NAIP_2008.jpg. Accessed December 10, 2010.

FIGURE 14-1B Aerial image after Kingston ash slide, December 23, 2008.

Source: Aerial image of Kingston ash slide 12/23/2008. http://www.tva.gov/kingston/photo_gallery/KIF_webMaps_PhotosOnly_-5x11_12_23_2008.jpg. Accessed December 10, 2010.

There are estimates of 400–1300 coal waste sites across the nation.[4,5] States with these sites regulate them in various ways. Like EPA, most regulate CCW as nonhazardous material. Some do not require a disposal permit, some require waste to be transported out of the state, some treat it as liquid waste while others treat it as solid waste.[6] These measures may be insufficient to fully protect human health and the environment.

During spring 2009, smaller CCW spills in Maryland and Alabama resulted in additional pressures for federal regulation. Numerous stakeholders made public statements, and a publicly released letter to the EPA administrator was signed by over 140 environmental advocacy groups. Advocacy groups practically demanded regulatory oversight.

The Sierra Club proclaimed, "Clearly the current [state-only] regulations are not adequate,"[1(para 8)] and "It also highlights the need for us to begin moving beyond coal to . . . keep our lights on without . . . damage to our communities."[7(para 6)]

The Environmental Integrity Project declared:

> The Tennessee eco-disaster has cast a spotlight on what is a very serious national problem— the existence of under-regulated toxic pollution coal dump sites . . . that pose a serious threat to drinking water supplies, rivers and streams. . . . this problem is truly national in scope . . .[8(para 9)]

FIGURE 14-2 Devastation from ground level, Kingston ash slide, December 2008.

Source: Tennessee Valley Authority. http://www.tva.gov/kingston/before_after_10-1-2010/IMG_0583_full.jpg. Accessed December 10, 2010.

It also stated, ". . . Tennessee may end up only being a warning sign of much more trouble to come."[4(p 2)]

Earthjustice asserted, "No amount of regulation can keep these wet ponds . . . from seeping dangerous toxins into groundwater and potentially collapsing like the TN impoundment."[3(para 20)]

As she worked toward a proposal on federal regulations, Administrator Jackson said:

> Environmental disasters like the one last December in Kingston should never happen anywhere in this country. That is why we're announcing several actions to help us properly protect families who live near these facilities and the places where they live, work, play and learn.[9(para 5)]
>
> What we've promised is to make new regulations governing coal ash, to propose them by the end of the year . . . but how you manage it, once it ends up in a community, and how you insure over time it's not neglected or forgotten—or . . . allowed to build to a point where it's physically unsafe. We owe that to the American people . . ."[10(paras 10, 12)]

In April, Congress held a public hearing to investigate coal ash regulatory options. During the House subcommittee hearing, Barry Breen, acting administrator of EPA's Office of Solid Waste and Emergency Response, testified as follows:

> "The failure of an ash disposal cell at the . . . Kingston plant . . . highlighted the issue of impoundment stability. . . . we are . . . considering whether to specifically include impoundment integrity as part of our CCR [coal combustion residue] regulatory development."[11(p 3)]

He added, "NPDES [the EPA's National Pollution Discharge Elimination System] regulatory requirements that address impoundment integrity include standard permit conditions . . . [and] best management practices. . ."[11(p 4)] and "EPA is developing model permit language and implementing guidance . . ."[11(p 5)]

During the spring of 2009, researchers led by Dr. Laura Ruhl stated contaminants within the Kingston coal ash had been identified as carcinogens; however, they did not assess whether exposures had occurred among Kingston area residents. EPA evaluated the risk of future impoundment spills by surveying existing sites, using the Federal Emergency Management Agency's (FEMA's) dam hazard potential ranking system.[12] This system's high hazard ranking depends upon probable immediate loss of human life if the impoundment should fail, but not on the risk of other human health impacts. Upon releasing a list of 44 high hazard impoundment sites based on FEMA's ranking system (out of 200 sites evaluated), Administrator Jackson observed, "The presence of liquid coal ash impoundments near our homes, schools and businesses could pose a serious risk to life and property in the event of an impoundment rupture."[13(para 4)]

BACKGROUND

The U.S. lifestyle is dependent on electricity. As more functions are moved from paper to a wide range of electronic platforms, the nation increases its economic and social dependence on electricity. The annual amount of electricity generated in the United States more than doubled between 1970 and 2000, and it increased 16% between 1997 and 2007. The U.S. power grid failure in the Northeast in August 2003 provides one example of how interdependent the U.S. power grid has become. More than 50 million people lost all power for up to 4 days due to a cascade of system failures.[14]

Can we continue to sustain increases in electricity generation? Where will all of the energy come from and at what cost? Electricity is produced through a variety of sources in the United States, but coal is the primary source of power production. According to the U.S. Energy Information Association, 48% of all U.S. electricity consumption in 2009 came from coal.[15] Other energy sources for electricity include nuclear power, natural gas, and hydroelectric power. Each source has advantages and disadvantages and its own set of benefits and risks. For example, nuclear power can provide significant amounts of energy, but operational accidents at the Chernobyl (Ukraine), Three Mile Island (Pennsylvania), and Fukushima (Japan) nuclear power plants raised important questions about whether nuclear power is worth the risks to human health and the environment. Further, many nuclear power plants are reaching the end of their functional life spans. The storage of nuclear waste—even at places like Yucca Mountain (Nevada), in a remote area where the surrounding geology should limit any potential releases—has caused significant controversies for communities and policy makers.[16]

The source-to-effects framework, used in community health problem analyses, is one way to organize the data and information about coal ash generation, environmental transport and fate, and the related human exposures and health effects.[iv] The following discussion has been structured based on this paradigm. Figure 14-3 has been designed to support the following sections.

Sources and Components of Coal Ash

When a power plant burns coal in a furnace to create electricity, the process initially produces heat, which, in turn, creates steam. The steam is then used to generate the desired electricity. Electricity, however, is not the only thing created by coal combustion. It is impossible to convert all of the coal into heat, steam, and electricity.

The coal combustion process creates a number of byproducts. These include bottom ash, boiler slag, fly ash, and flue gas desulfurization (FGD) materials. Of the 121 million tons of coal ash produced in the United States in 2003, fly ash was the main component (62%), followed by flue gas desulfurization material (19%), and boiler slag/bottom ash (18%).[14]

To understand the sheer volume of coal ash produced in the United States, consider the following analogy regarding the mass of coal ash produced in the United States in 2003 alone:

[iv] For an example of a source-to-effects framework, see Figure 3.1 on page 35 in Committee on Research Priorities for Airborne Particulate Matter, National Research Council. *Research Priorities for Airborne Particulate Matter: I. Immediate Priorities and a Long-Range Research Portfolio.* Washington, DC: National Academies Press; 1998. This report is available at http://www.nap.edu/catalog.php?record_id=6131#toc.

FIGURE 14-3 Source to effects framework.

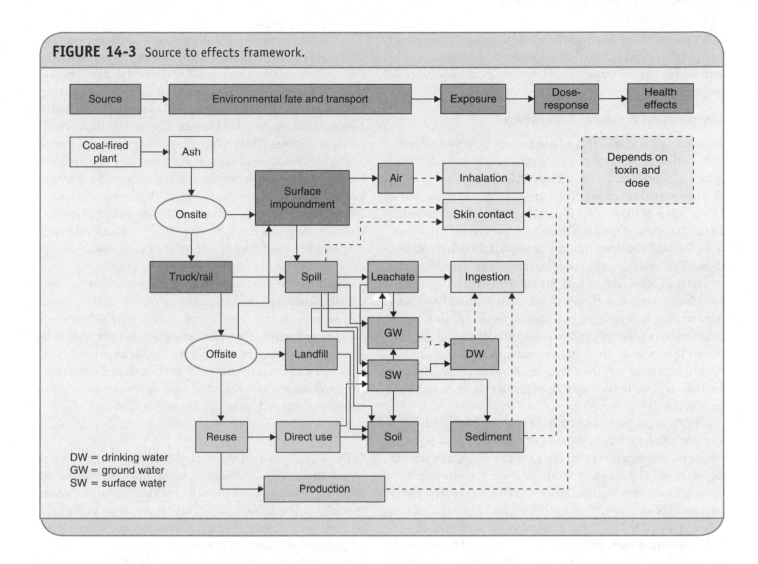

. . . approximately 890 pounds per capita, which is roughly the amount of municipal solid waste disposed in landfills throughout the U.S. per capita per year. . . . To paint a better picture, the amount of CCRs produced annually would fill about a million standard railroad coal cars, which, if hitched together, would create a train about 9,600 miles long . . . that would span the United States from New York City, New York to Los Angeles, California, 3.5 times."[14(pp14–15)]

In 2007, 131 million tons of coal ash were produced, so that train full of waste is growing longer every year.

The physical and chemical characteristics of coal ash can vary significantly; they depend on a number of factors including the chemical content of the coal burned, the chemical content of anything else burned at the same time, the type of technology being used to burn the coal, and the pol-

lution control technology being used to reduce air pollution emissions created during the coal combustion process.[14] The EPA-corporate partnership known as the Coal Combustion Products Partnership has stated:

> The concentrations of naturally occurring elements found in many fly ashes are similar to those found in naturally occurring soil. A mineral analysis of coal combustion products from coal-fired power plants indicates that they are composed of 95 percent iron oxides, aluminum, and silica. They also contain oxidized forms of other naturally occurring elements found in coal, such as arsenic, barium, cadmium, copper, lead, mercury, selenium, and zinc.[17]

In general, trace elements (like those in the previous quote) are concentrated in coal ash, because they are not easily transferred into heat and steam during the coal combustion process. They have nowhere else to go except into coal combustion byproducts. Although on-site pollution control technology serves important purposes, it can concentrate trace elements even further.

Environmental Fate and Transport

To comply with federal regulations enacted to reduce air pollution, coal-fired power plants must generally install additional pollution control technology. These technologies may result in changes to coal ash chemical composition. For example, while EPA's Clean Air Interstate Rule of 2005 focuses on reducing sulfur dioxide and nitrogen oxide, the necessary control technologies may result in flue gas desulfurization byproducts, thereby generating more concentrated sulfur, ammonia, and metals (mercury, arsenic, lead, etc.). Furthermore, regulations specifically targeting metals in air, such as the EPA's Clean Air Mercury Rule of 2005, may also increase mercury and/or other metals in coal ash and/or require handling and disposal of new byproducts. To be protective of the environment and health, monitoring of the changing chemical composition of coal ash will be needed during implementation of the 2005 regulations.[14]

With many millions of tons of coal ash produced annually, the material has to go somewhere. Some coal-burning power plants ship their coal ash (in a dry form) to a landfill for disposal. Others store it on site (near the power plant), usually by mixing the coal ash with water to create a slurry (wet form of coal ash) that is collected and stored in an area below ground level. These collection sites are called surface impoundments, and they exist as "natural depressions, excavated ponds, or diked basins."[14(p 20)] When a surface impoundment fails (e.g., one or more of the walls keeping the coal ash contained breaks), some or all of the coal ash slurry spills out onto the surrounding land and surface water (as in Kingston, Tennessee). The extent of the spill depends on the size of the break, the amount of coal ash stored, and the safeguards in place to deal with potential spills. At both surface impoundments and landfills, there is also the potential for the chemical components of the coal ash to become mobilized and leach out into nearby groundwater or surface water.[14]

The EPA has documented several instances where coal ash has caused environmental damage, including 24 proven environmental damage cases involving 16 groundwater and 8 surface water systems.[18] The agency also found 43 potential environmental damage cases, where there was less evidence of impact or the source of coal ash exposure was not fully understood.

The EPA estimates that in 2007, 36% of all coal ash produced was placed in landfills, while 21% was placed in surface impoundments, about 5% was used to fill in abandoned mines, and 38% was reused to create new products.[11] The main reuse for coal ash is in concrete, where coal ash replaces raw materials used to make portland cement (the basic building block of most concrete). This replacement avoids the use of energy needed to create portland cement. Ash-based concrete has been used to build a variety of structures—from the Milwaukee Art Museum to the Washington, DC subway system, to federal agency office buildings, to the Hoover Dam. Coal ash reuses in consumer products vary from grout and wallboard to snow and ice salt. (See Figure 14-4.) Coal ash is also used as embankment fill; e.g., for a golf course in Virginia.[19]

Even in the EPA's proven and potential environmental damage cases, the fate and transport of coal ash and its chemical components into ground and surface waters—and even into fish and wildlife[14]—is an extremely complex process to study and characterize. It can be very difficult to document, measure, and quantify the exact environmental concentrations and the pathways by which coal ash moves in the environment, potentially reaching human populations.

Exposure

In this case, *exposure* is the point of contact between a hazard and a human body. This contact may occur on the skin and/or in the respiratory and/or digestive tracts. Exposure is fundamentally different from dose, which is discussed in the next section. Further, federal agencies have different roles related to exposure. For example, in a variety of community cases, the Agency for Toxic Substances and Disease Registry (ATSDR) is responsible for determining whether human exposure is occurring, has occurred, or might occur.[v]

To evaluate the potential public health impacts and inform the regulatory process of coal ash, the worst-case exposure scenario should be constructed. Key factors in developing such a scenario include who is exposed, who may be at greater risk of adverse health impacts, to how much coal ash or toxic constituents they are exposed, how often, and over what duration. The scenario should include the potentially most harmful chemical contaminant and the potentially most harmful route of exposure. This most conservative public health scenario should be used for estimating the lowest exposure level at which adverse health outcomes would be expected, including among potentially high-risk populations. Because coal ash

---

[v] For the ATSDR exposure investigation process, see http://www. atsdr.cdc.gov/hac/products/ei.html.

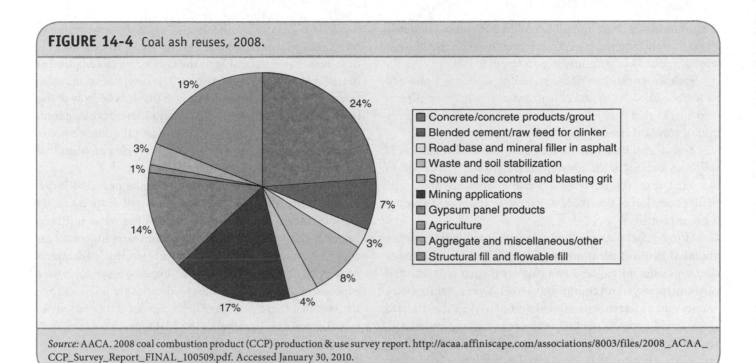

FIGURE 14-4 Coal ash reuses, 2008.

- Concrete/concrete products/grout
- Blended cement/raw feed for clinker
- Road base and mineral filler in asphalt
- Waste and soil stabilization
- Snow and ice control and blasting grit
- Mining applications
- Gypsum panel products
- Agriculture
- Aggregate and miscellaneous/other
- Structural fill and flowable fill

Source: AACA. 2008 coal combustion product (CCP) production & use survey report. http://acaa.affiniscape.com/associations/8003/files/2008_ACAA_CCP_Survey_Report_FINAL_100509.pdf. Accessed January 30, 2010.

varies in chemical composition, however, it is not possible to create one exposure estimate that would be appropriate for all communities.[20]

Residents are likely to be exposed for short periods of time and/or to low levels of coal ash constituents. Subpopulations such as children or people with preexisting health conditions are more likely to experience more serious impacts from coal ash exposure. Continuing with the source-to-effects framework shown in Figure 14-3, routes of exposure for communities include inhalation, ingestion, and skin contact.

Residents who live or play near coal ash waste sites that are uncovered or readily accessible may be exposed to airborne coal ash contaminants. Residents of Forward Township, Pennsylvania, lived near such a site and experienced a coal ash landslide in 2005. Their neighborhood was directly affected by large amounts of waste covering yards, roads, recreational areas, and a popular creek. Residents inhaled airborne ash following the landslide and during the cleanup when uncovered trucks were used to transport the ash; fine particle exposures presented the greatest community health risks. Residents with preexisting respiratory conditions would have been more sensitive to these exposures.[20]

Ingestion of coal ash–contaminated drinking water is another community exposure pathway. Of particular concern are the cases where the maximum contaminant limits for

drinking water standards have been exceeded, including for selenium and arsenic.[18,vi] Groundwater contaminations above EPA drinking water standards have occurred in Massachusetts, Wisconsin, Maryland, and Virginia.[14] Drinking water wells were affected in York Township, Virginia[21] and Pines, Indiana.[22] In the Chisman Creek, Virginia area, coal ash was deposited in former sand and gravel pits between 1957 and 1974; less than 10 years after these waste deposits stopped, a resident complained of discolored well water. Well and surface water samples revealed many metals characteristic of coal ash waste. This evidence caused Virginia Power to pay for public water supply lines, replacing 55 potentially affected private drinking water wells.[18] In Pines, Indiana, coal ash contamination of groundwater likely resulted in community exposures through drinking water. Over 100 residential wells and 13 landfill monitoring wells were sampled. Although manganese, boron, and arsenic were found, the complex nature of

---

vi According to NRC:

Also, in the EPA's review of monitoring data and damage cases, various drinking water standards were identified not to have been met, usually from wells on-site, downgradient, or from nearby surface waters impacted by surface impoundments or landfills containing CCR. While MCLs [maximum contaminant levels] were exceeded in cases that were not in public drinking water wells, and hence not violations, the EPA considered them examples of its concern.[14(p 96)]

the groundwater contamination made it difficult to accurately quantify drinking water exposure levels or to predict the potentially related community health impacts.[22]

Fish, frogs, and wildlife, including deer, are known to have been exposed to and consumed coal ash.[14] But there is no evidence that people have been exposed through consumption of contaminated species.

Young children who exhibit pica (elevated ingestion of soil) may be at risk for adverse health effects. The report of the ATSDR on the Forward Township landslide made particular mention of this route of exposure and ways to reduce these exposures.[20]

Skin contact with contaminated water and soil is another potential route of community exposure. In Forward Township, soil used for gardens and play areas such as residential yards, driveways, and community streets were contaminated. Adults and children who waded and played in the affected creek could come in contact with contaminated water, soil, and sediments. However, since the landslide occurred in January, it was thought that few dermal exposures would occur before the creek area was remediated. Although tracking of coal ash into vehicles and homes presented possible inhalation and dermal exposure pathways especially for children, there was no evidence that such exposures occurred.[20]

Dose Response

Dose refers to the amount of the toxin that reaches a target organ within the human body; it is fundamentally different from the toxin-human interface or point of contact (exposure). In this part of the source-to-effects paradigm, *response* refers to the subclinical level of human response to the toxin. Clinically detectable impacts are known as human health effects; these are discussed in the next section.

Relationships between toxins and human responses can be estimated based on animal and human studies. The toxic dose for a substance varies in part due to the substance's chemical characteristics. Variations in the human host—including the ways humans absorb, process, and remove the chemical—are important as well. Additionally, humans at different stages of development, in different states of health, or experiencing other exposures (including medications) metabolize toxins differently. Despite these variations, dose-response relationships can be used to evaluate the following:

- Causal association between a toxin and biological effects.
- Minimum dosages needed to produce a biological effect.
- Rate of accumulation of harmful effects.[23(p50)]

While there is an understanding of the dose-response relationship for many specific components in coal ash, the dose-response relationship of the entire mix of components in coal ash is less well understood. The components may also interact, creating different substances that may be more or less hazardous to humans. Given the many different possible combinations and interactions, understanding the dose-response relationship of coal ash exposure is a complex problem that requires further scientific study.[14]

Using the available exposure information, ATSDR calculated conservative or worst case scenario dose estimates for individuals exposed through drinking water in Pines, Indiana. The agency used the maximum sampling result for each contaminant tested as the exposure level to that contaminant. ATSDR then assumed that all exposed individuals were exposed to the maximum observed exposure levels, despite the fact that there may have been significant variations in actual exposures. To calculate the dose for each contaminant, ATSDR made standard assumptions about the body weight of exposed individuals and the amount of water consumed each day. Separate dose calculations for each contaminant were made for adults and then for children. The agency compared the estimated contaminant-specific values against health-based guidelines developed by ATSDR and the EPA. The results led ATSDR to conclude that the levels found "might pose a threat to residents and children in the area"[22(Discussion)] and recommended an alternative drinking water supply be provided to the community.[22]

Following the spill in Kingston, Tennessee, attempts were made to evaluate potential impacts on human health and the environment. One study examined radioactivity and concentrations of metals in various sediments and water samples collected around the spill area.[24] However, the authors were unable to calculate any dose estimates based on this information, due to the uncertainties about exposure levels.

Human Health Effects

The ability to link coal ash with potential human health impacts is directly related to the ability to verify exposure to coal ash at levels that could cause human health effects. Taken alone, a number of the chemical components found in coal ash have the potential to cause adverse health effects if individuals are exposed to high enough levels over a long enough period of time. With minimal exposure data, however, there are very few examples where an association between coal ash exposure and adverse health effects has been documented. Therefore, it becomes very challenging to show an association between a toxicant and adverse health effects, no matter how biologically plausible the association. These challenges are amply demonstrated by ATSDR's investigation of Pines, Indiana.[22] According to the Electric Power Research Institute:

> Ash produced from coal-fired power plants is much like volcanic ash. It contains trace quantities (in the parts-per-million range) of the . . . same elements [that] exist in soil, rock, and coal. . . . These elements can have adverse effects on human health if inhaled or ingested in sufficient quantity.[25(p 3)]

Without more exposure information and a greater understanding of the health impacts of the mixture of contaminants in coal ash, the ability to effectively link coal ash to adverse health effects is quite difficult.[14]

Some residents may be more sensitive to adverse health impacts associated with coal ash exposure. If pica-behaving children come in contact with coal ash, they may ingest a sufficient amount to cause irritation or more serious health effects. According to ATSDR:

> Children are shorter than are adults, and thus they breathe dust, soil, and vapors closer to the ground. A child's lower body weight and higher air intake rate results in a greater dose of hazardous substances per unit of body weight. If toxic exposure levels are high enough during critical growth stages, the developing body systems of children can sustain permanent damage.[20(p 20)]

Especially among sensitive subpopulations, low-level exposures over a long period of time may cause adverse health effects. However, these exposures are often hard to detect and may lead to a variety of health effects that are difficult to identify clinically. There is no direct evidence to date linking coal ash with adverse health effects in sensitive subpopulations.

Environmental Controls and Risk Management Approaches

There are many possible options for reducing or eliminating community health risks due to coal ash exposure. While some options were implemented fairly quickly at the Kingston site (e.g., evacuating homes, posting warning signs, banning waterway uses, controlling access to the site), these approaches did not require legislation and may be effective only temporarily.

However, other approaches require regulatory action, and the EPA administrator had committed to proposing new national regulations by the end of 2009. She had to consider options that would be effective and acceptable for hundreds of sites in various ecological settings and sustainable for many decades.

Fundamental principles of environmental health could guide the administrator in considering the strengths and weaknesses of risk management approaches. One foundation for environmental health decision making is the *precautionary principle*. Although there are many definitions of this fore-caring concept, it can be summarized as: "preventive, anticipatory measures . . . [should] be taken when an activity raises threats of harm to the environment, wildlife, or human health, even if some cause-and-effect relationships are not fully established."[26(p263)]

The intent of the principle is to guide decision makers toward erring on the side of anticipating and preventing harm. The mere presence of a hazardous substance may be a threat but does not necessarily constitute a risk to people; they must come in contact with (i.e., *be exposed to*) the toxin to be harmed. The precautionary principle indicates that action is needed to ensure that exposure does not occur, including when scientific evidence suggests but does not fully establish the potential for adverse consequences of exposure to a hazardous substance.

A three-step framework for mitigating environmental health risks includes assessing the situation, classifying the situation, and addressing the situation. These steps focus on gathering and organizing information as the basis for prioritizing concerns and identifying the most effective control options. In the spring of 2009, the EPA began the first two steps to fulfill the administrator's commitment to propose regulations (the third step).

Assess the Situation

EPA took the first step to assess the situation by carrying out a national survey of existing surface impoundments to determine the risk of harm in the event that these sites were to fail. FEMA's dam hazard potential ranking system[12] has three levels—low, significant, and high (Box 14-1). Those with a high hazard potential are those that have been determined to have probable immediate loss of human life *if* the surface impoundment were to fail. Based on this survey, 44 high-hazard-potential sites were identified in the spring of 2009.[27] The EPA committed to further assessment (including on-site inspections) for these high-hazard sites.[28]

The use of the FEMA ranking system raises many questions. For example, is this approach sufficiently protective of human health and the environment? Is this approach sufficiently anticipatory to prevent harm? Are there other approaches available to assess the situation more effectively for coal ash–related risks?

Classify the Situation

There are many dimensions to the coal ash disposal problem, and many options exist for classifying the information gathered in the assessment step. Some key questions to guide a classification choice are:

- Is coal ash a liquid or solid waste, or a mixture of the two?
- Are the chemical constituents of coal ash important to determining how the waste should be handled?
- Is coal ash hazardous or nonhazardous waste?

Coal ash could be classified based on its most hazardous component or on the basis of the properties of the overall mixture. The EPA has hosted a number of public sessions and discussions with industry, states, and communities to determine how to manage CCW. Since 1978, the EPA has exempted CCW from being classified as a hazardous waste. Most recently, in 2000, the EPA formally determined that CCW did not merit classification as a hazardous waste under Subtitle C of the Resource Conservation and Recovery Act (RCRA).[29] However, the EPA also decided that, when coal ash is disposed in surface impoundments, landfills, or mines, it should be regulated as a nonhazardous waste, under Subtitle D. Further, the agency determined that CCW reused in products did not present a sufficient risk to justify regulation.[29] Wastes considered hazardous are currently regulated by the EPA under RCRA Subtitle C, with more stringent handling and labeling requirements than are required under Subtitle D for nonhazardous wastes.[30] In the absence of federal regulations specifically for coal ash as a solid, liquid, or as a mixture, it has been managed under the more general Subtitle D regulations. After these rulings, many studies and reports were completed on a variety of coal ash topics (e.g., those discussed in Elcock and Ranek[6] and NRC[14]). The EPA also published a report evaluating coal ash environmental damage cases.[18]

In addition to the federal decisions, each state could develop its own CCW regulatory approach to meet state-specific needs and/or account for local geological conditions. Current state regulations have resulted in a variety of regulatory approaches within the same broad definition of nonhazardous waste. For example, in the case of dry coal ash disposal in landfills, these approaches range from complete exclusion from solid waste-permitting requirements (e.g., in Alabama) to designation as utility waste requiring specific permits for landfill disposal (e.g., in Missouri).[6]

These types of classification invariably lead to more complex questions about the levels at which the waste becomes hazardous to human health and how classification catego-

BOX 14-1 FEMA's Dam Hazard Potential Ranking System

Hazard potential classification	Loss of human life	Economic, environmental, lifeline losses
Low	None expected	Low and generally limited to owner
Significant	None expected	Yes
High	Probable. One or more expected	Yes, but not necessary for this classification

Source: Federal Emergency Management Administration (FEMA). Federal guidelines for dam safety: hazard potential classification system for dams. Available at http://www.fema.gov/library/viewRecord.do?id=1830. Print and online copies published April 2004; CD edition published September 2005. Accessed November 21, 2009.

ries should be defined. Other key questions are: What is the public health goal? Who should be protected? How are they exposed? How often and how much exposure do they have? Should their exposures be reduced, prevented, or eliminated? Answers to these questions guide how coal ash waste should be managed.

Address the Situation

The administrator's decisions may be driven by legal mandates and influenced by political contexts and/or societal expectations. The many options being used by states can inform her decision making.

The environmental controls available to mitigate the health risks associated with coal ash could be considered along a spectrum, ranging from controls that simply reduce the risks of coal ash exposure to controls that actually eliminate the risks. A widely accepted framework is known as the hierarchy of controls.[31] From least to most effective in managing human health risks, the hierarchy calls for personal protective equipment, administrative controls, engineering controls, substitution of the hazardous material, or elimination of the hazard or exposure. This paradigm was developed for workplace settings but can be useful for addressing community health risks as well. The last three approaches in the hierarchy of controls paradigm are discussed here; as with many community exposure situations, personal protective equipment is not feasible as a mitigation option.

Administrative Controls

These methods can be used to reduce exposures. In some states (e.g., Illinois and Indiana) proximity of the proposed disposal site to nearby communities, surface water, or groundwater is key to determining what type and extent of protective actions (such as groundwater monitoring) are necessary.[6]

Some states (e.g., Missouri and Wisconsin) have regulatory requirements for testing the chemical content of the coal ash[6]; the results are used to determine whether coal ash may be placed as a liquid slurry in a surface impoundment or as a dry solid in a landfill, reused as an ingredient in products, or handled in some other way. Regulations may require that a life cycle analysis be conducted, considering where the new product will be going and what the potential exposures would be to various populations and consumers, including in states other than where the product will be made.

Some states require trucks and railroad cars containing coal ash to be permitted and coal ash shipping containers to be labeled (e.g., California[32,33]). Permits may also be required to ensure that a surface impoundment or landfill has been safely built and to allow for state inspections for enforcing continuous, safe operations. Because dry placement in a landfill provides opportunities for coal ash to mix with other waste, regulations for additional monitoring (either above ground or below the surface) may be needed to detect potential mixing. Corrective action could be required if the mixing causes contamination at levels that are considered unsafe. As was done in Kingston, Tennessee, to limit community access to the concentrated coal ash slurry of a surface impoundment, signs can be posted and access controlled around contaminated sites. However, these approaches have limited effectiveness.

Engineering Controls

This set of control options focuses on reducing the probability of human exposures by implementing design and technical changes. When a surface impoundment or landfill is designed, a decision has to be made as to whether or not the impoundment will be lined; effective liners reduce the potential for coal ash to leach into the nearby environment. Ideal liners are im-permeable; clay liners are the preferred choice.[14] Groundwater monitoring devices can be installed to determine if leaching occurs and which corrective actions should be taken when issues are identified.[6]

Some states require coal ash shipping containers to be closed vessels, reducing the potential for the waste to be released into the environment and communities.

Substitution

Another approach could be burning coal containing fewer or less hazardous chemicals, resulting in fewer hazardous combustion by-products. However, this approach would be difficult and costly to monitor and infeasible to implement.

Long-Term Considerations—Elimination

Another risk-reduction option could be producing less coal ash by burning less or entirely eliminating coal as fuel for electricity generation. However, the early 21st century is a period in which there is increasing demand for electricity; there are a rapidly expanding number of electronic devices. Such energy source changes would require significant changes in current U.S. lifestyle and energy policy, and could result in major shifts toward alternatives such as wind and nuclear power. These alternatives carry substantial risks or costs that must be weighed against potential benefits from using less or no coal as an energy source. Although not using coal to fire power plants could be the ultimate solution, this option is not politically, technologically, or economically feasible at this time, nor is it within the administrator's authority.

THE CASE SCENARIO

In this case scenario, it is June 30, 2009. Administrator Jackson has made a public commitment to recommend federal regulations for coal combustion waste. To expand her understanding of the many concerns and issues, she is seeking input from EPA staff and external organizations and individuals. Your instructor/facilitator will provide you with additional instructions about your opportunity to contribute to the administrator's decision-making process. You will be advising Administrator Jackson about the best option for managing coal ash, and you must be prepared to defend your choice. *On June 30, 2009, the RCRA Subtitle D regulations were not yet drafted.*

Thought Questions
1. What are the primary reasons why coal ash is or is not a public health issue? Should coal ash be addressed as a public health issue? Why or why not?
2. Which characteristics of coal ash, generation/disposal sites, and fate and transport mechanisms increase the likelihood of exposure?

a. How is waste handled? (e.g., in liquid, solid, mixed waste, or other form; e.g., in containers, on land, in holding ponds, etc.)

b. Should coal ash be handled on site or transported off site?

c. Are there neighbors (e.g., people who live or recreate near the site)?

3. Who is exposed to coal ash? How are they exposed to it (by what route/s)?

a. What, if any, objective evidence of actual human exposures exists at any of the sites discussed in this chapter? What is the evidence?

b. If there is any evidence of exposure, have these exposures caused harm?

4. What are the most important problems and issues associated with managing coal ash? How do you think the EPA administrator should proceed with regulating coal ash?

a. For regulatory purposes, should coal ash be considered hazardous or nonhazardous waste?

b. Is the use of the FEMA dam hazard ranking system an appropriate mechanism for assessing the sites? (What issues were addressed or not addressed through the use of this system?)

c. What options should be considered for regulating coal ash?

5. Who are the stakeholders in this decision process?

a. Which stakeholder groups does Administrator Jackson *need to hear from*? What are their interests and priorities?

b. Which stakeholders *need to be involved* in the regulatory decision-making process?

About the Authors

Rebecca Parkin, PhD, MPH, retired in July 2010 as professor of environmental and occupational health and of epidemiology and biostatistics and the associate dean for research and public health practice at the School of Public Health and Health Services of The George Washington University. She continues her affiliation as a member of the part-time faculty. Previously she served as the assistant commissioner of occupational and environmental health in the New Jersey Department of Health and as an environmental epidemiologist at the Centers for Disease Control and Prevention. She earned her PhD in epidemiology and her MPH in environmental health from Yale University. She is a national associate of the National Academies and has served on numerous boards and committees there and at the U.S. Environmental Protection Agency.

Elizabeth Holman, MS, EdM, is a physical scientist at the U.S. Environmental Protection Agency. Previously she worked as a science educator at the Museum of Science in Boston, Massachusetts. She earned an MSc from the University of Rochester, specializing in geochemistry; an EdM from Harvard University; and a graduate certificate from the Gillings School of Global Public Health at the University of North Carolina-Chapel Hill. During the preparation of this case study, she was pursuing her DrPH at the School of Public Health and Health Services of The George Washington University.

REFERENCES

1. Rogers S. TVA spill update: worried residents and more coal spills. www.earthfirst.com/tag/tva-spill/. Published January 2009. Accessed October 2, 2009.

2. Bearden, T. Tenn. coal ash disaster raises concerns about similar sites nationwide. http://www.pbs.org/newshour/bb/environment/jan-june09/coalash_02-02.html. Accessed October 2, 2009.

3. Collins M. EPA designate Jackson vows to look at ways to regulate toxic sludge. http://www.knoxnews.com/news/2009/jan/15/epa-designate-jackson-vows-look-ways-regulate-toxi/. Posted January 15, 2009. Accessed October 2, 2009.

4. Clayton M. Coal-ash waste poses risk across the nation. *Christian Sci Monitor.* January 9, 2009. http://features.csmonitor.com/environment/2009/01/09/coal-ash-waste-poses-risk-across-the-nation/. Accessed Nov. 21, 2009.

5. Schlesinger R. Coal ash piles up. http://energycentral.fileburst.com/EnergyBizOnline/2009-2-mar-apr/fin_front_Coal_Ash.pdf. March-April, 2009. Accessed November 21, 2009.

6. Elcock D, Ranek NL. *Coal Combustion Waste Management at Landfills and Surface Impoundments, 1994–2004.* DOE/PI-0004, ANL-EVS/06-4. Report to the U.S. Department of Energy. http://www.ead.anl.gov/pub/doc/coal_waste_report.pdf. Published August 2006. Accessed December 4, 2009.

7. Nilles B, Hitt MA. Coal waste spills by the dozen? http://sierraclub.typepad.com/compass/2009/01/coal-waste-spills-by-the-dozen.html#more. Published January 2009. Accessed December 4, 2009.

8. Sustainable Business. Dozens of ash dumps pose similar threats as TN disaster. http://www.sustainablebusiness.com/index.cfm/go/news.display/id/17436. Published January 8, 2009. Accessed October 2, 2009.

9. Sheppard K. EPA announces plan to regulate coal ash. http://www.grist.org/article/Ash-and-ye-shall-receive. Published March 2009. Accessed October 2, 2009.

10. Burress J. Coal ash likely heading to Alabama, not Georgia. http://www.publicbroadcasting.net/wabe/news.newsmain/article/0/0/1516211/Atlanta./Coal.Ash.Likely.Heading.to.Alabama..Not.Georgia. Published June 10, 2009. Accessed on October 2, 2009.

11. Breen B. Testimony to the U.S. House subcommittee on water resources and the environment. April 30, 2009. http://www.epa.gov/ocir/hearings/testimony/111_2009_2010/2009_0430_bb.pdf Accessed November 25, 2009.

12. Federal Emergency Management Administration (FEMA). Federal guidelines for dam safety: hazard potential classification system for dams. Available at http://www.fema.gov/library/viewRecord.do?id=1830. Print and online copies published April 2004; CD edition published September 2005. Accessed November 21, 2009.

13. Environmental Protection Agency Region 3. EnviroBytes, a Summary of Issues and Events for Week Ending July 3, 2009. http://www.epa.gov/region3/ebytes/ebytes07_03_09.html. Accessed March 27, 2011.

14. National Research Council (NRC). *Managing Coal Combustion Residues in Mines.* Washington, DC: National Academies Press; 2006.

15. U.S. Energy Information Association (USEIA). Annual Energy Review: U.S. Primary Energy Flow by Source and Sector, 2009. http://www.eia.gov/emeu/aer/pecss_diagram.html. Accessed March 27, 2011.

16. Craig JR, Vaughn DJ, Skinner BJ. *Resources of the Earth: Origin, Use, and Environmental Impact.* Upper Saddle River, NJ: Prentice Hall; 1996.

17. Environmental Protection Agency. Using coal ash in highway construction: a guide to benefits and impacts. http://nepis.epa.gov/Exe/ZyPURL.cgi?Dockey=P100071H.txt Published April 2005. Accessed March 27, 2011.

18. Environmental Protection Agency. Coal combustion waste damage case. http://www.publicintegrity.org/assets/pdf/CoalAsh-Doc1.pdf. Published July 9, 2007. Accessed January 23, 2010.

19. McCabe R. Above ground, a golf course. Just beneath it, potential health risks. http://www.chesapeakeclimate.org/news/news_detail.cfm?id=542. Published March 30, 2008. Accessed November 21, 2009.

20. Agency for Toxic Substances and Disease Registry. Health consultation, coal fly ash landslide, forward township, Allegheny County, PA. http://www.atsdr.cdc.gov/HAC/pha/CoalFlyAshLandslide/CoalFlyAshLandslideHC060106.pdf. Published June 1, 2006. Accessed January 23, 2010.

21. Environmental Protection Agency. Chisman creek current site information. http://www.epa.gov/reg3hwmd/npl/VAD980712913.htm. Last updated January 2011. Accessed March 27, 2011.

22. Agency for Toxic Substance and Disease Registry. Health consultation town of Pines groundwater plume. http://www.atsdr.cdc.gov/hac/pha/pha.asp?docid=891&pg=0. Updated January 20, 2010. Accessed April 4, 2010.

23. Friis RJ. *Essentials of Environmental Health.* Sudbury, MA: Jones and Bartlett Publishers; 2007.

24. Ruhl L, Vengosh A, Dwyer G, et al. Survey of the potential environmental and health impacts in the immediate aftermath of the coal ash spill in Kingston, Tennessee. *Environ Sci Technol.* 2009;43(16):6326–6333.

25. Electric Power Research Institute (EPRI). *Coal Ash: Its Origin, Disposal, Use, and Potential Health Issues* [EPRI environmental focus issue paper]. Palo Alto, CA; Electric Power Research Institute, 1998.

26. Smith C. The precautionary principle and environmental policy: science, uncertainty, and sustainability. *Int J Occup Environ Health.* 2000;6(4):263–265.

27. Morford S. EPA releases secret list of 44 high-risk coal ash ponds. http://www.solveclimate.com/news/20090629/epa-releases-secret-list-44-high-risk-coal-ash-ponds. Published June 2009. Accessed October 2, 2009.

28. Environmental Protection Agency. Coal combustion residuals. http://www.epa.gov/osw/nonhaz/industrial/special/fossil/coalashletter.htm. Updated February 11, 2011. Accessed January 27, 2010.

29. Environmental Protection Agency. Fossil fuel combustion (FFC) waste legislative and regulatory time line. http://www.epa.gov/osw/nonhaz/industrial/special/fossil/regs.htm. Updated November 23, 2010. Accessed March 27, 2011.

30. Environmental Protection Agency. Laws and regulations. http://www.epa.gov/osw/laws-regs/index.htm. Updated September 9, 2008. Accessed April 4, 2010.

31. Centers for Disease Control and Prevention. Engineering controls. http://www.cdc.gov/niosh/topics/engcontrols. Accessed November 22, 2009.

32. California Department of Environmental Quality (CalDEQ). Managing hazardous waste. http://www.dtsc.ca.gov/HazardousWaste/. Accessed November 23, 2009.

33. National Energy Technology Laboratory (NETL). IEP—Coal utilization by-products current regulations governing coal combustion by-products—California. http://www.netl.doe.gov/technologies/coalpower/ewr/coal_utilization_byproducts/states/california.html. Accessed November 23, 2009.

The Diethylstilbestrol Story

An Investigation into the Evolving Public Health Policy for Pharmaceutical Products

MARGARET ANN MILLER, EMILY BLECKER, AND MEGHAL PATEL[i]

Regulatory agencies such as the United States Food and Drug Administration (FDA) play an important role in promoting and protecting public health by preventing or limiting exposure to unsafe products. Unfortunately, laws and regulations that protect public health are rarely proactive. Most current laws, regulations, and policies governing the manufacture and sale of pharmaceutical drug products (drugs) were enacted following a public health disaster. Understanding how public health disasters have impacted the development of health laws and regulations is critical for understanding current public health policy in the United States and for developing a proactive, rather than reactive public health framework. This case study describes the tragic story of the prescription drug, diethylstilbestrol (DES). It involves numerous players in the public health arena including research scientists, regulators, pharmaceutical companies, physicians, lawyers, advocates, and of course, patients.

INTRODUCTION

In 1971, several physicians noted an alarming increase in the development of clear cell adenocarcinoma in teenage girls and young women. This rare and potentially deadly form of vaginal and cervical cancer had previously occurred mainly in women over 50 years of age. The only treatment was major invasive surgery to remove the uterus (hysterectomy) or vagina (vaginectomy). This surgery was not only emotionally and physically painful but sometimes not a cure. A few

physicians began to search for the cause of this rare form of cancer, and one physician, Arthur Herbst, described a common link: all of the women developing clear cell adenocarcinoma were exposed to DES in utero.[1] The implications of this finding were terrifying for the American public—millions of children might develop cancer or some other reproductive problem after an unknown length of time because their mothers took this prescription medication during pregnancy. Today there is still no test for detecting DES exposure and it is impossible to know how many people were, or will be, affected by the medication. DES remains one of the most significant public health disasters of the 20th century.

THE BEGINNING

Starting in the mid-1920s, scientists understood the action of natural estrogens and their potential utility for treating numerous conditions from cancer to wrinkles. The natural estrogens identified at that time were not water soluble and showed no activity when given orally. Several research scientists (many of whom were supported by pharmaceutical companies) began their search for an orally active form of estrogen. In 1938, British physician and chemist Charles Dodds and his team of scientists published a paper describing the synthesis of DES, a compound that showed estrogenic activity when consumed orally in tablet or pill form. The synthesis of DES was relatively simple and inexpensive, and by publishing the formula, Dodds relinquished his patent rights. Although Dodds promoted the use of DES for the treatment of menopausal symptoms and encouraged the marketing of DES by pharmaceutical companies, he also voiced concerns about the potentially harmful effects of the medication.[2]

---

[i] The views expressed in this publication are those of the authors and do not necessarily represent of those of the United States Food and Drug Administration.

THE APPROVAL PROCESS

Prior to 1938, there was no federal law to prevent the marketing of pharmaceutical drugs—whether safe or hazardous, effective or useless.[ii] Any drug product could be marketed provided it was synthesized according to the standard compendia and properly labeled. At the time, drug companies were small manufacturers producing patent medicines[iii] that were sold over the counter at pharmacies, while most physicians prescribed pills and potions formulated from their own recipes. Beginning in the early 1930s, Congress considered strengthening the 1906 Pure Food and Drug Act, but support for legislation was inadequate until 1937, when a drug company introduced an untested formulation of sulfanilamide with a solvent that caused the death of over 100 people, many of them children.[3]

Starting in 1938, drug companies had to submit evidence of a drug's safety for its intended use to the FDA before it could go on the market. The FDA had 2 months to approve, reject, or request additional data from the firm, and failure to act on the application would lead to automatic approval of the drug. This mandate for premarket evidence of a drug's safety represented the birth of the new drug application (NDA).[iv,3]

Despite the lack of product exclusivity that would have been provided by a patent, several drug companies, including Eli Lilly & Company, took an interest in producing and marketing DES. In 1940, 13 drug companies filed NDAs for DES. In anticipation of this event, a number of scientists published studies showing that estrogens induced cancer in animals, and wrote editorials urging a thorough review of DES by the FDA. FDA informed the drug companies that it did not believe the current data supported a determination of safety for DES and that it would turn down the applications. The companies withdrew their applications but committed to work together to develop the clinical safety information needed for DES to obtain FDA approval. The following year, the drug companies again filed NDAs for DES. This regulatory submission focused on the safety of DES in human clinical studies—evidence that discounted the disturbing findings from several animal studies.

In 1941, DES was officially approved by the FDA for four indications: treatment of gonorrheal vaginitis, menopausal symptoms, senile vaginitis, and prevention of lactation in women who had given birth. The product label listed a number of side effects for estrogen treatment[v] as well as precautions and contraindications of use: "Diethylstilbestrol is contraindicated in patients with personal or familial history of breast or genital cancer (except in the treatment of cancer). Prolonged, continuous administration can lead to endometrial hyperplasia and to 'breakthrough' bleeding ..."[4(para 3),vi]

In 1943, two Harvard Medical School physicians, George and Olive Smith, began evaluating the use of DES to prevent and treat complications of pregnancy. Animal research suggested DES could stimulate the production of progesterone, and the Smiths hypothesized that increasing progesterone production would prevent many complications of pregnancy. In their study of approximately 600 pregnancies, DES was effective in preventing miscarriage, late pregnancy toxemia, intrauterine death, and premature delivery.[5] The Smiths advocated for the prophylactic use of DES in all pregnant women to prevent complications of pregnancy (also termed *accident of pregnancy*) associated with progesterone deficiency. In 1947, DES was approved by the FDA for use in preventing accidents of pregnancy.[6]

THE MAGIC BULLET

The FDA does not regulate the practice of medicine. Once DES was approved, physicians were legally allowed to use it for any purpose. The scientific and medical communities viewed orally active estrogen as a magic bullet that could be used to treat many medical conditions and improve the quality of life. In addition to the FDA-approved indications, DES was used by physicians for the treatment of acne, osteoporosis, heavy menstrual bleeding, female infertility, and prostate cancer, as an oral contraceptive, and as a morning-after pill. DES was given to teenage girls who were too tall in an attempt to stunt their growth and to male transsexuals to help prepare them for a sex change. DES was eventually used to treat over 100 conditions and was prescribed across the United States and throughout the world. DES was even given to livestock to promote rapid weight gain.[2]

Following World War II, Americans experienced a period of great social optimism. New suburban complexes were being developed, science and technology seemed to have no limits, and physicians were viewed as kings. As soldiers returned home from war, they were eager to get married and start

---

[ii] In 1906, Congress passed the Pure Food and Drug Act, which prohibited the sale of misbranded or adulterated food, drinks, and drugs.

[iii] Patent medicines are medicines, usually of low potency, protected by patent and available without a prescription.

[iv] To administer an unapproved new drug to humans, the manufacturer requested an investigational new drug application exemption from the FDA.

---

[v] Side effects include nausea, vomiting, fullness and congestion of the breasts, edema, uterine bleeding (either during or upon cessation of administration), and, rarely, various forms of abdominal distress or pain, anorexia, diarrhea, lassitude, vertigo, headache, anxiety, insomnia, thirst, scotomata, cutaneous rashes, purpura, and jaundice. Gynecomastia and loss of libido may occur in men.

[vi] Product labels are available online at www.pharmapendium.com.

families. The era known as the baby boom began.[vii] Despite a surge in pregnancies during this era, many women desperate to have children were struggling with miscarriages. These women were eager for suggestions from their physicians about any medications that would help them prevent miscarriages. FDA's approval of DES for accidents of pregnancy in 1947 led to a surge in DES use among pregnant women. Herbst et al. estimated that between 1946 and 1951, DES was prescribed for about 1 out of every 20 high-risk, pregnant patients at Boston's Lying-In Hospital.[7]

Physicians were encouraged by the drug company sales representatives to use DES not only in high-risk pregnancies but also as a "vitamin" for all pregnant women. Drug company sales representatives offered incentives for physicians and pharmacists to prescribe their company's product—including free samples, medical booklets, and an assortment of gifts for their personal and professional use. Pharmacists were offered incentive plans for buying DES products, including discounts on larger purchases. At that time, Eli Lilly & Company was one of the largest pharmaceutical companies in the world; it is estimated that Lilly produced 50 to 75% of all the DES products sold in the United States.[2] However, because several drug companies manufactured DES and because it was widely used, it is difficult to determine exactly how many people, including pregnant women and their offspring, were exposed to DES during this time.[viii]

FROM MAGIC BULLET TO TIME BOMB

Although doctors widely prescribed DES for pregnant women, some early clinical studies failed to show an increase in progesterone levels in pregnant women treated with DES. In the early 1950s, Dieckmann et al. noted that the Smiths' studies lacked an adequate control group and the benefits reported for DES could simply be due to improved medical care given to the study participants. Dieckmann's research group conducted a randomized, double-blind clinical trial (a study design that is still considered the gold standard by the FDA) to assess pregnancy outcomes in women who were assigned to receive either DES or a placebo. The study definitively showed that DES did not work to prevent miscarriages or any of the other indications proposed by the Smiths. In fact, although not statistically significant, there was a clear trend for the women taking DES to have more miscarriages, more premature deliveries, and lower birth weight babies than women

who took the placebo.[8] The Smiths provided comment on the study stating their belief that the negative findings were due to the heterogeneous sample of pregnant women, which masked the effect of DES.[9] Despite the lack of efficacy in the double-blind, placebo-controlled clinical study and the increasing evidence that DES caused reproductive tumors in animal models, DES continued to be widely prescribed to pregnant women throughout the 1950s and 1960s.

Beginning in the 1950s, some public health professionals suggested that drug product safety needed to be considered in light of product effectiveness. A congressional investigation and subsequent hearing launched by Senator Estes Kefauver in the late 1950s raised questions about drugs, including drug effectiveness. However, once again, Congress was not able to garner support for a stronger drug law until another tragedy occurred. This time it was thalidomide.[3]

Thalidomide was developed by a German pharmaceutical company, and was approved and widely used in Europe between 1957 and 1961 to treat morning sickness in pregnant women. In the late 1950s and early 1960s, more than 10,000 children in 46 countries were born with limb deformities. In 1961, a German pediatrician demonstrated a link between these birth defects and the use of thalidomide during the first trimester of pregnancy. Later that same year, thalidomide was removed from the market in Europe.[10] In the United States, the impact of thalidomide was minimized because the FDA insisted that additional studies were needed to demonstrate safety as mandated in the 1938 legislation and refused to approve the drug application. Although thalidomide was never approved for sale in the United States, millions of tablets were distributed to physicians as part of the investigational clinical testing program.[3]

In 1962, following on the heels of the thalidomide tragedy, the United States Congress amended the drug law to require, among many other items, that: (1) manufacturers establish the effectiveness of drugs through adequate and well-controlled clinical trials prior to marketing; (2) the FDA exert greater control over investigational studies; and (3) manufacturers test for safety during pregnancy before a drug received approval for sale in the United States.[3] For products such as DES that were approved prior to these amendments, the FDA engaged the National Academy of Sciences/National Research Council to convene panels of experts to review the published literature to determine if the results supported product efficacy for a particular indication. The results of the panel reviews were submitted to the FDA, which evaluated the findings and published its approval decisions in the *Federal Register*. If FDA determined that a

---

[vii] The U.S. Census Bureau defined the increased births between 1946 and 1964 as the baby boom.

[viii] Major manufacturers of approved DES products include: Abbott Laboratories, Ayerst, McKenna & Company, George A. Breon & Company, Charles E. Frost & Company, Eli Lilly & Company, Merck, Inc., William S. Merrell Company, Sharp & Dohme Inc., E.R. Squibb & Sons, Inc., The Upjohn Company, Winthrop Chemical, and Wyeth Laboratories.

drug was ineffective for a particular indication, the agency had to follow the legal administrative hearing process to withdraw the NDA.[11]

Following the passage of the 1962 amendments to the drug law, drug companies needed to provide the National Academy of Sciences/National Research Council review panel with published clinical studies to support the clinical efficacy of DES for each of its approved indications. The National Academy of Sciences/National Research Council panel concluded DES was effective in the treatment of menopause, senile vaginitis, postpartum breast engorgement, functional uterine bleeding, and controlling carcinoma of the breast and prostate. With regards to the accidents of pregnancy claim, the panel stated that *accidents of pregnancy* is a very vague term and probably includes a whole group of indications, and that the company should be asked to clarify exactly what indications it covered. The panel also stated that it "feels that this drug is not harmful in such conditions as threatened abortion, but that its effectiveness cannot be documented by literature or its own experience."[12(p 2)]

In 1970, Herbst and Scully published a paper describing adenocarcinoma of the vagina in seven adolescent females. This finding was especially concerning because these cancers were usually seen in women over 50 years of age.[1] Interestingly, two of the mothers suspected their DES use during pregnancy had caused the cancer in their daughters.[7] In early 1971, Herbst et al. published a study in *The New England Journal of Medicine* titled, "Adenocarcinoma of the Vagina: Association of Maternal Stilbestrol Therapy with Tumor Appearance in Young Women." This study described the association between clear cell adenocarcinoma of the vagina seen in seven women ages 15 to 22 and in utero exposure to DES.[13] Herbst next obtained the patient records from the Smiths to allow for the study of other mothers exposed to DES. In these studies, Herbst determined that the development of vaginal adenosis was dose dependent and related to the gestational age of exposure, with exposure prior to 18 weeks causing cancer. In addition, Herbst established a patient registry to study the clinical, epidemiologic, and pathologic aspects of clear cell adenocarcinoma in young women with and without DES exposure. From the registry data, it was determined that adenocarcinomas occurred with a cumulative incidence of approximately 1 in 1000 exposures to DES. DES became the first example of a chemical known to cause cancer in offspring following in utero exposure. Noncancerous alterations of the reproductive tract were an even more common finding, affecting 75% of the female offspring exposed to DES, which contributed to the overall concern regarding the use of any medication during pregnancy.[7] The young women facing the health problems as a result of DES exposure in utero became known as "DES daughters."

Shortly after the publication of the first paper by Herbst in 1971, the FDA sent a bulletin to all U.S. physicians advising them against the use of DES in pregnant women. In November, 1971, the FDA published a *Federal Register* notice stating that based on the findings of the National Academy of Sciences/National Research Council Drug Efficacy study, it would approve DES for the treatment of osteoporosis, disturbances of the menstrual cycle, suppression of lactation, and to lessen blood loss at surgery. However, based on concerns about the association between DES use in pregnant women and adenocarcinomas in the offspring, the FDA concluded that for pregnant women, the risk of treatment did not outweigh the benefits and thus DES was contraindicated for use during pregnancy.[14] Following a contentious comment period, the FDA withdrew the approval of DES for use in pregnant women in 1975.[15]

It has been estimated that between 5 and 10 million pregnant women and their offspring were exposed to DES worldwide from 1938 to 1971. It has now been proven that the DES daughters face a statistically small, but nevertheless significant, risk of developing clear cell adenocarcinoma. Additionally, they face an even greater risk of having a premature birth or other difficulties becoming pregnant due to DES exposure.[7]

While most of the initial attention given to DES was placed on the affected daughters, in the 1980s, attention was broadened to include the problems faced by DES sons. Assessing the biological impact of DES exposure on males was more difficult than it was for females. Many men rarely go to the urologist, and often they do not admit to having genital or reproductive problems. However, many DES-exposed sons experienced reproductive problems such as pain during sexual intercourse, a low sperm count, and a smaller than average penis.

THE EMOTIONAL AND SOCIAL IMPACT

Epidemiologic incidence numbers do not begin to capture the emotional and social impact of DES exposure. Many DES mothers felt guilty about taking a medicine while pregnant, resulting in harm to their children, while others objected to having their daughters examined. Cancer and surgical removal of the vagina and uterus had a very traumatic effect on the teenagers and young women who developed clear cell adenocarcinoma. After these surgeries, numerous young women felt angry about what had happened to them and struggled with their body image. Many young women and young men who faced problems due to DES exposure developed a fear of sexual relations and social rejection. Some couples were willing to discuss their experiences and difficulties in trying to get pregnant but still did not discuss the tension that occurred between them. Women often had trouble seeking support from their husbands whom they felt could not understand or respond to the emotional distress they were feeling. Infertility and other medical problems related to DES put a strain on many marriages and sometimes led to divorce.[2]

DES ADVOCACY

Many DES advocacy groups were formed to seek compensation from the drug companies responsible for manufacturing DES and to help the victims of DES exposure handle the physical and emotional consequences of their health problems. In 1977, Fran Fishbane became the first president of DES Action, National. The goal of DES Action, National was to identify all DES-exposed individuals, to provide referral and follow-up care, to develop networks of information, and to offer a newsletter on legal and other information pertaining to DES. Fran Fishbane later became the head of the Ralph Nader–funded Public Citizen's Health Research Group. The advocacy community pressured the drug companies and public health community to assume responsibility for the problems associated with DES exposure. This led to the development of a patient registry of women exposed to DES. Patient registries are observational studies designed to determine the safety of a drug in the real world by tracking the health of patients who have taken the medication. Patient registries, also referred to as phase IV studies, remain the best way to identify safety signals for marketed drug products and are now a common requirement for the approval of drugs used by pregnant women.

LEGAL ACTION

In civil law, an individual or an organization (plaintiff) sues another individual or group (defendant), claiming the defendant committed some wrong. Sometimes the plaintiff will join with other individuals or organizations that are making the same accusation. A specific branch of civil law is the product-liability field. When people claim to be injured by a product, they may sue the manufacturer of that product for damages. Thus, numerous lawsuits were filed against manufacturers of DES. However, one major problem in many of the lawsuits surrounding DES was that DES was never patented, and many different manufacturers produced the drug. Furthermore, many women did not know which company synthesized the pill that they or their mother took.

In one famous DES case, a lawyer named Jason Brent filed a lawsuit in 1976 on behalf of Judith Sindell against Abbott Laboratories, E.R. Squibb, and Eli Lilly & Company. The defendants were all leading drug companies and known manufacturers of DES. Since it was not known which company made the DES Sindell's mother had taken, the court decided that each defendant would be held responsible for a percentage of the total compensation based upon their portion of

the total DES market. This decision, upheld by the California Supreme Court in 1980, changed the course of legal history because the plaintiffs were now able to sue the manufacturers even if they didn't know which company manufactured the exact drug product they were given.[2]

CONCLUSION

DES products are no longer on the market in the United States and regulatory standards for FDA approval of medicine are now much more stringent than those used when DES was approved. However, the fact that so many scientists, physicians, and regulators failed to recognize the problem with DES until it was too late begs the question: could a public health disaster similar to DES happen again? Understanding laws and regulations and process of drug approval and postmarketing surveillance will help public health professionals engage proactively in ensuring the safety of pharmaceutical products.

About the Authors

Margaret Ann Miller, PhD, received her PhD in endocrinology-reproductive physiology from the University of Wisconsin-Madison in 1981 and was a postdoctoral fellow at the University of Illinois, Champaign-Urbana. In 1985, Dr. Miller accepted a position at Monsanto Agricultural Company working on the approval of recombinant products. In 1989, Dr. Miller joined the United States Food and Drug Administration (FDA) in the Center for Veterinary Medicine. She held several positions within the Center for Veterinary Medicine, including deputy director for human food safety. In 1999, Dr. Miller joined the FDA's Office of Women's Health as the manager of science programs. In this position, she initiated several successful research initiatives that promoted the health of women. In 2005, she accepted a 2-year detail to the World Health Organization, where she worked on food safety. Dr. Miller is currently the associate director of regulatory activities in the Washington office of the National Center for Toxicological Research and a professorial lecturer at The George Washington School of Public Health and Health Services.

Emily Blecker is majoring in sociology with a concentration in health and medicine at the University of Pennsylvania. She is interested in having a career in public health after she graduates. In 2010, Ms. Blecker received a summer internship from Oak Ridge Research Institute and worked at the National Center for Toxicological Research at the Food and Drug Administration.

Meghal Patel, MPH, is a graduate of Indiana University, where she received a bachelor of science degree in biology and a bachelor of arts degree in psychology. In 2010, she received her master of public health from The George Washington University School of Public Health and Health Services, concentrating in global health. She participated in writing this case while working at the National Center for Toxicological Research at the Food and Drug Administration under Dr. Margaret Ann Miller.

ADDITIONAL RESOURCES

Centers for Disease Control and Prevention. DES update home. http://www.cdc.gov/des/

National Cancer Institute. DES questions and answers. http://www.cancer.gov/cancertopics/factsheet/Risk/DES

REFERENCES

1. Herbst AL, Scully RE. Adenocarcinoma of the vagina in adolescence: a report of 7 cases including 6 clear-cell carcinomas (so-called mesonephromas). *Cancer.* 1970;25(4):745–757.

2. Meyers R. *D.E.S.: The Bitter Pill.* New York, NY: Seaview/Putnam; 1983.

3. United States of America. The Food and Drug Administration. *About FDA: summary of NDA approvals & receipts, 1938 to the present.* http://www.fda.gov/AboutFDA/WhatWeDo/History/ProductRegulation/SummaryofNDAApprovalsReceipts1938tothepresent/ucm2006085.htm. Updated February 16, 2011. Accessed July 9, 2010.

4. United States of America. The Food and Drug Administration. *New Drug Application: Diethylstilbestrol Tablets, U.S.P.* September 16, 1947.

5. Smith OW. Diethylstilbestrol in the prevention and treatment of complications of pregnancy. *Am J Obstet Gynecol.* 1948;56(5):821–833.

6. D.E.S. timeline. http://www.douglasandlondon.com/docs/DES-Timeline.pdf. Accessed July 15, 2010.

7. Herbst AL. Diethylstilbestrol and adenocarcinoma of the vagina. *Am J Obstet Gynecol.* 1999;181(4):1576–1578.

8. Dieckmann WJ, Davis ME, Rynkiewicz LM, Pottinger RE. Does the administration of diethylstilbestrol during pregnancy have therapeutic value? *Am J Obstet Gynecol.* 1953;66(5):1062–1081.

9. Smith, GvS. as quoted Dieckmann WJ, Davis ME, Rynkiewicz LM, Pottinger RE. Does the administration of diethylstilbestrol during pregnancy have therapeutic value? *Am J Obstet Gynecol.* 1953;66(5):1075–1076.

10. Miller MT, Stomland K. Teratogen update: thalidomide; a review, with a focus on ocular findings and new potential uses. *Teratology.* 1999;60:306–321.

11. Karst KR. Marketed unapproved drugs—past, present and future. *RA Focus.* February 2007:37–42.

12. National Academy of Science/National Research Council. Drug efficacy studies for diethylstilbestrol. Available at www.pharmapendium.com. Published 1969. Accessed July 20, 2010.

13. Herbst AL. Adenocarcinoma of the vagina: association of maternal stilbestrol therapy with tumor appearance in young women. *N Engl J Med.* 1971;282(16):878–881.

14. Food and Drug Administration. Certain estrogens for oral or parenteral use: drugs for human use; drug efficacy study implementation. *Fed Regist.* 1971;36(217):21537–21538.

15. Food and Drug Administration. Certain estrogens for oral use: notice of withdrawal of approval of new drug application. *Fed Regist.* 1975;40(25):5384.

PART III

Assurance Cases: Overview

Assurance is the last step in improving and protecting the public's health. Once problems have been identified via assessment and decisions have been made to mobilize efforts and resources through policy development, then assurance functions to make sure conditions are in place for crucial services to be provided. Four of the 10 essential public health services fall into the category of assurance:

- Enforcing laws, regulations, and rules that protect health and ensure safety
- Linking people to needed personal health services and assure the provision of health care when otherwise unavailable
- Assuring a competent public and personal health care workforce
- Evaluating effectiveness, accessibility, and quality of personal and population-based health services

As mentioned in the other chapter introductions, research is also an integral component of all of the essential public health categories.

This section includes six case studies that examine issues related to protecting and assuring the public's health. The cases are:

16. Beyond Measurement? Evaluating Environmental Public Health: Assessing the Effectiveness of Food Safety Programs
17. Cardiac Rehabilitation for the Elderly: A Public Health Perspective
18. The X-Pack Smoking Cessation Kit: A Social Marketing Case Study
19. Mumps Epidemic in Iowa: Lessons Learned from the Front Line of Testing
20. Big Brother Is Watching: Utilizing Clinical Decision Support as a Tool to Limit Adverse Drug Events
21. The 2009 H1N1 Influenza Pandemic: When You Make Mistakes, Don't Miss the Lessons

Enforcing rules to ensure health safety is perhaps the most commonly known public health function. Most people are familiar with laws, regulations, and standards that require food sold to the public to be safe. The *Beyond Measurement?* case examines a food safety program in Baton Rouge, Louisiana, amidst statewide budget cuts. The program director must come up with an evidence-based approach, in the face of sparse data, to determine which functions should be continued to assure food-borne illness is kept to a minimum in the community.

Cardiac Rehabilitation for the Elderly and *The X-Pack Smoking Cessation Kit* focus on connecting people to needed health services. The importance of broadening medical management to incorporate lifestyle issues and patient empowerment is emphasized through the experience of an internal medicine physician in *Cardiac Rehabilitation for the Elderly*. The physician must determine whether to recommend a patient participate in an interventional program after the patient has experienced an acute myocardial infarction. Is the evidence sufficient? Will the patient benefit? Could such interventions improve population-based health standards? All of these questions are considered in the case. Similarly, *The X-Pack Smoking Cessation Kit* recounts a research effort to create a specialized smoking cessation intervention for young smokers—a group for whom tailored resources were previously unavailable. Researchers reviewed existing evidence, conducted in-depth discussions with the population in need, and created partnerships to create a unique kit to help young smokers quit tobacco.

Building and maintaining the infrastructure of public health in local, state, national, and international communities is essential in order to continue to provide crucial population-based services. Training a competent public health workforce is a key component of that infrastructure and two cases are provided to consider different aspects of this essential service.

Mumps Epidemic in Iowa: Lessons Learned from the Front Line of Testing addresses management challenges faced by the state health laboratory in Iowa. A state health lab functions as a reference lab for analytical testing, and training facility for state and local public health professionals, healthcare providers, and citizens. How to manage a laboratory during an epidemic is a skill for which most coursework does not specifically prepare students. This case helps learners think through the challenges of operating a crucial element of the public health infrastructure, including how to train and retain talented and competent staff. *Using Clinical Decision Support as a Tool to Limit Adverse Drug Events*, in a related vein, provides the opportunity to think about how electronic tools might be created to enhance the ability of public health professionals, especially healthcare providers, to deliver safe and effective care.

The assurance section closes with a case examining lessons learned. Against a backdrop of the proverbial dodged bullet, *The 2009 H1N1 Influenza Pandemic: When You Make Mistakes, Don't Miss the Lessons* case provides detailed information on how to think through previous assurance activities in order to garner best practices. It also engages learners in identifying opportunities to improve processes in order to provide better services in future public health emergencies.

The *2009 H1N1* case is also a fitting end to the entire case study volume as it reminds public health students and practitioners alike that the 10 essential public health functions are a continuous cycle. After assurance activities are complete, the cycle should begin again. Experts must use research, including on previous experiences and failures, to activate new assessment activities. Well-functioning public health systems are always a work in progress. By continuously learning, the public health community, and public health at large, will also be continuously improving.

Beyond Measurement?

Evaluating Environmental Public Health: Assessing the Effectiveness of Food Safety Programs

LINDSEY REALMUTO AND SURILI SUTARIA[i]

BATON ROUGE, LOUISIANA, JANUARY 2010—STATE HEALTH DEPARTMENT FACES BUDGET THREATS

In January 2010, the environmental health director of Louisiana, John Smith, attended a director's meeting run by the state health commissioner in Baton Rouge. The meeting was called in response to the release of the preliminary annual state budget.

"The preliminary state budget was released yesterday and it looks like the Louisiana Department of Health is facing another round of cuts across the board. I am passing around a spreadsheet that has the proposed cuts to your individual departments and programs," the state health commissioner said.

On this spreadsheet, John noted the environmental health department faced a 20% budget reduction. This would force John to lay off personnel even though his entire department had been overworked and understaffed for quite some time. The food safety program had absorbed the largest reduction, which John attributed to a public perception that the program was not very effective and overly burdensome on restaurants and the food industry.

The state health commissioner continued, "The only way we're going to be able to fight this budget cut is by proving to the state legislature with solid facts that our programs are vital to the health and safety of Louisiana residents. You have 3 weeks to perform an evaluation of the programs that are on the chopping block."

---

[i] Disclaimer: All opinions and views expressed in this case study are of the authors and the authors alone. They do not represent the official position of the Association of State and Territorial Health Officials or the Louisiana Department of Health and Hospitals.

John was faced with an incredible task. How could he make the case that environmental health programs, especially food safety, are critical to protecting public health, and a reduction in financial resources could be detrimental to the health of state residents? He had never undertaken this kind of program evaluation before. He needed to answer some significant questions, including:

- How do restaurant inspections impact the public's health?
- How can his staff measure the impact to public health if it does exist?
- How much does the food safety program cost to implement?
- What is the estimated cost of food-borne illness in the state, from both direct medical expenditures and lost school and work days?

Question 1 What sort of roles and responsibilities do environmental health professionals have regarding food safety?

Question 2 What type of information would the environmental health director need to know to help make his case to the state legislature?

Question 3 From the farm to the plate, what are some of the ways food can become contaminated with pathogens?

BACKGROUND ON FOOD SAFETY

The U.S. Centers for Disease Control and Prevention (CDC) estimates 48 million food-borne illnesses occur every year— 128,000 people are hospitalized and 3,000 die from food-borne illness.[1] A majority of these food-borne illnesses are mild and, therefore, never reported. The most common pathogens responsible for food-borne illness include Campylobacter, *Salmonella*, and *Escherichia coli* 0157:H7.[2] These pathogens are found abundantly in nature and throughout the course of food processing. According to CDC, the foods most commonly associated with food-borne illness outbreaks are raw foods from animal origins, including meat, poultry, raw eggs, unpasteurized milk or cheese, and raw seafood. Processed foods that combine raw animal products, such as sausage or ground beef, also pose a high risk of contamination. In addition, raw vegetables and fruit are considered at high risk of contamination due to unsanitary processing conditions, such as using fecal contaminated water for washing and rinsing.[3] Upon reaching a processing facility or restaurant, food can be contaminated as a result of improper sanitary conditions, such as dirty equipment or poor personal hygiene, as well as close contact with other foods that are at high risk for contamination, such as raw meats. Thus, food contamination can occur during many points in the food production process.

State and local health departments use food safety inspections to prevent illnesses that can be caused by food contamination. The current food safety inspection system, based on the concept of Hazard Analysis and Critical Control Point (HACCP), is a preventive approach to food safety as opposed to a reactive approach.[4] The HACCP system is intended to prevent the occurrence of food safety issues "by assessing the inherent hazards attributable to a product or a process, determining the necessary steps that will control the identified hazards, and implementing managerial control practices . . ."[5(para 1)] The HACCP system identifies critical control points, which inform inspection guidelines that define critical versus noncritical violations. A critical violation, as defined by the U.S. Food and Drug Administration (FDA) 2001 *Food Code*, is a violation "that, if in noncompliance, is more likely than other violations to contribute to *food* contamination, illness, or environmental health *hazard*."[6(Listing of Terms: 19a)] The five general circumstances for food-borne illness include:

1. Food from unsafe sources—such as food past its expiration date
2. Inadequate cooking—for example, poultry or beef that is not cooked to the appropriate temperature to ensure pathogens are destroyed
3. Improper holding temperatures—for example, dairy products or seafood not stored in adequately cold temperatures to keep from spoiling
4. Contaminated equipment—such as dirty cooking implements or surfaces directly involved in food preparation
5. Personal hygiene—for example, employees not washing their hands after using the bathroom[7]

Evidence of these conditions or behaviors during an inspection indicates noncompliance with the *Food Code* and results in a critical violation.

According to the FDA, routine food safety inspections have been an integral part of food safety regulation since the early days of public health.[8] As Americans have increasingly eaten meals outside of the home, retail food inspections have become an essential component of the food safety system. However, the responsibility for food safety in the United States spreads beyond the FDA, across many agencies, at all levels of government.

> More than 3,000 state, local and tribal agencies have primary responsibility to regulate the retail food and foodservice industries in the United States. They are responsible for the inspection and oversight of over 1 million food establishments—restaurants and grocery stores, as well as vending machines, cafeterias, and other outlets in healthcare facilities, schools, and correctional facilities.[9(para 1)]

States vary according to where they house retail food programs. For example, responsibility may reside at the state-level agriculture department, state-level environmental health department, at the county level, or it may be a shared responsibility among multiple entities. In Louisiana, the retail food program is centralized within the Center for Environmental Health in the Louisiana Office of Public Health. The Center for Environmental Health ensures safety for almost 32,000 food establishments throughout the state of Louisiana. The term *food establishments* includes full-service restaurants, fast-food businesses, cafeterias in hospitals, prisons, nursing homes, and schools, concession stands, delis, bars, and grocery stores. The primary functions of the state food safety program include:

- Responding to consumer complaints and reports of food-borne illness
- Providing food safety certification
- Issuing permits
- Conducting food establishment inspections
- Performing food safety education[10]

These essential services are designed to ensure the food supply is adequately protected for Louisiana residents and visitors.

Another important component of the food safety system is food outbreak surveillance and response. According to the CDC, food-borne outbreak investigations help identify new pathogens, new routes of exposure, and potential gaps in the food safety system. They also help improve scientific understanding of the nature of food contamination and more effective strategies to prevent illness from occurring.[11] Public health professionals monitor the occurrence of food-borne outbreaks to be able to understand what caused an outbreak, control the source of the outbreak, minimize the number of people affected, and prevent future outbreaks from happening. There are seven primary steps that occur during an investigation of a food-borne disease outbreak (see Box 16-1).

The role of state public health agencies in a food-borne outbreak investigation depends on the size and scope of the outbreak. State health agencies will generally become involved if an outbreak spans several cities or counties but will also work with federal partners in the event of a multistate outbreak. Investigating a food-borne disease involves several professional disciplines within public health, including epidemiologists, microbiologists, environmental health specialists, or sanitarians, as well as regulatory compliance officers or inspectors.[13] In Louisiana, responsibility for food-borne disease investigations falls on the Infectious Disease Section within the Community Health Office—outside of John's office. Therefore, in the case of an outbreak, sanitarians and

food safety inspectors in John's office must work very closely with the epidemiologists and microbiologists in the Infectious Disease Section to find the source of the outbreak and minimize the risk to the population. However, the Community Health Office faces similar budget cuts as John's environmental health program and works with limited staff capacity and resources when responding to outbreaks. Deepening budget cuts will affect all aspects of the food safety system in Louisiana and could affect the agency's ability to adequately respond and protect public health in the event of an outbreak.

> **Question 4** What food safety practices would a health inspector look for during a routine restaurant inspection?
>
> **Question 5** What are examples of recent food-borne illness outbreaks that have taken place in the last 2 years? What was the cause of the outbreak?
>
> **Question 6** What actions can health inspectors take to mitigate or prevent an outbreak from occurring?

WORKFORCE SHORTAGES, FOOD SAFETY INSPECTIONS, AND HUMAN HEALTH: AN EVIDENCE BASE?

Across the United States, counties and states have recently been coping with similar budgetary challenges. According to a survey of state health officials conducted by the Association of State and Territorial Health Officials in 2009, 83% of state health departments suffered job losses between July 2008 and July 2009, and almost three quarters of state health departments made cuts to their fiscal year 2009 budget.[14] States are dealing with these budget cuts by eliminating entire programs and reducing services. Additionally, state health departments are incapable of filling some positions when staff leave or retire.

> John wanted to find out more about how other states' food safety programs had been affected by workforce shortages and how other states performed evaluations of their programs. To gather this information, John had one of his staff members review the scientific literature regarding the utility and effectiveness of food safety programs. She came across a few news articles from El Paso County, Colorado, where, for a number of years, the health department has lacked the staff resources to perform two inspections per year of restaurants and other food providers as required by law.[15] Additionally, a report released in 2008 on the healthcare infrastructure in Colorado Springs (in El Paso County), revealed complaints about restaurant cleanliness and employee hygiene increased from 60 in 2005 to 219 in 2007. The report went on to explain that the health department's annual budget was relatively low compared to other departments within the county, and that the Colorado

---

BOX 16-1 Steps for Investigating a Food-Borne Disease Outbreak

1. Detecting a possible outbreak
2. Defining and finding cases
3. Generating hypotheses about likely sources
4. Testing the hypotheses
5. Finding the point of contamination of and source of the food
6. Controlling an outbreak
7. Deciding an outbreak is over[12]

Outbreaks are identified through public health surveillance, informal and formal reporting, and laboratory testing and tracking. Once a possible outbreak has been identified, public health officials go through the subsequent steps to identify possible cases, find the point of contamination, and take action to prevent more cases from occurring. The steps do not necessarily have to happen in this sequence and often overlap one another in time or occur at the same time.

Department of Health and Environment's number of full-time-equivalent personnel was only two thirds the national average. This makes performing inspections in accordance with state regulations very difficult. The authors of the Colorado Springs report noted that although the county has not seen a major increase in food-borne outbreaks, complaints of sickness from food poisoning increased nearly threefold from 2005 to 2006.[16] While this association is not necessarily causative, the Colorado Springs report suggested that workforce shortages may present serious public health risks.

John's researcher also found several peer-reviewed articles discussing restaurant inspection frequency. Allwood, Lee, and Bordon-Glass published an article in 1999 comparing restaurant mean inspection scores in Bloomington, Minnesota, between 1987, when inspections were performed four times a year, and 1988, when the health department faced diminishing resources and was forced to decrease the frequency of inspections to three times a year. The study showed restaurant inspection scores were significantly higher (better) in 1987 when restaurants were inspected four times a year, compared to 1988, when frequency was decreased.[17] The authors concluded that routine "restaurant health inspections continue to play a vital role in protecting the public from foodborne disease."[18](Discussion, para 1)

In contrast, Canadian researchers performed a study to assess the impact of inspection frequency on compliance of food safety regulations in restaurants. The researchers identified high-risk restaurants and routinely inspected them three, four, or five times a year. They then compared inspection scores among the three frequency groups. The authors did not find a statistical difference between outcome measures based on inspection frequency.[19] The results of this research therefore shed doubt on the findings from the Allwood et al. study. Despite their findings, the authors from Canada concluded that "food premise inspections should continue to play an important role in protecting the public from food-borne illnesses by educating workers."[20](p 60)

In the peer-reviewed literature, the staff member came across several contradictory studies that analyzed the utility and effectiveness of restaurant inspections. The Seattle-King County Washington Health Department performed the first such study in 1987. It conducted a study to determine whether poor routine inspection scores were associated with reported outbreaks in restaurants. To conduct this study, the health department identified 28 case restaurants that reported a food-borne outbreak and two control restaurants per case that did not report an outbreak (56 control restaurants). The Seattle-King County researchers found, "restaurants with poor inspection results [were] *more* likely to have outbreaks,"[21](p 590) and that routine inspections by the health department could help identify restaurants with an increased risk of an outbreak. However, when epidemiologists from the Florida Department of Health tested the claims made by the Seattle-

King study by performing a similar analysis of routine restaurant inspections during 1995 in Miami-Dade County, Florida, researchers found that lower inspection results did not correlate with an increased risk of an outbreak.[22]

Despite variances in the literature regarding the frequency of retail food inspections and the ability to predict restaurant-induced outbreaks, the FDA still recommends that to sustain an effective risk-based food safety program, state agencies should maintain well-resourced programs. The FDA 2009 *Food Code*, a model document intended to provide government entities at all levels with scientifically sound guidance for regulating the retail and food service industry, recommends:

> ... regulatory agencies should have adequate funding, staff, and equipment necessary to support a risk-based retail food safety program designed to reduce the occurrence of food-borne illness risk factors. Program management should do everything they can to secure funding and resources to support regulatory food programs.[23](Section 3.D.)

The FDA also recommends every food safety program should have at least one full-time staff member devoted to food for every 280–320 inspections.[24] In Louisiana, the ratio of sanitarians to the number of expected food inspections is already much higher than the recommended FDA ratio; this does not even consider other inspection responsibilities of the sanitarians. Sanitarian inspection responsibilities cover a wide range of program areas, including: beach monitoring, building and premises, commercial seafood, disease/vector control, food and drug, infectious waste, milk and dairy control, mollusks and shellfish, on-site wastewater, and retail food establishments.[25] For example, in the East Baton Rouge area, only seven sanitarians perform all the inspections required by Louisiana regulations. There are approximately 2,775 food establishments in the East Baton Rouge area, which creates a ratio of 396 retail food establishments in need of inspection per sanitarian. In the current situation, East Baton Rouge sanitarians must perform nearly 25% more inspections than FDA recommends for an effective food safety program. This ratio does not even consider the other sanitarian program area inspections. Even now, it is difficult for John's sanitarian staff to perform the number of inspections required at the recommended frequency to protect public health. Continued cuts to the budget will result in decreased staff capacity and place greater inspection responsibilities on the remaining sanitarians, who will in turn have to reduce inspection frequency and quality.

Question 7 What have you learned thus far that could better inform your answer to question No. 2?

Question 8 The literature review illustrated the studies conducted were varied in methodology and are not recent publications; how do you think this would impact on John's current dilemma?

After reviewing the background literature, John is presented with several options for his program evaluation. He does not have the time or resources to carry out a lengthy prospective study like some of the studies from the literature. However, his department uses an online database to store and track the results of food safety inspections. In this database, John has access to all electronic inspections of food establishments from 2005 (the electronic system was not available before then). For each inspection record, John can access several key pieces of information, including the date of inspection, the type of inspection (e.g., routine, reinspection, or complaint), and critical and noncritical violation information. Through this electronic system, John can also track which restaurants received complaints and view the results of the inspections that followed from those complaints. Additionally, John can contact the Infectious Disease Section for information and data on recent outbreaks in the state.

Question 9 As John begins to design his program evaluation, what principal factors should be evaluated? Outline a suggested methodology. Consider its strengths and limitations. Keep in mind that John has a relatively small amount of time left to make his case to the governor.

Question 10 Assume that even in the best scenario, John will face some budget cuts and will need to balance the level of available resources while ensuring an adequate level of protection against illness. Is there a way he can glean insights from his program evaluation to begin to inform the following decisions?

1. Should he cut additional personnel?
2. Should he limit the scope of his department's environmental health services (for example, reduce the number of retail food inspections, or eliminate or cut back on some of his other environmental health programs)?

THE FUTURE OF PUBLIC HEALTH IN A BUDGET-CONSTRAINED WORLD

The current reality is that substantial budget cuts threaten the ability of all levels of government to provide an adequate level of public health protection. With increased budget cuts, many public health departments are experiencing workforce reductions and are not able to continue many public health programs. In a study conducted by the Association of State and Territorial Health Officials in 2010, the four primary measures state health departments are taking in response to the budget cuts include eliminating programs, reducing services, lowering administrative costs, and cutting back staff via layoffs, furloughs, and attrition. Since 2008, 87% of state health departments have suffered job losses, and they were expected to face another 16% in budget cuts by fiscal year 2011.[26] Local health departments echo the struggle faced by state health departments. The local health department workforce was hit by a 15% reduction in 2008 and 2009. Additionally, 38% of local health departments reported a lower budget in 2010 than the previous year. Local environmental health programs were ranked third in terms of hardest-hit programs, experiencing 17% of cuts, next to chronic disease screening and treatment programs at 19% and clinical health services at 21% of all cuts.[27] According to the Trust for America's Health Report, *Shortchanging America's Health: A State-by-State Look at How Public Health Dollars are Spent and Key State Health Facts*, CDC funds for state and local health environmental health programs saw a total of $87,680,289 in cuts during fiscal year 2009.[28] All three tiers of government face budgetary challenges, and as a result, workforce reductions.

Furthermore, the environmental health workforce in state health departments is shrinking rapidly. In addition to budgetary reductions, environmental health workforce shortages are a result of several other factors, including the accelerated rate at which environmental health professionals are retiring. There is also a lack of skill set and interest in environmental health, which health departments have to overcome in order to recruit and train new staff. This dilemma can be attributed to underqualified candidates, a lack of competitive salary for state health departments, and insufficient environmental health marketing efforts. The environmental health workforce must confront these challenges with better outreach and marketing to universities and trade schools to help recruit younger people into the field. Additionally, environmental public health professionals need strong science and data to validate the effectiveness of their programs, especially during lean financial periods.

About the Authors

Lindsey Realmuto, MPH, received her master of public health degree from The George Washington University in the spring of 2011. Her studies focused on environmental and occupational health. This case study was based on Lindsey's culminating project for her MPH, entitled, *State Health Agency Workforce Shortages and Implications for Public Health: A*

Case Study of Restaurant Inspections in Louisiana. Lindsey is currently an environmental health analyst for the Association of State and Territorial Health Officials (ASTHO). Her work portfolio areas include safe water, toxicology/chemical safety, and the State Environmental Health Directors peer group. Prior to joining ASTHO, she worked for The George Washington University as a research assistant for a pharmaceutical marketing research project in the Department of Environmental and Occupational Health. Before moving to Washington, DC, she worked at NO/AIDS Task Force, a nonprofit HIV clinic in New Orleans, Louisiana. She received her BA from Tulane University, where she majored in Latin American studies and Spanish. Lindsey currently resides in Washington, DC.

Surili Sutaria, MS, is a senior environmental health analyst at ASTHO. Her portfolios include climate change, vector and zoonotic diseases, environmental health workforce development and messaging, and state asthma legislation. Before working on the environmental health team, Surili worked on the ASTHO emergency preparedness team. Surili holds a master of science degree in biomedical science policy and advocacy from Georgetown University and bachelor's degrees in political science and biology from the University of Maryland, Baltimore County.

REFERENCES

1. U.S. Centers for Disease Control and Prevention. Estimates of Foodborne Illness in the United States. http://www.cdc.gov/foodborneburden/index.html. Updated December 22, 2010. Accessed April 3, 2011.

2. Centers for Disease Control and Prevention. Foodborne infections: what are the most common foodborne diseases? http://www.cdc.gov/nczved/divisions/dfbmd/diseases/foodborne_infections/#common. Updated December 13, 2010. Accessed April 3, 2011.

3. Centers for Disease Control and Prevention. Foodborne infections: what foods are most associated with foodborne illness? http://www.cdc.gov/nczved/divisions/dfbmd/diseases/foodborne_infections/#association. Updated December 13, 2010. Accessed April 3, 2011.

4. US Food and Drug Administration. FDA 2001 food code—annex 5: HACCP guidelines. http://www.fda.gov/Food/FoodSafety/RetailFoodProtection/FoodCode/FoodCode2001/ucm089302.htm. Updated April 2004. Accessed April 5, 2010.

5. Idem. US Food and Drug Administration. Annex 5. April 2004.

6. US Food and Drug Administration. FDA 2001 food code—chapter 1: purpose and definitions. http://www.fda.gov/Food/FoodSafety/RetailFoodProtection/FoodCode/FoodCode2001/ucm089124.htm. Updated April 2004. Accessed April 5, 2010.

7. Idem. US Food and Drug Administration. Annex 5. April 2004.

8. Idem. US Food and Drug Administration. Annex 5. April 2004.

9. FDA. Retail food protection: a cooperative program. http://www.fda.gov/Food/FoodSafety/RetailFoodProtection/default.htm. Updated February 9, 2011. Accessed April 3, 2011.

10. Louisiana Center for Environmental Health, Office of Public Health. Retail food program home page. http://www.dhh.louisiana.gov/offices/?ID=216. Accessed November 7, 2010.

11. Centers for Disease Control and Prevention. Preventing future outbreaks. December 2009. http://www.cdc.gov/outbreaknet/investigations/preventing.html. Accessed November 7, 2010.

12. Centers for Disease Control and Prevention. Investigating foodborne outbreaks. December 2009. http://www.cdc.gov/outbreaknet/investigations/investigating.html. Accessed November 7, 2010.

13. Centers for Disease Control and Prevention. Key players in foodborne outbreak response. December 2009. http://www.cdc.gov/outbreaknet/investigations/key_players.html. Accessed November 7, 2010.

14. Association of State and Territorial Health Officials. Impact of budget cuts on state public health. http://www.astho.org/Display/AssetDisplay.aspx?id=4818. Accessed November 7, 2010.

15. Auge K. Home of TABOR in a pinch. *The Denver Post*. March 1. 2009. http://www.denverpost.com/newsheadlines/ci_11810109.Accessed April 3, 2011.

16. Limbert WM and Beard S. Health care infrastructure in Colorado Springs—chapter 1: Public health. January 2008. Colorado Springs, CO: Western Strategies Institute.

17. Allwood P, Lee P, Borden-Glass P. The vital role of restaurant health inspections. *J Environ Health*. 1999;61(9):25–28.

18. Allwood et al, 1999.

19. Newbold KB, McKeary M, Hart R, Hall R. Restaurant inspection frequency and food safety compliance. *J Environ Health*. 2008;71(4):56–61.

20. Newbold et al, 2008.

21. Irwin K, Ballard J, Grendon K, Kobayashi J. Results of routine inspections can predict outbreaks of foodborne illness: the Seattle-King County experience. *AJPH*. 1989;79(5):586–590.

22. Cruz M, Katz D, Suarez J. An assessment of the ability of routine restaurant inspections to predict food-borne outbreaks in Miami-Dade County, Florida. *AJPH*. 2001;91(5):821–823.

23. U.S. Food and Drug Administration. FDA food code 2009: annex 5—conducting risk-based inspection. http://www.fda.gov/Food/FoodSafety/RetailFoodProtection/FoodCode/FoodCode2009/ucm187947.htm. Updated October 30, 2009. Accessed April 28, 2010.

24. Idem. U.S. Food and Drug Administration. Annex 5. October 30, 2009.

25. Sanitarian Services; Center for Environmental Health. Louisiana Department of Health and Hospitals. Title 51. Public health—sanitary code. http://www.dhh.louisiana.gov/offices/?ID=206. Accessed February 1, 2010.

26. Association of State and Territorial Health Agencies. Impact of budget cuts on state public health. http://www.astho.org/Display/AssetDisplay.aspx?id=4818. October 2010. Accessed November 5, 2010.

27. National Association of City and County Health Officials. Local health department job losses and program cuts: state-level tables from January/February 2010 survey. http://www.naccho.org/advocacy/upload/JobLossSurvey_State-level-tables-3-10.pdf. Published March 2010. Accessed November 5, 2010.

28. Trust for America's Health. Shortchanging America's health: a state-by-state look at how public health dollars are spent and key state health facts. http://healthyamericans.org/assets/files/TFAH2010Shortchanging05.pdf. March 2010. Accessed November 5, 2010.

Cardiac Rehabilitation for the Elderly:

A Public Health Perspective

LARRY F. HAMM

A PATIENT QUESTION LEADS TO HOMEWORK FOR DR. NELSON

Dr. Nelson is an internal medicine physician who has been in practice for only a year. His practice is in a metropolitan area, and he treats patients with a wide variety of chronic diseases; many of his patients are elderly and minorities.

About 3 weeks ago he was notified by an interventional cardiologist at the local hospital that one of his patients, Ms. Smith, was admitted emergently to the hospital with vague left shoulder pain and dyspnea. In the emergency room, her electrocardiogram and preliminary blood test results indicated that she was experiencing an acute myocardial infarction.

She was taken to the cardiac catheterization laboratory and significant atherosclerotic lesions were identified in two of her coronary arteries. She underwent urgent percutaneous transluminal coronary angioplasty, and two stents were inserted.

Ms. Smith had an uneventful recovery and she had one outpatient follow-up appointment with Dr. Nelson. During that appointment, she asked the physician his opinion about whether or not she should attend a cardiac rehabilitation program. She had received some literature about cardiac rehabilitation during her hospitalization but didn't know if she should consider being referred to and attending a program.

Being relatively new in practice and having previously managed only a few patients post–myocardial infarction, Dr. Nelson was uncertain as to the best answer to Ms. Smith's question. Is cardiac rehabilitation effective, or is it simply unnecessary medical care? Specifically, is it effective for secondary prevention of cardiac mortality and morbidity? Would it put Ms. Smith at risk for another heart attack? Would she be able to afford it? He suspected that, even if effectiveness was established in general, all cardiac rehabilitation programs were not created equal. How would they be able to identify a quality program? He didn't voice these concerns to Ms. Smith, but instead told her that he would look into the issue and they could discuss it again at her next follow-up appointment in 2 weeks.

Dr. Nelson developed the following list of questions concerning cardiac rehabilitation for Ms. Smith:

- What are the general benefits of cardiac rehabilitation?
- Is cardiac rehabilitation appropriate for this 79-year-old woman?
- What are the costs associated with cardiac rehabilitation services?
- Does Ms. Smith's health insurance cover cardiac rehabilitation?
- What is the reputation of the cardiac rehabilitation program at the hospital?

Dr. Nelson decided that he would have to do some literature research, network with colleagues within his local medical community, and briefly visit the program at the hospital in order to develop an informed opinion about cardiac rehabilitation and answer Ms. Smith's question.

MS. SMITH'S PERTINENT MEDICAL HISTORY

Ms. Smith is a 79-year-old, African American woman who is a widow. She has two adult children, one of whom lives in the immediate area. She stopped smoking cigarettes 20 years ago and has never used recreational drugs. She drinks wine on some social occasions only. She had no history of heart disease prior to this myocardial infarction.

Her risk factors for atherosclerotic heart disease include:

- A 22-year history of essential hypertension intermittently controlled with medications
- A 4-year history of type 2 diabetes mellitus controlled with a biguanide
- Class I obesity (body mass index = 33.9 kg/m^2)
- Physically inactive

Her primary health insurance is Medicare, and Ms. Smith has a secondary health insurance policy from her former employer, which she maintained after retirement.

THE HEALTHCARE ISSUES

Dr. Nelson identified several issues that are important for patients with atherosclerotic heart disease and are recovering from a myocardial infarction. He needed to:

1. Determine the strength of the clinical/scientific evidence for the efficacy of cardiac rehabilitation both in general and for elderly women.
2. Identify the current Centers for Medicare and Medicaid Services regulations concerning cardiac rehabilitation.
3. Assess the quality of the cardiac rehabilitation program at the local hospital.

On the basis of this list, Dr. Nelson would then develop a recommendation regarding a referral of Ms. Smith to cardiac rehabilitation.

CARDIAC REHABILITATION: CLINICAL AND POLITICAL BACKGROUND

Contemporary cardiac rehabilitation services are comprehensive, long-term programs involving medical evaluation, prescribed exercise, cardiac risk factor modification, education, and counseling. Programs are designed to limit the physiologic and psychologic effects of cardiac illness, reduce the risk for sudden death or reinfarction, control cardiac symptoms, stabilize or reverse the atherosclerotic process, and enhance the psychosocial and vocational status of selected patients.[1] Cardiac rehabilitation services are provided by a multidisciplinary team. The specific composition of the cardiac rehabilitation team will vary from program to program but is generally composed of some combination of physicians, nurses, clinical exercise physiologists, physical or occupational therapists, clinical dietitians, diabetes educators, pharmacists, and clinical psychologists. Cardiac rehabilitation is related to several public health goals, including:

- Promoting and encouraging healthy behaviors
- Informing, educating, and empowering people about health issues

- Assuring the quality and accessibility of health services

HOW DOES CARDIAC REHABILITATION RELATE TO THESE PUBLIC HEALTH GOALS?

Promoting and Encouraging Healthy Behaviors

A major goal of cardiac rehabilitation is secondary prevention of cardiovascular events. In order to achieve this, programs must provide educational information and counseling to assist patients with understanding their personal risk factors for cardiovascular disease and provide patients with strategies and a plan to effectively manage these risk factors so that the risk for future clinical events is reduced.

Informing, Educating, and Empowering People about Health Issues

Cardiac rehabilitation addresses more than cardiovascular disease. It also provides information to patients about diseases and lifestyle issues that are risk factors for cardiovascular disease. This requires that appropriate members of the multidisciplinary team provide education and intervention strategies for diabetes mellitus, hypertension, abnormal blood lipid values, obesity, smoking, physical inactivity, and diet. Patients are empowered to make lifestyle changes (making dietary modifications, engaging in physical activity, and reducing or eliminating obesity) that will positively impact their cardiovascular risk profiles.

Assuring the Quality and Accessibility of Health Services

Referral to a cardiac rehabilitation program for patients with select cardiac diagnoses has been approved as a quality measure by the National Quality Forum (NQF).[2] As described in Box 17-1, the NQF is a nonprofit organization that has a three-part mission to help improve the quality of health care in America.

In addition, referral to cardiac rehabilitation and selected program outcomes are included in published performance measures.[3] The American Heart Association and the American College of Cardiology have classified the scientific evidence for the use of cardiac rehabilitation as I-B, indicating that treatment should be administered, and the benefits greatly exceed any risks.

Cardiac rehabilitation programs have a relatively short history in American medicine since the first programs began to appear in this country in the late 1960s and early 1970s. Unfortunately, physicians in training for the internal medi-

BOX 17-1 The National Quality Forum

The NQF is a nonprofit organization supported by a contract with the Department of Health and Human Services to help establish quality and efficiency measures for reporting on and improving healthcare quality. The NQF's mission includes:

1. Setting national priorities and goals for performance improvement
2. Endorsing national consensus standards for measuring and publicly reporting on performance
3. Promoting the attainment of national goals through education

Sources: National Quality Forum. http://www.qualityforum.org/About_NQF/About_NQF.aspx. Accessed November 29, 2010.

cine specialty or the cardiovascular diseases subspecialty receive very little information about or training in cardiac rehabilitation. Thus, the questions facing Dr. Nelson in this case study are a common experience for many newly trained physicians.

DR. NELSON'S DECISION-MAKING PROCESS

Strength of Evidence for the Safety and Efficacy of Cardiac Rehabilitation in General and in Elderly Women

The first step Dr. Nelson took in his data-gathering efforts was to request a literature search of cardiac rehabilitation outcomes in order to assess the clinical and scientific evidence for possibly recommending cardiac rehabilitation to Ms. Smith. This search identified several articles that reviewed studies concerning the safety and clinical benefits for patients who received cardiac rehabilitation compared to those who did not.[4–10]

Cardiac rehabilitation is safe, with a major cardiovascular event occurring in 1 of every 50,000 to 120,000 patient-hours of supervised exercise. The reported frequency of fatal events was 2 per 1.5 million patient-hours of exercise. The prestigious Cochrane Collaboration has reviewed the clinical benefits of cardiac rehabilitation. In this systematic review, the authors concluded that the pooled effect for cardiac mortality in the exercise-only programs demonstrated a reduction

of 31% (OR [odds ratio] 0.69 95% CI [confidence interval] 0.51 to 0.94) and 26% (OR 0.74 CI 0.57 to 0.96) in the comprehensive cardiac rehabilitation programs. This magnitude of reduced mortality is similar to that for the majority of medications currently recommended for secondary prevention in patients with atherosclerotic heart disease. The position of the American College of Cardiology and the American Heart Association on exercise training and cardiac rehabilitation for the secondary prevention of atherosclerotic vascular disease was revised in 2006.[7]

In addition to becoming aware of any potential general benefits for all patients participating in cardiac rehabilitation, Dr. Nelson was also interested in assessing any issues specific to the fact that Ms. Smith is elderly, African American, and a woman. Dr. Nelson discovered that, similar to other areas of cardiovascular health disparities, elderly, minorities, and women are often underserved when it comes to cardiac rehabilitation.[11–13] Yet, the benefits of cardiac rehabilitation for patients participating in cardiac rehabilitation are applicable to the elderly. The 5-year cumulative mortality rate in elderly patients ($\geq$ 65 years of age) who participated in cardiac rehabilitation was statistically lower at 16.3% compared to 24.6% in elderly patients who did not use cardiac rehabilitation. A significant reduction in 5-year mortality was also reported in favor of women aged 75–84 years who used cardiac rehabilitation compared to those who did not (17.2% vs. 30.7%) and also for nonwhites (18.1% vs. 28.1%).[14] In the elderly patients, there was also a significant dose effect in that patients who completed the maximum of 36 cardiac rehabilitation sessions had a 47% lower risk of death and a 31% lower risk of having a subsequent myocardial infarction compared to patients who attended only one session.[15] Cardiac rehabilitation also increased functional capacity and improved the performance of activities of daily living in elderly patients.[16]

Because Ms. Smith is an African American woman, Dr. Nelson was interested to read that being a woman and a member of an ethnic minority often negatively affects referral to and utilization of cardiac rehabilitation.[12–14,17,18] Minority women have a more adverse prognosis following a cardiac event, and despite the fact that it has been widely documented that cardiac rehabilitation improves survival, fewer minority women are referred to cardiac rehabilitation compared to white women. Indeed, cardiac rehabilitation is specifically recommended for women following an acute cardiac event.[19]

Dr. Nelson read a few other articles indicating there is a generalized issue concerning referral to and utilization of cardiac rehabilitation programs.[13,17] Based on data from a large Medicare database, utilization of cardiac rehabilitation by Medicare patients after experiencing a myocardial infarction averaged 13.9%; following coronary artery bypass graft surgery, utilization was 31%. Dr. Nelson also identified additional relevant information related to this referral and utilization issue.[12,14,20]

Current Centers for Medicare and Medicaid Services Regulations for Cardiac Rehabilitation

After speaking with the clinical director of the cardiac rehabilitation program at the local hospital where Dr. Nelson has admitting privileges, he realized that the current Centers for Medicare and Medicaid Services coverage for cardiac rehabilitation services has been significantly and positively affected by both legislative[21] and regulatory[22] decisions during the last few years. With the passage of Public Law 110-275, cardiac rehabilitation became a mandated service for Medicare patients who have a covered cardiac diagnosis. These covered diagnoses include myocardial infarction, coronary artery bypass graft surgery, stable angina pectoris, percutaneous coronary interventions with or without stenting, heart valve repair or replacement, and heart or heart-lung transplantation.

New Medicare regulations developed as a result of this 2008 legislation provide payment for up to 36 cardiac rehabilitation sessions delivered within 36 weeks. With some slight geographic variation, the payment rate per cardiac rehabilitation session from Centers for Medicare and Medicaid Services to programs is approximately $68. The patient co-payment responsibility is $13.86 per session.

Assessing the Quality of the Local Cardiac Rehabilitation Program

While meeting with the program director of the cardiac rehabilitation program at the local hospital, Dr. Nelson learned more about providing a quality program. They discussed a scientific statement from the American Association of Cardiovascular and Pulmonary Rehabilitation (AACVPR) and the American Heart Association concerning core components for a comprehensive cardiac rehabilitation program.[23] These core programmatic components include a patient assessment, recommended interventions, and expected outcomes in the several clinical areas (see Box 17-2).

The program director showed Dr. Nelson that each of these recommended core components were included in his program's protocols. Dr. Nelson thought that having Ms. Smith attend this program could be an effective way to assist him in addressing her coronary artery disease risk factors—hypertension, type 2 diabetes mellitus, class I obesity, and sedentary behavior. The program director also discussed the multidisciplinary program staff, which was composed of a physician medical director, nurses, and clinical exercise physiologists. In addition, the program used a clinical dietician, a clinical psychologist, and a pharmacist on a part-time basis.

Dr. Nelson also discovered during this conversation that the program regularly measures clinical outcomes in each

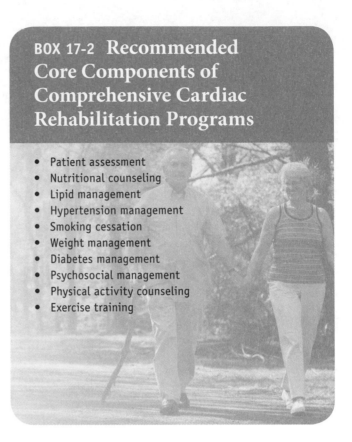

BOX 17-2 Recommended Core Components of Comprehensive Cardiac Rehabilitation Programs

- Patient assessment
- Nutritional counseling
- Lipid management
- Hypertension management
- Smoking cessation
- Weight management
- Diabetes management
- Psychosocial management
- Physical activity counseling
- Exercise training

patient and reports these outcomes to the referring physicians. Program outcomes are compiled by combining individual patient outcomes over a specified period of time. The program director shared some sample program outcomes from the last year with Dr. Nelson, who concluded that these outcome data could be helpful to him in determining if positive changes were occurring in a patient's health status and risk factor profile for atherosclerotic heart disease.

Related to this quality discussion, Dr. Nelson had read that there are published performance measures for cardiac rehabilitation.[3,24] These performance measures are part of an effort by the American Heart Association and the American College of Cardiology to provide tools for assessing and improving the quality of cardiovascular care. These performance measures were developed in response to the fact that a number of healthcare organizations have endorsed the use of cardiac rehabilitation in published practice guidelines and practice management papers. Additionally, the importance of these performance measures was increased by having them elevated to endorsement by the NQF as quality measures.[25]

The performance measures are both structure- and process-based measures and have been organized into two sets—set A and set B. Set A measures the referral of patients with appropriate cardiac diagnoses to a cardiac rehabilitation program. As a physician relatively new to private practice but attuned to performance evaluation, Dr. Nelson thought it might be helpful to prospectively collect this information in an effort to document one aspect of his quality of care for cardiac patients. The set B measures are related to the optimal structure and processes within cardiac rehabilitation programs. The measures are related to the published core components for programs and provide a structure for measuring and reporting program outcomes. The program director told Dr. Nelson that the program was using the set B performance measures for this purpose.

Finally, the program director told Dr. Nelson that the program has been certified by the AACVPR[25] for the past 7 years. Advantages to being a certified program include improving and meeting important standards of care; recognition by patients and family members that the program operates at a high standard; and recognition by some insurance companies that the essential standards required by the certification process can be used as performance measures of patient care.

What Will Dr. Nelson Recommend?

Once Dr. Nelson completed his research, it was time for him to decide whether or not to refer Ms. Nelson to cardiac rehabilitation. Point by point, he evaluated the information he had collected concerning cardiac rehabilitation and drew his conclusions:

- Is clinical efficacy established?
- What about quality assurance for cardiac rehabilitation programs?
- Would Ms. Smith have insurance coverage?
- What about the quality of the local program?
- What questions remain for Ms. Smith? Are there any barriers to her attending a cardiac rehabilitation program?

About the Author

Larry F. Hamm, PhD, is a professor of exercise science and director of the master's degree program in clinical exercise physiology in the School of Public Health and Health Services at The George Washington University Medical Center, Washington, DC. He has 35 years of experience in cardiac rehabilitation including as program director at the Toronto Rehabilitation Centre and other positions in hospital-based and private practice cardiology programs in Minneapolis, Minnesota, and Washington, DC. Dr. Hamm was the president of the American Association of Cardiovascular and Pulmonary Rehabilitation (AACVPR) for 2008–2009. He is a fellow of AACVPR and currently serves on its board of directors. He is also a fellow of the American College of Sports Medicine and has delivered more than 130 invited lectures at national and international venues on topics related to cardiac rehabilitation and clinical exercise physiology.

REFERENCES

1. Wenger NK, Froelicher ES, Smith LK, et al. *Cardiac Rehabilitation: Clinical Practice Guideline No. 17*. Rockville, MD: U.S. Department of Health and Human Services, Public Health Service, Agency for Health Care Policy and Research and the National Heart, Lung, and Blood Institute; October 1995:p 3. AHCPR Publication No. 96-0672.

2. National Quality Forum. http://www.qualityforum.org/About_NQF/About_NQF.aspx. Accessed November 29, 2010.

3. Thomas RJ, King M, Lui K, et al. AACVPR/ACC/AHA 2007 performance measures on cardiac rehabilitation referral to and delivery of cardiac rehabilitation/secondary prevention services. *J Cardiopulm Rehabil Prev.* 2007;27:260–290.

4. Leon AS, Franklin BA, Costa F, et al. Cardiac rehabilitation and secondary prevention of coronary heart disease: an American Heart Association scientific statement from the Council on Clinical Cardiology (Subcommittee on Exercise, Cardiac Rehabilitation, and Prevention) and the Council on Nutrition, Physical Activity, and Metabolism (Subcommittee on Physical Activity) in Collaboration with the American Association of Cardiovascular and Pulmonary Rehabilitation. *Circulation.* 2005;111:369–376.

5. Williams MA, Ades PA, Hamm LF, et al. Clinical evidence for a health benefit from cardiac rehabilitation: an update. *Am Heart J.* 2006;152:835–841.

6. Taylor RS, Brown A, Ebrahim S, et al. Exercise-based rehabilitation for patients with coronary heart disease: systematic review and meta-analysis of randomized controlled trials. *Am J Med.* 2004;116:682–692.

7. Smith SC, Allen J, Blair SN, et al. AHA/ACC guidelines for secondary prevention for patients with coronary and other atherosclerotic disease: 2006 update. *Circulation.* 2006;113:2363–2372.

8. Clark AM, Hartling L, Vandermeer B, McAlister FA. Meta-analysis: secondary prevention programs for patients with coronary artery disease. *Ann Intern Med.* 2005;143:659–672.

9. Lavie CJ, Thomas RJ, Squires RW, Allison TG, Milani RV. Exercise training and cardiac rehabilitation in primary and secondary prevention of coronary heart disease. *Mayo Clin Proc.* 2009;84:373–383.

10. Joliffe J, Rees K, Taylor RRS, et al. Exercise-based rehabilitation for coronary heart disease. *Cochrane Database of Systematic Reviews.* 2001;(1):Art. No. CD001800. DOI:10.1002/14651858.CD001800.

11. Jackson L, Leclerc J, Erskine Y, Linden W. Getting the most out of cardiac rehabilitation: a review of referral and adherence predictors. *Heart.* 2005;91:10–14.

12. Mazzini MJ, Stevens GR, Whalen D, et al. Effect of an American Heart Association Get with the Guidelines program-based clinical pathway on referral and enrollment into cardiac rehabilitation after acute myocardial infarction. *Am J Cardiol.* 2008;101:1084–1087.

13. Brown TM, Hernandez AF, Bittner V, et al. Predictors of cardiac rehabilitation referral in coronary artery disease patients. Findings from the American Heart Association's Get with the Guidelines program. *J Am Coll Cardiol.* 2009;54:515–521.

14. Suaya JA, Stason WB, Ades PA, Mormand S-LT, Shepard DS. Survival in older coronary patients. *J Am Coll Cardiol.* 2009;54:25–33.

15. Hammill BG, Curtis LH, Schulman KA, Whellan DJ. Relationship between cardiac rehabilitation and long-term risks of death and myocardial infarction among elderly Medicare beneficiaries. *Circulation.* 2010;121:63–70.

16. Audelin MC, Savage PD, Ades PA. Exercise-based cardiac rehabilitation for very old patients (> 75 years). Focus on physical function. *J Cardiopulm Rehabil Prev.* 2008;28:163–173.

17. Suaya JA, Shepard DS, Normand S-LT, et al. Use of cardiac rehabilitation by Medicare beneficiaries after myocardial infarction or coronary bypass surgery. *Circulation.* 2007;116:1653–1662.

18. Mochari H, Lee JR, Kligfield P, Mosca L. Ethnic differences in barriers and referral to cardiac rehabilitation among women hospitalized with coronary heart disease. *Prev Cardiol.* 2006;9:8–13.

19. Mosca L, Banka CL, Benjamin EJ, et al. Evidence-based guidelines for cardiovascular disease prevention in women: 2007 update. *Circulation.* 2007;115:1481–1501.

20. Mueller E, Savage PD, Schneider DJ, et al. Effect of a computerized referral at hospital discharge on cardiac rehabilitation participation rates. *J Cardiopulm Rehabil Prev.* 2009;29:365–369.

21. Medicare Improvements for Patients and Providers Act of 2008. Pub L No.110-275, 122 Stat. 2492, §144.

22. *Federal Register.* November 25, 2009;74(226):62004–62005.

23. Balady GJ, Williams MA, Ades PA, et al. Core components of cardiac rehabilitation/secondary prevention programs: 2007 update. A scientific statement from the American Heart Association Exercise, Cardiac Rehabilitation, and Prevention Committee, the Council on Clinical Cardiology; the Councils on Cardiovascular Nursing, Epidemiology and Prevention, and Nutrition, Physical Activity, and Metabolism; and the American Association of Cardiovascular and Pulmonary Rehabilitation. *J Cardiopulm Rehabil Prev.* 2007;27:121–129.

24. Thomas RJ, King M, Lui K, et al. AACVPR/ACCF/AHA 2010 update: performance measures on cardiac rehabilitation for referral to cardiac rehabilitation/secondary prevention services. A report of the American Association of Cardiovascular and Pulmonary Rehabilitation and the American College of Cardiology Foundation/American Heart Association Task Force on Performance Measures. *J Cardiopulm Rehabil Prev.* 2010;30:279–288.

25. American Association of Cardiovascular and Pulmonary Rehabilitation. The AACVPR certification center. http://www.aacvpr.org/Certifcation/tabid/63/Default.aspx. Accessed November 29, 2010.

The X-Pack Smoking Cessation Kit:

A Social Marketing Case Study

LORIEN ABROMS, BRENDA L. GLEASON, KATELIN LUCARIELLO, AND ALLISON MOBLEY

"What if young adults could have their own tools for quitting smoking, which would counter the barrage of marketing they get from the tobacco industry?" Lorien Abroms asked other members of the Harvard Tobacco Control Working Group at a monthly meeting in April 1998.

"Definitely. There need to be cessation products made just for young adults. Their clothes and music are designed just for them, so why not something so important and lifesaving as a smoking cessation aid?" Jonathan Winckoff, another student member of the Harvard Tobacco Control Working group agreed.

Three student members of the Harvard Tobacco Control Working Group—Abroms, Winckoff, and Laurie Fisher—approached Population Services International (PSI) in 1998, hoping to make their idea of a product for young adult smoking cessation into a reality. Since 1970, nonprofit PSI had used social marketing to empower low-income people to lead healthier lives. PSI had promoted behavior change by providing "accurate health information, [and] readily accessible health products and services that empower people to make informed and healthy choices."[1(para1)] Its work had earned it the position as the world's leading social marketing organization.

The Harvard Tobacco Control Working Group members felt that PSI's consumer orientation was just what they needed to create a smoking cessation product aimed at young adult smokers. Simultaneously, PSI was interested in exploring innovative ideas for behavior change in health areas outside of its current scope of work. The PSI United States program staff, Alexandra Lowell and Allison Mobley, in Portland, Oregon, had a growing interest in smoking cessation and were intrigued by the concept Ms. Abroms and the others presented. In May 2001, PSI granted the Portland office a budget of $80,000 to develop a first-of-its-kind smoking cessation kit and market it in the United States within 9 months.

BACKGROUND ON SMOKING AND CESSATION

Tobacco use and addiction usually begin in adolescence. Among adults in the United States who have ever smoked daily, 82% tried their first cigarette before age 18, and 53% became daily smokers before the age of 18.[2] Awareness of the negative effects of smoking cigarettes is widespread, yet individuals continue to smoke. While the overall prevalence of cigarette smoking has decreased over the past several decades, smoking rates have remained steady among young adults.[3]

Increased smoking rates are a potential response to intensified industry focus on youth smokers. In the late 1980s, tobacco companies conducted many promotional activities targeted toward young smokers. They used fruit-flavored cigarettes and cartoon characters like Joe Camel to make their products appeal to youth.[4] Studies reviewing the period between 1978 and 1998 found increased promotional activities to be a major reason for increased adolescent smoking rates.[5,6]

In 1998, 46 states and the 4 largest tobacco companies in the United States settled Medicaid lawsuits brought forth by the states. These states filed suit against the tobacco companies to recover Medicaid funding that had gone to support tobacco-related healthcare costs. As a result, the Master Settlement Agreement (MSA) required tobacco companies to make payments to the states and, among other conditions, compelled them to stop targeting youth under 18 in the promotion of tobacco products. Although the MSA stopped the tobacco companies from marketing to youth, the tobacco companies began targeting a new age group, young adults, the youngest group they could legally pursue.

In the United States, for the 3 years following the MSA tobacco company spending on marketing increased by 66%. In 2001, for example, tobacco companies spent $11.2 billion on marketing[7] to make sure smokers bought cigarettes and enjoyed the ritual of opening each pack. While many categories of tobacco marketing expenditures decreased—for example, newspaper advertising, outdoor advertising, sporting events, and coupons—most of the increase in spending was in retail store marketing, which has been shown to be highly effective at reaching youth.[8]

Tobacco companies invest substantial funding into their marketing by studying young adults' attitudes, social groups, values, role models, and activities to learn how to best infiltrate young adults' physical and social environments.[9] Despite attempts to change the reality, tobacco companies have become very influential on young smokers. Young smokers are more likely to be aware of tobacco promotions, to own promotional items like caps and T-shirts, and to be able to identify cigarette advertisements. They are also more likely to smoke brands of cigarettes that are heavily marketed.[10]

Despite attempts by the tobacco companies, young adult smokers, who are lighter smokers, are more interested in quitting their tobacco habits than older smokers are. Among daily smokers, adults aged 18–24 years are more likely to try to quit smoking than older adults.[11] The vast majority of these quit attempts occur without the support of evidence-based tobacco cessation treatments, such as counseling, telephone quit lines, or pharmacotherapy.[12] The underutilization of support may be due to a lack of cessation programs directed at young adults. Studies have found that only around 5% of smoking cessation programs serve people in this age group.[13] The lack of promising interventions aimed at young adults is recognized as a public health problem.[14–17] The fact that three out of four young smokers tries, but fails, to quit smoking is further testament to the need for smoking cessation programs directed at this age group.[8] Studies have suggested that differences in their stage of development and smoking characteristics imply that young adults may benefit from a smoking cessation program developed around the needs and preferences of young adults.[19]

BEHAVIOR CHANGE: WHAT DOES IT TAKE?

Why do people begin smoking in the first place? Can they be influenced to quit? Human behavior is a complex concept with multiple factors influencing actions and attitudes. Modeling health behavior has changed how public health professionals think about promoting health.[20] The stages of change

BOX 18-1   The Stages of Change Model

- *Precontemplation:* Not yet acknowledging that there is a problem behavior that needs to be changed
- *Contemplation:* Acknowledging that there is a change that needs to be made but not yet ready and willing to make a change
- *Preparation/determination:* Getting ready to change the behavior
- *Action:* Taking action to change the behavior
- *Maintenance:* Maintaining the behavior change over time

Source: Data from: DiClemente CC, Prochaska JO. Processes and stages of self-change: coping and competence in smoking behavior change. In: Schiffman S and Wills T (eds). *Coping and Substance Use: A Conceptual Framework.* New York, NY: Academic Press; 1985, pp 319–343.

model (Box 18-1) was developed by a psychologist studying the behavior of smokers who were trying to quit smoking.[21] The underlying assumption of the model is that behavioral change does not happen all at once. Instead, people progress through different stages on their way to meaningful behavioral change. Likewise, people progress through the stages at their own pace.

In smoking cessation, the stages of change model helps public health professionals tailor messages to an individual's stage in the change process. According to this model, precontemplators are not considering quitting, contemplators are considering quitting in the next 6 months, and preparators are planning to quit in the next 30 days; those in the action stage have achieved cessation within the last 6 months; and individuals in the maintenance stage have quit for at least 6 months.[22]

Moving from stage to stage is associated with a variety of influencing factors including increased support while quitting. While few studies exist on the preferred smoking cessation method for young adults, public health professionals can use the stages of change model to tailor interventions in smoking cessation to young adults by identifying ways to influence the factors that promote movement from one stage to another.

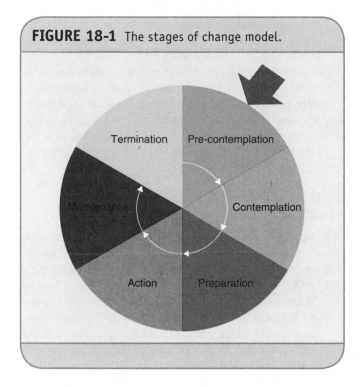

FIGURE 18-1 The stages of change model.

ESTABLISHING THE CASE FOR CHANGE

To start the project, PSI hired the smoking cessation experts—the Harvard Tobacco Control Working Group members—to write a report to document what was known about youth smoking and youth smoking cessation. The review examined psychosocial factors involved in smoking uptake and cessation and current programs that targeted young adult smokers. The report noted that while over 25% of young people were smokers, hardly any smoking cessation programs that were aimed at 18–24-year-olds existed. The literature review also found that young people are in a unique stage of the life cycle because they are in a time of transition in their lives, from high school to college, or from school to work, from being single to being married, etc. They were more likely to have an interest in quitting smoking at this time in their lives, but were less successful in their quit attempts.

USING MARKETING TO CREATE CHANGE

The American Marketing Association defines marketing as "the activity, set of institutions, and processes for creating, communicating, delivering, and exchanging offerings that have value for customers, clients, partners, and society at large . . ."[23(para 2)] Thus, marketing is not just about running ads on television, but it is also about communicating value through products and services. The primary aim of marketing in the commercial sector is financial gain.[24]

In the case of slowing or stopping tobacco use, the primary aim is not financial gain, but societal gain. Fewer smokers means longer lives, cleaner air, and lower healthcare costs. Therefore, a slightly different kind of marketing is needed—social marketing.

> **Social marketing** is the application of commercial marketing technologies to the analysis, planning, execution and evaluation of programs designed to influence the voluntary behavior of target audiences in order to improve their personal welfare and *that of their society.*[25(p91)]

The two definitions show the primary aims of social marketing and commercial marketing are different, but there is another significant difference as well. Commercial marketers are selling goods and services, but social marketers are selling behaviors. Kotler and Lee indicate public health professionals or other so-called change agents seek to change behavior in one of four ways. The recipient of the social marketing effort could be influenced to:

1. Accept a new behavior
2. Reject a potentially undesirable behavior
3. Modify a current behavior
4. Abandon a potentially undesirable behavior[26]

While social marketing typically takes the form of communication, campaigns can also distribute and promote products in order to encourage behavior change. Social marketing campaigns that distribute and promote condom and contraceptive use are examples.[27,28] Another is the distribution and promotion of bed nets to families in areas with high levels of malaria infections.[29]

SOCIAL MARKETING SMOKING CESSATION

The literature review provided PSI with a strong rationale for moving forward with the next step of developing and pilot testing a smoking cessation aid. PSI took the lead on carrying out a needs assessment and developing and testing of prototypes. The needs assessment was necessary to first ensure that there was in fact a need for the proposed product in Portland, to learn more about how young adults wanted to quit, and finally, to gain insight on the elements of a product that would be valued and used by young adult smokers.

Selecting the target market is a key component of successful social marketing campaigns. A three-step process is often used to determine the target market:

1. Segmenting the market
2. Evaluating the segments
3. Choosing one or more segments for targeting

Segmenting means trying to identify smaller groups within a larger population that will be targeted for the changed behavior. Geographic, demographic, psychographic, and behavioral variables are often used to segment consumer markets. For example, within the demographic domain, a researcher might want to consider the age, gender, income, education, race, and generation of the target market in order to best understand what motivates them. Psychographic variables include social class and lifestyle. Behavioral variables can sometimes be among the most important and include user status, usage rate, and readiness stage as mentioned previously.

In this case, the researchers had narrowed the target audience to young adults 18 to 22 years of age who smoked. During a needs assessment, researchers collect information to determine deficiencies within a population and use the information to develop a plan to address those needs. In this case, researchers looked for inadequacies in cessation programs that might be used by young adults. As part of the needs assessment, interviews were conducted with smoking cessation experts in the field. Talking to professionals already involved in smoking cessation programs would give the program team insight into a variety of issues, including:

- The products and services already available to meet the needs of the target market
- Previous successes and failures in working with the designated population
- Information on young adult smokers' behavior and habits
- A sense of how enthusiastic smoking cessation experts were about the proposed idea

Following the assessment, the team proposed that their cessation tool would provide tips and tools covering primarily the final three stages of the stages of change model—preparation, action, and maintenance. It was suggested that advice and tools to help young adults move through these stages could be packaged in some way, for example a tool kit.

From the start, PSI was intent on creating a product with a look and feel that resonated with the target audience. Essential to this goal was finding an experienced design firm that could create a product that would be just as attractive to young smokers as a pack of cigarettes was. PSI was lucky to have an award-winning design firm interested in working on the project and committed to seeing it through. Sandstrom Design, based in Portland, Oregon, had created brands and packaging for products such as Tazo Tea, Moonstruck Chocolate, Converse sneakers and clothing, and Levi Strauss Red Tab jeans.

"Cigarette companies spend a lot of money on packaging to make sure smokers enjoy opening each and every pack. That's the trouble. It's not just the nicotine that's addictive, it's the ritual," explained the program team. They presented a creative brief to Sandstrom, laying out the essentials of the young adult smoking cessation campaign. Box 18-2 provides an overview of a creative brief.

For the young adult smoking cessation program, the creative brief was informed by the literature review, the interviews conducted with smoking cessation experts, and of course, the insight gained from the target audience. Sandstrom took the creative brief and came up with two prototypes and accompanying materials including a booklet with information.

A DIFFICULT DECISION: INSIDE THE MINDS OF THE PROGRAM TEAM

In November 2001, two prototypes were shown to 27 smokers who were interested in quitting in the next 6 months. The prototypes had two themes. The first was called "Cold Turkey," named for the popular term for quitting without an aid and packaged to look like a pack of cigarettes. The second approach was packaged in a side-opening box and was called "Seven Minutes to Burn," a common phrase referring to the amount of time shortened off of one's life for each cigarette smoked.

The participants in the pilot test were responsive to both concepts, immediately picking up the kits and digging in to find out what was inside. As the interview process went on, a clear winner emerged. The imagery and feel of "Cold

BOX 18-2 A Creative Brief

A creative brief is a marketing tool that sets expectations between the team responsible for conceptualizing and executing the program and the team responsible for creating the materials that will help sell the product or service. The brief summarizes the program, what is to be achieved, and how success will be measured. Core components of a creative brief include:

- Target audience(s)
- Objective(s)
- Obstacles
- Key promise or reward to be provided
- Support statements/reasons why
- Tone
- Media
- Openings
- Creative considerations

Turkey" attracted these young adult smokers to grab the kit and learn more. They liked the look of the box and the way it flipped open from the top and how it resembled a pack of cigarettes. The box was familiar, yet promised them something different—the opportunity to quit. Of the two concepts, "Cold Turkey" was the hands-down favorite.

Excited to move on to production and distribution of the first-of-its-kind stop smoking kit for young adults, the PSI team shared the results with the Harvard Tobacco Control Working Group. Several of the tobacco cessation experts were not convinced that the winning prototype would actually work. Ms. Abroms explained, "The flip-top box looks like a box of cigarettes. It might be too much of a trigger for smoking, and may get in the way of quitting."

After 5 months of work, almost 50 interviews, and the target audience preference for "Cold Turkey" with the flip-top lid, there was no consensus about moving forward with this prototype. The collaborators had to decide what to do next. Should they follow the principles of social marketing and listen to the target audience, or should they heed the advice of the tobacco control experts?

THE SMOKING CESSATION KIT: FROM IDEA TO FRUITION

The team was faced with two main hurdles to overcome. First was the decision to be made about the flip-top box design. Second, and perhaps most importantly, was a problem the team hadn't anticipated but proved to be a significant roadblock in the development of the final smoking cessation intervention product—funding.

Question 1 How would you advise the product developers to proceed? Should they listen to the smoking cessation experts or should they create a product to which the target audience responds? What criteria might the creators use to make their decision?

WHAT HAPPENED NEXT

The first decision was whether to proceed with the flip-top box. In April 2002, PSI conducted 36 interviews with current and ex-smokers and cessation specialists and found that the top-opening box was clearly the most favored box design over a side opening box. PSI decided to proceed with the flip-top box.

PSI required that a trademark and copyright be obtained for the final product. Unfortunately because the phrase "Cold Turkey" is in common use, it was not possible to copyright or trademark "Cold Turkey." This forced the development team to go back to the drawing board. The creative team at Sandstrom Design came up with "X-Pack" (see Figure 18-2) to replace "Cold Turkey." This seemed to all team members like an appealing alternative.

The contents of the X-Pack were primarily aimed at helping a smoker who was thinking about quitting in the next month (preparation) make a successful quit attempt (action) and remain a quitter (maintenance). As such, the contents of the X-Pack were geared around these stages of the quitting process. The guidebook covered all three stages of change and gave instructions on how to move from one stage to the next. The Success-O-Meter/Ick-U-Lator—a slide card showing the harmful chemicals in cigarettes on one side and the money saved and health benefits of quitting on the other side—was aimed at preparation and increasing motivation to quit. The quit cards—which consisted of a strip of four pocket cards that listed a person's reasons for quitting, tips for getting through a craving without smoking, contact info of a friend to call for support, and a list of quitting truths—was aimed at action and getting a person through the first week of being cigarette free and beyond. Finally, the Hotlix cinnamon toothpicks, the Wrigley's Orbit chewing gum, and the Preoccupation Putty (stress putty) were designed to help people unlearn the cigarette habit and develop new habits and were aimed at action and maintenance.

The second major hurdle to be cleared, that of how to obtain and sustain funding, was more difficult. For the X-Pack to be widely distributed, significant funding would be needed. PSI had developed a website that was intended mainly to be used as a place to sell/distribute the X-Pack. The website was in much need of expansion to serve as a community resource for smokers. Funding was also needed to promote the X-Pack and let interested smokers know that the product was available. Furthermore, funding was needed to build the evidence base on the efficacy of the X-Pack. The group brainstormed a number of possible funders, such as foundations, public health agencies, and other nonprofit groups with an interest in smoking cessation—including the American Legacy Foundation. They wondered whether cause-related marketers such as MTV or Levi Strauss would be interested as part of youth health campaigns. Another possibility was to work with corporate sponsors, such as pharmaceutical companies. Some suggested talking with tobacco companies, since they are required to not encourage youth to smoke.

Question 2 How would you advise the X-Pack creators to proceed? What sources of funding should they pursue? How should they balance the need for sustained funds and their desire to stay true to their public health values?

EPILOGUE

The X-Pack was sold in a limited number of retail stores, on the Internet, and to the public health sector, including universities, county health departments, and private clinics. More than 20,000 X-Packs have been sold in the United States.

FIGURE 18-2 The final X-Pack product box and contents.

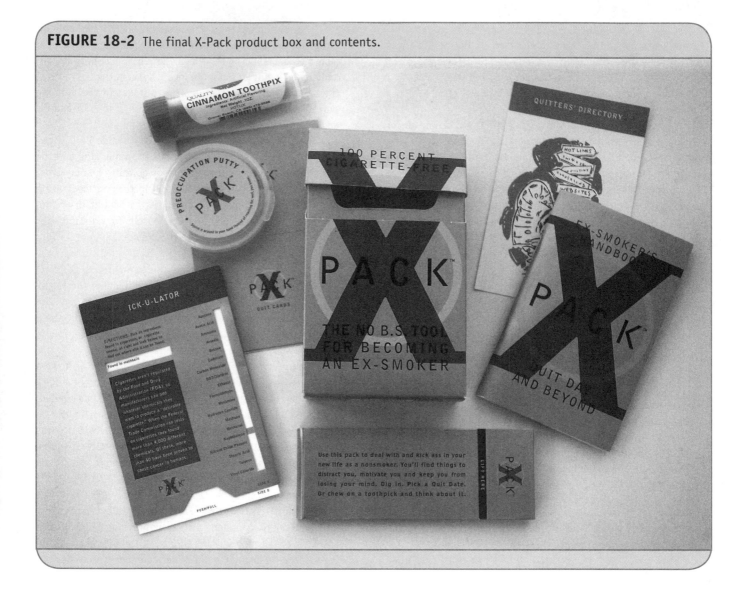

A National Institutes of Health–funded, randomized, control study tested the acceptability and efficacy of an X-Pack–based smoking cessation intervention combined with e-mail counseling from a peer. Results indicated that compared to a control group, participants in the X-Pack group were found to be more engaged in the program activities (e.g., calling up a friend or family member for support; reading their top reasons for quitting; considering pharmacotherapy), "to rate their treatment more favorably overall, and to have quit for more consecutive days at 3- and 6-month follow-ups."[30(p 31)]

The team achieved its original goal, to create a smoking cessation product aimed at young adult smokers. Despite the success of the intervention, both in terms of its appeal and preliminary indications that it could help a smoker quit, the group was ultimately not able to find funding to scale up the project in a way that would compete with either tobacco products or cessation products marketed by private industry.

About the Authors

Lorien Abroms, ScD, MA, is an assistant professor of prevention and community health in the public health communication and marketing program at The George Washington University School of Public Health and Health Services. Her research focuses on the application of social marketing for smoking cessation and other health behaviors. She participated in the development of and has evaluated the X-Pack, a smoking cessation kit for young adult smokers. Currently, she is conducting an evaluation of the Text2Quit Program, an interactive text messaging program for smoking cessation that evolved from her work on the X-Pack.

Brenda L. Gleason, MA, MPH, is the president and founder of M2 Health Care Consulting, a strategic policy and communications consulting firm with offices in Denver, Colorado, and Washington, DC. Beginning her career in health policy at the Massachusetts Department of Public Health, she has worked on issues at the intersection of business and policy for a range of industries for more than 15 years. She is a member of the adjunct faculty at The George Washington University School of Public Health and Health Services. She earned an MA from Boston College and an MPH from Boston University.

Katelin Lucariello, MPH, is a senior consultant at M2 Health Care Consulting, a strategic policy and communications firm with offices in Denver, Colorado, and Washington, DC. Her experience is concentrated in health policy research, development, and analysis, specifically in the areas of healthcare reform and state health policy. She earned her MPH degree from Boston University.

Allison Mobley, MHS, has 25 years of public and private sector marketing experience working on domestic and international programs for public health issues, including reproductive health (family planning, teen pregnancy prevention, emergency contraception), HIV/AIDS prevention, smoking cessation, and infectious disease control. She led the development of X-Pack, including formative research, creative development, prototype testing, and marketing. She has a master of health science degree in international health, with a specific focus on health communications, from Johns Hopkins University School of Hygiene and Public Health. She is the director of Behavior Works, a health communications nonprofit organization committed to developing messages and products to help people live healthier lives.

REFERENCES

1. Population Services International. Healthy lives. http://www.psi.org/our-work/healthy-lives. Accessed September 1, 2010.

2. U.S. Department of Health and Human Services. Healthy People 2010. With understanding and improving health and objectives for improving health, 2000. Vol 2, 2nd edition, pp 27–33.

3. Centers for Disease Control and Prevention. State-specific prevalence of cigarette smoking and quitting among adults—United States, 2004. *MMWR: Morb Mortal Wkly Rep.* 2005;54(44):1124–1127.

4. Carpenter C, Ferris WG, Connolly GN, et al. New cigarette brands with flavors that appeal to youth: tobacco marketing strategies. *Health Affairs.* 2005;24(6):1601–1610.

5. Pollay RW, Siddarth S, Siegel M, et al. The last straw? cigarette advertising and realized market shares among youths and adults, 1979–1993. *J Mark.* 1996;60:1–16.

6. Evans N, Farkas A, Gilpin E, Berry C, Pierce JP. Influence of tobacco marketing and exposure to smokers on adolescent susceptibility to smoking. *J Natl Cancer Inst.* 1995;87:1538–1545.

7. Federal Trade Commission cigarette report for 2001. http://www.ftc.gov/os/2003/06/2001cigreport.pdf. Issued 2003. Accessed September 1, 2010.

8. The Campaign for Tobacco Free Kids. Special report: big tobacco still addicting kids. http://www.tobaccofreekids.org/reports/addicting/. Published July 7, 2003. Accessed September 1, 2010.

9. Ling PM, Glantz SA. Why and how the tobacco industry sells cigarettes to young adults: evidence from industry documents. *Am J Public Health.* 2002;92(6):908–916.

10. Abroms L, Fisher L, Hillis V, Winickoff J. *Smoking Cessation in Youth: Literature Review for the Quitpack Project.* Submitted to Population Services International. September 7, 2001.

11. Centers for Disease Control and Prevention. *Behavioral Risk Factor Surveillance System Survey Data.* Atlanta, GA. U.S. Department of Health and Human Services.

12. Mermelstein R. Teen smoking cessation. *Tob Control.* 2003;12(Suppl 1):25–34.

13. Curry S, Emery S, Sporer A, et al. A national survey of tobacco cessation programs for youths. *Am J Public Health.* 2007;97(1):171–177.

14. Abroms L, Winickoff J, Lowell A, Mobley A. The acceptability of a self-help smoking cessation aid for youth. Presented at annual meeting of the Society for Research on Nicotine and Tobacco; 2003, New Orleans, LA.

15. Backinger C, Fagan P, Matthews E, Grana R. Adolescent and young adult tobacco prevention and cessation: current status and future directions. *Tobacco Control.* 2003;12(Suppl 4):iv46–iv53.

16. Curry S. Youth tobacco cessation: filling the gap between what we do and what we know. *Am J Health Behav.* 2003;27(Suppl 2):S99–S102.

17. Orleans C, Arkin E, Backinger C, et al. (2003). Youth tobacco cessation collaborative and national blueprint for action. *Am J Health Behavior.* 2003;27(Suppl 2):S103–S119.

18. Hines D. Young smokers' attitudes about methods for quitting smoking: barriers and benefits to using assisted methods. *Addict Behav.* 1996;21(4):531–535.

19. Andreasen A. *Marketing Social Change: Changing Behavior to Promote Health, Social Development, and the Environment.* San Francisco, CA: Jossey-Bass; 1995.

20. Maibach E, Abroms L, Marosits M. Communication and marketing as tools to cultivate the public's health: a proposed "people and places" framework. *BMC Pub Health.* 2007;7:88.

21. DiClemente CC, Prochaska, JO. *Processes and stages of self-change: coping and competence in smoking behavior change.* In Schiffman S and Wills T (eds). *Coping and Substance Use: A Conceptual Framework.* New York, NY: Academic Press; 1985.

22. DiClemente CC, Prochaska, JO, 1985.

23. American Marketing Association, Definition of Marketing, October 2007. http://www.marketingpower.com/AboutAMA/Pages/Definitionof-Marketing.aspx. Accessed April 9, 2011.

24. Kotler P, Lee NR. *Social Marketing: Influencing Behaviors for Good.* Thousand Oaks, CA: Sage Publications; 2008:13.

25. Andreasen A. *Social Marketing in the 21st Century,* Thousand Oaks, CA: Sage Publications; 2006:91.

26. Kotler P, Lee NR. *Social Marketing: Influencing Behaviors for Good.* Thousand Oaks, CA: Sage Publications; 2008:8.

27. Eloundou-Enyegue P, Meekers D, Calves A. From awareness to adoption: the effects of AIDS education and condom social marketing on condom use in Tanzania (1993–1996). *J Biosoc Sci.* 2005;37:257–268.

28. Harvey P. Let every child be wanted: how social marketing is revolutionizing contraceptive marketing around the world. Oxford, England: Greenwood Publishing; 1999.

29. Hanson K, Kikumbih N, Schellenberg J, Mponda H, Nathan R. Cost effectiveness of social marketing of insecticide-treated nets for malaria control in the United Republic of Tanzania. *Bull World Health Organ.* 2003;81:269–276.

30. Abroms LC, Windsor R, Simons-Morton B. Getting young adults to quit smoking: a formative evaluation of the X-Pack program. *Nicotine Tob Res.* 2008;10(1):27–33.

Mumps Epidemic in Iowa:

Lessons Learned from the Front Line of Testing

MICHAEL A. PENTELLA

MUMPS? OR THE SENIOR PROM?

As laboratorians, we have limited patient contact, but are trained to always remember that behind every specimen tested, there is a patient. Such was the case in the 2006 mumps outbreak in Iowa. One Friday afternoon, we received a call from a physician's office that wanted a patient test result, but the sample had not arrived in time to test it that day. The patient was a 17-year-old who needed a negative test result so she could attend her senior prom. The lab had been facing record workloads for several weeks, but things were finally slowing down and this was going to be the first Saturday off for many of us in some time. Fortunately, someone volunteered to come in and do the test on Saturday. Unfortunately the result was positive; the patient had mumps and had to be isolated, which meant missing her senior prom. While this was unfortunate, her isolation kept others from getting mumps. That is the purpose of public health—to prevent others from getting sickened.

How to manage a laboratory during an epidemic is a skill for which most course work does not specifically prepare students. In retrospect, like so many things in life, the management decisions made today may greatly impact a laboratory's capabilities tomorrow. The wrong decisions may place the laboratory in a position of not being able to respond to an event of public health importance. The seemingly unconnected decisions made during previous years greatly affected the ability of the State Hygienic Lab (SHL) at the University of Iowa to respond effectively when the largest U.S. mumps epidemic since 1988 hit Iowa in the winter and spring of 2006.

BACKGROUND: WHAT IS A STATE HYGIENIC LAB?

The SHL at the University of Iowa is the state of Iowa's environmental and public health laboratory, serving 3 million Iowans. The laboratory has been actively involved with the Centers for Disease Control and Prevention (CDC), participates in public health and emergency preparedness networks such as the Laboratory Response Network, and provides primary laboratory support for all disease outbreaks from food and water for the state of Iowa. The SHL has a staff of 260 and functions as a reference lab, analytical testing site, and training facility for state and local public health professionals, healthcare providers, and citizens of Iowa. The SHL can operate in surveillance mode or can serve as a high-capacity surge testing laboratory as it did in 2009 during the H1N1 pandemic, when it tested over 8000 specimens with a turnaround time of about 24 hours from the time the specimen was received in the lab. The SHL provides numerous training opportunities on topics such as the importance of influenza surveillance, test methods and interpretation, and biosafety, via regional workshops, teleconference, the Iowa Communications Network, on-site visits, web-based training, and other venues. SHL staff members regularly attend training provided by the CDC and Association of Public Health Laboratories on current methodology and best practice.

There are two SHL facilities in Iowa—one located in Iowa City, where most of the infectious disease testing is performed, and a second in Ankeny. The workforce is relatively small, with only three people dedicated to serology and another three

BOX 19-1 Core Functions and Capabilities of State Public Health Laboratories

1. Disease prevention, control, and surveillance
2. Integrated data management
3. Reference and specialized testing
4. Environmental health and protection
5. Food safety
6. Laboratory improvement and regulation
7. Policy development
8. Emergency response
9. Public health-related research
10. Training and education
11. Partnerships and communication

people routinely working in virology, where virus isolation and detection is performed.

Public health laboratories serve 11 core functions[1] to protect the health of the nation. These core functions are listed in Box 19-1.

THE ROLE OF THE MUMPS TEST IN PUBLIC HEALTH

The first management decision that impacted Iowa's response to the 2006 mumps outbreak actually came in the fall of 2005. The issue was whether the SHL should continue to offer a mumps test that was rarely performed. Prior to 2006, only about five mumps tests per year were conducted. In an era of cost cutting, low-volume testing offers a prime target for quick savings with minimal negative effects. Since the test was also available from commercial labs, eliminating mumps testing was an attractive choice, even though the turn-around time for positive results to be reported to the Iowa Department of Public Health would be slower than expected from the SHL. However, such a cut in costs could create a significant expense in an epidemic. To make the decision, we asked: how does mumps testing fit with the public health mission?

Mumps is an acute viral illness with symptoms including fever, headache, muscle aches, tiredness, and loss of appetite, followed by swelling of the salivary glands. It is caused by the mumps virus, which is a negative strand RNA virus of the Paramyxoviridae family. In mumps, the parotid salivary glands (which are located within the cheek, near the jaw line, below the ears) are most frequently affected. At the time of

the epidemic, mumps could be diagnosed in the laboratory by growing the mumps virus in tissue culture cells and by looking for antibodies to mumps virus from a blood sample. Whether virus culture or serology for antibodies is the most reliable test to use depends on the stage of the disease. Complications of mumps are rare, but can include meningitis, deafness, pancreatitis, orchitis, and first-trimester abortion.[2] Vaccines for mumps have been available since the 1960s, and live attenuated mumps Jeryl-Lynn strain is included in the MMR (measles, mumps, rubella) vaccine required for entry into U.S. schools. The measles, mumps, rubella vaccine is currently given on a two-dose schedule that is estimated to be 88% effective and has been shown to reduce the incidence of mumps virus by $\geq$ 97%. Due to the success of the two-dose measles, mumps, rubella vaccination program, relatively few cases have been reported in the United States in the last decade (an average of 265 cases per year since 2001).[3]

Decision 1: Keep the Test or Drop It?

Public health laboratories across the United States sustained major cutbacks between 2000 and 2010, and Iowa was not an exception. Therefore, management was constantly looking for a means to cut costs. A logical target is low-volume tests. Considerations to be analyzed before making a decision include cost of the product, retention of competent professionals to perform the test, availability of tests by other labs, and the turnaround time of the result if performed in the public health lab or referred to another lab. Public health labs aim to maintain their ability to perform the 11 core functions listed in Box 19-1. This decision exemplifies an issue that crosses into several of the core functions—namely, core function No. 1, disease prevention and control; core function No. 3, reference and specialized testing; and core function No. 8, emergency response. Cost, competency, availability, and turnaround time must be weighed against the public health significance of the test and the impact to public health if testing is not readily available.

A key question is how easily transmissible is the infectious disease agent for which the test is performed? That is, is disease spread likely while the results are pending? Measles, for example, is highly infectious and readily spread via an airborne route to those who are not vaccinated. Therefore, results are needed immediately because quick action—such as offering vaccinations—is needed to protect the health of the public. On the other hand, human papillomavirus is also infectious but not as easily spread. With measles, time is needed for investigation and emergency response, including vaccination and formulation and delivery of a message for the media.[4] While time is passing, more exposures will occur, in turn resulting in more expense as more vaccine will need to be delivered. Therefore, the sooner the lab is able to confirm a case of measles, the sooner the response can start and the less expensive it will be. In the summer of 2005, the Iowa SHL reviewed all infectious disease testing it offered by reviewing the volume of testing and the cost. The specific question was, at only five cases of mumps per year, why even offer mumps testing? Fortunately, the SHL management made a decision in the summer of 2005 to keep the test on the menu of services.

Decision 2: When to Implement the Emergency Response Plan

In December 2005, the mumps outbreak began in Iowa. By September 2006, a total of 1643 confirmed cases and 315 probable cases had been reported by the Iowa Department of Public Health. The mumps epidemic spread to neighboring states with over 1000 confirmed and probable cases reported by May of 2006 in Illinois, Kansas, Missouri, Nebraska, Pennsylvania, South Dakota, and Wisconsin. Followup with Iowa mumps cases revealed that most had received one or two doses of the vaccine.[3] It is unclear why this epidemic occurred in a highly vaccinated population.

The second major decision faced by the SHL pertaining to mumps came in early 2006, and concerned when to implement its incident response plan. Iowa's SHL emergency response plan was developed in 2004 for response to pandemic influenza or a bioterrorism event. The intent of having an emergency response plan is to have a tool to assist the lab in meeting an increase in test requests. An epidemic brings a surge of testing that can quickly overwhelm the resources of the lab. The emergency response plan is designed to assist the lab with additional resources, such as additional staffing to help meet the surge of testing. When did the mumps epidemic rise to the level of emergency needed to trigger execution of the response plan?

On April 1, 2006, the SHL implemented its emergency response plan—the first such time it had put this plan into practice. There is no magic formula that tells you that your test volume or case numbers are so high that the only way to manage a response to the surge in test requests is to implement your emergency response plan. For the SHL, activating the plan involved implementation of the incident command system (ICS),[5] which is a term used to describe the policies and procedures utilized to efficiently and effectively respond to an event. It is designed to reduce problems and allow for a single point of control—the incident commander. There was every indication that the mumps epidemic should not spread as far as it did because the population in Iowa had high vaccine coverage (that is, a large percentage of individuals were vaccinated). But as we later discovered, even those who were vaccinated could be infected.

Figure 19-1 displays the number of mumps tests that were processed by the SHL from January to June of 2006. Because of the graph's large scale, it is a little difficult to see from the figure that 57 mumps tests had been conducted by February 26, with an additional 388 by March 26. After a major event such as this epidemic, when incident command systems have been implemented, it is common practice to review the event in detail so that lessons may be learned. This is commonly called an after action report. From the after action perspective, implementation of the ICS should have been considered by March 1, 2006.

A major reason for the delay was the time it took for individuals involved with the ICS to master the skills required to effectively work with the ICS structure. It is understood that regularly exercising the ICS is essential to maintain the skills needed to respond during an event, and the SHL had not exercised enough to acquire the necessary skill level. Furthermore, since staff changes occur, it may be necessary to have a system in place to build ICS competency and maintain it.

Decision 3: Whether to Develop New Technology

The third decision the SHL faced was when to develop new technology to meet demand. At the start of the epidemic, there were two tests available to diagnose infection with mumps—serology and culture. While the serology test results were routinely available within 24 hours of receipt of the specimen, the virus culture could take up to 7 days for the virus to grow. When the serology test was positive, the physician could be assured that the patient had mumps. However, if the test was negative, it could be another 7 days to know for certain that the patient did not have mumps. This was far too long to keep individuals in quarantine if they did not have mumps. As the epidemic spread throughout Iowa and to other states, the need to have a test with a more rapid turnaround time was recognized. Therefore, the SHL worked with the CDC to develop a technologic solution through the development of a mumps polymerase chain reaction test, which is equivalent to virus culture in sensitivity and specificity. The SHL was fortunate to have an Association of Public Health Laboratories and CDC emerging infectious diseases fellow available to work on the development of this new test.[6] Through this collaboration, in a matter of weeks, a new test was validated. Since mumps was spreading to patients in other states, the SHL and CDC made the test available to other state public health labs. This synergy among state public health labs and CDC adds great strength to the public health system, and the national Laboratory Response Network[7] serves as an outstanding example of the great abilities of the U.S. public health system.

FIGURE 19-1 Mumps testing in Iowa, January through June 2006.

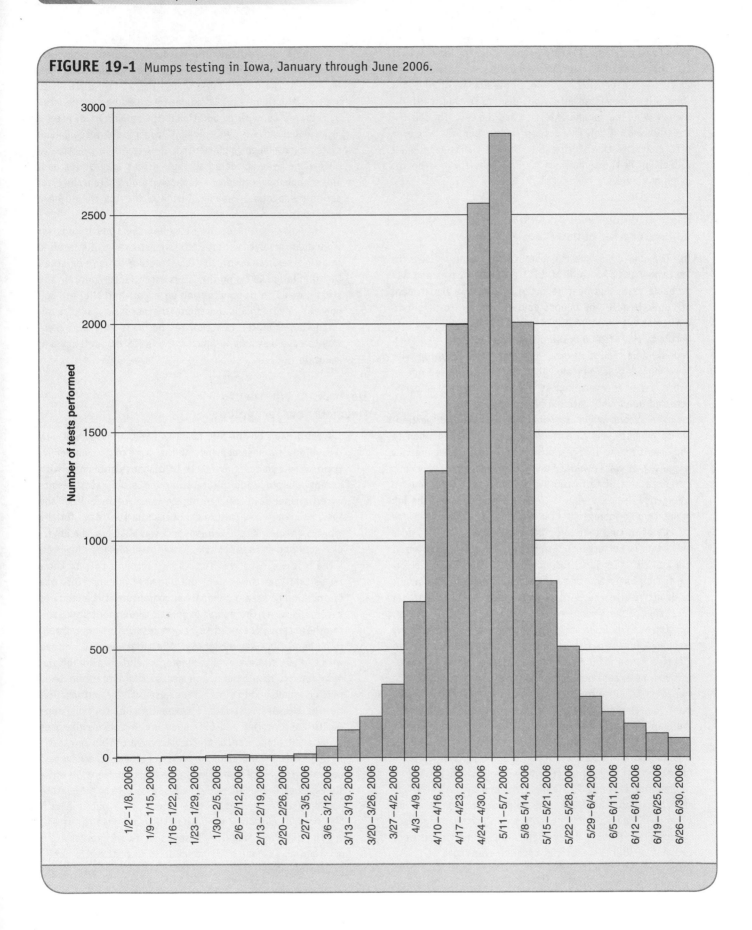

Power point extra credit

THE IMPORTANCE OF INFRASTRUCTURE

Providing testing services requires a competent workforce, laboratory space, instrumentation, reagents, supplies, and electronic communication capabilities. This is what is known as infrastructure. In order to mount a response to an epidemic, there has to be in place sufficient infrastructure to support the activities needed to collect specimens, perform the tests, report results, and meet the surge of testing demanded. The SHL had been building the infrastructure of the lab since the anthrax attacks of 2001. With the support of federal funding from the CDC in support of the National Laboratory Response Network initiative, emergency response activities have been emphasized and addressed. Those funds designated for terrorism preparedness allowed for the strengthening of the public health lab so that challenges such as the mumps epidemic could be met. Although the mumps epidemic and a bioterrorism event are entirely different, the emergency response infrastructure that responds to both is essentially very similar.

The SHL had worked with clinical lab partners in preparation for a bioterrorism emergency, so a network of communication had already been built. This network was called the "Iowa Laboratory Response Network" and consisted of every lab in Iowa that performs clinical laboratory tests. An e-mail mailing list was started in 2004 that allowed the SHL to send messages to the Iowa Laboratory Response Network. Instructions on collecting specimens were easily disseminated throughout the state. The interconnectivity of labs is sometimes overlooked. This can result in obstacles, for example, to surveillance, and cause further spread of the disease. Labs often fail to comply with voluntary guidelines of public health reporting processes and the submission of specimens, causing the laboratory system to fail. This requires training and relationship building to overcome. Strong collaborations and partnerships in all areas of the public health laboratory are essential for the success of the national laboratory system.

In retrospect, there were many other decisions that the SHL had made prior to the epidemic that served to mitigate the impact of the outbreak. In 2003, a courier system was implemented to serve the hygienic lab's newborn screening program and the biological/chemical terrorism response program for samples suspected to contain agents of bioterrorism. In 2005, the courier system was expanded to include delivery of clinical specimens to and from the laboratories in Iowa to the SHL's Iowa City and Ankeny labs. By the time of the 2006 mumps epidemic, specimen transport to the SHL was already well established with a daily courier system that operated throughout Iowa, delivering specimens from the 135 labs to the SHL the same day that the specimen was collected.

The hygienic lab's web-based reporting system also expedited access to test results. Created by the lab's information technology group, an Internet-based system allowed labs to retrieve results through a password-protected site on the SHL's home web page, thus replacing phoned and mailed results and significantly reducing time for health providers to receive test results. While this useful electronic result reporting had been developed, only about 50% of the labs were utilizing this service at the time of the outbreak. The others had to be quickly added so that the results did not have to be phoned or mailed. Using this service, the testing results of mumps samples received in the morning were available to providers that same afternoon. The program continues to add subscribers and functions successfully today.

Ultimately, the success of the hygienic lab's mumps response was dependent on the dedication of the laboratorians to complete testing, to develop a new test during the epidemic, and to provide an essential public health service for Iowans.

In addition to strides that were made during the mumps epidemic, many lessons were learned from the hygienic laboratory response. Plans that originally were created primarily for a terrorism event or pandemic influenza epidemic were strengthened. The experience demonstrates the need for a cohesive, integrated system that can respond quickly to threats to the public health.

BE GRATEFUL FOR DEDICATED PERSONNEL

While all the tests, infrastructure, and new technology were essential to the laboratory success, none of this was possible without dedicated staff who performed the work. Those individuals stayed late, worked weekends, deferred vacations, and made many sacrifices because testing needed to get done.

Laboratorians are truly unsung heroes, receiving little recognition for what they do. Yet it is critical to healthcare delivery that accurate laboratory testing be delivered. As previously mentioned, a small staff actually did the testing; the decision makers behind this story are mentioned in the acknowledgments. But they were supported by the couriers, the information technology staff who programmed the reports, the data entry staff who accessioned the specimens, the central service staff who packaged kits and took care of shipping and receiving, the client service staff who manned the telephones to answer questions, the secretaries who fielded calls and kept us organized, the housekeeping staff who kept the lab clean, the molecular biologist who designed a new test, the microbiologist who reviewed results and maintained the quality, and the managers and directors who tried to make data-driven decisions.

While the 17-year-old patient anxiously awaited her test results, she probably did not know that there was a small army of scientists and support staff making certain that the result was performed quickly and accurately for the benefit of the citizens of Iowa.

ACKNOWLEDGMENTS

The decision-makers behind the story of the 2006 mumps epidemic in Iowa include: Mary Gilchrist, laboratory director; Michael Pentella, program manager for virology; Lucy Desjardin, program manager for molecular diagnostics; Sandy Jirsa, virology supervisor; Tom Gahan, serology supervisor; Jennifer Boddicker, emerging infectious disease fellow; and, Bonnie Rubin, emergency response coordinator.

About the Author

Michael A. Pentella, PhD, SM(ASCP), CIC, D(ABMM), is the associate director for infectious disease at the University of Iowa hygienic laboratory and holds an associate professor clinical position with the University of Iowa College of Public Health. He received his BS degree in microbiology from Ohio State University, his MS degree in clinical microbiology from Thomas Jefferson University, and his PhD degree in infectious disease from the University of South Florida, College of Public Health. He has over 30 years' experience in the clinical microbiology laboratory and over 20 years' experience in hospital infection control and epidemiology. He is certified as a specialist in microbiology through the American Society for Clinical Pathology, in infection control through the Association of Professionals in Infection Control, and he is also certified as an American Board of Medical Microbiology diplomate. He has written over 20 articles and 4 book chapters. He is a member of several statewide committees, such as Iowa's Antibiotic Resistance Task Force, and national committees for infectious diseases and preparedness, such as the Association of Public Health Laboratories' Infectious Disease Committee. Dr. Pentella's interests are in infectious disease prevention, biodefense, antimicrobial resistance, food-borne pathogens, and emerging infectious diseases.

REFERENCES

1. Witt-Kushner J, Astles JR, Ridderhof JC, et al. Core functions and capabilities of state public health laboratories. *MMWR Morb Mortal Wkly Rep.* 2002;51(RR14):1–18.

2. Dayan GH, Quinlisk MP, Parker AA, et al. Recent resurgence of mumps in the United States. *N Engl J Med.* 2008;358:1580–1589.

3. Centers for Disease Control and Prevention (CDC). Update: multistate outbreak of mumps e—United States, January 1–May 2, 2006. *MMWR Morb Mortal Wkly Rep.* 2006;55:559–563.

4. Dayan GH, Ortega-Sanchez IR, LeBaron CW, Quinlisk MP. The cost of containing one case of measles: the economic impact on the public health infrastructure—Iowa 2004. *Pediatrics.* 2005;116:e1–e4.

5. United States Department of Homeland Security. National Incident Management System. Washington, DC: U.S. Department of Homeland Security, 2008. Accessed April 10, 2011.

6. Boddicker JD, Rota P, Kreman T, et al. Real-time RT-PCR assay for the detection of mumps virus RNA in clinical specimens. *J Clin Microbiol.* 2007;45:2902–2908.

7. Centers for Disease Control and Prevention (CDC). Biological and chemical terrorism: strategic plan for preparedness and response. *MMWR Morb Mortal Wkly Rep.* 2000;49(RR04):1–14.

Big Brother Is Watching:

Utilizing Clinical Decision Support as a Tool to Limit Adverse Drug Events

AARON ROBERTS

A CRISIS IN THE EMERGENCY ROOM

It was nearing 3 p.m. in the emergency department and the charge nurse was rapidly losing her daily battle to make the hands of the clock move more quickly. The day had proven to be somewhat busy for a Friday afternoon, and she couldn't wait for a chance to rest her weary feet. The most disappointing case of the day involved a kind, elderly gentleman that the attending physician was only barely able to stabilize. She remembered taking a peek at his chart and being stunned at how quickly a manageable situation had gotten out of hand. A little past 8 a.m., "Miller, Richard" had arrived in her unit after his routine morning finger prick had alerted him to an increased blood glucose level—high enough, he thought, to warrant some medical attention. The 78-year-old patient had recounted his current medication to the receptionist and the staff had checked multiple times to determine whether he had any drug allergies. After a brief stint in the waiting area and a decently short time in one of the emergency beds, he was out the door. In hand were two new prescriptions and an extra dose of comfort. However, 4 hours later, he was back in the emergency department, this time in critical condition with clear signs of an adverse drug reaction. The charge nurse could only wonder whether direct hospital error or some other cause had contributed to Mr. Miller's condition.

MEDICATION ERRORS

In the United States, medication errors account for 44,000 deaths and millions of hospitalizations and clinical visits a year.[1] These statistics are the consequences of adverse drug events (ADEs), which are any unexpected side effects attributed to the use of a combination of drugs. Researchers have estimated that 95% of adverse drug reactions go un-reported.[2] However, of those ADEs that are recognized, a substantial proportion can be attributed directly to mistakes made by hospital staff. Many health providers have turned to new health information technology as a way to reduce this burgeoning problem. In particular, the development of computer-decision support systems is a potential step toward reducing this problem and a step toward preventing people like Richard Miller from spending his night in the emergency department.

Costs

In 2003, U.S. spending on prescription drugs soared to over $200 billion, with spending for 40 popular drugs reaching $1 billion apiece.[3] The prevalence of suboptimal prescribing practices has been estimated to be as high as 30%.[4] Every year, $177.4 billion is wasted to cover morbidity and mortality caused by adverse drug events.[5] A drug reaction may lead to hospitalization and outpatient treatment, which can account for over a third of hospital visits for the aging population.[6] When combined, the direct costs for hospitalization for ADEs, the costs of poor prescribing practices, and calculated indirect costs amount to a sum that would reinvigorate an ailing U.S. healthcare system.

Health Disparities

Mr. Miller, as an elderly diabetic, belongs to a subgroup that experiences a disproportionate number of adverse drug events. Although increased age has been cited as a key risk factor for adverse drug reactions, other measures, such as the existence of comorbidities, better typify this issue.[7] Among older patients, the drugs insulin, warfarin, and digoxin contribute to a third of all adverse drug events.[8] Patients with chronic conditions, especially those that affect drug distribution, experience more adverse drug events.[9] Individuals taking anticoagulants or medications that interfere with the central nervous system are also at increased risk.[10] Additionally, whites and those with private insurance are more likely to face adverse drug reactions as their increased access to health services causes them to be at risk more often.[11]

Limited Research

The rush of new and increasingly popular drugs to the market has led to controversy regarding the effectiveness and appropriateness of certain treatment options. For example, statins, a class of drugs designed to reduce levels of low-density lipoprotein cholesterol, are widely prescribed. Every year, articles show strong evidence that these drugs are extremely effective at producing better health outcomes.[12] They are countered by equally striking evidence showing this class of drugs is largely ineffective.[13] The uncertainty demonstrated by scientific research hasn't slowed the increase in prescribing rates, with statins quadrupling in total use among ambulatory patients over 10 years and occupying 90% of the lipid-lowering market in 2002.[14] Researchers are unlikely to use older patients as subjects in trials to test new drugs.[15] So, one possibility in Mr. Miller's case is that the hospital staff may have administered the correctly indicated drug, but the research that contributed to its approval may not have been comprehensive. Additionally, physicians don't generally wait for the final verdict on effectiveness before choosing to prescribe new drugs, making adverse drug events and suboptimal prescribing a possibility.

Prescribing Errors

On the other hand, the physician in charge of Mr. Miller's case may have prescribed an incorrect medication—either one that negatively impacted his concurrent ailments or one that interacts poorly with other medications. Patients often see a variety of different specialists, who aren't always given accurate information about patient medication history.[16] Changes to drug regimens made by one provider may not always be relayed to other physicians caring for a shared patient.[17] Even when such prescribing information is shared, physicians and pharmacists may have limited knowledge about adverse drug events because they are not up to date on current findings. To limit prescribing errors, physicians should be using tools like the Beers criteria for potentially inappropriate medication use in

FIGURE 20-1 Medication appropriateness index.

Adapted tool to determine medication appropriateness			
To assess the appropriateness of the drug, please answer the following questions and circle the applicable rating:			
1. Is there an indication for the drug? Comments:	A Indicated	B	C Not Indicated
2. Is the medication effective for the condition? Comments:	A Effective	B	C Ineffective
3. Is the dosage correct? Comments:	A Correct	B	C Incorrect
4. Are the directions correct? Comments:	A Correct	B	C Incorrect
5. Are the directions practical? Comments:	A Practical	B	C Impractical
6. Are there clinically significant drug-drug interactions? Comments:	A Significant	B	C Insignificant
7. Are there clinically significant drug-disease/condition interactions? Comments:	A Significant	B	C Insignificant
8. Is there unnecessary duplication with other drugs(s)? Comments:	A Necessary	B	C Unnecessary
9. Is the duration of therapy acceptable? Comments:	A Acceptable	B	C Unacceptable
10. Is this drug the least expensive alternative compared with others of equal utility? Comments:	A Acceptable	B	C Unacceptable

Source: Hanlon JT, Schmader KE, Samsa GP, et al. A method for assessing drug therapy appropriateness. *J Clin Epidemiol.* 1992;45:1045–1051.

the elderly[18] and the Medication Appropriateness Index (see Figure 20-1) to limit prescribing errors.

Mistakes can occur elsewhere as well. Appropriately prescribed medication may not reach the patient due to poor handwriting or overuse of abbreviations. Telephone orders may be easily confused.[19] When healthcare providers overcome these barriers, patients are able to get the correct prescriptions and will hopefully be placed along the path toward improved health.

Medication Adherence

It's possible that Mr. Miller may have taken an incorrect dosage or combined his new prescription with some synergistic medium such as alcohol. Medication adherence requires proper understanding of proper dosage and when to take medications as well as a willingness to stick to drug regimens. Simple things, like remembering to take medication, also become more difficult as people age or succumb to disorders like dementia. The costs associated with many popular pharmaceuticals can also hinder medication adherence, as patients sometimes choose not to fill prescriptions in order to save money.

Strong provider-patient relationships, in which patients have their concerns answered, contribute to higher rates of adherence.[14] Patients take the medications they feel were prescribed correctly and will achieve the desired results. Assistance from physicians and pharmacists with prescription refills and medication schedules helps to improve patient comprehension and increase medication adherence. The minimal time available to hurried emergency physicians and nurses may not leave sufficient time to ensure patients like Mr. Miller understand their medication instructions.[20]

Challenges in Long-Term Care

Nursing homes continue to care for a substantial fraction of the population over 65. Some would argue Mr. Miller may need more directed care if he cannot manage his medication needs. Unfortunately, the choice to move an elderly patient to managed care doesn't completely protect him from adverse drug events. Studies have shown that nursing home patients take, on average, 8.8 medications daily, making nursing homes breeding grounds for medication error.[21] Patients have been found to receive the incorrect medication, to receive medication at the wrong time of day, or miss a treatment altogether. Nursing home workers have a high level of job strain, have to cope with poor staffing levels, and often feel guilty about not being able to adequately meet the needs of residents.[22] Within such a high-demand work environment, mistakes are not surprising. In a third of cases, however, medication

errors are made repeatedly.[23] Decreasing rates of adverse drug events not only provides better health outcomes among nursing home residents; it also helps to lower the already stifling costs of institutionalized care.

Polypharmacy as a Risk Factor

Mr. Miller's earlier trip to the emergency department and his current condition could be completely coincidental. It is possible his body had not withstood the effects of polypharmacy. Polypharmacy, the excessive prescription of medication, has begun to take a heavy toll on the elderly population. By 2000, 37 million doctor visits by people over the age of 65 (one quarter of all such visits) ended with patients being prescribed at least five different medications.[24] Excessive prescription can refer simply to the number of medications (usually five or more) or to cases in which drugs are inappropriately or unnecessarily prescribed. Patients taking more than five medications are more likely to have combinations that lead to adverse drug events.[14] The reaction that brought Mr. Miller back into the hospital could have been caused by one of his other combinations and may have had nothing to do with his new prescriptions. Nonetheless, the most effective approach to prevent his unfortunate situation would have been if the emergency department staff had taken steps to reassess his drug use.

ADVERSE DRUG EVENTS AS A PUBLIC HEALTH CONCERN

Adverse drug events are a concern for individuals as well as communities. Driving has been an area of particular concern for older adults. Many medications, especially antidepressants, alter the ability of an individual to stay focused behind the wheel. Very little research has been conducted on the effect of multiple medications on driving ability.[25] Considering the general decline in driving ability and reaction time associated with specific classes of drugs, this should be an area of concern for policy makers. It would have been most unfortunate if Mr. Miller had experienced his reaction while behind the wheel.

Falls are also associated with adverse drug events. Individuals prescribed numerous prescriptions are at high risk for falls and consequent debilitating injuries. Falls are a serious concern for the aging population as the associated injuries can often lead to a loss of independence or hasten individual decline toward death. Interventions designed to reduce the incidence of falls often aim to reduce adverse combinations of drugs among patients.[26] Patients who take fewer medications have fewer drug reactions that interfere with their daily activities.

HEALTH INFORMATION TECHNOLOGY—A SOLUTION?

New technologies are always emerging in health-related fields as older instruments are updated or a new product is designed to increase productivity. Electronic medical records (EMRs) emerged as a way to improve quality of care and increase efficiency. An EMR serves as a replacement for paper medical records by electronically storing critical patient information in a central location.[27] EMRs provide enhanced documentation and allow physicians to pool patient information. They may offer certain clinical tools, like medication ordering or patient assessments. Equipped with evidence for the effectiveness of this technology, 31% of emergency departments and 17% of physicians' offices had switched to EMRs in 2003.[28] Currently, 11% of hospitals have fully implemented systems, while 66% more have partially implemented systems.[29] Although a skeptical Mr. Miller may question the safety of health information being stored electronically, his physicians are more thankful for the clarity these systems can provide. Early support systems were programmed to provide reminders to hospital staff, to catch errors before they occur, or to perform basic diagnostic tasks.[30] These more progressive programs, termed *clinical decision support (CDS) systems*, have been utilized in attempts to reduce the occurrence of adverse drug events.

Three examples that follow describe research into the impact of clinical decision support programs. Could these systems have changed the circumstance at hand and prevented Mr. Miller's critical health crisis?

Case 1: CDS in Prescribing Practices

Researchers in the Pacific Northwest took notice of the high prevalence of adverse drug events nationwide and the thousands of deaths that can be attributed to preventable mistakes. Their study design attempted to reduce ADEs through the use of CDS. All 450,000 members of a health maintenance organization group were included in the study in an attempt to best represent the general population of this region. The primary care physicians, nurse practitioners, and physician's assistants recruited for the study were already acquainted with electronic medical record systems, allowing them to enter patient orders (for lab tests, medication needs, and treatment options) electronically. The quasiexperimental intervention began with a 12-month observational period designed to identify provider prescribing practices, followed by a 27-month intervention period. Using a computerized decision support system, researchers were able to alert providers of a preferred alternative when they prescribed a nonpreferred drug. The criterion for a nonpreferred drug was established as those that were not indicated for use in older patients, including a class of long-acting benzodiazepines and tertiary

amine tricyclic antidepressants. This technology alerted physicians when they prescribed one of the suboptimal drugs. It is important to note that even though these drugs were acceptable in younger patients, the technology raised alerts for all patients. Thus, alerts were drug specific and did not vary based on patient characteristics or any aspect specific to a patient's case. After receiving an alert, providers then had the option to change the medication or to ignore the alert. The number of medication alerts and data on dispensing rates were used to determine the effectiveness of the intervention.[31]

Patients whose cases evoked alerts were most likely to be older (22.9 alerts per 10,000 for patients over age 65 versus 8.2 alerts in patients under 65) and female (69.4% of elderly women but only 56.2% of elderly men triggered alerts). A 22% decrease from the initial prescribing rate of nonpreferred medications was seen after the first month of the intervention; this lower rate of prescription of 16.1 dispenses per 10,000 held for the duration of the trial. The use of preferred medications also spiked 20% after the first month of the intervention and then experienced a slight but steady increase throughout the course of the experiment. The most dramatic changes in prescribing pattern occurred in the elderly population. However, prescription of preferred medications also increased among nonelderly patients, an unexpected result for researchers. The subclasses of drugs that experienced the largest overall change in dispensing rates in favor of preferred drug classes were those for which physicians could see clear evidence for clinical equivalency and for which there was a consensus on drug effectiveness.[31]

Overall, the use of this new technology helped to limit the frequency of nonpreferred medications prescribed to elderly patients. The system appeared to be widely accepted by clinicians, as some were more likely to order the preferred medication after receiving an alert because the system automatically filled important parts of the prescription, thus saving the physician more time to allot to adequately treating patients.[31]

Could a system like this have helped improve Mr. Miller's situation?

Case 2: CDS in Medication Adherence

Respiratory therapies represent an area in which patients do not always employ the recommended treatment options. One approach designed to improve treatment utilization is to train more knowledgeable healthcare providers who can better communicate care management strategies to patients. One randomized intervention study was carried by Indiana University's medical group in an attempt to increase treatment adherence among respiratory patients. This intervention targeted patients seen by physicians across four hospitals with shared medical records. Seven hundred and six patients were initially enrolled in the study and about two thirds completed the final survey.[32]

Patients were randomized into four different intervention groups according to the physicians they saw, and were additionally randomized to obtain medication from a single pharmacist. In the first group, both the physician and the pharmacist received the intervention, while only the provider or the pharmacist received the intervention in the second and third. A final comparison group received no intervention. Patient-specific care suggestions were generated by a panel of expert clinicians and programmed into each physician's electronic workstations, with explanations and references. Care suggestions fit into several key categories that can be found in Table 20-1. As a member of the intervention group, Mr. Miller's physician would have been presented with a care suggestion on her workstation when she wanted to order new care options or review patient information. Members of the intervention groups were required to view all suggestions, with an option to order or omit the new care options. They were also presented with information being used in concurrent studies, such as medication warning alerts[32] (similar to the alerts from the Pacific Northwest intervention).

Researchers were left with somewhat less promising results than they would have liked. At the conclusion of the trial, there was no significant difference in patient adherence or satisfaction with providers across the experimental groups. There was an isolated improvement in emotional quality of life for those who received medication from a pharmacist in the intervention group. In this provider-centered approach,

---

TABLE 20-1 Potential Suggestions for Providers Used in Case 2—CDS in Medication Adherence

- Performing pulmonary function tests
- Giving influenza and pneumococcal vaccinations
- Prescribing inhaled steroid preparations in patients with frequent symptoms of dyspnea
- Prescribing inhaled anticholinergic agents in patients with chronic obstructive pulmonary disease
- Escalating doses of inhaled β-adrenergic agonists for all patients with persistent symptoms ·
- Prescribing theophylline for patients with chronic obstructive pulmonary disease and continued symptoms despite aggressive use of inhaled anticholinergic agents, β-agonists, and steroids
- Encouraging smoking cessation

Source: Data from Tierney W, Overhage M, Murray M, et al. Can computer-generated evidence-based care suggestions enhance evidence-based management of asthma and chronic obstructive pulmonary disease? A randomized, controlled trial. *Health Serv Res.* 2005;40(2): 477–498.

---

designed to create improvements in adherence, physicians expressed mixed opinions about the care suggestions. Some felt the suggestions were helpful and educational, while others believed they were too rigorous and infringed on physician autonomy. Physicians in the intervention groups also experienced significantly higher healthcare costs.[32]

Would a system like this have helped Mr. Miller's geriatrician convey health information more effectively, and thereby enhance Mr. Miller's medication adherence?

Case 3: North Carolina Initiative

The North Carolina Long-Term Care Polypharmacy Initiative used CDS to improve patient health outcomes in the nursing home setting. If fate did push Mr. Miller into a long-term care setting, his care would be greatly impacted by the changes enacted by this initiative. This intervention was developed by a Medicaid case management firm, Community Care of North Carolina, and involved both physicians and pharmacists. The study originated from a desire to lower medication costs for long-term care residents, but evolved into an effort to reduce polypharmacy and adverse drug events. This intervention built upon two previous pilot studies and began with an assessment of detailed baseline demographic and health information for over 8000 participants.[33]

Lengthy computer algorithms were used to determine five categories of medication profiles that should be brought to the attention of the pharmacists. The alert categories, listed in Table 20-2, were formed based on drug interactions, costs, and effectiveness. Using the alert system and Medicaid claims information, patient medication records were reviewed and flagged for further pharmacy services. The pharmacists would then make recommendations to providers, which, based on the discretion of the provider, could lead to a change in drug regimens. A prospective aspect was also added to the intervention, allowing pharmacists to take action when they received new medication orders that warranted concern. This two-pronged approach was designed to end a cycle of bad practice, by protecting new and existing patients from adverse medication combinations. An initial 90-day baseline period was followed by a 90-day intervention period and a 90-day postintervention period. Hospitalizations, drug alerts, and costs were tracked. The targeted group was compared with other Medicaid patients not enrolled in this program in order to provide a viable comparison group.[31]

For analysis, subjects were divided into 10 groups based on the services they received and whether those were retroactive or prospective actions. The most significant results were found among patients who received both prospective and retrospective services that eventually led to drug changes. On average, patients saved about $21 per month, which could translate to annual savings of about $2 million for everyone

TABLE 20-2 Description of Drug Alert Categories Used in Case 3: North Carolina Initiative

Alert category	Description
1	Drugs listed on the Beers list of medications not designed for the elderly population
2	Drugs that have a less expensive generic
3	Drugs that have a more effective alternative listed on clinical initiatives (created by long-term care pharmacy expert panel)
4	Drugs for short-term or acute use
5	Drugs that had detrimental effect due to their metabolic processing

Source: Data from Trygstad TK, Christensen DB, Wegner SE, et al. Analysis of the North Carolina Long-Term Care Polypharmacy Initiative: a multiple-cohort approach using propensity-score matching for both evaluation and targeting. *Clin Ther.* 2009;31(9):2018–2037.

in the initiative. Participants were immediately less likely to experience hospitalizations, and the reduction of drug alerts suggests better medical outcomes over longer periods of time. The total number of medications taken remained mostly constant throughout the study.[33]

If this system had been in place in the pharmacy where Mr. Miller had filled his prescriptions, what reviews of his existing and new medications might have been performed? To what effect?

A BRIGHTER TOMORROW WITH BIG BROTHER

All three of these studies illustrate interventions that attempt to address the myriad possible underlying causes of Mr. Miller's adverse drug event. The results found in the Pacific Northwest intervention are not atypical. Decision support systems in the clinical field tend to be met with little resistance by clinicians and produce moderate results. However, research also demonstrates that it's more challenging to deal with patients *already* receiving inappropriate medications. While CDS can often result in fewer prescribing errors, it may not reach those patients who are on stable medication regimens.

Although case 2 could ultimately prove to be a beneficial model, computer-decision support was unable to produce positive results in this attempt to address adherence with respiratory medications. Perhaps certain aspects of the case design or target population prevented researchers from reaching the target goals. The North Carolina Initiative produced much more promising results, yet it still had a few downsides to overcome.

It is also helpful to consider what happens to prescribing practices once intervention programs end. Once support systems are removed, have providers learned to order the correct drugs or will they simply revert to old mistakes? Making successful interventions sustainable is an important next step.

As healthcare systems implement these sorts of clinical decision support tools, the innovations will be largely invisible to the patients. Mr. Miller would never directly interact with the health information technology and would not be aware that Big Brother was watching. All he would experience is better health.

About the Author

Aaron Roberts grew up in Rochester, New York, and recently graduated from Brown University with a double concentration in human biology and community health. He developed his love for medicine at quite a young age. After working as a surgical technician in a women's care unit, he developed an interest in the health of vulnerable populations. Currently, his career focus is on outreach to urban youths and producing sustainable elder care while he works his way toward medical school and an eventual career in pediatrics.

REFERENCES

1. Institute of Medicine. *To Err Is Human: Building a Safer Health System*. Kohn LT, Corrigan JM, Donaldson MS, eds. Washington, DC: National Academy Press; 2000.

2. Hazell L, Shakir SA. Under-reporting of adverse drug reactions: a systematic review. *Drug Saf.* 2006;29(5):385–396.

3. Aitken M, Berndt E, Cutler D. Prescription drug spending trends in the United States: looking beyond the turning point. *Health Aff.* 2009;28(1):w151–w160.

4. Cannon KT, Choi MM, Zuniga MA. Potentially inappropriate medication use in elderly patients receiving home health care: a retrospective data analysis. *Am J Geriatr Pharmacother.* 2006;4(2):134–143.

5. Ernst FR, Grizzle AJ. Drug-related morbidity and mortality: updating the cost-of-illness model. *J Am Pharm Assoc (Wash).* 2001;41:192–199.

6. Page RL II, Ruscin F. The risk of adverse drug events and hospital-related morbidity and mortality among older adults with potentially inappropriate medication use. *Am J Geriatr Pharmacother.* 2006;4(4):297–305.

7. Beyth R, Shorr R. Epidemiology of adverse drug reactions in the elderly by drug class. *Drugs Aging.* 1999;14(3):231–239.

8. Budnitz D, Pollock D, Weidenbach K, Mendelsohn A, Schroeder T, Annest J. National surveillance of emergency department visits for outpatient adverse drug events. *JAMA.* 2006;296(15):1858–1866.

9. Chester M, Chen L, Kaski JC. Identification of patients at high risk for adverse coronary events while awaiting routine coronary angioplasty. *Br Heart J.* 1995;73:216–222.

10. Gurwitz JH, Field TS, Avorn J, et al. Incidence and preventability of adverse drug events in nursing homes. *Am J Med.* 2000;109:87–94.

11. Eric T, David S, Burstin H, et al. Incidence and types of adverse events and negligent care in Utah and Colorado. *Medical Care.* 2000;38(3):261–271.

12. Wilt TJ, Bloomfield HE, MacDonald R, et al. Effectiveness of statin therapy in adults with coronary heart disease. *Arch Intern Med.* 2004;164:1427–1436.

13. van der Harst P, Voors AA, van Gilst WH, et al. Statins in the treatment of chronic heart failure: biological and clinical considerations. *Cardiovasc Res.* 2006;71(3): 443–454.

14. Ma J, Sehgal NL, Ayanian JZ, et al. (2005) National trends in statin use by coronary heart disease risk category. *PLoS Med.* 2005;2(5):e123.

15. Hutchins F, Unger J, Crowley J, Coltman C, Albain K. Underrepresentation of patients age 65 years and older in cancer-treatment trials. *N Engl J Med.* 1999;341:2061–2067.

16. Gurwitz J, Field TS, Harrold LR, et al. Incidence and preventability of adverse drug events among older persons in the ambulatory setting. *JAMA.* 2003;289:1107–1116.

17. Staroselsky M, Volk LA, Tsurikova R, et al. (2008). An effort to improve electronic health record list accuracy between visits: patients' and physicians' response. *Int J Med Inf.* 2008;77(3):153–160.

18. Fick DM, Cooper JW, Wade WE, et al. Updating the Beers criteria for potentially inappropriate medication use in older adults: results of a U.S. consensus panel of experts. *Arch Intern Med.* 2003;163:2716–2724. [Published correction appears in *Arch Intern Med.* 2004;164:298].

19. Chase BA, Bennett NL. Medication safety, systems and communications. http://www.massmed.org/Content/NavigationMenu2/MedicationSafetySystemsandCommunication/CourseInformation/default.htm. Published 2006. Accessed September 25, 2010.

20. Williams AF, Manias E, Walker R. Adherence to multiple, prescribed medications in diabetic kidney disease: a qualitative study of consumers' and health professionals' perspectives. *Int J Nurs Stud.* 2008;45(12):1742–1756.

21. Handler SM, Nace DA, Studenski SA, Fridsma DB. Medication error reporting in long term care. *Am J Geriatr Pharmacother.* 2004;2:190–196.

22. Morgan DG, Semchuk KM, Stewart NJ, D'Arcy C. Job strain among staff of rural nursing homes: a comparison of nurses, aides, and activity workers. *J Nurs Adm.* 2002;32(3):152.

23. Crespin DJ, Modi AV, Wei D, et al. Repeat medication errors in nursing homes: contributing factors and their association with patient harm. *Am J Geriatr Pharmacother.* 2010;8(3):258–270.

24. Aparasu RR, Mort JR, Brandt H. Polypharmacy trends in office visits by the elderly in the United States, 1990 and 2000. *Res Soc Adm Pharm.* 2005;1(3):446–459.

25. Lococo KH, Staplin L. *Literature Review of Polypharmacy and Older Drivers: Identifying Strategies to Collect Drug Usage and Driving Functioning among Older Drivers.* Washington, DC: U.S. Department of Transportation, National Highway Traffic Safety Administration; 2006. Report no. DOT HS 810 558.

26. Moylan KC, Binder EF. Falls in older adults: risk assessment, management and prevention. *Am J Med.* 2007;120(6):493.e1–493.e6.

27. Allen D, Fenwick M. Continued progress: hospital use of information technology, *American Hospital Association.* www.aha.org/aha/research-and-trends/AHA-policy-research/2007.html. Published 2007. Accessed October 14, 2010.

28. Burt CW, Hing E. Use of computerized clinical support systems in medical settings: United States, 2001–03. *Advance Data.* 2005;353:1–8.

29. Wager K, Schaffner M, Foulois B, Swanson Kazley A, Parker C, Walo H. Comparison of the quality and timeliness of vital signs data using three different data-entry devices. *Comput Inform Nurs.* 2010;28(4):205–212.

30. Johnston ME, Langton KB, Haynes RB, Mathieu A. Effects of computer-based clinical decision support systems on clinician performance and patient outcome. A critical appraisal of research. *Ann Intern Med.* 1994;120(2):135–142.

31. Smith DH, Perrin N, Feldstein A, et al. The impact of prescribing safety alerts for elderly persons in an electronic medical record: an interrupted time series evaluation. *Arch Intern Med.* 2006;166(10):1098–1104.

32. Tierney W, Overhage M, Murray M, et al. Can computer-generated evidence-based care suggestions enhance evidence-based management of asthma and chronic obstructive pulmonary disease? A randomized, controlled trial. *Health Serv Res.* 2005;40(2):477–498.

33. Trygstad TK, Christensen DB, Wegner SE, et al. Analysis of the North Carolina Long-Term Care Polypharmacy Initiative: a multiple-cohort approach using propensity-score matching for both evaluation and targeting. *Clin Ther.* 2009;31(9):2018–2037.

The 2009 H1N1 Influenza Pandemic:

When You Make Mistakes, Don't Miss the Lessons

PIETRO D. MARGHELLA

PROLOGUE: THE NEW REALITY OF PANDEMICS

The historian and author John Barry was fond of telling interested readers that the most important part of his 2005 book, *The Great Influenza: The Epic Story of the Deadliest Plague in History,* was the afterword, in which he attempted to describe what a pandemic in the modern era might portend. Barry points out three major differences between what a highly pathogenic and lethal influenza pandemic outbreak might look like in the modern era when compared to the 1918–1919 influenza pandemic, which claimed up to 100 million lives worldwide.

1. The human population has tripled since the early part of the 20th century. We now have three times the global population at risk, most of whom are already competing for access to scant medical and public health resources.

2. Exacerbating the first point is that as a result of the HIV/AIDS pandemic, we now have geographically vast swaths (i.e., sub-Saharan Africa, Southeast Asia, and parts of the Caribbean and Latin America) of immunocompromised populations who already place a significant burden on public health resources. While these populations might not be as much at risk as healthier populations that tend to be hit hardest by novel viruses like H1N1, their ongoing health needs will likely limit access to critical public health resources during significant surge capacity events.

3. Finally—and perhaps, most ominously—our now-global-ized transportation system is a historically unprecedented facilitator of major disease outbreaks.[1]

The medical historian, Dr. RS Bray, points out there is one inexorable truth regarding the spread of disease: for time immemorial, disease has always spread via lines of communication, a military euphemism for lines of transportation. In other words, major disease outbreaks have always leveraged the most modern and rapid transportation modality of an era to facilitate disease outbreaks.[2] In 1918–1919, intra- and intercontinental travel was predominantly by rail and sea, respectively. The advent of the modern air travel industry may find itself unwittingly functioning as the vector accelerant of the modern era: air travel will undoubtedly facilitate the next great global disease event.

A novel strain of avian influenza virus first appeared in China in 1996, and within a year, outbreaks of the highly pathogenic H5N1 were reported in poultry and wet markets in Hong Kong. The virus quickly appeared to have jumped species, with 18 cases (and 6 fatalities) being reported among the first known instances of human infection with this virus. It wasn't until 2004, however, that these H5N1 outbreaks began to make appearances in domestic poultry in sufficient numbers throughout Asia that concern of a coming human pandemic began to be raised.[3] By late 2008, the World Health Organization (WHO) had reported 426 verifiable human H5N1 cases with a case fatality ratio of 63%. In comparison, global case fatality ratios associated with past 20th-century influenza pandemics have ranged from about 0.1% for the 1957 and 1968 pandemics to 2.5% for the 1918–1919 pandemic.[4] With H5N1, there was, indeed, much about which to be concerned.

H1N1 ARRIVES

The appearance of another novel influenza virus in Mexico in May 2009 appeared to validate the growing level of concern. Quickly characterized as a quadrivalent H1N1 virus containing human influenza A, an avian component, and two swine genetic components, it was dubbed the "swine flu." The 2009 H1N1 influenza soon proved itself to be highly pathogenic. By June 10, 2009, WHO officials officially declared a pandemic as cases had appeared on at least three continents. Initially relying on a tripartite plan of (1) containment; (2) the use of assumed-to-be-effective antivirals; and (3) the rapid development of a vaccine, WHO and public health officials worldwide braced themselves for a potentially devastating global outbreak.

Fortunately, the 2009 H1N1 influenza pandemic never reached its much-feared impact and was declared officially over on August 10, 2010. Although the WHO and national epidemiologic reporting agencies stopped counting the number of new cases by September 2009, it is believed the virus caused infections in more than 214 countries and ultimately caused some 18,000 deaths worldwide.[5,i] By any measure, the global impact of this event never came near that of its 20th-century predecessors, and government and public health officials worldwide collectively heaved a sigh of relief that their worst fears and darkest imaginings were never realized.

In the United States, there is no report card, per se, that adjudicates the successes or failures of the response. Many observations and lessons can, however, be extracted from this event, and they can inform strategic impact planning for future pandemics and incidents of national significance. There is no doubt that at some future time, a global disaster will require a U.S. management response across the operational perspective—from the microtactical level of individuals' homes to the institutional level of the healthcare system to the macrostrategic levels of international cooperation and collaboration.

FIRST, WE MUST CONTAIN

Public health officials at WHO staunchly maintained containment as a principal means for mitigating the scope and scale of a novel influenza pandemic.[6,ii] It was almost universally believed by scientists involved in pandemic planning and response that by relying on global epidemiologic surveillance systems and shared information resources, the notice of a focal outbreak would allow cooperative national agencies

to respond under the direction of WHO. Responding entities would use much the same strategy of the concentric ring construct of vaccination used for the eradication of smallpox shown in Figure 21-1. They would envelop the focal nodes, identify contacts from index clusters, vaccinate these populations, and subsequently prevent the spread to epidemic and pandemic proportion.

WHO scientists, in conjunction with scientists in the United States, convinced international and national policy makers, including the U.S. Department of Health and Human Services and the Centers for Disease Control and Prevention, that this model of smallpox response would work for novel influenza pandemics. Conceptually, it made sense. As outbreaks occur, people would be vaccinated quickly, preventing further outbreaks.

However, in 2009, less than one month after the H1N1 pandemic was declared, WHO dropped containment as a primary pandemic mitigation strategy. The reason was simple: Influenza (like many other highly pathogenic infectious diseases that are spread via human-to-human contact) has a latency period before onset of acute symptoms. During that period, infected persons are capable of shedding the virus via respiratory particulate matter. Given the fact that intercontinental travel is now facilitated by air, it is virtually impossible to contain any outbreak before infected individuals can have a chance to break the containment barrier. This fact as a lesson learned has profound implications not only for future pandemics, but also for bioterrorism preparedness, surveillance, and response.

Question 1 Was it reasonable for public health officials to use the concentric ring construct in planning for an influenza outbreak in 2009? Why or why not?

Question 2 Would it have been reasonable to recommend quarantine as a method of containment instead? Why or why not?

ON THE NOTION OF WAVES AND LENGTH OF PANDEMIC PERIOD

During the 2009 H1N1 pandemic, we assumed that a modern influenza pandemic capable of producing significant global morbidity and mortality would occur in multiple separate waves, each lasting 8–12 weeks. The pandemic was expected to last for approximately 18 months, effectively replicating the outbreak pattern of the 1918–1919 pandemic. Available empirical data did not actually support this theory. Preparedness planners did not consider the notion of the airline industry as a vector accelerant, which would facilitate a hyperwave outbreak—significantly compressing the outbreak period and the length of time influenza continued and/or reemerged in subsequent waves.

---

[i] The reported number of fatal cases is an underrepresentation of the actual numbers as many deaths are never tested or recognized as influenza related.

[ii] This strategy was widely promulgated through the WHO website both before and during the initial response to H1N1; for example, see WHO Interim Protocol: Rapid operations to contain the initial emergence of pandemic influenza (reference 6).

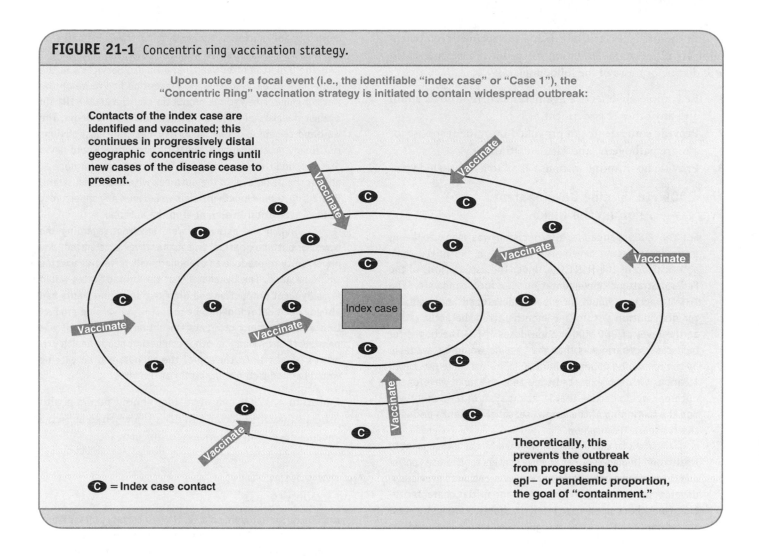

FIGURE 21-1 Concentric ring vaccination strategy.

Upon notice of a focal event (i.e., the identifiable "index case" or "Case 1"), the "Concentric Ring" vaccination strategy is initiated to contain widespread outbreak:

Contacts of the index case are identified and vaccinated; this continues in progressively distal geographic concentric rings until new cases of the disease cease to present.

Index case

C = Index case contact

Theoretically, this prevents the outbreak from progressing to epi— or pandemic proportion, the goal of "containment."

IF NOT CONTAINMENT, THEN VACCINATION

As scientists, public health experts, and policy makers around the world grappled with the failure of containment as an approach to slowing and perhaps even stopping the 2009 H1N1 flu outbreak, it was clear to most that vaccination would need to be a core component of any tactical plan. That said, experts were also keenly aware of the hurdles the routine vaccine development process might cause in the timing and success of this particular part of the plan.

The Vaccine Development Process for Influenza

The process for developing vaccines for routine seasonal human influenza A outbreaks normally takes 18 months and includes these four key steps:

1. Characterization of a projected circulating strain
2. Vaccine development
3. Vaccine production
4. Vaccine distribution

Faced with a novel (i.e., not previously identified) strain of influenza with pandemic potential, there are two courses of action which may be pursued:

1. Public health officials charged with the characterization of the emerging strain may choose to immediately begin to develop vaccine
2. They may choose to wait until a reassortment of the virus occurs, which advances it to a higher degree of pathogenicity and virulence.[iii]

[iii] Viruses are nothing if not adaptive to their hosts. It is not the least bit unexpected for viruses to go through an antigenic shift or reassortment sometime after gaining a foothold in a host species. When this occurs, the virus is predictably more dangerous and capable of taking greater advantage of the affected population by causing higher levels of illness and death.

In the first scenario, advancing to vaccine development upon an initial characterization will produce a vaccine which will do one or more of the following:

1. Be completely effective against the current novel strain and any other reassortment
2. Provide some degree of provoked immune response for a more pathogenic and virulent strain
3. Provide no immune response at all to a reassorted virus

The 2009 Flu Vaccine Development Process—Weighing the Risks

For the 2009 pandemic, the decision was made to begin immediate vaccine development based on the initial characterization of the H1N1 flu. Under the assumptions of the Federal Strategic Implementation Plan for a pandemic,[iv] the "H1N1 vaccine (would have been) developed and available for distribution within 3–6 months after characterization at the level of 300–600 million doses."[7(p 9)] The hoped-for best-case scenario was that the vaccine would be available by the beginning of September 2009. This estimate was timed to align with the expected time that the next wave of the outbreak would occur—that is, at the start of the school year and the beginning of the normal seasonal influenza period in the Northern Hemisphere.

The risks to this approach selected by the Department of Health and Human Services and the Centers for Disease Control and Prevention were manifold. First, as mentioned previously, development of a vaccine based on the initial characterization could have been completely ineffective against a reassorted virus that was more highly pathogenic and virulent; this was always a risk when developing a vaccine for a novel virus. Second, this would also mean significant resources would have been spent by government and private healthcare purchasers and by public health entities for a nonutilitarian vaccine production.

Third, accelerating the production capacity prior to a worsened reassortment of the virus would increase the risk of mistakes and problems associated with the vaccine.[v] Finally, the worst case: If estimates for the projected wave and time-line period were incorrect *and* escalation to a peak pandemic featured a highly pathogenic and virulent virus with high morbidity and mortality, the production of vaccine based on the initial characterization would be useless.

The Department of Health and Human Services and the Centers for Disease Control and Prevention had to weigh the risks of immediate vaccine production for the 2009 H1N1 flu against the risks of waiting for a reassortment to begin. The wait-and-see approach was also risky. First, the most obvious risk to any go-slow approach was that the virus would never reassort, and there would be insufficient vaccine (or none at all) for the peak level of the outbreak with the initial strain. By waiting, public health officials would miss any opportunity to use vaccination to slow or stop the outbreak.

Second, if the estimates were incorrect regarding the waves or outbreak period, and if the waves accelerated, any opportunity to produce an even marginally effective vaccine would be gone. The likelihood that the United States would actually meet production and distribution requirements had already been determined to be low; slowing vaccine production would further exacerbate this situation. Finally, it was possible that by waiting, other competing public health priorities could rise to the top of the agenda, and no vaccine would be produced for any strain of the virus.

Question 3 What considerations should public health officials take into account in deciding when to launch a vaccine development process for influenza?

The 2009 H1N1 Flu Vaccine Production Process

In 2008, prior to leaving office, then-Secretary of Health and Human Services Michael Leavitt made more than $5 billion in funds available for contracts for emergency vaccine development in the event a novel virus with pandemic potential emerged. Of the contracts made, only 30% of the production capacity was given to U.S. pharmaceutical companies. The remaining 70%—the vast majority of the vaccine needed for the U.S. population—was given to foreign production facilities. Had the virus been more virulent, it is entirely possible that the foreign governments where these production facilities were located would have refused to allow export of the vaccine until their own populations were fully protected.[8] In the end, H1N1 flu vaccine became available for the majority of the U.S. population some 10 months after the initial outbreak—a delay that could have been untenable in a highly virulent scenario.

Part of the reason that the contracts were given to foreign production companies is that they were using cell-based production to create influenza vaccine. Meanwhile, U.S.-based pharmaceutical companies were still required to use egg-based production because the FDA hadn't yet approved the cell-based technology for use in the United States. Cell-based vaccine production dramatically accelerates production time

---

[iv] The Federal Strategic Implementation Plan was a crisis action planning version of the national strategy for pandemic influenza. It was produced by the Operations Coordination and Planning Directorate at the Department of Homeland Security in coordination with the federal interagency planning team. The final approved product was dated July 15, 2009. Because it was labeled "For Official Use Only," it is not available publicly.

[v] This was one of the major lessons learned from the 1976 swine flu outbreak.

and the availability of sufficient quantities of vaccine for population requirements. While the decision to use foreign vaccine manufacturers may have seemed logical while not operating under the duress of a looming crisis, in hindsight, concerns about a likely export embargo under the conditions of a true international disease outbreak disaster should have been foreseeable.

HURRY UP AND WAIT: MANAGING MEDICAL LOGISTICS BEFORE A VACCINE IS AVAILABLE

Even though the Department of Health and Human Services chose the rapid development approach, it did so knowing vaccines would not be available for several months—and perhaps not in time for the first wave of flu outbreak. During vaccine development, it was essential for public health officials to be prepared with other interventions. At the national level, the Strategic National Stockpile (SNS; see Box 21-1) remained positioned to provide medical logistics and supply resources to states affected by the pandemic. The plan was to accomplish this support mainly through the provision of antiviral medications such as oseltamivir (Tamiflu) and zanamivir (Relenza) that were expected to have some degree of efficacy in reducing the acuity of symptoms related to the 2009 H1N1 flu. Additionally, the SNS would be the central distribution resource for personal protective equipment such as face masks and respirators that would be used to provide barrier protection from exposure. That said, there were two issues of national significance related to medical logistics and supply support for a pandemic outbreak in 2009.

Once states received SNS platform resources, it was up to them to determine how and to whom supplies were provided.

BOX 21-1 The Strategic National Stockpile

The Strategic National Stockpile (SNS) is the United States' national repository of antibiotics, vaccines, chemical antidotes, antitoxins, and other critical medical equipment and supplies. In the event of a national emergency involving bioterrorism or a natural pandemic, the SNS has the capability to supplement and resupply local health authorities that may be overwhelmed by the crisis, with response time as little as 12 hours. The SNS is jointly run by the Centers for Disease Control and Prevention and the Department of Homeland Security.

However, the states had no uniform or standard applications for these "hub and spoke" distribution plans to get medical supply resources into the hands of end users. Additionally, if degradations of the transportation and services-critical infrastructure and key resource sectors would have occurred as a result of an expanded impact of the pandemic, getting the very resources that potentially represented the most viable population sustainment assets into the hands of U.S. citizens would have been problematic.

The SNS had sufficient supplies of certain medications and personal protective equipment. However, neither the SNS nor the United States in general had the appropriate number of assisted breathing apparatus (ventilators) used in hospitals. The United States had a critical nationwide shortage of ventilators for providing mechanical ventilation to pulmonary-challenged patients. For those influenza cases that might have progressed to acute pneumonitis, access to a ventilator would have been critical to increase survivability. At the strategic level, the United States was not engaged in a requirements-determination process to assess the nation's tertiary care needs to support populations affected by a pandemic or any other incident of national significance. Without a requirements determination, planning resources for population sustainment needs was left to local communities and sometimes individual hospitals, creating conditions for systemic failure.

Question 4 How should public health officials prioritize the following scarce resources when it comes to pandemic preparedness: vaccine production, immediate intervention medical supplies, and lifesaving medical supplies?

HEALTHCARE OR PUBLIC HEALTH? SURGE CAPACITY EXPLAINED

A key assumption in the Department of Homeland Security Federal Strategic Implementation Plan was that medical surge capacity would be challenged during a pandemic. If an outbreak occurred, the general public would assume that hospitals and community and state-based public health resources would be sufficient to administer to the needs of affected individuals. However, as a by-product of our national managed care system, hospitals in the United States already operate at between 96.5% and 98% of maximum bed capacity on any given day.

Surge capacity is defined as encompassing "potential patient beds; available space in which patients may be triaged, managed, vaccinated, decontaminated, or simply located; available personnel of all types; necessary medications, supplies and equipment; and even the legal capacity to deliver health care under situations which exceed authorized capacity."[9(p 19)] In pandemic preparedness and disaster planning, it is a well-known truism that telling people not to go to the hospital is a sure recipe for having hundreds, if not thousands of people—many of whom are not ill and are not exhibiting symptoms—show up. Effective crisis communications messaging would recommend avoiding healthcare facilities and might even suggest leveraging shelter-in-place resources. ·

Populations affected by (or even thought to be affected by, i.e., the "worried well") a highly pathogenic and virulent strain of the H1N1 virus would likely have storm surged the healthcare infrastructure in the United States and quickly stressed it to the point of collapse.[10] Indeed, in some jurisdictions in the United States, hospitals were forced to create triage areas in parking garages to handle the flow of potential patients streaming in after they first heard about the so-called swine flu on the news. Arguably, the inability to handle surge capacity might have been the single biggest vulnerability to a pandemic or bioterrorism response, in part because of the predictable surprise driven, in large part, by well-known human behavior. As with medical logistics and supply, the only viable option for preventing this predictable surprise would be a national initiative to determine requirements based on state assessments of the population at risk against the strategic impact scenarios of the National Planning Scenarios.[11,vi]

A Note about Special Needs Populations

A severe pandemic would have required an almost complete paradigm shift from the traditional approach to managing special needs populations. Most special needs populations require either sustainment resources (e.g., medical support and pharmaceutical maintenance) or transportation requirements to evacuate them from a hazard threat area. Since a severe pandemic would have required a minimization of travel and movement, and instead relied on strategies like sheltering in place and social distancing to reduce the spread of the disease, identifying special needs populations in advance of a severe outbreak and developing strategies for home-based life support and sustainment of human needs (e.g., food, water, sanitary products) is paramount.

Question 5 In what ways could public health experts and policy makers better prepare for surge capacity? How would such plans vary or coincide with addressing the supply of ventilators and other medical supplies?

---

vi The National Planning Scenarios were created to domestically replicate the illustrative planning scenarios that are part of the *Defense Planning Guidance*, which drives planning requirements for each of the geographic combatant commands in the Department of Defense. For medical planners, scenario-based planning provides impact estimates against an associated population at risk, and those estimates are used to determine the requirements needed (e.g., medical supplies) to mitigate the impact of the event.

BEYOND HEALTH CARE: MASS FATALITY MANAGEMENT PLANNING

In the event the 2009 H1N1 flu virus had reassorted to a more highly pathogenic and virulent form, it is likely the United States and nations around the world would have seen significantly increased mortality. Currently, mortuary affairs are managed at the local level and are supported by the funeral service industry and the offices of local coroners and medical examiners. In times of disaster, the disaster mortuary teams of the Department of Health and Human Services' National Disaster Medical System are activated to provide mass fatality management surge resources.

Just as with medical supplies in hospitals and surge capacity, it is highly likely that local fatality management assets would have been overwhelmed if the pandemic scenario had worsened in 2009, as these assets were simply not prepared to conduct mass fatality management operations. It was assumed that responding disaster mortuary team resources would come from the state-level funerary service industry and local coroner and medical examiner assets. Expecting state and local resources to be available for a national mass fatality mission was tantamount to a "rob Peter to pay Paul" syndrome. Additionally, in the event the pandemic worsened, the locations of bodies would not be restricted to a geographical or jurisdictional level. In these types of situations, 50–75% of deaths would occur outside of the hospitals and would place additional stress on all local responders. The supplies for the care and management of the deceased would be in short supply due to staffing and manufacturing shortages. Barry pointed out in *The Great Influenza* that communities across the United States were completely unprepared to conduct adequate mass fatality management operations.[1] Why? Most local (i.e., town or county) mortuary infrastructures dealt with fewer than 10 fatalities per week and did not have the personnel, equipment, or supplies needed to handle large numbers of fatalities presenting in a rapid manner. Finally, while the media paid much attention to the disease dangers of large numbers of dead bodies, it was a misnomer from a disease vector perspective to say that massive fatalities represented a significant public health concern. However, mass fatalities posed enormous psychosocial, legal, and public confidence issues that should be addressed at all levels of the operational continuum for strategic impact events.

A NATION OF STATES, A MULTITUDE OF PLANS

Right up until the pandemic occurred in early 2009, the Centers for Disease Control and Prevention maintained a website for pandemic influenza (www.pandemicflu.gov) featuring a tab for state and local plans that included each of the 58 state and U.S. territory plans published since pandemic influenza planning had begun in earnest in 2005. None of those plans contained any commonality in their templates, approach to planning, or mission areas covered. Simply put, there was a wholesale lack of commonality on how the United States approached disaster preparedness planning and response across the operational spectrum. But did that matter?

In their 2006 book, *Disaster: Hurricane Katrina and the Failure of Homeland Security*, authors Cooper and Block point out that the inability to cooperate and collaborate back and forth along the silos of the operational continuum led to marked failures of incident management efforts for an event of national significance.[12] It is an axiom of planning that fractious and disparate preparation invariably leads to fractious and disparate response. Although the Department of Homeland Security and the Federal Emergency Management Agency have been working diligently to publish the integrated planning system and comprehensive planning guidance that will respectively give the various federal agencies and the states a common architectural framework for preparedness planning and response, the lack of one during the pandemic could have proved extremely difficult for national incident management efforts had the outbreak been more severe.

Question 6 At what level should pandemic preparedness occur? International? National? State? Local? Community?

A BULLET DODGED?

Public health experts, disaster planning managers, scientists, and policy makers struggled to plan and respond to the 2009 H1N1 outbreak, both in the United States and internationally. Still, because the virulence of this particular strain of influenza was not as severe as anticipated, the public's health was not significantly compromised. Dr. Bray, in his role as a medical historian, asks us in *Armies of Pestilence* to consider the following: In all of recorded history from which we are able to extrapolate important information on influenza pandemics, a consistent and inexorable pattern emerges, to wit, in every single pandemic of global significance (i.e., a highly pathogenic and virulent outbreak that produces significant morbidity and mortality among humans), the event is *always* proceeded by 1 to 2 years of outbreak that reaches pandemic proportion but does not produce casualty loads of significant—or in some cases, noticeable—import.[2]

While it may be argued that we dodged the proverbial bullet with the 2009 H1N1 pandemic, complacency is a risky response. When we make mistakes, we must not miss the lessons learned, for the next emergency may not be far down the road.

About the Author

Pietro (Peter) D. Marghella, DHSc(C), MSc, MA, CEM, FACCP, is a retired U.S. Navy plans, operations, and medical intelligence officer. His assignments included serving as chief of medical plans and operations for the Joint Chiefs of Staff and director of medical contingency operations for the Office of the Secretary of Defense. His national-level planning credentials include the national smallpox response plan and the nation's first catastrophic incident response plan. During the 2009 pandemic he served as a strategic advisor to senior leadership at the U.S. Department of Homeland Security. He currently consults on health care and public health disaster preparedness and response and teaches at The George Washington University School of Public Health and Health Services.

REFERENCES

1. Barry J. *The Great Influenza: The Epic Story of the Deadliest Plague in History.* New York, NY: Penguin Books; 2005.

2. Bray RS. *Armies of Pestilence: The Impact of Disease on History.* London, UK: Clarke, James and Company; 2004.

3. World Health Organization. H5N1 avian influenza: timeline. http://www.who.int/csr/disease/avian_influenza/timeline.pdf. May 8, 2006. Accessed December 1, 2010.

4. Li FC, Choi BC, Sly T, Park AW. (2008). Finding the real case-fatality rate of the H5N1 avian influenza. *J Epidemiol Community Health.* 2008;62(6):555–559.

5. World Health Organization Pandemic (H1N1) 2009 Update 112. WHO global alert and response (GAR). http://www.who.int/csr/don/2010_08_06/en/index.html. Posted August 6, 2010. Accessed December 1, 2010.

6. World Health Organization. WHO Interim Protocol: Rapid operations to contain the initial emergence of pandemic influenza, updated October 2007. http://www.who.int/csr/disease/avian_influenza/guidelines/draftprotocol/en/index.html. Accessed April 15, 2011.

7. U.S. Department of Homeland Security. The Federal Strategic Implementation Plan for the 2009 H1N1 Flu. Version 5. Washington, DC: U.S. Department of Homeland Security; 2009.

8. Barry J. Pandemic reality check [letter to the editor]. *The Washington Post.* June 22, 2009:A26.

9. Joint Commission for the Accreditation of Healthcare Organizations. Healthcare at the crossroads: Strategies for creating and sustaining community-wide emergency preparedness systems. http://www.jointcommission.org/assets/1/18/emergency_preparedness.pdf. 2003. Accessed April 13, 2011.

10. Marghella PD. Managing incidents of national significance. In: Hawley A, Matheson J. eds, *Making Sense of Disaster Medicine.* Oxford, UK: Oxford University Press; 2010:63–88.

11. Bazerman M, Watkins M. *Predictable Surprises: The Disasters You Should Have Seen Coming.* Cambridge, MA: Harvard University Press; 2004.

12. Cooper C, Block R. *Disaster: Hurricane Katrina and the Failure of Homeland Security.* New York, NY: Times Books; 2006.

Index

Boxes, figures, notes, and tables are indicated by b, f, n, and t following the page number.

A

AACVPR (American Association of Cardiovascular and Pulmonary Rehabilitation), 168
Abbott Laboratories, 149
Abortion statistics, 60, 113
Abstinence-only programs, 109–110
"Accidents of pregnancy," 146, 148
ACIP (Advisory Committee on Immunization Practices), 105, 105b
ADC (Asociación de desarrollo comunitario, Honduras), 69, 72
Administrative controls to mitigating health risks, 141
Adolescence
    risk factors in Latino population, 83
    as smoking cessation target group. *See* Smoking cessation kits
Adolescent and adult male vs. neonatal circumcision, 27, 28, 30
Adverse drug events, 187–192. *See also* DES (diethylstilbestrol) product safety
    background, 187
    electronic medical records, 190
    future of, 192
    medication adherence, 190–191, 191t
    medication appropriateness index, 188, 188f
    medication errors, 187–189
    North Carolina initiative, 191–192, 192t
    overview, 154
    prescribing practices, 190–191
    as public health concern, 189

Advisory Committee on Immunization Practices (ACIP), 105, 105b
Advocacy groups for victims of DES exposure, 149
Africa, circumcision and HIV infection, 24–28, 24f, 30. *See also specific countries*
African Americans
    asthma risk in, 123, 125
    cardiac rehabilitation benefits for, 167
    circumcision and HIV infection in, 30
    mental health services for, 83
    obesity initiatives for, 99
    public health initiatives for, 92
    women's heart disease in, 49, 55, 99
Agency for Toxic Substances and Disease Registry (ATSDR), 136, 137
AIDS. *See* HIV/AIDS
Airline industry as vector accelerant, 196
Alaskan Natives, 91, 107
Alianza de Sistemas de Agua Rural (ASAR, Honduras), 73
AMA (American Medical Association), 117
American Academy of Pediatrics, 30, 117
American Association of Cardiovascular and Pulmonary Rehabilitation (AACVPR), 168
American College of Cardiology, 166, 167, 168
American College of Obstetricians and Gynecologists, 117
American Congress of Obstetricians and Gynecologists, 117
American Heart Association, 166, 167, 168
American Life League, 116
American Marketing Association, 173
American Medical Association (AMA), 117
Antiretroviral therapies, 16
ASAR (Alianza de Sistemas de Agua Rural, Honduras), 73
Ash. *See* Coal ash

Asociación de desarrollo comunitario (ADC, Honduras), 69, 72
Assessment in public health, 2
Association of Public Health Laboratories, 181
Association of State and Territorial Health Officials, 159, 161
Asthma and the Environment (report), 124
Asthma outcomes, 123–130
    background, 123
    overview, 47
    policy recommendations, 123–124, 124*b*
    prevalence and cost of asthma, 124–127, 126*t*
    risk factors surrounding asthma, 125–127, 126*t*
    strategies for, 127–128
ATSDR (Agency for Toxic Substances and Disease Registry), 136, 137
Avian influenza, 195

B
Baton Rouge, Louisiana, food safety programs, 157
Behavioral risk factors
    cardiac rehabilitation goals for, 166–167
    for Latino youth, 83
    for Native Americans, 89
    smoking cessation changes in, 172–173, 172*b*, 173*f*
Biological plausibility of HIV in circumcised males, 26
Birth control, 114, 115*f*
Birth rates in U.S., 114, 114*f*
Black Women's Health Imperative, 99
Bloomington, Minnesota, food safety inspections in, 160
Body mass index, defined, 95*n*
Branding in public health arena, 51
British Library Index to Conference Proceedings, 35
Building on Strengths program. *See* School-based mental health programs
Bureau of Indian Affairs, 89

C
Canada
    food safety inspections report, 160
    SARS outbreak in. *See* SARS II
Canadian Medical Association Journal (CMAJ), 6
Cancer
    cervical, 104, 104*n*, 110, 110*n*, 145
    clear cell adenocarcinoma, 145, 148
    stages of, 110*n*
    types of from HPV, 104, 104*n*, 110, 110*n*
Cardiac rehabilitation for elderly, 161–170
    background, 165
    benefits of, 167
    clinical and political background, 166
    decision-making process for, 167–169, 168*b*

healthcare issues, 166
    medical history, 165–166
    overview, 154
    public health goals, 166–167, 167*b*
Cardiometabolic risk, 96
Cardiovascular events and Vioxx. *See* Vioxx and cardiovascular events
Case-control studies
    in cardiovascular risk, 40
    description of, 39
Case isolation, defined, 6*b*
Causal association, assessing, 40–41
CCA (Chandler Chicco Agency), 96
CCW (coal combustion waste), 131
Cell-based flu vaccine production process, 198
Center for Drug Evaluation and Research, FDA, 118, 120
Centers for Disease Control and Prevention (CDC)
    Advisory Committee on Immunization Practices and, 105*b*
    flu vaccine development process and, 198
    on HIV, 15, 16, 19, 25
    pandemic influenza website, 200
Centers for Medicare/Medicaid services regulations for cardiac rehabilitation, 168
Cervical cancer
    DES exposure and, 145
    HPV association with, 104, 104*n*
    personal story of, 110
    statistical data on, 110*n*
Chandler Chicco Agency (CCA), 96
Changing pO₂licy: The Elements for Improving Childhood Asthma Outcomes (report), 123, 124
Children
    asthma outcomes in, 47, 123–130, 124*b*, 126*t*
    deaths due to diarrhea, 70
    health data in Rhode Island, 90
Children's Health Insurance Program Reauthorization Act (2009), 127
China
    avian influenza outbreak in, 195
    SARS outbreak in, 6–7
Chlamydia pneumoniae, 7
Cigarette smoking
    as asthma trigger, 125
    cessation of. *See* Smoking cessation kits
Circumcision and HIV, 23–32
    background for, 23–24, 24*f*
    cultural considerations, 30
    description of problem, 24–25
    etiology/efficacy of program, 25–26, 25*t*
    evaluation of program, 29–30
    implementation of, 28–29

overview, 2
recommendations for, 26–28
Clean Air Interstate Rule of 2005 (EPA), 136
Clean Air Mercury Rule of 2005 (EPA), 136
Clear cell adenocarcinoma, 145, 148
Clinical care, quality of, 127
Clinical decision support systems, 190–192, 191–192*t*
Clinical heterogeneity, 37
Clinical standards compared to performance measures for
    asthma, 125, 126*t*
Clinical trials, description of, 39
ClinicalTrials.gov, 35
CMAJ (*Canadian Medical Association Journal*), 6
Coal ash, 131–143
    background, 134, 135*f*
    dose response considerations, 138
    environmental impacts/controls, 136, 137*f*, 139
    exposure considerations, 136–138
    human health effects, 138–139
    Kingston, Tennessee, coal slurry incident, 131–134,
        132–133*f*
    overview, 47
    risk management approaches, 139–141, 140*b*
    sources and components of, 134–136
    transportation of, 134–136
Coal Combustion Products Partnership, 135
Coal combustion waste (CCW), 131
Cochrane Collaboration, 166
The Cochrane Controlled Trials Register, 35
Cohort studies, 39, 40
Collaborative initiatives. *See also* Partnership initiatives
    in asthma outcomes task force, 123–124, 124*b*, 127, 128
    in public health laboratories, 181
Colorado Springs, Colorado, food safety inspections in,
    159–160
Commercial marketing, 173–174
Communications. *See also* The Heart Truth campaign
    with HIV patients regarding test results, 18–19
    between hospitals during SARS outbreak, 7
    between laboratories in Iowa mumps epidemic, 183
    to public in medical emergencies, 62–65
    during yellow fever outbreak in Paraguay, 62–65, 63–64*b*
Communities, building trust in, 89–93
    background, 91
    challenges, 91–92
    Narragansett Indians, statistical information on, 89–90
    overview, 46
    public health initiative, 92
    Rhode Island plan for minority care, 90–91
Community-based partnerships and programs, 51, 52
Community-based potable water system project, 69–79
    background, 69–71

community meetings, 73–76
decision making and considerations, 76–77
history of controversy, 71–72
overview, 46
partners and their priorities, 72–73
Community biases, 84
Community decision process for mandatory HPV vaccine,
    103–104
Community health problem analyses, 134, 135*f*
Concentric ring vaccination containment strategy, 196, 197*f*
Concerned Women for America, 116
Confirmatory testing infrastructure of HIV, 19–20
Contraception. *See* Plan B emergency contraception
Contraindications, medical, 109, 109*n*
Controls approach to mitigating health risks, 140–141
Core components of comprehensive cardiac rehabilitation
    programs, 168, 168*b*
Corporate partnership and programs, 52
Cost effectiveness of circumcision to prevent HIV, 28
Costs
    of asthma treatment, 124–127, 126*t*
    of HPV vaccinations, 107
    of potable water in Honduran community, 74, 76
    of prescription drugs, 187
    of school-based mental health programs, 86
Counseling for HIV testing, 16
Creative brief, marketing tool, 174
Cultural brokers, 82, 82*n*
Cultural competency training, 84–85
Cumulative meta-analysis, 38–39, 39*f*

D

Dade County, Florida, food safety inspections in, 160
Dam hazard potential ranking system, FEMA, 134, 139,
    140*b*
Data abstraction section of review reports, 35–36
Databases
    for food health inspections, 161
    for medical studies/trials, 35
    for systematic review selections, 35
Decision process
    for cardiac rehabilitation for the elderly, 167–169, 168*b*
    for HPV vaccine, 103–104
    for potable water system project, 76–77
    for smoking cessation kit product development, 175–176
Defense Planning Guidance (Department of Defense),
    200*n*
Demographic data
    of circumcision worldwide, 23–24
    of Latino population in United States, 23–24, 83
    of Narragansett Indian tribe, 89–90
    of San Gabriel, Honduras, 69–70

DES Action, 149
DES (diethylstilbestrol) product safety, 145–151
    background, 145–146
    effectiveness of, 147–148
    emotional and social impacts of, 148–149
    FDA approval process for, 146
    legal issues, 149
    overview, 47
    physical effects of, 147–148
    uses for, 146–147
    victims advocacy for, 149
Detailed protocol section of review reports, 35
Diarrheal disease, 70
Diplomacy in global health issues, 62, 62b
Disaster: Hurricane Katrina and the Failure of Homeland
        Security (Cooper & Block), 201
Disinhibition considerations in circumcision and HIV
        study, 30
District of Columbia, Washington
    AIDS incidence rate, 15
    pre/post HIV counseling requirements, 19
Drinking water
    coal ash contamination of, 138
    potable. See Community-based potable water system
        project
Driving and effects of drugs, 189
Drugs. See also Food and Drug Administration (FDA);
        Vaccines and vaccinations
    adverse events from, 47, 145–151, 154, 187–192, 188f,
        191–192t
    approval process for, 117–118, 117–118b, 119f
    errors in administration of, 188–189
    incentive offering for promotion of, 147

E

Early detection programs for HIV. See Emergency
        departments, routine screening for HIV
Earthjustice, 133
Economic ramifications of SARS outbreak, 5, 9, 12
Education Department (U.S.), 127
Egg-based flu vaccine production process, 198
Elderly population
    adverse drug events in. See Adverse drug events
    cardiac rehabilitation for, 154, 161–170, 167–168b
    health disparities in, 187–188
Electricity, dependence on, 134, 141
Electric Power Research Institute, 139
Electronic medical records (EMRs), 190–191
Electronic tools in public health systems
    databases, 35, 161
    medical records, 190–191
    reporting systems, 7, 183
Eli Lilly & Company, 149

El Paso County, Colorado, food safety inspections in,
        159–160
EMBASE (database), 35
Emergency contraception. See Plan B emergency
        contraception
Emergency departments, routine screening for HIV, 15–22
    background for, 15
    confirmatory testing infrastructure, 19–20
    history of HIV, 16
    lessons learned from, 20–21
    overview, 2
    pilot program, 17–20
    screening policy, 16
    screening test, 16–17
Emergency response plan for laboratories, 181
Emotional impacts of DES exposure, 148–149
Empirical data, importance of, 85–86
EMRs (electronic medical records), 190–191
Energy Information Association, 134
Engineering controls to mitigating health risks, 141
Engineers, Ltd., 70, 73, 77
Environment
    coal ash disasters. See Coal ash
    Native Americans in Rhode Island concerns for, 90
Environmental health risks
    childhood asthma and, 125
    mitigating framework for, 139–141
Environmental Integrity Project, 132–133
Environmental Protection Agency (EPA)
    childhood asthma collaborative effort, 123, 127
    Clean Air Interstate Rule of 2005, 136
    Clean Air Mercury Rule of 2005, 136
    health risk communication guidelines, 63, 63–64b
    National Pollution Discharge Elimination System, 134
    Office of Solid Waste and Emergency Response, 134
Environmental public health
    food safety and. See Food safety programs
    precautionary principles for, 139
    task force for, 123, 124b
Epidemics. See specific diseases
Epidemiologic links in SARS case, 8, 9
E.R. Squibb, 149
Estrogens, use of, 145
Ethical issues surrounding vaccines, 62
Ethnic disparities in pediatric asthma outcomes. See
        Asthma outcomes
Exposure impacts of coal ash, 136–138

F

Falls from drug reaction, 189
Family values, government intrusion on, 107–108
Fatality management, 200
FDA. See Food and Drug Administration

Federal Emergency Management Agency (FEMA)
  dam hazard potential ranking system, 134, 139, 140*b*
  strategic national stockpile, 199
Federal Strategic Implementation Plan, 198, 199
Female population
  cardiac rehabilitation benefits for, 167
  contraception options. *See* Plan B emergency
    contraception
  genital mutilation, 24
  heart disease awareness. *See* The Heart Truth campaign
  male circumcision impact on, 28
  obesity task force on, 99
  task force on, 99
Financial impacts. *See* Costs
Fixed effects meta-analysis model, 38
Florida, food safety inspections in, 160
Flu. *See* Pandemic outbreaks
Food and Drug Administration (FDA)
  Center for Drug Evaluation and Research, 118, 120
  DES approval, 146
  DES market withdrawal, 148
  Food Code, 158, 160
  Gardasil approval, 105
  new drug approval process, 117–118, 117*b*
  Office of Women's Health, 113, 118
  Plan B emergency contraception and, 117
  switching prescriptions to OTC status, 118, 118*b*, 119*f*
  Vioxx market withdrawal, 33
Food-borne diseases, 157–159, 159*b*
Food establishments, defined, 158
Food safety programs, 157–163
  background of, 157–159
  future of, 161
  inspector shortages, 159–161
  overview, 154
  state and local programs, 157, 159–160
Forest plots used in meta-analysis, 36–38, 37*f*, 39*f*

G
Gates Foundation, 25
GAVI Alliance (formerly Global Alliance for Vaccines and
    Immunization), 61
George Washington University, 15, 96
Gila River Indian Community, 91
Glaxo Welcome register of clinical trials, 35
Global Alliance for Vaccines and Immunization, 61
Government Accountability Office, 100
Government intrusion on family values, 107–108
Gray water, 71
The Great Influenza (Barry), 195, 200
Guangdong Province, China, SARS outbreak in, 6–7
Guideline tools for development and assessment policies,
    96

H
Harvard Tobacco Control Working Group, 171
Has America Reached Its Tipping Point on Obesity?
    (forum), 99, 100
Hazard Analysis and Critical Control Point (HACCP)
    concept, 158
HEALTH (Rhode Island Department of Health), 90
Health Affairs journal, 98
Health and Human Services Department
  Advisory Committee on Immunization Practices,
    105*b*
  on childhood asthma outcomes, 123, 127
  flu vaccine development process and, 198
  National Disaster Medical System, 52
  Office on Women's Health, 52
Healthcare
  access for Native Americans in Rhode Island, 90
  educators/advocates and The Heart Truth Champions
    Program, 52
  SARS outbreak in Toronto healthcare workers, 7, 9
Health Decision Makers Survey, 98
Health Department (District of Columbia), 16, 17
Health diplomacy, 62, 62*b*
Health disparities in elderly population, 187–188
Health effects of coal ash, 138–139
Health laboratory functions, 154, 179, 180*b*
Health risks
  asthma and, 125–127, 126*t*
  in cardiovascular disease, 40
  communications strategy for, 62–65, 63–64*b*
  framework for mitigating, 139–141
  task force on, 123, 124*b*
The Heart Truth campaign, 49–57
  background, 49–50
  future directions, 55
  implementation of, 51–53
  materials development, 53
  overview, 2
  planning and development of, 50–51
  results from, 53–55
The Heart Truth Champions Program, 52
Herd immunity, 106, 106*n*
Heterogeneity, 36, 37
H5N1 influenza, 195
Hindu population, circumcision and HIV infection in, 23,
    30
Hispanic population
  asthma risk in, 123
  circumcision and HIV infection in, 23, 30
  mental health program for. *See* School-based mental
    health programs
  obesity initiatives for, 99
  women's heart disease awareness in, 49, 53, 55

HIV/AIDS
    African Americans belief about, 92
    circumcision and, 2, 23–32, 24f, 25t
    routine screening in emergency departments for, 2, 15–22
Homeland Security. *See* Federal Emergency Management
        Agency (FEMA)
Honduras, community-based potable water system project
        in, 69–79
    background, 69–71
    community meetings, 73–76
    decision making and considerations, 76–77
    history of controversy, 71–72
    overview, 46
    partners and their priorities, 72–73
H1N1 influenza, 196
Hospital-acquired pneumonia, 5–6, 8
Housing and Urban Development (HUD) Department,
        127
HPV (human papillomavirus) vaccine, 103–112
    abstinence-only programs and, 109–110
    community decision process for, 103–104
    government intrusion on family values and, 107–108
    legal issues surrounding, 106–107, 108, 108b
    medical expert testimony on, 104–106
    overview, 47
    personal story of cervical cancer, 110
Human Life International, 116
Hygiene promotion projects, 71, 74–75

I

ICS (incident command system) for laboratories, 181
Illegal migrants, 83–84
Immunizations. *See* Vaccines and vaccinations
Immunofluorescent assay HIV testing method, 17
Improving Obesity Management in Primary Care (white
        paper), 99
Improving Obesity Management in Primary Care
        Roundtable, 99
Incident command system (ICS) for laboratories, 181
India, circumcision and HIV infection in, 23, 30
Indiana, drinking water contamination in, 138
Indiana University, 190
Indian Health Services Department, 89
Influenza. *See* Pandemic outbreaks
Informed consent process for HIV testing, 16, 17
Infrastructure in public health care structure, 183
Institution International, on Honduras potable water
        system, 73, 74
Intention-to-treat analysis method, 26
Iowa. *See* Mumps epidemic in Iowa
Iowa Laboratory Response Network, 183
Isolation guidelines, 9

J

JAMA report of meta-analysis on cardiovascular events and
        Vioxx usage, 34
Jungle yellow fever, 60
Juni 2004 study, 34, 36–39, 43

K

Kenya, circumcision and HIV study in, 25, 30
King County, Washington, food safety inspections in, 160
Kingston, Tennessee, coal slurry incident, 131–134, 132–133f
Korea, Republic of, circumcision in, 28–29

L

Laboratory Response Network, 181
Lancet report of meta-analysis on myocardial infarction
        and Vioxx usage, 33–34
Legal issues
    DES exposure, 149
    HPV vaccine, 106–107, 108, 108b
    tobacco companies, 171
Let's Move campaign, 95
Long-term care facilities, 189
Louisiana, food safety programs in, 157

M

Male population
    circumcision in. *See* Circumcision and HIV
    HPV vaccine recommendations for, 105, 105n
Marketing to create change, 173–174, 174b
Master Settlement Agreement (MSA) in tobacco lawsuit,
        171
Maternal health data in Rhode Island, 90
McGettigan & Henry 2006 study, 34–35, 39–40, 43
Media relations/partnerships
    with Obesity Alliance, 99–100
    in women's heart disease awareness, 51, 52–53
Medical contraindications, 109, 109n
Medical Expenditures Panel Survey, 125
Medical expert testimony on HPV vaccine, 104–106
Medical surge capacity, 199–200
Medicare/Medicaid
    cardiac rehabilitation, services regulations for, 168
    tobacco lawsuit and, 171
Medication Appropriateness Index, 188–189, 188f
Medications. *See* Drugs
Medline (database), 35
Mehlman Vogel Castagnetti Inc., 96
Mental health programs. *See* School-based mental health
        programs
Merck & Co., Inc., 33
Meta-analysis in epidemiology
    analyzing data from, 36–39

description of, 34
of observational epidemiologic studies, 39–40
protocol for, 35–36
Mexico, swine flu outbreak in, 196
Miami-Dade County, Florida, food safety inspections in, 160
Migration issues surrounding mental health systems, 83–84
Minnesota, food safety inspections in, 160
Miscarriages, 147
Mitigating environmental health risks, framework for, 139–141
MSA (Master Settlement Agreement) in tobacco lawsuit, 171
Mumps epidemic in Iowa, 179–185
    background, 179–180, 180*b*
    dedicated personnel, importance of, 183
    infrastructure, importance of, 183
    overview, 154
    testing for mumps, role of, 180–181, 182*f*
Muslim population, circumcision and HIV infection in, 23, 30

N
Narragansett Indian tribe in Rhode Island, 89–92
Narrative-type research summaries, 34
National Academy of Sciences/National Research Council, 147–148
National Asthma Education and Prevention Program, 125, 127
National Disaster Medical System, 200
National Eating Disorders Association, 99
National Family Planning and Reproductive Health Association, 116–117
National Health Interview Survey, 125
National Heart, Lung, and Blood Institute (NHLBI), 49, 96, 125, 127
National Hispanic Medical Association, 99
National HIV screening policies, 16
National Indian Health Board, 99
National Institutes of Health, 25
National Laboratory Response Network, 183
National Planning Scenario, 200, 200*n*
National Pollution Discharge Elimination System (EPA), 134
National Quality Forum (NQF), 166, 167*b*
National Wear Red Day, 52
National Women's Law Center, 120
Native Americans
    obesity initiatives for, 99
    Rhode Island as home of, 89–92
    vaccine funding for, 107
Natural estrogens, use of, 145

Natural family planning (NFP), 116
Neonatal vs. adolescent and adult male circumcision, 27, 28, 30
Net sensitivity, defined, 20
Net specificity, defined, 20
New England Region Conference for the Elimination of Health Disparities, 90
NFP (natural family planning), 116
NHLBI. *See* National Heart, Lung, and Blood Institute
Nonpreferred drugs, 190
North Carolina Long-Term Care Polypharmacy Initiative, 191–192, 192*t*
NQF (National Quality Forum), 166, 167*b*
Nuestra Comunidad mental health center, 82–83
Nursing homes, 189

O
Obesity Alliance, 95–102
    activities of, 98–99
    background, 95
    coalition operating through consensus, 98
    early stages of, 96
    establishment of, 96–98
    future of, 100
    impact of, 99–100
    objectives of, 98
    overview, 46
Obesity GPS (Guide for Program and Policy Solutions), 98
Observational epidemiologic studies, 39–40
Office of Solid Waste and Emergency Response (EPA), 134
Office of Women's Health (FDA), 113, 118
Office on Women's Health (HHS), 52
Ogilvy Public Relations Worldwide, 49
Opt-out screening for HIV, 16
Orange Farm, South Africa, HIV study, 25–26
OraQuick Advance HIV1/2 Antibody Test, 16–17, 19

P
Pan American Health Organization (PAHO) in yellow fever outbreak, 59, 60, 62
Pandemic outbreaks, 195–202
    background, 195
    containment efforts, 196, 197*f*
    H1N1 influenza, 196
    mass fatality management planning, 200
    medical logistics, 199, 199*b*
    national and state level unified plans, 200–201
    overview, 154–155
    period lengths of of, 196
    surge capacity of healthcare system, 199–200
    vaccinations for, 197–199
Paraguay, yellow fever outbreak in, 59–67

background, 59
communication issues, 62–65, 63–64*b*
description of, 60–61
overview, 46
vaccination availability of, 61–62
Partnership initiatives. *See also* Collaborative initiatives
Coal Combustion Products Partnership, 135
in Honduras potable water project, 72–73
for immunizations, 106
in Obesity Alliance, 96, 97*f*, 99
in Paraguay's yellow fever outbreak, 61
in school-based mental health program, 82
in women's heart disease awareness campaign, 51–53
Patient Protection and Affordable Care Act (2010), 100, 124
Patient registries, defined, 149
Per-protocol analysis results of circumcision study, 26–27
Personnel, importance in public health care system, 183
Pharmaceutical companies, 147, 149. *See also* Drugs
Phase IV studies, defined, 149
Physicians for Reproductive Choice and Health, 117
Plan B emergency contraception, 113–122
approval process, 117–118*b*, 117–120, 119*f*
background, 113
controversial aspects of, 116–117
description of, 113–116, 114–115*f*
overview, 47
Pneumonia
Chlamydia pneumoniae, 7
hospital-acquired, 5–6, 8
postoperative, 6
SARS vs. general, 5
Policy development
guideline tools for, 96
in public health, 2
Political ramifications of SARS outbreak, 9, 12
Polypharmacy, 189
Population Services International (PSI), 171
Postoperative pneumonia, 6
Potable Water For All (PWFA, Honduras), 72, 73, 76
Precautionary principle for environmental health decisions, 139
Predictive value negative/positive (PVN/PVP) calculations, 17–18, 18*b*
Pregnancy
accidents of, 146, 148
DES used during. *See* DES (diethylstilbestrol) product safety
HIV screening recommendations for, 16
U.S. statistics on, 113–114, 114*f*
Prescription drugs. *See* Drugs
President's Task Force on Environmental Health Risks and Safety Risks to Children, 123, 124*b*
Pretest counseling for HIV testing, 16

Prevention counseling for HIV screening programs, 16, 19
Preventive intervention concerns, 27, 28–29
Privatization of mental health system, 84
PSI (Population Services International), 171
Public Citizen's Health Research Group, 149
Public health
laboratory functions, 154, 179, 180*b*
Native Americans in Rhode Island, issues for, 89–90, 92
SARS case study response, 7–8
screening programs, principles of, 21, 21*b*
services of, xvi, xvi*b*, xvi*f*
state agencies role in food-borne outbreak investigations, 199
Pure Food and Drug Act (1906), 146
PVN/PVP (predictive value negative/positive) calculations, 17–18, 18*b*

Q
Quantitative summary of data across epidemiologic studies. *See* Meta-analysis in epidemiology
Quarantine
case definitions vs., 6
defined, 6*b*
guidelines for, 9

R
Racial disparities in pediatric asthma outcomes. *See* Asthma outcomes
Random effects meta-analysis model, 38
Randomized clinical trials
of circumcision and HIV, 25–26, 25*t*, 27
description of, 39–40
using meta-analysis for, 34, 36
Rapid test for HIV, 16–17
Red Dress branding for women's heart disease awareness, 50–51
Red Dress Collection fashion show, 52
Reference laboratories, 154, 179
Relative risk calculation in HIV study, 26
Religious stance on circumcision, 23–24, 30
Research-based campaign for women's heart disease awareness, 50–51, 53
Research synthesis. *See* Vioxx and cardiovascular events
Resource Conservation and Recovery Act of 1976 (RCRA), 134
Respiratory papillomatosis, 104, 104*n*
Reuse of coal ash, 136, 137*f*
Rhode Island and Narragansett Indian tribe, 89–92
Rhode Island Department of Health (HEALTH), 90
Ring vaccination strategy, 61
Risk compensation considerations in circumcision and HIV study, 30
Risk factors

coal ash exposure management and, 139–141
   for Latino youth, 83
   for yellow fever, 61
Routine screening for HIV. *See* Emergency departments, routine screening for HIV

S

Safety issues surrounding HPV vaccine, 108–109
Sandstrom Design, 174
SARS II, 5–13
   case definitions for, 5, 6*b*
   concluding analysis of, 9–12
   initial outbreak, 5–7
   lessons learned from, 8–9
   overview, 2
   public health response to, 7–8
   quarantine vs. case definitions, 6, 6*b*
   time line for, 10–11*b*
School-based mental health programs, 81–88
   background, 81–82
   Building on Strengths program, 82
   case scenario, 86–87
   change adjustment issues, 85
   cultural competency issues, 84–85
   limited data and organizational challenges, 85–86
   migration issues, 83–84
   Nuestra Comunidad program, 82–83
   overview, 46
   risk factors facing Latino youth, 83
School requirement for HPV vaccine. *See* HPV (human papillomavirus) vaccine
Screening
   HIV, national and local policies, 16–17
   statistics calculation, 17, 18*b*
Seattle-King County, Washington, food safety inspections in, 160
Segmenting a market, 174
Seminal National Institutes of Health, 128
Senegal, circumcision and HIV study in, 27–28
Serial screening statistics calculations, 19
Severe acute respiratory syndrome. *See* SARS II
SHL (State Hygienic Lab), University of Iowa, 179
Sierra Club, 132
Smoking, as asthma trigger, 125
Smoking cessation kits, 171–178
   background, 171–172
   behavior change, 172–173, 172*b*, 172*f*
   decision process, 174–175
   marketing, 173, 173*b*
   overview, 154
   results, 175–176, 176*f*
   social marketing, 173–174, 174*b*
Social impacts of DES exposure, 148–149

Social marketing, 50, 50*b*, 173–174
Social media marketing, defined, 52
Socioeconomic indicators for Native Americans, 89
Source-to-effect framework for community health problem analyses, 134, 135*f*
South Africa, Orange Farm, HIV study, 25–26
Stages of change model, 172, 172*b*, 173*f*
State Hygienic Lab (SHL), University of Iowa, 179
State public health laboratory functions, 154, 179, 180*b*
Statistical data
   on abortions in United States, 60, 113
   on asthma among children, 125
   on cervical cancer, 110*n*
   on coal combustion process byproducts, 134–135
   on electricity usage in United States, 134
   on electronic medical records, 190
   on environmental damage due to coal ash, 136
   on HIV screening, 15
   on human papillomavirus, 104
   on mandated immunizations, 106
   on Native Americans in Rhode Island, 89–90
   on obesity, 95
   on pregnancies in United States, 113–114, 114*f*
   on tobacco use, 171
Statistical heterogeneity, 37
STOP (Strategies to Overcome and Prevent) Obesity Alliance, 95, 98–99
Strategic National Stockpile, 199, 199*b*
Stratified analysis, 38
Studies selection section of review reports, 35
Substitution approach to mitigating health risks, 141
Surveillance data for AIDS in US, 16, 17, 20–21
Swine flu, 196
Systematic reviews in epidemiology, 34–36, 34*b*
Systems thinking approach in circumcision and HIV study, 29–30

T

Target market, 173–174
Task Force on Women, 99
Technology developments. *See also* Electronic tools in public health systems
   for laboratories, 181
   for preventing adverse effects from drugs, 190–192, 191–192*t*
Tennessee, Kingston, coal slurry incident, 131–134, 132–133*f*
Testing
   for HIV, 16–17
   for mumps, 180–181, 182*f*
Thalidomide, adverse effects of, 147
317 program for vaccines, 105
Toronto, Canada, SARS outbreak. *See* SARS II
Transportation of coal ash, 134–136, 141

Travel advisory for Toronto SARS outbreak, 5
Treated analysis results of circumcision study, 26–27
Trial flowcharts, 35, 36f
Trials selection section of review reports, 35
Trust for America's Health Report, 161

U

Undocumented migrants, 83–84
Unintended pregnancy statistics (U.S.), 113–114, 114f
United Nations Children's Fund (UNICEF)
   diarrheal disease and, 70
   yellow fever vaccine and, 61
United States
   abortion statistics in, 60, 113
   AIDS surveillance cases in, 16
   birth rates in, 114, 114f
   circumcision and HIV infection in, 30
   electricity usage in, 134
   pregnancy statistics in, 113–114, 114f
University of Iowa, 179
Unpublished studies used for systematic review selections, 35
Urban yellow fever, 60
U.S. Department of. *See name of department*

V

Vaccine Court, 108, 108b
Vaccine Injury Compensation Program, 108, 108b
Vaccines and vaccinations, 197–199
   concentric ring containment strategy for, 196, 197f
   development and production process for, 197–199
   HPV affordability and cost, 105, 106–107
   legal issues surrounding mandatory, 106–107, 108, 108b
   for mumps, 180–181
   yellow fever availability and strategy, 59, 61–62
Vioxx and cardiovascular events, 33–44
   background, 33–34
   causal association and, 40–41
   meta-analysis in
     analyzing data from, 36–39
     description of, 34
     of observational epidemiologic studies, 39–40
     protocol for, 35–36
   overview, 3

systematic reviews in, 34, 34b, 35–36
Vioxx Gastrointestinal Outcomes Research Study (VIGOR), 33, 43
Viruses, 197n

W

Washington (state), food safety inspections in, 160
Washington, D.C., AIDS incidence rate in, 15
Water
   gray, 71
   potable. *See* Community-based potable water system project
Western blot assay HIV testing method, 17, 19
Women. *See* Female population
Women's Capital Corporation, 118
Workforce shortages for food safety inspections, 159–161
World Bank, 28
World Health Organization (WHO)
   on circumcision and HIV, 23, 25
   on diarrheal disease, 70
   H1N1 pandemic declared, 196
   H5N1 cases reported, 195
   pandemic flu outbreak containment strategy, 196, 197f
   SARS outbreak and, 2, 5, 6, 7, 9
   yellow fever vaccine and, 60, 61

X

X-Pack. *See* Smoking cessation kits

Y

Yellow fever outbreak in Paraguay, 59–67
   background, 59
   communication issues, 62–65, 63–64b
   description of, 60–61
   overview, 46
   vaccination availability of, 61–62
Youth
   risk factors in Latino population, 83
   as smoking cessation target group. *See* Smoking cessation kits

Z

Zambia, circumcision and HIV study in, 27